Fissures in EU Citizenship

This book argues that core concepts in EU Citizenship law are riddled with latent fissures traceable back to the earliest case law on free movement of persons, and that later developments simply compounded such defects. By looking at these defects, not only could Brexit have been predicted, but it could also have been foreseen that unchecked problems with EU Citizenship would potentially lead to its eventual dismantling during an era of widespread populism and considerable challenges to further integration. Using a critical constructivist approach, the author painstakingly outlines the 'temple' of citizenship from its foundations upwards, and offers a deconstruction of concepts such as 'worker', the role of non-economic actors, the principle of equal treatment and utterances of citizenship. In identifying inherent fissures in the concept of solidarity and postnational identification, this book poses critical questions and argues that we need to reconstruct EU Citizenship from the bottom up.

Martin Steinfeld is an Affiliated Lecturer at the Faculty of Law and the University Advocate, University of Cambridge. He is also a Director of Studies in Law, College Lecturer and Dean at Hughes Hall, University of Cambridge.

Cambridge Studies in European Law and Policy

The focus of this series is European law broadly understood. It aims to publish original monographs in all fields of European law, from work focusing on the institutions of the EU and the Council of Europe to books examining substantive fields of European law as well as examining the relationship between European law and domestic, regional and international legal orders. The series publishes works adopting a wide variety of methods: comparative, doctrinal, theoretical and interdisciplinary approaches to European law are equally welcome, as are works looking at the historical and political facets of the development of European law and policy. The main criterion is excellence, that is, the publication of innovative work, which will help to shape the legal, political and scholarly debate on the future of European law.

Books in the Series

Fissures in EU Citizenship: The Deconstruction and Reconstruction of the Legal Evolution of EU Citizenship
Martin Steinfeld

The Boundaries of the EU Internal Market: Participation without Membership
Marja-Liisa Öberg

The Currency of Solidarity: Constitutional Transformation during the Euro Crisis
Vestert Borger

Empire of Law: Nazi Germany, Exile Scholars and the Battle for the Future of Europe
Kaius Tuori

In the Court We Trust: Cooperation, Coordination and Collaboration between the ECJ and Supreme Administrative Courts
Rob van Gestel and Jurgen de Poorter

Beyond Minimum Harmonisation: Gold-Plating and Green-Plating of European Environmental Law
Lorenzo Squintani

The Court of Justice of the European Union as an Institutional Actor: Judicial Lawmaking and Its Limits
Thomas Horsley

The Politics of Justice in European Private Law: Social Justice, Access Justice, Societal Justice
Hans-W Micklitz

The Transformation of EU Treaty Making: The Rise of Parliaments, Referendums and Courts since 1950
Dermot Hodson and Imelda Maher

Redefining European Economic Integration
Dariusz Adamski

Human Rights in the Council of Europe and the European Union: Achievements, Trends and Challenges
Steven Greer, Janneke Gerards and Rosie Slowe

Core Socio-Economic Rights and the European Court of Human Rights
Ingrid Leijten

Green Trade and Fair Trade in and with the EU: Process-based Measures within the EU Legal Order
Laurens Ankersmit

New Labour Laws in Old Member States: Trade Union Responses to European Enlargement
Rebecca Zahn

The Governance of EU Fundamental Rights
Mark Dawson

The International Responsibility of the European Union: From Competence to Normative Control
Andrés Delgado Casteleiro

Frontex and Non-Refoulement: The International Responsibility of the EU
Roberta Mungianu

Gendering European Working Time Regimes: The Working Time Directive and the Case of Poland
Ania Zbyszewska

EU Renewable Electricity Law and Policy: From National Targets to a Common Market
Tim Maxian Rusche

European Constitutionalism
Kaarlo Tuori

Brokering Europe: Euro-Lawyers and the Making of a Transnational Polity
Antoine Vauchez

Services Liberalization in the EU and the WTO: Concepts, Standards and Regulatory Approaches
Marcus Klamert

Referendums and the European Union: A Comparative Enquiry
Fernando Mendez, Mario Mendez and Vasiliki Triga

The Allocation of Regulatory Competence in the EU Emissions Trading Scheme
Jospehine van Zeben

The Eurozone Crisis: A Constitutional Analysis
Kaarlo Tuori and Klaus Tuori

International Trade Disputes and EU Liability
Anne Thies

The Limits of Legal Reasoning and the European Court of Justice
Gerard Conway

New Governance and the Transformation of European Law: Coordinating EU Social Law and Policy
Mark Dawson

The Lisbon Treaty: A Legal and Political Analysis
Jean-Claude Piris

The European Union's Fight against Corruption: The Evolving Policy towards Member States and Candidate Countries
Patrycja Szarek-Mason

The Ethos of Europe: Values, Law and Justice in the EU
Andrew Williams

State and Market in European Union Law: The Public and Private Spheres of the Internal Market before the EU Courts
Wolf Sauter and Harm Schepel

The European Civil Code: The Way Forward
Hugh Collins

Ethical Dimensions of the Foreign Policy of the European Union: A Legal Appraisal
Urfan Khaliq

Implementing EU Pollution Control: Law and Integration
Bettina Lange

European Broadcasting Law and Policy
Jackie Harrison and Lorna Woods

The Transformation of Citizenship in the European Union: Electoral Rights and the Restructuring of Political Space
Jo Shaw

The Constitution for Europe: A Legal Analysis
Jean-Claude Piris

The European Convention on Human Rights: Achievements, Problems and Prospects
Steven Greer

Social Rights and Market Freedom in the European Constitution: A Labour Law Perspective
Stefano Giubboni

EU Enlargement and the Constitutions of Central and Eastern Europe
Anneli Albi

Fissures in EU Citizenship

The Deconstruction and Reconstruction of the Legal Evolution of EU Citizenship

Martin Steinfeld
University of Cambridge

CAMBRIDGE
UNIVERSITY PRESS

CAMBRIDGE
UNIVERSITY PRESS

University Printing House, Cambridge CB2 8BS, United Kingdom

One Liberty Plaza, 20th Floor, New York, NY 10006, USA

477 Williamstown Road, Port Melbourne, VIC 3207, Australia

314–321, 3rd Floor, Plot 3, Splendor Forum, Jasola District Centre, New Delhi - 110025, India

103 Penang Road, #05–06/07, Visioncrest Commercial, Singapore 238467

Cambridge University Press is part of the University of Cambridge.

It furthers the University's mission by disseminating knowledge in the pursuit of education, learning, and research at the highest international levels of excellence.

www.cambridge.org
Information on this title: www.cambridge.org/9781108490894
DOI: 10.1017/9781108859165

First published 2022

A catalogue record for this publication is available from the British Library.

ISBN 978-1-108-49089-4 Hardback

Institutions and states will perish, if those who love them do not criticize them, and if those who criticize them do not love them.

Luzius Wildhaber (2012)

Contents

Acknowledgments

This book is in many ways both the endpoint of a long project and perhaps even the starting point of others. It is the result of literally years of painstaking work and necessitated reading verbatim every free movement of persons' case (as well as equal treatment cases) from the Court of Justice of the European Union's infancy until 1992. At one point (in Chapter 4) it also required reading multiple versions of the same cases in different languages. It required the skills of a political scientist immersed in constructivist theory with the nuts and bolts pragmatism of a trained lawyer. 'Tracing' the European Citizen to its origins has revealed fissures within some of the most basic concepts of EU law that have become particularly exposed in an era of Brexit, populism, radical restrictions in free movement as a result of a global pandemic and even serious questions now being posed about the merits of constructing postnational Citizenship on the basis of Europe itself, with its inherent colonial legacy. It is hoped that this book helps scholars of EU law and politics to think critically about seemingly sacrosanct concepts and perhaps even inspires further constructivist or discourse theoretical work in any concrete body of case law.

This is the author's first book and getting to this point has required huge amounts of help from others to whom I will be eternally indebted and cannot thank enough.

First, I would like to thank those who believed in me as a young political scientist many years ago now – in particular Matthew Watson at the University of Warwick (previously Birmingham) for inspiring me to be my best self all those years ago and, of course, Thomas Diez at the University of Tübingen (also previously Birmingham), who turned me into a critical scholar and has literally been there from the start of my academic career until the present day.

In addition, huge thanks go to Alan Dashwood, Eleanor Sharpston and Graham Virgo at the University of Cambridge, as well as Tony Arnull at the University of Birmingham. Alan was prepared to supervise an audacious attempt at an LLM dissertation many years ago, which turned into doctoral work and eventually a book. It took a long time, a lot of patience, meticulous supervision and a lot of inspiration to get me to this point. In relation to the UK's last advocate general at the Court, it meant a huge amount to me that Eleanor took so much time to read my research and be genuinely interested in it. It also means a huge amount that a copy of my PhD, at the time of writing, is still hopefully sitting in Eleanor's chambers in Luxembourg. In relation to Graham, a private lawyer who might be surprised to get an acknowledgement in a book on EU law, the help that he gave me when I was at Downing College to enable me to teach for the first time and finally get my PhD will never be forgotten. In relation to Tony, he was one of the first people to tell me that he felt my work should become a book, which I will also never forget.

Equally, I would like to thank the Arts and Humanities Research Council, who funded my original doctoral research, Cambridge University Press for allowing me to write this book, and many others who have helped me to get to this point. My enormous gratitude must go to Finola O'Sullivan at Cambridge University Press for believing in my book, being extremely patient and being fundamentally one of the most thoroughly decent and kind editors at any publishers.

Finally, I would like to thank a few fellow academics in particular, as well as my parents, wife and children. I owe both Markus Gehring at the University of Cambridge and Antje Wiener at the University of Hamburg an enormous debt of gratitude. You have both gone above and beyond the call of duty, and considerably so. You are model citizens! Without Markus, and his proposal to turn my work into a book, this project would not have got off the ground. In addition, the hundreds of hours that he must have now devoted to helping me in my career over fifteen years now will never be forgotten. In relation to Antje quite simply in addition to being one of the most inspirational academics I have ever met, there would be no book at all and words cannot really encapsulate my gratitude for reading my work in painstaking detail prior to proposing this book to CUP.

Words also fail to describe how grateful I am to my father Alan, without whom I would not have got to this point in so many ways and will always be a source of huge inspiration not only to me but I have no doubt to many others over the years. I will always remember the diligence he showed in reading through my PhD prior to its submission and having to get his head around an area of law and a theoretical approach he literally knew nothing about.

Equally, words also fail to describe my wonderful and inspirational wife Charlotte who always believed in my potential as an academic when we first met at the Inns of Court School of Law as budding barristers. Without your constant support and encouragement I would not have got to this point. Thank you for always being there for me.

The final word goes to my equally wonderful and inspirational daughters Emily and Abigail. I hope they like the book, read it one day and perhaps will be encouraged to undertake critical scholarship themselves in the future. There was many a day when writing this book, as well as my doctoral work, that was lit up by your never-ending enthusiasm and happiness.

Preface

From the perspective of EU citizenship, the departure of the UK from the EU in January 2020 was a radical event. At a stroke, millions of then EU citizens lost a host of basic citizenship rights. What was it, however, that they lost on that day? How did EU citizenship evolve into the series of ideas and associated rights that became a central part of the Brexit debate? While Martin Steinfeld's compelling book is not primarily about the Brexit process, it provides us with a deep set of tools to understand how EU citizenship, and the ideas underlying it, have framed European integration's most central political debates. By deconstructing EU citizenship, his book casts a critical eye on a concept whose positive features are often taken for granted.

At the core of Steinfeld's book is the notion that EU citizenship was 'contaminated' from the beginning. As a concept grounded in the political economy and legal structure of the original Treaty, it has struggled to shake-off its original link to a particular idea of the 'worker'. While, therefore, new narratives (most notably, equal treatment) have been placed on the citizenship concept, mobile and active workers have remained privileged in the application of citizenship rules, neglecting more static forms of discrimination. These early fissures in the concept of citizenship emerging from the Rome Treaty and its later judicial interpretation were then carried-over into the well-known 'introduction' of citizenship into the Maastricht Treaty. By digging deeply into the historical debate, Steinfeld shows us that Maastricht's notion of citizenship was less a revolution that a constitutionalisation of decades of existing discourse.

Discourse is central to Steinfeld's argument. His book therefore also carries methodological and theoretical value in bringing debates about social constructivism most active in international relations and public administration directly into contact with current scholarship on EU law and governance. As Steinfeld argues, citizenship is highly bound-up with notions of collective identity. Understanding legal change requires therefore an account of social and ideational change for which social constructivism provides relevant tools. By deconstructing citizenship, Steinfeld's book also therefore extensively deconstructs EU law as an academic discipline, questioning the prevalence of doctrinal methodology within it. His book thus suggests closer attention to the role law and Courts play in subtly shaping social and political identity (while themselves being shaped by predominant social ideas in turn).

In the book's final part, Steinfeld offers some broad proposals for 'decontamination', drawing on a wide-range of case-law involving litigants cast as 'deserving' or 'undeserving' of legal protection under EU law. As Steinfeld shows, a tentative way forward for EU citizenship in an era of increasing political polarization may depend on anchoring citizenship more closely in the concept of solidarity (for example in the contributions mobile and non-mobile citizens make to each other, most poignantly evidenced in the British Prime Minister's recent recovery with the assistance of a Portuguese nurse). As Steinfeld concludes, while his analysis points to the deep path-dependencies that drive EU law, Brexit may offer an opportunity to go back to the drawing board on citizenship, putting to one side the historical baggage EU citizenship has had to carry from its formative decades.

Steinfeld's critical and inter-disciplinary book offers a novel perspective in understanding both how EU citizenship came to be such a foundational concept in EU law and politics, and how it could be reconstructed in the coming decades. We are very pleased to welcome it as the newest addition to the *Cambridge Studies in European Law and Policy series*.

Mark Dawson

Laurence Gormley

Jo Shaw

Introduction: Contaminated Citizenship

It is possible that had a vote by one of the largest Member States of the European Union on the very membership upon which Citizenship is predicated not taken place in June 2016 during an era of Pan-European populism, a critical deconstructivist approach to the evolution of free movement of persons law might have had purely academic relevance. Whilst European Union Citizenship was 'born' in 1992 after the original Treaty of Rome was amended to include Articles 17 and 18, its roots can be excavated to a much earlier period and this book, in a sense, seeks to replicate the Greek Temple façade envisioned by the Maastricht Treaty and examine the structure from its foundations upwards. As early as 1976, Plender famously stated that European Citizenship was 'incipient'.[1] Likewise, in 1982, Evans defined citizenship as being in an 'embryonic' state of development.[2] The law on free movement of persons is one of the core foundations of the Union. Sitting on top of the pillars that created it is citizenship itself and its very existence distinguishes it from other international or regional organizations and its supranational nature the subject of enormous political conjecture and academic commentary. What so-called Brexit has served to do is to put such a structure under a microscope to examine whether, after all, what were thought to be foundations and pillars made of stone were actually merely compacted sand in reality containing multiple unresolved and not properly examined fissures. In this book, the standard narrative on ctizenship will be critically re-examined and deconstructed through the use of Foucaultian discourse methodology. In a truly Foucaultian sense, what started off as an archaeological attempt to dust off cases perhaps

[1] Richard Plender, 'An Incipient Form of European Citizenship', in Francis Jacobs (ed.), *European Law and the Individual* (Amsterdam: North Holland Publishing, 1976), p. 39.

[2] Andrew Evans, 'European Citizenship' (1982) 45(5) *Modern Law Review*, 497–515 at 497.

considered to be irrelevant and confined to the dustbin of history have actually been exposed to be 'exquisite and glaring'[3] and highly relevant in a context not only including Brexit but considerably beyond it. Perhaps, if anything, the nebulous quest for postnational citizenship (at least in its current form in Europe) needs to be fundamentally re-examined. In addition, somewhat ironically, the substantive reality of Brexit (with the rights and obligations that flow from the Treaties absent of the title 'Citizenship' for UK nationals during an interim period), was itself preceded by prolific border closures (some, such as Hungary, in controversial circumstances) constituting the most significant impediment to free movement of persons (with goods continuing to move unencumbered) in the history of EU free movement law.[4] Thus, from the perspective of all the Member States, not simply the UK, flexible free movement has had to be radically questioned. The premise of this book is that the early case law of the Court on free movement of persons provides fertile ground for Citizenship's unravelling and, ultimately, dismantling; and this problem is, if anything, exacerbated by the later case law specifically on EU Citizenship, particularly that on solidarity. Unravelling and deconstructing citizenship does, though, serve a particular double purpose, one that needs to be stated from the outset. Thym states, at the outset of a chapter entitled 'Judicial Deconstruction of EU Citizenship':

> Against this backdrop, the title to this introduction employs the term 'deconstruction' not as a normative bias that supranational citizenship is bound to fail or that the alleged judicial retrenchment should be criticised. Rather, it uses the 'deconstruction' metaphor as an investigative device to encourage an examination of the legal, political and social practices and forces which may influence the outcome of legal disputes.[5]

[3] Adrienne Chambon, 'Foucault's Approach: Making the Familiar Visible', in Adrienne Chambon, Allan Irving and Laura Epstein (eds.), *Reading Foucault for Social Work* (New York: Columbia University Press, 1995), p. 60.

[4] See, in particular, Alberto Alemanno, 'We Lived the European Dream. Will Any Politician Stand Up for Open Borders?' (*The Guardian*, 22 May 2020) www.theguardian.com/world/commentisfree/2020/may/22/european-dream-politician-stand-up-for-free-movement accessed 10 September 2020. On the issue of both restrictions to free movement and potentially excessive restrictions by Hungary see also Sophie Robin-Olivier, 'Free Movement of Workers in the Light of the Covid-19 Sanitary Crisis: From Restrictive Selection to Selective Mobility' (2020) 5(1) *European Papers*, 613–619.

[5] Daniel Thym, 'Judicial Deconstruction of the EU', in Daniel Thym (ed.), *Questioning EU Citizenship: Judges and the Limits of Free Movement and Solidarity in the EU* (Oxford: Hart, 2017), pp. 1–14 at p. 4.

This book will essentially 'deconstruct' to achieve both purposes Thym outlines, with the caveat that to critique judicial retrenchment is not born of normative bias but, by contrast, out of painstaking analysis of a cumulative body of case law. Deconstruction is most certainly an investigative device which can uncover the inherent subjectivity of judicial creativity. Thus, this book will attempt to suggest that in the light of considerable challenges to the very notion of EU Citizenship, most specifically typified by, but not unique to, 'Brexit', what deconstructivist analysis of the early free movement of persons law (itself the bedrock of the later notion of EU Citizenship) reveals is that the entire edifice of EU Citizenship was/is perhaps bound to fail – an ever-increasing set of fissures will engulf it – because it was built on uncertain foundations and that critical questions need to be posed now projecting towards its future development.

What is undeniable is that the (then) newly inserted citizenship provisions of the Treaty were ultimately used by the Court of Justice of the European Union ('the Court' or 'the ECJ') commencing with the renowned case *Sala* in what Jacqueson terms the '*Sala* Revolution' until the present day.[6] However, the point that both Plender and Evans were making was that European (then Community) Citizenship itself existed in an incipient form by virtue of the emerging case law on free movement of persons: that the concept's roots go back much further than 1992. As Shaw put it:

> The idea of the link between a community of citizens and a political authority was not really the starting point for EU citizenship. [. . .] Most of this work predated the formal establishment of the legal concept of the citizen.[7]

The governing criterion of this book is to trace the origins of the Citizen – examining such 'work' – and to do so in a way that conventional legal approaches do not do by adopting a Social Constructivist perspective to the case law. The specifics of such a perspective – including justification for its use – will be outlined in the remaining part of this introductory chapter. The underlying point being made, though, is that, if Evans is adamant that the 'embryonic Citizen' can be seen to have emerged from thirty years of jurisprudence of the Court, then there is an incumbent duty to outline this development in explicit terms but that in so doing a rather gaping chasm of fissures emerges.

[6] Catherine Jacqueson, 'Union Citizenship and the Court of Justice: Something New Under the Sun? Towards Social Citizenship' (2002) 27(3) *European Law Review*, 260–281 at 264.

[7] Jo Shaw, 'EU Citizenship: Still a Fundamental Status?', in Rainer Bauböck (ed.), *Debating European Citizenship* (Cham: Springer, 2019), pp. 1–17, p. 3.

Without impinging extensively on future chapters, it is clear that thirty years of developing jurisprudence led to the point in 1992 (and indeed increasingly towards the end of the 1980s) where it was collectively understood both within the Court and beyond that it was its role to protect vast categories of individuals who were considerably distanced from the definition of the word 'worker' as conventionally understood, such that it became acceptable to talk of the emergence of a genuine citizenship that, in turn, could become radically decoupled from the Treaty's initially purely economic base. This book will, then, focus specifically on the emergence of various norms or discourses within the text of Court judgments that clearly relate, and critically so, to contemporary legal and political debates concerning citizenship.

The underlying premise of the book, divided in three parts, is that citizenship is contaminated, and has been from the outset and in this respect each chapter is cumulative. In Part I, the Foundations of the Greek Temple façade will be outlined. In Chapter 1, the concept of the 'worker', clearly foundational to the evolution of EU free movement of persons law, will be examined and it will be suggested that not only does it constitute a powerful discourse but also that its development closely relates to the emergence of the later EU Citizen because of its context-specific and novel understanding of the concept of 'work'; one that is perhaps so alienated from its ordinary definition that the evolution towards a so-called Community worker was inherently controversial. In Chapter 2, the Court's dynamic and evolving treatment of both the explicitly economically inactive and socially excluded categories of individuals will also be maintained to have played a highly significant role in providing the normative basis for the formal creation of EU Citizenship but one that, by definition, had several fissures at its core due, in particular, to the emphasis on providing substantive protection to non (or marginally) economic actors.

Part II of the Book focusses on the pillars upon which the edifice of citizenship itself was placed and focusses on the role of utterances in the evolution of discursive construction in two contexts. In Chapter 3, the principle of equal treatment will be examined because, firstly, it constitutes a prevailing norm within Union law and, secondly, there is an evident interrelationship between such a principle and citizenship projects more generally. It will be suggested that equal treatment can equally be classified as discursive but that the evolution of such a discourse is inherently loaded, particularly favouring economic actors that move to the exclusion of other (more static) forms of discrimination. In Chapter 4, specific utterances of the 'citizen' will be examined in both a quantitative and qualitative (or context-specific) sense. Mere utterances of citizenship in the case law are of particular significance, as, prior to 1992, the word itself had no formal legal basis for its own existence, was reliant on various national understandings of the concept and thus was equally underpinned by hidden fissures when it did eventually emerge formally in a supranational context.

Part III of the book – constituting an examination of the roof of the temple upon which citizenship was placed – consists of one chapter and focusses upon the potential for the dismantling of the citizenship project in a substantive sense based upon debates within the early free movement case law that are highly relevant today and will remain so for many years to come. In a sense, what will be discussed will then be the shape and form of the roof structure of the temple façade upon which citizenship has been placed. Chapter 5 is divided in three parts. First, it will be argued that a fissure of solidarity, a concept that arose in particular in the post-*Grzelczyk* citizenship case law, was around from the outset and needs to be critically exposed. It will also, and secondly, be claimed that an inherent and perhaps unresolvable dissonance is evident in any attempt to engender some form of postnational identification by virtue of and contrasting with national identification and construction which remain evident and glaring in the early case law. The final part of the chapter (and conclusion to the book) will provide conceptual space, as a starting point for discussion, for a sustainable EU Citizenship project that might, only might, outlast the buffetings of the contemporary climate, in which one significant Member State has left, the other Member States appear to be partly submerged with waves of populism, where free movement itself has historically literally been prevented due to a global pandemic and, finally, where many of the Member States have to deal with the post-colonial implications of constructing a citizenship project based upon the imagined territory of Europe. In other words, the book will conclude with trying to outline at least some potential to decontaminate citizenship.

The Use of Social Constructivist Methodology in Assessing the Law on Free Movement of Persons

Social Constructivism (SC) is a sociopolitical approach that, in part, proclaims that ideas are important in social life. It would seem, therefore, that such an approach should stay well clear of the 'inner-sanctum' of the courtroom in Luxembourg. Yet, it is the chief contention of this book that SC should be used to examine the case law on free movement of persons. Part of this claim is a negative one; that conventional approaches, laudable though they are, in strict legal terms, just simply are not capable of examining the impact of the case law in all its social complexity and the first part of this introductory chapter will attempt to explain why that is. Having done so, it will be argued that, for several reasons, SC adds value to conventional understandings of the case law. Before doing so, though, it is necessary to both define SC and then outline how it approaches the case law on free movement and this will be undertaken for two reasons. First, because it is difficult to claim that SC adds value to conventional approaches without defining what it is in the first place. Second, because there are certain key concepts that underpin it that will serve as methodological tools to be used in the substantive analysis that will take place in the following chapters; particularly through its set of related claims that ideas, institutions and identity 'matter'. Having both defined and outlined SC, it will then be argued that it adds value to the law on free movement for three key reasons. First, that what has been revealed by defining SC and outlining how it approaches the case law is that it is a qualitatively different methodological approach – particularly in the role that it attributes to ideas – and this in itself adds value. Second, that by claiming that identity 'matters', SC is capable of recognizing the notion of citizenship for what it is; an identity practice as well as a legal concept and therefore that any debate on the development of Union Citizenship from within the pre-1992 cases on free movement of persons has to be able to recognize both of these aspects of it. Finally, it will be claimed that all of the aspects of SC that will be outlined are used as a way of theorizing social change in even legal environments, something which conventional legal approaches simply are not capable of doing. It will be concluded that SC is a theoretical approach that is uniquely capable of assessing the law on free movement in all its sociopolitical and legal complexity and it is for this reason that it should be used.

What is Wrong with a Conventional (Legal) Approach to Free Movement of Persons Law?

It is a core claim of this book that conventional approaches, whilst undeniably of value, are not capable of holistically examining the law on free movement in all its complexity; there is something missing from them. It will then be argued that SC has attempted to grapple with the problems of conventional approaches and offer an alternative to them. There are five key problems with conventional approaches that need to be recognized. First, there is often no recognition that all approaches 'tacitly presuppose' certain assumptions about the world in order to engage in any form of analytical endeavour.[8] Second, because of this, the world is ostensibly and unthinkingly reduced to one consisting solely of autonomous, rational individuals (or agents) acting with a 'given' set of interests and fixed unchanging identities and in which, crucially, ideas play little or no role in constituting 'reality'.[9] It is noticeable, for instance, how often the Citizenship provisions of the Treaty were (initially) dismissed as 'a symbolic plaything', or as 'grand rhetoric'.[10] For SC, 'rhetoric' and 'symbolism' should not be so readily cast aside; they are both highly significant potential causal factors worth studying in their own right. Third, little or no attempt is made to explain how social change comes about even within legal contexts except in terms of the development of legal principles within case law. Fourth, identity plays little role in conventional approaches. This is something that is particularly relevant to any debate on the extent to which citizenship can be seen to have partially emerged from the early case law on free movement as it cannot simply be viewed as: 'a formal ... elaboration of ... rights attaching to a particular category of persons', there is ultimately an inexorable link to debates on an emerging European identity.[11] We need to recognize that true citizenship involves: 'a psychological sense of attachment between the peoples of Europe and ... Union ... citizenship ... cannot just be created through legal enactment; it is dependent to a significant extent on the society in which the law exists'.[12] Finally, conventional methods arguably make

[8] Alexander Wendt, *Social Theory of International Politics* (Cambridge: Cambridge University Press, 1999), p. 371 (quoting Alfred North Whitehead).

[9] Wendt, *Social Theory*, p. 371.

[10] Hans Ulrich Jessurun D'Oliveira, 'Union Citizenship: Pie in the Sky', in Allan Rosas and Esko Antola (eds.), *A Citizen's Europe: In Search of a New Order* (London: Sage, 1995), p. 82; Sionaidh Douglas-Scott, *Constitutional Law of the European Union* (London: Longman, 2002), p. 371.

[11] Jo Shaw, 'Citizenship of the Union: Towards Post-National Membership?', in *Collected Courses of the Academy of European Law – 1995 European Community Law, Vol VI, Book 1, European University Institute, Florence, Academy of European Law* (Hague: Martinus Nijhoff Publishers, 1998), p. 248.

[12] Nicholas Barber, 'Citizenship, Nationalism and the European Union' (2002) 27(3) *European Law Review*, 241–259 at 247.

little attempt to recognize the inherently social context within which the Court operates. The problem is ultimately a methodological one. Haltern contends that the law is: 'too often taught as a highly technical set of rules, a dense doctrinal thicket hardly extending beyond "black letter law"'.[13] It is a literal and descriptive approach; portraying law as establishing 'objective facts' with the end-result being the appearance of a seemingly ideologically neutral assessment being conducted in a seemingly ideologically neutral legal terrain.[14] This has resulted in the Court being portrayed as existing in an 'hermetically closed' environment; which, of course, it is not.[15] Thus, for all of the above-mentioned reasons, conventional legal and sociopolitical approaches lack the ability to *holistically* assess citizenship, in particular because they are methodologically incapable of seeing it in its inherently social context; so much so that Haltern pleads that it 'virtually cries out to be understood by means of an interdisciplinary approach to law' and one that, according to Wincott, 'very few scholars' do.[16] It is this that this book will attempt to do.

What is Social Constructivism?

Before an attempt is made to explain why SC is being used to assess the case law on citizenship it is necessary to (briefly) define it. Social Constructivism encompasses a set of theoretical perspectives that claim to occupy a 'middle ground' in the so-called positivist/post-positivist debate.[17] What this means is that SC attempts to use the critical deconstructivist insight gained from postmodern theorists but to have also 'left the stage of meta-theorising and entered the realm of concrete

[13] Ulrich Haltern, 'Integration through Law', in Antje Wiener and Thomas Diez (eds.), *European Integration Theory* (Oxford: Oxford University Press, 2004), p. 178.

[14] Ibid., p. 192; Anne-Marie Burley and Walter Mattli, 'Europe before the Court: A Political Theory of Legal Integration' (1993) 47(1) *International Organization*, 41–76 at 45.

[15] Ibid. Before concluding this section, it is important to note, at this point, that this is a criticism of the theoretical framework that tacitly has to underpin conventional approaches, that is, of legal scholars, not necessarily practising lawyers. This point will be expanded upon later; though at this point it should be noted that the ECJ is exemplary of how it is not so easy to distinguish between theory and practice as many of the representatives before the Court also teach the legal principles it establishes.

[16] Haltern, 'Integration through Law', p. 178; Daniel Wincott, 'Political Theory, Law and European Union', in Jo Shaw and Gillian More (eds.), *New Legal Dynamic of European Union* (Oxford: Clarendon Press, 1995), p. 293, p. 299.

[17] Emanuel Adler, 'Seizing the Middle Ground: Constructivism in World Politics' (1997) 3 (3) *European Journal of International Relations*, 319–363 at 320.

empirical work'.[18] By suggesting that reality is socially constructed, SC claims to both recognize that material factors (such as natural disasters) and human agency matter, but also that we should recognize that human life is inherently *social*, and therefore that ideas equally 'matter'. For SC, 'ideas' is a generic term to describe discourse and social 'norms' and therefore by contrast with conventional approaches: 'we need to take words, language and communicative utterances seriously'.[19] Termed 'intersubjectivity', SC claims that individuals ultimately subjectively create and re-create discourse but that, having done so, discourse takes on a life of its own that cannot be pinned down to one particular individual in a truly dialectical relationship.[20] This can be seen as an attempt to theorize how a subjective assertion becomes a social truth. Individuals create discourse through articulating subjective principles but then these principles (sometimes) become understood and accepted by others and it is at this point that it becomes intersubjective, a norm or discourse.[21] For Johnstone, law is not immune from this process: 'legal discourse within an interpretive community is necessarily an intersubjective enterprise'.[22] Agency is important in this process as 'well placed individuals, with entrepreneurial skills' still make an enormous difference in dictating whether what they say becomes normalized.[23] Nonetheless, SC recognizes that individuals do not operate prior to society; they are deeply and inexorably immersed in it and individuals must be recognized as ultimately cognitive ever-changing beings. As Ruggie put it: 'Constructivism is about human consciousness and its role in international life'.[24] Identity, in other words, also 'matters' and the methodological individualism that tends to underpin conventional approaches cannot recognize that identities constantly change.[25] SC claims that this happens through

[18] Thomas Risse, 'Social Constructivism and European Integration', in Wiener and Diez (eds.), *European Integration Theory*, p. 173.

[19] Ibid., p. 164.

[20] Ibid.

[21] Ibid.

[22] Ian Johnstone, 'The Power of Interpretive Communities', in Michael Barnett and Raymond Duvall (eds.), *Power in Global Governance* (Cambridge: Cambridge University Press, 2005), pp. 185–204 at p. 191.

[23] Jeffrey T. Checkel, 'Social Construction and European Integration', in Thomas Christiansen, Knud Erik Jørgensen and Antje Wiener (eds.), *The Social Construction of Europe* (London: Sage, 2001), p. 56.

[24] John Ruggie, 'What Makes the World Hang Together? Neo-Utilitarianism and the Social Constructivist Challenge' (1998) 52(4) *International Organization*, 855–885 at 856.

[25] Ibid.

discourse in specific contexts; normally a multiplicity of institutional fora. In other words, institutions also 'matter' as they are social environments in which individuals interact and where identities (as well as ideas themselves) are formed.[26] Institutions (which would naturally include the Court) are considered to be fundamental to SC theory because they both act as 'conveyor belts for the transmission of norms' which would include 'legal discourse' and are 'effective agents of social construction'.[27] SC also defines institutions broadly as 'a relatively stable collection of practices and rules defining appropriate behaviour for specific groups of actors in specific situations'.[28] A fundamental aspect of institutions as understood by (some) constructivists is the concept of an epistemic community. Haas maintains:

> An epistemic community is a network of professionals with recognized expertise and competence in a particular domain and an authoritative claim to policy-relevant knowledge within that domain or issue area.[29]

[26] Thomas Risse and Antje Wiener, 'The Social Construction of Social Constructivism', in Christiansen, Jørgensen and Wiener (eds.), *The Social Construction of Europe*, p. 202. As Adler maintains: 'Constructivists understand institutions as reified sets of intersubjective constitutive and regulative rules that, in addition to helping coordinate and pattern behaviour and channel it in one direction or another, also help establish new collective identities and shared interests of practices'. Emanuel Adler, 'Constructivism in International Relations', in Walter Carlsnaes, Thomas Risse and Beth Simmons (eds.), *Handbook of International Relations* (London: Sage, 2002), pp. 95–110 at p. 104.

[27] Michael Barnett and Martha Finnemore, *Rules for the World: International Organizations in Global Politics* (New York: Cornell University Press, 2004), p. 33; Johnstone, 'The Power of Interpretive Communities', p. 201; Martha Finnemore and Kathryn Sikkink, 'Taking Stock: The Constructivist Research Program in International Relations and Comparative Politics' (2001) 4 *Annual Review of Social Science*, 391–416 at 400.

[28] James March and Johan Olsen, 'The Institutional Dynamics of International Political Orders' (1998) 52(4) *International Organization*, 943–969.

[29] Peter Haas, 'Introduction: Epistemic Communities and International Policy Coordination' (1992) 46 *International Organization*, 1–35 at 3. Likewise, Finnemore and Sikkink state: 'Groups with specialized knowledge often have a common set of norms and world views; many scholars would argue that technical knowledge is never value neutral and always comes with an array of shared normative understandings that make it meaningful, therefore powerful, in social life. As they deploy their knowledge, these epistemic communities often disseminate new norms and understandings along with technical expertise. Consequently, they can act as powerful mechanisms of social construction'. In a more critical way, in keeping with the Foucaultian analysis that will be specifically used in this book, Finnemore and Sikkink also claim (in an earlier article) 'Professions often serve as powerful and pervasive agents working to internalize norms among their members. Professional training does more than simply transfer technical knowledge; it actively socializes people to value certain things above others . . . lawyers all carry different normative biases systematically instilled by their professional training'. Finnemore and Sikkink, 'Taking Stock', 402; Martha Finnemore and Kathryn Sikkink, 'International Norm Dynamics and Political Change' (1998) 52 *International*

Likewise, as Mutschler put it (paraphrasing Haas): 'Epistemic communities have a shared set of normative and principled beliefs, shared causal beliefs, shared notions of validity and a common policy enterprise'.[30]

In this context, law, lawyers and courts/courtrooms can be seen to be considerably more than physical buildings but inherently social enterprises within which powerful discourses or norms are created. As Finnemore and Sikkink contend:

> Lawyers have been shown to do extensive social construction again, often in conjunction with international institutions that consolidate and formalize the new social facts lawyers create. Burley & Mattli's (1993) analysis of the efforts of community lawyers to empower the then-new European Court of Justice illustrates the ways in which professional groups can translate their own shared understandings into formalized organizations and legal structures.[31]

SC is therefore concerned with examining and theorizing all of these factors (ideas, identity and institutions) that constitute social life in combination and it is through doing so that SC claims, perhaps uniquely, to be able to holistically assess and examine social change. Collectively, the social *context* within which the ECJ (or any other institution) works, 'matters'.

However, there are three key related factors that stand SC apart from other methodological approaches. First is its ability to lay bare social life for what it is: inherently contingent. Thus what is ultimately meant by the very phrase, 'Social Constructivism' is that reality is what we make of it and that it is therefore 'reformable'.[32] Change is seen to come about through a process of what has been termed 'social learning'; a claim that individuals' identities evolve over time through interaction with others and discourse in a multiplicity of institutional environments.[33] Crucially, though, it is important to recognize that individuals change slowly. The concept of social learning is about theorizing the *incremental* evolution of individual identities through a plethora of hitherto unrecognized and

Organization, 887–917 at 905. See also Emanuel Adler and Peter Haas, 'Conclusion: Epistemic Communities, World Order, and the Creation of a Reflective Research Program' (1992) 46(1) *International Organization*, 367–390 at 380.

30 Max Mutschler, *Arms Control in Space: Exploring Conditions for Preventive Arms Control* (London: Palgrave Macmillan, 2013), p. 54.

31 Finnemore and Sikkink, 'Taking Stock', 401.

32 Alexander Wendt, 'Anarchy Is What States Make of It: The Social Construction of Power Politics' (1992) 46(2) *International Organization*, 391–425 at 410; Dora Kostakopoulou, *Citizenship, Identity and Immigration in the European Union: Between Past and Future* (Manchester: Manchester University Press, 2001), p. 2.

33 Checkel, 'Social Construction', p. 31.

seemingly mundane day-to-day practices and routines.[34] In other words, ideas are seen to have material effects. Second, once inherent contingency is recognized a whole new social world is opened up in which SC offers a qualitatively different view on the notion of citizenship. For a start, identities need not be monopolized by 'the state'; for Kostakopoulou, 'multiple identity is now normal', and Union Citizenship is therefore perfectly possible.[35] Citizenship must therefore be recognized for being an identity practice like any other; it 'entails more than rights . . . it also contains a context specific meaning which has been developed through social . . . practice' (which can include the free movement cases) and is 'continually contested and rebuilt over time'.[36] Finally, SC simply views the EU differently. All theorists recognize the 'unique *sui generis* nature of the Community', but SC goes further and sees it as a perfect example of an enormously complex process of 'social learning in action'.[37] It 'is the most likely case for international institutions to have constitutive effects . . . it is an institutionally dense environment . . . with high levels of transnational . . . normative activity'.[38] Thus, there are several aspects of SC that make its approach qualitatively different from conventional approaches, in particular its claim that ideas, institutions and identity 'matter'.

Why Use Social Constructivism in Assessing the Case Law on Free Movement of Persons?

It is a key contention of this book that SC's approach to the ECJ differs from conventional legal approaches and therefore constitutes a novel approach to a significant body of case law. It does so for several reasons, the most important of which is a view shared with neofunctionalists; namely that the Court operates in a subtle yet inherently political way.[39] Moreover, there are several key aspects of this view that will specifically underpin the substantive approach to the case law that will be taken in the following chapters. The first aspect is its use of technical

34 Ibid.

35 Kostakapoulou, *Citizenship, Identity and Immigration*, p. 2.

36 Antje Wiener, *'European' Citizenship Practice: Building Institutions of a Non-State* (Boulder: Westview Press, 1998), pp. 26–28.

37 Michelle Everson, 'The Legacy of the Market Citizen', in Shaw and More (eds.), *New Legal Dynamics of European Union*, pp. 73–90 at p. 79 (quoting Diedre Curtin).

38 Checkel, 'Social Construction', p. 59.

39 Burley and Mattli, 'Europe before the Court', 91–92.

legal language. For SC, seemingly mundane day-to-day practices have a much greater social effect than has hitherto been acknowledged – the Court creates discourse as well as 'law' – and the Court's use of technical legal language is an example of this. For Burley and Mattli: 'law functions as a mask for politics ... [with the Court] camouflag[ing] controversial decisions in technical legal garb which has the effect of making it appear to be "independent" and "non-political," which must be met by a counterargument on its own terms'.[40] In other words, the seemingly trivial and technocratic nature of the Court operates as a powerful form of an exclusionary language game; separating off the 'high politics' of the Union's institutions and its Member States from the 'law' or 'low politics' of the Court and masking the profound political developments that the Court has been heavily involved in, in the process.[41] Second, the Court also creates discourse in a more overt way by making normative 'sweeping statements' and even 'invent[ing] out of thin air'.[42] In other words, the constitutionally controversial nature of the Court's interpretative method should be laid bare and we should recognize that ECJ judges act as *de facto* politicians and examples of this should be examined. Third, as has been implied, the agency of the Court – more specifically the 'cleverness and political acumen of the judges' – is fundamental in this process.[43] A form of discursive judicial discretion is crucial. The Court needs to perform a very delicate balancing act, recognizing, on the one hand, that the political project of integration will continue to be dependent on its activist role in advancing the principles of Union law; whilst, on the other, needing to retain political credibility through both appearing to be apolitical and being sensitive to the desire of Member States to preserve their own essential characteristics; therefore equally recognizing – though not always adhering to – the limits which the Treaty has placed upon integration. This involves simply knowing when the political climate is, or perhaps more importantly is *not*, right to advance a particular area of EU law at a particular time.[44]

40 Ibid., 70–72.
41 Wincott, 'Political Theory', p. 305.
42 Haltern, 'Integration through Law', pp. 181–185.
43 Daniel Wincott, 'The Court of Justice and the European Policy Process', in Jeremy Richardson (ed.), *European Union, Power and Policy Making* (London: Routledge, 2001), p. 193.
44 Indeed, no more is this cleverness better explained than by one of the Court's former judges, Mancini, when he maintains that: 'what makes a judge "good" is his awareness of the constraints of judicial decision making and the knowledge that the rulings must be convincing in order to evoke obedience'. See ibid.

Moreover, a fourth aspect of an SC approach to the case law on free movement goes further than neofunctionalism by claiming that discourse plays a crucial role in this process. This involves two interrelated claims. First, that the Court has had, and continues to have, a subtle political influence by incrementally changing the discursive terrain of political debates on the Union; rendering what appeared thirty years ago to be 'unacceptable' both 'legitimate' and 'acceptable'. Second, that law is itself discourse. Wincott argues that: 'pure persuasive force of the arguments of ECJ judges alone cannot wholly explain their influence on the integration process' and there is a 'normative power of the legal form ... the "pull of formalism"'.[45] For SC, a powerful intersubjective discourse is created by the ECJ by subtly interweaving the technocratic with the principled, or overtly normative, statement. The two work in tandem: the principled statement forms the keystone, or foundational basis, of a socio-legal discourse and a plethora of technocratic statements give it uncontroversial content; in a sense the building bricks or 'nodal points' underneath the keystone.[46] The final aspect of an SC approach is a critical recognition that, because the Court does not exist in an ideologically neutral hermetically sealed 'bubble' we need to critically assess the relationship between the Court and wider social world beyond it. 'Black letter law' is seen to have a discursive effect both within and beyond the courtroom and the Court cannot help but be influenced by sociopolitical factors outside of the Court.[47] At the same time, as has been stated earlier, it can equally have a subtle influence on the outside world; changing the discursive terrain over time and thereby effecting genuine sociopolitical change. What this therefore reveals about an SC approach to the case law is an attempt to map out the complex and dialectical material and discursive processes in which the Court's collective agency operates; (re)creating discourse within it but being equally influenced by the cultural and material confines within which it operates. This book will thus use these key aspects of SC approaches to the ECJ in the substantive assessment that will follow.

Perhaps it is worth mentioning one specific aspect of how the Court operates that is conceptually interesting to Social Constructivists; that of the relationship between the Court and its Advocates-General (AGs). It is true to say that conventional approaches are equally aware of this

[45] Ibid.

[46] Thomas Diez, 'Europe as a Discursive Battleground – Discourse Analysis and European Integration Studies' (2001) 36(1) *Cooperation and Conflict*, 5–38 at 14–15.

[47] Wincott, 'Court of Justice', p. 194.

unique relationship; one where AGs, on the one hand, make often highly politically charged statements, whereas the Court, in the same case uses much more restrained and technocratic language.[48] Reich and Harbacevica argue that this is because: 'obviously Court practice cannot make such bold statements, but has to develop Citizenship more incrementally ... [whereas] Advocates-General enjoy more freedom in the making of sweeping statements approaches'.[49] However, once discourse is brought into the equation this relationship takes on an altogether more significant role. This is because it can be characterized as one in which AGs can, to a certain extent, freely create discourse, through overtly principled normative assertion, within the institutional environment of the Court but in a way that is perceived as politically acceptable. This is a subtle but crucial relationship that needs to be assessed as AGs can both operate within and outside of the structural confines of the Court. On the one level what an AG says, neither forming part of the judgment of the Court nor being legally binding, makes it appear that what the Court is doing is uncontroversial; whatever an AG says, a judgment will be accepted by Member States so long as the ECJ itself does not repeat what its AGs say. Yet on another, discursive, level, an AG's opinion still forms part of the court report and once a subjective utterance is made, no matter who is making it, it is out in the open and could be seen as part of a complex incremental process of norm development resulting, at some later stage, in the discursive terrain being somehow changed. This can be seen as part of the process in which what was unacceptable for the Court to state in one case becomes acceptable over time.[50] Therefore, as well as focussing on the aspects outlined earlier, perhaps this book will shed an entirely different light on this relationship.

Why Use Social Constructivism? Its 'Value Added'

It is also a key claim of this book that SC theory constitutes a 'value added' to conventional approaches to the case law on free movement: it does not

48 Helen Toner, 'Judicial Interpretation of European Union Citizenship - Transformation or Consolidation?' (2000) 7(2) *Maastricht Journal of European and Comparative Law*, 158–182 at 175.

49 Norbert Reich and Solvita Harbacevica, 'Citizenship and Family on Trial: A Fairly Optimistic Overview of Recent Court Practice with Regard to Free Movement of Persons' (2003) 40(3) *Common Market Law Review*, 615–638 at 617.

50 Haltern, 'Integration through Law', p. 187.

replace them. Indeed, the origins of SC theory were quite explicitly a value-added theory. Risse, for instance, foresaw constructivism as an emerging theory capable of complementing pre-existing theories through better explaining and understanding the end of the Cold War.[51] In this context, conventional methods are not dismissed: 'Constructivism does not challenge science, rationalism and modernity; it merely makes science more compatible with the constructivist understanding of social reality, by so doing, it is an explicitly value-added theory'.[52] Fundamentally, it is perhaps implicit from all that has already been outlined that its approach is different from a conventional one and this, in itself adds value. As Torfing put it (in response to mainstream criticism of the approach):

> The reaction of mainstream political theory to the emerging 'discursive turn' has shifted from down-right rejection to grudging tolerance and, latterly, critical dialogue. This means that discourse theorists are, to an increasing extent, asked what value the discourse approach adds to the study of politics. The first response to this question is that discourse theory poses other kinds of research questions than those generated by behaviourist, institutionalist, and rational choice perspectives.[53]

In other words, merely 'posing' different questions in a qualitative sense adds value.

Moreover, it is hoped that that further value will be added to legal research specifically in two ways. First, to conventional legal scholars' work by trying to persuade conventional theorists that it is important to understand that the law on free movement is potentially a social, as well as a legal phenomenon. As Torfing continues: 'discourse theory has persuaded many mainstream theorists to pay attention to new issues such as knowledge paradigms, identity formation, and the discursive construction of sedimented norms, values, and symbols'.[54] Such 'mainstream theorists' also undeniably include legal scholars. Second, to practising lawyers within the Court by providing them with a critical awareness of the extra-legal role that they perform. As Adler states: 'constructivism can make practitioners more sensitive to the

[51] Thomas Risse, 'Ideas Do Not Float Freely: Transnational Coalitions, Domestic Structures, and the End of the Cold War' (1994) 48(2) *International Organization*, 185–214 at 213.

[52] Adler, 'Constructivism', p. 96, p. 102.

[53] Jacob Torfing, 'Discourse Theory: Achievements, Arguments and Challenges', in David Howarth and Jacob Torfing (eds.), *Discourse Theory in European Politics: Identity, Policy and Governance* (Basingstoke: Palgrave Macmillan, 2005), pp. 1–32 at p. 22.

[54] Ibid., p. 4.

functions, practises and discourses of transnational epistemic communities and transnational advocacy networks'.[55] What is clearly different is its claim that not only do 'ideas matter' but that they matter in novel and perhaps even previously unthought-of ways, according an independent causative role to previously under-theorized social practices.[56] By claiming that 'ideas matter', so-called symbolic window dressing takes on an altogether more important role. Equally, merely because an articulation in a formal legal setting is termed 'law' and is shrouded in legal formalism does not prevent what is said in the ECJ from having a discursive social impact both within the Court and beyond it; legal settings are no less breeding grounds of discourse than any other institutionalized setting. The value that SC adds to conventional legal approaches is that it makes clear that discourse, unlike legal precedent, follows *no clear-cut rules* and it has a methodological approach that at least attempts to 'trace' a discursive 'path' *wherever* it may lead.[57] It adds a totally different dimension to our understanding of how the ECJ operates by virtue of its claim that 'law' has as much a social effect as a legal one. Perhaps a case-in-point is, as has been outlined earlier, that a complex and highly interesting relationship potentially exists between the Court and its AGs which cannot be adequately theorized by conventional approaches. Equally, SC adds value because it is capable of assessing the relationship between the Court and the outside world and, most importantly, in a complex, holistic and dialectical way. It is like tracing a process of linguistic diffusion in which individuals are seen to create norms in particular institutional environments. In this context, legal rules still matter but so do discourses, institutions and identities. Similarly, it is a unique contention that ideas are capable of having material effects; they can make individuals act in particular ways. This has two further critical implications that, again, add to our understanding of the case law. First, there is a recognition that all human beings are inherently social and questions of identity formation are therefore crucial even within the Court; it does not exist in a social vacuum. As Risse maintains:

[55] Adler, 'Constructivism', p. 102.

[56] Checkel, 'Social Construction', p. 56. As Van Dijk maintains: 'Discourse analysis provides us with rather powerful, while subtle and precise, insights to pinpoint the everyday manifestations and displays of social problems in communication and interaction'. Teun Van Dijk, 'The Role of Discourse Analysis in Society', in Teun Van Dijk (ed.), *Discourse Analysis in Society: Handbook of Discourse Analysis Volume 4* (London: Academic Press, 1985), p. 7.

[57] See 'Introduction' for an elaboration of this point in the context of contingency and the use of the Foucaultian method.

> It is a truism that social reality does not fall from heaven, but that human agents construct and reproduce it through their daily practices but at the same time human agents do not exist independently from their social environment and its collectively shared systems of meanings ('culture' in a broad sense) . . . the social environment in which we find ourselves, defines ('constitutes') who we are, our identities as social beings.[58]

Moreover, SC clearly adds to conventional legal understandings of Union Citizenship by recognizing the inexorable link between Citizenship and identity which, because of its socially holistic nature and focus on the fluid role of ideas, is particularly applicable to attempts to trace the embryonic citizen to the early law on free movement of persons. By doing so, the Court can again be laid bare for doing more than subtly (and even unsubtly) extending the rights of nationals of EU Member States through the use of the free movement (and other) provisions in the Treaty. There was clearly the potential for a supranational 'European-ness' to have emerged from what the Court was doing and what the Court was doing, then, was more than just establishing 'any old' case law, instead playing a key role in constructing citizenship itself out of the case law. Finally, and most importantly, SC adds value by attempting to theorize social *change*. As Adler comments:

> Constructivism is about . . . change in world politics . . . rather than using history as a descriptive method, constructivism has history 'built in' as part of theories. Historicity, therefore, shows up as part of the contexts that make possible social reality, the path-dependent processes involving structural and agent change, and the mechanisms involved in the explanation of change.[59]

In a sense, conventional approaches are either entirely descriptive, stating what the law 'is', or prescriptive, stating what the law should be; in between which social change takes place – people change, society changes. It is therefore important for there to be a methodological approach that recognizes, and attempts to map out the social processes within which change takes place; as opposed to 'view[ing] Citizenship either as something that exists, but is in need of promotion, or something that the Union lacks'.[60] It needs, instead, to be 'seen as something

[58] Risse, 'Social Constructivism', p. 161. Likewise, 'by ontological assumption, constructivists understand that actors are shaped by the social milieu in which they live'. Finnemore and Sikkink, 'Taking Stock', 394.

[59] Adler, 'Constructivism', p. 102.

[60] Kostakopoulou, *Citizenship, Identity and Immigration*, p. 7.

that is in the process of formation'.[61] It is exactly this that this book will now attempt to do. It is this point that appears to have been lost in the very wording of Article 17 of the Treaty when it was amended at Maastricht to state: 'Citizenship of the Union is hereby established'. This is not a criticism of the wording of the Treaty. In a sense, enshrining it within a Treaty does establish it. The point an SC approach makes, though, is that the mere statement of it does not establish *genuine* Citizenship. In a sense, the Treaty is treating it as something that already exists. Alternatively, by dismissing Article 17 as mere symbolic 'window dressing', conventional approaches clearly view it as something the Union lacks. Approaching the early case law on free movement of persons differently makes it possible to assess whether the Court subtly (and perhaps even unintentionally) radically changed the discursive terrain within which it, and the then Community as a whole, operated. It is Social Constructivism that is capable of theorizing how this may be happening in all its complexity:

> Constructivism's added value, therefore, is that it helps explain why people converge around specific norms, identities and cause-effect understandings, and thus where interests come from. It also adds value by being concerned with outlining change in world politics, is concerned with social communication, and spelling out the role of language in social life.[62]

Thus, SC clearly potentially adds value to conventional approaches to not only the early case law on free movement but also to the later case law on EU Citizenship (and linkages that can be made between the two bodies of jurisprudence).

The Methodological Scope of This Book

Social Constructivism encompasses a broad spectrum of theoretical approaches ranging from perspectives more closely aligned to mainstream systemic neoliberal and neorealist standpoints in International Relations to those more comparable to poststructuralist discourse theory. In other words, whilst, as Adler famously stated (above) SC attempted to seize a middle ground between two seemingly irreconcilable approaches, the 'middle ground' itself takes various forms. Regardless, what SC theorists claim is that there is a fundamental

[61] Ibid.
[62] Adler, 'Constructivism', p. 102.

need to draw particular strands of such a set of perspectives together to form a methodological basis for empirical work. In so doing, though, individual pieces of research are given conceptual space in which to develop a particular method based upon a particular set of *a priori* assumptions. As Finnemore and Sikkink maintain:

> There is no single constructivist method or research design. Constructivism opens up a set of issues, and scholars choose the research tools and methods best suited to their particular question. In some cases, quantitative methods yield particular insight. In other cases, qualitative and interpretative methods are more appropriate. Many research projects have used a combination of these methods to illuminate different parts of a larger puzzle. In this sense, designing constructivist research is not fundamentally different from designing other kinds of research. Constructivists, like any other researchers, use the full array of available tools.[63]

Fundamentally, this has taken place in this book and this particular piece of research is based upon a Foucaultian understanding of discourse theory and methodology, combining both qualitative and quantitative research methods dependent upon the particular circumstances of statements made within the Court's judgments, something which is perfectly conceivable in SC methodology.[64] Based upon Foucault's archaeological and genealogical conception of the origins of discourse and the way in which societies are governed by it, the book makes an attempt to 'trace' the subjective origins of particular discourses within the context of free movement cases and follow their development to the point where they become a form of social common sense.[65] This method has several fundamental aspects to it. First, this book takes a particular stance on discourse (and therefore implicitly the role of ideology in social life); with points of comparison and contrast with

[63] Finnemore and Sikkink, 'Taking Stock', 396. Indeed, Torfing takes issue with one criticism of discourse theory from mainstream scholars in suggesting that there might be a problem with having such flexible set of approaches. As he put it: 'A last response to this challenge is to problematize the idea of an all-purpose method with the character of a "complete user's guide to discourse analysis," and to question the very idea of "applying a rule." Discourse theory should not aim to develop a general set of methodological rules that can and should be used in all kinds of discourse analysis. The aspiration for a rigid decontextualized method is absurd, as a problem-driven analysis of discourse will require a constant invention and adjustment of particular methodological rules'. Torfing, 'Discourse Theory', p. 27.

[64] Finnemore and Sikkink, 'Taking Stock', 395–396.

[65] Jason Powell, 'The Development of Post-Structuralism and Aging', in Jared Jaworski (ed.), *Advances in Sociology: Volume 3* (New York: Nova Science Publishers, 2006), 53–68 at 57–58.

other SC perspectives and other theoretical perspectives – particularly post-structuralism – manifesting itself in a number of ways. Second, the context within which statements or utterances are made will be emphasized. Third, at times, an overtly critical discourse theoretical approach will be adopted. Finally, and relatedly, attempts will be made to examine (and critique) the social construction of prevailing norms or social common sense within EU free movement law, placing a particular emphasis on the role of agency in their construction and the inherent contingency embedded within the socialized process of norm diffusion.

The Conception of Discourse Adopted in This Book

From the perspective of this book (and a number of SC theorists), critical analysis of language within case law is fundamentally necessary, in addition to deriving legal principles from it. As Risse contends: 'If we want to understand and explain social behaviour, we need to take words, language, and communicative utterances seriously'.[66] It is the particular use of language that literally constructs reality and a courtroom is as much part of this process as any other institution. As Finnemore and Sikkink maintain:

> Speech can also persuade; it can change people's minds about what goals are valuable and about the roles they play (or should play) in social life. When speech has these effects, it is doing important social construction work, creating new understandings and new social facts that reconfigure politics. In one of the pioneering works of the field, Kratochwil (1989) examined the role of legal reasoning in persuasion and other social construction processes.[67]

Whilst the notion of language being an important conceptual variant in social life lends itself to comparisons with linguistic approaches to case law, what distinguishes SC and discourse theoretical approaches is a fundamental emphasis on language *as* discourse. Kendall and Wickham, for instance, warn of the 'danger' of confusing the term 'discourse' with 'language'.[68] In part, the distinction between 'language' *per se* and discourse is structural. From a Foucaultian perspective, discourse can be understood as 'a corpus of statements whose organisation is regular and systematic'.[69] Likewise, Waever suggests: 'Discourse can be defined as a system that regulates the formation of

[66] Risse, 'Social Constructivism', p. 164.
[67] Finnemore and Sikkink, 'Taking Stock', 402.
[68] Gavin Kendall and Gary Wickham, *Using Foucault's Methods* (Guildford: Sage, 1999), p. 42.
[69] Ibid.

statements'.[70] Furthermore, it is the structural nature of discourse that itself constitutes reality. As Ferguson put it: 'discourse is a practice, it is structured, and has real effects which are much more profound than simply "mystification"'.[71] Moreover, this conception of discourse then has a practical application in terms of examining the interrelationship between texts (which would include different court judgments) and patterns of language within texts. In terms of examining the use of language between texts, Paltridge maintains:

> Discourse analysis focuses on knowledge about language beyond the word, clause, phrase and sentence that is needed for successful communication. It looks at patterns of language across texts and considers the relationship between language and the social and cultural contexts in which it is used. Discourse analysis also considers the ways in which the use of language presents different views of the world and different understandings. It examines how the use of language is influenced by relationships between participants as well as the effects the use of language has upon social identities and relations. It also considers how views of the world, and identities, are constructed through the use of discourse.[72]

Likewise, in terms of patterns of language within texts, Torfing claims that discourse analysis examines the 'form of a chain of statements/ expressions, the manner in which they came about (archaeology) . . . [as well as] rule-governed behaviour that leads to a chain of similarly interrelated system of statements'.[73] Thus, aspects of the analysis in this book will focus on patterns of statements and expression, their interrelationship with statements in different cases and the potential social impact that such statements have upon the epistemic community

[70] Ole Waever, 'Discursive Approaches', in Wiener and Diez (eds.), *European Integration Theory*, pp. 197–215 at p. 199.

[71] James Ferguson, *The Anti-Politics Machine: Depolitization, and Bureaucratic Power in Lesotho* (Cambridge: Cambridge University Press, 1994), p. 18.

It should also be noted that discourse can be construed more broadly than simply text on a page. It is simply that for the purposes of this book, the actual wording of court reports is the focus of substantive analysis. As Torfing maintains: 'Discourse is defined as an empirical collection of practices that qualify as discursive in so far as they contain a semiotic element. Hence, discourse is reduced to a subset of a broader range of social practices. It includes all kinds of linguistically mediated practices in terms of speech, writing, images, and gestures that social actors draw upon in their production and interpretation of meaning. Discursive practices are said to be ideological in so far as they contribute to the naturalization of contingently constructed meanings'. Torfing, 'Discourse Theory', p. 7.

[72] Brian Paltridge, *Discourse Analysis: An Introduction* (London: Continuum, 2006), p. 2.

[73] Torfing, 'Discourse Theory', p. 26.

of the Court. Indeed, this is a point made by Paltridge when outlining the interrelationship between discourse and identity in the above quote. In this respect, comparisons can also be made with cognitive psychological approaches to the social sciences because 'constructivism is about human consciousness and its role in international life'.[74] This point is also made by Finnemore, who contends: 'Constructivists have turned to research in cognitive and social psychology (the same research on which much of the mediation literature implicitly or explicitly rests) to understand these processes [of norm production and their social impact]'.[75] Focussing on the cognitive impact of discourse is clearly, then, a fundamental aspect of critical SC theory. However, merely because SC has turned to aspects of cognitive psychology does not make SC a purely psychological theory. It is distinct from a purely cognitive approach:

> Discourse analysis should be clearly distinguished from cognitive approaches, which analyse what people perceive and think. If cognitive approaches sometimes use public texts these serve as indicators for perceptions, thoughts and beliefs, realising all kinds of problems regarding the validity of discourse as a source of knowledge about people's minds. Discourse analysis focusses attention on discourse as interesting in itself. It is not an indicator for something else and thus questions about whether 'they really mean what they say' are irrelevant. A discourse analysis tries to find the structures and patterns in or statements what regulate political debate so that certain things can be said while other things will be meaningless or less powerful of reasonable.[76]

Thus, the approach taken in this book places a fundamental emphasis on the use of language within texts (and its nuances). This approach is structural in the sense of examining patterns of predominant language within texts and is cognitive in terms of examining the social impact of language on the utterer but at the same time focussing on the fundamental role of discourse within institutional environments in and of itself.

The Importance of the Context in which Utterances Are Made

In addition to focussing on the specifics of words uttered within the text of court reports, the approach adopted in this book is also context-specific. This is what is meant by the concept of a discursive 'snapshot' being adopted, as part of a broader scheme of analysis, in the

[74] Ruggie, 'What Makes the World Hang Together?', 856.

[75] Martha Finnemore, 'Are Legal Norms Distinctive?' (2000) 32 *NYU Journal of International Law and Politics*, 699–710 at 700.

[76] Waever, 'Discursive Approaches', p. 199.

substantive chapters that follow.[77] This is therefore an overtly qualitative approach in the sense of examining the nuances in detail in the context of particular utterances and then comparing and contrasting such an utterance with a statement often made several years later. The context-specific holism of SC is both cognitive and institutional. In cognitive terms, certain phrases retain a particular 'hold' within particular environments. As Ulbert and Risse put it: 'arguments have to "resonate" with prior knowledge, agreed-upon principles and norms, or commonly held world views in order to become persuasive'.[78] This book will, in part, attempt to identify particular statements that 'resonate' (as evident from the text of jurisprudence of the Court) and trace such statements to their ultimately subjective origins. In addition, such an approach focusses on the context of statements uttered within institutions. As Titscher, Meyer, Wodak and Vetter maintain: 'Discourses occur, on the one hand, in macro-contexts, in organizations and institutions … but on the other hand they occur at a particular time, in a particular place, with particular participants, and so on (that is, micro-context)'.[79] Thus, in this book, the focus will be on the micro-context of utterances, situating them within the context of the free movement of persons case law, though within the macro-context of the Court and the institutional framework within the EU that the Court forms part of.

The Fundamental Importance of Taking a Critical Approach

As has already been outlined, SC constitutes a spectrum of approaches, from approaches that are more closely aligned with mainstream approaches in law and politics to approaches that could be compared with post-structuralism (or postmodernism). This book overtly adopts a 'value-added' approach and, in this context constitutes an approach that attempts to 'compete' with mainstream (and more status-quo orientated) empirical work. However, aspects of the method adopted in this book are also overtly critical and, it is submitted, unavoidably so. Parts of the substantive examination of the case law that follows focus, at times, not solely on what has been uttered within texts but also on what has been (deliberately) not uttered.[80] For Risse, there is a fundamental need

[77] Kendall and Wickham, *Using Foucault's Methods*, p. 45.

[78] Cornelia Ulbert and Thomas Risse, 'Deliberately Changing the Discourse: What Does Make Arguing Effective?' (2005) 40(3) *Acta Politica*, 351–367 at 361.

[79] Stefan Titscher and others, *Methods of Text and Discourse Analysis* (London: Sage, 2000), p. 27.

[80] For instance, in Section 4.3, what has been noticed within the free movement case law is a comparative reticence in using the word 'citoyen' in the French language version of

for a critical approach within constructivist empirical work because 'discourse is a process of construction of meaning allowing for certain interpretations while excluding others ... [in] which constructions of meaning become so dominant that they are being taken-for-granted'.[81] In this respect, this book is particularly devoted to 'tracing' the social construction of so-called common sense: the 'taken-for-granted' or 'dull' aspects of the case law that are often overlooked by conventional approaches. Thus, an aspect of the Foucaltian method is to focus on the 'the background understandings – shaped by general culture, science, and normative understandings – that people use to make sense of the world'.[82] This is partly an acknowledgement that common discourses within the framework of EU law *should* be traced to their subjective origins. For Finnemore and Sikkink, when 'norm internalization occurs, norms acquire a taken-for-granted quality and are no longer a matter of broad public debate'.[83] Through tracing, therefore, the mundane features as part of public debate. This methodological approach, though, goes further than simply trying to trace common sense to its subjective origins: it is concerned with being critical at the same time. This involves a further acknowledgement of the power of such prevailing norms or discourses and a normative attempt at deconstructing such prevailing norms. In terms of power, what cannot be denied is the power of social common sense. As Finnemore and Sikkink continue:

> At the extreme of a norm-cascade, norms may become so widely accepted that they are internalized by actors and achieve a "taken-for-granted" quality that makes conformance with the norm almost automatic. For this reason, internalized norms can be both extremely powerful (because behaviour according to the norm is not questioned) and hard to discern (because actors do not seriously consider or discuss whether to conform). Precisely because they are not controversial, however, these norms are often not the centrepiece of political debate and for that reason tend to be ignored by political scientists".[84]

It is for this reason that, for instance, in researching for this book, a fundamental assessment of not only every overt free movement of

the Court reports (with the powerful resonance that the word has in the French language) by comparison with the seemingly more liberal use of the word 'citizen' in the English language version.

[81] Risse, 'Social Constructivism', p. 165.

[82] Emanuel Adler and Steven Bernstein, 'Knowledge in Power: The Epistemic Construction of Global Governance', in Barnett and Duvall (eds.), *Power in Global Governance*, pp. 294–318 at p. 296.

[83] Finnemore and Sikkink, 'International Norm Dynamics', 904.

[84] Ibid.

persons case from the Court's inception until 1992 has taken place but also every social security case, as a number of such cases are rarely commented on by conventional legal commentators. Instead, a normative aspect of this book – a focus on deconstruction – at times critiques such 'common sense' and this is because what is presented as 'value-neutral' is often far from so. As Paltridge maintains: 'The norms and values which underlie texts are often "out of sight" rather than overtly stated ... the aim of a critical approach to discourse analysis is to help reveal some of these hidden and "often out of sight" values, positions and perspectives'.[85] Therefore, part of the Foucaultian method is devoted towards shedding light on aspects of any subject area that was hitherto not forming part of mainstream analysis. By so doing the 'normal' becomes almost surreal. As Chambon put it: 'Foucault often selected the least expected features, those that tend to be overlooked as insignificant, the details that "don't matter." Through dissection, ordinary features of routine activity become exquisite and glaring – at times unbearable'.[86] For example, attempts are made, at times, to examine the concept of 'othering' within the text of Court judgments in the context of examining the social construction of borders.[87] 'Othering' is a fundamental aspect of critical discourse theory and Foucaultian discourse analysis specifically:

> The hegemonic articulation of meaning and identity is intrinsically linked to the construction of social antagonism, which involves the exclusion of a threatening Otherness that stabilizes the discursive system while, at the same time, preventing its ultimate closure ... Foucault convincingly demonstrated that the limits and unity of discourse cannot be constructed by reference to an inner essence, in terms of a particular theme, style, conceptual framework, etc. Alternatively, we have to look for something outside the discourse in order to account for its limits.[88]

Europe and the European Union are considered by some to be fertile ground for 'othering' in the sense of the construction of a threatening 'other' beyond Europe's borders such that the famous post-structural theorist Derrida himself wrote an article specifically on this subject.[89] It

[85] Paltridge, *Discourse Analysis*, p. 178.
[86] Chambon, 'Foucault's Approach', p. 60.
[87] See Section 2.2. See also Chapter 5 for further analysis on the implications of constructing an 'other' to 'Europe' in a post-colonial context.
[88] Torfing, 'Discourse Theory', p. 15.
[89] Jacques Derrida, *The Other Heading: Reflections on Today's Europe* (Indiana: Indiana University Press, 1992). See end of Section 5.4.3 for an outline of this concept.

can also be used in a practical sense, in terms of examining specific texts as part of what Wodak terms the 'discourse-historical approach ... focussing foremost on the construction of "us" and them'.[90] Naturally, a core aspect of 'othering' in a modern political context relates to borders: the physical demarcation of 'us' versus 'them'. For SC, whilst borders themselves do exist, they are as much socially constructed through derived meanings and bureaucratic processes as they manifest themselves in a material sense.[91] Issues relating to borders are therefore an important aspect of a critical approach as: 'In a concrete analysis of discourse, social antagonism shows itself through the production of political frontiers, which often invoke stereotyped pictures of friends and enemies'.[92] As will be outlined (in part) in both Chapter 2 and Chapter 5, aspects of 'othering' in the context of issues relating to borders and, ironically, the construction of supranational citizenship, did arise in the free movement case law, something that mainstream legal approaches have not specifically analysed.

It should be noted, though, that the particular method adopted in this book does not engage in acts of deconstruction for the sake of so doing. Instead, the focus is both practical and emancipatory (or normative). In a practical sense, attention will be drawn to both the structure of language on pages of Court judgments and the way in which particular words are emphasized within the text. This approach is exemplified by Paltridge, who states:

> A ... way of doing a critical analysis is to examine the way in which the context of a text is framed; that is, the way in which the content of the text is presented to its audience, and the sort of perspective, angle and slant the writer or speaker is taking. Related to this is what is foregrounded and what is backgrounded in the text: that is, what the author has chosen to emphasize, de-emphasize or, indeed, leave out of the text.[93]

In emancipatory terms, an aspect of this book is devoted towards the intellectual space that emerges from critical analysis in order to offer potential alternatives to prevailing norms. In this respect, the method adopted partially derives from critical social theory as

[90] Ruth Wodak, 'National and Transnational Identities: European and Other Identities Oriented to in Interviews with EU Officials', in Richard Hermann, Thomas Risse and Marilynn Brewer (eds.), *Transnational Identities* (Maryland: Rowman and Littlefield, 2004), pp. 97–128 at p. 125.

[91] Ibid.

[92] Torfing, 'Discourse Theory', p. 16.

[93] Paltridge, *Discourse Analysis*, p. 187.

espoused by Giddens, Habermas and Foucault himself.[94] From such a critical perspective, it is not enough to deconstruct; deconstruction *should* be followed by a process of reconstruction. As Finnemore and Sikkink suggest: 'the task of the critical scholar is both to unmask … ideational structures of domination and to facilitate the imagining of alternative worlds'.[95] Likewise, Kratochwil (in the context of outlining a constructivist approach to international law) advocates reconstruction through the use of Rorty's 'therapeutic re-description' method which:

> Provides us with the possibility of 'seeing' the old in a new way and in creating new opportunities for practices and experiences which sidestep old vocabulary standing in the way … new ways of conceptualisation presuppose two steps: one of 'unlearning' by deconstructing the problem, and one of construction by utilizing new conceptual tools in the analysis.[96]

Thus, this reconstructive form of discourse theory can be used to advocate alternative emancipatory concepts in a number of different substantive areas. For example, Asen attempts 'a discourse theory of citizenship' which:

> Takes discourse seriously. This seemingly tautological statement is important because in both scholarly and popular assessments discourse is too often regarded as prefatory to genuine action. According to this view, talk is cheap, and talk is a bargain only insofar as its ways lead to activities such as voting and volunteering. Citizenship should not be reserved for special occasions, however. Discourse practices present potentially accessible and powerful everyday enactments of citizenship.[97]

In Chapter 5 of this book, attempts are made to do just that; namely to 'present potentially accessible and powerful everyday enactments of citizenship' not on the basis of the subjective ideas of academic theorists but through utterances in the free movement case law itself. Thus, for a number of reasons, a critical constructivist approach has been adopted in this book.

94 Finnemore and Sikkink, 'Taking Stock', 398. Particularly Harbermas' concept of 'communicative rationality'. See Torfing, 'Discourse Theory', p. 8.

95 Ibid.

96 Friedrich Kratochwil, 'How Do Norms Matter?', in Michael Byers (ed.), *The Role of Law in International Politics* (Oxford: Oxford University Press, 2000), pp. 35–68 at p. 45.

97 Robert Asen, 'A Discourse Theory of Citizenship' (2004) 90(2) *Quarterly Journal of Speech*, 189–211 at 207.

The Fundamental Role of Agency in Discourse Analysis

An evident consequence of a theoretical framework devoted to the critical examination of taken-for-granted concepts within the free movement cases is to place an emphasis on the inherent contingency of human existence. As has previously been stated, norms (and the entire process from their subjective creation to widespread diffusion) do not follow straightforward rules in the way that, perhaps, legal rules do. For Torfing, 'social phenomena' can be described as 'discursive because their meaning depends upon a decentred system of contingently constructed rules and differences'.[98] Therefore, 'the accounts of norm origins in most studies stress human agency, indeterminacy, chance occurrences, and favourable events, using process tracing or genealogy as a method'.[99] Discourse, in this sense, is not a passive concept. As Stillar put it:

> Discourse is "action": It does things for social agents in the real contexts of their living. No discourse takes place outside the situated, embodied experiences and interest of the participants involved in an exchange. Discourse is an integral part of the complex goings-on that make up social life.[100]

In this context, critical constructivists assess institutions (whether manifested in a purely social sense or in terms of a material structure within which norms emerge) in terms of demonstrating that: 'even our most enduring institutions are based on collective understandings; that they are reified structures that were once upon a time conceived *ex nihilo* by human consciousness; and that these understandings were subsequently diffused and consolidated until they were taken-for-granted'.[101] By so doing, emphasis is placed on the critical role of human agency in constructing profound discourses that impact upon institutional and broader societal environments. It is this suggestion that both distinguishes even critical SC approaches from a 'pure' poststructuralist one in that discourse is not conceived of in a purely structural sense in which individuals are simply cognitive recipients of prevailing norms, with the relationship instead being a dialectical one between structure/culture and agent.[102] Instead, critically assessing individuals (or 'norm

[98] Torfing, 'Discourse Theory', p. 8.
[99] Finemore and Sikkink, 'International Norm Dynamics', 896.
[100] Glenn Stillar, *Analyzing Everyday Texts: Discourse, Rhetoric and Social Perspectives* (California, Sage, 1998), p. 5.
[101] Adler, 'Seizing the Middle Ground', 322.
[102] Finnemore, 'Are Legal Norms', 700.

entrepreneurs') is seen to be at the heart of discourse creation.[103] As Finnemore and Sikkink state:

> Norm entrepreneurs are critical for norm emergence because they call attention to issues or even "create" issues by using language that names, interprets, and dramatizes them. Social movement theorists refer to this reinterpretation or renaming process as "framing." The construction of cognitive frames is an essential component of norm entrepreneurs' political strategies, since, when they are successful the new frames resonate with broader public understandings and are adopted as new ways of talking about and understanding issues.[104]

This concept has a number of different aspects to it that will be utilized in the substantive analysis that follows. For instance, emphasis is placed by Finnemore on how language is framed such that particular norms 'resonate' widely. The fundamental point being made by Finnemore is that there is considerable normative judgment exercised by individuals when attempting to construct a discourse – hence the use of the word 'entrepreneurs'. As she contends: 'Norms do not appear out of thin air; they are actively built by agents having strong notions about appropriate or desirable behaviour in their community'.[105] Equally, emphasis is also placed on the skill of the individual in choosing particular language in particular contexts that becomes intersubjective. Such skilled individuals, in addition to being termed entrepreneurs, have also been described as 'meaning managers' or 'meaning architects'.[106] For instance, in Chapter 4, space has been devoted to examining the famous statement 'civis europeus sum' made by AG Jacobs in *Konstantinidis*.[107] In addition, such individuals can be seen to be part of a *process* of embedding discourses. Finnemore and Sikkink outline two phases of this process. In the first phase – where the norm emerges: 'the characteristic mechanism … is persuasion by norm entrepreneurs. Norm entrepreneurs attempt to convince a critical mass of states [here people] to embrace new norms'.[108] Furthermore, the second stage constitutes a move beyond the instrumental art of persuasion and focusses more on the skill of repetition and subtle changes within the already established norm: what has been termed 'dynamic imitation'.[109] Finally,

[103] Ibid.
[104] Finnemore and Sikkink, 'International Norm Dynamics', 897.
[105] Ibid., 896.
[106] Lawrence Lessig, in Ibid., 897.
[107] See Section 4.4.
[108] Finnemore and Sikkink, 'International Norm Dynamics', 895.
[109] Ibid.

emphasizing the fundamental role that individuals play in the construction of discourse has an equally critical edge to it. By placing the individual at the heart of social construction, so-called taken-for-granted concepts can be traced back to their inherently contingent and therefore contestable origins. Exemplary of this notion was the underlying point made by Wendt in *Social Theory of International Politics*. The book itself (and the related article) constituted a watershed moment in International Relations because of its trenchant critique of neorealist theory's attempt to 'present' itself as an objective systemic method designed to simply reflect the world 'as it is' – a world (at the time) seemingly only prevented from destroying itself by the mutual (and self-interested) assurance of destruction that would follow should a nuclear weapon be launched.[110] For Wendt, such theorists were not value-neutral and, instead, were constructing the reality that they were merely purporting to describe; in the process perpetuating a climate of misery and fear on a global scale.[111] Instead, for Wendt 'Anarchy is What States Make of It', arguing that such behaviour is 'a self-fulfilling prophecy'.[112] Thus, one final aspect of the particular methodological approach undertaken in this book is to stress the fundamental role of agency in discourse construction (thereby examining not only what has been uttered but who has uttered it) and this method at times, then, critically examines the inherently contingent subjectivity that is involved in their creation.

The Methodological 'Toolkit' to Be Adopted in This Book

In addition to the particular standpoint within SC theory that has been adopted in this book, specific practical aspects of its methodological scope have been developed and tailored for assessing the free movement case law. Such a methodological tailoring is considered to be fundamentally necessary in adapting discourse theory to practical empirical work. As Torfing maintains:

> Discourse theory aims to describe, understand, and explain how and why particular discursive formations were constructed, stabilized, and transformed. In order to reveal the necessary and sufficient conditions for discourse to be shaped and reshaped in a particular way, discourse theory employs a

110 Wendt, *Social Theory*, p. 75.
111 Ibid.
112 Wendt, 'Anarchy', 410.

contextualized conceptual tool kit that includes important concepts like dislocation, hegemony, social antagonism etc.[113]

The particular 'toolkit' to be adopted in this book has several aspects to it. First, as has already been outlined, the particular stance taken on the notion of discourse is structural, in part. As Waever put it: 'Discourse analysis looks for structures of meaning. "Things" do not have meaning in and of themselves, they only become meaningful in discourse'.[114] In this book, attempts will be made to assess language in terms of examining the point at which it becomes structural or, as has already been stated, a series of statements with a 'corpus' to it.[115] By so doing it is possible to identify various different aspects – or 'nodal points' – of pervasive discourses within the text of Court judgments.[116] Second, attempts will be made to examine the types of language used and emphasis placed by particular 'meaning architects' in order to embed particular discourses within the institutional environment of the Court. As Finnemore and Sikkink suggest:

> The meanings of any particular norm and the linkages between existing norms and emergent norms are often not obvious and must be actively constructed by proponents of new norms. Activists work hard to frame their issues in ways that make persuasive connections between existing norms and emergent norms.[117]

Thus, one aspect of intelligent discourse construction relates to the way in which a new discourse can be developed through being continually associated with pre-existing and pervasive norms that had existed for many years. This is particularly pertinent to attempts to derive contemporary meaning for Union Citizenship from early free movement of persons case law. For example, Chapter 3 examines the nature of equal treatment in terms of it constituting a self-contained discourse but also examines the 'discourse of equal treatment' in relation to the later development of Union citizenship. Likewise, Chapter 2 examines the manner in which the non-economically active are both legally and discursively outlined by the Court in order to make fundamental linkages with the later citizenship cases in the post-'*Sala* revolution'.[118] In addition to linkages made both within and between discourses,

[113] Torfing, 'Discourse Theory', p. 19.
[114] Waever, 'Discursive Approaches', p. 198.
[115] Ibid.
[116] See n. 70.
[117] Finnemore and Sikkink, 'International Norm Dynamics', 908.
[118] Jacqueson, 'Union Citizenship', 264.

attempts will be made to examine the types of words used and other rhetorical strategies which tend to emphasise the importance of particular concepts within the text. For instance, Stillar maintains that it is important to examine the 'devices that are used to relate parts of one sentence to parts of another across spans of text'.[119] Indeed, Torfing suggests that this is part of a practical application of discourse theory:

> At a more concrete level, discourse can be analysed as an ensemble of cognitive schemes, conceptual articulations, rhetorical strategies, pictures and images, symbolic actions (rituals), and structures (architectures), enunciative modalities, and narrative flows and rhythms. All these things should be analysed both in terms of their ability to shape and reshape meaning.[120]

Thus, in a number of chapters, attempts will be made to examine not only what has been uttered in particular judgments but also where within the physical structure/appearance of the judgments particular utterances appear. For instance, do particular utterances referenced in bold at the beginning or end of judgments have the consequence of emphasizing their importance within the text? In addition, how often are words that are used to emphasize the importance of a particular concept used in relation to specific discourses that will be outlined in the various chapters that follow? Particular attention will be devoted to the use of the word 'fundamental' in this regard. It should be noted that the importance of putting particular words or phrases under a discursive microscope is that the successful use of such 'devices' leads to textual 'cohesion' which is, in turn, structural and then discursive.[121] As Stillar continues: 'Cohesion gives text unity, enabling it to be interpreted as a whole, rather than as an unorganized collection of words'.[122] Likewise, Titscher, Meyer, Wodak and Vetter maintain: 'by means of lexical elements, sentence components and other linguistic elements, text structures are formed'.[123]

Third, and relatedly, repetition is considered to be fundamental to establishing discourse and therefore instances of repetition of particular phrases or concepts will be examined. Repetition is fundamental in the context of a holistic approach to norm diffusion as it emphasizes both structure and agency in so doing. As has already been outlined, a

[119] Stillar, 'Analyzing Everyday Texts', p. 49.
[120] Torfing, 'Discourse Theory', p. 14.
[121] Stillar, 'Analyzing Everyday Texts', p. 49.
[122] Ibid.
[123] Titscher and others, *Methods of Text*, p. 22.

core tenet of SC theory is that a concept is subjectively uttered but then becomes sufficiently pervasive to become intersubjective (i.e. discursive). Finnemore and Sikkink, as has been stated earlier, outline two phases in the process of norm creation, the first of which deals specifically with subjective utterances. It is the second phase, though, that is of most concern to SC theorists in that an assessment of how subjective utterance becomes pervasive simultaneously justifies the *a priori* use of the theory itself: it is part of its 'value-added'. An aspect of this 'second phase' has, as has been outlined earlier, been termed 'dynamic imitation'.[124] By using the phrase 'dynamic', emphasis is then placed upon the instrumental use of repetition by well-placed individuals in order to consolidate subjective utterances such that they can have the potential to become discursive. In addition, repetition has a structural aspect to it in that it is also important to examine repetition that is made almost unthinkingly not by 'norm entrepreneurs' but by a number of less dynamic actors within the Court environment. For Risse in particular, 'the dispersal of cultural values works through mimetic imitation'.[125] It should be noted that such an approach is both quantitative and qualitative in its implications. It is quantitative in the sense that, at times in this book, space will be devoted to the sheer repetition of a particular phrase within a text. However, in addition to so doing, attempts will be made to examine the context in which particular repetitions are made and thus repetition is examined also in a qualitative sense. For example, in Chapter 4, attempts are made to examine every utterance of the word 'citizen' used in the English version of the early free movement cases. However, as will become apparent in the chapter, the repetition of the 'citizen' is examined in both a quantitative and qualitative sense, something which, as has already been outlined, is perfectly acceptable within SC theory.

Fourth, at times, attempts will be made to illustrate the development of a discourse through attempting various discursive 'snapshots' at particular times: what Powell terms a 'slice through the discursive nexus'.[126] This is also qualitative in the sense that attempts will be made to compare statements made within the text of Court judgments often many years apart in order to demonstrate the fundamental change of the context within which the Court operates over time. This discursive 'snapshot' concept also has an additional practical aspect to it

[124] Finnemore and Sikkink, 'Taking Stock', 895.
[125] Risse, 'Social Constructivism', p. 611.
[126] Kendall and Wickham, *Using Foucault's Methods*, p. 45.

in that the book itself is then limited to examining words on the page of court judgments as they appear, whilst acknowledging, implicitly, that there is life beyond the framing of a camera lens. In other words, what is not being denied is that various actors may or may not have an influence on the text of a report without being directly mentioned. Obvious examples of these are the référendaires within the cabinet of a particular judge or advocate general (AG). The views of these actors by necessity can only be credited to that of the particular judge or AG (whose role it is to ultimately write and be accountable for a particular opinion or judgment in any case). It may well be, for instance, that highly significant acts of subjective creation commenced with highly confidential discussions and reports within a particular cabinet or, indeed, over lunch at the Court's cafeteria. However, such discussions are by definition either confidential and/or un-reportable, and thereby unresearchable. Ultimately what matters are the words as they appear on the page of a particular judgment irrespective of their extra-textual background and it is in this context that the concept of a 'snapshot' provides a useful practical limitation to the substantive areas of law being examined.

Finally, aspects of this book will also focus on what can be termed 'failures and resistance'. In terms of failures, Finnemore and Sikkink acknowledge that 'many emergent norms fail to reach tipping point'.[127] In other words, some subjective utterances fail to become intersubjective or alternatively some early discourses lose resonance over time and remain essentially confined to linguistic history. It is important to still examine such 'failures' as they also demonstrate the instrumental contingency that is at the heart of discourse creation. In other words, an alternative 'reality' could perhaps have led to an entirely different outcome. Indeed, such an examination can be seen to be fundamentally in keeping with the essence of Foucault's method as aspects of Court judgments that are now considered to be 'irrelevant' may prove to be far from so in a discursive sense. Likewise, resistance to the emergence of a discourse equally demonstrates the role of agency and contingency. As Finnemore and Sikkink put it: 'People who dislike existing norms and rules . . . often band together and try to change them'.[128] In this respect, what will become apparent from the chapters that follow is that a number of protagonists within the Court environment (particularly the Member States) were overtly resistant to not only the radical

[127] Finnemore and Sikkink, 'International Norm Dynamics', 895.
[128] Finnemore and Sikkink, 'Taking Stock', 400.

development of legal principles within the Court but were also particularly attentive to and resistant towards the use of particular language or phrases. Nonetheless, resistance to a particular discursive development is still an important aspect of its development because: 'No discourse can be protected from contestation and contamination as their boundaries are continuously breached and redrawn'.[129] This dialectical process of contamination, contestation and recontestation is fundamental to analyzing discourse because by so doing, for instance, a discourse of EU Citizenship has developed in a specific context that can simply not be understood in a sense abstracted from its context and generically compared to other citizenship models. Conversely, resisting voices within the text of the Court's jurisprudence can, ironically, further validate and consolidate the creation of a discourse through simply uttering it, what could be termed being 'entrapped by one's own rhetoric'. Risse, for, instance outlines the concept of 'entrapment ... to denote that EU member states might comply with certain rules to which they have committed even if these norms contradict their preferences or current interests'.[130] For Risse, what is evident in an EU context is that certain initially resistant Member States become entrapped into uttering concepts that they would not ordinarily have agreed with because the entire context of the utterance has already been 'strategically framed' by other actors, particularly the Commission.[131] Thus, examining both discursive failure and discursive resistance forms part of the methodological 'toolkit' that will be adopted in this book.

[129] Torfing, 'Discourse Theory', p. 19.
[130] Risse and Wiener, 'The Social Construction', p. 196.
[131] Ibid.

Part I

Fissures in the Foundations of the Temple

1 Is a 'Worker' Really a Worker?

A Discursive Assessment of the Substantive Evolution of the Concept of the 'Community Worker'

1.1 Introduction

A fundamental tenet of Plender's contention that the 'incipient' citizen can be seen to have emerged from the early case law on free movement is that the 'worker' can be construed as the early prototype of the citizen. This ties in particularly with the linkages made between market citizenship and EU Citizenship.[1] The legal evolution of the 'worker' has arguably been the foundation stone of all free movement of persons law upon which the later temple of citizenship was built. This is particularly so as the concept of the 'worker' has been incorporated to include large parts of the law or, in the alternative, has been used as a counterpoint to either dovetail with or juxtapose against other aspects of free movement law (such as on establishment). Even in relation to the later legal creation of the Citizen, it would be impossible to imagine key cases on EU Citizenship had the earlier case law not existed (which will be examined in some detail in Chapter 5). This chapter outlines the way in which the 'worker' has been outlined in the early case law of the Court ultimately maintaining that the Community 'worker' is as much a discourse as a legal concept. Both contingency and agency are at the heart of the following analysis in that, as will be examined, the nature of the discourse of the 'worker' evolved over the course of thirty years of jurisprudence and did so on the basis of both initial subjective articulation and subsequent repetition. Initially, the Court needed to establish its own basis for being able to define the 'worker' in the first place, and, in this context, this chapter first examines the principle outlined in *Unger* (1969)

[1] See Section 5.2.4 for an outline of this concept.

that the 'worker' itself had a Community definition.[2] After so doing, what is evidenced from an examination of the case law are essentially two core phases in the evolution of the 'worker'. In the first phase, the Court constructed a progressive understanding of the Community worker and, crucially, did so in tandem with now repealed Regulation No. 3/58.[3] As will be a recurrent theme in this book, there is a dialectical or an iterative relationship between discourse within the case law and legislative evolution. However, what distinguishes the approach in this chapter from more conventional approaches to the 'worker' is its context-specific focus on Regulation No. 3/58 because, in addition to providing an important legal basis for the Court in its early case law on the 'worker', it is now a piece of legislation that is rarely referred to by 'commentators'.[4] What therefore may be considered to be irrelevant for legal approaches to the worker is now highly relevant from an SC perspective.[5] In this first phase, a very specific Community understanding of the 'worker' evolved, placing particular emphasis on the broadness of categories of individuals that 'counted' as 'workers' for the purposes of Community law. It will then be maintained that whilst core aspects of this doctrine remained in the 'second phase' of the evolution of the discourse of the 'worker', the 1982 case *Levin* (in tandem with *Lawrie-Blum* in 1986) fundamentally changed the linguistic emphasis of the discourse of the worker.[6] It will then be concluded that it was this

[2] Case 75/63, *Mrs M. K. H. Hoekstra (née Unger)* v. *Bestuur der Bedrijfsvereniging voor Detailhandel en Ambachten (Administration of the Industrial Board for Retail Trades and Businesses)* [1964] ECR 177.

[3] Council Regulation No. 3/58 of 16 December 1958 concerning social security for migrant workers [1958] OJ 30/561.

[4] With a few notable exceptions as will be outlined, see subsequently (Sections 1.3.4 and Section 1.3.7).

[5] It should also be noted at this point that because this chapter (and indeed this book in general) is intended to outline the discursive evolution of particular concepts in (then) Community law, it is not intended to devote time to outline the case law on the 'worker' from a conventional legal perspective as such commentary is prolific and the chapter would then follow a well-trodden path. See, in particular, Dennis Martin and Elspeth Guild, *Free Movement of Persons in the European Union* (London: Butterworths, 1996); Robin White, *Workers, Establishment and Services in the European Union* (Oxford: Oxford University Press, 2004); John Handoll, *Free Movement of Persons in the EU* (Chichester: John Wiley, 1995); Catherine Barnard, *The Substantive Law of the EU: The Four Freedoms* (Oxford: Oxford University Press, 2010); Mark Bell, *Anti-Discrimination Law and the European Union* (Oxford: Oxford University Press, 2002); Nicholas Green, Trevor Hartley and John Usher, *The Legal Foundations of the Single Market* (Oxford: Oxford University Press, 1991); Freidl Weiss and Frank Wooldridge, *Free Movement of Persons within the European Community* (The Hague: Kluwer Law International, 2002).

[6] Case 53/81, *D. M. Levin* v. *Staatssecretaris van Justitie* [1982] ECR 1035; Case 66/85, *Deborah Lawrie-Blum* v. *Land Baden-Württemberg* [1986] ECR 2121.

change of emphasis that led to a crystallized, deeply embedded and context-specific discourse of the worker. This arguably constitutes the first of many fissures in citizenship, particularly seen from the perspective of the hidden constituency of static or immobile citizens.

1.2 Power and Language: Who Defines? The Need for the 'Community Worker'

From the outset a definition of the Community worker – the 'worker' – emerged that differs considerably from how the worker is conventionally understood. The first worker's case, *Unger* (1964), set the tone for the next thirty years of development. One of the early juridico-political 'battles' the Court had was in relation to who defined words in the Community – namely, the Member State courts or the Court itself? If it was the former that had the power to define a word, then it is left to the whims of individual Member States' legal processes and would lead to a complete lack of legal uniformity.[7] Alternatively, if it is the Court that has the jurisdiction to define (and as a consequence is considered to have the parallel discursive authority to make such a definition), in this case, the worker, then the Court is given the power (one that is accepted by the Member States and their referring courts) to construct a definition that can be applied uniformly throughout the Community and, more crucially, given the authority to add legal content to the definition of the worker that goes beyond the simple 'ordinary' definition of the worker. Ultimately, this battle was won by the Court (and authority taken by it) in *Unger* when it established that the worker has a 'Community meaning' and that 'Articles 48 to 51 of the Treaty, by the very fact of establishing freedom of movement for "workers," have given [the] Community scope to [define] this term'.[8] Furthermore, the

[7] *Unger*, para. 1. See also *Levin*, para. 11; Federico Mancini, 'The Free Movement of Workers in the Case-Law of the European Court of Justice', in Deidre Curtin and David O'Keefe (eds.), *Constitutional Adjudication in European Community and National Law: Essays for the Hon. Mr Justice TF O'Higgins* (Dublin: Butterworths, 1992), p. 69; A. Pieter Van Der Mei, *Free Movement of Persons within the European Community: Cross-Border Access to Public Benefit* (Oxford: Hart, 2003), p. 35; Charlotte O'Brien, 'Social Blind Spots and Monocular Policy Making: The ECJ's Migrant Worker Model' (2009) 46(4) *Common Market Law Review*, 1107–1141 at 1115; Siofra O'Leary, *The Evolving Concept of Community Citizenship* (The Hague: Kluwer Law International, 1996), p. 80.

[8] *Unger*, pp. 184–185. 'Community meaning' is repeated several times within the text of the Court judgement (the first page (177), para. 1 of the judgement (184 & 185), para. 2 of the judgement (185) and the concluding summary in bold (187; para. 1). The use of the Treaty was a cleverly constructed and subtle euphemism for the Court allowing itself

question posed by the referring court was 'whether the concept of a "wage-earner or assimilated worker" … is defined by the legislation of each Member State or by Community law as having a supranational meaning'.[9] The referring court therefore sees having a 'Community meaning' as being synonymous with having a 'supranational' one. The importance of such a synonym should not be underestimated. If the referring court is correct in equating Community law with having a 'supranational' existence, then it is truly *sui generis* – a unique entity being neither solely a matter of domestic law nor 'another' *inter*-national Treaty merely governing relations between nation-states; something that is perhaps taken for granted or 'common sense' today but would certainly have been a radical notion at that time.[10]

Moreover, having established that the 'worker' has a Community meaning, the Court in *Unger* then uses a typical rhetorical discursive device to establish its importance[11] when it maintains:

> The establishment of as complete a freedom of movement for workers as possible, which thus forms part of the 'foundations' of the Community, therefore constitutes the principal objective of Article 51 [of the Treaty] and thereby conditions the interpretation of the regulations adopted in implementation of that Article.[12]

It is the use of the word 'conditions' that is particularly important in that, as will be outlined in Chapter 3, a continual practice of the Court is to use key 'welding' phrases in order to establish the importance of particular concepts, such as the 'worker'.[13] This was an opportunity to reinforce in the minds of all parties the fact that this *sui generis* legal entity was in the process of creating distinct and powerful legal concepts, which will then entirely change the legal landscape within

(being, in effect, the Community) the power (or scope) to define the Treaty). Mancini (writing extrajudicially) described this as the Court establishing a 'hermeneutic monopoly' for itself. Mancini, 'Free Movement', p. 68.

9 *Unger*, p. 179.

10 See, for instance, Barrington, on the important role the Court played in ensuring that the (then) EEC evolved into a *sui generis* entity. Donal Barrington, 'The Emergence of a Constitutional Court', in James O'Reilly (ed.), *Human Rights and Constitutional Law: Essays in Honour of Brian Walsh* (Dublin: Round Hall Press, 1992), p. 251.

11 See 'Introduction' for an outline of the importance of rhetorical devices in the context of SC theory.

12 *Unger*, para. 1.

13 See Section 3.6 for a detailed discussion of the concept of 'welding' and see 'Introduction' for an outline of the inherently contingent nature of the social construction of discourse.

Europe more generally. Putting it differently, what the Court was in effect suggesting was that it was now creating one of many supranational concepts, that it can normatively justify this by suggesting that it was a logical corollary of the aim of free movement and that this aim 'conditions' everything else. Equally, it is 'foundational'. The Court is, to a certain extent, masking the subjectivity of its own creation by suggesting that the supranational concept of a Community worker was part of the Community's foundations as if it was there all along. If that was genuinely the case, then it would beg the question as to why, in *Unger*, the German government argued to the contrary that a worker should be defined by the law of individual Member States.[14] The Court doing what it did in *Unger* was foundational in that, as has already been outlined, it was fundamentally necessary for it to define key concepts such as the worker otherwise the entire Community project would perhaps have taken a different (and more intergovernmental) direction if definitions were left solely to different Member States in accordance with provisions of either domestic law or, worse still, policy decisions of national governments.[15]

1.3 The Early Discourse of the Worker: From *Unger* to *Levin*

1.3.1 *A Preliminary Point*

How the 'worker' was described roughly follows a pattern up until *Levin* (1982), after which a clearly solidified discourse of the worker emerged and was persistently consolidated by the Court. There are perhaps two points that the initial pre-*Levin* depiction of the worker and the post-*Levin* worker have in common. First, a very specific definition of the

[14] *Unger*, pp. 181–182. Indeed, Mancini alludes to the fact that the Court's ruling in *Unger* 'provoked harsh criticism in political circles', not least from the former French Prime Minister, Michel Debré, who claimed that the Court was 'suffering from "morbid megalomania"'. Mancini, 'Free Movement', p. 68.

[15] See Sections 1.5.1 and 2.6. Indeed, it should also be noted that this early seizing of jurisdiction by the Court has attracted contemporary academic criticism on the grounds of democratic deficit. Shaw, for instance, states that the fact that 'authoritative interpretation and application' of the treaties is 'handed over' to the CJEU 'has the effect of over-emphasising the role of the judiciary, both at the supranational and national level' and that since the Court is not elected, this 'unnecessarily subverts the role of elected institutions' and democracy'. Shaw, 'EU Citizenship: Still a Fundamental Status', p. 7. See also Pedro Caro de Sousa, *The European Fundamental Freedoms: A Contextual Approach* (Oxford: Oxford University Press, 2015).

worker emerged – a 'worker' that in a Community context was inter-subjectively understood – that differed considerably from the manner in which a worker was conventionally understood. It is worth bearing in mind *a priori* the worker's 'ordinary' or obvious meaning as conventionally understood: namely 'a person who works' especially a 'manual or industrial employee'.[16] From the outset it was made clear that the Community worker was a qualitatively different concept from the ordinary definition of the worker (indeed it is a 'concept' more than a simple word).[17] There are several different aspects to this qualitatively different understanding that were legislatively enshrined prior to a specific discourse of the 'worker' emerging in the Court's jurisprudence. For instance, pensioners and widows/widowers of workers and/or pensioners can also be seen to be part of the broader understanding of a 'worker' that emerged.[18] Likewise, one rare occasion in which the Community definition (in the form of a derogation) is narrower than its ordinary definition is in relation to employment in the public service.[19] Even a civil servant at the heart of central government is still a worker; however, such civil servants clearly do not count in terms of the Community worker.[20] Finally, by definition, a Community worker

[16] Robert Burchfield (ed.), *The Oxford English Dictionary* (Oxford: Clarendon, 1994), p. 1263.

[17] *Unger*, p. 179.

[18] This is because, in part, (ex) Article 48(d) of the Treaty makes provision for workers remaining on a territory after ceasing employment (albeit whilst needing to fulfil certain conditions as contained within Council Directive 1251/70/EEC). This right to free movement was then explicitly extended to family members and dependents by virtue of Article 11 of Regulation No. 15/61 (repealed by (Part 1 of) Council Regulation No. 1612/68/EEC. Council Regulation No. 3/58 EEC (subsequently repealed by Council Regulation No. 1408/71/EEC) then made specific provision for entitlements to social security benefits for surviving spouses (Article 2 (1) (c), (d) and, in particular, Article 4 (1) makes provision for assimilated workers and (2) extends such an entitlement to social security benefits to surviving spouses). See also commentary on the position of retired persons in Greve.

Treaty establishing the European Community [2002] OJ C325/1 (EC Treaty), p. 51; Council Directive 1251/70/EEC; Regulation No. 15/61; Council Regulation No. 1612/68/EEC of 15 October 1968 on free movement of workers within the Community [1968] OJ L257/2; Council Regulation No. 3/58 EEC; Council Regulation No. 1408/71/EEC of 14 June 1971 on the application of social security schemes to employed persons and their families moving within the Community [1971] OJ L149/2; Bent Greve, 'Economics and Social Security in Europe', in Danny Pieters (ed.), *Social Security in Europe: Miscellanea of the Erasmus-programme Social Security in the EC* (Brussels: Bruylant, 1991), pp. 191–216 at pp. 191–199.

[19] By virtue of (ex) Article 48(4) of the EC Treaty.

[20] Case 149/79, *Commission of the European Communities* v. *Kingdom of Belgium* [1980] ECR 3881, p. 3900, para. 11. In other words, this is the logical corollary of (a) necessitating 'direct or indirect participation in the exercises of powers . . . designed to safeguard the general

needs to move from one Member State to another: it is this basic tenet that marks out the Community worker as distinct.[21] Thus, from the outset a very specific definition of what a 'worker' meant in a Community context was created by virtue of the Treaty and subsequent secondary legislation. Second, this equally constituted a context-specific discourse as it is in part a series of collective assumptions and associations that combine to form a unified (though ever-changing whole).[22] Putting it differently, take the basic understanding of a Community worker as it became defined over decades to any other part of the world and it simply would not be understood as meaning the same concept as a worker in its ordinary definition. Perhaps, though, the problem in a contemporary Brexit context with this early definition is that it may not have been understood within the then Community by the vast majority of then Community nationals, let alone any other part of the world.

1.3.2 *The Pre-*Levin *Discourse Itself: To be 'Engaged in Economic Processes' and the Principle of Assimilation*

The pre-*Levin* discourse of the worker was subjectively created, to a certain extent, in *Unger* and set the tone for jurisprudential development over the next thirty years as well as provided its crucial litmus test. Advocate General (AG) Lagrange states in the case that in order to count as a 'worker', an individual had to be 'actively concerned in the economic processes'.[23] This rather loose definition at least provides a limit to how the 'worker' can be defined; namely the individual has to be ultimately construed as an economic contributor in some form.

interests of the State' and (b) requiring 'a special relationship of allegiance to the State' as the number of public sector jobs that could satisfy such a test in substance is rather limited. See also Derrick Wyatt, 'Article 48(4) EEC: Scope of the Public Service Proviso' (1981) 6(6) *European Law Review*, 459–463.

21 Indeed, ironically, it is this basic tenet that also became the source of so much controversy in the later free movement cases and then citizenship cases in terms of attempts by litigants to reverse the 'wholly internal situations' rule. See (Section 4.3.5, 195–196, esp. n. 120) for further analysis of this concept.

22 See 'Introduction' for an outline of the nature of discourse.

23 *Unger*, pp. 189–190. The applicant, a Dutch national living in the Netherlands, had paid into a compulsory sickness insurance scheme, ceased employment, and then continued paying into the scheme on a voluntary basis. She then fell ill whilst staying with her parents in Germany, received medical attention, attempted to claim a reimbursement of her medical expenses upon her return to the Netherlands, and was refused on the grounds that she was not a worker.

However, the tone was also set when AG Lagrange continues by maintaining that individuals who are protected by the Treaty are those:

> Whose working relationship, although these persons may not carry on an activity within the framework of a contractual wage-earning relationship, is *expressly* assimilated to the position of a wage-earner *by means of legislative interpretation by national legislation* of the Member State concerned, *with a view to applying* one or more social insurance laws.[24]

From the outset, then, a qualitatively different understanding of what is meant by a 'worker' was outlined by the Court and by virtue of both Regulation No. 3/58 and the soon-to-emerge jurisprudence on the worker, in certain limited circumstances, non-workers can be treated as if they were workers. Such circumstances were, at least initially, legislatively limited to those who are 'expressly assimilated' to being a worker by virtue of national legislation.[25] In *De Cicco*, the limitations of such a process of assimilation arose in relation to craftsmen.[26] For the Sozialgericht:

> This category of small independent contractors has, according to general European legal theory, a position analogous to that of workers, is exposed to essentially the same risks as the latter, and may be assimilated to them in the field of social security, in spite of its economic and social characteristics.[27]

This is, then, an example of 'theory' becoming reality in that what the Sozialgericht is attempting to do is to linguistically make craftsmen into 'workers' as understood in the broader context of (then) Community law. The concept of assimilation is both fundamental and controversial, as well as being rather ingenious. It is fundamental because it was a building block upon which a novel concept of the 'worker' was developed, in which ultimately an assimilated worker was simply conflated with the 'worker' and became part of a much broader definition and underlying integrative project.[28] It is also ingenious in that it gives the

[24] Ibid.

[25] Article 4(1) of Regulation No. 3/58. See also commentary on this in Philippa Watson, *Social Security Law of the European Communities* (London: Mansell Publications, 1980), pp. 58–63.

[26] Case 19/68, *Giovanni de Cicco* v. *Landesversicherungsanstalt Schwaben.* [1968] ECR 473.

[27] *De Cicco*, p. 484 (cited by AG Gand).

[28] See in particular Derrick Wyatt, 'The Social Security Rights of Migrant Workers and their Families' (1977) 14(4) Common Market Law Review, 411–433 at 416. Whilst the literature on the repealed Regulation No. 3/58 is not prolific because it was replaced by Regulation No. 1408/71, for Wyatt there was a clear relationship between how the 'worker' was understood in the former Regulation, and how it later evolved in the case

impression that the Member States themselves, not the Court, are making the implicit decision to extend the categories of those who count as 'workers' by virtue of their own internal legislation.

However, this impression of Member State empowerment is rather misleading. As far as the Court was concerned, in *Janssen*, on the question as to how 'assimilated' within the meaning of Article 4 of the Regulation No. 3/58 was to be interpreted, it 'follows a general tendency of the social law of Member States to extend the benefits of social security in favour of new categories of persons by reason of identical risks'.[29] The court continues:

> 7 However, the exact measure of this assimilation can only be determined in terms of the national legislations to which Regulation No 3 refers.
>
> 8 Such an assimilation takes place on every occasion on which, as the result of the effect of national legislation, the provisions of a general scheme of social security are extended to a category of persons other than the wage-earners referred to by the said Regulation, whatever may be the forms or methods employed by the national legislature.[30]

This form of reasoning by the Court is far from immune from criticism.[31] It firstly makes a sweeping statement of a 'general tendency' of the social law of all of the Member States to assimilate various categories of individuals to the position of worker without appearing to back such a claim up with any empirical studies on the matter.[32] It then appears to

law on the latter. Regulation No. 3/58, in Wyatt's view, effectively extended the remit of (ex) Article 48 of Treaty by virtue of Article 4(1) of the Regulation. See also Jean-Claude Séché, 'The Revision of Regulations Nos. 3 and 4 (Social Security of Migrant Workers) in the Light of their Interpretation by the Court of Justice' (1969) 6(2) *Common Market Law Review*, 170–192.

29 Case 23/71, *Michel Janssen* v. *Landsbond der christelijke mutualiteiten* [1971] ECR 859, p. 864, para. 6.

30 Ibid., p. 864, 866. The applicant was a Belgian national who worked as 'helper' on his father's farm in Belgium after having previously worked on a farm in France. After his wife became ill, the local authorities refused to reimburse him for her treatment on the grounds that (a) he had not resided in Belgium for six months and (b) could not be classified as a 'worker' as in Belgium 'helpers' were explicitly determined to be self-employed. See also Gabriel Perl, 'Règlement no 3 du Conseil de la C.E.E. relatif à la sécurité sociale des travailleurs migrants' (1972) *Revue belge de sécurité sociale*, 591–595.

31 As Paskalia maintains, there were significant consequences to the Court's approach here as 'the emphasis placed from the beginning on the criterion of social security rather than the criterion of paid employment [meant that] . . . the nature of the economic activity, i.e. whether it is paid employment or any other professional activity . . . lost its relevance'. Vicki Paskalia, *Free Movement, Social Security and Gender in the EU* (Oxford: Hart, 2007), pp. 140–141.

32 *Janssen*, p. 864.

pay deference to national legislation on the matter (in paragraph 7), but yet paragraph 8 appears to give ultimate power to the Court, once again, to define. It is not the exact wording – its 'forms and methods' – of the legislation that matters but its 'effect', and the ultimate determinant of such an 'effect' would be the Court.[33] This, then, gives the Court a great deal of power and it is also, therefore, equally controversial as the principle of assimilation had the potential to launch a discourse of the worker that became far more extensive than the Member States might have envisaged.[34] Illustrative of this point is *De Cicco* (1968), in that craftsmen are clearly not workers as ordinarily understood (there is no master/servant relationship nor is there remuneration in the form of a wage) and are, in reality, self-employed.[35] Indeed, for this reason, AG Gand in *De Cicco* was reticent to establish a broader Community-wide principle in the case because it would be 'going too far' to assimilate craftsmen to the position of worker because some Member States do not classify craftsmen as workers for the purposes of their social security legislation.[36] The Court, though, offers no such reservation in the case. Whilst acknowledging that there is still a dependence on national legislation in order for the principle of assimilation to apply, the Court ruled that craftsmen were 'to be considered assimilated to wage-earners' without offering any additional caveats.[37] The case clearly was legally significant as it established that a new category of individuals' occupations could be assimilated to the position of a worker. However, from a discursive perspective, irrespective of the legal mechanism used to incorporate such a grouping of Community nationals into the provisions of (ex) Regulation No. 3/58, a collective understanding of a context-specific Community 'worker' was emerging that was considerably more extensive than workers as conventionally understood.[38] Furthermore, the discursive aspects of the principle of assimilation were bolstered through repeated emphasis.[39] As AG Gand states (once again in *De Cicco*) 'we are thus led to a formula which more or

33 Ibid.

34 See Van Der Mei, *Free Movement*, pp. 22–28 (a general discussion of what the original conservative intentions of the Member States were for the free movement provisions of the Treaty).

35 And thereby entitled to protection under (ex) Article 52 of the EC Treaty in any case.

36 *De Cicco*, p. 485.

37 Ibid., p. 481.

38 See 'Introduction' for a discussion of the interrelationship between collective grouping and identification and discourse.

39 See 'Introduction' for an outline of the importance of repetition in the process of establishing a discourse.

less repeats and develops that which Mr Advocate-General Lagrange proposed in the case of [*Unger*]'.[40] Thus, even at this point a very powerful and now 'repeated formula' – with both legal and discursive implications – has been developed.

1.3.3 *A Non-worker as a 'Worker'? The Paradox of the Early Definition*

Thus far, the 'worker' can already be collectively understood as referring to something qualitatively different from conventional definitions. The 'worker' is either engaged in an economic process of some sort or is a pensioner or is 'assimilated' to the position of a worker by virtue of national legislation and is not employed in the public service. These are the key component parts of the discourse or, in other words, the collective set of assumptions that are made when the word is uttered or stated in a Community context.[41] The discourse then developed, and, in tandem with the principle of assimilation, came to be understood, in part and paradoxically, as involving those that do not work or cannot be defined as workers. It is paradoxical, clearly, for a 'worker' to be understood as one who is not actually employed but yet it became an increasingly prevalent understanding as to what the 'worker' meant. Once again, this trend was set in *Unger* and consolidated, repeated and developed in subsequent cases. Immediately after the above citation on being 'actively concerned in the economic processes'[42] AG Lagrange refers to the 'worker' as encompassing those who 'may not carry on an activity within the framework of a contractual wage-earning relationship' but who can become assimilated to the worker by virtue of national legislation.[43] This then leads to the Court in *Unger* making the rather extraordinary statement – seen from a linguistic perspective – that a '"worker" is not exclusively one who is currently employed'.[44] Likewise, what was at issue in *Murru* was whether 'the claimant's unemployment ... may be assimilated to a period of employment'.[45] Indeed, in *Pierik*, the Dutch social security

[40] *De Cicco*, p. 487.
[41] Ibid., paras. 16–17.
[42] See Section 1.3.2.
[43] *Unger*, p. 191.
[44] Ibid., p. 185, para. 2.
[45] Case 2/72, *Salvatore Murru* v. *Caisse régionale d'assurance maladie de Paris* [1972] ECR 333, p. 336 at para. 1, p. 334 and p. 337 (facts). The applicant was a migrant worker who had worked in both France and Italy, ceased employment, then resided in Italy for a year and then filed a claim for an invalidity pension in France. French law was prepared to assimilate his year of employment to that of employment in order to obtain the pension had he resided in France. However, in Italian law he would not have been able to apply the principle of assimilation to his circumstances. The Court ruled that the period of

body went one step further when it claimed that in order to define the 'concept of the "worker" ... the decisive factor ... is that the person concerned should be "insured," and it is immaterial whether or not he actually pursues an activity'.[46] This is quite an extraordinary claim and appears to contradict even *Unger* as by this interpretation an individual need not even be engaged in any kind of economic process; a claim though, that is highly indicative, in 1979, of a development in which the 'worker' has clearly now been understood conceptually differently from its standard definition.[47]

The facts of *Pierik* are highly illustrative of this in that the applicant was an incapacitated worker who wanted to go to another Member State for relatively controversial medical treatment (hydrotherapy) and was asking for her home state to fund the treatment.[48] With the exception of moving across a border, she was clearly not a worker. However, she was 'insured' under her home social security system. Equally, a case-specific understanding of the 'worker' was outlined that had an impact on the broader discourse of the 'worker' that eventually emerged from the jurisprudence of the Court. The Netherlands government maintains: 'one of the essential objectives of the EEC Treaty is to promote freedom of movement in particular for "active" workers'.[49] In addition, the Italian government then claims that 'any person ... [can]be regarded as a "worker" ... whether he is an active worker or a passive worker'.[50] There are three implications of this interplay between the two governments. First, that there is such a thing as a Community worker – the 'worker' – as a distinct concept.[51] Second, that a 'worker' can be either 'active' or 'passive'. Taking a conventional understanding of a worker, a passive worker appears to be a contradiction in terms.[52] Indeed, as has been cited earlier, seen from the perspective of the Dutch social security

assimilation should take place on the territory where he had most recently been employed (France), thereby entitling him to the benefit.

46 Case 182/78, *Bestuur van het Algemeen Ziekenfonds, Drenthe-Platteland, Zwolle*, v. *Mrs G. Pierik* [1979] ECR 1977, p. 1983. See subsequently for an outline of the facts of the case.

47 See, for example, 'the Community notion of "employed" stretches well beyond the group of typical full-time employees'. Paskalia, *Free Movement*, p. 157.

48 Case 182/78 *Bestuur van het Algemeen Ziekenfonds, Drenthe-Platteland, Zwolle*, v. *Mrs G. Pierik* [1979] ECR 1977, p. 827. Note the full summary of the facts is available in the first reference by the Dutch court on behalf of the applicant in 1977, whereas the material statements on the worker are made in the second reference in 1979.

49 *Pierik*, pp. 1986–1987.

50 Ibid.

51 Ibid.

52 Ibid.

body in *Pierik*, it seems to be irrelevant – 'it is immaterial' – as to whether a 'worker' actually works.[53] Third, there is then a further repetition of this specific distinction – between active and passive – by the Italian government and then twice by the Commission.[54] This clearly had a cognitive effect on the Court as it then uses the rather tautological phrase 'inactive pensioners' in paragraph 5 of its own judgment.[55] Therefore, at least within the case itself, a new phrase, the 'inactive worker' has emerged, following a pattern of repetition.

Moreover, indicative of the discursive aspects of the trend to classify, in effect, non-workers as 'workers' is the UK's reaction to it in *Pierik*. It argues that:

> The whole structure of Regulation 1408/71 is based upon the assumption that 'workers' and 'pensioners' are two separate categories of persons, even if some pensioners have formerly been, and in some case may again become, 'workers' in the narrower sense.[56]

The UK's attitude is very typical in both legal and discursive terms as it appears to be attentive not only to legal developments within the Court (and, as will be examined, is usually resistant to them) but also its use of language.[57] Legally, naturally, the UK was concerned with the development of the 'worker' to incorporate people that were not really workers.[58] Linguistically, though, it is submitted that the above citation is illustrative of both an acute awareness of the importance of language and a guarding against a casual conflation of different 'categories' to form a 'fuzzy' (and perhaps slightly legally incoherent) whole.[59] Discourse is, though (as has already been outlined in the Introduction), built up on a whole set of assumptions that are collectively understood, and the UK by stating the above is indicating a concern about such a development taking place. Nonetheless, as will later be outlined, such attempts at compartmentalization are bound to fail against a rising tide of discursive development in which several categories of individuals are intentionally conflated.[60]

[53] Ibid. See also Derrick Wyatt, 'Current Survey: Contrasting Cases on Non-Discrimination' (1981) 6(1) *European Law Review*, 42–51.
[54] *Pierik*, p. 1989.
[55] Ibid., p. 1993.
[56] Ibid., p. 1987.
[57] See Chapter 3 (n. 138) and Section 5.4.1 for an outline of the UK's approach to the EU.
[58] Ibid.
[59] See 'Introduction' for an analysis of the notion of conflation in the context of discourse creation.
[60] See Section 3.2.

1.3.4 A 'Worker' as Being 'Not Strictly' a Worker

Furthermore, the discourse of the worker developed to include what may appear to be contradictory but equally fundamental terminology, namely a repeated assertion that the 'worker' does not need to be a worker as 'strictly' construed. This was first articulated in *Singer*, where AG Gand refers to the applicant not being a 'migrant worker *stricto sensu*'.[61] It is this particular phrase that accumulated linguistic resonance but before its development is examined, it is worth pointing out that the facts of the case demonstrated a tenuous link to work as conventionally understood. Here the issue was not in actual fact work, but insurance,[62] in which a French company's employee crashed into a German national whilst simply being on holiday in France.[63] Seen from a narrow and strict perspective, there arose no issue of Community law and this was a point that the defendant made.[64] It was not denied that both parties to the crash worked. The defendant was a company, Maison Singer et Fils, its employee was clearly a worker and the German third party, Mr Gassner, worked in Germany as a miner.[65] However, what is also clear is that the third party was clearly not working when the accident occurred, nor had he ever moved borders to work.[66] As counsel for the defendant therefore submitted, on a strict interpretation of the regulation, Community law was seemingly irrelevant to the dispute.[67] The Court's response to this issue is telling in that not only did it allow the third party, Mr Gassner, to 'count' as a migrant worker but it also ruled that: 'It would not be in conformity with [the] spirit [of the Treaty] to limit the concept of "worker" to migrant workers *stricto sensu* or solely to workers required to move for the purpose of their employment'.[68] Thus, circumstances, not merely people – *ratione materiae* in addition to *personae* – which ordinarily have nothing to do with work, also allowed individuals to count as 'workers' for certain purposes. This then opened up the door for an additional category of individuals to derive rights on the basis of being migrant

[61] Case 44/65, *Hessische Knappschaft* v. *Maison Singer et fils* [1965] ECR 965, p. 977.
[62] A point also made in *Pierik*. See Section 1.3.3.
[63] *Singer*, p. 974 (summarized by AG Gand).
[64] Ibid., p. 968.
[65] Ibid., p. 974.
[66] Ibid.
[67] Ibid., p. 968.
[68] Ibid., p. 971.

workers; namely national workers (i.e. non-moving) who were merely on a holiday.[69] As the Court later states in *Entr'aide médicale*:

> Far from referring solely to migrant workers within the strict meaning of the term, the regulation is applicable to any wage-earner or assimilated worker who finds himself in one of the situations involving international elements as provided for in the said regulation.[70]

Even at this point, then, an understanding of the 'worker' had arisen appearing to suggest that the Court is more concerned with whether an individual has crossed a border than whether they could be classified as a worker for the purposes of their movement, or indeed at all. This point is then reiterated in *Frilli*[71] where AG Roemer maintains: 'the Court [in *Singer*] has expressly stated that this concept is not limited solely to migrant workers *stricto sensu* or solely to workers required to move for the purpose of their employment'.[72] Equally, the latinism *stricto sensu* is then used by AG Mayras in *Michel S.* in tandem with the concept of assimilation when he states: 'This principle of assimilation extends beyond working relationships "*stricto sensu*"'.[73] Furthermore, what is also noticeable is that the utterance of the phrase '*stricto sensu*' by AG Mayras is also done in tandem with several classic 'welding' phrases as will be outlined in the Chapter 3. In the paragraph prior to the above statement, AG Mayras refers to 'achieving complete equality of treatment of Community workers' and then immediately after the above sentence utters: 'Thus the equality of treatment required by Article 48 of the Treaty forms the very foundation of Regulation 1612/68'.[74] The 'worker' thus was associated with the 'principle of assimilation' and

[69] For a commentary of the incorporation of holiday makers in the concept of the 'worker', see Séché, 'Revision of Regulation', 174.

[70] Case 27/69, *Caisse de maladie des C. F. L. 'Entr'aide médicale' and Société nationale des chemins de fer luxembourgeois* v. *Compagnie belge d'assurances générales sur la vie et contre les accidents* [1969] ECR 405, p. 410, para. 3, p. 414. The case itself concerned a Luxembourger railway worker who was killed in a car crash in Belgium and the issues were similar to *Singer* in that what mattered was whether the deceased driver could be classified as a worker at the time.

[71] Case 1/72, *Rita Frilli* v. *Belgian State* [1972] ECR 457, p. 468. A case concerning a Italian pensioner denied a legislatively guaranteed income on the grounds of nationality.

[72] Ibid., p. 472.

[73] Case 76/72, *Michel S.* v. *Fonds national de reclassement social des handicapés* [1973] ECR 457, p. 466, p. 468. The applicant was the son of a migrant worker denied access to a disability fund on the grounds that his condition was diagnosed prior to his father moving to Belgium to work. See also Derrick Wyatt, 'The Scope of "Equal Treatment" under Articles 7 and 12 of Regulation 1612/68' (1975) 1(1) *European Law Review*, 62–63.

[74] Ibid.

the phrase '*stricto sensu*' in addition to being sandwiched between two classic 'welding' phrases.[75] Indeed, in addition to referring to equal treatment and 'foundations', the Community 'worker' is also very explicitly stated. Thus, further to the 'worker' being collectively understood as not being one '*stricto sensu*', what is also noticeable is how the phrase has been uttered in the context of terminology in relation to the principle of equal treatment, itself a core aspect of the later development towards citizenship.[76]

1.3.5 *The 'Worker' as 'Broadly' Construed*

Moreover, there is one key aspect of the pre-*Levin* discourse on the worker that is perhaps its defining characteristic, and that is the repeated reference to the concept of the 'worker' being a 'broad' or 'wide' one. AG Gand in *Bertholet* maintains that what has arisen is: 'a very wide definition which is obviously much wider than that of a migrant worker in the strict sense'.[77] Whether using the Latin *stricto sensu* or the English 'strict sense' what is immediately apparent is that the use of the word 'wide' is used in tandem with the 'worker' not being a worker in a strict sense. In addition, there is an implicit recognition of the epistemic community and cultural context in which the 'worker' emerges by using the word 'obvious'.[78] For those within this community it is simply 'obvious' that the 'worker' was not only qualitatively different from normal understandings of it but also that the stage was set for an extensive expansion of its definition, enabled, to a large extent, by the repeated emphasis on a 'wide' definition. The Court, in *De Cicco*, likewise refers to both wideness and a lack of strictness, where it states:

> [Regulation No 3/58] is based on a wide conception of the persons to whom it applies inasmuch as it subjects to the provisions of the regulation not only wage-earners within the strict sense of the word but in addition all those assimilated to such workers.[79]

[75] See Section 3.6 for a detailed discussion of the concept of 'welding'.

[76] See Section 3.1 for an expansion on this point.

[77] Case 31/64, *'De Sociale Voorzorg' Mutual Insurance Fund* v. *W. H. Bertholet*. [1965] ECR 81, p. 92, p. 90. The applicant in *Bertholet* crashed into a Belgian/Netherlands frontier worker in Belgium and the victim was seeking compensation. What was at issue in the case was whether the victim could be classified as a worker on the grounds that he resided and worked in the Netherlands but went through Belgium on his route to work.

[78] See 'Introduction' for an outline of the relationship between epistemic communities, culture and 'common sense'.

[79] *De Cicco*, p. 480.

Indeed, the principle of assimilation is also tied in with the other two concepts (i.e. 'wide' and 'strict sense'). Equally, what is noticeable is that the use of the phrases 'wide' or 'broad' can be seen to be discursive in its nature. In *Duffy*, AG Roemer maintains that: 'this body of case-law might in fact be said to favour the notion ... [of a] wide definition of the scope of Regulation No 3'.[80] He reiterates and expands this statement in *Janssen*, where he states:

> This is also the tenor of the judgment [in *De Cicco*] ... [where] the Court ... emphasised that the provisions of Regulation No 3 are based on a wide conception of the persons to whom they apply since they covered not only wage-earners in the narrower sense but, in addition, all those assimilated to such workers.[81]

At this point there has been no deviation from the regulation itself (it was early on in the jurisprudence of the Court) but what is evident is the perception of there being a 'body' of case law or 'tenor' constructing a very broad image of the 'worker' articulated in tandem with the principle of assimilation, and a non-strict interpretation of the concept of the 'worker as previously' outlined. From an SC perspective, what can be observed by such a statement by AG Roemer in *Duffy* is the point at which a core aspect of the discourse of the 'worker' has become intersubjective through continual linguistic emphasis (i.e. the notion of broadness creates both the underlying 'tenor' of an individual judgment (*De Cicco*) and has emerged out of a 'body' of case law.[82] Thus, 'broadness' can be seen at this point to be both a core aspect of the early pre-*Levin* understanding of the 'worker' and it can be defined as discursive in its nature.

Furthermore, this understanding of the' worker', having started initially in *Bertholet* in 1965 as an interpretation in the context of Regulation No. 3/58 then had a wider linguistic impact on other provisions of (then) European Economic Community (EEC) law. In *Entr'aide médicale*, AG Gand claims: 'The interpretation of Article 52 - which moreover does not employ the term "migrant worker" - results from the very wide notion which you have conceived of the scope *ratione personae* of Regulation No. 3'.[83] AG Gand's statement above was in effect arguing that such a broad definition of the

[80] Case 34/69, *Caisse d'assurance vieillesse des travailleurs salariés de Paris* v. *Jeanne Duffy* [1969] ECR 597, pp. 606–607, p. 601. A plurality of benefits case concerning the receipt by the applicant of a pension in Belgium in addition to a widow's pension in France.

[81] *Janssen*, p. 868.

[82] See 'Introduction' for an outline of the importance of emphasis in the context of discourse creation.

[83] *Entr'aide médicale*, p. 415.

worker in Regulation No. 3/58, as interpreted by the Court in its jurisprudence, has swept into the Treaty itself, even if its origins were elsewhere (the regulation). Equally, in *Frilli*, the Italian government claims that:

> Every specific provision of secondary Community law concerning the treatment to be accorded to nationals of the Member States within the Community ought to be based on Article 7 of the EEC Treaty. The prohibition against any discrimination based on nationality laid down by this article is a fundamental principle.[84]

The Italian government then concludes that:

> The fact that the guaranteed income is granted regardless of the existence of a state of employment is irrelevant. So also is the fact that in the present case the plaintiff is retired because in Community law a wide meaning should be given to the concept of the worker.[85]

This citation is significant for a number of different reasons. First, it is a Member State in effect contributing to the substantive discursive development of Community law.[86] Second, the principle of equal treatment is implicitly referred to by citing non-discrimination and (ex) Article 7 of the Treaty. Third, this once again concerns an individual who is not a worker but has retired. Fourth, this is then tied in with the 'wide meaning' of the 'worker'. Here the Italian government is referring to the Treaty as opposed to Regulation No. 3/58 and so is making the point that such 'broadness' can go above and beyond the regulation. Indeed, the overall focus of both citations appears to be less concerned with the issue of *bona fide* work and more with the principle of equal treatment. This, then, is an example of an agent playing a role in the perpetuation of a discourse in that this particular (re)articulation was made by the Italian government.[87] The influence of the Italian government can equally be seen in two subsequent cases. In *Marsman*, AG Roemer states: 'this is made even clearer if one adopts the view of the Italian Government that Article 48 of the Treaty must be *broadly* interpreted'.[88] Finally, the notion of 'broadness' played a critical role

[84] *Frilli*, p. 462.

[85] Ibid., p. 466.

[86] Italy had a particular interest in protecting migrant workers as it had a considerable diaspora working, in particular, in northern Europe. See Section 5.5.1 and end of Section 3.6.7 for specific analysis of this particular issue.

[87] See 'Introduction' for an elaboration of the role of agency in the construction of discourse.

[88] Case 44/72, *Pieter Marsman* v. *M. Rosskamp* [1972] ECR 1243, pp. 1250–1251 (emphasis added). A case concerning a Dutch frontier worker who worked in Germany and was

in the development of the 'worker' to such a point that it is barely recognizable from the original definition of the worker. In *Watson and Belmann*, AG Trabucchi maintains: 'The widest possible interpretation has, as we know, been placed on the prohibition of discrimination by the case-law of the Court, which has extended the principle to cover provisions and circumstances which are unconnected with the master and servant relationship'.[89] Thus, for AG Trabucchi, the cumulative effect of the emerging discourse of the 'worker' is inexorably linked to adopting a 'wide' interpretation of the principle of non-discrimination more generally.

Ultimately, this aspect of understanding the 'worker' became deeply embedded. In *Commission* v. *Italy (reduced rate mortgages)*, over a decade later (in 1987), AG Da Cruz Vilaça states:

> Let us not forget, too, that the EEC Treaty includes among the fundamental principles on which the Community is based the freedom of establishment, a fundamental freedom on a par with the free movement of persons and the freedom to provide services . . . Th[e] Court has held that Article 52 is 'one of the fundamental provisions of the Community'.[90]
>
> The court has interpreted those fundamental provisions and the requirements flowing from them broadly.[91]

Thus, by 1987 the notion of construing the 'worker' broadly (both within Regulation No. 3/58 and (ex) Article 48 of the Treaty) had been extended to all the free movement provisions of the Treaty.[92]

1.3.6 *The 'Other' of Broadness*

Finally, the broadness of the Community worker can be contrasted with its bipolar opposite, namely narrowness. AG Capotorti in *Walsh*, for instance, states: 'I would add that if one were to favour a narrower construction of the term "worker" by making that status subject to

not entitled to legislative protection on the grounds of disability as he was not a resident of Germany.

89 Case 118/75, *Lynne Watson and Alessandro Belmann* [1976] ECR 1185, p. 1208, p. 1203. A case concerning a mandatory obligation in Italy to report the presence of a foreigner on Italian soil within three days of arriving. See also Derrick Wyatt, 'Alien's Duty to Notify National Authorities of His Presence' (1976) 1(6) *European Law Review*, 556–560.

90 Referring to Case 79/85, *D. H. M. Segers* v. *Bestuur van de Bedrijfsvereniging voor Bank- en Verzekeringswezen, Groothandel en Vrije Beroepen* [1986] ECR 2375, p. 2387, para. 12.

91 Case 63/86, *Commission of the European Communities* v. *Italian Republic* [1988] ECR 29, p. 44, paras. 54–55 (*Commission v. Italy (reduced rate mortgages)*).

92 See Van Der Mei, *Free Movement*, pp. 10–13 (for a commentary on the broadness in which the Court has construed the free movement provisions of the Treaty more generally).

the condition that the person be still paying compulsory contributions, Regulation 1408/71 could not apply to pensioners or the unemployed'.[93] Narrowness, then, is the 'other' to a broad understanding of 'worker'.[94] The Court in the case, likewise, reinforces the normative justification for the adoption of 'broadness' by stating that it would be 'contrary to the spirit' of the regulation 'to give a restrictive interpretation to the definition of the term "worker"' to define 'certain categories of people' who are not in actual fact workers as 'workers'.[95] Moreover, this contrast is equally applicable in relation to the Treaty articles themselves. As AG Lenz outlines in *Mutsch*: 'The Court has never interpreted [Article 48] of the Treaty narrowly. It has even given a restrictive interpretation to the exception contained in Article 48 (4)'.[96] What is not being denied here is that there is a clear legal aspect to the emergence of the Community worker; collectively the Court has tended to adopt a broad interpretative approach to provisions of the Treaty, Regulation No. 3/58 and subsequent pieces of secondary legislation especially in relation to protecting individual rights; this is much commented upon.[97] However, it is maintained that there is also a clear discursive aspect to it. Immediately preceding the above citation in *Mutsch,* AG Lenz refers to freedom of movement of workers as 'one of the foundations of the Community' and as 'one of the fundamental liberties of the system'.[98] As will be concluded in this book, all of these concepts combine ultimately to form a coherent and clearly understood collective set of assumptions which delineated the exact contours of a Community-specific understanding of Citizenship.

[93] Case 143/79, *Margaret Walsh* v. *National Insurance Officer* [1980] ECR 1639, p. 1660, p. 1649. The case itself concerned a UK national who, having worked in both the UK and Ireland, gave birth in Ireland, then returning to the UK and being subsequently denied maternity benefit on the grounds that she was not a 'worker' for the purposes of Regulation No. 1408/71.

[94] On 'othering' see 'Introduction'.

[95] *Walsh*, p. 1652.

[96] Case 137/84 *Criminal proceedings against Robert Heinrich Maria Mutsch* [1985] ECR 2681, pp. 2685–2686, p. 2683. The applicant, a Luxemburg national, was being prosecuted in a German speaking municipality within Belgium – Saint Vith – and was refused permission for his trial to be conducted in his mother tongue on the grounds that he was not a Belgian national. See further Anthony Arnull, 'Social Advantages and the Language Barrier' (1985) 10(5) *European Law Review*, 346–348.

[97] See, for example, Paskalia, *Free Movement*, pp. 158–159; White, *Workers, Establishment and Services*, pp. 32–33; Massimo Condinanzi, Allessandra Lang and Bruno Nascimbene, *Citizenship of the Union and Freedom of Movement of Persons* (Leiden: Brill, 2008), pp. 68–71. In the latter, Condinanzi, Lang and Nascimbene claim this to be an 'eagerness to expand the categories of beneficiaries of the right to free movement'.

[98] *Mutsch*, pp. 2685–2686.

Furthermore, as has been outlined in the Introduction, 'othering' is (often) a fundamental (albeit negative) aspect of establishing a discourse in that the contrast between a normatively justifiable concept (here the 'worker' as broadly construed) and one that, by contrast, appears reprehensible (to construe narrowly legislative provisions on the 'worker') further establishes and solidifies the discourse of (here) the 'worker' based open such a broad understanding. Indeed, it is submitted that implicitly the contrast between the two words encourages, to a certain extent, the Member States to cease any objections to the jurisprudential development of the 'worker' on the grounds that to do so would be 'narrow'-minded. Thus, the linguistic contrast between a negative concept (narrowness) and a positive one (broadness) played as fundamental a role in establishing the discourse of the 'worker' as mere utterances of broadness.

1.3.7 *A Preliminary Assessment of the (Pre-*Levin*) Discourse of the 'Worker'*

Prior to *Levin* in 1982, a context-specific understanding of a Community 'worker' emerged. In general terms, this manifested itself in a socially inclusive understanding of the 'worker' in which a variety of individuals could be construed as Community workers even if in reality they could not be defined as workers in the classic or ordinary sense.[99] By the time of *Brack*, in 1976, the applicant had formed the view that several years of jurisprudential development 'lead to the conclusion that the principle of freedom of movement for workers is not confined to those who are or were employed, with the result that the term "worker" ... refers to any person capable of taking up employment whether he was formerly employed, unemployed or self-employed'.[100] In specific terms, the legislative interplay between (ex) Article 48 of the Treaty and the (now repealed) Regulation No. 3/58 created a collective understanding or

[99] See, for example, O'Leary where she opines: 'The Court's progressive judicial approach in the field of free movement may be congratulated for championing the socio-political rights of Member State nationals and their families and for affording them judicial protection detached from purely national considerations'. O'Leary, *Evolving Concept*, p. 66. Also, see (Section 1.3.1; 33–34) on the ordinary definition of a worker.

[100] Case 17/76, *M. L. E. Brack, widow of R. J. Brack*, v. *Insurance Officer* [1976] ECR 1429, p. 1437. The applicant in the case was a UK national who was refused sickness benefits on the grounds of having moved temporarily to France for a period of convalescence. See further, John Forman, 'R. J. Brack v. Insurance Officer. Case 17/76. Preliminary Ruling of September 29, 1976 on request of the National Insurance Commissioner' (1977) 14 *Common Market Law Review*, 231–240 at 235–240.

discourse of the worker and it did so through a process of subjective utterance and continual emphasis. For White, these early social security cases 'had a profound influence on the development of Community social security law' and the main reason behind such an influence was the Court's 'liberal interpretation of the scope of Regulation 3'.[101] Thus, in general terms, emerging from the early jurisprudence of the Court came an understanding of 'worker' that differed considerably from its ordinary definition.[102]

Furthermore, the jurisprudence on Regulation No. 3/58 played a pivotal role in the emergence of the discourse of the 'worker' independently of the regulation itself through repeated emphasis. The core aspects of the discourse of the worker that have been outlined were, firstly, the inclusion of a category of individuals that could not be classified as workers by virtue of the principle of assimilation, secondly, the need for the individual to not be 'exclusively employed', thirdly, to not 'strictly' need to be a worker and, fourthly to be 'broadly' understood. *Unger* in 1964 first discussed the concept of the 'worker' in the context of the principle of assimilation in Regulation No. 3/58.[103] This was then further articulated in *De Cicco* in 1968 and *Janssen* in 1971.[104] Second, content was added to the principle of assimilation (and therefore the 'worker') through an emphasis on not needing to be

[101] Robin White, *EC Social Security Law* (London: Longman, 1999), p. 23. See also Watson, *Social Security Law*, p. 63; Paskalia, *Free Movement*, pp. 157–161; Erika Szyszczak, *EC Labour Law* (Harlow: Longman, 1980), pp. 59–62 (for an assessment of such a 'liberal' interpretation).

[102] This was not without controversy. For a critical assessment of this, see Section 5.2. In particular, O'Brien essentially claims 'liberal interpretation' still meant 'liberal [market] interpretation and thus equal treatment as a concept was still 'subsidiary to the higher objectives of the market' and ultimately this form of 'market citizenship instrumentalises and alienates' since rights 'can only be utilised by the privileged'. Charlotte O'Brien, *Unity in Adversity: EU Citizenship, Social Justice and the Cautionary Tale of the UK* (Oxford: Hart, 2017), pp. 4 and 259–260. Arguably from this perspective (and contrast with the views of O'Leary earlier (n. 99) the liberal nature of this legal development benefited a privileged elite of movers and paradoxically alienated the non-moving majority. Recchi then continues this point but in a statistical sense when making the point that non-movers constitute 97 per cent of the majority in most Member States (and thus partly the cause of Brexit) with the seemingly elite movers constituting the 'horsepower' behind any attempts at postnational identification. Ettore Recchi, 'The Engine of "Europeanness"? Free Movement, Social Transnationalism and European Identification', in Daniel Thym (ed.), *Questioning EU Citizenship: Judges and the Limits of Free Movement and Solidarity in the EU* (Oxford: Hart, 2017), pp. 138–148.

[103] See Sections 1.3.2–1.3.5 for the specific analyses of these cases.

[104] Ibid.

'exclusively employed' in *Unger* in 1964 and then repeated in *Murru* in 1972 as well as *Pierik* in 1979.[105] Third, AG Gand in *Singer* in 1965 subjectively articulated that a 'worker' need not be a worker as strictly understood.[106] This was then repeated by the Court in *Singer*, as well as in *Entr'aide médical*, *Frilli* in 1972 and *Michel S.* in 1973. Fourth, the notion of the 'worker' as broadly construed subjectively emanated from *Bertholet* in 1965 and was then rearticulated in *De Cicco* in 1968, *Duffy* in 1969 and *Janssen* in 1971. Importantly, this notion was extended beyond Regulation No. 3/58 itself to include more general provisions of the Treaty in *Entr'aide medical* in 1969, *Frilli* in 1972, *Marsman* in 1973 and *Watson & Belmann* in 1976. All of the above aspects of the discourse of the 'worker', it should be noted, can be seen as originating from a subjective articulation followed by rearticulation in a number of subsequent cases thereby evidencing a process from subjectivity to intersubjectivity.[107]

Finally, in relation to the fourth aspect of the discourse of the 'worker', AG Da Cruz Viląca in *Commission* v. *Italy (reduced rate mortgages)* in 1987 then reflects back on a then established understanding of the Treaty provisions on free movement of persons.[108] In other words, by 1987 this understanding of the worker had become solidified as an unchangeable aspect of the discourse of the worker. Therefore over a relatively short period of jurisprudential development, from 1964 to 1987, the 'worker' emerged as a concept that both on many occasions had little relationship with work and gave the impression that there was an implicit understanding that the Community worker was destined for loftier heights than being a mere factor of production.[109] Prior to *Levin* in 1982, the jurisprudence of the Court on the 'worker' related not to Article 48 of the Treaty but as specifically understood in the context of Article 4(1) Regulation No. 3/58. In linguistic terms, though, a Community worker was specifically understood in this context as an individual not really working as such but as someone considerably

[105] Ibid.

[106] Ibid.

[107] See 'Introduction' for detailed discussion on this point.

[108] In a sense, therefore, this citation acts as a form of discursive 'snapshot'.

[109] For a specific outline of this see Sections 2.3.2, 3.5.1 and 4.4. See also O'Keeffe where he states that the Court ensured that the 'worker' 'came to be seen not as factor of production but rather an individual capable of invoking a constitutional protection which was not necessarily related to his or her economic activity or status'. David O'Keeffe, 'Judicial Interpretation of the Public Services Exception to the Free Movement of Workers', in Deidre Curtin and David O'Keeffe (eds.), *Constitutional Adjudication in European Community and National Law* (Dublin: Butterworths, 1992), p. 267.

above and beyond conventional understandings of a worker: a 'worker' is not 'strictly' (or really) a worker.[110] Putting it differently, the 'worker' became so divorced from the original concept that it took on a life of its own (i.e. became a discourse) and made it acceptable for the citizen to emerge later on.

Moreover, as a question of linguistic interpretation, it was perfectly conceivable for these various aspects of the discourse of the 'worker' to be treated entirely separately. In other words, there was instrumental contingency involved in the creation of the early discourse of the 'worker'. Prior to the jurisprudential development in *Levin*, the jurisprudence on the 'worker' centred on the definition of 'wage-earner or assimilated worker' within the meaning of Article 4(1) of Regulation No. 3/58. 'Wage-earner' is evidently more closely connected to a conventional understanding of a worker than 'assimilated worker'. Equally, the two phrases could be seen to be linguistically separate in that a 'wage-earner' is not the same as an 'assimilated worker'. Moreover, in definitional terms even an 'assimilated worker' is not the same as a worker because if that were the case then the use of the word 'assimilated' would be superfluous. Thus, it is conceivable to treat all of these concepts independently and retain a more conventional definition of a worker.[111] Seen in this manner, the extension of the principle of assimilation to include new categories of individuals (even if by virtue of national legislation) can be seen as a separate line of jurisprudence from attempts to define the 'worker' in 'broad' terms as has been outlined earlier. In discourse theoretical terms, though, an entirely different approach is fundamentally posited in that discourse, as has already been outlined earlier, can be seen to be a series of collective linguistic strands that combine to create a context-specific understanding of a term – here the 'worker' – which differs considerably from an 'objective' or dictionary definition.[112] In SC terms, then,

[110] See, for example, O'Leary for a detailed analysis of a 'weak' link to an 'economic element' and an equally tenuous link to 'work' that appears to dominate much of the jurisprudence of the Court on free movement of persons. O'Leary, *Evolving Concept*, pp. 65–99.

[111] Indeed, as Pennings points out, Regulation No. 3/58 never actually contained any direct reference to the worker, simply referring to 'employed person', 'wage-earner' and 'assimilated worker'. Equally, Martin and Guild maintain that in actual fact the concept of 'worker' as defined in (ex) Article 48 of the Treaty is not actually the same as that as elaborated in the jurisprudence of the Court on social security. Frans Pennings, *Introduction to European Social Security Law* (Antwerp: Intersentia, 2003), p. 35; Martin and Guild, *Free Movement of Persons*, p. 26.

[112] See 'Introduction' for a detailed description of the nature of discourse and its creation.

the extended principle of assimilation combines with attempts to construe the worker 'broadly' to form an intersubjective and distinct understanding of a 'worker' in a Community context. In other words, it has been demonstrated that a core aspect of the way in which the 'worker' was defined in its early years was because the liberal interpretation of Regulation No. 3/58 created an equally liberal understanding of the 'worker'.

1.4 The Reaction of Various Parties (in Turn Further Moulding the Discourse)

As has already been outlined in the Introduction, what distinguishes SC theory from discourse theory more generally is that individual agency is placed at the heart of discourse creation (hence reality being seen to be socially constructed).[113] In the context of the jurisprudence of the Court on the 'worker', agency can be seen to play a role in four different ways. First, an individual plays a role in subjectively creating discourse (AG Gand in *Singer*, for instance (see above)). Second, an individual can play a role in consolidating a discourse through its rearticulation (what in SC terms can be classified as the process of intersubjectivity).[114]As has been outlined earlier, various agents have done so in the context of the early jurisprudence of the Court on the 'worker'. For the most part this has consisted of utterances by the Court itself in its judgments and the AGs in their opinions (with the exception of the Italian government in *Frilli*).[115] However, two sets of voices that are not as frequently cited in conventional legal analysis (by contrast with Court judgments or AGs' opinions) are the applicants and the Member States (their views are always cited in the summary of case by the Judge-Rapporteur). In addition to the first two points that have been outlined in the previous sections of this chapter, the importance of agency in the context of discourse construction can be seen, third, in relation to the applicants and, fourth, in relation to the views of (some of) the Member States. In relation to the

113 Ibid.

114 Ibid.

115 See Sections 1.3.4 and 1.3.5. Though it should be noted that this was not surprising as Italy was one of the major protagonists for the advanced implementation of the free movement provisions of the Treaty from the outset in order to solve its own unemployment problems. See Federico Romero, 'Migration as an Issue in European Interdependence and Integration: The Case of Italy', in Alan Milward, Frances Lynch and Ruggero Raniero (eds.), *The Frontier of National Sovereignty: History and Theory 1945–1992* (London: Longman, 1993), pp. 33–58.

former, their approach to litigation at the Court can be seen as evidence of a paradigm shift within the institutional environment of the Court in which a qualitatively different understanding of the word 'worker' had emerged. In relation to the latter, certain Member States were not necessarily in accord with the Court's 'liberal' approach to Regulation No. 3/58 and can, in discursive terms, be seen to be attempting, within the text of Court judgments, to break up or prevent a wide-ranging discourse of the 'worker' emerging.[116] Nonetheless, as will be outlined, they played a different yet equally important role in the construction of the discourse of the 'worker' because their utterances were made subsequent to the repeal of Regulation No. 3/58 and ensured that, notwithstanding the coming into force of Regulation No. 1408/71, the legacy of the Court's discourse of the 'worker' continued until *Levin* in 1982.

1.4.1 *The Applicants*

It is submitted that the applicants (or more specifically their counsel) played an important role in the rearticulation of the discourse of the 'worker' and can also be used to evidence a sociocultural shift within the epistemic community of the Court. Moreover, counsel for the applicants were lawyers instructed by the various applicants in their home jurisdictions and can therefore be seen to partly demonstrate the impact of the jurisprudence of the Court on the 'worker' beyond the courtroom in Luxembourg.[117] In terms of the applicants, what is particularly noticeable is the simple audacity of many of them. Such audacity, though, is, it is maintained, born of an emerging contextual understanding of an increasingly loose and tenuous link to work, which, as will become clear in Chapter 5, will prove to be particularly controversial in the context of the concept of solidarity.[118] Putting it differently, the nature of the pleadings of some of the applicants appears to demonstrate an intersubjective awareness of an adventurous development by the Court and that it might

[116] As Watson maintains, there were profound consequences in terms of immigration law because of the early social security cases on Regulation No. 3/58 which was contrary to the intention of the Member States when enacting both the Treaty and the regulation: 'There was no intention to . . . encourage the general flow of persons, for whatever reason, throughout the Community. Yet these are the consequences of the interpretation by the Court of Justice of Article 51 and Regulation No. 3/58'. Watson, *Social Security Law*, p. 64.

[117] See, for example, Lawrence Gormley, 'The Application of Community Law in the United Kingdom' (1986) 23 *Common Market Law Review*, 287–323 (for an outline of the impact of the jurisprudence of the Court more generally in national legal cultures).

[118] See n. 33.

be within the realms of acceptability to plead cases that had little or nothing to do with work as properly understood. There are various cases that illustrate this point. In *Costa*, the applicant (Mrs Mazzier (née Costa)) admitted that 'her only occupation is that of housewife' but she was denied a handicapped allowance.[119] She was Italian and married a Belgian and resided in Belgium.[120] For AG Reischl, 'it is clear that the plaintiff … is not a worker within the meaning of the social security regulations … and that she has never been gainfully employed'.[121] It is not surprising that the AG was rather blunt about the circumstances of the applicant. In Mrs Mazzier's case she was clearly not a worker even if she had moved. Likewise, her husband may have been a worker but he was not a 'worker' as he had never moved. Arguably, the personal circumstances of her case – the scope *ratione personae* – therefore fell entirely outside the remit of Community law.[122] However, it is the reasoning that she gave in her pleadings that is of particular interest:

> The plaintiff considers that it is sufficient for someone to be recognised as a member of the family by social security provisions of a Member State as a whole, and that it does not matter whether such members of the family are entitled to rights that can be derived from the rights of the worker.[123]

This is, of course, a gross distortion of the principle of assimilation, but what is significant is that the language of assimilation has been used. Indeed, such an attempt was not entirely far-fetched because if it is the case, according to the Court – that anyone affiliated to a worker under national law is a 'worker' – then it is submitted that it would not be taking an enormous conceptual leap to suggest that members of the family more generally could be in effect assimilated to the members of the family of a worker exercising his/her freedom of movement.[124]

119 Case 39/74, *Luciana Costa, spouse Mazzier* v. *Belgian State* [1974] ECR 1251, p. 1263.
120 Ibid.
121 Ibid., p. 1265.
122 A point strongly made by the Belgian government when it stated: 'In the present case the interested party stated she was a "housewife." Moreover, nothing appearing on the Court file makes it possible to call her a former worker. Consequently, the interpretation given by the Court to Regulation Nos. 3 and 1612/68 can have no bearing on the possible award of benefits provided for'. Ibid., p. 1254.
123 Ibid., p. 1266 (as summarized by AG Reischl).
124 Ex Article 51 of the Treaty was an enabling provision designed to allow future legislative development to 'make arrangements … for migrant workers and their dependents' and under Article 51, Regulation No. 3/58 was enacted. Article 1(n) of Regulation No. 3/58 enabled dependents of workers to be entitled to the same benefits

Legally, this is, though, an example, it is suggested, of ill thought-out and 'woolly' reasoning as the governing criterion is that such rights have to be derived from someone's 'rights' as a worker (whether Mrs Mazzier or her husband) and neither of them were. Nonetheless, the fact that the applicant used such an argument is indicative, it is maintained, of an awareness of an emerging discourse amidst a rising tide in which individuals who clearly were not workers appeared to derive rights. Moreover, to a certain extent the applicant's audacity paid off. The Belgian government's view on this reference for a preliminary ruling was that it should really have been struck out for having 'no bearing' on Community law as she was not a worker and the benefit in question had nothing to do with work.[125] The Court itself ignored the issue as to whether Mrs Mazzier was a worker or not and simply focused on the question as to the scope *ratione materiae* of the allowance.[126] However, as AG Reischl maintained, the only way of making such an assessment is to make the *a priori* assumption that the applicant was a worker.[127] Equally, the text of the Court's judgment ultimately produced a considerable amount of words on a page in response to the circumstances of an applicant which, at least according to the Belgian government, had nothing to do with Community law and, in SC theory, the physical appearance and quantity of words on a page matter irrespective of their legal relevance.[128] Indeed, it is maintained that the Court could clearly have made this point but chose to utter literally nothing on this issue, instead choosing to focus on whether the benefit in question fell within the scope *ratione materiae* of the Treaty. This type of approach therefore gives the impression to these types of litigant that they 'count'[129] as their reference was not struck out, any issue relating to the scope *ratione personae* was ignored and, instead, several pages of the text are devoted to discussing the applicant's reference, albeit in the

as workers themselves. However, the applicant's submissions, whilst appearing to try and broaden the principle of assimilation, were fundamentally flawed because, as the Court made clear in *Kermaschek*, a member of the family of a worker 'can only claim derived rights acquired through their status as a member of their family'. Case 40/76, *Slavica Kermaschek* v. *Bundesanstalt für Arbeit* [1976] ECR 1669, pp. 1677–1678, para. 7. See also Watson, *Social Security Law*, pp. 82–84.

125 *Costa*, p. 1254.

126 Ibid., p. 1260, para. 3.

127 Ibid., p. 1265.

128 See 'Introduction' for an outline of the cognitive impact of words on a page.

129 See 'Introduction' in relation to the epistemological implications (and the power structures that are inherent in particular standpoints) of determining who (or what) is or is not relevant.

context of outlining the scope *ratione materiae* of the particular benefit being claimed.

Furthermore, *Costa* headed a long list of applicants with dubious claims to fall within the scope *ratione personae* of Community law. In *Kuyken*, the applicant was a Belgian student claiming discrimination by his own state on the grounds that he was denied unemployment benefit by virtue of his studying in the Netherlands.[130] The Court roundly dismissed his application as it was a 'case of an unemployed person who has never been in employment and has never been treated as an employed person under national legislation applicable to employed persons'; but yet the applicant still managed to secure a reference to the Court and a judgment was actually given.[131] As has been outlined in the Introduction, trivial though this may sound, the fact that words on a page are produced on this matter is still of significance from a discursive perspective even if a particular case is bound to fail legally.[132] In *Laumann*, AG Reischl claimed that the applicants' mother 'had never been employed and plainly did not intend to pursue a professional activity in Belgium . . . [and therefore her case was] clearly unrelated to the free movement of *workers* within the Community'.[133] Yet, once again, the justification for making such an application was that it must be seen in the context of 'a series of cases . . . concerning the persons covered by Regulation No 3 ... [which] were very liberally interpreted' (ibid.).[134] It was clearly understood by these applicants,

130 Case 66/77, *Petrus Kuyken* v. *Rijksdienst voor Arbeidsvoorziening* [1977] ECR 2311, p. 2312. See further Derrick Wyatt, 'Recent Cases on Regulation No. 1408/71. Unemployment Benefit for School-Leavers' (1978) 3 *European Law Review*, 398–399.

131 *Kuyken*, p. 2818, para. 14.

132 See n. 73.

133 Case 115/77, *Gert Laumann and Anja Laumann* v. *Landesversicherungsanstalt Rheinprovinz* [1978] ECR 805, p. 819, pp. 813–814. The status of the applicants' mother was fundamental to determining the success of their case as it concerned two applicants who were minors and German nationals. Upon the divorce of their German parents, the children then moved to reside in Belgium with their mother who then married a Belgian national but had never actually worked. Their father then died in Germany and the applicants were denied the payment of an orphan's pension to which they would ordinarily have been allowed on the grounds that they were now members of the family of a worker under Regulation No. 1408/71 (i.e. their stepfather in Belgium) and that, then, enables them to claim a family allowance in Belgium instead. This therefore constituted a rare occasion in which a Member State was attempting to use a provision of Community law to narrow the benefits available to a Community national. Derrick Wyatt, 'Regulation No. 1408/71: Duplication of Orphans' Benefits and Family Allowances' (1978) 3 *European Law Review*, 371–373.

134 A point made in commentary by White, *EC Social Security Law*, p. 23; and Watson, *Social Security Law*, p. 63. Also, see n. 62.

whether legally correctly or not, that the 'worker' was now so divorced from the real definition of a worker that a wide range of individual circumstances may have a possibility of success in front of the Court. A case to demonstrate this point was *Moser*. In *Moser*, a German national was refused a teaching contract in Germany on the grounds of his political affiliation.[135] The Court understandably dismissed the application as being a purely internal situation of no relevance to Community law.[136] The German government contended that the reference was inadmissible and claimed that the referring court 'clearly misunderstood the ambit of Community law, so that it is unnecessary for the Court to ask the questions'.[137] This 'misunderstanding' though is not a surprise as clearly at this point a social truth had emerged in which the 'worker' had become so broadly defined that it had become 'acceptable' to pose the question as to whether Mr Moser could likewise, 'count'.[138] Indeed, the arguments raised by counsel for the applicant are indicative of such a context. He first submits that individuals should be able to 'enjoy domestically the freedoms which are contained in the Treaty' and, secondly, that not allowing Mr Moser to complete his training by being offered a contract at a school after his academic training would potentially impede his ability to take up employment in another Member State.[139] These two submissions are then roundly dismissed by AG Slynn where he simply replied, in relation to the first point, that 'that contention can simply not be accepted', and the Court, in relation to the second point, ruled that 'a purely hypothetical prospect of employment in another Member State does not establish a sufficient connection with Community law to justify the application of Article 48 of the Treaty'.[140] It is clear that counsel for Mr Moser was being audacious in making such submissions. Nonetheless, the fact that these questions were posed are once again illustrative of a paradigm shift occurring within the jurisprudence of the Court. Likewise, in *Meade*, counsel for the applicant attempted to claim that 'even a housewife contributes in any event to the economic life of the country'.[141] Once

[135] Case 180/83, *Hans Moser* v. *Land Baden-Württemberg* [1984] ECR 2539, p. 2549.
[136] Ibid., pp. 2547–2548, paras. 19–20.
[137] Ibid., p. 2550.
[138] See 'Introduction' for an outline of the nature of social truths.
[139] *Moser*, p. 2542.
[140] Ibid., p. 2550, p. 2547, para. 18.
[141] Case 238/83, *Caisse d'Allocations Familiales de la Région Parisienne* v. *Mr and Mrs Richard Meade* [1984] ECR 2631, p. 2634. See further Phillipa Watson, 'Family Allowance: Persons Covered' (1984) 9 *European Law Review*, 434–435.

again, this is an audacious, but not ill-conceived, argument to raise in the circumstances. In the case, there were three categories of individuals that did not 'count' for various reasons. Mr Meade (the father) was a third country national.[142] His son was a student and his wife did not work.[143] Because Mrs Meade was a national of a Member State, counsel for the applicant clearly felt that it was at least worth running an argument that a housewife was a 'worker'.[144] The fact that a lawyer appearing before the Court felt that it was 'appropriate' to make such submissions is indicative, though, of an approach taken by the Court in which either mere 'lip service' was being paid to the concept of the worker or, in addition, an ever-expanding set of categories of individuals were claiming rights from the Treaty on the basis of a 'broad' construction of the principle of assimilation.[145] Thus, not only had there been a clear discursive development but also this development resulted in a change of the context or rules of the game in which the Court operated.[146]

In short, what is evident from some of the pleadings of the applicants is that they were legally adventurous (or had at least been provoked into being so), attempting to push the limits of the 'worker' into new frontiers. However, for SC, fundamentally, lawyers would have been cognitively aware of the boundaries of linguistic acceptability within the epistemic community of the Court.[147] Even if to push to their limits, an agent is consciously aware of what is or is not appropriate in a given context.[148] Thus the audacity of the above pleadings made by some of the applicants is evidence of a paradigm shift within the legal culture of the Court in which a new understanding of the 'worker' had emerged. This can also be demonstrated in chronological terms. As has been outlined earlier, a specific understanding of the 'worker' had been developed by 1976 when the applicant in *Brack* reflected on this.[149] All the previous cases that were cited commenced with *Unger* in 1964 and then appear in a cluster at the beginning of the 1970s (*Janssen* in 1971, *Murru* in 1972, *Frilli* in 1972 and *Michel S.* in 1973), followed by the reflection in *Brack* in 1976. By contrast, the cases that have been cited

[142] *Meade*, p. 2632.
[143] Ibid.
[144] Ibid., p. 2634.
[145] See Section 1.3.2.
[146] See 'Introduction' for an outline of 'rules of the game' seen from an SC perspective.
[147] Ibid.
[148] Ibid.
[149] See Section 1.3.7.

earlier as evidence of the audacity of the applicant's counsel appeared to take place after this point (i.e. when the definition of a 'worker' had become increasingly crystallized). *Costa*, for instance, was reported in 1974, *Kuyken* in 1977, *Laumann* in 1978, *Moser* in 1984 and *Meade* in 1984. Thus, the fact that some of the submissions made by the applicants were even deemed to be within the realms of linguistic acceptability within the institutional environment of the Court is reflective of an earlier discursive change that had taken place from *Unger* in 1964 until the various cases in the early 1970s.

1.4.2 *The Long-Term Consequences of the Court's 'Liberal' Approach to the 'Worker' and the Reaction of the Member States*

Ultimately, Regulation No. 3/58 was repealed and replaced by Regulation No. 1408/71. One aspect of the discourse of the 'worker' that (at least overtly) disappeared upon the coming into force of the new regulation was the principle of assimilation.[150] Article 4(1) of Regulation No. 3/58 was not replicated by Article 1(a) of Regulation No. 1408/71 (which defined a 'worker') and contained no reference to a 'wage-earner or assimilated worker'.[151] The legacy, though, was one of judicial radicalism. In *Frilli*, AG Roemer reflects:

> Coming now to the case-law of this Court, I think it is sufficient to take a quick look at the most typical of the judgements delivered on this subject to come to the conclusion that the Court itself has given Regulation No 3 a liberal, if not even far-reaching interpretation.[152]

As has been previously outlined, a great enabling mechanism for this 'far-reaching interpretation' was the principle of assimilation.[153] The Court in *Janssen* maintains there to be: 'a general tendency of the social law of Member States to extend the benefits of social security in favour of new categories of persons by reason of identical risks'.[154] The significance of this statement is twofold. First, this is a consequence of the principle of assimilation. It became established jurisprudence of the Court that a Community national can be assimilated to the position of

[150] Though this did not mean that the principles that underpinned the jurisprudence on assimilated workers disappeared. See Section 1.4.2.

[151] Regulation No. 3/58; Council Regulation No. 1408/71/EEC of 14 June 1971 on the application of social security schemes to employed persons and their families moving within the Community [1971] OJ L149/2.

[152] *Frilli*, p. 474. See n. 104.

[153] See Section 1.3.2.

[154] *Janssen*, p. 481, para. 6.

a worker if an insurance or social security scheme of a Member State does so for home nationals and therefore an extension of national law leads to an extension of the remit of assimilation.[155] Second, authority is implicitly derived for an extension of social security protection to 'new categories of person' from the Member States themselves as it is their own (collective) legislative processes that are making such extensions, not the Court. In other words, it is submitted that because the extension of the definition of 'assimilated worker' was being enacted through national law, the Member States were effectively stopped from profoundly objecting to the Court's 'liberal' interpretation of Regulation No. 3/58, at least in part.[156]

However, this is not to suggest that there were no objections by some of the Member States and the creation of a discourse of the 'worker' in a manner that had become so divorced from its natural meaning was not entirely accepted.[157] AG Mayras in *Brack* claimed that the Court's jurisprudence on the principle of assimilation can be seen as a 'generalization of the trend towards protection of the whole of the population'.[158] In other words, in practical terms, the consequences of the Court's case law on Regulation No. 3/58 was that it would have been hard to find a Community national (exercising a right to move) who would not be able to derive an entitlement to social security benefits on the basis of being a wage earner or assimilated worker, particularly bearing in mind the initiative being taken by the Member States (as outlined earlier) to extend the categories of individuals entitled to protection. The Danish government objected to this generalization and asserted, in *Brack*, that it feared that:

> The consequence of conceding that a person retains his status as a worker in every respect would … be that virtually the entire adult population of the Communities would have to be regarded as a worker within the meaning of the Regulation.[159]

155 *De Cicco*, pp. 480–481 (the Court). See also *Janssen*, p. 859.

156 See Pennings, *Introduction to European Social Security Law*, pp. 34–36 (for a discussion of the interrelationship between the principle of assimilation and national legislation).

157 See Section 1.3.7. Indeed, as Van Der Mei argues 'it does not seem very likely that the Member States which signed and ratified the EEC Treaty ever intended to translate the theoretical notion of a free factor mobility into practical reality'. Van Der Mei, *Free Movement*, p. 25.

158 *Brack*, p. 1462, p. 1430. A case concerning a UK national who had contributed to a National Insurance scheme as both an employed and self-employed person, had to receive urgent medical attention whilst on holiday in France and was (partly) denied access to a sickness cash benefit on the purported grounds that he was not a 'worker'.

159 Ibid., p. 1467.

For the Danish government, then, this was clearly a worrying development and, in linguistic terms, denudes the word 'worker' of considerable meaning in substantive terms if in effect all Community nationals could be classified as 'workers'. Equally, no distinction is made by the Danish government between an assimilated worker and a worker; clearly for it a 'worker' can be seen as a collective edifice incorporating all of the various strands of the Court's jurisprudence on Regulation No. 3/58. Therefore, such an objection by the Danish government must be read in tandem with those that have already been outlined in this chapter such as *Costa* where the Belgian government objected to the applicant's reference on the grounds that she was simply not a worker[160] and *Pierik* where the UK Government made the explicit point of distinguishing workers from pensioners.[161] Thus, the expansive definition of the 'worker' was not universally accepted.

Despite this any objections to the emerging discourse of the 'worker' were not, prior to *Levin*, sufficient to impede its expansive development. In Chapter 2, it will be maintained that a combination of the Court's definition of the 'worker' from *Levin* onwards and the emergence of the Community student in *Gravier* did lead to a reaction of the Member States in the form of the three residency directives.[162] This is not to suggest that early expressed scepticism in relation to the liberal understanding of the 'worker' was not without later effect in the *Levin* jurisprudence itself.[163] However, the enactment of Regulation No. 1408/71 can, instead of being seen to be a reaction to the Court's liberal interpretation of Regulation No. 3/58, be portrayed as one of linguistic and discursive continuation. In *Brack*, the issue was whether the applicant was a 'worker' and whether the jurisprudence on the 'worker' derived from Regulation No. 3/58 could be used when interpreting Regulation No. 1408/71. AG Roemer determines: 'I consider that it is quite possible for the case-law which you developed in relation to Regulation No 3 to be transposed in the context of Regulation 1408/71'.[164] In other words, all of the prior language that had been carefully crafted could be neatly transposed onto the new regulation. The Court itself acknowledged that

160 See Section 1.4.1.
161 See Section 1.3.3.
162 See Chapter 2 for a discussion, from an SC perspective, of the impact of the jurisprudence of the Court on the later residency directives.
163 See Section 1.5.7 for an elaboration on this point.
164 *Brack*, p. 1465. See also White, *EC Social Security Law*, pp. 25–26; Watson, *Social Security Law*, pp. 68–71 (for commentary on this issue).

the new regulation 'no longer employs the expression "wage-earners or assimilated workers" and merely refers . . .. to "employed persons", but then also claims that it 'also applies to certain categories of person who . . .. do not have the status of "employed persons" within the meaning of the law of employment' and then states:

> Consequently the provision must be understood as referring also to persons who are not 'employed persons' within the meaning of the law of employment but who must be treated as such for the purposes of [the new regulation] taking into account the objectives and spirit of this Regulation and [the Treaty].[165]

Thus, as far as the Court was concerned, the new regulation would make little or no difference to the expansion of the 'worker' as it can employ a different rhetorical justification – the 'spirit' and aims of the Treaty – to implicitly incorporate the principle of assimilation into the regulation even though it was deliberately omitted. Thus, irrespective of the repeal of Regulation No. 3/58, the Court's early discourse of the 'worker' did not cease because of the implementation of Regulation No. 1408/71 and, therefore, prior to *Levin* in 1982, a context-specific understanding of the phrase 'worker' had emerged that became well established within the institutional framework of the Court. Moreover, any objections that the Member States may have made did not appear to affect this development.[166]

1.5 *Levin* and *Lawrie-Blum*: A Profound Change of Direction for the Discourse of the Worker

In *Levin* (1982) and *Lawrie-Blum* (1986), a profound linguistic shift in emphasis took place within the discourse of the 'worker'. 'Worker' talk simply changed considerably after that point or, putting it differently, the discourse of the 'worker' continued to evolve in a context specific and inherently contingent manner.[167] This subjectively created understanding of the 'worker' became the predominant understanding

[165] Ibid., pp. 1451–1452.

[166] Though, to repeat what has been maintained earlier, this is not to suggest that such objections did not play a role in the manner in which the discourse of the 'worker' was then remoulded after *Levin*.

[167] By this what is meant is that the Court subjectively developed a powerful concept that it either need not have done or at least in the manner in which it did. For example, in relation to Regulation No. 3/58, Watson claims that the Court's approach was 'a rather more extensive approach to the problem of the personal scope of the Regulation than was strictly necessary. The Court could conceivably have viewed the

of the 'worker' in the immediate period prior to the incorporation of the Citizenship provisions into the amended Treaty at Maastricht and, as will be explained, the specific manner and form of its development paved the way for a seemingly inevitable legal creation of the EU Citizen.

1.5.1 *The Controversial Circumstances of the Applicant in* Levin

In *Levin*, the applicant was a UK national, married to a South African national, who, in 1979 was refused a residence permit by the Dutch police authorities on the grounds that she had not been in work since 1978 and did not have sufficient resources to support herself.[168] Subsequent to the refusal to grant such a permit, the applicant undertook a form of employment, giving the impression that she was solely undertaking it in order to obtain the permit.[169] This impression appeared to be further compounded by the fact that, by the applicant's own admission, because she owned property and other investments in tandem with her husband, she had sufficient resources to support herself (i.e. whatever employment she undertook was not her real means of financial support).[170] The case therefore represented a significant bridging case between the worker and the citizen because this was the first case in which the issue of own resources (and therefore not being a burden on the state) arose.[171] This was as a result of Council minutes and a subsequent declaration in which the situation of work-seekers arose and it was agreed that a work-seeker should be allowed a limited period of three months to go to another Member State and seek work 'on condition that [(s)he] does not become a burden on public funds'.[172] Equally, though, the applicant was forthright about using the provisions of the Treaty as a ruse in that there was no intention to

matter more narrowly and confined the benefits of the Regulation to workers who were employed under a contract of employment'. Watson, *Social Security Law*, p. 61.

168 Case 53/81, *D. M. Levin* v. *Staatssecretaris van Justitie* [1982] ECR 1035, p. 1036.

169 Ibid., p. 1035, p. 1055. The employment itself was not specified in the summary of the facts by the Juge-Rapporteur, nor by the Court, but AG Slynn states this to be a hotel chambermaid.

170 Ibid., p. 1035.

171 See Chapter 2 for an outline of the Court's expansion to include non-economic contributors and Section 5.2.8 for a specific discussion on the controversial issue of own resources. See also David O'Keeffe, 'The Free Movement of Workers: An Annotation of the *Levin* Case' (1984) 3(1) *Journal of the Irish Society for Labour Law*, 17–22; Brenda Sufrin, 'When is a Worker a Worker?' (1983) 46(4) *The Modern Law Review*, 495–499.

172 *Levin*, p. 1056 (referred to by AG Slynn).

undertake genuine work. Even though she had her own resources, Mrs Levin was perfectly upfront with her intention behind taking up part-time employment; namely 'as a precaution' designed to ensure a residual right for both Mr and Mrs Levin to remain in the Netherlands should the 'own resources' argument fail.[173] AG Slynn therefore determined that the applicant's 'chief motive for residing in that Member State is for a purpose other than the undertaking of limited employment or the provision of services'.[174] Thus, in addition to an applicant attempting to seek protection on the basis of (ex.) Article 48 of the Treaty on the grounds of being economically self-reliant, the applicant also raised a hitherto unheard-of issue of motive.

Moreover, what was particularly controversial in *Levin* was not simply the fact that the applicant was essentially using the Treaty provisions as a ruse in order to obtain a panoply of benefits but that a precedent was being set that other litigants could follow. The applicant in *Brown*, for instance, tried to claim an entitlement to a substantial benefit on the basis of a short period of work. The applicant, a dual UK and French national brought up in France, had worked for several months as a trainee engineer in Edinburgh, a job that was specifically designed as preparatory to the imminent commencement of an engineering degree at the University of Cambridge.[175] The applicant, though, attempted to use this short period of employment as means to avoid the usual residency requirement in the UK for an exemption from tuition fees and access to a maintenance grant during the course of his studies on the grounds that, even for a short period of time, he was a 'worker' within the meaning of EEC law.[176] Counsel for the applicant in *Brown* defined his position in the following terms: 'Once a worker, he is a worker for all purposes and no period can be prescribed before he can be regarded as a worker either for the purpose of Article 48 or for the purposes of the regulation'.[177] The problem for the applicant, though, was two-fold. First, it was never denied that he was a worker for the short period of time prior to commencing his degree (he was paid a wage and made National Insurance contributions).[178] Had he, for

[173] Ibid.
[174] Ibid., p. 1054.
[175] Case 197/86, *Steven Malcolm Brown* v. *The Secretary of State for Scotland* [1988] ECR 3205, p. 3207.
[176] Ibid., p. 3208.
[177] Ibid., p. 3232.
[178] Ibid., p. 3225.

instance, been discriminated against in some way on the grounds of nationality in the course of his employment, then he would have been entitled to protection under (ex) Article 48 of the Treaty. What the applicant was claiming, though, was access to social welfare benefits that did not relate to his employment nor were they ever going to be received whilst he was employed. Second, had the applicant's claim been allowed, it would have involved setting a legal precedent involving a considerable amount of Member State expenditure.[179] Thus, not only was the applicant's claim also controversial in terms of what was being claimed but his motive for undertaking a brief period of employment in Scotland was at issue.[180]

1.5.2 *The Negative Reaction of Many of the Member States to the Applicant's Claim in* Levin

For the Danish and Dutch governments in *Levin*, the economic criterion, reflecting back on the conception from *Unger* of being 'involved in an economic activity' was paramount and, by contrast, the case concerned:

> A national of a Member State [who] move[d] to another Member State in order to pursue an activity devoid of economic interest with the sole aim of thus being able to enjoy the advantages conferred upon persons to whom the provisions on freedom of movement for workers apply.[181]

In other words, there was a partial revolt by the Member States, born out of concern that the workers provisions of the Treaty and secondary legislation had been construed so broadly by the Court that there was a real, and for them very worrying, possibility of a 'worker' emerging that simply referred to any member of the population more generally.[182] Thus for both the Danish and Dutch governments the provisions of the Treaty were simply: 'not for nationals of Member States in general, or those who engage in no economic activity or

[179] See Section 5.2.6 for an SC analysis of the so-called Taxpayer principle. See also Catherine Barnard, 'Case C-209/03, *R (on the application of Danny Bidar)* v. *London Borough of Ealing, Secretary of State for Education and Skills*' (2005) 42(5) *Common Market Law Review*, 1465–1489; Noreen Burrows, 'Wandering Scholars' (1989) 34(1) *The Juridical Review*, 99–102; Mark Gould, 'Equality of Access to Education' (1989) 52(4) *Modern Law Review*, 540–550.

[180] *Brown*, p. 3223. It should be noted that case also concerned the extended principle of access to vocational training under (ex) Article 128 as established at *Gravier* (1985), which will be specifically analysed in Section 2.5.3.

[181] *Levin*, p. 1040.

[182] See Section 1.4.2.

whose economic activity is insignificant'.[183] There was an important reason for such concern; namely, that the types of rights which 'workers' could claim were so extensive and the 'worker' itself being construed so broadly that a considerable amount of taxpayers' money of the various Member States would be devoted towards paying out social security benefits (such as unemployment benefits) to individuals who had barely ever worked in any meaningful sense.[184] In this sense, the 'worker' was being claimed to be narrower than its ordinary meaning because of what was financially at stake in terms of its definition.

Moreover, the Member States attempted to use the language of economic engagement derived from *Unger* to redefine this new category of litigants attempting to use the Treaty for instrumental purposes and in the process the very nature of the 'worker'. For the Netherlands, it was, in effect, attempting to create a 'counter-discourse' in which the focus should revert back to 'genuine' workers. For the Netherlands in *Levin*, a 'real' worker is one 'performing work in the fullest sense of the word [by] contribut[ing] to the economic development of the Community' and whose work is 'full and complete ... which enables the worker at least to provide for himself with means of support'.[185] For the Netherlands government, then, a 'real' worker needs to be 'of importance to the economic life of the Member States, or who contribute by their economic activity to the development of the Community'.[186] Equally, once again there is an issue of who gets to define – i.e. who has the power – when both the Danish and Dutch governments argue that:

> In the absence of a definition in Community legislation of a "worker" national criteria may be adopted to decide both the minimum wage and the minimum number of hours. It is suggested that only in this way can the category of worker be kept within bounds and such grounds as full-time students and pensioners be excluded from the category, even if they do a few hours' paid work each week.[187]

There are three key points to be made in relation to the above citation. First, this is a clear attempt by the two Member States to wrest back the power to define, which was bound to fail. Second, there was a clear 'floodgates' argument at stake here in that there was evidently

[183] *Levin*, p. 1058.
[184] See Section 5.3.2 for criticism of this.
[185] *Levin*, p. 1040.
[186] Ibid., p. 1058 (as summarized by AG Slynn).
[187] Ibid.

a prevailing concern on the part of the Member States that the manner in which the Court was defining the 'worker' would inevitably lead to students and pensioners deriving an entire panoply of rights on the basis of a token amount of work being undertaken, costing different Member States a considerable amount of taxpayers' money and possibly even leading to social security forum shopping around the Member States.[188] Third, there is a discursive element to this as the response by the two Member States to an increasingly expanding discourse of the 'worker' was to 'keep it within bounds'. Thus, the controversial circumstances of *Levin* evidently precipitated a strong reaction on the part of the Member States within the text of the Court judgment. Furthermore, prior objections made by some of the Member States to the expansive definition of the worker under Regulation No. 3/58 eventually bore fruit in *Levin* in that the above points being made in *Levin* by the Member States can also be seen to have emerged out of the previous context prior to 1982.

1.5.3 *The Emergence of a Refashioned Discourse of the 'Worker'*

It is ultimately as a result of the resistance of the Member States that a modified discourse of the 'worker' emerged. Faced with such strong criticism within the case, AG Slynn and the Court reacted in a manner that fundamentally changed the nature of how the 'worker' was intersubjectively understood. AG Slynn responds: 'the worker must show that he wishes to enter and reside for the purposes of employment. Such a purpose must be a genuine purpose and a substantial purpose' and continues:

> The person whose only real purpose in entering is to study, or to retire, to do nothing which can genuinely be called employment, may not be entering for the purpose of employment even if as a device he takes on a few hours work each week or from time to time ... The fact that only a few hours are worked may be relevant in deciding whether work is the genuine and substantial purpose of the application to reside. The fewer hours worked, the more difficult it may be to establish that work is such a genuine and substantial purpose.[189]

The AG could have chosen to co-opt the language of the Member States and emphasize the need for a 'worker' to work in its 'fullest' sense or,

[188] Szyszczak, *EC Labour Law*, p. 59. See also Chapter 5 and O'Leary, where she outlines the greatest concern of the Member States as being 'migration detached from employment'. The Danish government were particular concerned about this potential development in Community law as it is 'renowned for its anxious protection of comparatively lucrative Danish welfare benefits'. O'Leary, *Evolving Concept*, pp. 81–82.

[189] *Levin*, p. 1061.

likewise, have focused on the 'substantial purpose' of the individual moving but clearly chose not use this particular terminology.[190] What AG Slynn clearly did choose to focus on was the genuineness of the work and this can be elicited from both the nature of the work (its duration etc.) and the intention of the person doing the work.[191] In a sense this was a brilliantly pragmatic and needed response by AG Slynn as it appeared to both satisfy the clear concerns of the Member States and provide the groundwork for future development. As the Dutch and Danish governments demonstrated, there was continual emphasis by the Member States on the need for a Community national to make a meaningful economic contribution to the host Member State with the resulting *quid-pro-quo* of being entitled to claim back in the form of social security payments what (s)he in effect put in to the economy.[192] What AG Slynn's reaction then demonstrates is a two-fold contribution by two sets of agents to a soon-to-emerge remoulding of the discourse of the 'worker'. What has been demonstrated is that the Member States voiced objections within the text, AG Slynn took these objections into account (it was never the case that, as counsel for the applicant in the later case of *Brown* tried to argue, motive was simply irrelevant) and the AG in turn offered his own interpretation of the matter.[193] In terms of an SC interpretation of agency, then, what can be seen to have taken place is that the Member States lodged a profound objection and this is then partly taken into account in terms of the legal interpretation of case and what was articulated by AG Slynn.[194] AG Slynn, then, can be seen to be taking into account the viewpoints of the Member States and, in turn, further moulding a refashioned discourse of the worker (the details of which will be outlined below).

In legal terms, the applicant's circumstances in *Levin* were unusual and presented the Court and AG Slynn with a controversial dilemma to resolve.[195] On the one hand, the conventional understanding of the worker would seem to suggest that she was clearly a worker: if an individual earns a wage and is employed in any capacity then the applicant was clearly a worker (which the applicant did).[196] Indeed, as

[190] See Section 1.4.2 for the reaction of the Danish and Dutch governments in *Brack* (1976).
[191] *Levin*, p. 1061.
[192] See Section 4.4 for a further example of the often controversial relationship between AGs and Member States.
[193] *Levin*, p. 1061.
[194] See 'Introduction' for a discussion of the relationship between agency and discourse.
[195] See Section 1.5.1 for a summary of the facts.
[196] See Section 1.3.1 for a description of the ordinary definition of the 'worker'.

AG Slynn states: 'where no words of limitation have been expressed the Court should be slow to introduce them in order to cut down the ordinary and natural meaning of the word "worker"'.[197] In other words, the ordinary meaning of the worker would clearly classify Mrs Levin as a worker and, in this respect, the intention behind her work was irrelevant. As AG Slynn continues:

> A person may wish to work in a particular country principally because his wife's family lives there, or because he wants his children to benefit from a particular system of health, or for cultural or health reasons. The fact that this is the initial, principal motivation does not prevent the pursuit of work from being a genuine or substantial one.[198]

Thus, in simple terms, the intention behind whatever work a Community national undertakes is seemingly irrelevant and on one level the applicant was a 'worker' for the purposes of Community (now Union) law.

On the other hand, though, the fact that the intention behind the work the applicant was undertaking was even an issue in the first place was reflective of an awareness by AG Slynn of the objections of the Member States. Immediately prior to the above citation, AG Slynn does also maintain that, for a number of reasons, intention was relevant in determining whether a Community national was a worker and, at least on one reading of his opinion, the applicant could not be classified as a 'worker' (though he is not explicit on the matter).[199] As has been cited earlier, for AG Slynn, a 'worker' has to demonstrate a 'genuine and substantial' intention to work and this can therefore exclude someone who 'as a device takes on a few hours work each week' (i.e. the applicant in *Levin*).[200] Likewise, the applicant in *Brown* was also pre-emptively excluded by AG Slynn in *Levin* when he determined that a 'worker' did not include someone entering a territory 'whose only real purpose in entering is to study'.[201] AG Slynn then confirms his view in *Brown* itself when he states:

> A person who has the fixed intention of going to a Member State in any event as a student, and who has a place in a university or school for a fixed date and period, but who in order to gain useful experience does a short term job does not

[197] *Levin*, p. 1059.
[198] Ibid., p. 1061.
[199] Ibid.
[200] Ibid.
[201] Ibid.

in my view qualify ... as a person who can claim a grant in his capacity as a worker.[202]

Thus, an understanding of the 'worker', in which the intention behind work was relevant, evolved as a result of the interaction between some of the Member States and AG Slynn in *Levin*.

Furthermore, it is maintained that, as a result of the influence of both the Member States and AG Slynn's opinion in *Levin*, the Court reacted, producing one of the most powerful statements made in Community law. In *Levin*, the Court reiterated what had been first established in *Unger* when it maintained that the 'worker' 'may not be defined by reference to the national laws of the Member State but [has] a Community meaning' and it then makes what is now a familiar statement:

Whilst part-time employment is not excluded from the field of application of the rules on freedom of movement for workers, these rules cover only the pursuit of effective and genuine activities, to the exclusion of activities on such a small scale as to regarded as marginal and ancillary.[203]

Part of the Court's judgment appears to satisfy aspects of the objections of the Member States when it elaborates upon what the new test of 'effective' and 'genuineness' meant when it further states that (ex) Article 48 of the Treaty can only apply to those who 'pursue or are desirous of pursuing an economic activity'.[204] It then rules that 'the advantages which Community law confers in the name of that freedom may be relied upon only by persons who actually pursue or seriously wish to pursue activities as employed persons'.[205] By placing an emphasis on the 'seriousness', 'effectiveness' and 'genuineness' of the intention of a Community national to undertake work the objections of the Member States were taken into account. However, it is also maintained that in substance the Court appeared to take a different stance from AG Slynn in *Levin*. The Court firstly (at paragraph 11) makes it clear that, without explanation, neither rules on minimum working hours nor whether the work itself is enough for minimum subsistence were relevant to determining whether the applicant was or was not a 'worker'.[206] It then explicitly determines that part-time work also

202 *Brown*, p. 3233.
203 *Levin*, p. 1044, p. 1050, para. 17.
204 Ibid.
205 Ibid., p. 1052, para. 21.
206 Ibid., p. 1049.

constitutes work for the purposes of the Treaty.[207] Finally, the Court then states:

> No distinction may be made between those who wish to make do with their income from such an activity and those who supplement that income with other income, whether the latter is derived from property or from the employment of a member of their family.[208]

In effect the above statement constitutes the Court suggesting (in the context of a preliminary reference) that the applicant was a 'worker'. Thus, whilst the Court appeared to take into account some of the rhetoric uttered by the Member States and AG Slynn, the first application of its created test of 'effective' and 'genuineness' appeared to ensure that Community nationals in circumstances such as the applicant in *Levin* 'count' as 'workers' thereby continuing, rather than preventing, the socially inclusive expansion of the Community 'worker'.[209] In other words, the Court purported to adopt a stricter test and then applied it in a loose fashion.

1.5.4 *The Discursive Impact of* Levin

Furthermore subjective statements made in Levin had an equally socio-legal and discursive impact. This can, initially, be demonstrated within the case itself. Firstly AG Slynn's emphasis on the need for work undertaken by a Community national to be 'genuine and substantial' did have an impact on statements made by the Court itself. As has been cited earlier, AG Slynn subjectively created a new test of 'genuine and substantial' work.[210] However, what has yet to be outlined is the frequency of the utterance of the phrase within the text of the AG's opinion. An emphasis on 'genuineness' is made on ten occasions over the course of his opinion.[211] In particular, the penultimate paragraph refers to the phrase five times and twice within the last (shorter) paragraph.[212] Thus, the phrase is highly visible within the text of the opinion.

[207] Ibid., p. 1050, para. 16.

[208] Ibid.

[209] See, for example, O'Leary, *Evolving Concept*, p. 69. She asserts that 'the Court is generally renowned for its "human" approach to the issues which have arisen in the context of free movement of persons and its rulings are said to have gone far beyond the Treaty's economic underpinnings'.

[210] *Levin*, p. 1061.

[211] Ibid., pp. 1054–1062.

[212] Ibid., pp. 1060–1061.

Furthermore, the test subjectively uttered by AG Slynn in his opinion in *Levin* played an important role in determining the Court's own language on the matter. The 'effective and genuine' aspect of the statement cited earlier is of particular relevance in a discursive sense. Paragraph 17 of the Court's judgment constitutes the first subjective utterance of a new test to determine who 'counts' as a 'worker' by placing an emphasis on the need to undertake 'effective and genuine work'.[213] However, what is particularly noticeable is the frequency of the statement's repetition. At paragraph 18 the Court then repeats that an individual is a 'worker' so long as he/she: 'pursues an activity as an employed person which is effective and genuine'.[214] This 'effective and genuine' aspect is then repeated at paragraphs 21, 23 and paragraphs 1 and 2 of its conclusions in bold.[215] As will be outlined later, this particular terminology became pervasive and hence discursive but what should also be noted is that AG Slynn's continual emphasis on 'genuineness' appears to be partly reflected in the text of the Court judgment. It is evident that a new emphasis had been placed on the 'worker' as a result of the Court in *Levin*. It is maintained, though, that the Member States played an important yet ironic role in the evolution of the 'worker'. The phrase ('effective and genuine') emerged as an attempt to deal with a backlash from the Member States and, as a question of interpretation, the phrase places an additional level of scrutiny to determining the scope of the 'worker' (in which intention was also relevant) and therefore can be seen to be more narrowly construed than the ordinary meaning of the worker.[216] The irony, though, is that by effectively determining that the applicant was a 'worker', the newly re-fashioned understanding of the 'worker' appears to allow for the continuation of a broad understanding of the 'worker', a point the Court itself made in *Levin* when it reemphasized that the free movement provisions of the Treaty must not be interpreted 'restrictively'.[217]

[213] Ibid., p. 1050.
[214] Ibid.
[215] Ibid.
[216] For a trenchant criticism of the *Levin/Lawrie-Blum* criteria see O'Leary who claims it to be an 'unsatisfactory definition of the worker'. She also maintains that 'The Court's present consolidation of its position arguably applies a new and stricter approach to the question of who is a worker in Community law' and uses *Bettray* (where the applicant was ultimately unsuccessful after applying the *Levin* criteria) to illustrate this point. O'Leary, *Evolving Concept*, p. 66, p. 99.
[217] *Levin*, p. 1049, para. 13.

1.5.5 *'Effective and Genuine' as the Dominant Paradigm*

Moreover, it is evident that the phrase 'effective and genuine' became the dominant paradigm in which to describe the 'worker' beyond the text of the judgment in *Levin* (in tandem with the terminology used in *Lawrie-Blum*, see later). What is noticeable is, first, the sheer volume of its repetition; second, that the manner in which the phrase is used in actual fact appears to extend the concept of the 'worker' rather than curb its development; and, third, the phrase itself is used in relation to issues that do not deal directly with the definition of the worker. All of these viewed together, it is submitted, give credence to the notion of discursivity.

1.5.6 *'Effective and Genuine' in* Kempf

In terms of sheer repetition what is noticeable is how 'ordinary' the use of the phrase 'effective and genuine' became. In *Kempf*, the judgment is littered with references to it. AG Slynn alludes to the phrase 'effective and genuine as opposed to marginal and ancillary' eight times in his opinion.[218] The Court, likewise, makes multiple utterances of the phrase, referring to it ten times.[219] Equally, the case can also be seen to extend the breadth of the concept of the 'worker'. Despite the repetition of such a (seemingly self-limiting phrase), what should not be ignored are the facts of the case as there is an argument that the applicant would certainly not have satisfied the requirements of work in its 'fullest' sense as espoused by the Netherlands in *Levin* nor even the 'effectiveness' criterion as outlined by the Court.[220] The applicant in *Kempf* was a German national who had worked as a part-time music teacher in the Netherlands undertaking a minimal amount of work per week (twelve hours) and subsequently became incapacitated from work due to illness, as a result of which he received sickness and social security benefits.[221] He subsequently applied for a residence permit and was refused on the grounds that he was neither a worker nor a work-seeker.[222] For the Danish and Dutch governments his status as a worker was rather dubious for a number of reasons.[223] First, on one level of analysis, the work that he did undertake was clearly not 'effective', otherwise he would not have

[218] Case 139/85, *R. H. Kempf* v. *Staatssecretaris van Justitie* [1986] ECR 1741, pp. 1743–1745.
[219] Ibid., pp. 1748–1751, paras. 5, 6, 7, 8, 10, 11, 14, 16.
[220] Ibid., pp. 1750–1758. For commentary on *Kempf* more generally, see White, *Workers, Establishment and Services*, pp. 34–35.
[221] Ibid., p. 1747, paras. 2–3.
[222] Ibid., p. 1748, para. 4.
[223] Ibid., p. 1749, para. 7.

needed to claim the supplementary allowance.[224] Second, the work that he did undertake was so minimal that in reality it was the various different forms of state benefits that sustained him, not the part-time work.[225] Finally, he was on the one hand claiming that he was a work-seeker and on the other hand he was in receipt of sickness benefits on the grounds of an incapacity to work.[226] The two statements clearly contradict each other. Despite this the Court used the 'effective and genuine' criteria to, in effect, determine that he was a 'worker' within the meaning of the Treaty and entitled to all of the above-mentioned benefits by viewing the context in which 'effective and genuine' work should be determined differently.[227] For the Court, 'effectiveness' was determined by the nature of what was being undertaken not the remuneration received and, in this context, he was clearly an 'effective and genuine' part-time worker.[228] Thus, the phrase 'effective and genuine' was uttered repeatedly throughout the text of the judgment in *Kempf*. Equally, it was uttered in circumstances where the Member States attempted to use the language of 'effective and genuine'(ness) to determine that an applicant who needed to claim benefits to supplement his income could by definition not be engaged in 'effective and genuine' work and the Court, by contrast, further expanded the concept of the 'worker' by ruling that the applicant was. In other words, the apparently self-limiting criteria adopted in *Levin* appeared to do the opposite.

1.5.7 *Cases Subsequent to* Kempf

In subsequent cases, the phrase 'effective and genuine' was repeatedly stated, irrespective of the successful application or not of the test established in *Levin* to the facts of particular applicants' cases or indeed whether its application was necessary to determine the case. In *Lebon*, AG Lenz states:

> Let me *cite once again* the judgment in [*Levin*] where it is *stressed* that the provisions of freedom of movement for workers concerns only the pursuit of effective and genuine activities, to the exclusion of activities on such a small scale as to be regarded as marginal and ancillary.[229]

[224] Ibid.
[225] Ibid.
[226] Ibid.
[227] Ibid., pp. 1750–1751, para. 14.
[228] Ibid. For a discussion of the application of the application of the 'effective and genuine' test in the Court's case-law, see Martin and Guild, *Free Movement of Persons*, pp. 23–25.
[229] Case 316/85, *Centre public d'aide sociale de Courcelles* v. *Marie-Christine Lebon* [1987] ECR 2811, p. 2830 (emphasis added).

What is of particular relevance here is that there is a perceived need to stress this phrase and cite it; or, in other words, a very conscious attempt is being made to render this particular phrase important.[230] It is therefore unsurprising that AG Slynn then cites *Lebon* itself in *Commission* v. *Belgium (tuition fees)* when he asserts that an individual needs to be 'available for effective and genuine work and not merely ancillary work'.[231] Moreover, crucial acts of rearticulation took place and were continued in *Lair* (where the phrase is used twice by AG Slynn and once by the Court),[232] and in *Lenoir* (where the Commission refers to it).[233] In *Brown*, the Headnote reiterates the phrase, along with the Commission (twice) and the Court.[234] In *Steymann*, AG Darmon uses the phrase, as well as the Commission and the Court where it asserts 'everything must be effective and genuine',[235] and together with a reference to the principle of equal treatment, the Court refers to it in *Matteucci*.[236] Likewise, in *Van Heijningen*,

[230] In *Lebon*, the applicant (the daughter of French pensioner in Belgium), was refused the *minimex* on the grounds that she did not appear to engage in any form of work (she resided in a homeless hostel during the week in Liège in order to receive treatment in a hospital and then returned to the parental home in Courcelles at weekends). The Court never actually determined the case on the basis of the *Levin* criteria, ruling against the applicant on the grounds of no longer being a dependent of a worker. *Lebon*, p. 2834 at para. 4, p. 2840. See further Rosa Greaves, 'Who is a Dependent Member of a Worker's Family' (1988) 13 *European Law Review*, 270–275.

[231] Case 293/85, *Commission of the European Communities* v. *Kingdom of Belgium* [1988] ECR 305, p. 340 (*Commission* v. *Belgium (tuition fees)*).

[232] Case 39/86, *Sylvie Lair* v. *Universität Hannover* [1988] ECR 3161, pp. 3181–3182, p. 3199 at para. 33, p. 3180 and p. 3197 at paras. 22–24 (facts). A case concerning a French national and former work in Germany that was charged the *minerval* in order to take up a course in Hannover. The case turned not an application of the 'effective and genuine test' but, in part, on whether the applicant's previous status as a worker entitled her to equal treatment in relation to an educational grant with a view to career improvement (which the Court determined that it did). See also Barnard, 'Case C-209/03', 1465–1489.

[233] Case 313/86, *O. Lenoir* v. *Caisse d'allocations familiales des Alpes-Maritimes* [1988] ECR 5391, p. 5404, p. 5420. The applicant in *Lenoir* was a pensioner that moved from France to the UK and for that reason was deducted an aspect of his pension. Once again, the case did not concern the definition of the 'worker'.

[234] *Brown*, p. 3245. See Section 1.5.1 for the facts, and analysis in Section 2.5.

[235] Case 196/87, *Udo Steymann* v. *Staatssecretaris van Justitie* [1988] ECR 6159, at p. 6167; p. 6165; p. 6172, para. 13; facts at p. 6170 and p. 6173, para. 14. The case itself directly concerned (and extended) the application of the *Levin* test. The applicant was a member of a religious Community (the Bhagwan Community) who performed various tasks for them (such as plumbing work) in return for board and lodging. The Court held that the applicant was 'worker' on the basis of his board and lodging being the 'indirect quid-pro-quo' for his work (the national Court had (fortunately for the Court) already determined that his work was 'effective and genuine').

[236] Case 235/87, *Annunziata Matteucci* v. *Communauté française of Belgium and Commissariat général aux relations internationales of the Communauté française of Belgium* [1988] ECR 5589,

AG Tesauro makes reference to the phrase four times in the case,[237] and in *Antonissen*, AG Darmon determines that in order to define 'the field of application of the rules on free movement of workers the Court stressed that they covered only the pursuit of an effective and genuine activity'.[238] The AG then continues 'When it comes to seeking employment, the right of residence should in some way be linked with "effectively and genuinely seeking an effective and genuine activity"'.[239] Perhaps his comments speak for themselves! It is clear that the use of the phrase 'effective and genuine' has become deeply ingrained and the governing paradigm in which to both describe and limit the worker. This trend then also appears in *Bettray* (where the Headnote refers to it, along with the Commission (three times)),[240] as well as *Factortame* – a case that was not about defining the 'worker'.[241] In *Factortame*, AG Mischo summarized the free movement provisions of the Treaty: 'the rules of the Treaty on free movement of persons cover only the pursuit of effective and genuine activities, to the exclusion of activities on such a small scale as to be regarded as purely

pp. 5609–5610, para. 9–10; facts at p. 5596. The applicant, an Italian national, was a dance teacher in Belgium who applied and was refused access to a scholarship (agreed under a bilateral agreement) in order to do a course in singing in Berlin. The issue of effective and genuine work never arose as the national court never asked the Court to determine that issue, the Court simply assumed that she was.

237 Case C-2/89, *Bestuur van de Sociale Verzekeringsbank* v. *M. G. J. Kits van Heijningen* [1990] ECR I 1755, pp. 1765–1766; facts at p. 1776. The case concerned a frontier worker between Belgium and the Netherlands who, upon retirement, continued teaching for two hours a week. The referring court asked the Court whether the applicant's work was effective and genuine within the meaning of *Levin* and the Court effectively determined that it did (though on the basis of Regulation No. 1408/71 rather than the Treaty itself).

238 Case C-292/89, *The Queen* v. *Immigration Appeal Tribunal, ex parte Gustaff Desiderius Antonissen* [1991] ECR I 745, p. 769, p. 775 and p. 779 (facts). The applicant in the case, a German national, was a convicted cocaine dealer who, upon his release from prison in the UK, was deported. The applicant tried to argue that he was a work-seeker and should therefore have been entitled to remain. The Court ruled that, if he had not found employment within six months of his release, the UK was entitled to deport him unless he could provide evidence that there was a 'genuine chance' that he would be employed. See also Carole Fox, 'European Community Migrant Workers: The Right to Remain and Look for Work' (1991) 13(2) *The Journal of Social Welfare Law*, 85–89; Dominik Lasok, 'Deporting Unemployed Immigrants' (1991) 88(17) *The Law Society's Gazette*, 17–18.

239 *Antonissen*, pp. 769–770.

240 Case 344/87, *I. Bettray* v. *Staatssecretaris van Justitie* [1989] ECR 1621, p. 1621, p. 1632 and p. 1646 at para. 17 (facts). A case concerning a German drug addict who had taken part in a rehabilitative scheme which involved a form of work for those 'unable to enter the normal job market'. The Court ultimately determined that the scheme did not constitute effective and genuine work because of its rehabilitative purpose.

241 Case C-221/89, *The Queen* v. *Secretary of State for Transport, ex parte Factortame Ltd and others* [1991] ECR I 3905.

marginal and ancillary'.[242] In other words this particular set of terminology is how the 'worker' has now become collectively known.

In summary, what has been particularly noticeable has been the considerable and repeated use of the phrase 'effective and genuine' such that that it became a pervasive understanding of the 'worker'. What is equally apparent is the timing of such a phenomenon in that such an understanding of the worker emerged within sets of cases that were heard relatively closely together; an epistemic community of sorts.[243] Whilst the phrase 'effective and genuine' was first uttered in *Levin* in 1982, it appears that it was then first rearticulated in *Kempf* in 1986, followed by *Lebon* in 1987. It was, though, prolifically repeated in 1988 as *Lair, Lenoir, Brown, Steymann, Commission* v. *Belgium (Tuition Fees)* and *Matteucci* were all reported in the same year. Finally, the phrase was also uttered in *Bettray* in 1989, *Van Heijningen* in 1990, *Antonissen* in 1991 and *Factortame* in 1991. Indeed, it is the phrase's use in the final case, *Factortame* that is of particular significance. *Factortame*, whilst clearly a free movement case determining the rights of fishermen, did not need to define the 'worker' in order to determine the case.[244] Seen in this context, the phrase 'effective and genuine' was being uttered by AG Mischo in circumstances that were more of repetitive rhetorical effect rather than legal relevance. In discursive terms, it is maintained that this is indicative of an understanding of the worker that had become predominant by 1991, such that it was almost unthinkingly being uttered. Equally, the case itself, reported in 1991, can be seen to be linguistically reflective of prolific references to the phrase made in 1988 in particular such that it became a norm to refer to 'effectiveness and genuineness' in a case that did not involve determining whether an applicant was a 'worker'. Thus, by 1991, in the immediate build-up to the incorporation of the Citizenship provisions into the Treaty, a clear intersubjective understanding of the 'worker' had developed.

Moreover, the development of the discourse of the 'worker' to incorporate 'effective and genuine'(ness) can be seen to have been co-opted by the Member States whilst at the same time continuing to radically

[242] Ibid., p. 3945.

[243] See 'Introduction' for an outline of the nature of epistemic communities.

[244] Factortame, p. 3907. See further Robin Churchill, 'Case 221/89, R v. Secretary of State for Transport ex p. Factortame; Case 246/89, Commission v. United Kingdom; Case 93/89, Commission v. Ireland' (1992) 29 Common Market Law Review, 405–414 (note); Catherine Noirfalisse, 'The Community System of Fisheries Management and the Factortame Case' (1992) 12(1) Yearbook of European Law, 325–351.

develop in a manner contrary to the understanding of the phrase as articulated by such Member States. What has already been outlined is that the phrase 'effective and genuine' arose in circumstances where the Member States profoundly objected to the applicant's attempt in *Levin* to claim that she was a 'worker'.[245] It has also been maintained that the phrase is a self-limiting one in which scrutiny of the 'genuineness' of a particular job is necessitated.[246] This point can be illustrated by the UK's view in *Lair*, where it stated:

> As regards the concept of 'worker', the U.K., like the Danish Government, refers to the judgement in [*Levin*] and considers that emphasis must be placed on 'effective and genuine' activities, by contrast with those which are marginal and ancillary.[247]

By stating that 'emphasis must be placed on "effective and genuine activities"' the UK is effectively suggesting that individuals can only derive protection from the Treaty on the basis of undertaking 'real' work. This, then, can be seen to be claiming the phrase 'effective and genuine' to incorporate an understanding of the worker based upon Danish and Dutch governments in *Levin* emphasizing the need for work to be undertaken in the 'fullest sense'.[248] Whilst emphasizing work in its 'fullest sense' never caught on to become discursive the Member States were clearly prepared to accept the terminology of 'effectiveness and genuineness' as an alternative.

Nonetheless, the language of *Levin* was harnessed by the Court to further extend the categories of individuals that could be classified as 'workers'.[249] In part, whilst the language to describe the 'worker' may have evolved, the Court appears, in *Lair*, to suggest that the substance of the concept of the 'worker', in which the concept was construed increasingly broadly, continued unabated by the supposed qualification in *Levin* when it states two paragraphs before the Court makes its seemingly obligatory allusion to effectiveness and genuineness, that to be a 'worker' it 'do[es] not necessarily depend on the actual or

[245] See Sections 1.5.1 and 1.5.2.
[246] Ibid.
[247] *Lair*, p. 3170.
[248] *Levin*, p. 1058.
[249] As O'Leary comments, because of the Court's jurisprudence 'in such diverse fields of activity as tourism, education, medicine, the activities of religious communities, traineeships and employment and retraining schemes for the unemployed, the essential definitions of "effective and genuine" employment, remuneration, services and economic activity have become obscured'. O'Leary, *Evolving Concept*, p. 67.

continuing existence of an employment relationship'.[250] Likewise, as has already been examined earlier, the applicant in *Kempf* was a part-time music teacher who subsequently became incapacitated entirely from work.[251] The Court, though, ultimately determined him to be a 'worker'.[252] *Kempf* was one of many cases in which the phrase 'effective and genuine' was used in the context of applicants on the periphery of what could be classified as a worker in the sense of substantive economic contribution as envisaged by the Danish government in *Levin*.[253] In other words, the Court ultimately used the discourse of 'effectiveness and genuineness' against the Member States rather than to adopt a more narrow understanding of the 'worker' in which the self-limiting nature of the phrase could have been applied. Equally, in *Lair*, as summarized earlier, the applicant had previously been in employment but had been unemployed for quite some time and was attempting to use the worker provisions of the Treaty in order to obtain an exemption from student fees; something seemingly wholly unrelated to work.[254] Indeed, at one extreme, in *Steymann* (as also summarized earlier) the Court formed the view that a member of a spiritual community who receives bed and board within the Community and in return performs various household tasks within it could be classified as a worker if bed and board was the 'indirect quid pro quo' for the work that he had undertaken.[255] The controversies of the continuation of an extended concept of the 'worker' will be examined in Chapter 5 in the context of the normative justification for the later EU Citizen but it should be stated at this point that this is what the inherently contingent vision of the 'market citizen', with all its fissures yet to be exposed, became.

What is equally of significance in terms of the emergence of the 'effective and genuine' aspect of the 'worker' at this point are the cases in which the Court ruled negatively against an applicant. It has already been outlined earlier that the audacity of the pleadings of lawyers for some of the applicants played an important role in both continuing to extend the concept of the 'worker' and can also be seen to be reflective of sociocultural change within the epistemic community

[250] *Lair*, p. 3199.
[251] See Section 1.5.6 for a summary of the facts.
[252] *Kempf*, pp. 1750–1751 at para. 14.
[253] *Levin*, p. 1058.
[254] See Section 1.5.7 for a summary of the facts.
[255] *Steymann*, p. 6173, para. 14. See Section 1.5.7 for a summary of the facts.

of the Court such that such pleadings were even entertained by the Court.[256] For instance, in *Lebon* (as also summarized earlier), it would be difficult to suggest that the applicant was engaged in genuine and effective work.[257] The applicant was French and residing in Belgium. She had at some stage in the past worked for two years in France and was claiming the minimum subsistence allowance – the *minimex* – whilst being initially hospitalized and then living in a homeless hostel.[258] Whilst the Court ultimately found against the applicant the fact that the application was made was indicative of the fact that applicants clearly viewed the concept of the 'worker' as continuing to expand enormously.[259] A similar point could be made in relation to the applicant in *Bettray* as he was a drug addict attending a scheme in Eindhoven that was explicitly for people 'unable to compete in the normal labour market' but yet the Court was at least prepared to entertain the idea that he might potentially be a worker (he performed service for remuneration) whilst ultimately conceding that all depended upon the purpose of the scheme and if the purpose of it was rehabilitative then ultimately the work he was undertaking was not sufficiently 'normal' to be effective and genuine.[260] What is therefore apparent is a collective paradigm shift in the linguistic understanding of the 'worker' and this has been outlined in terms of the initial subjective utterance of 'effective and genuine'(ness) in *Levin*, followed by repeated references to the phrase in multiple cases. It has also been suggested that this can be evidenced by the Member States' adoption of the phrase 'effective and genuine'. From a discursive perspective, though, this aspect of the discourse of the 'worker' was perpetuated and strengthened irrespective of the Court ruling in favour of an applicant (as in *Steymann*) or against him (as in *Bettray*). Equally, it is maintained that the 'broad' concept of the 'worker' continued to develop. Additionally, what is particularly important to take into account is that the discourse of the 'worker' changed and thereby evolved after *Levin* and was moulded into something that linguistically sounded different from the *Unger*-type understanding of it.

[256] See 'Introduction' for an elaboration of an SC understanding of conceptualizing sociocultural change.
[257] See Section 1.5.7 for a summary of the facts.
[258] Ibid.
[259] Ibid.
[260] *Bettray*, p. 1646, para. 17; p. 1636. See Section 1.5.7 for a more detailed summary of the case. Indeed, the Commission was prepared to conceive of the applicant as a 'worker'.

1.5.8 *The Linguistic Addition in* Lawrie-Blum

Finally, the language of 'effective and genuine'(ness) in *Levin* was expanded to incorporate additional linguistic criteria in *Lawrie-Blum*. The case itself could be seen to be adding the discursive 'finishing gloss' to twenty-five years of jurisprudential development as what might previously have been classified as a 'worker' took an entirely different turn afterwards (see Chapter 2). This, then, marks the final piece of discursive tapestry of the 'worker' prior to Maastricht. In *Lawrie-Blum*, the applicant, a UK national, was refused admittance to a preparatory stage of teacher training in Germany on the grounds that a teacher was a civil servant in Germany and civil servants were required to be German nationals.[261] In dismissing the German authority's attempt to invoke the public service exception in (ex) Article 48(4) of the Treaty and determining that the applicant was a 'worker', the Court ruled that:

> The term 'worker' covers any person performing for remuneration work the nature of which is not determined by himself for and under the control of another, regardless of the legal nature of the employment relationship.[262]

There are two key aspects of this definition that became recurrent: 'remuneration' and 'control'.[263] Equally, the way that the Court chose to clarify or define the 'worker' may seem obvious but in reality it is the particular use of this phrase that is of relevance, not the 'obvious' point: that a worker gets paid to undertake employment under the supervision and authority of his employer. This point could be expressed in a multiplicity of ways but what is noticeable is that this particular terminology, together with the 'effective and genuine' terminology of *Levin* became the predominant paradigm in which to describe the 'worker'. One manner of doing this is to 'weld' these particular phrases together by classifying them as fundamental, and what is noticeable is that the Court in *Lawrie-Blum*, immediately prior to asserting that the 'worker' must have a Community definition, states that 'freedom of movement of workers constitutes one of the fundamental principles of the Community'.[264]

[261] *Lawrie-Blum*, p. 2140 at para. 2.

[262] Ibid., p. 2143 at para. 12.

[263] For academic commentary on the test in *Lawrie-Blum*, see O'Leary, *Evolving Concept*, p. 83; Robin White, 'A Round-up of Cases of Free Movement of Workers' (1987) 12(2) *European Law Review*, 147–153; John Handoll, 'Article 48(4) EEC and Non-National Access to Public Employment' (1988) 13 *European Law Review*, 223–241.

[264] *Lawrie-Blum*, p. 2144 at para. 16. See Chapter 3 for a detailed analysis of the discursive concept of 'welding'. Suffice it to say that it involves the interrelationship between the

Equally, it refers to the need to define the worker 'broadly', thus tying it in with the pre-*Levin* discourse of the 'worker'.[265] Moreover, what is equally fundamental to a discourse is the continual reiteration of its component parts, with consistent linkages between each of them.[266] In *Lair*, in addition to referring to the need to be 'effective and genuine' the Court also immediately after alluding to *Levin* then maintains that the 'essential characteristic' of a 'worker' 'is that during a certain period of time he performs services for and under the direction of another in return for remuneration'.[267] Thus, in both *Lawrie-Blum* and *Lair*, the criterion of control is both outlined and linked to all the various pre-existing characteristics of the discourse of the worker.

1.6 The Final 'Snapshot' of the 'Worker' Prior to the Birth of the Citizen

Furthermore, in the immediate build-up to Maastricht, several reported cases appeared to make repeated references to both the pre-*Levin* discourse of the 'worker' and the *Levin* and *Lawrie-Blum* criteria seen as inexorably intertwined. In other words, several statements were made in which the development of the discourse of the 'worker' was reflected. In *Raulin*, in 1992, the applicant, a French national, worked, part-time, as a waitress in the Netherlands and one of the issues in the case was whether this constituted 'genuine and effective' work in order to entitle her to claim a study grant.[268] AG Van Gerven summarizes the discursive

repetition of core aspects of discourse together with key words that are designed to denote their importance.

265 Ibid.

266 See Section 3.3 for a detailed discussion of the concept of 'welding'.

267 *Lair*, p. 3181.

268 Case C-357/89, *V. J. M. Raulin* v. *Minister van Onderwijs en Wetenschappen* [1992] ECR I 1027, p. 1042, p. 1060 at paras. 13–14. It should be noted that a mere act of articulation is always relevant from the perspective of discourse theory, irrespective of whether a litigant actually 'wins' or 'loses' in a given case (see 'Introduction'). In *Raulin*, the guidance which the Court gave to the referring national court appeared to cast doubt on whether the applicant was a 'worker'. Whilst re-emphasizing the point first made in *Levin* that part-time work can *per se* count as 'work' for the purposes of the Treaty, account has to be made of the 'irregular nature and limited duration' of the work actually performed (i.e. by the applicant) and that this may be 'an indication that the activities concerned are purely marginal and ancillary'. See further David O'Keeffe, 'Case C-357/89, *Raulin* v. *Netherlands Ministry of Education and Science*, and Case C-3/90, *Bernini* v. *Netherlands Ministry of Education and Science*, Judgments of 26 February 1992' (1992) 39 *Common Market Law Review*, 1215–1228.

development of the 'worker' in an exemplary fashion. Firstly, he summarizes the pre-*Levin* discourse of the 'worker':

> The Court has held on many occasions that the concept of migrant worker has a specific Community meaning because otherwise national legislation would be able arbitrarily to exclude certain categories of person from the scope of the EEC Treaty.[269]

It is now noticeable that, in referring to the original definition of the worker in *Unger*,[270] AG Van Gerven refers to the deeply embedded nature of this in his use of the words 'many occasions'. The AG then continues:

> The Court has consistently held that a migrant worker includes anybody pursuing (or wishing to pursue) effective and genuine paid activity which is not on such a small scale as to be purely marginal and ancillary.[271]

Thus, the development of the worker from *Levin* includes both the 'effective and genuine' criteria from *Levin* itself in addition to the Community definition of it from *Unger* as part of a collective whole. Finally, AG Van Gerven then maintains that: 'the essential feature of an employment relationship is that for a certain period of time a person performs services for and under the direction of another person for which he receives remuneration'.[272] Furthermore, what is also of note in *Raulin* is the fact that the Member States and the Court also rearticulate the core collective components of the discourse of the 'worker'. The Netherlands, for instance, refers to the 'essential feature of an employment relationship' as being that derived from the specific understanding of the worker as outlined in *Lawrie-Blum* and *Levin* and, in addition, the Court refers to both 'effective and genuinely' and performing 'services for and under' the direction of another.[273] Thus, in *Raulin*, repeated reference is made to the definition of the 'worker' as adopted in both *Levin* and *Lawrie-Blum*.

Moreover, such acts of repetition also take place in a number of other cases prior to 1992. In *Bernini*, the applicant was an Italian national who had been brought up and schooled within the Dutch educational system since the age of two.[274] The applicant, after leaving school, then

[269] *Raulin*, p. 1043.
[270] See Section 1.2.
[271] *Raulin*, p. 1043.
[272] Ibid.
[273] Ibid., p. 1033, p. 1059 at para. 10.
[274] Case C-3/90, *M. J. E. Bernini* v. *Minister van Onderwijs en Wetenschappen* [1992] ECR I 1071, p. 1074.

commenced an occupational training course, ten weeks of which consisted of being a paid trainee in a furniture factory.[275] She subsequently wanted to study architecture in Naples, applied for study finance from the Dutch authorities and was refused on the grounds, *inter alia*, that she was not a 'worker'.[276] The Court appeared to express scepticism as to whether this was enough to allow the applicant to retain the status of 'worker' when applying for study finance by ruling that the applicant should have 'completed a sufficient number of hours in order to familiarize himself with the work'.[277] Despite this, from a discursive perspective, the *Levin/Lawrie-Blum* concept of the 'worker' was comprehensively rearticulated by AG Van Gerven when he states:

> In accordance with the case-law of the Court a migrant worker must be deemed to be any person actually engaged in effective and genuine salaried employment to the exclusion of activities on such a small scale as to be regarded as purely marginal and ancillary. In accordance with these judgements, the essential feature is that for a certain period of time a person performs services for and under the direction of another person in return for remuneration.[278]

Thus understood, as far as AG Van Gerven is concerned, this is the 'worker' and therefore it is clear that a combination of these two cases has redefined its discursive nature. Thus, in *Bernini*, once again, the *Levin/Lawrie Blum* conception of the 'worker' was rearticulated.

It should be noted, though, that a collective picture of the 'worker' in the immediate build-up to the coming into force of the TEU can still be seen to be an amalgamation of the discourse of the 'worker' prior to *Levin* and its linguistically amended form as a result of *Levin* and *Lawrie Blum*. In *Le Manoir*,[279] the Court summarized the concept of the 'worker' as a tripartite concept involving 'broadness', 'effectiveness and

[275] Ibid.

[276] Ibid.

[277] Ibid., p. 1105 at para. 16.

[278] Ibid., p. 1089.

[279] Case C-27/91, *Union de Recouvrement des Cotisations de Sécurité Sociale et d'Allocations Familiales de la Savoie (URSSAF)* v. *Hostellerie Le Manoir SARL* [1991] ECR I 5531, pp. 5539–5541. In the case, the applicant was the employer of an Irish national working in France who was sent by her employer to undertake a brief period of vocational training in Ireland. The French social security authorities demanded a greater amount of social security contributions from the applicant company than would have been required had the period of training taken place in France. One of the issues in the case was, therefore, whether the applicant was a 'worker' whilst undertaking this period of training. The Court ruled that, on this matter, the fact that a person performs those services under a traineeship contract does not prevent him from being regarded as a worker.

genuineness', 'remuneration' and finally the development in *Lawrie-Blum* when it stated:

> In order to reply to the question referred . . . it should be stated *in limine* that the concept of worker . . . has a Community meaning. As the Court has already held, any person who pursues an activity which is effective and genuine, to the exclusion of activities on such a small scale as to be regarded as purely marginal and ancillary, is to be treated as a worker. The essential characteristic is that for a certain time a person performs services for and under the direction of another person in return for which he receives remuneration.[280]

For the Court, then, it is submitted that the entire context within which it operates is based upon a powerful and pervasive understanding of the 'worker' that dictates what it thinks. Moreover, this understanding is also evident in academic literature. Van Der Mei, for example, when summarizing the 'worker', states:

> The concept has a Community meaning. From the case law, and the rulings in *Levin* (1982) and *Lawrie-Blum* (1986) in particular, it follows that the status of Community worker can be obtained by nationals of the Member States who are pursing effective and genuine economic activities under the direction of an employer established in another Member State and who, in return for their activities, receive remuneration. The Court's definition is quite broad.[281]

This is both discursive and normative. As the Court itself states, it feels that it 'should' be stated '*in limine*' (i.e. before anything else is stated), thereby making it normative. Likewise, it is discursive as it delineates the entire parameters within which it operates.[282] Indeed, perhaps an implicit reference to the discursive nature of the 'worker' is made by AG Tesauro in *Singh*.[283] The case itself has little or nothing to do with

[280] *Le Manoir*, p. 5541 at para. 7.

[281] Van Der Mei, *Free Movement*, p. 36. Equally exemplary of this is Wouters, writing in 1994 and at the time Legal Secretary at the Court, when he states that 'it is well established case-law' that the 'worker' has a 'Community notion' (as stated in *Unger*) and then outlines the *Levin/Lawrie-Blum* criteria. O'Leary maintains that in the end all the Court did in its case-law was to 'juggle . . . these two criteria and variously accept . . . or den[y] the individual's status as a community worker'. Jan Wouters, 'European Citizenship and the Case-Law of the EC Court of Justice on the Free Movement of Persons', in Epaminondas Marias (ed.), *European Citizenship* (Maastricht: European Institute of Public Administration, 1994), pp. 25–61 at p. 27; O'Leary, *Evolving Concept*, p. 66. See also Weiss and Wooldridge, *Free Movement of Persons*, pp. 46–47; Szyszczak, *EC Labour Law*, p. 59.

[282] See 'Introduction' for a discussion of the interrelationship between pervasive discourses and cognition.

[283] Case C-370/90, *The Queen* v. *Immigration Appeal Tribunal and Surinder Singh, ex parte Secretary of State for Home Department* [1992] ECR I 4265.

a 'worker' as conventionally understood and more to do with UK immigration law.[284] The applicant, an Indian national, married a UK national, then undertook a period of employment in Germany and, upon returning to the UK, attempted to set up a business.[285] The applicant then divorced his wife and an order for deportation was made against him by the Home Office.[286] The applicant argued that he was entitled to leave to remain in the UK on the basis of his wife having previously exercised her right to free movement and subsequently attempting to set up a business back in her home state, the UK.[287] The case therefore related to the right to establishment, not the definition of the 'worker' and the Court itself made no reference to the concept of the 'worker'.[288] Despite this, AG Tesauro stated:

> Moreover, the Court's case-law to the effect that in order to be regarded as such an occupational activity must be effective and genuine, and not purely marginal and ancillary, *may prove a useful point of reference* for the national authorities in seeking to prevent abuses.[289]

This statement has profound implications. It is clear that at this point an understanding of the 'worker' had developed that was deeply embedded. For AG Tesauro, it is almost unthinkingly the 'useful point of reference for the national authorities'. Moreover, this is clearly now the dominant paradigm being used in unusual circumstances. Here the norm of 'effective and genuine'(ness) was not being used to determine whether someone was a worker but whether a marriage was 'genuine and effective'.[290] Seen in this manner, it is maintained that the discursive nature of the *Levin/Lawrie Blum* criteria is inherent, as what is clear is that the language of the 'worker' can move laterally into other areas and to describe different factual scenarios.[291] The evolution of discourse

[284] See, for example, White, *Workers, Establishment and Services*, pp. 158–161 (for a commentary on a series of cases towards the end of the 1980s in which Community law was claimed to be used in order to circumvent national immigration law). See also Philippa Watson, 'Free Movement of Workers: A One Way Ticket?' (1993) 22(1) *Industrial Law Journal*, 68–77; Holly Cullen, 'Spouses' Right to Free Movement – Community Rules Prevail' (1993) 15(1) *Journal of Social Welfare Law*, 77–82.

[285] *Singh*, p. 4290.

[286] Ibid.

[287] Ibid.

[288] Ibid.

[289] Ibid., p. 4286 (emphasis added).

[290] Ibid.

[291] See 'Introduction' for an outline of the impact of discourse being seen in its use in different scenarios.

can, then, be evidenced in its language emanating in context 'A' but, because of its pervasiveness, flowing through subjective utterance, into context 'B'. Thus, the development of the discourse of the 'worker' can be seen to have developed further by virtue of the additional language inherited from *Lawrie-Blum*.

1.7 Conclusion

By 1992, a clear picture of the 'worker' had emerged incorporating a number of dominant concepts that were sufficiently pervasive to be used in novel (and indeed controversial) circumstances that did not actually relate to the definition of the 'worker' and provided a fundamental backdrop to the formal creation of EU Citizenship. What this chapter has sought to do is to trace the 'worker' to its subjective origins and it has done so in both a qualitative and quantitative sense in order, in particular, to illustrate the important interplay between subjective utterance and norm diffusion through repetition and rearticulation. What is evidenced through the text of early court judgments is that a discourse of the worker emerged in which Community nationals were entitled to derive protection on the basis of liberal interpretations of the Court that were considerably distanced from conventional understandings of the concept of 'work'. In addition to such subjective interpretations what was also evidenced was a cognitive internalization process in which later on in the case law it had simply become 'common sense' to construe the concept of the 'worker' broadly. This, in turn, effected social change as can be seen in the increasingly audacious attempts by a number of litigants to claim that they could also be construed as 'workers'. In addition, the critical response by certain Member States to this discursive evolution had also, it is maintained, led to a refashioned discourse of the 'worker', placing emphasis on the criteria set out in *Levin* and *Lawrie-Blum*, which appear, on the surface, to limit the Community-specific understanding of the 'worker'. Ultimately, despite such a limitation, what appears to have happened was that the Court purported to adopt a stricter test and then applied it in a loose fashion, allowing the substance of its liberal interpretation to continue unabated.

However, the final 'snapshot' of the 'worker' prior to the formal creation of the Citizen evidenced a profoundly embedded discourse that constituted a Community-specific understanding of the 'worker': the 'market citizen' but fundamentally one that is problematic. From the moment the Court established the 'worker' as a supranational concept it set itself the task of elaborating a concept at times seemingly divorced from the ordinary notion of 'work'. Within the emerging grundnorm of the epistemic community of EU lawyers this evolution made sense. The Treaty had a normative 'spirit' to it which it was the Court's job to elaborate on through the case law and, if anything, any attempt to encourage cross-border movement was one step on the way to creating a European polis. Even at this point, though, it remains entirely unclear as to whether the hidden constituency of the immobile citizen would be content with a supranational legal construct so divorced from the ordinary meaning of work (and deriving a panoply of benefits therefrom) that a further discursive evolution in *Levin* had to evolve to seemingly stem the tide (and still fail). What is clear, though, from the very wording of the texts of some of the cases (and invariably overlooked in conventional commentary) are the initial objections of some of the Member States to this radical innovation. It may well be the case that elites within the objecting Member States simply accepted this legal and discursive evolution but in a contemporary (post-Brexit) environment it is clearly the case that large contingents of the UK population at the very least did not. Fundamentally, it made sense for the Court to construe the 'worker' in a supranational sense. To do otherwise would have left the concept to the vagaries of differing definitions within national law. The logic would therefore also seem to suggest, given the predisposition of the (then) Treaty to closer integration, that the Court should adopt a broad vision of the worker in order to entitle millions of Community nationals (at the time) to extensive legal protection. However, such a 'logic' is arguably critically flawed in the sense that at least some of the Member States (on one level representing the constituency of the immobile as well as the mobile) formed the view that at the very least (if not allowed to adopt national definitions) the concept of work should have been restricted to a more conventional understanding of work, rather than becoming increasingly divorced from it. If anything, the attempt to stem the tide via the 'effective and genuine' paradigm achieved the reverse effect. Thus, the fissures were there from the outset, constituting a core part of the foundations of EU free movement of persons law but were clearly not seen.

2 The Role Explicitly Economically Inactive and Potentially Socially Excluded Categories of Individuals Played in the Subjective Creation of EU Citizenship

2.1 Introduction

If Chapter 1 can be understood as the incipient citizen being partially seen through the social construction of the worker, then, because its 'final form' was well defined in a discursive sense, understanding it is relatively straightforward. This chapter, by contrast, focusses on the complex, the contingent and, ultimately, the controversial. More specifically, it constitutes a nuanced and qualitative attempt to examine strands which, woven together, partially constitute Union Citizenship in a contemporary and contextual sense but yet is also a chapter that further illustrates a series of fissures within its very foundations. What was outlined in Chapter 1 was a rather large fissure that had formed in relation to the very essence of the 'Community worker' from the outset. What remained unresolved (particularly after the development in *Levin/ Lawrie-Blum*) was where those who simply could not be classified as workers conceptually fit within the framework of free movement of persons law. Today, EU Citizens derive protection whether explicitly economically active or within socially excluded categories of individuals or not.[1] Whilst one may point to the rights derived directly from EU Citizenship itself, the infancy of protection for these various categories of individuals also derived from the early case law of the Court prior to the formal creation of the Citizen. If anything, though, this is part of an undertheorized problem in the contemporary environment. What arguably constituted an attempt to paper over the cracks of a rather large

[1] It should be noted that even the principle of equal treatment does not necessarily create de facto parity with home nationals. O'Brien, for instance, outlines the administrative and legal obstacles that EU Citizens actually face when trying to exercise their *de jure* right to freedom of movement. O'Brien, *Unity in Adversity*, p. 4.

fissure created by the deficiencies of the discourse of the worker arguably ended up creating multiple fissures which remain unresolved today.

There will be two recurrent themes throughout this chapter. First, an attempt will be made to trace the origins of the three residency directives in 1990 (Directives 90/364, 90/365 and 90/366), and there is an important reason for doing so in that the origins of Directive 2004/38 – 'on the right of citizens of the Union' – can, in turn, be traced to these directives.[2] These directives preceded the Treaty of Maastricht only by two years. In other words, in a Union-specific context, these directives were foundational building blocks upon which the later Citizen was built. Second, it will be suggested that the discourse of the 'worker', emancipatory though it was in many ways, was also linguistically self-limiting and, in tandem with a number of other factors, created a linguistic impetus for a 'new' phrase upon which various conceptual strands can hang. In the opening part of this chapter a number of different elements will be exposed from within the text of the case law that made a significant contribution to a sociocultural momentum towards a generalized right of residence. In the first instance, a comparison will be made between the social construction of borders within the North American Free Trade Agreement (NAFTA) and the EU. It will then be suggested that borders, as well as their social construction, must now simply be understood differently because of the way in which expulsion is, likewise, understood in a qualitatively different sense within the Union's borders. In a Brexit context, this issue has become toxic. In addition, momentum towards such a generalized right will be claimed to be evidenced through the focus in a substantive sense on cases concerned with issues of residence and not work.

The second part of the chapter is devoted to examining two core aspects of the Court's later development of its jurisprudence that, likewise, played a significant role in establishing a momentum towards

[2] Council Directive 90/364/EEC of 28 June 1990 on the right of residence [1990] OJ L180/26; Council Directive 90/365/EEC of 28 June 1990 on the right of residence for employees and self-employed persons who have ceased their occupational activity [1990] OJ L180/28; Council Directive 90/366/EEC of 28 June 1990 on the right of residence for students [1990] OJ L180/30; Directive 2004/38/EC on the right of Citizens of the Union and their family members to move and reside freely within the territory of the Member States amending Regulation (EEC) No. 1612/68 and repealing Directives 64/221/EEC, 68/360/EEC, 72/194/EEC, 73/148/EEC, 75/34/EEC, 75/35/EEC, 90/364/EEC, 90/365/EEC and 93/96/EEC [2004] OJ L158/77 ('The Citizenship Directive'). Note that Directive 90/366 was legally challenged and was replaced by Directive 93/96 (see Section 5.3).

the three residency directives: the case law on the 'tourist' and the student, respectively. It will be maintained that initially attempts were made to compartmentalize both tourists and students within the pre-existing framework of the 'worker' but that such attempts were doomed to fail, particularly because of the self-limiting nature of the discourse of the worker after *Levin*. It will, instead, be argued that, in a contextual sense soon after *Levin*, the landmark cases of *Cowan* and *Gravier* (both of which will be holistically examined) created a further impetus towards legislative change. It will finally be claimed that the image of the 'citizen' as understood specifically in the context of the *Citizenship Directive* was partially crystallized into legislative form as a result of a reaction towards an evident momentum from within the case law to create a seemingly unencumbered right of residence. By so doing, it will be concluded that the 'embryonic' citizen can also be seen to be an inherently contingent one – a complex, at times jumbled, but inherently controversial tapestry of concepts evolving over many years that have one aspect of commonality in the form of a focus on individuals that could not be construed as workers. There is an underlying logic or 'social common sense' behind these various overlapping developments in the protection of Community nationals, but it will fundamentally suggest hidden fissures lay right at the heart of them.

2.2 A New Social Construction of Borders

One key aspect of the progression inherent to the process of European integration is how a Community national is treated at the border of another Member State by contrast with third-country nationals ('TCNs').[3] Yet the border is also a key visible element of a desire to 'take back control'. Understanding the evolution of internal borders within the EU is fundamental to understanding the evolution towards (and controversy behind) Citizenship beyond the notion of the worker. Borders are a fundamental aspect of a state's identity; it is what, in part, defines each state and distinguishes 'self' from 'Other'.[4] It is at the border where very visible signs of national identity are present, such as flags, official documents and border officials, being the representatives of the state and its immigration policy.[5] Any change to the nature,

[3] See n. 36.
[4] See 'Introduction' for a further discussion of the 'Other'.
[5] As Guild outlines: 'Borders delineate areas within which certain types of order and activities take place and identities are formulated ... the border from movement of an

routine and 'rules of the game' in terms of the treatment of Community nationals at the border could have led to an entirely different conceptual understanding of national identities within the then EEC that was more closely aligned to a conventional understanding of national identities and borders beyond the EU.[6] Putting it differently, it was perfectly feasible for the various border authorities of the Member States (prior to the Schengen Agreement) to have adopted an entirely different and more restrictive approach to the manner in which Community nationals were let in at the border than in actual fact took place.[7] Free movement rights were primarily intended for workers and the national authorities could have insisted on proof of employment being demonstrated at the border. It is true to say that Community law also encompasses work-seekers and the self-employed, but even in those circumstances individuals could have been questioned about the genuineness of both at the border. By way of illustration, the contrasting position of the 'NAFTA Professional' will be examined. This will then be contrasted with the nature of borders as outlined by the Court in *Pieck*, and it will then be maintained that this evidences a *sui generis* social construction of borders.

individual is the place where a control takes place which is constitutive of whether the individual can pass or not'. Elspeth Guild, 'The Border Abroad – Visas and Border Controls', in Kees Groenendijk, Elspeth Guild and Paul Minderhoud (eds.), *In Search of Europe's Borders* (The Hague: Kluwer Law International, 2002), pp. 87–105 at p. 87.

6 See 'Introduction' for an outline of the interrelationship among identity evolution, discourse and borders.

7 The point being made here is that the context in which the core principles on free movement as elaborated by the Court emerged ensured that the Community became a *sui generis* entity and without such a context the Union may not have developed to become such a distinct organization. The context was one in which there was, to a certain extent, a collective commitment to a shared set of integrative ideals and one shared by the Court intended on creating substantive rights by inferring the 'spirit' of the Treaty. Likewise, as early as the 1970s the Commission made a proposal for a Passport Union designed to considerably reduce restrictions at borders within the Union and also to include non-economic actors. In other words, a holistic sociological understanding of the context of Community law is a necessary and a fundamental aspect of SC theory (see 'Introduction'). The method of reasoning used by the Court has not been without its critics (see Section 2.4.2). This collective set of ideals contrasts with the views of some of the Member States in the early days of the Court's jurisprudence who viewed the Treaty as merely one of many international agreements that were not intended to create enforceable rights in national courts. As the Netherlands government maintained in *Van Gend*: 'the EEC Treaty does not differ from a standard international treaty' and the Belgian government had similar views. John Crowley, 'Locating Europe's Borders', in Groenendijk, Guild and Minderhoud (eds.), *In Search of Europe's Borders*, pp. 27–44 at pp. 34–36; Case 26/62, *van Gend en Loos (NV Algemene Transporten Expeitidie Onderneming)* v. *Nedelandse Administratie der Belastingen* [1963] ECR 1, pp. 6–8.

2.2.1 *The Contrasting Position of the 'NAFTA Professional'*

In NAFTA, non-US nationals (in reality Mexican) had a more extensive right to free movement than other TCNs in order to work in the United States.[8] However, in order to exercise that right, such nationals had to obtain a NAFTA visa beforehand, and the genuineness of the work that they were undertaking was heavily scrutinized. There was technically no legislatively enshrined right to free movement of persons within the NAFTA area. Article 101 of the NAFTA Agreement merely establishes a 'Free Trade Area'.[9] Provisions relating to labour were contained within the supplementary agreement: the North American Agreement on Labor Cooperation ('NAALC'). The NAALC, likewise, only refers to movement of persons obliquely. The preamble to the NAALC alludes to attempting to foster improved working standards within rather than between states. Likewise in the 'Objectives' of the NAALC as set out in Part One of the agreement, the emphasis was on a need to 'Improve working conditions and living standards in each Party's territory'.[10] There was, though, an implicit reference to movement of labour. One of the other Objectives set out in Part One of the NAALC was to 'Pursue cooperative labor-related activities on the basis of mutual benefit'.[11] In reality, though, movement of workers within NAFTA to the United States was governed by governmental policy on the basis of the two agreements. In guidance notes issued by the Department of State, the equivalent of the Community 'worker' in NAFTA was classified as a 'NAFTA Professional'.[12] Whilst

[8] US Department of State, 'Visas for Canadian and Mexican NAFTA Professional Workers' (*Travel State Gov*, 2014), https://travel.state.gov/content/travel/en/us-visas/employment/visas-canadian-mexican-nafta-professional-workers.html, accessed 6 August 2020. It should be noted that NAFTA has been chosen as a point of comparison because it came into force a year after the citizenship provisions were added to the Treaty at Maastricht, on 1 January 1994. Whilst it is acknowledged that NAFTA has been replaced by the United States–Mexico–Canada Agreement, the underlying points of comparison with NAFTA remain. Office of the United States Trade Representative, 'Agreement between the United States of America, the United Mexican States and Canada 12/13/19 Text' (2020), https://ustr.gov/trade-agreements/free-trade-agreements/united-states-mexico-canada-agreement/agreement-between, accessed 14 September 2020.

[9] NAFTA Secretariat, 'North America Free Trade Agreement' (2014), www.nafta-sec-alena.org/Default.aspx?tabid=97&ctl=FullView&mid=1588&language=en-US, accessed 4 November 2014.

[10] Secretariat of the Commission for Labor Cooperation, 'North American Agreement on Labor Cooperation between the Government of the United States of America, the Government of Canada and the Government of the United Mexican States, September 13, 1993' (2014), www.naalc.org/naalc/naalc-full-text.htm, accessed 4 November 2014.

[11] Ibid.

[12] US Department of State.

making a specific link between 'NAFTA Professionals' and NAFTA, it is also immediately obvious that such an approach was considerably more restrictive by comparison with the Community 'worker':

> North American Free Trade Agreement (NAFTA) created special economic and trade relationships for the United States (U.S.), Canada and Mexico … The nonimmigrant NAFTA Professional (TN) visa allows citizens of Canada and Mexico, as NAFTA professionals, to work in the U.S. in a prearranged business activity for a U.S. or foreign employer.[13]

As is immediately obvious, a visa was required in order to move to the United States and such a visa would only have been issued for a 'prearranged business activity'.[14] In other words, work-seekers are immediately excluded. Indeed, a further examination of the policy as adopted by the Department of State demonstrates that the right for NAFTA Professionals was even more restricted than at first glance. First, a visa would only have been granted if the profession concerned was on an approved 'NAFTA list'. Second, there were additional requirements including the need to have a 'baccalaureate degree' in which 'experience cannot be substituted' and, further, in some professions 'experience is required in addition to a degree'.[15] Moreover, a prearranged interview at a US consulate is mandatory and prior to that interview a detailed letter is required to be written by the applicant's employer evidencing genuine employment, as well as proof of educational qualifications.[16] However, having satisfied such an extensive set of requirements, an additional level of scrutiny took place at the border itself. The Department of State advised 'applicants should be aware that a visa does not guarantee entry into the U.S.' and, for Mexican citizens, proof of employment is required and could be inspected by an immigration official at the border.[17] It should also be noted that the rules on NAFTA Professionals also uniquely applied to Mexican citizens as, ordinarily, a NAFTA Professional visa was not required for Canadian citizens.[18] Equally, a visa fee was payable in order to obtain a NAFTA Professional visa. Finally, to contrast markedly with the nature of European integration 'applicants must show their intended stay is temporary, without the intent to establish

[13] Ibid.
[14] Ibid.
[15] Ibid.
[16] Ibid.
[17] Ibid.
[18] Ibid.

permanent residence'.[19] In short, at every stage of a NAFTA Professional's attempt to exercise a right to movement there was a considerable level of scrutiny and this included an inspection at the border in order to determine the genuineness of the work that was intended to be undertaken. In addition, NAFTA Professionals were explicitly not intended to integrate themselves within the United States.

2.2.2 *The Construction of Borders in* Pieck

The issue of inspections of individuals at borders arose in *Pieck* (1980) where the UK authorities appeared to be trying to adopt a restrictive approach to Community nationals entering into the United Kingdom. It had adopted a practice of issuing six-month visas, thereby almost treating Community nationals as if they were tourists on tourist visas with a limited stay to be scrutinized by the Home Office.[20] In the case the applicant was a dual Netherlands and New Zealand international who lived and worked in the United Kingdom and every time he entered into the United Kingdom he was issued with the above-mentioned six-month visa, the validity of which he challenged.[21] In effect what the United Kingdom was trying to do was to assimilate Community law rights into the pre-existing framework of UK immigration law without acknowledging the fundamental change in the status of nationals from other Member States (by comparison with non-Community nationals) resulting from the Treaty as developed by the Court.[22] Nonetheless, the UK

[19] Ibid. By contrast, an underlying purpose of the free movement provisions of the Treaty was to facilitate long-standing integration of Community nationals throughout the Union. See Section 5.5.1.

[20] Case 157/79, *Regina* v. *Stanislaus Pieck* [1980] ECR 2171, p. 2176.

[21] Ibid.

[22] This 'one size fits all' approach to immigration by the United Kingdom was also evident in the negotiations for the new Article 8A of the Treaty that was to be inserted into it at Maastricht. For O'Keeffe, the United Kingdom simply did not want to allow TCNs to move freely within the Community along with EU Citizens because, in part, it fundamentally did not want to alter its pre-existing immigration regime. For Barav, *Pieck* and related cases (such as *Bouchereau*) had a significant impact upon the immigration law in the United Kingdom, which the United Kingdom had to take some time to acclimatize to. As Ward put it, 'border controls seem to matter in one distant corner of the Union, even if they do not seem to matter quite so much everywhere else'. Likewise, Wyatt concluded that *Pieck* 'poses considerable difficulties for the United Kingdom's system of immigration control, which relies on point of entry scrutiny to a greater extent than most, if not all, of the Member States'. O'Keeffe, 'The Free Movement', 8–10; Ami Barav, 'Court Recommendation to Deport and the Free Movement of Workers in EEC Law' (1981) 6(3) *European Law Review*, 139–161 at 146–150; Ian Ward, *A Critical Introduction to*

approach was not inconceivable. It was at least feasible for there to have been a restrictive approach taken at the border in which a national of another Member State would be subject to considerable scrutiny as to whether they were working *and* to have a visa issued of limited duration to enable the Member State to continually subject the individual's status to near-on continuous review. Thus, such an approach could have been taken towards Community nationals at the border, which would, in turn, have led to a more restrictive understanding of the 'worker'.

However, it is clear that this restrictive approach was never allowed by the Court in *Pieck* to take place. The legislation at issue in *Pieck* was Directive 68/360 on residence – a piece of legislation that came into force in the middle of the considerable (and 'broad') jurisprudential creation and development of the 'worker' by the Court as outlined in Chapter 1. The preamble to the directive stated that its provisions were intended to apply to workers, and Article 1 of the directive limited its application to those who were entitled to protection under Regulation No. 1612/68 (i.e. workers).[23] However, the directive itself had to be seen within the juridical and legislative context in which it was enacted and as part of a process in which Community law developed from being concerned with protecting workers to initially other forms of economic actors and, subsequently, non-economic actors.[24] As AG Warner maintains in *Pieck*:

> The authors of the directive must have been aware that it and the successive directives relating to free movement of persons in connexion with freedom of establishment and freedom to provide services would, between them, cover many if not most nationals of Member States travelling to other Member States. They cannot have intended that all should be delayed at the internal frontiers of the Community while the sheep were sorted from the goats.[25]

As AG Warner has outlined, there were clearly pragmatic reasons for such an expansion. For inherently practical reasons, since the EEC's inception, it would have been not impossible but difficult and time-

European Law (Cambridge: Cambridge University Press, 2009), p. 148; Derrick Wyatt, 'Article 48: Permissible Entry Formalities for Nationals of Member States' (1980) 5(5) *European Law Review*, 380–388 at 386.

[23] Council Directive 68/360/EEC of 15 October 1968 on the abolition of restrictions on movement and residence within the Community for workers of Member States and their families [1968] OJ L257/13.

[24] See Section 5.2.7.

[25] *Pieck*, p. 2201.

consuming to sort the 'sheep' (workers) from the 'goats' (non-economically active Community nationals) at the border.

AG Warner's point can be further illustrated by the legislative context in which Directive 68/360 was one small part. Ex Article 48 of the Treaty made it clear that a Community national was allowed to move to another Member State to work; however, Title III of Regulation No. 1612/68 also explicitly enabled a Community worker to move his or her family (who are not economically active themselves) to another Member State.[26] Pensioners, likewise, had a limited and implicit right to free movement. Regulation No. 1251/70 enshrined not only a right to move but also a right to permanent residence for a retired worker (as well as his or her family).[27] Whilst an entirely free-standing right for a pensioner (seen specifically as a non-economic contributor without having previously worked in the host state) to move and reside in another Member State was not legislatively enshrined until Directive 90/364 (and on the basis of not being an unreasonable burden on state resources),[28] a worker, on reaching a pensionable age, was, according to Article 2(1)(a) of the regulation, entitled to permanently remain within his or her host state subject to having been employed for at least twelve months (in the host state) and resided there for at least three years. In addition, the self-employed were (and still are) entitled to move to set up a business (ex Article 52 of the Treaty) and individuals were entitled to move to provide services (ex Article 59). In the case of both categories of Community nationals (as well as their families), Directive 64/220 formally abolished restrictions on movement and residence (Article 1).[29] Indeed, Article 1(b) of the directive formally created such an entitlement to recipients of services in addition to providers, something not

[26] In addition, Regulation No. 1408/71 facilitated such a movement by ensuring access to state social security benefits for them and their families (such as sickness pay in Articles 19–24 and family benefits and family allowances in Articles 72–76 of the regulation). Council Regulation No. 1612/68/EEC of 15 October 1968 on free movement of workers within the Community [1968] OJ L257/2; Council Regulation No. 1408/71 of 14 June 1971 on the application of social security schemes to employed persons and their families moving within the Community [1971] OJ Spec Ed. 416.

[27] Regulation No. 1251/70 of 29 June 1970 on the right of workers to remain in the territory of a Member State after having been employed in that State [1970] OJ Spec Ed. 402.

[28] Council Directive 90/364/EEC of 28 June 1990 on the right of residence [1990] OJ L180/26, Article 1(1).

[29] Directive 64/220/EEC of 25 February 1964 on the abolition of restrictions on movement and residence within the Community for nationals of Member States with regard to establishment and the provision of services [1964] OJ Spec Ed. 115.

explicitly referred to in the Treaty. This position was then consolidated by Directive 73/148, which formally established an entitlement for the self-employed, providers and recipients of services and their families (Article 1) to enter onto the territory of the host Member State upon the mere production of a passport or other form of national identification (Article 2).[30] Finally, an unemployed work-seeker was (and still is) entitled to a limited right to move.[31] Indeed, the position of the work-seeker, even prior to the enactment of the *Citizenship Directive* made the job of 'sifting the sheep from the goats' even more complicated despite the fact that ex Article 48 of the Treaty made no reference to work-seekers.[32]

Likewise, the majority of Regulation No. 1612/68 is concerned with individuals already in possession of a contract of employment or being close to being so (Articles 1–4 and Article 6 of Title I). However, Article 5 of the regulation entitled an individual seeking employment in another Member State to equal treatment in relation to assistance in finding employment, logically presupposing, therefore, a prior right to enter onto the territory of the host state to seek work.[33] Furthermore, Article 2 of Directive 68/360 refers to a right to free movement at the border (on the mere production of a valid passport or other lawful identification in Article 3 (see subsequent sections for further analysis of this point)) for those not only taking up an activity as an employed person but pursuing employment. For the avoidance of doubt, though, the Council made a declaration at the meeting in which both Directive 68/360 and Regulation No. 1612/68 were adopted explicitly allowing a work-seeker to move to another Member State to seek work but on the proviso that they did not become dependent upon social assistance in the host state.[34] In short, even prior to Directive 90/364 and the later *Citizenship Directive*, a wide variety of individuals, in addition to workers understood in a straightforward sense, were entitled to move to and reside in another Member State; *de jure* these categories of individuals were entitled to move.

[30] Council Directive 73/148/EEC of 21 May 1973 on the abolition of restrictions on movement and residence within the Community for nationals of Member States with regard to establishment and the provision of services [1973] OJ L172/14.

[31] *Lebon*, para. 26 (the Court).

[32] This is because of the 'liberal' interpretation that the Court gave to Directive 68/360 for work-seekers in which some considerable time has to elapse before a Community national can be deported for not genuinely seeking work. See Condinanzi, Lang and Nascimbene, *Citizenship of the Union and Freedom of Movement of Persons*, p. 82.

[33] Handoll, *Free Movement*, p. 109.

[34] *Levin*, p. 1043 (note also, a case reported in the same year is *Pieck*).

However, de facto, it would have been a thankless task for border officials to determine the status of the remaining categories of individuals that were not technically covered by the Treaty and secondary legislation. This state of affairs was then consolidated by AG Warner's interpretation of Directive 68/360 in *Pieck* (discussed earlier) because he emphasized that the border was not the place to scrutinize the 'worker', his or her family or any individual who fitted into any of the above categories.[35] In the Directive, Article 2, as outlined earlier (and mirrored by Article 2 of Directive 73/148), made it clear that no proof was required that an individual either worked or was the member of a family of a worker; all that was needed was a passport or identification card of a Member State and the authorities were obliged to let all Community nationals enter the territory of the host state. There was in effect no discretion on their part at the border itself.[36] Thus, the evolution and enactment of an increasingly complex web of secondary legislation (as briefly outlined earlier) incorporating a wide variety of economic actors, along with their potentially non-economically active dependent family members, rendered it practically impossible to 'sort the sheep from the goats' at the border itself. The consequence, therefore, was that borders within the then EEC became fluid by comparison with, for example, those within the former NAFTA regime.[37]

Furthermore, the combination of enacted secondary legislation and its judicial interpretation (of which AG Warner in *Pieck* played a small

[35] *Pieck*, p. 2201.

[36] This is not to suggest that the Member States were not entitled to scrutinize the status of Community nationals entering their territory; merely that the border was not the place in which to do it. See Section 2.3.1 for an elaboration on this point. See also Condinanzi, Lang and Nascimbene, *Citizenship of the Union and Freedom of Movement of Persons*, pp. 79–80.

[37] As Guild maintains: 'the traditional relationship in international law of the individual alien subject to the control of the State ... no longer applies within the European Union'. Indeed, for Wilsher, the evolution of borders within the Union has provided a stark contrast with the position of TCNs and 'exacerbated' the gap between Union Citizens and conventional migrants. This is a view shared with Geddes, who takes a critical approach to the emergence of EU Citizenship on the grounds that it takes no account of the 'sixteenth Member State' (at the time of writing there were only fifteen Member States), namely the nine million TCNs on Community territory. Elspeth Guild, *Immigration Law in the European Community* (The Hague: Kluwer Law International, 2001), p. 36; Daniel Wilsher, 'Economic Migration into the European Union: Standing at the Crossroads' (2001) 21(1) *Yearbook of European Law*, 163–193 at 169; Andrew Geddes, 'Immigrant and Ethnic Minorities and the EU's "Democratic Deficit"' (1995) 33 *Journal of Common Market Studies*, 197–217 at 203–204. See also Martin Baldwin-Edwards, 'Immigration and Migrants in the Europe of the 1990s' (1992) 3 *European Access*, 14–16.

but important part) did considerably more than simply respond to the practical problem of how to sort 'sheep' from 'goats' and ultimately led to an ontological paradigm shift as to how borders were conceptualized within the EEC. What has already been outlined (above) is that borders themselves are inherently socially constructed and, as has been detailed in the Introduction, a core tenet of SC theory is that because reality itself is socially constructed, it can also be deconstructed and, fundamentally, change.[38] Moreover, if it is reality itself that has changed, then this represents an ontological shift in relation to, in this instance, national borders within the EEC. It has been submitted (above) that legislative change itself played a key role in such an evolution. However, aspects of reality within the EU were (and arguably still are) judicially constructed,[39] and part of such a construction can be evidenced by AG Warner in *Pieck*. In addition to the AG outlining (as examined earlier) the practical problem associated with determining, at the border, which remaining categories of Community nationals are not able to exercise a right to free movement, he also constructs a novel practice for border officials themselves when confronted by a Community national at the border. AG Warner maintained that when presented with a passport or identity card of another Member State at the border, a border official need not 'necessarily remain mute or passive' (though of course that is also a possibility) and could be allowed to give 'at least a smile, a nod, or a wave of the hand'.[40] Nonetheless, what is obvious in both cases is that the 'rules of the game' are entirely different for Community nationals by contrast with TCNs.

If an individual were trying to enter the UK from a non-EU country (such as Nigeria or the USA) then he/she would have to apply for a visa in three sets of circumstances: work, studying or tourism. In all three cases, administrative formalities are a prerequisite and paperwork would be required to be scrutinized by border agency staff. Tourists from Nigeria are classified as 'general visitors' to the UK and, as such, are required to overcome several administrative hurdles in order to obtain a visa to gain entry.[41] Prior to arriving at the border or at the border itself documentary evidence must be provided to demonstrate the intention to only visit for six months, to leave the UK at the end of

[38] See 'Introduction'.

[39] Alec Stone-Sweet, *The Judicial Construction of Europe* (Oxford: Oxford University Press, 2004), p. 3.

[40] *Pieck*, p. 2220.

[41] Please note that in a post-Brexit environment the 'General Visitor visa' has been reclassified as a 'Standard Visitor visa'. Home Office, 'UK Visas'.

the visit and to 'have enough money to support and accommodate yourself without working or help from public funds and to be able to meet the costs of the return journey'.[42] In addition, an applicant must also demonstrate a lack of intention to, *inter alia*, work or study.[43] For tourists from the United States, a visa is not required for a stay of up to six months and, instead, an 'entry certificate' is issued.[44] However, border officials equally play a key role in scrutinizing US nationals entering the UK as tourists as they are not entitled to a visa waiver if the intention of entry is either to work or study.[45] Therefore, in order to even obtain an entry certificate, a border official is entitled to ask questions about a US national entering the UK as a tourist such as information about the entrant, the purpose of the visit and where the visitor will be staying.[46] Moreover, documentary evidence might be required to prove the *bona fide* nature of the visit as a tourist.[47]

In relation to workers, a non-Economic Area (EEA) national could have, prior to Brexit, gain(ed) entry to the UK in order to work either as a short term 'Business Visitor' or to undertake a 'permitted paid engagement' and as a long-term visitor under a points-based system.[48] Whilst the complexities of UK immigration law are beyond the scope of this book, what takes place, as a summary, at the border to the UK is, in relation to short-term workers, firstly, a detailed scrutiny by border officials of the *bona fide* nature of the work and secondly, a determination as to whether the work itself fits within the established categories of short-term workers.[49] In relation to longer-term workers, evidence of sponsorship by an employer needs to be demonstrated and, in addition, a determination has to have been made by the Home Office prior to attempting to gain entry to the UK that an individual applicant has satisfied the points-based criteria and that a quota for the particular tier of visa being applied for has not been filled.[50] In relation to students, a points-based system also operates in order to obtain a 'Tier 4' visa and such 'points' are satisfied if an academic institution provides a 'Confirmation of Acceptance for Studies' letter and, in addition, proof is required of the ability to finance fees and living costs.[51]

[42] Ibid.
[43] Ibid.
[44] Ibid.
[45] Ibid.
[46] Ibid.
[47] Ibid.
[48] Ibid.
[49] Ibid.
[50] Ibid.
[51] International Student Team, University of Cambridge, 'Tier 4 Visas'.

Moreover, both core aspects of required proof will also be scrutinized at the border.[52] In short, in relation to TCNs entering into the UK, border officials clearly engage in a great deal more than a 'smile', 'nod' or 'wave'.[53]

With Community nationals, on the other hand, according to AG Warner in *Pieck*, a qualitatively different approach should be taken at the border, irrespective of the purpose of a Community national for being in another Member State. The result of such subjective articulations was an almost metaphysical (or ontological) sea change in the way that a Community national is treated at a border.[54] Putting it differently, as far as Community nationals were concerned, reality itself changed at the internal borders of the then EEC. A mere wave of the hand, at least initially, is considerably different from all of the above in relation to TCNs. This will, in turn, have created a sense of awareness amongst individuals all around the Community that they belong to a collective which enables them to cross borders with ease, in turn, a sense of empowerment and, indeed, a sense of entitlement that border officials are solely entitled to 'wave' them through at a border as, ultimately, it is all 'their' territory.[55] It is therefore not a surprise that blue lanes were subsequently created to enable all Community nationals to not have their luggage inspected at airports and, equally, it would not seem to be much of a step further to abandon borders entirely as eventually took place in the form of the Schengen Agreement, signed five years after *Pieck* in 1985.[56] As has been outlined earlier, the initial

52 Please note that, in addition to a change in the terminology of the 'General Visitor visa', in a post-Brexit environment the 'Tier 4' student visa has been reclassified as simply as 'Student visa'. Home Office, 'UK Visas'.

53 See n. 40.

54 Crowley, for instance, sees one of the defining characteristics of 'European "citizenship"' as being merely 'whether one has to wave one's passport at a border' (as opposed to detailed scrutiny) and that this sociological change had a 'hugely symbolic character'. Likewise, the changing nature of treatment at a border was a formative part of Durand's early prediction of European Citizenship, an article written at a similar time to *Pieck* and was part of a momentum towards the creation of a generalized right of residence. Crowley, 'Locating Europe's Borders', p. 36; Andrew Durand, 'European Citizenship' (1979) 4 *European Law Review*, 3–14 at 13.

55 This is what Dougan, Shuibhne and Spaventa term 'a novel "European" dimension to our senses of geography, membership and belonging'. Michael Dougan, Niamh Nic Shuibhne and Eleanor Spaventa, 'Introduction', in Michael Dougan, Niahm Nic Shuibhne and Eleanor Spaventa (eds.), *Empowerment and Disempowerment of the European Citizen* (Oxford: Hart Publishing, 2012), pp. 2–7 at p. 2.

56 For detailed analysis of the Schengen Agreement and its implications, see David O'Keeffe, 'The Schengen Convention: A Suitable Model for European Integration' (1991) 11(1) *Yearbook of European Law*, 185–219 at 185–205; Diedre Curtin and Herman Meijers,

legislative framework was designed principally to enable workers to move freely within the Community. However, what can also been seen through juridical and legislative development is a parallel sociological development in which an entirely different and ontological understanding as to what a border actually means emerged.[57] Thus, an attempt to compartmentalize Community nationals, as the UK did in *Pieck*, into an existing legislative framework of immigration law was bound to fail.

However, it could be suggested that this development, lauded by many as evidence of the evolution towards an emancipatory supranationalism, was an inherently problematic contingency: a large fissure was evident in plain sight. It is clear that seven years into the UK's membership of the EEC it still struggled to categorize the movement of Community nationals at the borders. Clearly the view of the UK Government as late as 1980 was that the 'sheep' should have been sifted from the 'goats' at the border, irrespective of status and territorial origin. Legal elites within the epistemic Community of EU lawyers clearly had accepted an evolution towards a qualitatively novel conception of borders and arguably AG Warner was expressing that view in plain language to the UK Government. It remained entirely unresolved, though, as to whether the UK Government (indeed successive ones) truly accepted that outcome, let alone the population of one of the EU largest Member States. Perhaps evidence of how problematic the UK

'The Principle of Open Government in Schengen and the European Union: Democratic Retrogression' (1995) 32 *Common Market Law Review*, 391–442 at 391–407; Sabina Mazzi-Zissis, 'Les Accords de Schengen et la libre circulation des personnes dans l'Union européenne: exemple á suivre ou dangereux precedent?', in Claus Ehlerman (ed.), *Multi-Speed Europe: the Legal Framework of Variable Geometry in the European Union* (Bonn: Bundesanzeiger, 1999), pp. 47–66; Georgia Papagianni, 'Free Movement of Persons in the Light of the New Title IV TEC: From Intergovernmentalism towards a Community Policy' (2001) 21(2) *Yearbook of European Law*, 107–162.

[57] Romero, after careful statistical analysis, maintains that there has been an enormous increase in cross border movement within the Community as a result of the changing nature of borders within it (in Spain, for instance, there was a 58.25 per cent growth in internal movement since it joined the EEC). Romero conceptualizes it as a: 'privileged inner space whose lack of restrictions affects … the possibility of combining various types of movement. In a common space of intense, evolving and multifarious flows of people, the abolition of [borders] … allows for greater elasticity and an increasing overlap among the diverse determinants of flows'. Federico Romero, 'Cross-Border Population Movements', in William Wallace (ed.), *The Dynamics of European Integration* (London: Pinter, 1990), pp. 171–191 at pp. 188–189. See also Malcolm Anderson and Didier Bigo, 'What are EU Frontiers For and What Do They Mean?', in Groenendijk, Guild and Minderhoud (eds.), *In Search of Europe's Borders*, pp. 7–26; Rey Koslowski, 'Intra-EU Migration, Citizenship, and Political Union' (1994) 32(3) *Journal of Common Market Studies*, 369–402.

Government found this development is the refusal to ever accede to the Schengen convention. Its preference in the late 1970s was to compartmentalize free movement within a pre-existing visa regime. Thus all Brexit is doing is to return to an issue that was unresolved from the outset. In the era of 'taking back control' there is clearly a desire to sift the 'sheep' from the 'goats'. Essentially free movement was simply too straightforward to be publicly acceptable and, by contrast, the NAFTA regime appears more attractive. What *Pieck* reveals is that movement at the border itself could at least conceivably have been different and more straightforwardly appear as a simple international border. Perception in a Brexit context (over substance) has arguably proven to be crucial and to a certain extent was engendered by cases such as *Pieck*.[58]

2.2.3 *A Reconceptualization of Expulsion*

Furthermore, a change equally took place in relation to the expulsion of Community nationals from the territory of the host Member State. In *Pieck*, AG Warner alludes to two categories of individuals that are not entitled to unencumbered free movement; namely non-workers and those for whom a Member State is entitled to prevent entry on public policy/security grounds.[59] However, this might give the misleading impression that in relation to these two categories the rules were somehow relatively similar to ordinary domestic immigration law. This view was taken by the Italian government in *Testa* when it asserted:

> The position of the unemployed person is to a certain extent comparable with that of a worker to whom his employer grants paid leave for the purpose of

[58] A core tenet of SC theory is that a social truth need not be 'rational' and this issue has proven to be particularly the case in an era of populism combined with widespread and unverified social media. As Marxen put it, 'Discourse theory of law in times of populism' means that 'traditional media no longer reach significant parts of society' creating 'detached and self-reliance bubbles' in which populist movements are 'unfolding dominant influence on the public discourse'. This 'bubble' feeds directly into the reasons behind Brexit. As Kochenov put it, after Brexit, 'Britain awoke to a new, much less rational world of inexplicable mysticism and the self-inflicted mutilation of citizenship' with the only desire of those at least that voted Brexit to regain sovereignty. The perception of the need for borders to appear more conventional was arguably right at the head of this 'bubble'. Christian Marxen, 'Discourse Theory of Law in Times of Populism' (2019) 25 *European Law Journal*, 480–486 at 485–486. Dimitry Kochenov, 'EU Citizenship and Withdrawals from the Union: How Inevitable is the Radical Downgrading of Rights?', in Carlos Closa (ed.), *Secession from a Member State and Withdrawal from the European Union: Trouble Membership* (Cambridge: Cambridge University Press, 2017), pp. 257–286 at p. 284.

[59] *Pieck*, p. 2201.

studying abroad for three months. If at the expiry of the leave the worker does not return to his employment, the employer may terminate the employment without prior notice.[60]

What is of note here is the comment that a non-worker could have his position 'terminated without prior notice'. This gives the impression that any non-national other than a 'worker' is in a vulnerable position and liable to be deported at the whim of the host Member State. In reality, though, this was far from the case because there has never been a reported case before the Court involving an unemployed person who was successfully deported from a host Member State for the sole reason of being unemployed.[61] One practical reason for such a paucity of cases is because the broadly constructed concept of the 'worker' meant that it was not onerous for a Community national to be construed as a 'worker' if all that was needed was to claim a loose connection to work as conventionally understood (such as in *Steymann*) to ensure their ability to remain within a host Member State.[62]

Nonetheless, even in relation to an applicant who could not be described as a 'worker' as broadly construed, expulsion was also not an issue. In *Hoeckx*, the applicant was a Dutch national who resided in Belgium and was receiving unemployment benefit in her host state.[63] She subsequently moved to France, receiving unemployment benefit there and then returned to Belgium to claim the *minimex*.[64] She was denied access to the *minimex* on the grounds of not having resided in Belgium for five continuous years.[65] In legal terms, the case solely concerned a residency requirement as a prerequisite for the receipt of a social security benefit. However, in conceptual terms the case evidences a paradigm shift in relation to Community nationals as at no point in the report of the case was the issue of the applicant's apparent lack of engagement in any economic activity raised. By contrast, she was

[60] Joined Cases 41/79, 121/79 and 796/79, *Vittorio Testa, Salvino Maggio and Carmine Vitale* v. *Bundesanstalt für Arbeit* [1980] ECR 1979, p. 1986, p. 1981 (facts). In the case the applicant was an Italian national who had worked in Germany and subsequently applied for unemployment benefit from the German authorities, despite having returned to Italy to seek work.

[61] See Section 2.4.2. Unemployment was an issue in relation to claims to social security, not an issue as grounds for deportation.

[62] See Section 1.5.7.

[63] Case 249/83, *Vera Hoeckx* v. *Openbaar Centrum voor Maatschappelijk Welzijn, Kalmthout* [1985] ECR 973, p. 983.

[64] Ibid.

[65] Ibid.

able to receive social welfare provisions in two Member States despite such a lack of economic contribution and her treatment was clearly different from that of a TCN, who would have been liable to be deported.[66] Once again, perception matters. The perception that EU Citizens often aspire to take advantage of so-called benefit tourism has been refuted by statistical evidence.[67] Nonetheless, it was one of the factors that not only led to the then Prime Minister David Cameron seeking to renegotiate the UK's membership of the EU with stricter controls by Member States on this issue but also was a key factor in the 2016 referendum result.[68] The issue here is partly cognitive: at no point within the structure of the case did the issue of engagement with an economic activity arise, despite the law at the time arguably requiring it. This additional perception was also problematic seen in contemporary light. The then Home Secretary of the UK (subsequently Prime Minister) Theresa May is credited with having created a 'hostile environment' towards non-nationals in general and one aspect of this is whether the UK took a light touch in determining whether a non-economic contributor was self-sufficient under the Citizens Rights Directive (CRD) which then appeared to be reversed during the Prime Ministership of May after the 2016 referendum.[69] In other words, the

[66] See Section 2.2.5.

[67] For instance, a 2014 study at UCL concluded that Eastern European migrant workers contributed £5bn to the UK public finances but are disproportionately less likely to claim state benefits (43 per cent) than UK nationals and 7 per cent less likely to live in social housing. UCL Centre for Research and Analysis of Migration, 'Positive Economic Impact of UK Immigration from the European Union: New Evidence' (2014) www.ucl.ac.uk/news/2014/nov/positive-economic-impact-uk-immigration-european-union-new-evidence, accessed 15 September 2020.

[68] In the build-up to reaching the so-called Tusk accord on 18 February 2016 Cameron stated that one of the purposes of entering into such a negotiation process (prior to a proposed UK referendum) was to 'crack down on the abuse of free movement' which included 'reducing the draw that our welfare system can exert across Europe'. Prime Minister's Office, 'PM Letter to President of the European Council Donald Tusk' (2015) www.gov.uk/government/publications/eu-reform-pms-letter-to-president-of-the-european-council-donald-tusk, accessed 15 September 2020. European Council, 'Decision of the Heads of State or Government, Meeting within the European Council, Concerning a New Settlement for the United Kingdom within the European Union' in 'Conclusions – 18 and 19 February 2016' (2016), pp. 8–24. www.consilium.europa.eu/media/21787/0216-euco-conclusions.pdf, accessed 15 September 2020.

In terms of the issue being a key factor in the 2016 referendum see Adrian Favell and Roxana Barbulescu, 'Brexit, "Immigration" and Anti-Discrimination', in Patrick Diamon, Peter Nedergaard and Ben Rosamond (eds.), *The Routledge Handbook of Politics of Brexit* (Routledge, London, 2018), pp. 118–133.

[69] On the creation of a hostile environment more generally see Colin Yeo, 'Theresa May's Immigration Legacy' (2019) www.freemovement.org.uk/theresa-mays-immigration-leg

perception of being economically parasitic was clearly constructed in the build-up to Brexit and can be traced to cases such as *Hoeckx*.

2.2.4 *Expulsion of the Unemployed*

Furthermore, what the case law of the Court reveals is an additional aspect of a much greater paradigm shift, this time in relation to the treatment of the unemployed. The issue in relation to the unemployed was not one of immigration at the border. In particular, as has already been outlined earlier, a mere work-seeker, even prior to the ruling in *Antonissen*, was entitled to unencumbered entry to and residence in a host state for at least three months, thereby precluding border officials from making such a determination.[70] Instead a conceptual shift took place in which unemployment was considered to be a reason for the denial by several Member States of social welfare benefits within the host state. For instance, several cases concerned unemployment benefit and it was only in that context that the issue of whether the applicant was a worker arose. In *Murru*, for instance, what was at issue was whether a period of unemployment can be assimilated, for social security purposes, to one of employment.[71] Likewise, *D'Amico* concerned a claim to an entitlement to an early retirement pension on the grounds of unemployment.[72] Moreover, *Bonaffini* (1975), *Kermaschek* (1976), *Di Paolo* (1977), *Testa* (1980), *Baccini* (1982), *Deak* (1985), *Cole* (1985), *Miethe* (1986) and *Bergemann* (1988) all concerned a denial of unemployment benefit.[73] What all these cases have in common is that at no stage was there an issue of deportation in relation to the various applicants in the references to the Court and mass-scale

acy/, accessed 15 September 2020. On the issue of taking a stricter stance on the interpretation of the CRD, see Benjamin Kentish, 'Brexit: Deportations of EU Citizens Soar Since Referendum' *The Independent* (London, 2017) www.independent.co.uk/news/uk/politics/brexit-latest-eu-citizens-deportations-rise-uk-home-office-referendum-a7935266.html, accessed 15 September 2020.

[70] See Section 1.5.7 for a summary of the facts of *Antonissen*.

[71] Case 2/72, *Salvatore Murru* v. *Caisse régionale d'assurance maladie de Paris* [1972] ECR 333, p. 336.

[72] Case 20/75, *Gaetano d'Amico* v. *Landesversicherungsanstalt Rheinland-Pfalz* [1975] ECR 891, p. 891.

[73] Case 27/75, *Gaetano Bonaffini and others* v. *Istituto Nazionale della Previdenza Sociale* (INPS) [1975] ECR 971; Case 40/76, *Slavica Kermaschek* v. *Bundesanstalt für Arbeit* [1976] ECR 1669; Case 76/76, *Silvana di Paolo* v. *Office national de l'emploi* [1977] ECR 315; *Testa*; Case 79/81, *Margherita Baccini* v. *Office national de l'emploi (ONEM)* [1982] ECR 1063; Case 94/84, *Office national de l'emploi* v. *Joszef Deak* [1985] ECR 1873; Case 122/84, *Kenneth Scrivner and Carol Cole* v. *Centre public d'aide sociale de Chastre* [1985] ECR 1027; Case 1/85, *Horst Miethe* v. *Bundesanstalt für Arbeit* [1986] ECR 1837; Case 236/87, *Anna Bergemann* v. *Bundesanstalt für Arbeit* [1988] ECR 5125.

deportation of Community nationals simply did not take place. This contrasts markedly with non or peripherally economically active TCNs where an order for deportation would be highly likely,[74] and peripheral types of work such as a part-time piano teacher or a member of a cult would not have been enough to satisfy ordinary work visas.[75] In any case, seeking to obtain a visa on the grounds of seeking work is simply not possible under domestic immigration law.[76]

2.2.5 *Expulsion of Others Not Seen to Be Conducive to the Public Good*

Moreover, in relation to actual or suspected criminals or other categories of individuals construed by a Member State as a threat to the public and liable to be deported on those grounds in accordance with (ex) Directive 64/221, the situation became completely different for Community nationals by comparison with TCNs. In *Van Duyn*, in 1974, the Court appeared, at least initially in its jurisprudence, to adopt a position that can compare, to an extent, with the approach that could have been taken in relation to TCNs. The applicant, a Dutch national, was a practising member of the Church of Scientology, an organization not, at the time in the UK deemed to be unlawful, but which the UK Government had determined to be contrary to the public good.[77] She had obtained employment in the UK as a secretary at the headquarters of the church in East Grinstead. Upon her arrival in Gatwick airport, she was refused entry to the UK on the grounds that her exclusion would be 'conducive to the public good'.[78] The applicant argued that this

[74] The recipient of a work visa who ceases employment in the UK (a scenario roughly analogous to the position of many of the Community national applicants referred to in both Chapter 1 and Chapter 2) would subsequently be classified as an 'Overstayer' and liable for deportation. Home Office, 'UK Visas'.

[75] Whilst it is not within the scope of this book to conduct a comparative analysis of the various immigration laws of the Member States, the UK's position in relation to work-seekers is illustrative of the position of TCNs. To reiterate the points made above, a TCN is allowed to obtain a short-term visa as a 'business visitor' and for 'permitted paid engagements', as well as a long-term visa on a points-based system (see Section 2.2.2). However, none of these visas entitles a TCN to obtain a visa solely on the grounds of seeking work. Moreover, on a points-based system, an application for a long-term visa on the grounds of being a part-time (self-employed) piano teacher would be bound to fail as to obtain a Tier 2 Visa (the visa that would be the most applicable to this particular illustration), sponsorship by a full time employer is mandatory and it needs to be demonstrated that the skill being exercised cannot be more readily undertaken by a home national. Home Office, 'UK Visas'.

[76] Ibid.

[77] Case 41/74, *Yvonne van Duyn* v. *Home Office* [1974] ECR 1337, p. 1339.

[78] Ibid., p. 1340.

exclusion contravened Article 48 of the Treaty read in tandem with Directive 64/221.[79] The case then turned on how to interpret Article 3 (1) of the Directive which allowed for measures to be taken on the grounds of public policy 'exclusively on the personal conduct of the individual concerned'. The Court took a conservative approach to the Member State derogation under the directive meaning that, in practice, the applicant was excluded from the UK without even getting to the point of needing to be deported; a situation that may appear, on the surface, to not differ greatly from the position of TCNs.[80] The Court firstly ruled that the activity of a particular organization which was considered by the UK government to be socially harmful need not be unlawful and, secondly, that this being so means that merely because UK nationals were entitled to both practise as scientologists and be employed by the Church of Scientology does not mean that the principle of non-discrimination is infringed.[81] This therefore meant that the present membership of an organization deemed subjectively by a Member State to be socially harmful was enough to constitute personal conduct of the applicant in order to exclude her from its territory.[82] Therefore, at least initially in the Court's jurisprudence, some discretion was given to the Member States to exclude or expel individuals on public policy grounds.

However, it is also evident that the Court's jurisprudence developed in relation to exclusion on public policy grounds in such a manner that a paradigm shift can equally be evidenced in relation to such categories of individuals. Whilst the Court in *Van Duyn* clearly made allowances for the Member States' determination of matters of public policy, it did also make it clear that deportation in these circumstances was the exception rather than the norm because any derogation from the 'fundamental' principle of free movement 'must be interpreted strictly'.[83] Even at this point, then, there is a conceptual difference between the treatment of Community nationals and TCNs as it is the Court that determines the scope of a derogation from an *a priori* right to free movement as opposed to being simply excluded at the discretion of a UK immigration official

[79] Ibid.

[80] Ward is particularly critical of the Court's interpretation of restrictions on free movement, describing such restrictions as 'notorious'. Ward, *Critical Introduction*, p. 146.

[81] *Van Duyn*, p. 1350 at paras. 19–21.

[82] *Van Duyn*, p. 1351 at para. 24.

[83] Ibid., p. 1350 at para. 18.

who was exercising a subjective and unfettered decision taken by the UK government in relation to the Church of Scientology.[84]

Moreover, subsequent case law on Directive 64/221 considerably circumscribed a Member State's ability to deport on public policy grounds. In *Bonsignore*, an Italian national residing and working in Cologne was convicted of a firearms offence for accidently causing the death of his brother by firing a pistol without having a licence for retaining the firearm in any case.[85] The German authorities attempted to deport him on the grounds that, whilst the offence he was convicted of was a technical one (possessing a firearm without a licence), he needed to be deported as a deterrent against social unrest and crime that might be committed by immigrant communities.[86] The Court ruled that the applicant could not be deported on the grounds that Article 3 of Directive 64/221 could only be satisfied if it was the applicant's personal conduct which would be the direct cause of social unrest, which it clearly was not.[87] Likewise, in *Watson and Belmann*, the Court ruled that the deportation of a migrant for failing to report within three days of arrival that she was staying in Italy could also not be justified under the Directive as it was completely disproportionate to attempt to deport a Community national for a minor infringement of the criminal law.[88] Similarly, in *Roux*, the applicant, a French national working in Belgium, was being prosecuted and had a deportation order made against her simply on the grounds of having a residence permit that was intended for self-employed persons; whereas she actually was employed.[89] In *Bouchereau*, the Court further curtailed a Member State's ability to deport in relation to a French national working in the UK who had been twice convicted for drug possession.[90] Whilst the Court determined that the ultimate decision to deport was still a matter for the national court to decide (it is therefore not known whether in actual fact the applicant was deported) the Court ruled that the mere breach, by virtue of the second offence, of a conditional discharge handed down to the applicant on committing the first offence was not sufficient to justify exclusion on public policy grounds.[91] Moreover, personal conduct for the

[84] Ibid., p. 1339.
[85] Case 67/74, *Carmelo Angelo Bonsignore* v. *Oberstadtdirektor der Stadt Köln* [1975] ECR 297, p. 309.
[86] Ibid., p. 310.
[87] Ibid., p. 307 at para. 6.
[88] Case 118/75, *Lynne Watson and Alessandro Belmann* [1976] ECR 1185, p. 1185 at para. 21.
[89] Case C-363/89, *Danielle Roux* v. *Belgian State* [1991] ECR I 273, p. 282.
[90] Case 30/77, *Regina* v. *Pierre Bouchereau* [1977] ECR 1999, p. 2001.
[91] Ibid., p. 2012–2013 at para. 28.

purposes of Article 3 of the directive would mean that the applicant's actions had to constitute a 'present threat to the requirements of public policy' by showing a likelihood of committing similar offences on another occasion.[92] In *Adoui and Cornuaille*, two French prostitutes in Belgium were threatened with expulsion on the grounds of engaging in behaviour contrary to public morals, despite prostitution itself not being a criminal offence in Belgian law.[93] The Court ruled, overruling *Van Duyn*, that it was 'arbitrary' to make a distinction between home nationals and nationals of other Member States in relation to their conduct as home nationals were not subject to any sanction whereas other Community nationals were faced with the threat of deportation.[94]

Indeed, even in relation to individuals convicted of serious criminal offences, a Community national that was a work-seeker would still be difficult, if not impossible, to deport. In *Antonissen*, the Court ruled that the ability to deport on the sole ground of unemployment was heavily precluded.[95] The applicant was a Belgian national who had entered the UK in 1984 to seek work but had been unable to obtain employment.[96] Instead the applicant was convicted of drugs offences, spent time in prison and, upon his release, was made the subject of a deportation order.[97] UK immigration rules (as has been alluded to in part in *Pieck* above) allowed for a period of no more than six months in order to seek employment and this law was itself challenged before the court by the applicant.[98] The Court held, ignoring the 1968 Declaration (referred to above) which it determined to have no legal significance, that, whilst a six month period was sufficient to ensure the effectiveness of the principle of free movement, the right to seek employment could be continued beyond that point so long as the person concerned can provide evidence of genuinely seeking employment.[99] Thus, even in relation to an applicant who has been convicted of a criminal offence, so long as genuine attempts are being made to secure employment whilst unemployed, a Member State cannot deport an individual on the grounds of simply not being employed.

92 Ibid., para. 29.

93 Joined Cases 115 and 116/81, *Rezguia Adoui* v. *Belgian State and City of Liège; Dominique Cornuaille* v. *Belgian State* [1982] ECR 1665, p. 1714.

94 Ibid., p. 1707 at para. 7.

95 *Antonissen*, p. 745.

96 Ibid.

97 Ibid.

98 Ibid.

99 Ibid.

The result of the Court's jurisprudence on Directive 64/221 is that the power of Member States to expel non-nationals on public policy grounds is considerably curtailed in relation to the treatment of Community nationals.[100] This has led to a conceptual change in the way that EU Citizens, even those who have committed criminal offences, are treated by contrast with TCNs. For Barnard, the consequence of the Court's case law in this area has been that 'the migrant EU citizen is treated like a national in all but name'.[101] Thus in reality, the Italian government in *Testa* was simply not correct to suggest Community nationals, be they non-economically active or those deemed to be a potential existential threat to a Member State, were under the perpetual threat of immediate deportation; in particular the comparison between Community nationals who had ceased employment in the host state and an employee having a contract terminated was simply not appropriate in the context of Community law. This would result, ultimately, in an entirely different conceptual understanding as to how *all* Community nationals, irrespective of whether they work, were to be treated within various host Member States: Community nationals were to be treated differently from TCNs in *all* circumstances; they were just simply 'different'.[102] Nonetheless, it could be suggested that one of the reasons behind the vote in the UK in 2016 was that there was a perception amongst some that EU Citizens should not be treated in a way that differs from TCNs and cases such as *Antonissen*, ultimately concerning an EU Citizen committing a serious crime in the UK, are particularly controversial in that a Member State's ability to deport individuals who it may regard as not conducive to the public good was heavily circumscribed by a combination of secondary legislation, judicial interpretation and self-serving statements from litigants about their desire to seek to work. Indeed what has been particularly noticeable is that a UK Cabinet under Boris Johnson's prime ministership consisting of several prominent Brexiters appeared to have exponentially increased the number of deportation flights for TCNs in circumstances similar to that of *Antonissen*.[103] Thus, if anything,

[100] See Frank Wooldridge, 'Free Movement of EEC Nationals: Limits Based on Public Policy and Public Service' (1977) 2(2) *European Law Review*, 191–206.

[101] Barnard, *Four Freedoms*, p. 487.

[102] For Wooldridge, the Court's jurisprudence on Directive 64/221 is evidence of its 'integrationist approach to the free movement of persons' which, in turn 'accords well with the adventurous line which the Commission is taking over the question of European Citizenship'. Wooldridge, 'Free Movement of EEC Nationals', p. 207.

[103] See Diane Taylor, 'Jamaican-Born Deportees mount last-minute challenges against the Home Office' *The Guardian* (London, 2020), www.theguardian.com/uk-news/2020/feb/

the issue of expulsion (or lack thereof) of those seen by the UK at least as not being conducive to the public good was extremely controversial and had been so within the Court's case law from its infancy. Furthermore, it should also be noted that several of the cases outlined involved core Member States such as France, Italy and Germany and thus at least partly illustrates a dissonance between the views of the Member States in terms of retaining competence to expel in circumstances where an EU Citizen has committed a criminal offence and that of the Court. Thus the UK was certainly not alone in having doubts about the development of this particular area of EU law.

2.3 The Momentum towards a More Generalized Right of Residence and Movement

2.3.1 A Focus on Residence

In Chapter 1, a novel approach to the 'worker' was examined which, it was maintained, played a key role in the subjective creation of a distinct concept of EU Citizenship. However, in this chapter (and the remainder of this book), it will be argued that the emergence of a discourse of EU Citizenship can also be attributed to legal and linguistic developments in a number of different (though closely related) substantive areas of EU free movement of persons law. Thus far it has been contended that the treatment of Community nationals by contrast with TCNs demonstrated both a legal conceptual difference and social change within the jurisprudence of the Court. It has firstly been claimed that a novel form of social reconstruction of borders can be evidenced in relation to the practice of border officials as outlined in *Pieck*. It has subsequently been submitted that, likewise, the ability for Member States to expel Community nationals on any grounds (be it for lack of engagement in an economic activity or for reasons of public policy) was considerably restricted by contrast with the treatment of TCNs. It is further maintained that the practical difficulty of 'sorting sheep from goats' at the border meant that such sorting did, in effect, take place, except at some considerable distance from the border itself.[104] The cases that have been cited above dealt, in part, with the denial of various claims to social security by the economically inactive by Member State social security

10/jamaican-born-deportees-mount-last-minute-challenges-against-home-office accessed 15 September 2020.

[104] See Section 2.2.2.

bodies. In addition, aspects of the jurisprudence of the Court were devoted to examining such categories of individuals' entitlement to unimpaired movement and residence. For instance, as has already been previously outlined, in *Hoeckx*, the issue for the applicant was the denial of the *minimex* on the grounds of not having resided in Belgium for a period of five years and, by virtue of having moved between France and Belgium, her prior entitlement to the *minimex* was lost.[105] What *Hoeckx* also demonstrates is that because such categories of individuals were no longer in danger of deportation, their primary concern (as was the case with the applicant in *Hoeckx*) was the scrutiny of a Community national's status not at the border, but upon arrival at the intended place of residence.[106] In *Hoeckx*, such scrutiny led to the denial of a social welfare benefit on the grounds of not having complied with the administrative formality of having resided for five continuous years in Belgium.[107] The case can therefore be seen as playing an important role in creating momentum for a more generalized right of residence because the primary issue in the case was one of residence, not of work; itself somewhat controversial from the perspective of the Member States.[108] As has previously been outlined, the applicant claimed unemployment benefit in Belgium, then moved to France where she also claimed unemployment benefit, moved backed to Belgium and obtained the *minimex*, then moved to France (again), finally returning to Belgium and being denied the *minimex*.[109] At no point was it ever suggested that the applicant worked and therefore she could be

105 See Section 2.2.3; *Hoeckx*, p. 983, p. 987 at para. 14, pp. 988–989 at paras. 17–25. Legally, what was at issue in the case was, firstly, whether the *minimex* could be classified as social security or a social advantage and, secondly, whether the conditions of entitlement to the *minimex* (which did not require Belgian nationals to have resided in Belgium but did require other Community nationals to do so) infringed the principle of equal treatment as contained in Article 3(1) of Regulation No. 1408/71 and Article 7 of Regulation No. 1612/68. The Court ruled, firstly, that the *minimex* was not social security as it was a 'general social benefit' without a specific link to work or any social security regime and, secondly that it was a social advantage which infringed the principle of equal treatment because it specified a residency requirement that did not apply to Belgian nationals.

106 This was the preferred approach by many of the Member States; namely to require that an individual report their presence to the local authorities within a Member State after a certain period of time. David O'Keeffe, 'The Free Movement of Persons and the Single Market' (1992) 17(1) *European Law Review*, 3–19 at 8.

107 See Section 2.2.3.

108 See Section 5.2 for an examination of this issue in the context of the principle of solidarity.

109 See Section 2.2.3.

classified as an economic 'freeloader' that had been the subject of much Member State criticism in the build-up to the drafting of the three residency directives.[110] However, the case can also be seen to highlight a protective lacuna in Community law whereby workers and their dependents would have been entitled to reside and have access to social welfare provisions such as the *minimex* as a social advantage; whereas explicitly economically inactive individuals could potentially be denied the former and would be denied the latter.

In relation to a residency permit, as has already been outlined earlier, only the employed (under Article 2 of Directive 68/360) and the self-employed (Article 3 of Directive 73/148) were allowed to obtain a 'Residence Permit for a National of a Member State'. Having therefore been implicitly denied a residence permit, economically inactive individuals would also be denied access to social welfare provisions as Regulation No. 1612/68 only allows workers access to host state social advantages (Article 7(1)) and Regulation No. 1408/71, likewise, makes provision for solely workers to be entitled to receive social security (Article 3(1)), a point explicitly made by the Court in *Hoeckx* itself.[111] In other words, given the fact that at no stage in the report of the case is it mentioned that the applicant was a worker, absent evidence of such, she still might not have been entitled to either a residence permit or the *minimex*. In addition, what *Hoeckx* also demonstrates is that, irrespective of the work status of individual applicants, the subject matter of many cases, in both conceptual and quantitative terms, concerned issues of residence, not work; thus, creating a further impetus towards the creation of a general right of residence.[112] Thus, issues relating to the failure to grant a residence permit arose in *Sagulo* (1977), *Pieck* (1980), *Adoui and Cornuaille* (1982), *Levin* (1982), *Kempf* (1986), *Echternach and Moritz* (1989), *Commission* v. *Germany* (1989) and, post enactment of the three residency directives, *Roux* (1991) and *Raulin* (1992).[113] Putting it in Social Constructivist terms, if issues of residence

[110] O'Leary, *Evolving Concept*, pp. 134–138.

[111] *Hoeckx*, p. 988 at para. 20.

[112] Anthony Whelan, 'Union Citizenship and The Free Movement of Persons' (2000) 5 *Bar Review*, 179–185 at 181.

[113] The issues relating to residence in *Levin* and *Kempf* are summarized in Sections 1.5.1 and 1.5.6. Likewise, *Pieck*, *Adoui and Cornuaille* and *Roux* are outlined above. *Sagulo* concerned the nature of the residence permit itself as the applicant, an Italian national working in Germany was being prosecuted for not possessing one. In both *Echternach and Moritz* and *Raulin* the applicants were both denied access to student finance on the basis of not having a valid residence permit (itself dependent upon them being construed as either workers or dependents of workers). Finally, in *Commission* v. *Germany*, what was at issue was whether the German authorities were entitled to insert

and movement are continually uttered, the legal culture within the Court itself can change to focus less on 'work' as the subject matter of substantive discussion and more on simply moving and residing, itself creating an impetus for legislative change.[114]

2.3.2 *Evidence of a Momentum towards a General Right of Residence*

The previous sections of this chapter can be seen, from an SC perspective, to provide reasons, both practical (for instance in terms of borders) and theoretical, for creating a general right of residence for all Community nationals irrespective of engagement in an economic activity. This thereby underpinned the Court's later case law on interpreting the citizenship provisions of the amended Treaty at Maastricht in order to infer such a right and the subsequent enactment of the Citizenship Directive as a response.[115] This final section attempts to provide a discursive 'snapshot' as evidenced through the text of court judgments of the culmination of the momentum towards the creation of such a general right of residence.[116] In *Morson and Jhanjan*, AG Slynn points to a gap in the Treaty – one which he concludes is 'possible and perhaps inevitable' – in which a home national that moves to another Member State and returns with a family consisting of TCNs would be entitled under Community law to have his family join him but a national that never moves would not be able to.[117] Importantly, the Commission offers a solution to such a gap: 'the resultant problems may be resolved only in the context of a generalised right of residence attaching to the status of citizen of the EEC'.[118] This clearly prophetic statement has significance for a number of different reasons. First, as has already been submitted, a case was clearly being made for such a generalized right. Second, this type of fundamental human right attaches not to a worker but to a citizen, showing a perceived development from one to the other, with the concept of the citizen clearly having a much more direct relationship with human rights. Third, the

a 'suitable housing' proviso into the renewal of residence permits for families of worker. *Sagulo*, p. 1497; Joined Cases 389/87 and 390/87, *G. B. C. Echternach and A. Moritz* v. *Minister van Onderwijs en Wetenschappen* [1989] ECR 723, pp. 756–757; *Raulin*, pp. 1056–1057; Case 249/86, *Commission of the European Communities* v. *Federal Republic of Germany* [1989] ECR 1263, p. 1287.

[114] See 'Introduction'.

[115] See Section 5.3.5.

[116] See 'Introduction' for a description of the concept of a discursive 'snapshot'.

[117] Joined Cases 35 and 36/82, *Elestina Esselina Christina Morson* v. *State of the Netherlands and Head of the Plaatselijke Politie within the meaning of the Vreemdelingenwet; Sweradjie Jhanjan* v. *State of the Netherlands* [1982] ECR 3723, p. 3742.

[118] Ibid., p. 3731.

circumstances of the case were controversial in that rights derived from the Treaty were being claimed in circumstances designed to subvert domestic immigration law.[119] The applicants were TCNs from Suriname whose children were Dutch nationals and had never moved from the Netherlands.[120] In theory, then, this was a wholly internal situation that had nothing to do with Community law and should never have made it through the Court door in Luxembourg, but, once again, it did.[121] Indeed, the Court in the case was at least prepared to ask a 'preliminary question . . . [as to] whether it may be inferred from the context of the provisions and the place they occupy in the Community legal system as a whole that they have a right of entry and residence'.[122] Fourth, therefore, even if the Court were to ultimately conclude negatively against the applicants, the mere fact that such a question is being posed is evidence that a momentum had been created towards a generalized right of residence. Such a juridical debate clearly formed an important backdrop to the subsequent enactment of the three residency directives, even though the ultimate directives concerned specific categories of individuals. Moreover, such 'talk' within the text of the Court's judgments can also be seen to be a prototype of a later debate within the Court's jurisprudence, leading to the eventual enactment of the Citizenship Directive, creating such a generalized right. In other words, an important facet of the context-specific emergence of EU Citizenship can be traced to cases such *Morson and Jhanjan.*

2.4 The Community Tourist

The 'Community tourist' occupies a unique place in the discursive structure and hierarchy of Community law and plays an important role in establishing the later discourse of citizenship.[123] It is clear that the vast majority of people that moved and continue to move across borders within

[119] For an elaboration of this point, see Christopher Greenwood, 'Free Movement of Workers under EEC Law and English Law' (1983) 133 *New Law Journal*, 933–934; Nigel Gravells, 'Article 177 EEC: References in Interlocutory Proceedings' (1983) 8(4) *European Law Review*, 250–251.

[120] *Morson and Jhanjan*, p. 3725.

[121] This issue is still controversial even after the implementation of the Citizenship provisions of the Treaty. See Niamh Nic Shuibhne, 'Free Movement of Persons and the Wholly Internal Rule: Time to Move On?' (2002) 39 *Common Market Law Review*, 731–771 at 731.

[122] *Morson and Jhanjan*, pp. 3735–3736 at para. 13.

[123] Reich and Harbacevica, 'Citizenship and Family on Trial', 616. See also Federico Mancini, 'The Making of a Constitution for Europe' (1989) 26 *Common Market Law Review*, 595–614 at 608.

then EEC and now Union were/are tourists;[124] yet from the perspective of Community law they were hard to conceptualize given the fact that there was no specific provision of the Treaty or secondary legislation to (at least overtly) deal with them.[125] As will be concluded, such a uniqueness actually aided the progression towards citizenship and this is largely derived from the radicalism of the Court in *Cowan* (1989) in its interpretation of the (then) Article 59 of the Treaty on services in which tourists were construed as actual or potential recipients of services.[126] The majority of the following analysis will be devoted to examining the social construction of the Community tourist in the context of the *Cowan* case law. However, as will be outlined below, the way in which the Court described 'the tourist' prior to the radicalism of *Cowan* is also important from a discursive perspective as it is from this case law that the subjective origins of 'the Community tourist' can be derived.

124 Bogdan, for instance, alludes to the 'explosive rise of international tourism in recent years', something which would not have been envisaged by the original Treaty makers and continues: 'Today, the enormous sums spent by foreign tourists clearly indicate that the tourist ... is an economic factor of primordial importance'. Likewise, Romero, after careful statistical analysis, states: 'Movements of people across European borders have mushroomed over the past three decades ... [and] the vast majority [of them] each year are tourists, they are estimated to account for 75% of all travelers'. By contrast, after the implementation period of the free movement provision of the Treaty had expired, movement of workers within the Community actually fell in statistical terms. Plender's explanation for this statistic was that the Member States were actually more interested in employing TCNs simply because they would not be able to apply the principle of equal treatment and therefore be entitled to social security benefits. Michael Bogdan, 'Free Movement of Tourists within the EEC?' (1977) 11(5) *Journal of World Trade*, 468–475, 6–7; Romero, 'Cross-Border Population Movements', p. 171; Wolf Böhning, *The Migration of Workers in the United Kingdom and the European Community* (Oxford: Oxford University Press, 1972), p. 81; Plender, 'An Incipient Form of European Citizenship', p. 40.

125 As Van der Woude and Mead maintained: 'At first glance it might appear doubtful whether the provisions of the EEC Treaty provide any protection for the individual travelling abroad in the Community'. This is because Ex Article 60 (3) TEC applied only to the free movement of the provider of a service, not the recipient. Similarly, Bogdan comments that because a plain reading of Article 59 of the Treaty might lead to the conclusion that tourists were simply 'not covered' by rules relating to free movement, the Council felt the need to enact Directive 73/148 making the position of tourists as a recipients of services explicitly clear (in Article 1(2)).

It was arguably only when the Court in its later jurisprudence interpreted (then) Article 18 (1) of the amended Treaty at Maastricht that effectively a free-standing right to free movement was created that would of necessity have included tourists (See *Grzelczyk* (2001) and *Baumbast* (2002)).

Marc Van Der Woude and Phillip Mead, 'Free Movement of the Tourist in Community Law' (1988) 25 *Common Market Law Review*, 117–140 at 139, 129; Bogdan, 'Free Movement of Tourists within the EEC', 471.

126 See Section 2.4.3.

2.4.1 *The Tourist as a 'Worker'?*

The tourist originally appeared as part of the Court's early jurisprudence on the social security benefits that could be derived by Community nationals by virtue of their status as a 'worker' in an extended sense.[127] On one level, it may seem absurd to suggest that a tourist could be construed as a 'worker' but what was clear is that, at least initially, this appeared to be implicitly the line taken by the Court in its interpretation of the applicability of Regulation No. 3/58. In *Singer*, Mr Gassner, a German national on holiday in France, was struck by a car driven by an employee of Maison Singer.[128] The case was in reality an issue of subrogation as an out-of-court settlement was reached between Gassner's estate and Maison Singer but the German social security body (that had already paid out to Gassner's successors) was trying to claim the repayment of such a payment from Maison Singer.[129] However, the body's claim in France was initially dismissed on the grounds that Mr Gassner was not a worker exercising an evident right to free movement.[130] Maison Singer, likewise, made the simple point that in order for Gassner to be a 'worker' he would have to have travelled in 'connexion with ... employment' and that a 'migrant worker [is] ... required to move for the purpose of their employment'.[131] Ultimately Gassner was not a migrant worker as he had not moved in the course of his employment but, nonetheless, the Court was prepared to classify Gassner as a 'worker' as 'it would not be in conformity with [the Treaty] ... to limit the concept of "worker" to migrant workers *stricto sensu*'.[132] Thus the pre-*Levin* discourse of the 'worker' was applied to Gassner's circumstances.[133] This, though, also had extensive repercussions as by that logic almost the entire population of the Community could have been construed as a 'worker' for the purposes of the Treaty as almost all tourists either work in their home states or are members of the families of workers.[134] Likewise, in *Entr'aide médicale*, a Luxemburgish railway worker was killed in a car crash in Belgium in what was explicitly stated

[127] See Section 1.3.
[128] Case 44/65, *Hessische Knappschaft* v. *Maison Singer et fils*. [1965] ECR 965, p. 967.
[129] Ibid.
[130] Ibid.
[131] Ibid., p. 968.
[132] Ibid., p. 971.
[133] See Section 1.3.4.
[134] See Section 1.4.2. For further analysis of the *Singer* case, see Derrick Wyatt, 'The Social Security Rights of Migrant Workers and Their Families' (1977) 14 *Common Market Law Review*, 411–433 at 418–421.

to be 'in the course of a pleasure trip'.[135] Once again, he was classified as a 'worker' by AG Gand on the basis of the 'very wide notion' that had been given to Article 52 of Regulation No 3 in which the '"term" migrant worker … should not be limited to migrant workers *stricto sensu*'.[136] From a strictly legal perspective, this early area of case law may not seem either radical or distinct from the early jurisprudence on the 'worker' as the legal issue in these cases was whether social security benefits should not have been payable simply because the accident occurred in another Member State.[137] Nonetheless, these cases, seen from a discursive perspective, are indicative of an increasingly radical conceptual understanding of the 'worker' in which, paradoxically, the tourist was compartmentalized within the pre-existing discursive structure of the 'worker' and dependent upon even a tenuous link to work. These cases may appear to be legally unproblematic because what was at issue was simply that of insurance payments in the context of Regulation No. 3/58.[138] Nonetheless, from a conceptual perspective an 'image' of the worker was being constructed in which tourists were simply treated as if they were 'workers'.

However, this was clearly not a satisfactory state of affairs for a number of reasons. Most importantly, there is an air of unreality about these cases; perhaps mitigated to a certain extent by the fact that they were ultimately cases between social security bodies in one Member State and insurers in another and therefore at one step removed from the parties directly affected. Ultimately the victims in both cases happened to be fortunate enough to be protected by Community law simply by virtue of being employed in their own states. This would lead to an unsatisfactory situation where tourists were not protected by Community law simply because they could not be construed as worker in their home states for various reasons (such as the elderly on holiday for instance). Moreover, in *Entr'aide médicale*, with the exception of moving across a border for the purposes of going on holiday, almost every aspect of the victim's circumstances was

[135] Case 27/69, *Caisse de maladie des C. F. L. 'Entr'aide médicale' and Société nationale des chemins de fer luxembourgeois* v. *Compagnie belge d'assurances générales sur la vie et contre les accidents* [1969] ECR 405, p. 407.

[136] Ibid., p. 411 at para. 7 (and the Court), p. 415.

[137] White, *EC Social Security Law*, p. 92.

[138] What was at issue, therefore, was not the free movement of a worker but the territorial application of an insurance scheme intended for workers, irrespective of movement. Vicki Paskalia, 'Co-ordination of Social Security in the European Union: An Overview of Recent Case Law' (2009) 46 *Common Market Law Review*, 1177–1218 at 1181.

wholly internal.[139] Thus, compartmentalizing the tourist within the 'worker' resulted in a restrictive linguistic 'ill-fit' and that a different label was needed to describe tourists for the purposes of Community law.

2.4.2 *The Birth of the Tourist as a Potential Recipient of Services*

There was, therefore, a clear need to conceptualize the tourist in a different manner and it is in this context that construing the tourist as a potential recipient of services could be considered to be a conceptual and discursive alternative to attempts to envisage tourists as 'workers' even as broadly construed. In *Watson and Belmann*, as has already been outlined, an au-pair was considered to be a 'worker'; yet AG Trabucchi examined the alternative proposition, that the applicant was a mere 'ordinary tourist' in order to determine whether 'freedom of movement for workers applies to her'.[140] He then comes up with a rather ingenious alternative form of rights protection when he states 'the EEC Treaty refers only to those providing services but makes no reference to the person for whom the services are intended' and it is from that point that the 'idea' of seeing the tourist as potential recipient of services was subjectively created and, crucially, that could only be so on the basis of a very 'wide interpretation' of services.[141] Thus, the concept of 'broadness' has been extended to other provisions of the Treaty aside from Article 48.[142] Nonetheless, what is noticeable about AG Trabucchi's claims in *Watson and Belmann* is that they were, firstly, inherently contingent and, secondly, not responded to by the Court. AG Trabucchi's reasoning was somewhat opaque. He starts off on the basis of the suggestion that 'there can be no doubt that tourists normally make use of

[139] It should be noted that this is not to deny the important contribution that these early Community tourists made to the eventual emergence of the Citizen; merely that finding a need to construe a tourist as worker in some form was also self-limiting. For Plender, both *Entr'aide médicale* and *Singer* played a highly significant role in establishing a wide definition of the 'worker' which, in turn, provided the 'basis for a common European definition of a class of persons akin to citizens'. Likewise, as Jacobs asserts, the consequence of the Court's desire to 'protect imaginatively the social security rights of migrant workers under virtually the first EEC legislation Regulations 3 and 4' was a broad notion of the 'worker' which, in turn 'paved the way for the development of the concept of Community citizenship'. Plender, 'An Incipient Form of European Citizenship', pp. 41–42; Francis Jacobs, 'The Evolution of the European Legal Order' (2004) 41 *Common Market Law Review*, 303–316 at 308.

[140] Case 118/75, *Lynne Watson and Alessandro Belmann* [1976] ECR 1185, p. 1202.

[141] Ibid., p. 1203.

[142] See Section 1.3.5.

services in the places which they visit'.[143] This starting point (while evidently true) is, though, at least for some, rather tenuously linked to the services provisions of the Treaty.[144] Ex Article 58 of the Treaty alludes to 'nationals of Member States who are established in a State of the Community other than that of the person for whom the services are intended' and ex Article 61 states that 'the person providing a service may, in order to do so, temporarily pursue his activity in the State where the service is provided, under the same conditions as are imposed by that State on its own nationals'. One reading of this, as paraphrased by AG Mancini in *Luisi and Carbone*, is that the services provisions of the Treaty were intended for 'a specific category of traders ... [and are] concerned therefore with the providers of services and not with the recipients thereof'.[145] Indeed, a strict interpretation of the above provisions could easily lead to the conclusion that Article 58 seems to envisage the provider of the service moving to provide a service and Article 61 merely makes it clear that he/she should have equal treatment with nationals in relation to the provision of such a service; no mention is made of the recipients of such a service. As AG Trabucchi suggests in *Watson and Belmann*, there is complete 'silence of the Treaty on this subject'.[146] There are two consequences of this silence in terms of the potential emergence of the Community tourist. First, in reality, as the AG continues:

> If a broad interpretation is placed upon this provision, namely, by including all those who are likely to be recipients of services ... the practical effect is to extend the right of freedom of movement to all nationals of the Member States because everyone is actually or potentially a recipient of services.[147]

In other words, if a development were to take place in which tourists have a right of freedom of movement, in effect all nationals of the Community 'count' and the path to the eventual judicial creation of the

143 *Watson and Belmann*, p. 1203.

144 See Section 2.4, particularly n. 125.

145 Joined Cases 286/82 and 26/83, *Graziana Luisi and Giuseppe Carbone* v. *Ministero del Tesoro* [1984] ECR 377, p. 415, p. 396 (facts). The case itself concerned two tourists that were fined for exceeding the limits that were imposed by Italian law for the export of currency. The Court ruled that tourists fell within the scope of the Treaty as recipients of a service. The case itself, whilst not as acclaimed as *Cowan*, was a vital forerunner for it. For more detailed analysis of the case, see Jean-Victor Louis, 'Free Movement of Tourists and Freedom of Payments in the Community: The Luisi-Carbone Judgment' (1984) 21 *Common Market Law Review*, 625–637 at 625.

146 *Watson and Belmann*, p. 1203.

147 Ibid., p. 1204.

EU Citizen in the post '*Sala* revolution' seems inevitable.[148] Second, to do so would undoubtedly amount to an entirely new Court-created right, pointing therefore to the inherently contingent subjectivity of doing so in the first place. As AG Trabucchi maintains:

> It is for the Court to decide whether it ought to look at the present state of Community law on this point on the basis of the wording of the Treaty as I have interpreted it, or whether it is possible to indentify [*sic*] elements which suffice to create a new right . . . In any case, it would be a sound rule to avoid the fiction of using the actual wording of the Treaty to justify the extension to all citizens of the Community of a right to freedom of movement which the Treaty intended to apply only to clearly defined categories of persons.[149]

What is then clear is that to extend the services provisions of the Treaty would, in AG Trabucchi's words, be to create a new right and to do so would be exactly as AG Trabucchi surmises, namely borne out of a 'fiction' in which the Court would construe a right based upon on a tenuous reading of the Treaty.[150] Crucially, though, the emphasis was placed on whether it was possible to do this on the basis of 'the present state of Community law'. Ultimately AG Trabucchi himself decided negatively on this point and the Court made no mention of this issue.[151] Arguably the reason for this was the socio-legal context in which this statement was made. The case was in 1976, after a period in which the discourse of the 'worker', derived in part from *Unger*, had only just been created.[152] In these circumstances, the context was not yet ready for such a radical expansion of the remit of the Treaty on the basis of a rather tenuous interpretation of the Treaty. However, AG Trabucchi rather prophetically spells out the time in which the context had sufficiently changed for the creation of such a right; namely when it was 'appropriate' to talk of extending 'to all citizens of the Community a right of freedom of movement'.[153] In other words,

[148] Jacqueson, 'Union Citizenship', 264.

[149] *Watson and Belmann*, p. 1205.

[150] For further analysis on the Court's (often controversial) method of legal reasoning, see Hjalte Rasmussen, *On Law and Policy in the European Court of Justice: A Comparative Study in Judicial Policymaking* (Dordrecht: Martinus Nijhoff, 1986); Mauro Cappelletti, 'Is the European Court of Justice "running wild"?' (1987) 12(1) *European Law Review*, 3–17; Takis Tridimas, 'The Court of Justice and Judicial Activism' (1996) 21(3) *European Law Review*, 199–210 at 210.

[151] *Watson and Belmann*, p. 1205.

[152] See Section 1.2.

[153] Martha Finnemore, *National Interests in International Society* (Ithaca: Cornell University Press, 1996), p. 156; *Watson and Belmann*, p. 1205. See 'Introduction' for a more detailed analysis of norms more generally.

such a development would have to emerge out of a context in which the 'worker' had sufficiently developed into the market citizen at the very least prior to creating rights that expand considerably beyond the 'worker'.

Furthermore, such a change did take place considerably later on in the development of the jurisprudence of the Court and almost immediately before the creation of the TEU. In *Luisi and Carbone*, in 1984, the Court explicitly established that tourists were potential recipients of services. AG Mancini refers to the 'novelty' of so doing on the basis of there being no 'exact precedents' to then conclude that 'the rules of the Treaty are concerned *also* with the recipients of services and with the provision of services involving travel by those persons'.[154] The Court likewise claims that the 'necessary corollary' of referring to the provider of services moving is that the recipient should, likewise, be allowed to move to then conclude, forcefully and repeatedly, that the tourist is a potential recipient of services and should therefore be protected by the Treaty.[155] The timing of this pronouncement should not be missed. The case came almost immediately after *Levin* in 1982. As has already been outlined, *Levin* changed the structural alignment of the discourse of the 'worker' in the course of so doing emphasizing 'genuine and effectiveness' which precluded construing the tourist as a 'worker'; another label had to be ascribed to him/her. What should also equally be noted is that the boundaries of acceptability had clearly changed such that in 1984 it was acceptable to construe the tourist as a potential recipient of services whereas it was not in 1976.[156]

2.4.3 Cowan *as a Key Turning Point*

Moreover, the timing (1989) of what is widely regarded to be the seminal and radical case of *Cowan* should also not be missed.[157] The case can be considered to be a development from *Levin* (1982) and *Lawrie-Blum* (1986) as then extended in cases such as *Lair* (1988) and *Lebon* (1987). Putting it

154 Joined Cases 286/82 and 26/83, *Graziana Luisi and Giuseppe Carbone* v. *Ministero del Tesoro* [1984] ECR 377, p. 416.

155 Ibid., pp. 402–403.

156 See 'Introduction' on changing context in SC theory.

157 Whilst *Luisi and Carbone* also concerned tourists being construed as recipients of service, what made *Cowan* distinct is that the judicial reasoning of the Court was 'much bolder' simply because 'the case nearly amounts to a generalized right of free movement and residence'. Wouters, 'European Citizenship', 1994, p. 32. For additional discussion of the radicalism of *Cowan*, see Takis Tridimas, *The General Principles of EC Law* (Oxford: Oxford University Press, 1999), p. 84; Jutta Pomoell, *European Union Citizenship in Focus: The Legal Position of the Individual in EC Law* (Helsinki: The Erik Castrén Institute of International Law and Human Rights Research Reports), p. 50.

differently, all of these key cases were taking place (along with *Gravier* (1985) as will be examined below) in the immediate build-up to *Cowan* and *Cowan* itself was being decided under the shadow of the soon to emerge Treaty of Maastricht. Furthermore, what took place in *Cowan* was irrefutably radical and would certainly not have been possible to countenance in the early days of the Court's jurisprudence; considerable contextual change had to take place.[158] The reason that the case was so radical was because of the nature of the applicant's claim; leading to the suggestion that if he was to be successful (which he was), a fundamental paradigm shift would have to have taken place in Community law.[159] In *Watson and Belmann,* the applicant was an au-pair and thus clearly did 'work' in some way, albeit in rather unconventional fashion.[160] Equally, what was being claimed was a restrictive measure relating to residence, something that is clearly within the scope *ratione materiae* of Community law.-[161] Likewise, in *Luisi and Carbone*, the applicant took issue with being subjected to restrictions on the amount of currency he transported across intra-Community borders.[162] The applicant tried to plead on the basis of either the free movement of capital or his own capacity as a tourist; but, crucially, his submissions were that it was with that currency that he would pay for services.[163] In both cases, therefore, what was being claimed was evidently within the scope *ratione materiae* of Community law.

In *Cowan*, on the other hand, what was at issue was a residence criterion for the receipt of compensation for being robbed on the Paris metro. Thus, the case did not relate to some form of discrimination in the receipt of a service, as such compensation was clearly not a 'service';

[158] Weatherill, for instance, sees *Cowan* as the culmination of several juridical developments which collectively were 'in effect an extension of the margin of Community competence'. Stephen Weatherill, 'Case 186/87, *Cowan* v. *Le Tresor Public*' (1989) 26 *Common Market Law Review*, 563–581 at 571 (note).

[159] For Mancini, *Cowan* marked a turning point towards citizenship because the consequence of the case was that it would in fact be somewhat difficult to construe oneself as not falling within the scope of Community law as it would be practically 'impossible' to be a tourist without making use of a service in a host country. He further claims that the case gave 'rise to a form, albeit still imperfect, of European citizenship'. Weatherill, likewise, formed the view that 'the decision constitutes a step towards the creation of a de facto Community citizenship'. Mancini, 'Making of a Constitution', 607–608; Weatherill, 'Case 186/87', 575.

[160] *Watson and Belmann*, p. 1188. The applicant never received a wage for looking after an infant, instead receiving free board and lodging.

[161] Ibid., p. 1195 at para. 5.

[162] *Luisi and Carbone*, p. 394.

[163] Ibid.

by contrast the issue was whether the conditions behind the applicant receiving other services would be impeded by this provision.[164] Indeed, AG Lenz's view was that the sole form of impediment to the applicant's free movement was that he would be forced to take out insurance to cover the same risk that a French national or resident would get compensated for by the state.[165] The 'service' being received was therefore rather remote and indirect.[166] It is therefore not surprising that AG Lenz formed the view that the only way in which Cowan could derive rights were in circumstances where 'a recipient of services must be capable of being an independent subject of Community rights and obligations'.[167] In other words, an entirely new free-standing right for tourists needed to in effect be created in order to facilitate this type of free movement. What AG Lenz has also crucially therefore implicitly suggested is that this type of right needs to be subjectively created: an entirely new right created almost out of 'nothing' by the Court. This much is, to a certain extent, admitted by AG Lenz when he maintains that 'no comprehensive framework for the freedom to provide services has yet been developed' and then claims: 'there are cases in which either the person providing services goes to another Member State or the recipient of services received them in another Member State. These movements are not covered by freedom of movement for persons as it has usually been defined'.[168] Thus at this point, with the Court on the cusp of creating a radically new type of right, its inherently contingent subjectivity should not be forgotten.

However, the creation of such a right was not without its controversy leading to the eventual emergence of a nuanced and possibly even flawed understanding of the (EU) Citizen. What is also noticeable is that this type of right also has obligations which, as will be examined in Chapter 5, more closely aligns the development of the Community tourist with the development of the Citizen. For the Court, this new right can only be created through the use of Article 7 of the Treaty, an

[164] Case 186/87, *Ian William Cowan* v. *Trésor Public* [1989] ECR 195, p. 210 (AG Lenz).

[165] Ibid.

[166] Weatherill, whilst being broadly supportive of the Court's judgement for being in keeping with the spirit of the Treaty, alludes to the somewhat artificial nature of the Court's reasoning because Community law then 'is capable of extending rights to any Community citizen who crosses a border and makes a purchase' and therefore could be seen to be 'an absurdly bold extension of the personal scope of Community law'. Weatherill, 'Case 186/87', 571–573.

[167] *Cowan*, p. 205.

[168] Ibid., pp. 205–206.

ever-present trend in almost all freedom of movement cases by this point.[169] For the Court, the freedom to provide services is merely 'the application of the general principle set out in [Article 7] ... and given concrete form in specific situations'.[170] Thus, it would arguably have only been possible to create a strong right to free movement for tourists in a climate in which, as will be examined in Chapter 3, Article 7 of the Treaty itself had been used to in effect create new rights by being used in tandem with other articles of the Treaty in which the specific right was not actually overtly created (such as that on services).[171] Moreover, the use of Article 7 in such a manner clearly related to the development of the Citizen as what is at issue is mere discrimination irrespective of participation in any economic activity in the post '*Sala* revolution'.

Ultimately, though, the controversy in the case is that what was being asked for was compensation by the state funded by French taxpayers. The law itself was not directly discriminatory as French citizens and (non-French) residents were both entitled to be paid. For the French government: 'it is a system of national solidarity financed by taxes and therefore intended principally for French nationals and resident foreigners'.[172] On one level the argument has some force, so much so that the Commission was prepared to accept this argument. It firstly claimed that Article 7 of the Treaty cannot be relied on by the applicant 'solely [by] virtue of being a Community national' and then continues by

[169] Weatherill also alludes to a trend (something that is clearly highly relevant from a discursive perspective) to utilize then Article 7 on non-discrimination as a 'source of rights' in tandem with more specific rights of the Treaty, something that had already taken place in *Gravier* (see subsequently). Likewise, Arnull maintains that '*Cowan* provides yet another example of how powerful weapon [Article 7] has become'. Weatherill, 'Case 186/87', 565; Anthony Arnull, 'Metropolitan Misfortune' (1989) 14(3) *European Law Review*, 166–169 at 169. See also Reich and Harbacevica, 'Citizenship and Family on Trial', 615–638.

[170] *Cowan*, p. 200 at para. 14.

[171] This is well summarized (once again) by Weatherill when he described the case as being at the 'outer margins' of Community law reached by virtue of it being a 'dynamic tool for pursuing further integration'. This type of analysis of socio-legal change is at the heart of SC theory. In 1989, the Court was able to push the limits of the concept of the Community tourist by virtue of it being a 'culmination' of the previous case law, including *Luisi and Carbone*. Once social change has been affected by virtue of seminal moments in the Court's jurisprudence, it then becomes possible to push the 'outer limits' yet further such that the original 'limit' seems commonplace (see 'Introduction' for a theory of social change). For instance, Reich and Harbacevica allude to *Cowan* as the established precedent and source of inspiration for the later '*Sala* revolution'. Weatherill, 'Case 186/87', 574; Reich and Harbacevica, 'Citizenship and Family on Trial', 616.

[172] *Cowan*, p. 199.

making a distinction between 'those persons ... integrated into the society of the host country, with all the consequential rights and obligations' and those who 'remain integrated in the society of their country of origin ... [and] cannot therefore be regarded as having to be assimilated and integrated into the society of the host country'.[173] Putting it differently, the former category have deeply integrated themselves into the society of the host country, have spent many years contributing to the tax and social security system (their duty) and *should* therefore have the right to in effect get back what they put in both financially and socially.[174] By contrast, the tourist is construed as somewhat of an economic freeloader and undeserving of this type of compensation.[175] The Court was at least prepared to refer to and deal with this argument when it states that:

> [The compensation provision] concerns a right which is a manifestation of the principle of national solidarity. Such a right presupposes a closer bond with the State than that of a recipient of services, and for that reason it may be restricted to persons who are either nationals of that State or foreign nationals resident on the territory of that State.[176]

Thus, what is immediately at issue is a soon-to-emerge principle of solidarity.[177] The Court, crucially, dismisses these arguments when it maintains:

> That reasoning cannot be accepted. When Community law guarantees a natural person the freedom to go to another Member State, the protection of that person from harm in the Member State in question, on the same basis as that of nationals and persons residing there, is a corollary of that freedom of movement. It follows that the prohibition of discrimination is applicable to recipients of services within the meaning of the Treaty as regards protection against the risk of assault and the right to obtain financial compensation provided for by national law when that risk materialises. The fact that the compensation at issue is financed by the Public Treasury cannot alter the rules regarding the protection of the rights guaranteed by the Treaty.[178]

This above citation clearly sets out this newly derived right; no longer is there reference to the 'worker' but now a 'natural person' has freedom

[173] Ibid., p. 201.
[174] For a discussion of the relation between citizenship and financial solidarity, see Section 5.2.
[175] For a discussion of the concept of a 'freeloader' in Community law, see Section 5.2.
[176] *Cowan*, p. 220 at para. 16.
[177] See Section 5.2.
[178] *Cowan*, para. 17.

of movement. Moreover, Article 7 specifically allows for the creation of rights for intended recipients of services which includes this type of financial measure and, as far as the Court was concerned, issues relating to solidarity and contribution towards the public purse were seemingly irrelevant.

However, AG Lenz is not as convinced as the Court clearly was that such ultimately moral arguments could be ignored; in particular any suggestion that the Court should be rewarding economic freeloaders. For instance, there is no suggestion that workers from other Member States working in France would not be entitled to such compensation; the issue is whether tourists should be so entitled. The AG, by contrast with the Court, maintains that: 'a Community citizen who does not belong to a privileged category under Community law enjoys a reduced level of protection with regard to his most personal rights'.[179] Thus AG Lenz, perhaps rather deliberately, creates the Citizen as the default position for those that are not either economically active or 'workers' and who should therefore enjoy some freedom and protection under Community law but not the panoply of benefits that a 'worker' would be entitled to.[180] He then makes five (rather unsubtle) references to the 'Community citizen' and thus it can but be assumed that for AG Lenz this is the specific nature or form of a future citizen, one that cannot quite fit into standard categories within the four fundamental freedoms. Crucially, though, this could only have come about because of discourse of the worker in which it was restricted to the *Levin/Lawrie-Blum* criteria. Forced to derive rights from elsewhere, the 'tourist' arguably emerged to form part of the later development of a discourse of EU Citizenship.

2.5 The Student as a 'Worker'?

To a certain extent the emergence of the 'Community student' was the crucial and final stage towards the emergence of the later Citizen. Subsequent chapters will focus on the development of citizenship in the context of the increasingly powerful use of the principle of equal treatment (Chapter 3) and direct references to citizenship (Chapter 4) or

179 Ibid., p. 212.

180 O'Brien, for instance, terms citizenship a 'gap filler, failing to offer much solace to those falling between traditional economic groups'. O'Brien, 'Social Blind Spots', 1108. See also Reich and Harbacevica, 'Citizenship and Family on Trial', 615–616; Whelan, 'Union Citizenship', 179–184.

core components of it such as rights (Chapter 5). However, the jurisprudential treatment of the student proved to be a key turning point in the evolution of EC law towards recognizing the (limited) rights of categories of individuals who could not be classified as workers because the development of the case law in this area immediately preceded substantive legislative change (in the form of the three residency directives) and arguably was precipitated by it.[181] This, then, served as a prototype for the later enactment of the Citizenship Directive which, whilst beyond the scope of this book, arguably emerged as a result of the Court's subsequent use of the then enacted citizenship provisions of the Treaty in order create free-standing rights for non-economic contributors in cases such as *Grzelczyk* (2001) and *Bidar* (2005).[182] Indeed, the Citizenship Directive explicitly merged the three prior residency directives and therefore, as far as the Union legislature itself was concerned, 'Citizenship' evidently concerned the treatment of non-economic contributors.[183] In a practical sense, what was at stake in both juridical debates (i.e. the case-law relating to students prior to the enactment of the three residency directives and the later case-law and subsequent enactment of the Citizenship Directive) was the tricky conundrum of students being a burden on the host state without necessarily doing all that much in return which will be examined in Chapter 5 in the context of the principle of solidarity.[184]

However, from a discursive perspective, what can be outlined is the end-point of an important collective development, in tandem with the 'worker' (as eventually settled upon by *Levin*/*Lawrie-Blum*), a more generalized right to move and reside and the tourist, prior to the enactment of

[181] See O'Leary, *Evolving Concept*, pp. 111–115.

[182] For a more detailed commentary on this line of case law, see A. Pieter Van der Mei, 'Union Citizenship and the "De-Nationalisation" of the Territorial Welfare State. Comments on Case C-456/02 *Trojani* and Case C-209/03 *Bidar*' (2005) 7(2) *European Journal of Migration and Law*, 207–211; Catherine Barnard, 'Of Students and Babies' (2005) 64 *Cambridge Law Journal*, 560–563; Michiel Brand, 'Case Law: Case C-209/03, *the Queen (on the Application of Dany Bidar)* v. *London Borough of Ealing, Secretary of State for Education and Skills*, 2005 E.C.R. I-2119' (2005) 12(1) *Columbia Journal of European Law*, 293–304.

[183] See Dougan for an analysis of the interrelationship between the residency directives and the citizenship directive. Indeed, the latter directive was specifically enacted to codify the former three directives into one single text. The links, therefore, between the *Gravier* line of cases (for which the three directives was a response) and the Directive which bears the name 'Citizenship' are inexorable. Michael Dougan, 'The Constitutional Dimension to the Case Law on Union Citizenship' (2006) 31(5) *European Law Review*, 613–641 at 615–633; O'Leary, *Evolving Concept*, p. 136.

[184] See Section 5.2.

the three residency directives. Prior to *Levin*, as has already been outlined, it appeared that a conscious attempt was being made to try and compartmentalize as many individuals as possible within the paradigm of the 'worker'.[185] Thus, for the tourist, early cases such as *Singer* (1965) were based upon the victim of the car accident either being a worker or assimilated to the position of one by virtue of being insured.[186] The opening part of this section will examine attempts to construe students as 'workers' prior to both *Levin* and *Gravier*. Nonetheless, as has also been maintained, the discourse of the 'worker' developed from *Levin* and *Lawrie-Blum* made it clear that students could not be classified as workers (*Brown*) on the basis of the remoulded discourse of the 'worker'.[187] As with the 'tourist', the 'student' was then left to find another label to describe itself and it is not surprising that the key case of *Gravier* (1985) emerged soon after *Levin* (1982), immediately preceded *Lawrie-Blum* (1986), and a few years prior to *Cowan* (1989) – itself almost immediately prior to the process of creating the TEU. In other words, in order to delineate the contours of the later EU Citizen, the prior case law on the 'worker' and other non-explicitly economic categories of individuals needs to be viewed both collectively and holistically in which for instance, the ultimate demarcation of the worker in *Levin/Lawrie-Blum* created a linguistic and legal incentive to create free-standing rights for non-workers. What the tourist, the worker and the Community national simply moving all have in common is a collectively perceived need to create such free-standing rights for all three whilst equally taking into account the sensitivities of the Member States on this issue. The second part of this section will thus be devoted to assessing the emergence of the student post *Levin* as a result of *Gravier*.

2.5.1 *The Student: Pre-*Gravier

Prior to both *Levin/Lawrie-Blum* and *Gravier*, attempts were clearly made to compartmentalize the student into either the framework of the 'worker' or one of the other fundamental freedoms of the Treaty.[188] However, what is particularly noticeable in relation to such cases is the moral or empathetic edge to such cases, with an emphasis on the more social aspects of the Treaty. In *Casagrande*, the facts and issues at stake were, in many ways, almost identical to *Bidar* (2005), a key later

185 See Section 1.3.
186 See Section 2.4.1.
187 See Sections 1.5.1 and 5.3.5.
188 See Chapter 1.

citizenship case, except that it took place in 1974.[189] The applicant, an Italian national, had applied for and was refused (on grounds of nationality) an education grant in Bavaria.[190] Arguably what was at issue was a clash between the moral case for the applicant and, ultimately, the amount of money at stake, payable by the host state should a precedent have been set in the case.[191] On the one hand, the applicant was clearly a very deserving case. Whilst he was technically Italian, he had 'lived since his birth in Munich' and, because he did not get the particular grant that he had claimed, he had to quit higher education altogether.[192] In other words, he was so heavily integrated into his host state that he was in many ways German in all but name. The situation in his circumstances was clearly unjust given the fact that the sole difference between himself and a German national getting the same grant was his nationality.[193] It is therefore not surprising that the 'softer' side to Community law came to the fore in the case.[194] AG Warner refers to the right to freedom of movement needing to be exercised 'in freedom and dignity' and 'requir[ing] equality of treatment'.[195] Thus, what is emphasized is the need to respect the applicant's 'dignity' and the rhetoric of human rights is tied in with that of equal treatment. Moreover, the Court was prepared to accept that Article 12 of Regulation No. 1612/68 (allowing for equal treatment in the sphere of education for the children of workers) could be construed as a derivative right of the general policy within the Treaty to encourage, in a cultural sense, equal treatment in the areas of education and training and thus the Court ruled that the applicants should

189 Case C-209/03, *The Queen (on the application of Dany Bidar)* v. *London Borough of Ealing, Secretary of State for Education and Skills* [2005] ECR I 2119; Case 9/74, *Donato Casagrande* v. *Landeshauptstadt München* [1974] ECR 773.

190 *Casagrande*, p. 782.

191 See Chapter 5 and note 51. For a discussion of the relationship between the burden on the taxpayer in the host Member State and the principle of solidarity, see Alexander Somek, 'Solidarity Decomposed: Being and Time in European Citizenship' (2007) 32(6) *European Law Review*, 787–818.

192 *Casagrande*, p. 782.

193 In *Bidar*, the applicant was denied a maintenance grant on the grounds that he was not 'settled' in the UK, this despite the fact that he was living with his grandmother and had completed his entire secondary education in London. *Bidar*, p. 2161.

194 For a detailed commentary on the link between the extension of the free movement provisions of the Treaty by the Court in order to facilitate social integration, see Siofra O'Leary, 'The Social Dimension of Community Citizenship', in Allan Rosas and Esko Antola (eds.), *A Citizen's Europe – In Search of a New Order* (London: Sage, 1995), pp. 160–163; O'Leary, *Evolving Concept*, pp. 126–136.

195 *Casagrande*, p. 782.

be entitled to this grant.[196] Thus, not only was the applicant entitled to receive a maintenance grant but also the softer more social aspect of the Court's reasoning was very much emphasized.[197]

However, on the other hand, for the Member States, this was a dangerous test case and, as AG Warner paraphrased, the point being made by the Member States was that although this case only concerned a 'relatively small sum', a considerable amount of state expenditure was riding on this case: 'it seems that there are in Bavaria so many children of migrant workers in the same or in a similar position that a decision in his favour would entail for that State expenditure running into millions of DM'.[198] Moreover, what was made explicitly clear in the case was that what was at issue were parasitic rights in that the applicant was the child of a worker entitled to the same benefits as a home national under Regulation No. 1612/68 who had therefore made a significant contribution to the German tax system. Thus, the case was not as radical as *Gravier* as it did not involve the Court in effect creating a free-standing right for students;[199] nor could that have been possible in the context of the development of Community law in 1974 as the socio-legal conditions were not yet ready for such a radical development.[200]

In *Kuyken*, the problems with limiting this 'softer' approach by the Court to the children of migrant workers were evident. The applicant, a Belgian national, undertook an engineering degree in the Netherlands, then returned to Belgium and was denied an entitlement to unemployment benefit by virtue of the fact that he had studied elsewhere.[201] Morally, this was clearly an unfair state of affairs. As AG Capotorti stated: 'I need hardly stress the distressing nature of the subject at the

[196] Ibid., p. 779 at para. 12.
[197] See Ibid.
[198] *Casagrande*, p. 783.
[199] See Section 2.5.3.
[200] For Flynn, the major distinction between *Casagrande* and *Gravier* is that the former concerned the right to education of the child of a 'worker' under Regulation 1612/68 – which at the time would not have been radical – whereas in *Gravier* the applicant had no connection to Belgium other than going to Belgium for the purposes of study. To create a right for the applicant in *Gravier* was a significant development and was necessarily 'foreshadowed' by considerable juridical development in the intervening period.

James Flynn, 'Vocational Training in Community Law and Practice' (1988) 8(1) *Yearbook of European Law*, 59–85 at 62. See also O'Leary, *Evolving Concept*, p. 154.
[201] Case 66/77, *Petrus Kuyken* v. *Rijksdienst voor Arbeidsvoorziening* [1977] ECR 2311, pp. 2312–2313.

present time'.[202] Yet, tough though this was for the applicant, he was ultimately neither a worker nor a member of the family of a migrant worker and thus AG Capotorti concluded:

> It is clear that Regulation 1408/71 is intended to apply to persons in paid employment who move about in the Community, or, to be more accurate, as the fourth recital makes clear, 'to all nationals of Member States insured under social security schemes for employed persons'. In principle, therefore, students cannot in that capacity avail themselves of it unless there are national laws which, for the purposes of granting social security benefits which are covered by the regulation, treat a student or former student on the same footing as an employed person.[203]

Thus, the applicant was not working nor could he be construed as one by virtue of the principle of assimilation because he was not insured under any social security schemes. The Court, likewise, concluded that he simply was not a 'worker' because his was 'the case of an unemployed person who has never been in employment and has never been treated as an employed person under national legislation applicable to employed persons'.[204] In other words, in 1974, students did not 'count' as part of the broader discourse of the 'worker'.

Indeed, in *Meade*, the applicant attempted to run an alternative argument that students were recipients of services in a case in which there were three different categories of individuals that did not, likewise, 'count'. The applicant was the son of a US Citizen and a British mother, all of whom lived in France prior to the applicant attending boarding school in the UK, and was denied payment from a French family allowance fund on the grounds that he had been construed as no longer residing in France because he had attended boarding school in the UK.[205] His father clearly did not 'count' as he was a TCN and his mother did not work, despite having moved. What was left, then, was the applicant's status and AG Mancini examined two alternatives:

> Let us begin with Article 48. The freedom of movement guaranteed by that article applies only to "workers of the Member States". The Court is aware of the identity of the person to whom that formula refers. The fact that Articles 48 to 51 contain numerous references to the *employment* of those to whom it applies and that the Treaty contains other, independent, rules relating to movement

[202] Ibid., p. 2321.
[203] Ibid., p. 2322.
[204] Ibid., p. 2818 at para. 14.
[205] Case 238/83, *Caisse d'Allocations Familiales de la Région Parisienne* v. *Mr and Mrs Richard Meade* [1984] ECR 2631, p. 2633.

which deal with self-employed persons, shows in the clearest possible way that the provision in question refers only to employed persons. Obviously students, who pursue no professional or trade activity, do not come into that category.[206]

This constitutes a definitive statement that students cannot be construed as workers; they simply cannot 'count' as workers. Crucially, AG Mancini also states that the Court (or indeed anyone within the epistemic Community of the Court) is perfectly 'aware of the identity of the person to whom that formula refers'. AG Mancini has thus inadvertently revealed the discursive aspects of the worker. There is a 'formula' to it (discourse), people are 'aware of it' (intersubjectivity) and it identifies people. Moreover, what cannot be ignored is the timing of this case as it comes soon after *Levin* (this was the 'formula') and in accordance with the newly shaped discourse of the 'worker' it would simply not be possible to define students as 'workers'.[207] Indeed, such a 'formula' is now so pervasive that AG Slynn was not prepared to construe the applicant in *Brown* as a worker, this despite the fact he had actually worked, but what ultimately lost the case for Brown was his intention behind such work (short term with a view to the commencement of his studies immediately after) and the nature of what he was claiming (a maintenance allowance whilst he was studying).[208] Thus, as has already been outlined in Chapter 1, *Levin* and *Lawrie-Blum* led to the definition of a 'worker' that was clearly broader than its ordinary definition in certain circumstances (such as *Steymann*) but also narrower in others (such as in *Brown*) and the views of AG Slynn in *Brown* illustrate the difficulty which the Court faced in conceptualizing students within the framework of Community law.[209] As an alternative to construing

[206] Ibid., p. 2641.

[207] See Section 1.5.1 and *Brown* in particular. See also Section 5.3.5.

[208] Case 197/86, *Steven Malcolm Brown* v. *The Secretary of State for Scotland* [1988] ECR 3205, p. 3233, pp. 3247–3248. The Court was, by contrast, prepared to construe the applicant in *Brown* as a worker; however, this did not entitle him to claim a maintenance grant.

[209] The limits of such an attempt were illustrated by *Forcheri*, a case which was heard by the Court two years before *Gravier* in 1983. The applicant was charged the *minerval* but was actually married to a Community official and the Court held that, whilst the Community official was not technically a migrant worker, he should be entitled to the same benefits which flow from the case law on free movement. This included the ability for his wife to not be discriminated against on grounds of nationality in access to vocational training. The problem that the applicant in *Gravier* faced was that she could not in any way be construed as either a migrant worker or as being in the family of one. Case 152/82, *Sandro Forcheri and his wife Marisa Forcheri, née Marino*, v. *Belgian State and asbl Institut Supérieur de Sciences Humaines Appliquées – Ecole Ouvrière Supérieure* [1983] ECR 2323, p. 2323; Flynn, 'Vocational Training', 62.

students as 'workers', AG Mancini in *Meade* claimed that: 'At the very most, students can enjoy a right of movement only as a person for whom services are intended'.[210] Yet, this alternative never took off linguistically and legally and the Court makes no mention of it in its judgment. Thus, prior to *Gravier* (and indeed arguably exacerbated by *Levin/Lawrie-Blum*), a significant section of the population of the EEC could not derive any rights directly from the Treaty.

2.5.2 *The Student: Post-*Gravier

What was left, then, was an ill-fitting category of individuals, struggling to find a label to attach to them, certainly within the four fundamental freedoms themselves. It was in this context – an absolutely fundamental one – that the 'Community student' truly emerged as a result of *Gravier*. What is distinct about *Gravier* is that the applicant was attempting to obtain rights derived from the Treaty solely on the basis of being a student, not based upon any prior period of residence.[211] Likewise, what distinguishes the facts of *Gravier* from *Meade* and *Kuyken* is that in the latter two cases the students were being penalized by their Member State of origin because they had moved to another Member State. In *Gravier*, by contrast, the issue was whether a student would be entitled to derive rights in his/her host Member State. On this basis, she could not obtain redress under conventional legal avenues. For instance, she tried to submit that 'education is a service', which was roundly dismissed by AG Slynn when he maintains: 'The fact that the student pays something is not enough to convert it into a service'.[212] Likewise, by contrast with *Casagrande*, AG Slynn also makes it clear that the applicant was 'neither a worker nor the child nor the spouse of a worker'.[213] Thus, for the applicant to derive rights an entirely novel legal avenue had to be construed and it was in this context that the hitherto relatively untouched policy of vocational training came to the fore.[214] AG Slynn claimed that

> It is contrary to Article 7 of the EEC Treaty, read with Articles 48, 52 and 59, for institutions providing vocational training (but not other forms of educations) in one Member State to discriminate on the grounds of nationality in respect of

210 *Meade*, p. 2641.
211 Case 293/83, *Françoise Gravier* v. *City of Liège* [1985] ECR 593, p. 607.
212 Ibid., p. 597, p. 603.
213 Ibid., p. 599.
214 As Flynn claims: 'until quite recently, Article 128 of the EEC Treaty was all but a dead letter'. Flynn, 'Vocational Training', 59.

fees charged against nationals of other Member States of the Community who are there for the sole purpose of undertaking such vocational training.[215]

Whilst the case itself proved to be a watershed moment in the development of Community law, the AG's legal reasoning was inherently subjective and not immune from criticism.[216] The only basis upon which the applicant could derive rights was to 'read' Article 7 of the Treaty (itself not overtly containing any identifiable rights) with the free movement provisions of the Treaty collectively, with vocational policy as a seemingly formative background.[217] In other words, a right, which could potentially impose a severe financial burden on the Member States was being construed out of no free movement right in particular, merely as a collective. The Court likewise, states:

The first remark which must be made in that regard is that although educational organization and policy are not as such included in the spheres which the Treaty has entrusted to the Community institutions, access to and participation in courses of instruction and apprenticeship, in particular vocational training, are not unconnected with Community law.[218]

To reiterate the above point, to create a legal right, with a considerable amount of money being at stake, on the basis of something that is 'not unconnected' with Community law is radical and was certainly not the view of the Member States. For Belgium, there was, by contrast, simply no such right as 'a national of one Member State has no right under the Treaty to enter another Member State for the purposes of education or to be admitted to a course on the same terms, as to fees and grants, as

[215] *Gravier*, p. 605.

[216] In terms of the case's radicalism, a number of commentators hailed its significance. As Flynn summarized: 'The ruling was received with great excitement in Community legal circles. To some, it seemed the foundation stone of a Community education system guaranteeing access to courses without consideration of nationality'. Likewise, for Steiner, *Gravier* 'established a significant principle' and, as Wouters asserted: 'Since the *Gravier* judgement, it is well-established case-law that students who are nationals of a Member State have a right of equal treatment under the EC Treaty as regards the conditions for access to professional education in another Member State'. Flynn, 'Vocational Training', 65; Josephine Steiner, 'Recipients of Services – Some More Equal than Others' (1985) 10 (5) *European Law Review*, 348–352 at 352; Wouters, 'European Citizenship', p. 33. For criticism, see subsequent footnote.

[217] Flynn, 'Vocational Training', 72. Rasmussen, for instance, as part of a work in which the reasoning of the Court more generally was heavily criticized on the grounds of judicial activism, commented: 'All too many judgments [of the Court] were constitutive of law, including *Gravier*'. Hjalte Rasmussen, *The European Court of Justice* (Copenhagen: GadJura, 1998), p. 366.

[218] *Gravier*, p. 612 at para. 19.

that Member State's own nationals'.[219] Despite this, the Court was prepared to allow the applicant to succeed on the basis of the fact that, firstly, the common vocational policy 'is thus gradually being established',[220] that 'access to vocational training is in particular likely to promote free movement of persons', that it 'constitutes discrimination on grounds of nationality contrary to Article 7 of the Treaty' and therefore that 'it follows from all the foregoing that the conditions of access to vocational training fall within the scope of the Treaty'.[221] Moreover, the Court then went on to say 'it [further] follows that any form of education' counts for the purposes of vocational training.[222] Once again none of the above reasoning necessarily follows but, crucially, what matters is that students who were nationals of a Member State of the Community were now entitled to not be discriminated against on the grounds of nationality.[223] Moreover, what undoubtedly had taken place was the creation of a free-standing right with radical repercussions.[224] AG Slynn, in *Commission* v. *Belgium (the 'minerval' case)* admits as much: '*Gravier* was a totally new development in Community law, since it recognized rights in respect of persons who could not be regarded as economically active' and then terms this new category of individuals 'Community students'.[225] Indeed, to avoid any shadow of doubt, the Court states overtly, in *Barra*, that 'in general all universities fulfil [the] ... criteria [of vocational training]'.[226] Thus, a clearly radical development had taken place in Community law – one reflected on later within the case law of the Court as being so – in which an effectively Court-created right for Community students emerged for a category of individuals – the student – who by definition are not economic actors.

Furthermore, the context in which *Gravier* was decided was crucial for a number of reasons. First, a free-standing right was created on the basis

219 Ibid., p. 596 (summarized by AG Slynn).
220 Ibid., p. 612 at para. 23. It should be noted that a core component of SC theory is that it is individuals or agents that construct a reality that, at times, they appear to be merely purporting to describe. Arguably this type of statement illustrates this point. See 'Introduction' for further analysis.
221 *Gravier*, para. 26, para. 25.
222 Ibid., p. 614 at para. 30.
223 See Section 2.5.3.
224 As Steiner stated: 'the European Court [has] opened the door to an altogether wider application [of the principle of non-discrimination], with serious implications for the Member States'. Steiner, 'Recipients of Services', 349.
225 Case 293/85, *Commission of the European Communities* v. *Kingdom of Belgium* [1988] ECR 305 (*Commission* v. *Belgium (the 'minerval' case)*), p. 331.
226 Case 309/85, *Bruno Barra* v. *Belgian State and City of Liège* [1988] ECR 355, p. 405 at para. 23.

of combining a policy of the Community – Article 128 – which is explicitly stated to be an enabling provision designed to facilitate secondary legislation to emerge but for which no concrete rights could be attached – with Article 7 of the Treaty itself being the statement of an aim rather than being intended to be the source of a right.[227] Nonetheless, this is exactly what happened in *Gravier* and in this respect, the explosion of the discourse of the principle of equal treatment, as will be examined in Chapter 3, played an important role. As will be suggested, there is a symbiotic interrelationship between the principle of equal treatment and Article 7 of the Treaty. By the time of *Gravier*, the principle had gathered such great momentum that it had become seen as ordinary to focus more attention on whether the principle had been infringed and less on whether there was any relationship with 'work' in a given case. The focus had become less on the 'worker' and more on the 'person' in free movement of persons and it is only by doing so that it was possible to see Article 7 as capable of facilitating the creation of free-standing rights independently of the workers provisions of the Treaty. Indeed, this point also ties in with the opening section of this chapter as what was examined was a conceptual shift within the jurisprudence of the Court towards protecting the right for individuals to move across borders and reside within the Community.

Moreover, in Chapter 1, what was outlined was a context that had developed in which workers had been construed so widely that it would not seem to be an enormous step to incorporate students within the Treaty, whether as 'workers' or through the creation of a novel right. The value in an SC theoretical analysis of such a development is that it is capable of delineating the boundaries of social acceptability within evolving epistemic communities, such that the context was appropriate for such a radical development in 1985; whereas it was not earlier on in the Court's jurisprudence.[228] For instance, to a certain extent, the *minerval* and the *minimex* combine. In *Hoeckx*, the applicant was claiming a minimal subsistence allowance on the basis that the minimal amount of work she was doing was not capable of actually sustaining her in real terms.[229]

[227] Adrienne De Moor, 'Article 7 of the Treaty of Rome Bites' (1985) 48 *Modern Law Review*, 452–459 at 452. O'Leary describes the use of (then) Article 6 of the Treaty as 'innovative'. O'Leary, *Evolving Concept*, p. 160. See also Enrico Traversa, 'L'Interdiction de Discrimination en Raison de la Nationalité en Matière d'Accès á l'Enseignement' (1989) 25(1) *Revue Trimestrielle de Droit Europèen*, 45–69 at 67–68.

[228] See 'Introduction'.

[229] See Section 2.3.1.

Prohibiting the denial of the *minimex* might not, then, be seen as such a radical development in the circumstances. In other words, there had been a considerable parallel development in which the types of benefits being claimed bore little or no relation to work anymore. Instead, by focussing on mere presence or residence on a territory, the abolition of restrictions relating to the receipt of the *minimex* seemed inevitable.[230] Finally, what cannot be ignored is the development of the jurisprudence on tourists as potential recipients on services, indeed *Carbone* is mentioned in *Gravier* itself.[231] Thus, on one level the only time in which the Community student could have emerged was in *Gravier* itself and not any earlier; the entire context within Community law operated had to change before the Community student could emerge.

2.6 Member State Revolt Leading to the First 'Image' of the Citizen Emerging

In the context of all three of this chapter's essential components (namely the creation of a momentum towards a more generalized right of residence, and the evolution of both the Community tourist and the Community student), the three residency directives were enacted. Such a profound legislative change came about as a result of a pragmatic attempt by the Member States to resist and limit a momentum in which the Treaty was being increasingly used by applicants, with varying degrees of success, to obtain rights that had little or nothing to do with work.[232] This section will examine the input of the Member States into the discursive evolution towards Citizenship. As has already been examined in the Introduction, resistance is a fundamental aspect of discourse creation as it plays a key role in delineating its specific manner and form. Whilst the enactment of the residency directives was designed, in part, to prevent non-economic contributors being a burden on the state, the three directives in turn formed a vital component of the later Citizenship Directive.[233] It is therefore worth examining such resistance within the text of the Court's judgment.

230 Ibid.

231 *Gravier*, p. 597 (AG Slynn).

232 Rasmussen summarizes the build-up to the enactment of the three residency directives as follows: 'faced with the choice of rolling back the judge-made Community powers in this field to point zero and peacefully acquiescing what the Court had done – the [Member States at the] IGC preferred the latter solution'. Rasmussen, *European Court of Justice*, p. 332.

233 See Section 2.3.3.

2.6.1 *Objections to a Potential Generalized Right of Residence*

The cause for concern as far as the Member States were concerned, was outlined by AG Mayras in *Brack* as early as 1976 in the context of the principle of assimilation when, as has already been referred to in Chapter 1, he alludes to a 'generalisation of the trend towards the protection of the whole of the population'.[234] If this were the case, then, almost the entire population of the Community could be assimilated to the status of worker. Whilst the principle of assimilation effectively disappeared after the repeal of Regulation No. 3/58, the notion that underpinned such a statement by AG Mayras in *Brack* – that Community law was developing in a direction towards a right of residence absent of participation in an economic activity – was clearly of great concern to the Member States.[235] Indeed, the concern by certain Member States was sufficiently serious that they had to categorically state that such a development was *not* taking place. In *Levin*, the Danish government claimed that:

> The right to freedom of movement is conferred only on those persons who play a role in the economic life of the Member States, whereas persons who do not or have pursued an occupation have under the Community rules applicable at present no right of residence in another Member State.[236]

Likewise, in *Lair*, an attempt to create rights for students, as indeed took place in *Gravier*, was a clear concern for the German government when it maintained that:

> [The *Gravier* approach] would result in an extension of that right to an indeterminable category of persons and thus an extension of the concomitant right of residence. Such a right of residence is not in fact granted by Community law as it stands at present.[237]

However, on both occasions, they both emphasize that a generalized right of residence did not exist 'at present' leaving room for there to be an eventual progression towards one. Thus, whilst the views of the Member States in *Levin* and *Lair* were not a direct response to AG Mayras' statement in *Brack*, it is clear that there was a concern about a development towards a generalized right of residence within the text of

[234] Case 17/76, *M. L. E. Brack, widow of R. J. Brack*, v. *Insurance Officer* [1976] ECR 1429, p. 1462.

[235] For this reason, for Rasmussen, the enactment of the directives in which emphasis was placed on individuals not being a burden on the host state was the result of profound protest by the Member States against the activism of the Court 'making it clear that enough was enough'. Rasmussen, *European Court of Justice*, p. 332.

[236] *Levin*, p. 1041.

[237] Case 39/86, *Sylvie Lair* v. *Universität Hannover* [1988] ECR 3161, p. 3166–3167.

Court judgments that were central to the evolution and delimitation of the 'worker'.

Moreover, in *Commission* v. *Netherlands* (1991), such concern was expressed overtly by two Member States contrary to the views of AG Tesauro and the Commission, whilst at the same time making a direct link to citizenship. The case was brought against the Netherlands as a result of a complaint brought by a German national that he was questioned by border officials as to the purpose and duration of his trip to the Netherlands, as well as the financial means at his disposal.[238] The officials were acting in accordance with a Dutch law and the Commission brought the case against the Netherlands on the ground that the law itself impeded free movement.[239] AG Tesauro states, firstly, that 'it is apparent ... that the more recent directives adopt ... albeit under certain specified conditions, a right of residence to all Community citizens'.[240] However, what is also noticeable is the reasoning he gives for making such a statement concerning this perceived development. He continues: 'Community law at present already grants, for various reasons, a right to enter and stay in other Member States to nearly everyone possessing the nationality of a Member State'.[241] The 'various reasons' could be suggested to be two-fold: first, the problem of sifting the 'sheep' from the 'goats' as has been examined above and, second, this stems, ultimately, from the jurisprudence of the Court in relation to the 'worker' to incorporate several categories of individuals that would not ordinarily be termed workers. This point is illustrated by AG Tesauro, when he states that free movement rights can be summarized as follows:

> In addition to the case of someone who goes to another State to work there, the conceivable possibilities are manifold: people may travel in order to seek work, to consult a professional practitioner, to enjoy an excursion and go to a restaurant or, to give an extreme example, even without carrying any means of payment, simply in order to visit shops with a view to returning at a later stage to make purchases.[242]

Ultimately the entire case was based on a complaint made by the complainant that a Member State should not even be entitled to enquire

[238] Case C-68/89, *Commission of the European Communities* v. *Kingdom of the Netherlands* [1991] ECR I 2637, p. 2644.
[239] Ibid.
[240] Ibid., p. 2647.
[241] Ibid.
[242] Ibid.

as to the purpose of his visit or whether he had adequate financial means: his mere status as a national of another Member State gives him the right to move and reside unencumbered and un-scrutinized.[243] Both the UK and the Netherlands strenuously objected to this interpretation of the Community law. As the UK contended:

> The EEC Treaty does not grant a right of residence to everyone. It cannot therefore be said that the mere status of national of one of the Member States confers on the person possessing that status a right to enter and reside in another Member State. The finding that a person possesses the nationality of a Member State of the EEC does not automatically afford that person a right of residence since there is at least one category of EC nationals who cannot claim a right of residence under the Treaty, namely those who are not working.[244]

Likewise, the Netherlands maintains:

> The status of citizen of a Member State does not automatically confer the right to enter and stay in other MS, since there is at least one class of Community nationals – those who are not in gainful employment – who do not, under the Community legislation in force, enjoy an independent right to enter and remain in a country.[245]

However, comparing and contrasting the two statements, it is clear that the UK merely reiterates a perceived orthodoxy that those that do not work do not 'count' for the purposes of the Treaty as has already been outlined in Chapter 1. In this respect, the Netherlands appears to be rearticulating the same orthodoxy. Nonetheless, there is an important difference as the Dutch government refers to a different status, that of the 'citizen of a Member State'. It is clear, then, that the case was being decided under the shadow of the soon-to-be incorporated citizenship provisions of the Treaty and was trying to pre-empt a potential future argument that these new provisions created such independent rights. Thus, even if the views of the Netherlands government represented a resistance to a development towards a generalized right of residence, its mere protest was articulated in the context of citizenship, itself a linguistic development.

2.6.2 *Objections to* Gravier*-type Rights*

Given how much money was literally at stake as a result of the creation of the Community student, many Member States revolted against its

[243] Ibid., p. 2645.
[244] Ibid., p. 2642.
[245] Ibid., p. 2645.

creation which, ironically, in turn facilitated the specific form of the Community Citizen.[246] The Belgian government in *Gravier* described as 'unthinkable' the idea that it should be forced to financially assist individuals who had made no direct or indirect (i.e. as a family member of a worker) contribution to the state.[247] In *Brown*, the German government asserted:

> The Treaty has not yet established a social union. Accordingly, Community law does not confer a general right on Community nationals of access to students' allowances in a Member States other than their own; that is something that would require practical steps towards political integration.[248]

Likewise, the Danish government (in *Brown*) maintains

> In view of the considerable expenditure which education represents, it would be quite unacceptable if nationals from other Member States were to be allowed to demand access to education without having first resided in the State concerned for a certain period.[249]

Finally, in *Raulin*, the Dutch government also adds: 'the EEC Treaty does not grant the right of residence to students who have no status other than that of students'.[250] It was in this context that an emphasis was placed upon all Community nationals being allowed to retain the rights created by the Court in not just *Gravier* but *Cowan* and more generally 'only if the persons concerned will not become a burden for the public purse'.[251] The UK in *Brown* then makes a distinction between 'worker rights' and '*Gravier* rights' to make the point that whilst acknowledging this clearly radical development in Community law, entirely different principles and priorities apply to the Community students than to workers.[252] Thus it is clear that *Gravier* was met with considerable resistance by the Member States.

[246] The point being made here is that by effectively proclaiming 'enough was enough', the Member States added the proviso in all three directives that non-economic migrants must not be a burden on the social security system of the host state. These directives were then repealed and replaced by the Citizenship Directive, the formative part of which was, likewise, to not be a burden on the host state. This issue then is the keystone of contemporary debates on EU Citizenship in the context of the principle of solidarity. See Section 5.2. See, for instance, Condinanzi, Lang and Nascimbene, *Citizenship of the Union and Freedom of Movement of Persons*, pp. 31–33.

[247] *Gravier*, p. 597.

[248] *Brown*, p. 3217.

[249] Ibid., p. 3219.

[250] *Raulin*, p. 1036.

[251] *Commission* v. *Belgium [1988]*, p. 323 (Belgium's position as summarized by AG Slynn).

[252] *Brown*, p. 3219.

2.6.3 *Embryonic Citizenship in the Form of Legislative Change*

Nonetheless, in this very specific context the embryonic Citizen emerged and what all of the Member States were clearly pointing towards was vital legislative change.[253] If a continual emphasis was being placed upon the Community student, as created by *Gravier*, not being a burden on public funds if he/she was to derive rights, then this arguably demanded further legislation. Likewise, if a distinction is to be made between 'workers' and those that can derive '*Gravier*-type rights', then this needed to be spelled out. It was therefore no surprise that the three Residency Directives eventually emerged (in turn then forming the vital legislative background to the later Citizenship Directive),[254] making it clear that all Community nationals had a right to move and reside so long as they were not a burden on the public purse.[255] Directive 90/364 created a right of residence for 'nationals of Member States who do not enjoy this right under other provisions of Community law' so long as they were covered by sickness insurance and, crucially, 'avoid becoming a burden on the social assistance system of the host Member State' (Article 1).[256] Directive 90/365 entitled former workers to a right of residence with, once again, the proviso of not being a burden on the host state (Article 1).[257] Finally, Directive 90/366 created a right of residence for students 'in order to facilitate access to vocational

[253] For a detailed analysis of the difficult and protracted process that led to the enactment of the three directives (one of which, Directive 90/366, was actually annulled by the Court on the grounds of not being enacted on the proper legal basis), because of the objections of the Member States to the Court's case law in cases such as *Gravier* and *Cowan*, see H. Taschner, 'Free Movement of Students, Retired Persons and other European Citizens – A Difficult Legislative Process', in Henry Schermers (ed.), *Free Movement of Persons in Europe: Legal Problems and Experiences* (Dordrecht: Kluwer Academic Publishers, 1993), pp. 427–436.

[254] Directive 2004/38/EC of 29 April 2004 on the right of Citizens of the Union and their family members to move and reside freely within the territory of the Member States amending Regulation (EEC) No 1612/68 and repealing Directives 64/221/EEC, 68/360/EEC, 72/194/EEC, 73/148/EEC, 75/34/EEC, 75/35/EEC, 90/364/EEC, 90/365/EEC and 93/96/EEC [2004] OJ L158/77 ('The Citizenship Directive'). The Citizenship Directive, in turn, repealed the three residency directives.

[255] The Belgian government, for instance, attempted to limit the effects of the *Gravier* ruling by enacting a new law, part of which meant that, in certain circumstances, a foreign student would have to produce proof of adequate resources in order to be exempted from the *minerval*. Flynn, 'Vocational Training', 66.

[256] Council Directive 90/364/EEC of 28 June 1990 on the right of residence [1990] OJ L180/26.

[257] Council Directive 90/365/EEC of 28 June 1990 on the right of residence for employees and self-employed persons who have ceased their occupational activity [1990] OJ L180/28.

training' (i.e. *Gravier*-type rights) on the proviso that not only are such students not a burden on the state but also that they make a prior declaration assuring the host state that they will not become so (Article 1).[258] Moreover, as has just been referred to, the German government in *Brown* claimed that one reason for not allowing for the establishment of such a free-standing right for students was that the Treaty had not yet established a social union. Yet, in a matter of a few years that proviso by Germany became reality with the creation of a Union (with clearly social as well as economic undertones) in which the Citizen was formally legally created. Thus, one key piece of the linguistic and legal jigsaw of citizenship was provided by the creation of rights for students, which in turn demanded radical legislative change.

In the build-up to the enactment of the three directives, the legislative basis of one of them (the proposed directive on students) was challenged in *European Parliament* v. *Council* (1992).[259] The dispute related to the proposed residence directive for students. However, what was also mentioned were proposals for two other directives formally giving a right of residence to non-economically active actors and collectively they would have all been entitled to a 'Residence permit for a national of a Member State of the EEC'.[260] Arguably the fact that such legislative proposals were being discussed is indicative of a watershed moment in the development of the Community.[261] Thus, the entire nature of the Community law was on the cusp of a radical change. In *Singh*, AG Darmon states:

> Until the adoption of [the new residency directives] ... which make that right more widely available, the free movement of persons within the Community was determined – and delimited – by the economic character of the Treaty. It follows that freedom of movement granted to Community nationals is deemed to involve movement *for the purposes of an economic activity*.[262]

Putting it differently, then, when this legislative change did take place, the entire character of the Community had changed and a more

258 Council Directive 90/366/EEC of 28 June 1990 on the right of residence for students [1990] OJ L180/30.

259 Case C-295/90, *Council of the European Communities* v. *European Parliament, Commission of the European Communities, United Kingdom and Kingdom of the Netherlands* [1992] ECR I 5299.

260 *European Parliament* v. *Council*, p. 4219.

261 Taschner, for instance, describes the enactment of the three directives as 'dramatic' and ushered in an era in which there was a 'new European citizen's right of residency'. Taschner, 'Free Movement of Students', p. 435.

262 *Singh*, p. 459.

generalized right of residence for mere nationals of another Member State – the Citizen – has been created.[263]

2.7 Conclusion

In this chapter it has been suggested that a number of complex conceptual strands were woven together to create a momentum for a generalized right of residence as legislatively enshrined in the residency directives. Throughout it has been claimed that the relationship with the worker has been symbiotic and, particularly as a pervasive discourse of the worker was constructed as a result of *Levin/Lawrie-Blum*, the 'worker' became an increasingly ill-fitting label for non-economic or peripherally economically active migrants within the then Community. Therefore, it was further submitted that the emergence of a discourse of EU Citizenship can also be attributed to legal and linguistic developments in a number of different (though closely related) substantive areas of EU free movement of persons law. In the opening part of the chapter it was maintained that borders began to look qualitatively different from other parts of the world (particularly in the treatment of individuals that would be ordinarily excluded in 'ordinary' domestic immigration law) and that this represented a socio-cognitive shift in the way that borders were understood within the Union. In addition, the origins of residency directives can also be traced more specifically to the emergence of the Community tourist and student after both *Cowan* and *Gravier* respectively but this chapter did so in a specifically constructivist sense in examining the complex interrelationship between both strands of case law, the cultural and structural evolution of borders in the opening part of the chapter and the self-limiting nature of the 'worker' as it became crystallized in Chapter 1. Thus, whilst the wording of Directive 2004/38 may appear to be simple, its origins can be traced to a number of complex factors which, when woven together, enable the reader of the text of judgments of the Court during this time to see a different, and (partly) non-economic aspect, of the 'incipient' citizen.

[263] As Koslowski claims: '*Gravier* and *Cowan* have not only affirmed certain social and civil rights, they have effectively enabled any citizen of a member state to claim rights through a de facto expansion of the definition of rights bearers under the treaty from "workers" to those receiving services as commonplace as a metro ticket'. Rey Koslowski, *Migrants and Citizens – Demographic Change in the European State System* (Ithaca: Cornell University Press, 2000), p. 120.

As will be outlined in Chapter 5, the CRD could be somewhat naively portrayed as an almost quasi constitutional document containing a body of rights that the Citizen is entitled to. What this chapter has sought to do is to focus on the inherently contingent and contested origins of such a seemingly fundamental document. Seen in this way, a more subtle fissure (or set of fissures) is evident right at the heart of the development towards a more generalized right of residence. The Court's jurisprudence on non or marginally economic actors is as important to the development of EU law as that of the worker in Chapter 1: it is part of its very foundations. As has been outlined an attempt was made by the Court to compartmentalize two obvious examples – the tourist and the student – into that category and it ultimately failed. What arguably followed was an alternative line of case law leading directly to citizenship in a substantive sense. However, this development was far from beyond controversy. Firstly, this chapter attempted to outline how the Court reconstructed internal borders within the EU in a manner that was unique in the world and where it has become hard, if not impossible in some cases, to deport EU Citizens if a Member State felt that that person's presence was not conducive to the public good. This appears emancipatory in many ways and very much on the way to AG Jacobs' vision in *Konstantinidis*.

Nonetheless, the consent of the Member States in this is not as obvious. Seen in this manner, the momentum towards a generalized right of residence is less a path towards citizenship and more one of its many hidden fissures. For instance, on one level to construe a tourist to be a recipient of services for the purposes of protection under EU law is based upon a somewhat artificial and strained interpretation of primary law. The Treaty did not even overtly refer to service recipients deriving protection, let alone tourists (which would in reality mean any EU Citizen moving from one Member State to another in order to do anything other than work or become established). Furthermore, what cannot be forgotten is that what the tourist in *Cowan* was asking for was for a compensatory sum derived ultimately from a fund provided by the domestic taxpayer in France. If anything, the development towards providing students with protection was even more controversial in the sense that the Court's interpretation of apparent rights that derived from the Common Vocational Policy (which on plain reading appeared simply to be an enabling provision for further legislation) was even more strained than the Court's interpretation of the remit of ex Article 52 TEC on services. It is for this reason that the Member States revolted against such developments by the Court, particularly because of how much taxpayers' money would need to be provided in order to allow for such court-created rights to be protected. Seen in this way the evolution towards the three residency directives (in turn eventually becoming the CRD) was less emancipatory and more begrudging acceptance by the Member States of the Court's jurisprudence with a view to providing restrictions on the exercise of such rights. The fissure at the heart of the development of this radical area of law was the lack of obtaining overt consent from the Member States prior to such a development rather than forcing them collectively into a *post hoc* response.[264] Ultimately, one of the Member States chose to leave the radicalism of such a regime altogether.

[264] It could be suggested that this is partly at the heart of the presentation of EU law's development being based on integration through law. As Dr Witte put it 'law is both the agent and object of integration, and is used to push through the objectives of integration even in the presence of political objection on the national or supranational level'. Perhaps the process may well have been better served by pausing to listen to such voices rather than simply 'push [ing] through'. Floris De Witte, 'Freedom of Movement Needs to Be Defended as the Core of EU Citizenship', in Rainer Bauböck (ed.), *Debating European Citizenship* (Cham: Springer, 2019), pp. 93–99 at p. 98.

Part II

The Crumbling Pillars of the Temple

3 A Discourse of Equal Treatment?

3.1 Introduction

The reform to the Treaty structure at Maastricht was frequently likened to that of a temple façade with pillars. This book has likened the core tenets of free movement of persons law (upon which the later citizenship specific law was based) to that of an edifice built upon foundations of sand. Chapters 1 and 2 were akin to describing inherent fissures within the foundations of such a temple. Chapters 4 and 5 constitute an inspection of inherent problems within the pillars upon which the roof of citizenship was ultimately laid. This chapter will focus specifically on utterances of equal treatment, making the inherent point that such utterances are worthy of assessment in and of themselves. Equal treatment is one of the core principles of Union law and is frequently linked to citizenship both more generally and in a Union-specific context.[1] Exemplary of this is Part Two of the Treaty on the Functioning of the European Union (TFEU) which is entitled 'non-discrimination and citizenship of the Union'. This chapter will therefore be devoted to examining a core tenet of EU Citizenship as conventionally understood but from an explicitly discursive perspective. Prior to doing so, though, it will be necessary to both limit and define the scope of the material that has been examined in this chapter. What this book examines is the case law on free movement of persons and, indeed, what this chapter is devoted to examining is the evolution of the principle of equal treatment on the grounds of nationality

[1] As Caro de Sousa put it: 'At its lowest level of definition – and, hence, at its most consensual – citizenship can be said to relate to a certain bundle of rights and duties which are attributed in terms of equality to an individual as a result of belonging to a certain community'. Caro de Sousa, *The European Fundamental Freedoms*, p. 73.

specifically. In other words, other areas of Union law also concern equal treatment and, indeed, contain a more substantive discussion of the principle of equality more generally and the opening part of this chapter outlines such a necessary limitation to the substantive analysis that follows. The rest of the chapter is then devoted to claiming that equal treatment constitutes a powerful discourse within the framework of Court judgments and does so for three key reasons. First, it will be maintained that prior to 1968 non-discrimination was the prevailing paradigm within the case law. Second, it will then be submitted that the subjective origins of the principle of equal treatment more specifically lay not in the Treaty itself but in Regulation No. 1612/68 and that that these origins are then reflected in the subsequent case law of the Court.[2] Third, though, it will then be claimed that a process can be examined whereby equal treatment went from subjective utterance to intersubjective dominance. In particular, the case law of the Court in the 1970s will be considered to be the vital linguistic proving ground in which various actors used a number of linguistic techniques throughout this period. The chapter will examine utterances of the phrase 'equal treatment' throughout the 1980s in order to provide various 'snapshots' from within the case law demonstrating how pervasive the phrase had become within the text of court judgments. It will then be concluded that the fissure at the heart of such a discursive construction is, somewhat ironically, the hegemonic articulation of nationality as the governing criterion of what constitutes equal treatment.

3.2 The (Limited) Contribution of the Early Free Movement Cases to the Momentum towards a Principle of Equality more Generally

This chapter attempts to assess the contribution, from an explicitly SC perspective, that the early cases on free movement of persons prior to Maastricht made to the establishment of a general principle of equality in EU law which, in turn, made a partial yet significant contribution to the evolution of EU Citizenship.[3] The essence of this chapter is that

[2] Council Regulation 1612/68/EEC of 15 October 1968 on free movement of workers within the Community [1968] OJ L257/2 (subsequently repealed by Regulation No. 492/2011 of 5 April 2011 on freedom of movement for workers within the Union [2011] OJ L141/1).

[3] As Bernard maintains: 'Citizenship evokes the idea of a commonality of rights and duties between the citizens and thus incorporates a notion of equality. In a federal or proto-federal

a linguistic evolution can be evidenced in the cases from a non-discrimination paradigm to that of equal treatment.[4] This is also based upon a core set of tenets of SC theory that, firstly, words have important connotations or derived meanings and that the mere utterance of one word rather than another is significant and, secondly, that a prevailing understanding or discourse structures a text.[5] The chapter is therefore limited in its scope and its substance. In terms of its scope, the book itself attempts to 'trace' the 'incipient citizen' to the early cases on free movement.[6] Therefore other areas of substantive Community law do not form an explicit part of this chapter or the overall book. In substance, therefore, it is important, in a holistic sense, to acknowledge the important contribution that other areas of law have made to such a momentum towards a general principle of equality. In particular, the prolific case law on discrimination on the grounds of gender (in which ex Article 119 of the Treaty and the Equal Treatment Directive (Directive 76/207) have been interpreted extensively[7]) arguably operated as a line of case law at one step removed from the free movement cases but in which a principle of equal treatment also emerged.[8]

structure, there is a close affinity between citizenship of the Union and non-discrimination between the citizens of the states making up the Union'. Nicolas Bernard, 'Discrimination and Free Movement in EC Law' (1996) 45(1) *International and Comparative Law Quarterly*, 82–108 at 91–92.

4 Whilst many authors use the two phrases interchangeably (see n. 9), the two concepts are, in actual fact, different, though closely related. As Barnard put it: 'equality provides no internal guidance as to the relevance of particular characteristics of individuals or groups [whereas] the principle of non-discrimination helps to fill this vacuum'. Catherine Barnard, 'The Principle of Equality in the Community Context: P, *Grant*, *Kalanke* and *Marshall*: Four Uneasy Bedfellows?' (1998) 67 *Cambridge Law Journal*, 362–373 at 363.

5 See 'Introduction'.

6 See 'Introduction'. O'Leary maintains that the application of the principle of equal treatment in the free movement cases is 'well documented' and makes specific reference to *Cowan* and *Gravier* as examples of the use of the principle. O'Leary, *Evolving Concept*, p. 106. See also Barnard, 'The Principle of Equality', 94–96; John Usher, *General Principles of EC Law* (London: Longman, 1998), pp. 16–18; Anthony Arnull, *The General Principles of EEC Law and the Individual* (Leicester: Leicester University Press, 1990), pp. 25–61.

7 In particular, see Case 80/70, *Gabrielle Defrenne* v. *Belgian State* [1971] ECR 445; Case 129/79, *Macarthys Ltd* v. *Wendy Smith* [1980] ECR 1275; Case 12/81, *Eileen Garland* v. *British Rail Engineering Limited* [1982] ECR 359; Case 184/83, *Ulrich Hofmann* v. *Barmer Ersatzkasse* [1984] ECR 3047; Case 222/84, *Marguerite Johnston* v. *Chief Constable of the Royal Ulster Constabulary* [1986] ECR 1651; Case C-208/90, *Theresa Emmott* v. *Minister for Social Welfare and Attorney General* [1991] ECR I 4269; Case C-9/91, *The Queen* v. *Secretary of State for Social Security, ex parte Equal Opportunities Commission* [1992] ECR I 4297.

8 See Evelyn Ellis, 'Gender Discrimination in the European Community', in Janet Dine and Bob Watt (eds.), *Discrimination Law: Concepts, Limitations and Justifications* (London:

Moreover, the sex discrimination cases clearly also made a significant contribution to the idea of a convergence of grounds of equality.[9] Besides sex discrimination cases, other areas of substantive law also played an important role in the development of the principle of equality, particularly those relating to the Common Agricultural Policy (CAP) because it was from within that line of case law that equality as a general principle of Community law was derived.[10]

Furthermore, this chapter also works on two related *a priori* assumptions, both of which have been subjected to academic scrutiny. First, it is maintained that the phrase 'equal treatment' can, in the context of Community law, be seen as a development from non-discrimination even if various actors within the Court and academic commentators alike tend to use the phrases interchangeably.[11] Non-discrimination is

Longman, 1996), pp. 14–30; Arnull, *General Principles*, pp. 236–258; Takis Tridimas, *The General Principles of EC Law*, 3rd edn. (Oxford: Oxford University Press, 2006), pp. 112–116; Bob Hepple, 'The Principle of Equal Treatment in Article 119 EEC and the Possibilities for Reform', in Alan Dashwood and Siofra O'Leary (eds.), *The Principle of Equal Treatment in EC Law* (London: Sweet & Maxwell, 1997), pp. 137–152.

[9] As Bell comments: 'a solid body of law governing discrimination on the grounds of nationality and gender has been constructed'. Bell, *Anti-Discrimination Law*, p. 32. See also Gráinne de Búrca, 'The Role of Equality in European Community Law', in Alan Dashwood and Siofra O'Leary (eds.), *The Principle of Equal Treatment in EC Law* (London: Sweet & Maxwell, 1997), pp. 137–152; Catherine Barnard, *EC Employment Law* (Chichester: Wiley, 1996), p. 74.

[10] It was in *Ruckdeschel* where the Court first stated that non-discrimination in the context of (ex) Article 40 (3) of the Treaty was 'merely a specific enunciation of the general principle of equality which is one of the fundamental principles of Community law'. Joined Cases 117/76 and 16/77, *Albert Ruckdeschel & Co. and Hansa-Lagerhaus Ströh & Co.* v. *Hauptzollamt Hamburg-St. Annen; Diamalt AG* v. *Hauptzollamt Itzehoe* [1977] ECR 1753, p. 1753.

The principle was also reiterated in Joined Cases 103 and 145/77, *Royal Scholten-Honig (Holdings) Limited* v. *Intervention Board for Agricultural Produce; Tunnel Refineries Limited* v. *Intervention Board for Agricultural Produce* [1978] ECR 2037; Case 810/79, *Peter Überschär* v. *Bundesversicherungsanstalt für Angestellte* [1980] ECR 2747; Joined Cases 201 and 202/85, *Marthe Klensch and others* v. *Secrétaire d'État à l'Agriculture et à la Viticulture* [1986] ECR 3477; Case 84/87, *Marcel Erpelding* v. *Secrétaire d'État à l'Agriculture et à la Viticulture* [1988] ECR 2647. See also Sotirios Manolkidis, 'The Principle of Equality from a Comparative Constitutional Perspective: Lessons from the EU', in Alan Dashwood and Siofra O'Leary (eds.), *The Principle of Equal Treatment in EC Law* (London: Sweet & Maxwell, 1997), pp. 80–104 at pp. 88–89; Bernard, 'Discrimination and Free Movement', 78–83; Tridimas, *General Principles*, pp. 78–94.

[11] Jacobs (writing extrajudicially), for instance, states: 'generally the provisions of the EC Treaty address the issue of discrimination, rather than guaranteeing equality . . . although it is sometimes said that non-discrimination and equality are simply different ways of expressing the same idea'. He then continues: 'although the principle of non-discrimination on grounds of nationality was, in its historical context, essential, there may now be doubts about whether, in at least some contexts, it is sufficient. A more

essentially prohibitory in nature – a minimum prerequisite – whereas to treat an individual as an equal is more closely aligned to the vision set out in the preamble to the Treaty of an 'ever closer union of peoples'.[12] The second assumption that is made is that the evolution towards a principle of equal treatment encompassing both nationality and gender also creates further momentum towards a general prohibition of discrimination on a number of other grounds, such as race, and that this is what is understood by some to mean a 'general principle of equality', particularly in the context of EU Citizenship.[13] However, this is not to

broadly based principle of equal treatment may be necessary for some purposes'. Likewise, Whiteford examines the development of EC pensions law as evidencing progress 'from non-discrimination to equality'.

On the other hand, de Búrca, in response to the question 'over the different meanings which can be attributed to the different terms used' maintains that 'the terms "equality" "equal treatment" and "non-discrimination" will [in her writings] be used interchangeably'.

Francis Jacobs, 'An Introduction to the General Principle of Equality in EC Law', in Alan Dashwood and Siofra O'Leary (eds.), *The Principle of Equal Treatment in EC Law* (London: Sweet & Maxwell, 1997), pp. 1–12 at pp. 1–3; de Búrca, 'Role of Equality', p. 13. See also Janet Dine and Bob Watt, 'Introduction', in Janet Dine and Bob Watt (eds.), *Discrimination Law: Concepts, Limitations and Justifications* (London: Longman, 1996), pp. 3–13; O'Leary, *Evolving Concept*, p. 105; Barnard, *EC Employment Law*, p. 65; Warwick McKean, *Equality and Discrimination Under International Law* (Oxford: Clarendon, 1983), pp. 204–205; Wouter Vandenhole, *Non-Discrimination and Equality in the View of the UN Human Rights Treaties* (Antwerp: Intersentia, 2005), p. 33; Usher, *General Principles of EC Law*, p. 16.

12 See Vernon Van Dyke, *Human Rights, Ethnicity and Discrimination* (Westport: Greenwood Press, 1985), pp. 193–194.

13 AG Jacobs, for instance, projects into a future 'beyond the application of the principle of non-discrimination or equal treatment in the specific fields of gender or nationality, which have been the traditional focus of Community legislation, case-law and academic literature'. Arguably, the implication of this statement is that AG Jacobs is acknowledging the important role that that prior case law on free movement played in establishing a basis in which a future general principle of equality can flourish. Likewise, Hepple claims that there should be 'a comprehensive right to equality of ... treatment without distinction an any arbitrary ground including sex or gender, marital status or family responsibilities', Guild advocates the cause of a principle to incorporate racism and xenophobia, and Brown claims that 'much has still to be done to ensure the right to non-discrimination for *all* the peoples of Europe'. Monaghan also charts a development of the principle of equal treatment from that based on nationality and gender to the implementation of the Race Directive (Directive 2000/43) and the Charter of Fundamental Rights.

Jacobs, 'General Principle of Equality', p. 10, p. 12; Hepple, 'The Principle of Equal Treatment', p. 137; Elspeth Guild, 'EC Law and the Means to Combat Racism and Xenophobia', in Alan Dashwood and Siofra O'Leary (eds.), *The Principle of Equal Treatment in EC Law* (London: Sweet & Maxwell, 1997), pp. 189–213; Christopher Brown, 'The Race Directive: Towards Equality for All the Peoples of Europe?' (2001) 21(1) *Yearbook of European Law*, 195–227 at 227; Karen Monaghan, *Equality Law* (Oxford: Oxford University

deny or fail to acknowledge that the origins of the principle of equality actually lay in the early CAP cases and the meaning of 'equality' in this context was that of formal legal equality; in other words the notion of failing to treat like cases alike and different cases differently or simply the refusal of arbitrariness.[14]

Nonetheless, the type of equality that is being referred to has been classified as substantive or de facto equality;[15] the phrase itself encapsulating a normative attempt to achieve sociopolitical aims[16] which, in turn, is closely related to fundamental rights.[17] This type of definition of equality is particularly important from a discursive perspective. As has already been outlined in the Introduction, discourses have a resonance in particular social contexts (and in society more generally) and what is of particular importance to SC theorists is the process of embedding particular phrases to become societal norms or forms of social truths and from an SC perspective, the evolving principle of equality has considerable normative potential. This contrasts markedly with the view of some legal academic commentators. For Westen, equality is an 'empty idea' which has taken on a confusing sociopolitical momentum involving 'suspect classifications' by which he means attempting to unify discrimination on various grounds under the banner 'true equality'.[18] In Westen's analysis of the evolution of the principle, what has effectively happened is that equality cases have been

Press, 2007), p. 99, pp. 113–135; Council Directive 2000/43/EC of 29 June 2000 implementing the principle of equal treatment between persons irrespective of racial or ethnic origin [2000] OJ L180/22.

14 See Jacobs, 'General Principle of Equality', p. 8; Takis Tridimas, 'The Application of the Principle of Equality to Community Measures', in Alan Dashwood and Siofra O'Leary (eds.), *The Principle of Equal Treatment in EC Law* (London: Sweet & Maxwell, 1997), pp. 214–242; Vandenhole, *Non-Discrimination and Equality*, p. 33.

15 For a discussion of the distinction between the two types of equality, see Gavin Barrett, 'Re-examining the Concept and Principle of Equality in EC Law' (2003) 22(1) *Yearbook of European Law*, 117–153 at 121–129.

16 As Barrett maintains: 'the pursuit of a notion of equality in the Community context is becoming that of an ideal broader than this, closely linked to a number of other ideals such as dignity, participation in society, and perhaps the idea of the redress of historical disadvantage'. Barrett, 'Re-examining the Concept', 150.

17 Rasmussen, for instance, characterizes the gender discrimination cases as being instigated by 'equal treatment activists'. Rasmussen, *European Court of Justice*, p. 210. Also, see below in the same paragraph, Westen's view that equality cases effectively 'collapse' into rights cases.

18 Peter Westen, 'The Empty Idea of Equality' (1982) 95(3) *Harvard Law Review*, 537–596 at 564. Bernard, likewise, sees the phrase as vacuous. Bernard, 'Discrimination and Free Movement', 79. See also Lammy Betten, 'New Equality Provisions in European Law: Some Thoughts on the Fundamental Value of Equality as a Legal Principle', in

'collapsed into rights cases and cannot be separated from the textual embrace of equality'.[19] Nonetheless, what appears to be (ironically) universally acknowledged in relation to equality is that there is no one definition of it. As Bell, maintains: 'equality is a pluralistic concept, one which is capable of bearing a number of different interpretations of it'.[20] From an SC perspective, the inherent linguistic flexibility of the term means that it has the potential to have subjective content added to it in different contexts and, significantly, Bell continues: 'The precise meaning of [the principle] is often difficult to pin down, especially in the context of the ... [EU] where it has adopted [its] own form of equality-speak [*sic*]'.[21] In other words the principle of equality can be classified as a discourse and that the European Union (and its institutions) has (have) been the site(s) of a nuanced form of its creation. Indeed, this much is in effect admitted by Westen when he defines the principle as 'a "form" for stating moral and legal propositions ... a "form" of discourse with no substantive content of its own'.[22] However, for SC theorists, a supposed 'empty' or 'vacuous' term in actual fact has considerable normative and transformative potential.[23] As Barrett comments:

Kim Economides, Lammy Betten, John Bridge, Andrew Tettenborn and Vivien Shrubsall (eds.), *Fundamental Values* (Oxford: Hart Publishing, 2000), p. 69.

19 Westen, 'The Empty Idea of Equality', 565. This therefore is equally significant from an SC perspective as an important link is made between the principle of equal treatment as outlined in this chapter and fundamental rights as will be outlined in Chapter 5. What is also of note in this citation is the fact that Westen sees the principle of equality as having 'textual embrace'.

20 Mark Bell, *Racism and Equality in the European Union* (Oxford: Oxford University Press, 2008), p. 27.

21 Ibid. See also Barrett, 'Re-examining the Concept', 149. Barrett characterizes equality as being like a 'prize which each man seeks to bestow on the qualities of his own choice'.

22 Westen, 'The Empty Idea of Equality', 577–578. Schaar, likewise, defines the principle as 'a protean word ... one of those political symbols into which men have poured the deep urgings of their own hearts' and Tridimas claims that it 'has perhaps greater resonance than any other legal concept'. 'Symbols' and 'resonance' are constituent aspects of an SC understanding of discourse (see the Introduction). John Schaar, 'Equality of Opportunity and beyond', in J. Roland Pennock and John Chapman (eds.), *Nomo IX: Equality* (New York: Atherton Press, 1967), pp. 228–249; Tridimas, *General Principles*, p. 59.

23 On this substantive understanding of equality, the development of the principle itself has the potential for radical 'social reorganisation'. Evelyn Ellis, 'The Principle of Equality of Opportunity Irrespective of Sex: Some Reflections on the Present and Future Development of European Community Law', in Alan Dashwood and Siofra O'Leary (eds.), *The Principle of Equal Treatment in EC Law* (London: Sweet & Maxwell, 1997), pp. 172–188 at p. 180.

If the concept of equality truly is, metaphorically speaking, an empty vessel, then it may be said to be one which, in the Community context ... is rapidly being filled with a powerful new cocktail of more potent and varied flavour than that which has been tasted before. The story of equality, both as a concept and in terms of the operation of the Community law principle, seems very far from its end.[24]

In other words, the story or narrative is an evolving or continuing one and it is in this context that the progression towards a general principle of equality can be seen to emanate from the solid basis created for it by the prior case law on non-discrimination on both the grounds of nationality and gender, of which the evolution towards the dominant paradigm of equal treatment is one significant part.[25]

Finally, merely because this chapter is focussing on the evolution of the jurisprudence of the Court from non-discrimination to equal treatment in the cases on free movement of persons does not mean that there was no discussion of the principle of equality meant in its broadest sense, merely that the origins of this particular general principle of EU law lay elsewhere.[26] For instance, AG Mischo in *Factortame* claims that the free movement provisions of the treaty are: 'merely an expression ... of the general principle of equality. The latter principle is broader in scope than the principle of non-discrimination on grounds of nationality, which, however, is the only general principle at issue here'.[27] Likewise, in one of the final cases before the coming into force of the TEU, *Wirth*, a German student had been refused a German study grant to go and study in the Netherlands.[28] His case was weak in that it looked particularly ripe for the suggestion that it was, for the most part, wholly internal.[29] However, the applicant still

[24] Barrett, 'Re-examining the Concept', 153.

[25] The starting point, for Usher, was that of nationality; which, broadly though it was interpreted, also had its limitations, for which the development of a general principle of equality, can be seen as a response. Likewise, Bell characterizes the evolution towards a general principle of equality as a 'hierarchy of equality' in which discrimination on the grounds of nationality was prioritized, followed by discrimination on the grounds of gender (both of which 'traditionally have been privileged categories') and finally discrimination on other grounds. Usher, *General Principles of EC Law*, p. 20; Bell, *Anti-Discrimination Law*, pp. 32–33. See also Ward, *Critical Introduction*, pp. 170–175.

[26] See n. 9.

[27] Case C-221/89, *The Queen* v. *Secretary of State for Transport, ex parte Factortame Ltd and others* [1991] ECR I 3905, p. 3941.

[28] Case C-109/92, *Stephan Max Wirth* v. *Landeshauptstadt Hannover* [1993] ECR I 6447, p. 6457.

[29] Ibid., p. 6459. For further analysis of this point, see N. Hopkins, 'Education and the European Community: Education as a Service and the Principle of Non-Discrimination' (1994) 16(4) *The Journal of Social Welfare and Family Law*, 486–491.

pleaded this case as being a breach of the principles of equality and then submitted that he can do this because the principle 'demonstrates a breadth of interpretation of what is meant by the "general principle of equality as a fundamental principle of Community law" which seems to go beyond the scope of Article 7 of the Treaty'.[30] Thus, this chapter can but be seen as a small part of a much greater whole (beyond the free movement case law) in the context of a general principle of equality. Nonetheless, this chapter will examine the significant role that equal treatment understood in terms of discrimination on the grounds of nationality played in the evolution towards citizenship.[31]

3.3 The Discursive Nature of the Principle of Equal Treatment

As has been outlined earlier, the main contention in this chapter is that the principle of equal treatment can be classified as a discourse. This can be evidenced in a number of ways that reflect the conceptual understanding of the evolution of discourse within SC theory. First, it is maintained that equal treatment became a dominant paradigm or 'label' in which to describe, in part, the normative basis of the free movement provisions of the Treaty[32] and that this can be partly illustrated by examining some of the early case law in which the use of the phrase 'non-discrimination', by contrast, appeared to be the prevailing paradigm. Second, after having examined a prior prevailing understanding based upon non-discrimination, an attempt to trace the

[30] *Wirth*, p. 6461.

[31] As de Búrca outlines: 'It is frequently said that the principle of equal treatment or non-discrimination occupies a central role in EC law'. Docksey likewise characterizes it as 'one of the basic principles which underpin the whole of Community law' and Barnard describes it as the 'cornerstone of the four freedoms'. Indeed, as Jacobs put it: 'it has even been suggested that the entire EC Treaty is simply the principle of equal treatment for nationals "writ large" . . . The prohibition of discrimination on grounds of nationality is also of great symbolic importance, inasmuch as it demonstrates that the Community is not just a commercial arrangement between the governments of the Member States but is a common enterprise in which all the citizens of Europe are able to participate as individuals'.

de Búrca, 'Role of Equality', p. 13; Chris Docksey, 'The Principle of Equality between Women and Men as a Fundamental Right Under Community Law' (1991) 20(4) *Industrial Law Journal*, 258–280; Barnard, *Four Freedoms*, p. 18; Jacobs, 'General Principle of Equality', pp. 1–2.

[32] See Hopkins, 'Education and the European Community', 486–491.

subjective origins of the principle of equal treatment will be made. Third, after having traced such subjective origins, a comprehensive attempt will be made to examine utterances of the principle in order to illustrate the process whereby equal treatment became a dominant discourse within the free movement of persons cases. It should finally be noted that the methodological approach that will be adopted is both quantitative (in the sense of examining the number of utterances of the phrase 'equal treatment') and qualitative (by examining the context in which some of the utterances were made).[33] In commenting on the evolution of the principle of equal treatment, Bamforth claims that 'the mere incantation of the word "equality" is not enough on its own to explain anti-discrimination law in a satisfactory fashion'.[34] On one level, it is maintained that Bamforth's comment has veracity in it in that, firstly, as has already been outlined earlier, 'equality' and 'equal treatment' also evolved in cases beyond those of free movement and, secondly, a context-driven (and qualitative) attempt to understand the evolution of the principle is fundamentally necessary. Nonetheless, it is contended that 'mere incantation' of a principle should not be so readily dismissed and that discourses are partly constituted through their sheer repetition.[35]

3.4 Non-discrimination as the Original Prevailing Paradigm

Whilst references to the principle of non-discrimination have repeatedly been made throughout the case law of the Court on free movement of persons, what is evident from the early days of the case law is that it was a dominant paradigm within the text of Court judgments.[36] This is because non-discrimination was one of the original founding principles contained in the original Treaty (Article 7) which, in turn, governs the administering of the free movement of workers provisions of the Treaty (Article 48(2)). It was therefore not surprising that non-discrimination

[33] SC theory does not take a purely quantitative methodological approach and thus a mixture of the two forms of analysis is essential. See 'Introduction'.

[34] Nicholas Bamforth, 'Limits of Anti-Discrimination Law', in Janet Dine and Bob Watt (eds.), *Discrimination Law: Concepts, Limitations and Justifications* (London: Longman, 1996), pp. 49–63 at p. 49.

[35] See 'Introduction'.

[36] This is, in part, because it was considered to be the 'corner-stone' of the provisions on free movement (see n. 30).

was a dominant feature within many of the cases on free movement. Whilst references to the principle are too prolific to comprehensively outline, in *Walrave*, for instance, the Court states: 'Articles 7, 48, 59 have in common the prohibition, in their respective spheres of application, of any discrimination on grounds of nationality'.[37] This seemingly innocuous statement has significance from a discursive perspective because, firstly, it refers, through the use of the phrase 'in common', to it in effect as a unifying principle – the hallmark of discourse – and, secondly, because it seems to have been written specifically for rhetorical effect as it is a self-contained and very short paragraph of the judgment. Moreover, in some cases, the utterance of the principle was structurally prioritized within the linguistic framework of Court judgments. It is, firstly, 'welded' to the word fundamental, and repeatedly so.[38] The Italian government in *Fossi* for instance characterizes it as 'one of the fundamental principles of the EEC Treaty',[39] and both the Court and the headnote in *Fearon* refer to it as a 'fundamental rule'.[40] Indeed, and secondly, the importance of this rule or principle is made abundantly clear by its repeated emphasis in very often the first few lines of headnote of particular cases. In *Sotgiu*, for instance, the case is summarized in italics as '*1. Freedom of movement – Workers – Principle of non-discrimination*' and this exact phrase is then repeated in paragraphs two and three.[41] Thirdly, therefore, repetition is crucial to ingraining a discursive trait and the principle of non-discrimination is repeatedly uttered and emphasized within many judgments. As an example, in

[37] Case 36/74, *B. N. O. Walrave and L. J. N. Koch* v. *Association Union cycliste internationale, Koninklijke Nederlandsche Wielren Unie and Federación Española Ciclismo* [1974] ECR 1405, p. 1417 at para. 16, p. 1405 (facts). The case concerned a nationality provision inserted into employment contracts in a competitive cycling team. See also Geoffrey Morse, 'Direct Applicability of Main Treaty Provisions and Scope of Safeguard Clauses' (1975) 1 (1) *European Law Review*, 67–69; Neville March-Hunnings, 'European Community Law: Nationality Discrimination' (1975) *The Journal of Business Law* 168–171.

[38] The nature and importance of linguistic 'welding' has been outlined in 'Introduction' and also Section3.6.5.

[39] Case 79/76, *Carlo Fossi* v. *Bundesknappschaft* [1977] ECR 667, p. 674, p. 670 (facts). An Italian miner's pension case.

[40] Case 182/83, *Robert Fearon & Company Limited* v. *Irish Land Commission* [1984] ECR 3677, p. 3677. The case itself concerned a close residency provision that prevented the compulsory sale of farm land in Ireland and the applicant, a UK national, claimed that this was a form of covert discrimination.

[41] Case 152/73, *Giovanni Maria Sotgiu* v. *Deutsche Bundespost* [1974] ECR 153, p. 153. In the case, the applicant, an Italian postal worker in Germany, received a separation allowance (from his family) that was less than the amount he would have received had his family resided in Germany. See also Wyatt, 'Scope of Equal Treatment', 62–63.

Walrave, the Court refers to it eight times over thirty-four paragraphs and in the operative part in bold at the end of the case two out of five paragraphs refer to it.[42] Thus, whilst the principle of non-discrimination is in many ways very clearly prioritized by the black letter of the Treaty itself, its use by the Court not only adds to that black letter but also has discursive aspects to it. It is ultimately the Court that brought the principle to life by its repetition and it is also the Court that attaches the label 'fundamental' to it, not the Treaty itself. In the end, it is one of the most uttered principles by the Court and various agents within it; it constitutes the 'traditional' narrative upon which all other principles are based, such as equal treatment.[43]

3.5 The Subjective Origins of the Principle of Equal Treatment

3.5.1 *In Legislation*

As has already been outlined, Article 7 of the EEC Treaty refers to non-discrimination and therefore not equal treatment. The first linguistic reference to the principle was made in Regulation No. 1612/68. Prior to this point there was no reference within the Court reports to this principle. The coming into force of this regulation directly changed the legal landscape of the Court – a reflection perhaps of a change of political will affecting the Court – and an important paradigm shift took place, from a *de minimis* prohibitory approach to a positive almost encouraging approach designed to establish equality for all Member State nationals.[44] Indeed the text of its preamble appears to reflect this development. The regulation starts off on the basis of non-discrimination, maintaining that freedom of movement entails abolishing discrimination[45] but it then leads to the following statement:

[42] *Walrave*, pp. 1405–1425.

[43] As Bell states: 'Anti-discrimination law has been a central element of social policy from the earliest stages of European integration' and as Prechal maintains: 'Discrimination on grounds of nationality was, and still is, a tool par excellence for market integration.' Bell, *Anti-Discrimination Law*, p. 32; Sacha Prechal, 'Equality of Treatment, Non-Discrimination and Social Policy: Achievements in Three Themes' (2004) 41 *Common Market Law Review*, 533–551 at 548.

[44] See n. 47.

[45] The specific wording of the regulation was 'whereas the attainment of this objective entails the abolition of any discrimination based on nationality between workers of the Member States'.

> Whereas the right of freedom of movement, in order that it may be exercised, by objective standards, in freedom and dignity, requires that equality of treatment shall be ensured in fact and in law in respect of all matters relating to the actual pursuit of activities as employed persons and to eligibility for housing, and also that obstacles to the mobility of workers shall be eliminated, in particular as regards the worker's right to be joined by his family and the conditions for the integration of that family into the host country.[46]

This aim in the preamble reflects a much softer or human edge than the wording of the original Treaty; the concern appears to be not so much for the worker as a factor of production but the worker as a human being.[47] What should firstly be noted is the reference to 'freedom and dignity'. This reflects a development to a new 'softer' paradigm and relates inexorably to the development of the citizen because the preamble to the regulation quite specifically gives the impression that the concern for the worker is not merely in relation to his/her pure economic rights but his/her welfare: his very essence.[48] His/her 'essence' is more fully expressed in the form of his/her family and the focus is less on pure conditions relating to work (which would be covered by ex-Article 48 in any case) but every aspect of his/her persona.[49] This can all be summarized by the principle of equal treatment and clearly

[46] Council Regulation 1612/68/EEC of 15 October 1968 on free movement of workers within the Community [1968] OJ L257/2.

[47] This contrasts with the wording of Article 48 EEC which was concerned with the abolition of discriminatory barriers in terms of 'employment, remuneration and other conditions of work and employment' (Art. 48(2)), that is, was primarily market focused. This is not to suggest that the Treaty was not concerned with the worker as human being, merely that Article 48 did not necessarily reflected that grander normative aim. For instance, the Treaty's preamble expresses the desire for 'an ever-closer union among the peoples of Europe' and, indeed, Regulation No. 1612/68 was specifically enacted by the enabling provision in Article 49 and therefore this certainly suggests that the Treaty had the potential to allow for developments towards a more social edge. Treaty establishing the European Community [2002] OJ C325/1.

[48] Prechal maintains that 'economic market integration was given a human face by' the regulation and that it demonstrated that 'already relatively early on, it became clear that Community law would not treat workers as being mere factors of production. The law on free movement of workers also includes important social and human aspects'. Prechal, 'Equality of Treatment', 548. See also Caroline Laske, 'The Impact of the Single European Market on Social Protection for Migrant Workers' (1993) 30 *Common Market Law Review*, 515–539 at 515; Harm ter Heide, 'The Free Movement of Workers in the Final Phase' (1969) 6 *Common Market Law Review*, 466–477 at 466; Wyatt, 'Social Security Rights of Migrant Workers and Families', 411.

[49] For Barrett, the Court's jurisprudence on family reunification goes considerably beyond 'merely constituting what is necessary in order to secure the free movement rights of the primary beneficiary of Community law. Instead, they seem to bespeak objectives on the part of the Community legal system which are as much rooted in fundamental

therefore reflects a development from the non-discrimination paradigm. Ultimately, this reflected back on the principle of non-discrimination and changed it. The preamble continues: 'the principle of non-discrimination between Community workers entails that all nationals of Member States have the same priority as regards employment'. The language here is softer and more substantive, the task of Community law is no longer primarily concerned with tackling overtly discriminatory laws, it is about treating non-nationals as equals; nor is it any longer about 'prohibiting discrimination on the grounds of nationality' as contained in Article 7 of the Treaty, reflecting, instead, a much more proactive approach to get Member States and employers to see non-nationals as equals.[50] This is then reflected into the substantive provisions of the regulation itself. Title II very explicitly in bold refers to 'Employment and equality of treatment' and Article 7(1) refers to not treating non-nationals differently (i.e. they must be treated the same) and Article 7(2) refers to being treated the same in the field of social and tax advantages and, once again the word 'same' is used in Article 7(3). In addition, the only occasion in which discrimination is actually referred to is in Article 7(4) referring to collective agreements. Equally, it should be noted that there is a real emphasis made to encourage vocational training. Article 7(3) refers to being treated the same in relation to it and in the preamble the reasoning behind such an emphasis is in order to facilitate workers taking up offers of employment 'from other regions of the Community'. What both the discrimination and vocational provisions of the regulation show is a subtle change that has taken place

rights as in economics'. Indeed, Costello maintains that Regulation No. 1612/68 itself played a highly significant role in the evolution from the 'worker' to the Citizen because family reunification (including for TCNs) was expressed as a '"fundamental right" to be exercised in "freedom and dignity"' in its preamble. Barrett, 'Re-examining the Concept', 419; Cathryn Costello, '*Metock*: Free Movement and "Normal Family Life" in the Union' (2009) 46 *Common Market Law Review*, 587–622 at 588. See also Eugenia Caracciolo di Torella and Annick Masselot, 'Under Construction: EU Family Law' (2004) 29(1) *European Law Review*, 32–51 at 33; Karin Lundström, 'Family Life and Freedom of Movement of Workers in the European Union' (1996) 10(3) *International Journal of Law, Policy and the Family*, 250–280 at 276; Diego Acosta-Arcarazo and Andrew Geddes, 'The Development, Application and Implications of an EU Rule of Law in the Area of Migration Policy' (2013) 51(2) *Journal of Common Market Studies*, 179–193 at 179; Jeremy Bierbach, 'European Citizens' Third-Country Family Members and Community Law' (2008) 5(2) *European Constitutional Law Review*, 344–362 at 346.

50 As Prechal put it, this form of equal treatment, understood in a substantive sense: 'involves not only eliminating discrimination but also actively taking steps to promote greater equality. In other words, it requires positive and proactive measures', Prechal, 'Equality of Treatment', 537. See also n. 46.

over ten years. In relation to discrimination, it is maintained that Member States clearly now know full well that they themselves cannot overtly discriminate, and thus the battle has, in a sense, moved on and is focused on more subtle forms of covert or indirect discrimination, much more closely akin to the meaning of equal treatment itself.[51] Likewise in relation to vocational training, Regulation No. 1612/68 appears to reflect less a position of protecting those who have already moved to work in another Member State and more at positively encouraging pan-European migration more generally.[52]

3.5.2 *In the Case Law: The First Subjective References to the Principle in the Early Case Law*

Almost immediately after the coming into force of the regulation, the language changed within the text of Court judgments and there then commenced a series of subjective assertions, to a certain extent designed to make this new principle the predominant overarching theme of the Court. The phrase was first used in *Ugliola*.[53] Indeed, perhaps, surprise

[51] Now, as Oliveira asserts: 'most often, in the field of free movement of workers, the Court concentrates on establishing whether or not a measure of the State of employment treats a worker . . . in an indirectly discriminatory manner'. See also Esther Johnson and David O'Keeffe, 'From Discrimination to Obstacles to Free Movement: Recent Developments Concerning the Free Movement of Workers 1989–1994' (1994) 31 *Common Market Law Review*, 1313–1346 at 1327–1334; Stephen Weatherill, 'Case Comment: The Scope of Article 7 EEC' (1990) 15(4) *European Law Review*, 334–340 at 334–336; Anastasia Iliopoulou and Helen Toner, 'Case Comment: A New Approach to Discrimination against Free Movers?' (2003) 28(3) *European Law Review*, 389–397 at 390–394; White, *Workers, Establishment and Services*, pp. 54–56; Arnull, *General Principles*, pp. 38–57; Barnard, *Four Freedoms*, pp. 239–241.

[52] As Barnard outlines, the regulation gave 'rights not only to workers but also their families in an attempt to encourage them to move'. Barnard, *Four Freedoms*, p. 265. See also David O'Keeffe, 'Equal Rights for Migrants: The Concept of Social Advantages in Article 7(2), Regulation 1612/68' (1985) 5(1) *Yearbook of European Law*, 95–123 at 94–95; À. Castro Oliveira, 'Workers and Other Persons: Step-by-Step from Movement to Citizenship - Case Law 1995-2001' (2002) 39 *Common Market Law Review*, 77–127 at 110–124; Jean-Claude Séché, 'Free Movement of Workers under Community Law' (1977) 14 *Common Market Law Review*, 385–420 at 389–398; Wellem Molle and Aad Van Mourik, 'International Movements of Labour under Conditions of Economic Integration: The Case of Western Europe' (1988) 26(3) *Journal of Common Market Studies*, 317–340 at 320–321.

[53] Case 15–59, *Württembergische Milchverwertung-Südmilch AG* v. *Salvatore Ugliola* [1969] ECR 363, p. 373. A case concerning an Italian national working in Germany who was forced to do military service in Italy. His period of time doing so was not calculated for purposes of working out social security benefits; whereas it would have been had he been a German national serving in the Wehrmacht.

might be expressed that it was only in 1969 that the phrase was first used in the text of Court judgments when AG Gand in *Ugliola* claims:

> Although the provisions relating to the eligibility for employment of the nationals of the Member States have become more liberal as the Council has adopted new regulations, the principle of equal treatment for an existing contract of employment was established from the outset. It was already expressed in Regulation No 15/61 of the Council, it was enunciated again by Article 9 of Regulation No 38/64.[54]

There is, though, a sense of irony in this statement and it is submitted that AG Gand himself is aware of the fact that something new has been subjectively created. Not only does he overtly refer to a new era of proactive legislation – reflecting the fact that change has clearly taken place – but also he seems to be concerned with establishing historic authenticity for the principle.[55] However, the phrase had never been used by the Court until *Ugliola* and this is where its origins in the form of the text of Court judgments can be traced. AG Gand himself then later on refers to the principle without anchoring it to Regulation No. 1612/68 in which it is specifically referred to and the Court then appears to reflect AG Gand's newly created principle equally detached from the regulation.[56] Initially it refers to non-discrimination, asserting that 'the regulations are based upon Article 48 which . . . prescribes the abolition of any discrimination based on nationality' but then the Court itself refers to the principle in bold.[57] Equally, the Commission appears to get this entire trend in motion by referring to it twice.[58] Therefore the Court itself both added life to the text of the regulation and created a life for the principle of equal treatment independently of it.

Furthermore, a number of different actors within the text of the Court judgment in *Ugliola* appear to reflect back on the Treaty and suggest that the principle of equal treatment was contained within it, which, as has

[54] Ibid.

[55] Both Regulation 15/61 and Regulation 38/64 refer to equal treatment (the former as a title to Chapter 3 and the latter as a title to Chapter 2). However, neither preambles refer to equal treatment; whereas it is quite explicitly referred to in Regulation 1612/68. It is therefore submitted that the enactment of the latter regulation was considered by many to be a seminal moment in the evolution of the law on free movement of persons and that this was reflected in the language used by the Court in *Ugliola*, a case report in the same year as the coming into force of the regulation. See n. 42.

[56] *Ugliola*, p. 376.

[57] Ibid., p. 368 at para. 3, p. 370 at para. 6.

[58] Ibid., p. 366.

already been outlined, it was not.[59] The Commission, for instance, alludes to 'the principle of equal treatment laid down by Article 48 of the EEC Treaty and referred to in Regulations Nos 38/64 and 1612/68'.[60] Likewise, the Court itself mimics this approach when it states in paragraph 6 of its judgment: 'Article 48 of the Treaty does not allow Member States to make any exception to the equality of treatment and protection required by the Treaty for all workers within the Community'.[61] It is maintained that this constitutes a form of *post hoc* labelling in which the phrase 'equal treatment' is ascribed to the Treaty as if had been so from the outset. It is this that makes the principle discursive in that it conditions a mindset at a particular time and indeed changes the very linguistic narrative of the history of Community law itself.[62] Moreover, whilst the first reference to the principle of equal treatment was made in *Ugliola*, this type of attempt at *post hoc* labelling was also made in several other subsequent cases. In *Michel S.*, for instance, AG Mayras maintains: 'the equality of treatment required by Article 48 of the Treaty forms the very foundation of Regulation 1612/68'.[63] This process of 'reflecting back' is also in effect admitted by the Commission in *Marsman* where it states that there is a 'duty to give workers equality of treatment contained in Art 48(2) of the Treaty and Article 7(1) of Regulation 1612/68 applies – as stated *ipsis verbis* in the said Article 7 – to any conditions of employment and work'.[64] Putting it differently, the phrase is clearly very firmly anchored in the regulation but the specific wording – *ipsis verbis* – is actually not contained in the Treaty at all. Therefore, at least according to the subjective assertions of the Commission, AG Gand and the Court, there is a principle of equal treatment that existed not from the moment of utterance but from the original Treaty itself. Thus, whilst the first subjective utterance of the principle of equal treatment was made in *Ugliola*, the Commission and the Court in the case appeared to mask the subjectivity inherent in making such utterances by giving it the historical

59 See above (3.5.1).

60 *Ugliola*, p. 366.

61 Ibid., p. 369.

62 See 'Introduction'.

63 Case 76/72, *Michel S.* v. *Fonds national de reclassement social des handicapés* [1973] ECR 457, p. 468, p. 458 (facts). In the case, the applicant, an Italian national, was denied a benefit in Belgium for his disabled son on the grounds that he had not resided in Belgium when his son was born. See also Wyatt, 'Scope of Equal Treatment', 62–63.

64 Case 44/72, *Pieter Marsman* v. *M. Rosskamp* [1972] ECR 1243, p. 1245, p. 1244 (facts). In the case, the applicant, a Dutch frontier worker working in Germany, was made redundant in circumstances where he would have had legislative protection had he resided in Germany.

authenticity of having been contained in the original Treaty, a form of 'labelling' that also took place in subsequent cases.[65]

3.6 The 1970s as an Intermediate Phase

In SC theory, a discourse is a dominant paradigm or understanding that emerged from subjective origins.[66] Section 3.5 was devoted to examining the subjective origins of the use of the term 'equal treatment' in both the case law and legislation. The final section of this chapter will consist of an examination of the prolific use of 'equal-treatment speak' in many of the free movement of persons cases throughout the 1980s, particularly in the build-up to Maastricht. It will then be claimed that this is evidence of the discursive nature of equal treatment. However, it is the phase in between the principle's subjective origins and its proliferation that is critical to examine from an SC perspective as it is during this period (which could be roughly equated to the 1970s) that the process can be outlined whereby an utterance progresses from being initially subjective to becoming intersubjective.[67] In the process of examining this 'intermediate phase' in the 1970s a number of factors were evident. First, that, initially, equal treatment was used purely as a synonym for the principle of non-discrimination and there appeared to be no discussion on whether there is a distinction between the two within the text of the Court judgments.[68] Nonetheless, secondly, there were voices within the text of Court judgments that were prepared to conceive of the two principles as not only distinct but also to portray equal treatment as a progression from non-discrimination. Third, techniques designed to convey the importance of a particular utterance are used that are important in discourse creation; particularly (what has already been termed) 'welding' equal treatment to the word 'fundamental', the 'foundations' of the Community or fundamental rights. Finally,

[65] As stated somewhat ironically by Rasmussen, this method has been used in this book to derive a principle that had hitherto been 'well hidden in the Treaty'. Rasmussen, *European Court of Justice*, p. 334. See also Burley and Mattli, 'Europe before the Court', 41–76; Gregory Caldeira and James Gibson, 'The Legitimacy of the Court of Justice in the European Union' (1995) 49(2) *International Social Science Journal*, 356–376; Trevor Hartley, 'The European Court, Judicial Objectivity and the Constitution of the European Union' (1996) 112(1) *Law Quarterly Review*, 95–109 at 95.

[66] See the Introduction.

[67] See 'Introduction'.

[68] Indeed, it should be noted that a number of academic commentators also treat the two principles synonymously. See n. 10.

as has already been outlined in the Introduction, sheer repetition is an important aspect of embedding a discourse and it will be claimed that the repetition of the phrase that did take place in the 1970s, whilst not as prolific as what took place in the 1980s, can be isolated to particular periods of phases within the Court's report, suggesting a linguistic interconnection between the cases.

3.6.1 *The Principle of Non-discrimination and Equal Treatment Treated within the Cases as Synonyms*

In this intermediate period, non-discrimination and equal treatment are often treated synonymously in a number of ways. First, the synonym is at times implicit by virtue of the two phrases either being used in tandem with each other or in the same paragraph or sentence. For example, the Commission in *Marsman*, immediately after the citation made above in which equal treatment was referred to, subsequently refers to non-discrimination twice, then 'inequality of treatment' and finally returning to the 'principle of Equal Treatment'.[69] Likewise, in *Gillard*, the Court refers to the 'principle of equality of treatment' and, four paragraphs later, reverts to 'the principle of non-discrimination'.[70] What is also common is to conflate the two concepts into the same sentence. For instance, the Court in *Sotgiu* states the following:

> The rules regarding equality of treatment, both in the Treaty and in Article 7 of Regulation no 1612/68, forbid not only overt discrimination by reason of nationality but also all covert forms of discrimination which, by the application of other criteria of differentiation, lead in fact to the same result.[71]

Indeed, occasionally, there are references to the two concepts as being not merely synonyms, but the same principle. AG Mayras in *Van Duyn*, for instance refers to: 'the principle of non-discrimination, in other words, that of equality of treatment with nationals';[72] and he once again makes

[69] *Marsman*, p. 1246.

[70] Case 9/78, *Directeur régional de la Sécurité sociale de Nancy* v. *Paulin Gillard and Caisse régionale d'assurance maladie du Nord-Est, Nancy* [1978] ECR 1661, p. 1666 at para. 3, p. 1667 at para. 7, p. 1662 (facts). In the case, the applicant, a Belgian national, was refused access to a pension intended for prisoners of war on the grounds of nationality. See also Derrick Wyatt, 'Discrimination on Grounds of Nationality: Schemes for the Victims of War or its Consequences' (1979) 4(5) *European Law Review*, 369–371.

[71] *Sotgiu*, p. 164 at para. 11.

[72] *Van Duyn*, p. 1358, p. 1337 (facts). Whilst the case is a seminal one in the development of EU law, the facts, to recap, were that the applicant, a Dutch national, was refused entry to the UK in order to take up employment at the headquarters of the Scientologists.

this point in *Reyners* where he maintains: 'Doubtless the terminology used is not strictly adequate: it is a question not so much of freedom of establishment as of the right of equality of treatment in the professional establishment, that is to say a prohibition on any direct or disguised discrimination based on nationality'.[73] Thus, it is clear that, for some, the two principles can be both conflated and treated synonymously and, more generally, for other actors within the Court, non-discrimination and equal treatment were treated as interchangeable synonyms.

3.6.2 *Equal Treatment and Non-discrimination as Distinct from Each Other*

Nonetheless, AG Mayras' own terminology in both *Van Duyn* and *Reyners* is discursively important but also equally 'not strictly accurate'. For instance, the headnote in *Sotgiu* that has been cited above refers not only to free movement and the principle of non-discrimination but also continues to refer to the equality of treatment in addition, twice.[74] This then raises the question as to whether they can truly be described as synonyms or are in actual fact conceptually different, albeit with a considerable overlap? If it were the case that the two concepts were exactly the same, then it begs the question as to why the Court would pronounce them separately in the headnote? The answer to this question is complex. On the one hand, there is repeated conflation of the two phrases. On the other hand, often a very deliberate attempt is made to make the reader aware of the differences. For instance, AG Warner in *Bonaffini* alludes, concurrently, to 'the principles of equal treatment and of non-discrimination enshrined in the Treaty'.[75] Moreover, AG Mayras makes the difference clear in substantive terms in *Michel S.* when he states that Regulation No. 1612/68 'aims at the abolition in their favour of any

[73] Case 2/74, *Jean Reyners* v. *Belgian State* [1974] ECR 631, p. 659, p. 632 (facts). In the case, the applicant was a Dutch national, born in Belgium, who was refused admittance to the Belgian bar on the grounds of nationality. See also Morse, 'Direct Applicability', 67–69; Natalie Beyless, 'Recent Developments – EEC Court of Justice: *H. P. Bulmer, Ltd.* v. *Bollinger, S. A.*, (1974) 2 ALL ER 1226 (CA)' (1975) 10(2) *Texas International Law Journal*, 419–428.

[74] *Sotgiu*, p. 153.

[75] Case 27/75, *Gaetano Bonaffini and others* v. *Istituto Nazionale della Previdenza Sociale* (INPS) [1975] ECR 971, p. 982, p. 971 (facts). The case concerned a group of Italian workers that had previously worked in Germany, then returned to Italy to claim unemployment benefit and were denied on the grounds that it should be the German authorities that paid it.

discrimination based on nationality and achieving complete equality of treatment',[76] and the Court, likewise, in *Reyners* alludes to 'perfect equality of treatment'.[77] Furthermore, the Italian government in *Alaimo* claims the need to 'achieve substantial equality in all sectors',[78] and, likewise, AG Trabucchi in *Farrauto* alludes to 'real equality'.[79] Finally, the German government in *Van Binsbergen* refers to 'requiring the full realization of the principle of equality of treatment'.[80] Thus, contrary to the prevailing understanding of the principle of equal treatment considerably later on in the development of the Court's jurisprudence,[81] the principle of equal treatment can be seen, within the text of Court judgments, as constituting a subjective development from the principle of non-discrimination and, as will be maintained, it required discursive work to make it into such a dominant paradigm.

3.6.3 *Making Equal Treatment a Discourse*

The discursive work required to truly establish equal treatment as the prevailing paradigm, even over the principle of non-discrimination, was a methodological process that has previously been outlined in the Introduction, namely, welding it with the label 'fundamental', using it in a multiplicity of contexts, more generally prioritizing it within the texts of judgments and, finally and crucially, sheer repetition within specific texts.[82]

3.6.4 *Welding the Principle as 'Fundamental'*

In relation to the use of the word 'fundamental' one rhetorical device used by the Court is to link the principle of equal treatment to it which, in turn, gives the impression that such statements are almost designed

76 *Michel S*, p. 467. See Section 3.5.2 above for summary of facts.

77 *Reyners*, p. 640 at para. 14.

78 Case 68/74, *Angelo Alaimo* v. *Préfet du Rhône* [1975] ECR 109, p. 168, p. 109 (facts). In the case the applicant, an Italian national, was denied a grant in secondary education in France on the grounds that non-French citizens should not be entitled to receive it as they were putting the education system under too much financial strain.

79 Case 66/74, *Alfonso Farrauto* v. *Bau-Berufsgenossenschaft* [1975] ECR 157, p. 167, p. 157 (facts). The case concerned an applicant who received a legal notice in a language that he did not understand.

80 Case 33/74, *Johannes Henricus Maria van Binsbergen* v. *Bestuur van de Bedrijfsvereniging voor de Metaalnijverheid* [1974] ECR 1299, p. 1319, p. 1299. A case in which a Dutch national was denied an entitlement to practise law in the Netherlands on the grounds that he resided in Belgium. See also March-Hunnings, 'European Community Law', 168–169.

81 See Section 3.7.

82 See 'Introduction'.

for rhetorical effect.[83] For example, the Court states in *Frilli*, 'the rule of equality of treatment ... is one of the fundamental principles of Community law',[84] and, once again, in *Sotgiu* it is described as 'one of the fundamental principles of the Community'.[85] Likewise, in *Reyners*, the Court makes a double reference to the principle. In a single contained paragraph, it maintains that: 'The rule on equal treatment with nationals is one of the fundamental legal provisions of the Community' and then later on in the judgment it asserts: 'having regard to the fundamental character of freedom of establishment and the rule on equal treatment'.[86] These matter-of-fact statements from a discursive perspective are significant because of the linguistic linkages being made with the word fundamental.

3.6.5 *Continual Linkages in a Multiplicity of Contexts and the Linguistic Structural Prioritization of Equal Treatment within the Cases*

Furthermore, attempts are also made within the text of Court judgments to link equal treatment to a number of other fundamental principles of Community law whilst, at the same time, structurally prioritizing the principle. On one level there is repeated emphasis on the principle's apparent origin, in the Treaty and Regulation No. 1612/68. For instance, in *Sotgiu* the Court refers to the 'the rules regarding equality of treatment, both in the Treaty and in Article 7 of the Regulation no 1612/68'.[87] Likewise, in *Michel S.*, AG Mayras asserts that: 'the equality of treatment required by Article 48 of the Treaty forms the very foundation of Regulation no 1612/68'.[88] In this respect, another 'welding word is used' in the form of the use of the word 'foundation' which then facilitates a process of 'reflecting back' on the original Treaty as if the phrase had been there from the outset.[89]

83 For an outline of the importance of statements designed for rhetorical effect, see 'Introduction'.

84 Case 1/72, *Rita Frilli* v. *Belgian State* [1972] ECR 457, p. 466. See Section 1.3.4 for an outline of the facts.

85 *Sotgiu*, p. 11.

86 *Reyners*, p. 24, p. 43.

87 *Sotgiu*, p. 11.

88 *Michel S.*, p. 468.

89 A subtle sign of the evolution of the principle of equal treatment in the later period of the 1980s to that of a prevailing discourse is a statement made by the Commission in *Prodest* where it alludes to 'the fundamental character of the principle of equality of treatment embodied in the Community legal order'. In legal terms, the case concerned a Belgian posted worker, working for a French company in Nigeria, which prompted the French social security authorities to refuse payment to him on the grounds that he

In *Michel S.*, AG Mayras also terms equal treatment a 'right'.[90] Finally, in *Sotgiu*, AG Mayras adds further powerful normative content to the principle when he asserts: 'Must we not, in such cases, going beyond appearances, condemn a violation of equality of treatment which may be compared with a true misuse of powers within the meaning of Community law?'.[91] Thus, the manner in which equal treatment, ultimately an initially subjective assertion, became discursive can be credited to methods – whether conscious or not by those utilizing them – of making continual linkages to other key words in Community law whilst at the same time structurally prioritizing this new principle within the framework of cases and adding powerful normative content to it.

3.6.6 *An Early Pattern of Infrequent Use in the 1970s Jurisprudence*

Sheer repetition, in both a qualitative and a quantitative sense, plays a fundamental role in the emergence of a discourse, no more so than in relation to the principle of equal treatment. After having assessed the number of times in which the phrase 'equal treatment' was used in the cases throughout the 1970s several traits were evident.[92] First, the use of the phrase was, by comparison with the 1980s, relatively infrequent. Second, the use of the phrase appears to be made in waves whereby utterances are made in a series of cases decided relatively closely together. Third, the AGs and other parties to the case appear to be less cautious with the use of the phrase than the Court.

was working outside of the territory of the Community. From a discursive perspective, though, the statement is illustrative of a changing context from the 1970s where the discourse of equal treatment had become deeply embedded. Here, the use of the word 'character' and 'embodied' arguably equally conveys a more discursive aspect to the phrase. Equally, it is 'embodied' with the fundamental normative 'character' of human rights norms. Finally, the principle appears to be stated entirely independently of any particular legislative provision. Case 237/83, *SARL Prodest* v. *Caisse Primaire d'Assurance Maladie de Paris* [1984] ECR 3153, p. 3158, p. 3154.

90 *Michel S.*, p. 468. Indeed, in *Castelli*, a case involving an attempt by an Italian national to export the receipt of a pension from Italy to Belgium, the Italian government claims that Belgium was 'committing a breach of the principle of equality of treatment' using strong language akin to a criminal offence. This statement, strongly worded that it is, is also illustrative of a change of emphasis in the 1980s such that the principle had become a firmly established discourse. Case 26/83, *Carmela Castelli* v. *Office National des Pensions pour Travailleurs Salariés (ONPTS)* [1984] ECR 3199, p. 3208.

91 *Sotgiu*, p. 160.

92 The methodological approach taken in this book is both qualitative and quantitative. However, for a purely quantitative outline of utterances of equal treatment throughout the Court's jurisprudence, please consult the table in Appendix I.

As has been outlined earlier, the first case in which the phrase 'equal treatment' was used was *Ugliola* in 1969. However, it was next used in 1972 by AG Roemer in *Merluzzi,* and no reference to the principle was made in the intervening period.[93] After that point, the use of the phrase 'equal treatment' – whilst not prolific by comparison with the 1980s –[94] was referred to in waves in that in certain years, repeated reference was made to equal treatment; whereas in others utterances either did not take place or were relatively infrequent. In 1972, for instance, the principle was uttered in three cases: in *Marsman* (six times), *Frilli* and *Merluzzi.* By contrast, in 1973, only one case referred to equal treatment – *Michel S.* – though it was stated on eight different occasions. In 1974 (*Sotgiu, Van Duyn, Reyners* and *Van Binsbergen*) and 1975 (*Bonaffini, Alaimo, Farrauto* and *F*) references were made in a number of cases. Whereas in 1976 (*Inzirillo*), 1977 (*Fossi*) and 1978 (*Gillard* and *Kenny*), utterances of the phrases were not as frequent. Finally, in 1979, the principle was stated in three cases (*Rossi, Even* and *Toia*). Therefore the references to equal treatment during this early period of the Court's jurisprudence were, in quantitative terms, infrequent and characterized by certain years in which a number of cases featured utterances of the phase and certain years where there was a relative paucity of such references.[95]

Furthermore, what was noticeable about the second reference that was made to the principle in *Merluzzi* was the structural difference in its usage as compared with *Ugliola.* In *Ugliola,* both the Court and AG Mayras frequently used the phrase.[96] In *Merluzzi*, though, the Court made no reference to the principle whatsoever and this reflects a reoccurring trend of the Court to often, though not always, be cautious in its usage as compared with other parties within the Court judgments. Exemplary of this is *Michel S.*, where equal treatment is referred to repeatedly by AG Mayras (eight times) whereas the Court does not refer to it all.[97] The Court, by contrast with AG Mayras, ties the principle in more closely with the principle of non-discrimination where, in paragraph three of the judgment, it refers to Article 7 of Regulation No. 1612/68 – which very explicitly refers to equal

[93] Case 80/71, *Adalgisa Merluzzi* v. *Caisse primaire centrale d'assurance maladie de la région parisienne* [1972] ECR 175, p. 183.

[94] See Section 3.7.

[95] For references to all such utterances, see Sections 3.6.7 and 3.6.8 below where such statements will be outlined and examined in qualitative terms.

[96] See Section 3.5.2.

[97] *Michel S.*, pp. 467–477.

treatment – but eschews its usage in favour of referring to conferring a 'right to take advantage, under the same conditions as Belgian nationals'.[98] Here, the Court could easily have referred to the principle of equal treatment because it was actually contained within the regulation but did not. Indeed, the closest it got was when it alluded to 'the equality of nationals of the Member States' which is more closely aligned to the paradigm of non-discrimination by mentioning nationality.[99]

Moreover, a pattern of non-reference to the principle of equal treatment when other parties have uttered it is also evident in other cases reported at around the same time as *Michel S.* in 1973. In 1972, for instance, the principle is uttered by AG Roemer in *Merluzzi*, *Frilli* and *Marsman*.[100] Equally, the Italian government uses the phrase in *Frilli*, as does the German government and the Commission (twice) in *Marsman*.[101] The Court does refer to the principle in *Frilli*, but in *Marsman* couches the entire judgment in the language of non-discrimination and, once again, when referring to Article 7 of the regulation refers to putting non-nationals on an 'equal footing' as opposed to simply using the phrase 'equal treatment'.[102] Not only is the non-usage of the phrase 'equal treatment' by the Court indicative of a pattern within the text of Court judgments, but also such a pattern is illustrative of a continuing narrative or discussion because such utterances all occurred in 1972.[103]

This pattern of non or less prolific reference to equal treatment by the Court also took place in two further phases in the 1970s, in 1975 and 1979. In 1975, a number of parties made repeated reference to the principle of equal treatment when, conversely, the Court made no such reference. In *Alaimo*, AG Warner refers to the principle twice (as well as, once again, the Italian government), as does AG Trabucchi in *Farrauto*.[104] Indeed, in *F*, AG Trabucchi repeatedly emphasizes the phrase, referring to it five times and, revealingly, on one of those

98 Ibid., p. 462.
99 Ibid., p. 466 at para. 15.
100 *Merluzzi*, p. 183; *Frilli*, p. 479; *Marsman*, p. 1252.
101 *Frilli*, p. 460; *Marsman*, p. 1245.
102 *Frilli*, p. 466 at para. 19; *Marsman*, p. 1254 at para. 5.
103 The judgment in *Merluzzi* was made on 7 March 1972 (reported at page 175 of the Court reports), the judgment in *Frilli* was made on 6 June 1972 (reported at page 475 of the Court reports) and, finally, the judgment in *Marsman* was on 13 December 1972 (reported at page 1243 of the Court reports). *Michel S.* was then reported on 4 April 1973.
104 *Alaimo*, p. 111, p. 112, p. 168.

occasions, states: 'I must emphasise that the foundation of this body of case-law is the need to provide for the Community worker full equality of treatment'.[105] In addition, the Belgian government alludes to the phrase twice in *F* as does AG Warner in *Bonaffini*.[106] This gives the impression that at this point a subjective effort was being made by a number of actors (see below) to structurally embed the principle of equal treatment. On the other hand, the Court makes no mention of the principle in *Farrauto* and *Bonnafini* but it does do so in *Alaimo* and *F*. In both *Alaimo* and *F*, the Court refers to it once and in the case of the latter it is termed a 'fundamental principle'.[107] In 1979, the pattern was, likewise, very similar to 1975. In *Rossi*, the principle is mentioned twice by the Italian government and once by AG Capotorti but yet the Court makes no mention of it at all.[108] Likewise, in *Even*, AG Mayras refers to it three times and the Commission five times but yet once again no allusion is made to it by the Court.[109] It is therefore maintained that what this pattern demonstrates is not that the Court is categorically opposed to the principle, simply that there was a tendency, at this stage in the case law of the Court, to utter the principle considerably less than other actors within the text of its judgments.

[105] Case 7/75, *Mr and Mrs F. v. Belgian State* [1975] 679, p. 696, p. 680 (facts). The case also concerned the denial of a disability allowance; in this instance an Italian worker residing in Belgium was denied access to the allowance on behalf of his disabled son, on the grounds that he had not resided in Belgium for fifteen years, a condition that was not required of Belgian nationals.

[106] *F*, p. 684; *Bonaffini*, p. 982.

[107] *Alaimo*, p. 113 at para. 3; *F*, p. 690 at para. 15. *Alaimo* was decided on 29 January 1975 (reported on page 109 of the Court reports), *Farrauto* was decided on 18 February 1975 (reported on page 157 of the reports), *F* was decided on 17 June 1975 (reported on page 679 of the reports) and *Bonaffini* was reported on 10 July 1975 (reported on page 971 of the reports). In particular, *Farrauto* was reported immediately after *Alaimo* in the reports.

[108] Case 100/78, *Claudino Rossi* v. *Caisse de compensation pour allocations familiales des régions de Charleroi et Namur* [1979] ECR 831, p. 841, p. 851, p. 833 (facts). In the case, the family of the applicant (all of whom were Italians resident in Belgium) were denied access to social security funds in both Belgium and Italy. The husband of the applicant, a worker in Belgium, was denied access to the fund in Belgium on the grounds that his wife worked in Italy. Conversely, the applicant was denied access to the fund in Italy on the grounds that she could not be classified as 'head of household' because she was female.

[109] Case 207/78, *Criminal proceedings against Gilbert Even and Office national des pensions pour travailleurs salariés (ONPTS)* [1979] ECR 2019, pp. 2036–2038, p. 2038, p. 2021 (facts). In the joined cases, the applicants were citizens of Belgium and France, residing in France and Belgium and both were denied early access to the state pension in circumstances where a home national would have been. See Wyatt, 'Current survey', 42–47.

3.6.7 *The Actors Uttering 'Equal Treatment'*

What has also been observed is that certain agents would make repeated reference to the principle of equal treatment over others. For instance, whilst many of the AGs refer to it (as has been noted earlier), AG Mayras in particular appears to be the most frequent in terms of stating it. Throughout the 1970s, AG Mayras refers to it 14 times in several cases (in *Frilli*, *Michel S.*, *Sotgiu*, *Reyners*, *Van Binsbergen*, *Van Duyn*, *Kenny*,[110] *Gillard* and *Even*).[111] Moreover, in many of these cases he mentions equal treatment on multiple occasions: in *Michel S.* on four occasions, *Van Duyn*, *Kenny* and *Gillard* (all twice) and *Even* (three times). In addition, the Commission is a frequent articulator of the phrase: in *Marsman*, *Reyners*, *Van Binsbergen*, *Inzirillo*[112] and *Even* (five times).[113] Moreover, two Member States in particular appear to utter the phrase frequently: Germany and Italy. In terms of Germany, it is referred to twice in *Marsman*, *Van Binsbergen* and *Fossi*.[114] In terms of the Italian government, as has already been outlined, it uses the phrase in *Frilli*, *Alaimo*, *Fossi* and *Rossi*.[115] Thus, what is also evident is that particular

[110] Case 1/78, *Patrick Christopher Kenny* v. *Insurance Officer* [1978] ECR 1489, p. 1500. The case itself concerned not discrimination but an argument of reverse discrimination made by the UK. In the case the applicant, an Irish national resident in the UK, was sent to prison for assaulting his wife and the UK social security authorities refused to count this period of time for the purposes of calculating incapacity benefit because they had created a legislative exception for these sets of circumstances. The problem the UK faced was that no such exception was provided for in Regulation No. 1408/71 and the UK argued in reply that this was effectively a form of reverse discrimination as UK nationals would have been subjected to such an exception.

[111] *Frilli*, p. 479; *Michel S.*, p. 467; *Sotgiu*, p. 173; *Reyners*, p. 652; Case 33/74, *Johannes Henricus Maria van Binsbergen* v. *Bestuur van de Bedrijfsvereniging voor de Metaalnijverheid* [1974] ECR 1299, p. 1328; *Van Duyn*, p. 1358; *Kenny*, p. 1504; *Gillard*, p. 1669; *Even*, pp. 2036–2038. Indeed, AG Mayras' opinions in both *Van Binsbergen* and *Van Duyn* were handed down to the Court on the same day: 13 November 1974.

[112] Case 63/76, *Vito Inzirillo* v. *Caisse d'allocations familiales de l'arrondissement de Lyon* [1976] ECR 2057, p. 2069. In the case, the applicant, the son of an Italian worker residing in France, was denied access to a disability fund on grounds of nationality.

[113] *Marsman*, p. 1245; *Reyners*, p. 638; *Van Binsbergen*, p. 1319; *Inzirillo*, p. 2070; *Even*, pp. 2036–2038.

[114] *Marsman*, p. 1246; *Van Binsbergen*, p. 1306; Case 79/76, *Carlo Fossi* v. *Bundesknappschaft* [1977] ECR 667, p. 672, p. 669 (facts). The applicant in *Fossi*, an Italian national residing in Germany, was denied the ability to apply a provision of domestic pension law that was intended for ethnic Germans who had been forced to move during the Second World War.

[115] *Frilli*, p. 460; *Alaimo*, p. 168; *Fossi*, p. 674; Case 100/78, *Claudino Rossi* v. *Caisse de compensation pour allocations familiales des régions de Charleroi et Namur* [1979] ECR 831, p. 841.

actors within the text of the Court's judgments repeatedly referred to the principle of equal treatment.

Whilst an in-depth assessment of the reasons why such actors uttered the phrase more frequently than others is beyond the scope of this book, it is at least possible to offer tentative reasons. In relation to the frequent use of the phrase by AG Mayras and the Commission, a number of academic commentators have alluded to various Community actors within the Court being closely aligned to the 'project' of integration and attempting to pursue such a project within the environment of the Court.[116] This point is reinforced by the claim made in the earlier part of this chapter that equal treatment can be seen as a development from non-discrimination.[117] It is therefore not surprising that the Court's AGs and the Commission can be seen to be chief instigators of a new linguistic pattern.[118] In relation to the German government's apparent attentiveness to using the phrase 'equal treatment', whilst there appear to be no overt statements by it that equal treatment must develop from non-discrimination, what is clear is that the principle of equality is enshrined in Article 3 of the German Basic Law and is clearly considered to be fundamental to it.[119] Therefore, it is not surprising that it chose to

[116] See, for instance, Rasmussen, *European Court of Justice*, p. 22; Hartley, 'European Court, Judicial Objectivity', 95; Federico Mancini and David Keeling, 'Democracy and the European Court of Justice' (1994) 57 *Modern Law Review*, 175–190 at 175; Wincott, 'Political Theory', pp. 583–602; Burley and Mattli, 'Europe before the Court', 41–76; Pierre Pescatore, 'The Doctrine of "Direct Effect": An Infant Disease of Community Law' (1983) 8 (1)*European Law Review*, 155–177 at 157; and Ward, *Critical Introduction*, pp. 78–80.

[117] See Section 3.4.

[118] The Court's Advocates-General have historically, because of their relative independence from the rest of the actors within the Court, had the ability to write much more adventurous and philosophical texts than the Court would be able to do. In effect they operate as a highly significant yet subtle influence on the Court. Likewise, the Commission has historically played an important role in the evolution of EU law within the text of Court judgements as it (as well as the AGs) both displayed 'entrepreneurship' designed to create the momentum towards later judicial activism by the Court. Rasmussen, *European Court of Justice*, p. 67; Takis Tridimas, 'The Role of the Advocate General in the Development of Community Law: Some Reflections' (1997) 34 *Common Market Law Review*, 1349–1387 at 1349; Dora Kostakopoulou, 'Ideas, Norms and European Citizenship: Explaining Institutional Change' (2005) 68 *Modern Law Review*, 233–267 at 245.

See also Noreen Burrows and Rosa Greaves, *The Advocate-General and EC Law* (Oxford: Oxford University Press, 2007); Alan Dashwood, 'The Advocate General in the Court of Justice of the European Communities' (1982) 2(2) *Legal Studies*, 202–216 at 202.

[119] Article 3 actually encompasses all three aspects of equal treatment as has been previously outlined. Article 3(1) prohibits unequal treatment in a procedural sense; whereas Article 3(2) deals with gender discrimination and Article 3(3) encompasses all

dress the principle of non-discrimination up in the language of equality. In relation to the Italian government's repeated use of the phrase, attentive to the possibility of the principle of equal treatment being conceived to be a development from non-discrimination, the government's use of the phrase was pragmatic. What is evident from the case law of the court is that Italian nationals at the time were in particular need of the assistance of the Court in integrating themselves within mostly France, Belgium and Germany and, indeed, many social security cases dealt with issues that arose involving Italian nationals working in Germany, France or Belgium (often in mines).[120] The implications of

other forms of discrimination. It is evidently a central lynchpin of the German constitution given the fact that it features as its third article and is widely considered to be a highly significant principle in German public law. Indeed, like the principle of equal treatment itself in EU law, it is the content that has been added to it by the German Supreme Court (as opposed to the ECJ in the context of EU law) that has engendered its importance. As Heun maintains: 'Although the equality clause itself looks like an empty norm [sic], in Germany under the guidance of the Court it has gained enormous importance and influences the enactment of statutes as well as the administration of the laws to a great extent'. Christian Starck, 'Constitutional Definition and Protection of Rights and Freedoms', in Christian Starck (ed.), *Rights, Institutions and Impact of International Law according to the German Basic Law* (Baden-Baden: Nomos Verlagsgesellschaft, 1987), pp. 54–55; Werner Heun, *The Constitution of Germany: A Contextual Analysis* (Oxford: Hart, 2011), p. 212. See also Sabine Michalowski and Lorna Woods, *German Constitutional Law: The Protection of Civil Liberties* (Dartmouth: Ashgate, 1999), pp. 161–183; Margaret Crosby, *The Making of a German Constitution: A Slow Revolution* (London: Bloomsbury Publishing, 2008).

120 There were dozens of references to the Court throughout the 1960s and 1970s from Italian nationals working in either Belgium, Germany or France. In total, 43 such references were made; a very high number. In addition to the cases that have already been referred to (*Ugliola*, *Frilli*, *Michel S.*, *Sotgiu*, *Alaimo*, *Farrauto*, *F*, *Bonaffini*, *Inzirillo*, *Fossi* and *Rossi*), other cases include: Case 18/67, *Argia Pagotto (née Cossutta)* v. *Office National des Pensions pour Ouvriers* [1967] ECR 309; Case 19/68, *Giovanni de Cicco* v. *Landesversicherungsanstalt Schwaben* [1968] ECR 473; Case 32/70, *Union nationale des mutualités socialistes* v. *La Marca Stéphanie* [1970] ECR 987; Case 2/72, *Salvatore Murru* v. *Caisse régionale d'assurance maladie de Paris* [1972] ECR 333; Case 140/73, *Direction régionale de la sécurité sociale de la région parisienne and Caisse régionale d'assurance maladie de Paris* v. *Carmela Mancuso and Caisse nationale d'assurance vieillesse des travailleurs salaries* [1973] ECR 1449; Case 9/74, *Donato Casagrande* v. *Landeshauptstadt München* [1974] ECR 773; Case 24/74, *Caisse régionale d'assurance maladie de Paris* v. *Giuseppina Biason* [1974] ECR 999; Case 39/74, *Luciana Costa, spouse Mazzier* v. *Belgian State* [1974] ECR 1251; Case 67/74, *Carmelo Angelo Bonsignore* v. *Oberstadtdirektor der Stadt Köln* [1975] ECR 297; Case 32/75, *Anita Cristini* v. *Société nationale des chemins de fer français* [1975] ECR 1085; Case 24/75, *Teresa and Silvana Petroni* v. *Office national des pensions pour travailleurs salariés (ONPTS)* [1975] ECR 1149; Case 36/75, *Roland Rutili* v. *Ministre de l'intérieur* [1975] ECR 1219; Case 33/75, *Benito Galati* v. *Landesversicherungsanstalt Schwaben* [1975] ECR 1323; Case 49/75, *Camilla Borella* v. *Landesversicherungsanstalt Schwaben* [1975] ECR 1461; Case 76/76, *Silvana di Paolo* v. *Office national de l'emploi* [1977] ECR 315; Case 8/77, *Concetta Sagulo, Gennaro Brenca and Addelmadjid Bakhouche* [1977] ECR 1495; Case 64/77, *Mario Torri* v. *Office*

this is that comparatively speaking at the time, much of Italy was poor (particularly the South); whereas most of Northern Europe was relatively wealthy.[121] In other words, there was a great deal of migration of

national des pensions pour travailleurs salaries [1977] ECR 2299; Case 83/77, *Giovanni Naselli* v. *Caisse Auxiliaire d'Assurance Maladie-Invalidité and l'Institut National d'Assurance Maladie-Invalidité* [1978] ECR 683; Case 126/77, *Maria Frangiamore* v. *Office National de l'Emploi* [1978] ECR 725; Case 134/77, *Silvio Ragazzoni* v. *Caisse de compensation pour allocations familiales "Assubel"* [1978] ECR 963; Case 26/78, *Institut national d'assurance maladie-invalidité and Union nationale des fédérations mutualistes neutres* v. *Antonio Viola* [1978] ECR 1771; Case 139/78, *Giovanni Coccioli* v. *Bundesanstalt für Arbeit* [1979] ECR 991; Case 237/78, *Caisse régionale d'assurance maladie de Lille (CRAM)* v. *Diamante Palermo, née Toia* [1979] ECR 2645; Case 266/78, *Bruno Brunori* v. *Landesversicherungsanstalt Rheinprovinz* [1979] ECR 2705.

In addition, there were eight cases that were referred by Italian nationals working in mines in Belgium: Case 6/67, *Teresa Guerra, widow of Pietro Pace* v. *Institut national d'assurance maladie-invalidité* [1967] ECR 219; Case 45/72, *Giuseppe Merola* v. *Nationaal Pensioenfonds voor Mijnwerkers* [1972] ECR 1255; Case 17/75, *Antonio Anselmetti* v. *Caisse de compensation des allocations familiales de l'industrie charbonnière* [1975] ECR 781; Case 108/75, *Giovanni Balsamo* v. *Institut national d'assurance maladie-invalidité* [1976] ECR 375; Case 112/76, *Renato Manzoni* v. *Fonds national de retraite des ouvriers mineurs* [1977] ECR 1647; Case 22/77, *Fonds national de retraite des ouvriers mineurs* v. *Giovanni Mura* [1977] ECR 1699; Case 36/77, *Azienda di Stato per gli interventi sul mercato agricolo (AIMA)* v. *Rocco Michele Greco* [1977] ECR 2059; Case 32/77, *Antonio Giuliani* v. *Landesversicherungsanstalt Schwaben* [1977] ECR 1857.

121 Italy has, since its inception, traditionally been regarded as one of the world's most significant 'sending states' where at one time a sixth of the entire country had migrated abroad (Choate). The main reason for doing so was to attempt to resolve considerable poverty in the south of the country in particular which, in turn, could prevent a perceived fear of social unrest (Smith). The Italian government has historically devoted an enormous amount its state apparatus to encouraging such migration and protecting its Diaspora citizens (such as establishing a chambers of commerce, the first being in Paris in 1911 and second being in Brussels in 1912) (Smith). Indeed, the Italian entry into the EEC created an even bigger incentive for the government to protect its workers because it changed the destination of many Italian emigrants from (usually) the new world to four key countries in Europe (Switzerland, Germany, France and Belgium), resulting in over two million Italians working in the four states, often in 'harsh' conditions in the steel, chemicals or construction industry (80 per cent of whom were men sending money back to their families in Italy) (Gabaccia).

The preferred destination was within Europe simply because the distances involved were not sufficiently long to impede the migrants' potential return, whilst at the same time sending money back to impoverished communities, in turn boosting the Italian economy (Choate). For the Italians, then, 'transnationalism [had become] a way of working class life' and countries such as France, Belgium and Germany were the net beneficiaries in terms of workers willing to undertake gruelling infrastructure projects (such as roads and tunnels) and working in mines because: 'In an astonishing number of cases the answer was the same. People born and living in economic insecurity in some far-away village would do almost all these tasks' (Gabaccia). Until the closure of coal mines in Belgium towards the end of the 1970s, Italian migrants were the first significant migrant community in the country and remain the largest community by some margin (Phalet and Swyngedouw). For example, in 1991, 240,000

Italian workers from Italy, and the Italian government, protecting its own citizens, had an incentive to push for the Court to accept a newly fashioned principle of equal treatment.[122] Thus, the impression is then

Italians were residing in Belgium. The next largest immigrant community was Moroccan (142,000) and, by comparison, France (93,000) and Germany (28,000), with common borders, had considerably fewer immigrants living in Belgium (ibid.) Indeed, the Belgian authorities very specifically recruited over 121,000 Italians to work in mines between 1945 and 1957 (Martens). In Germany, Italian migrants were also the most significant contributors to the migrant population from within the EU, after emigrants from Turkey and Yugoslavia (Worbs).

Mark Choate, '"Sending States" Transnational Interventions in Politics, Culture, and Economics: The Historical Example of Italy' (2007) 41(3) *International Migration Review*, 728–768 at 728, 735; Robert Smith, 'Diasporic Memberships in Historical Perspective: Comparative Insights on the Mexican, Italian und Polish Cases' (2003) 37(3) *International Migration Review*, 724–759 at 738, 739–742; Donna Gabaccia, *Italy's Many Diasporas* (London: University College London Press, 2000), pp. 154–156, p. 81; Karen Phalet and Marc Swyngedouw, 'Measuring Immigrant Integration: The Case of Belgium' (2003) XL(152) *Studi Emigrazione*, 773–803 at 775–778; Albert Martens, *25 jaar Wegwerparbeiders. Het Belgisch Immigratiebeleid na 1945* (Leuven: KULeuven, 1973), p. 101; Susanne Worbs, 'The Second Generation in Germany: Between School and Labor Market' (2003) 37(4) *International Migration Review*, 1011–1038 at 1014.

See also Pasquale Verdicchio, 'Bound by Distance: Rethinking Nationalisms through the Italian Diaspora' (Madison: Fareligh Dickinson University Press, 1997), pp. 149–154.

122 From the outset, with a few qualified exceptions, the Italians have been passionate enthusiasts of closer integration and an enormous element of that, viewed by both the Italian population at large and political elites, was that there was a net benefit to Italy of the free movement provisions of the Treaty (Gallo and Hanny). In terms of political rulers, it was the Italians who were the most vocal proponents of the free movement provisions at Messina where: 'the country demanded that that certain specifically Italian needs be taken into consideration. Primarily it felt that the principle of free circulation should be applied not only to goods but also to labor and capital. This first objective corresponded to the traditional Italian need to favour emigration for its laborers, while the second one revealed the government's special regard for Italy's South: it hoped that financial resources would flow throughout the peninsula, thereby contributing to the nation's overall development' (Fabbrini and Piattoni). In terms of the Italian population, Cotta maintains: 'Italians have always been among the most favourable to European integration; they are among those who are more convinced that their country has benefited from it and among those who would be more sorry if the European Community were not continued' (citing the Eurobarometer).

Flaminia Gallo and Birgit Hanny, 'Italy: Progress behind Complexity', in Wolfgang Wessels, Andreas Maurer and Jürgen Mittag (eds.), *Fifteen into One? The European Union and Its Member States* (Manchester: Manchester University Press, 2003), pp. 271–297 at p. 271; Sergio Fabbrini and Simona Piattoni, *Italy in the European Union: Redefining National Interest in a Compound Polity* (Lanham: Rowman & Littlefield, 2008), p. 5.

See also Sylvia Kritzinger, Francesco Cavatorta and Raj Chari, 'Continuity and Change in Party Positions Towards Europe in Italian Parties: An Examination of Parties' Manifestos' (2004) 11(6) *Journal of European Public Policy*, 954–974 at 957–958; Riccardo Faini and André Sapir, 'An Obsolete Model? Growth and Specialisation in the

given that a particular set of agents (an epistemic Community in effect) felt the normative desire to use the language and terminology of equal treatment over and above non-discrimination. In other words, what took place was a subjective attempt by certain interested individuals to make equal treatment a predominant principle over and above that of non-discrimination.

3.7 The Increasingly Prolific Utterances of Equal Treatment in the 1980s

In the 1980s, by comparison with the infrequent usage of the phrase 'equal treatment', a sea change was evident in which, within the single texts of Court judgments, often multiple references are made to the principle and by a number of parties. In *Reina* (1982), the structure of the cases has evidently changed, clearly prioritizing the principle.[123] The headnote contains multiple references to equal treatment in italics, saying '*Free movement of persons – Workers – Equality of treatment*' repeatedly in paragraphs 2, 3 and 4.[124] Here no mention is even made of non-discrimination. In *Forcheri*, non-discrimination is mentioned, but now the italicized headnote prioritizes 'equality of treatment' over 'discrimination on the grounds of nationality'.[125] Equally, the principle is no longer at the stage of subjective creation; it appears to be now universally accepted as 'fundamental'.[126] The Court itself asserted, in *Marshall*: 'However, in view of the fundamental importance of the principle of equal treatment, which the court has reaffirmed on numerous occasions' and this statement is reiterated in the headnote, along with two references to the principle of equal treatment.[127] Likewise, in *Biehl*, AG Darmon states: 'In my view, therefore, the provision at issue disregards both the fundamental principle of the free movement of persons and

Italian Economy', in Marco Buti (ed.), *Italy in EMU – The Challenges of Adjustment and Growth* (Basingstoke: Palgrave Macmillan, 2009), pp. 1–36 at pp. 1–2;
Kenneth Dahlberg, 'The EEC Commission and the Politics of Free Movement of Labour' (1967) 6(4) *Journal of Common Market Studies*, 310–333 at 331.

[123] Case 65/81, *Francesco Reina and Letizia Reina* v. *Landeskreditbank Baden-Württemberg* [1982] ECR 33, p. 35 (facts). The case involved another Italian migrant in Germany who, on this occasion, was denied access to a childbirth loan that a home national would have been entitled to.

[124] Ibid., pp. 33–34.

[125] *Forcheri*, p. 2323. See Section 2.5.2 for a summary of the facts.

[126] Ibid.

[127] Case 152/84, *M. H. Marshall* v. *Southampton and South-West Hampshire Area Health Authority (Teaching)* [1986] ECR 723, p. 746 at para. 36, pp. 723–724.

the principle of equal treatment which it entails', following no less than five different references to it in the headnote.[128] In qualitative terms the point that is being made here is that whereas references were made to the principle of equal treatment by various actors in the 1970s, the principle is evidently more visible within the text in the 1980s in that it is clearly structurally prioritized and repeated within the judgments in a way that did not take place in the prior period. Exemplary of this is *Marshall*, as has been cited above, because not only is the Court stating that equal treatment is fundamentally important but also the structure of the case is such that the statement by the Court is repeated in the headnote in bold, with two additional references to the principle also being made. It is claimed that this form of structural prioritization within the text was novel and indicative of a changing context within which the Court operated in the 1980s in which by that point the discourse of equal treatment had become deeply embedded within the epistemic Community of the Court. This point is equally illustrated by the Court's reference to the fact that, by 1986, the principle had been 'reaffirmed on numerous occasions'. Thus, in qualitative terms what is noticeable is how accepted what was an initially subjective assertion or set of assertions – particularly during the 1970s – has become the dominant paradigm in which to describe the free movement provisions of the Treaty.

Moreover, such dominance is equally evident in purely quantitative terms within the texts of particular judgments. In *Commission* v. *UK* (1983), the case contains multiple utterances of the principle. The headnote refers to it as the title to the case and in italics and the Commission refers to it six times, and the Court once.[129] However, what is remarkable about the case is that the UK government is said to have used the phrase five times in one page.[130] This arguably marks an important change in its usage because this illustrates the fact that the phrase was now in

[128] Case C-175/88, *Klaus Biehl* v. *Administration des contributions du grand-duché de Luxembourg* [1990] ECR I 1779, pp. 1784–1787, p. 1791 (facts). In the case, a German worker in Luxembourg was refused a tax refund for an overpayment he made because he had ceased to reside in the host state. See also Jan Wouters, 'The Case-Law of the European Court of Justice on Direct Taxes: Variations upon a Theme' (1994) 1(2) *Maastricht Journal of European and Comparative Law*, 179–220; Timothy Lyons, 'Discrimination against Individuals and Enterprises on Grounds of Nationality: Direct Taxation and the European Court of Justice' (1995) 1(3) *EC Tax Journal*, 27–51.

[129] Case 165/82, *Commission of the European Communities* v. *United Kingdom of Great Britain and Northern Ireland* [1983] ECR 3431, p. 3431, p. 3449.

[130] Ibid., p. 3453.

common usage and uttered by actors who had not made prolific reference to the principle in the 1970s. It is, in SC terms, a classic example of becoming entrapped by the rhetoric of equal treatment.[131]. Indeed, in *Castelli*, the UK once again referred to it four times in a very short paragraph.[132] By the time of *Lebon* (1987), the dominance of equal treatment was almost complete. AG VerLoren van Themaat in his opinion makes multiple references to 'a claim to equality of treatment' (three times) and the 'right' to equal treatment.[133] Nonetheless, what is most remarkable about the case is what the Court said in the judgment. The 'right to equal treatment guaranteed by Community law' is stated in paragraphs 10, 11, 13, 14, 20, 25, 26 and 27 of the judgment.[134] 'Equality-speak' is now rife at the Court and, as has been outlined before, what is particularly noticeable is that this new dominant paradigm has reflected back on the original Treaty. As the Court maintained in paragraph 10 of the judgment in *Lebon*, 'It must be pointed out that the principle of equal treatment is derived in the first place from Article 7 of the EEC Treaty'.[135] By 1987, non-discrimination simply *was* equal treatment. In *Lebon*, it is maintained that at least here the Court was prepared to say 'derived from', being perfectly aware of the fact that Article 7 does not mention equal treatment; whereas in *Commission* v. *Greece*, the Commission simply states 'equal treatment as set out in Article 7 of the Treaty'.[136] Finally, what is perhaps heavily indicative of the principle of equal treatment becoming structurally embedded is its use, once again, by the UK government in *Commission* v. *UK*, in 1983. In the case, the UK refers to it five times in several short paragraphs and, on one occasion, it was stated two sentences in a row.[137] This, in a sense, is 'proof' of what was initially subjective becoming intersubjective because the UK is hardly likely to overtly be advocating the use of a word that could be seen to mark a key stage in the development of European integration.[138] This is a marked

[131] See 'Introduction'.

[132] *Castelli*, p. 3210.

[133] Case 316/85, *Centre public d'aide sociale de Courcelles* v. *Marie-Christine Lebon* [1987] ECR 2811, pp. 2822–2831. See Section 1.5.7 for outline of the facts of the case.

[134] Ibid., pp. 2836–2839.

[135] Ibid., p. 2836 at para. 10.

[136] Case 305/87, *Commission of the European Communities v Hellenic Republic* [1989] ECR 1461, p. 1465, p. 1462 (facts). The case concerned a rule effectively making it impossible for a non-national to own property in Greece.

[137] *Commission* v. *UK*, pp. 3437–3438, p. 3438.

[138] Arguably the most famous description of the UK's relationship with the EU has been that of an 'awkward partner'. Whilst care needs to be taken in making such a simplistic assumption for the interaction of a number of governments with the

contrast with previous cases in the 1970s where there is no reference by the UK to the principle of equal treatment in the case law of the Court. Finally, indicative of the evolution of the principle of equal treatment from subjective utterance to intersubjective discourse is a statement made by AG Mancini in *Commission* v. *France* in 1986 when he asserts:

I would say, however, that in the case-law of the Court that principle [of equal treatment] has been developed, perfected and has been applied with increasing rigour. Thus, in *Sotgiu*, the Court held that [this was the case] in

Union's institutions over a prolonged period of time, for George the reputation for awkwardness was something that commenced when it became a Member State and continues to this present day. George also claims that one of the problems that the UK faced was 'handling the terminology of political debate that had developed among the original members' and that it took the UK some time to engage with a *Communautaire* approach and Miers maintains that it has always been in a position of having to internalize the 'ground rules' created by others. Likewise, May claims: 'a consistent pattern has emerged since 1945 . . . of British governments initially standing aloof from the latest thrust of integration, then finding themselves on the sidelines, then being forced to join in when the mould had been set [sic]'. This is also reflected in the use of language by the UK in the Court and that this is evidenced by the use of the phrase 'equal treatment' much later on than Italy or Germany. For instance, Aspinwall maintains that 'much agreement exists among academics and policymakers that Britain takes a persistently negative approach to European integration' and that this manifests itself particularly in what he terms 'rhetorical negativism' which is also reflected in its use of language at the Court. For Aspinwall, therefore, the attitude of the UK can be characterized as 'utilitarian' and 'pragmatic' by contrast with the ideological approach taken by a number of other Member States.

Stephen George, *An Awkward Partner: Britain in Europe* (Oxford: Oxford University Press, 1998), pp. 275–278; David Miers, 'Britain in Europe – Community to Union: 1973-2001', in Phillip Giddings and Gavin Drewry (eds.), *Britain in the European Union: Law, Policy and Parliaments* (Basingstoke: Palgrave, 2004), pp. 12–36 at p. 14; Alex May, *Britain and Europe Since 1945* (London: Routledge, 2009), p. 93; Mark Aspinwall, *Rethinking Britain and Europe – Plurality Elections, Party Management and British Policy on European Integration* (Manchester: Manchester University Press, 2004), p. 5, p. 19.

See also Andrew Gamble, 'The European Issue in British Politics', in David Baker and David Seawright (eds.), *Britain for and against Europe* (Oxford: Clarendon, 1988), pp. 11–30 at p. 13; Simon Bulmer, 'Britain and European Integration: of Sovereignty, Slow Adaptation, and Semi-Detachment', in Stephen George (ed.), *Britain in the European Community* (Oxford: Clarendon, 1992), pp. 1–30 at p. 2; David Gowland, Arthur Turner and Alex Wright, *Britain and European Integration Since 1945 – on the Sidelines* (Abingdon: Routledge, 2010), p. 77 ('uncooperative' relationship); Michael Franklin and Michael Wilke, *Britain's Future in Europe* (London: Pinter, 1990), p. 7; Duncan Watts and Colin Pilkington, *Britain in the European Union Today* (Manchester: Manchester University Press, 2005), pp. 286–287; Hugo Young, *The Blessed Plot* (London: Macmillan, 1998), p. 472; David Baker and David Seawright, 'Introduction', in David Baker and David Seawright (eds.), *Britain for and against Europe* (Oxford: Clarendon, 1998), pp. 1–11 at p. 1.

view of the 'fundamental nature' of the principles of freedom of movement and equality of treatment.[139]

Thus, what is evident is the rise of a new paradigm in which almost all parties now express themselves and by the time of the coming into force of the SEA and subsequent TEU; equal treatment was now a predominant discourse used by the court.

3.8 The Fissures within Equal Treatment

However, one fundamental issue that perhaps needs to be outlined is whether the pervasive articulation of equal treatment understood on nationality grounds alone is itself inherently problematic. If anything, reverting back to describing the phenomenon as simply reflective of the principle of non-discrimination illustrates that the principle of non-discrimination on nationality grounds is purely one of nationality, by definition and is more easily understood as being one of many grounds of discrimination. By contrast, the principle of equal treatment, from a discursive perspective, masks more than it reveals, and thus lacks transparency. Whilst it is the case, as has been outlined earlier in this chapter, that equal treatment was also understood, outside of the context, for the most part, of free movement of persons law, on gender and due process grounds, the prevailing understanding within the body of one of the most powerful areas of EU law was that of nationality. The implications of this suggestion are perhaps much greater than might be initially thought of without a genealogical exploration of the inherent contingency of such a discursive evolution. After all, this was ultimately a pillar upon which citizenship was built and one that has a loaded and exclusionary legacy. For instance, by definition, the principle is predisposed to being applied only in the context of movement. The immobile are thus excluded from the embrace of such a principle with a number of implications. In the context of Brexit, and in particular given the fact that this issue is not unique to the UK, equal treatment does not look or feel so 'equal' from the perspective of those that do not move. Bauböck claims there to be a 'new cleavage' between the mobile and immobile with the immobile not 'perceiving' a citizenship model predisposed to movement as either of 'value' or that can be

[139] Case 307/84, *Commission of the European Communities* v. *French Republic* [1986] ECR 1725, p. 1729.

identified with.[140] In quantitative terms there are in effect two Europes, as Favell outlines, one of mobility (which he terms 'Eurostars') and one without it where 'the stayers vastly outnumber the movers'.[141] Consequently, no other forms of discrimination, with the exception of gender, at least historically, are properly within the remit of the body of case law which formed the bedrock of citizenship. Even in the context of gender, it is not always the case that the emancipatory evolution of the case law on the Equal Treatment Directive is credited to EU law specifically. For instance, some Brexiters in the UK suggested that as the Equal Pay Act 1970 preceded the UK joining the then EEC, the UK itself is where the origins of gender equality law lay.[142] Indeed, even in the context of nationality not all discrimination on the grounds of nationality is incorporated under the principle of equal treatment. For instance, sub-state nationality (such as within the UK) does not 'count' for the purposes of the principle, neither does TCN nationality or, more broadly, racial and ethnic discrimination more generally. It is in effect a hegemonic discourse with cognitive dissonance at its heart. It thus does not come as much of a surprise that the EU is yet to fully embrace a holistic Equal Treatment Directive conferring wide-ranging and directly effective rights for EU Citizens for discrimination on many grounds, despite several attempts by the EU's legislature to pass it.[143] Finally, the immobile remain almost entirely unprotected by the principle by virtue of the successively tough stance that the Court

[140] Rainer Bauböck, 'The New Cleavage between Mobile and Immobile Europeans', in Rainer Bauböck (ed.), *Debating European Citizenship* (Cham: Springer, 2019), pp. 125–127 at p. 127.

[141] Adrian Favell, *Eurostars and Eurocities: Free Movement and Mobility in an Integrating Europe* (Oxford: Blackwell, 2008), p. ix.

[142] This is arguably a post-hoc populist fantasy and is far from immune to criticism. This is what Azmanova and Dakwar term 'The inverted postnational constellation' where populist movements appropriate postnationalist rhetoric while negating its 'normative spirit' through 'exclusionary protectionist claims: "our" democracy, "our" capitalism, "our" welfare state. Thus, the inclusionary ideals of cosmopolitan liberalism and democracy that were meant to nourish the advent of humanistic postnationalism have been transformed into goods to be distributed, elements of a privileged life-style to be protected from "intruders"'. Albena Azmanova, and Azar Dakwar, 'The Inverted Postnational Constellation: Identitarian Populism in Context' (2019) 25 *European Law Journal*, 493–501.

[143] See, for instance, ILGA Europe, 'Equality for All – Joint NGO Statement' (2015), www.ilga-europe.org/sites/default/files/Attachments/2015-0617_joint_ngo_statement_on_horizontal_directive_before_junes_epsco_council.pdf, accessed 16 September 2020.

has taken on the issue of reverse discrimination and wholly internal situations, despite AG Sharpston's impassioned plea in *Walloon* to the contrary.[144] Seen from this perspective, as O'Brien put it, a discursive structure predicated on movement is inherently problematic:

> Equal treatment on the grounds of nationality is an illusion. Clients faced severe welfare rights cliff-edges … The class contingent nature of market citizenship meant that many of the exclusions targeting the economically inactive actually affected EU national workers because of their fluid work statuses, or because of the detrimental effects of living under the threat of exclusion, or because of the heightened administrative burdens imposed on all EU nationals. Equal treatment 'just' for the economically inactive proved to be equal treatment for no one.[145]

Thus, the hegemonic and inherently contingent discourse of equal treatment as it emerged from the case law is thus in reality, perhaps, not so equal.

3.9 Conclusion

It is undeniably trite to claim that equal treatment is an important principle in free movement of persons law prior to 1992 and, indeed, later EU Citizenship law. This chapter, though, attempts to undertake something entirely different with this principle by making the suggestion that it operates as a principle that is as much discursive as it is legal by undertaking a holistic and chronological assessment of utterances of equal treatment (along with non-discrimination) from within the case law and it does so in a way that reflects the inherent contingency that is at its heart. The opening part of this chapter examined a period prior to 1968 where utterances of equal treatment did not exist in the case law.

[144] Case C-212/06, *Government of Communauté française and Gouvernement walloon v. Gouvernement flamand* [2008] ECR I 1683, pp. 1687–1729.

[145] O'Brien, *Unity in Adversity*, p. 178. See also Iglésias Sanchez, who states: 'the balance of interests in free movement cases has traditionally been tailored to respond to the needs of movers, notwithstanding the potential negative effects on static citizens' and Oberman who questions whether perhaps no focus has been put on whether freedom of movement should include 'the freedom to stay'. Sara Iglésias, Sanchez, 'A Citizenship Right to Stay? The Right Not to Move in a Union Based on Free Movement', in Dimitry Kochenov (ed.), *EU Citizenship and Federalism: The Role of Rights* (Cambridge: Cambridge University Press, 2017), pp. 371–393 at p. 372. Kieran Oberman, 'What to Say to Those Who Stay? Free Movement is a Human Right of Universal Value', in Rainer Bauböck (ed.), *Debating European Citizenship* (Cham: Springer, 2019), pp. 145–148 at p. 147.

The contingency of the principle was, though, exposed, in a number of different ways, with particular focus on the case law in the 1970s. For example, it has been suggested that a number of actors claimed that equal treatment existed at the outset of the creation of the Community as it was enshrined in Article 48; whereas in actual fact no such reference was made. It was therefore suggested that by simply 'reflecting back' in this manner a number of protagonists constructed a narrative of the principle's historic authenticity. Equally, it has been maintained that a number of actors within the text of the judgments had played a significant role in uttering equal treatment but that such actors were not necessarily value-neutral in making such utterances. The final part of this chapter examines a period in the 1980s in which it is evident from the text of the case law that equal treatment had become a dominant norm within the jurisprudence and demonstrates such a dominance in both a quantitative sense through examining sheer repetition of 'equal treatment' and a qualitative sense in examining the context of such utterances. Furthermore, this chapter constitutes one of two pillars between the core legal principles that have been outlined from an SC perspective in the first two chapters and the specific legal concept of EU Citizenship as it evolved post-Maastricht. In this context, this chapter concluded by suggesting that the hegemonic utterance of equal treatment on the grounds of non-discrimination (and one predisposed to movement across a border) created a problematic fissure that, to an extent, can be seen in later legal and legislative developments and where, perhaps, equal treatment might not appear to the immobile in particular to be so 'equal'.

Appendix I

A Table of References to Equal Treatment

Year	Case	Number of references within the case	Number of references per year in total
1969	*Ugliola*	6	6
1972	*Merluzzi*	1	
	Marsman	6	
	Frilli	2	9
1973	*Michel S.*	8	8
1974	*Sotgiu*	4	
	Van Duyn	1	

(cont.)

Year	Case	Number of references within the case	Number of references per year in total
	Reyners	3	
	Van Binsbergen	1	9
1975	*Bonaffini*	2	
	Alaimo	4	
	Farrauto	1	
	F	6	13
1976	*Inzirillo*	1	1
1977	*Fossi*	1	1
1978	*Gillard*	2	
	Kenny	1	3
1979	*Rossi*	3	
	Even	8	
	Toia	1	12
1982	*Reina*	5	5
1983	*Forcheri*	1	
	Commission v. *UK*	12	13
1984	*Prodest*	1	
	Castelli	5	6
1986	*Marshall*	4	
	Commission v. *France*	1	5
1987	*Lebon*	12	12
1989	*Commission* v. *Greece*	1	1
1990	*Biehl*	1	1

4 The Citizen Is Born – Literal Utterances to the Citizen Prior to 1992

4.1 Introduction

Citizenship is clearly considered to be integral to free movement of persons law within the European Union, but yet it technically did not legally exist until 1992. This chapter asserts that mere utterances of the phrase prior to the Citizen's legal creation are not only worthy of analysis in their own right but that such utterances provided one of at least two vital discursive pillars upon which to situate the 'roof' of citizenship when it eventually emerged. This book began by examining in effect two key moments in the development of Community (now Union) law. First, as has been repeatedly mentioned, there was clearly significance in the formal inclusion of Union Citizenship into the Treaty on European Union (TEU) at Maastricht, even if it was initially dismissed as a merely symbolic plaything.[1] There has been a two-fold premise to this book; namely both to examine the emergence of the Union citizen and to do so on the basis of a methodological approach that can add value to conventional legal approaches through examining the jurisprudence of the Court qualitatively differently.[2] In other words, the Citizenship provisions of the Treaty did not emerge out of a legal, political and social vacuum and, as has already been outlined, a build-up to such a radical development can be pinpointed through a closer examination of thirty years of jurisprudence by the Court. In this context, the second key moment for the emergence of the Citizen is when AG Jacobs famously stated in *Konstantinidis* that an individual is 'entitled

[1] Hans Ulrich Jessurun D'Oliveira, 'European Citizenship: Its Meaning, Its Potential' in Renaud Delhousse (ed.), *Europe after Maastricht: An Ever Closer Union?* (Munich: Law Books in Europe, 1994) pp. 126–149 at p. 147. See Section 5.2.1.

[2] See 'Introduction'.

to say "*civis europeus sum*"'.[3] Crucially, it is the context in which this statement was made that matters in that it was one of the final cases prior to the formal incorporation of Citizenship into the Treaty at Maastricht.[4] In this respect, it is what Jacobs states prior to '*civis europeus sum*' that equally matters, namely an 'entitlement' to 'say'. By referring to 'say', this makes it clear that this is a statement but by referring to an 'entitlement', there is also a discursive undertone in that statement in that it reflects an increasingly widely held belief amongst Community nationals of an 'entitlement' to exercise a broad right of free movement[5] and such a sense of entitlement is a fundamental aspect of citizenship as conventionally understood.[6] In other words, the fact that there is now a sense of 'entitlement' to make such a statement is crucial in that it is reflective of a watershed moment in European integration.

The underlying essence of this book, though, has been to 'trace' the emergence of two such key moments.[7] In the previous chapters, it has been claimed that the Citizen can be traced, often implicitly, through the emergence of the doctrines of equal treatment, a specific discourse of the worker and the interrelationships between it and categories of individuals that could not be classified as 'workers'. Each doctrine had an impact on the emergence of the later citizen for different reasons. In the case of equal treatment, as has already been outlined, there is a clear interrelationship between it and citizenship more generally. In other words, a 'citizen' expects to be treated equally with other citizens and have their rights respected. Chapters 4 and 5, though, are reflective of the emergence of an EU-specific concept of Citizenship, one in which it was collectively understood that the Citizen had to paradoxically incorporate

[3] Case C-168/91, *Konstantinidis* v. *Stadt Altensteig* [1993] ECR I 1191, p. 1212. For further analysis of the case see Rick Lawson, 'Case C- 168/91, *Christos Konstantinidis* v. *Stadt Altensteig-Standesamt*' (1994) 31(2) *Common Market Law Review* 395–412 (note); Michael O'Neill, 'The Expansion of the ECJ's Fundamental Rights Jurisdiction: A Recipe for Tensions with Strasbourg?' (1995) 129 *Irish Law Times and Solicitors' Journal*, 168–170; Ulrich Haltern, 'The Dawn of the Political: Rethinking the Meaning of Law in European Integration' (2004) 14(4) *Schweizerische Zeitschrift für internationales und europäisches Recht*, 585–614. See also Section 4.4 and Section 5.2.4.

[4] AG Jacob's opinion was handed down on 9 December 1992 (the judgment of the case then being handed down on 30 March 1993). The TEU came into force on 1 November 1993 and was in the process of being ratified when the case was being heard.

[5] See Sections 2.5 and 2.6.

[6] See Section 5.2.1.

[7] See 'Introduction' on tracing.

a Community-specific understanding of the worker and a whole series of categories of non-working individuals searching for a collective label to better describe themselves.

The final piece of a complex jigsaw, though, is an assessment of the impact of direct references to the Citizen as well as the broader citizenship-type debates that preceded the emergence of EU Citizenship and clearly had an impact on the specific emergence of EU Citizenship in the '*Sala* revolution'.[8] This chapter will therefore be devoted to such direct references because a core aspect of SC theory is that mere utterance of a term can potentially have a profound discursive impact.[9] In the opening part of this chapter, a number of competing phrases will be examined prior to outlining utterances of the 'citizen' itself as the citizen can be seen to have progressed from such phrases. It will firstly be suggested that the original linguistic orthodoxy within the text of the early case law on free movement was the phrase 'national of a Member State'. It will then be maintained that evolution took place in these early days from such a limiting phrase to the 'Community national' (and, indeed, worker and student) and that the linguistic 'end-point' of such a progression was the Community citizen. After having outlined such 'competing' phrases, attention will then be devoted to examining utterances of the 'citizen' over thirty years of developing jurisprudence on free movement. It will be claimed that progression towards citizenship can be seen by simply examining such utterances in a quantitative and qualitative (or contextual) sense. An opening phase in the 1970s of infrequent references to the citizen will be outlined in which, at times, citizenship was conceived of as a mere synonym for Member State nationality. A vital intermediate phase in the 1980s will then be examined and it will be claimed that this period was important in terms of the development of citizenship because it was during this that the

[8] Jacqueson, 'Union Citizenship and the Court of Justice' 265. For a more specific analysis of the substance of the *Sala* case see Chapter 5. See also Albertina Albors-Llorens, 'A Broader Construction of the EC Treaty Provisions on Citizenship?' (1998) 57 *Cambridge Law Journal*, 461–463; Sybilla Fries and Jo Shaw, 'Citizenship of the Union: First Steps in the European Court of Justice' (1998) 4(4) *European Public Law*, 533–559; Siofra O'Leary, 'Putting Flesh on the Bones of European Union Citizenship' (1999) 24(1) *European Law Review*, 68–79; Whelan, 'Union Citizenship and The Free Movement of Persons' 179–185; Christian Tomuschat, 'Case C-85/96, *María Martínez Sala* v. *Freistaat Bayern*, Judgment of 12 May 1998, Full Court. [1998] ECR I-2691' (2000) 37 *Common Market Law Review* 449–457; Christiaan Timmermans, '*Martínez Sala* and *Baumbast* revisited' in Miguel Poiares Maduro and Loïc Azoulai (eds.), *The Past and Future of EU Law: The Classics of EU Law Revisited on the 50th Anniversary of the Rome Treaty* (Oxford: Hart, 2010), pp. 345–355.

[9] See 'Introduction'.

context changed from subjective utterance to intersubjective reality. It will be contended that during this period utterances of the citizen increased considerably such that citizenship became part of the Court's everyday language in a way that it was not in the 1970s. In addition, utterances of the 'citizen' were made in a number of significant cases that have been examined in previous chapters (such as *Levin*) and often in controversial circumstances (such as in cases where attempts were being made to circumvent reverse discrimination). The chapter will then examine three key cases – *Commission* v. *France*, *Micheletti* and *Konstantinidis* – in which the Court's AGs played a highly significant role in subjectively articulating a new role for citizenship, one which differed considerably from simply being seen to be a synonym for other established phrases. This chapter will then conclude by maintaining that AG Jacobs' '*civis europeus sum*' statement in particular did not appear out of the subjective ether but emerged out of an inherently problematic context as outlined in the 1970s and 1980s in which its radicalism was at least acceptable in a way that it would not have been thirty years previously but in which, as has already been stated, there was a fissure at its core.

4.2 Utterances and the Citizen: The Impact of Statements of the Citizen and Words Relating to or Opposing It

As this chapter is devoted to specific references to the citizen, the exact wording of such utterances is important because a particular phrase can have a loaded meaning in the context in which it is uttered (i.e. what is being said, how can such a phrase be understood, who is saying it and why?). In the course of several decades of jurisprudence of the Court prior to 1992, a set of utterances on citizenship is evident from what were initially tentative and infrequent references to a more frequent usage. Seen in this manner, there are similarities between the development of the discourse of equal treatment from that of non-discrimination as described in Chapter 3 and utterances of the citizen. With equal treatment it has been submitted that the early governing paradigm was non-discrimination and that a subtle development had to take place in order to ensure that equal treatment became the more dominant discourse. What has also been maintained is that there are linguistic politics behind the use of the two phrases: 'non-discrimination on grounds of nationality' cannot as easily be conflated with other forms of discrimination by contrast with the principle of equal treatment.[10] The latter, therefore, can be used in a normative sense to precipitate closer integration, whereas the former cannot be as easily. Similarly, in relation to citizenship, there are sets of phrases to describe it (or indeed that contrast with it), each of which has nuanced and politicized meaning and in which certain phrases can be seen as a development leading to further integration whereas certain phrases are more status-quo orientated. This part of the chapter will focus on the use of such phrases.

Finally, what should also be taken into account is the concept of becoming 'entrapped by one's own rhetoric'.[11] As has also been maintained in Chapter 3, certain agents would have an incentive to use a less integration-focused phrase such as non-discrimination (such as certain Member States) whereas other agents would have an incentive to do the opposite (such as the Commission, the Court and certain AGs).[12] However, various agents may not be aware of the nuances of particular phrases and may simply use them as a convenient, though loaded, shorthand to describe in effect one and the same concept or phenomenon.[13] Seen in this manner, equal treatment and non-discrimination have been used interchangeably to describe the same concept, with the agent making the statement not necessarily being aware of such nuances. As will be outlined in this chapter, 'Community citizenship' (or its variants) prior to their formal legal enactment in 1992 can be used as a convenient (and clearly highly symbolic) shorthand in which to label pre-existing rights (such as of the worker). However, as will also be argued, mere utterances (particularly in a repeated manner) in and of themselves play an important role in the process of further integration through 'Communitising' key words or concepts, especially those which traditionally were considered to be the sole preserve of nations (or in other words the Member States) and such a linguistic harnessing cannot be better illustrated than in relation to the Citizen.[14]

[10] See Section 3.4.
[11] See 'Introduction' on this concept.
[12] See Section 3.6.1.
[13] Ibid.
[14] See n. 36.

4.2.1 *The Use of the Phrase 'Nationals of a Member State'*

In part, an 'other' to the EU Citizen is the above phrase. On one (legal) level, it could be suggested that not much could be read into the use of the phrase 'national of a Member State'. Article 8(1) of the Treaty as amended in 1992 makes it clear that in order to qualify as an EU Citizen an individual has to be a national of a Member State. On one reading of the phrase, then, one could be equated as being synonymous with the other and could not be seen to be almost antithetical to it (a 'thin' conception of citizenship).[15] However, even a cursory attempt to read slightly further into this phrase reveals the two concepts to be far from synonymous. At the very least having the nationality of one of the Member States is a mere portal for an additional supranational layer of identification, even if this layer is (or was) a legal and discursive void to be filled in incrementally over time.[16] Moreover, as *Kaur* demonstrated, there is power inherent in who gets to define nationality of the Member States (in order to then qualify as an EU Citizen) as this remains, for the most part, the sole preserve of individual Member States.[17] In other words, the phrase 'national of the Member States' is a loaded one and the Member States in particular have an incentive to

[15] See Willem Maas, *Creating European Citizens* (Lanham: Rowman and Littlefield, 2007), p. 3.

[16] See Section 5.4.

[17] Case C-192/99, *The Queen* v. *Secretary of State for the Home Department, ex parte: Manjit Kaur, intervener* [2001] ECR I 1237, p. 1251. A power in many ways that was reinforced by Article F (1) of the TEU in which it was stated that 'the Union shall respect the national identities of its Member States'. See also Case C-135/08, *Janko Rottman* v. *Freistaat Bayern* [2008] ECR I 1449. For further commentary see Prakash Shah, 'British Nationals under Community Law: The *Kaur* Case' (2001) 3(2) *European Journal of Migration and Law*, 271–278; Stephen Hall, 'Determining the Scope *ratione personae* of European Citizenship: Customary International Law Prevails for Now' (2001) 28(3) *Legal Issues of Economic Integration*, 355–360; Helen Toner, 'Case C-192/99, *R* v. *Secretary of State for the Home Department, ex parte Kaur*' (2002) 39 *Common Market Law Review* 881–893 (note); Anja Seling, 'Case C-135/08 *Janko Rottmann* v. *Freistaat Bayern*, Judgment of the Court of Justice (Grand Chamber) of 2 March 2010, nyr – Towards a direct "droit de regard"?' (2010) 17(4) *Maastricht Journal of European and Comparative Law*, 470–478; Hans Ulrich Jessurun D'Oliveira, 'Decoupling Nationality and Union Citizenship?' (2011) 7(1) *European Constitutional Law Review*, 138–149; (2011; 138–149), Gerard-René De Groot and Anja Seling, 'The Consequences of the *Rottman* Judgment on Member State Autonomy: The European Court of Justice's Avant-Gardism in Nationality Matters' (2011) 7(1) *European Constitutional Law Review*, 150–160; Kristine Kruma, 'How Do We Get More out of the EU Citizenship? Which Integration Policies for Migrants? Interaction between the EU and its Member States' in Yyves Pascouau and Tineke Strik (eds.), *Which Integration Policies for Migrants? Interaction between the EU and its Member States* (Nijmegen: Wolf Legal Publishers, 2012), pp. 185–207.

continually use it in circumstances where different terminology may be used by other parties (see further on such terminology).

On one level, then, the most cautious terminology to use is 'nationals of a Member State', as it was the original terminology that was used upon which other phrases could develop. This is very much evidenced by the original wording of the Treaty. The early part of the original draft of the Treaty (i.e. Part One on principles) makes no reference to an individual who is the national of a Member State being entitled to derive rights from the Treaty in a similar way to how citizenship was presented in the amended Treaty in 1992. Perhaps such an assumption was implied or 'obvious' in the general context of the Treaty. The first mention of the phrase was in Article 37 of the Treaty on state monopolies. However, the phrase then appears and is repeated in Title III of the Treaty which contains individuals' derived rights. Article 52 on establishment refers to 'nationals of a Member State' twice in the same paragraph. It is also referred to in Article 54(3)(e), Article 58 and Article 59 on services (as well as Article 132 on Association agreements). The closest the original Treaty gets to Article 8(1) of the amended Treaty is actually in Article 157 where it is stated: 'Only nationals of Member States may be members of the Commission' with an additional reference to the phrase following in the same paragraph. In this respect, it could be suggested that being a member of the Commission was an early prototype to the EU Citizen (particularly as its members were supposed to not be governed by national preferences in Article 157(2)) and what was in effect being maintained was that in order to become a member of this rather exclusive supranational community, an individual had to be a national of a Member State.

However, this phrase is far from value-neutral and has its obvious limitations. Article 53 of the Treaty alludes to 'nationals of other Member States'. This particular turn of phrase has a subtle and nuanced meaning to it that should perhaps be examined a little further. Legally and practically, it implicitly outlines the principal use of the Treaty by individuals as it refers to the situation in which a national of Member State A moves to Member State B in order to establish him/herself. There is, though, also a discursive meaning to the phrase in that the practical situation as described in the previous sentence labels the national of Member State A almost continually as an 'other' to/in his host state. It is therefore a cautious phrase lacking genuine inclusiveness, which contrasts markedly with the phrase 'citizenship'.[18]

[18] See 'Introduction' for an outline of the concept of the 'other'.

Moreover, Articles 52 and 60 reveal an additional limitation to the phrase. Article 52 refers to the need to be treated, as regards the conditions of establishment, in the same way as for a Member State's 'own nationals' and Article 60 makes a reference to the same phrase.[19] This gives the impression that nationality is the exclusive preserve of the Member States – they literally 'own' it – and is clearly therefore not a phrase upon which supranational identity can be developed.[20]

Nonetheless, in what is evidently a politically sensitive issue, it was, to a certain extent, initially the phrase 'national of a Member State' that was the original orthodoxy in the early years of the Court's jurisprudence.[21] For instance, it is alluded to by the National Fund in *Michel S.*,[22] the applicant in *Coenen*,[23] and AG Mayras in *Royer* refers to a 'national of a Member State of the Community'.[24] Moreover, what is also mentioned by the applicant in *Coenen* is the phrase 'national of the "other" Member States'.[25] Thus, in the early stages of the Court's jurisprudence the orthodoxy as specifically outlined in the Treaty is alluded to.

However, the substantive use of this particular turn of phrase by all agents within the text of Court judgments was short-lived, even though it was the exact wording used in the Treaty. As will be examined later, other phrases became more common, though its use lived on and was used instrumentally by various parties. In *Pieck*, for instance, the Court refers to 'nationals of Member

[19] As well as Articles 220 and 221.

[20] See Section 5.3.

[21] For a general (and rather unique) discussion of the nature of the translation process at the Court see Federico Mancini and David Keeling, 'Language, Culture and Politics in the Life of the European Court of Justice' (1995) 1(3) *Columbia Journal of European Law*, 397–414.

[22] Case 76/72, *Michel S.* v. *Fonds national de reclassement social des handicapés* [1973] ECR 457, p. 460. The phrase used in the original French was 'les ressortissants des États membres de la Communauté'. See also Chapter 1 (n. 43) for specific analysis of the case.

[23] Case 39/75, *Robert-Gerardus Coenen and others* v. *Sociaal-Economische Raad* [1975] ECR 1547, p. 1551, p. 1554 (facts). Ibid. (in terms of the wording in the original French). The applicant in the case, a Dutch national, was an insurance broker who resided in Belgium and fell foul of a requirement in Dutch law requiring residency in the Netherlands. See also Geoffrey Morse, 'Residence Requirements and the Provision of Services' (1976) 2(4) *European Law Review*, 227–229.

[24] Case 48/75, *Jean Noël Royer* [1976] ECR 497, p. 525. The original wording was 'ressortissants des pays membres de la Communauté européenne'. For further analysis of the case, see Derrick Wyatt, 'Rights of Employment and Residence: Some Further Clarification' (1976) 1(6) *European Law Review*, 406–410.

[25] *Coenen*, p. 1550. 'Ressortissants des « autres » États membres' in the original French.

States'.[26] However, it did so in a context in which it appeared to be reiterating the traditional way of describing a concept that was being expressed differently by others. Similarly, the headnote twice refers to 'Community workers'.[27] However, the title summary of the case stated that, by contrast, the case concerned the 'Right of residence of Community Citizens'.[28] Thus, the turn of phrase used by the Court (or its translators) is very far from the seemingly radical statement of the title summary. Perhaps the most obviously deliberate use of the most conservative phrase that could be used to describe the same person or concept, in effect, was by the UK in *Adoui*. In the case, the UK alludes to 'nationals of Member states within the Community',[29] a phrase which in itself may seem unremarkable taken out of context. However, in the context, it was clear that in 1982 when the case was reported that every other party appears to have used a different and more advanced phrase to describe the same concept in the English translation of the case. The applicants, for instance, refers to 'Community citizens' five times, as well as 'Community national'.[30] In terms of the other Member States, Belgium alludes to 'European nationals',[31] and the French government refers twice to Community citizens.[32] In addition, the Court and Commission make reference to 'Citizens of the community' (the Court) and 'Community nationals' (the Commission), respectively.[33] Indeed, the Court's statement of the

[26] Case 157/79, *Regina* v. *Stanislaus Pieck* [1980] ECR 2171, p. 2184. Whilst the case is an English case, the phrase used in the French version of the judgment is 'les ressortissants des États membres'. See Section 2.2.2 for further analysis of the case.

[27] *Pieck*, pp. 2171–2172. 'Travailleurs communautaires' in the French version.

[28] Ibid., p. 2171. 'Ressortissants des « autres » États membres' in the original French.

[29] Joined Cases 115 and 116/81, *Rezguia Adoui* v. *Belgian State and City of Liège; Dominique Cornuaille* v. *Belgian State* [1982] ECR 1665, p. 1698. 'Ressortissants des États membres' in the original French. Note that this is still differently phrased from the views attributed to the other parties even in French.

[30] *Adoui*, pp. 1680–1682, p. 1686. Community citizen is 'ressortissant communautaire' in the original French, including the reference to a 'Community national' in the English translation.

[31] Ibid., p. 1686. 'Ressortissant européen' in the original French.

[32] Ibid., p. 1689. 'Ressortissants des États membres' in the original French.

[33] Ibid., p. 1712, p. 1702, p. 1681 (below). It is interesting to note the complete lack of use of the word 'citoyen' in the original French (with one notable exception) in the case. As will later be contended, the word in French carries with it a much greater resonance in the context of the French state itself than 'citizen' in the English language. The one notable exception is worth outlining. In the English translation of the case the plaintiffs allude to 'affecting citizens' freedom of movement'. However, the French version also states: 'la liberté d'aller et de venir des citoyens'. The context, though, is different from

Citizen is actually in summary and in bold at the end of the judgment.[34] It is clear, therefore, that by 1982 the preponderance of the phrase 'national of the Member States' was in marked decline (to re-emphasize, in the English versions of Court judgments) in favour of more integrative and advanced phrases and seen in this light the continual use of the 'orthodoxy' attributed to the UK can but lead to the assumption that its use was deliberate. Thus, whilst the original phrase 'national of the Member States' dominated discussions of the free movement provisions of the Treaty, it had been reduced much later on in the development of the Court's jurisprudence to its marginalized and instrumental use by parties attempting to stem a seemingly inevitable linguistic flow towards the citizen.

4.2.2 *The Process of 'Communitizing'*

The phrase 'communitizing' has been used in both a political and legal sense to describe a process whereby a policy such as legislation previously within the remit of JHA (Justice and Home Affairs) in the Third pillar under the Maastricht Treaty incrementally developed into a matter of Community policy in the first pillar, hence being 'communitized'.[35] It can also, though, be used to describe a deepening of the process of European integration more generally through incremental evolution on a policy by policy basis.[36] However, what is meant here is that an evolutionary process also took place during this period that was as much linguistic as it was legal in which concepts were increasingly labelled as Community ones and, as has been outlined earlier, there is nuanced significance in every word that is used to in effect describe the same concept.

the above citations in that there is no reference to the 'Community' and the phrase is sufficiently generally phrased to refer to national citizens and civil liberties (i.e. to not give the impression that Community Citizenship had been created in the French language version of the judgment).

[34] Ibid.

[35] Claudia Major, 'Europeanization and Foreign and Security Policy: Undermining or Rescuing the Nation State?' (2005) 25(3) *Politics*, 175–190 at 176.

[36] Ibid. For Major, the concept can also now be used more broadly (and discursively) to describe: 'a growing convergence of national policies through commonly defined norms, directives and laws'. See also Tanja Boerzel, 'Toward Convergence in Europe? Institutional Adaptation to Europeanisation in Germany and Spain' (1999) 37(4) *Journal of Common Market Studies*, 573–596; Alistair Cole and Helen Drake, 'The Europeanization of the French polity: continuity, change and adaptation' (2000) 7(1) *Journal of European Public Policy*, 26–43; Christoph Knill, *The Europeanisation of National Administrations. Patterns of Institutional Change and Persistence* (Cambridge: Cambridge University Press, 2001).

What will be examined in this section is the emergence of the 'Community national' along with 'Community worker' and the 'Community student'.

Two points, though, should perhaps be made prior to such an examination. First, that what ties all three of these phrases together is a direct link between the Community and individuals: a crucial first step. This may seem unremarkable in the sense that the Treaty makers clearly envisaged individuals as not just being entitled to derive rights directly from the Treaty but also that such individuals would *perceive* themselves as such. However, several Member States did not necessarily envisage that the then EEC would evolve into a *sui generis* supranational entity in which, to a certain extent, an individual could derive legislative protection in a manner that in many ways bypasses the legislative and administrative sovereignty of the Member States.[37] It therefore makes sense that, seen in this manner, the phrase 'national of a Member state of the Community' is a phrase that could very deliberately have been used by certain Member States. In that phrase, the relationship between the individual and the Community is indirect in that an individual is the national of a Member State and that Member State is a member of the Community, not the individual. This is one reading of that phrase. By contrast, the above-mentioned three phrases, whilst perhaps being used by some as a rather convenient shorthand for 'national of a Member State of the Community', has a meaning that is much more integrative in its nature in that the link to the individual is direct.

[37] For instance, in the seminal case *Van Gend*, even the Dutch and Belgian governments did not see the Treaty of Rome as containing rights that could be distinguished from any other treaty in international law. Case 26/62, *van Gend en Loos (NV Algemene Transporten Expeitidie Onderneming)* v. *Nedelandse Administratie der Belastingen* [1963] ECR 1, pp. 6–8. See also Bruno De Witte, 'The Continuous Significance of *Van Gend en Loos*, The Past and Future of EU Law' in Miguel Poiares Maduro and Loïc, Azoulai (eds.), *The Classics of EU Law Revisited on the 50th Anniversary of the Rome Treaty* (Oxford: Hart Publishing, 2010), pp. 9–15; Morten Rasmussen, 'The Origins of Legal Revolution: The Early History of the European Court of Justice' (2008) 14(2) *Zeitschrift für Geschichte der Europäischen Integration*, 77–98; Pierre Pescatore, 'Van Gend en Loos, 3 February 1963: A View from within, The Past and Future of EU Law' in Miguel Poiares Maduro and Loïc, Azoulai (eds.), *The Classics of EU Law Revisited on the 50th Anniversary of the Rome Treaty* (Oxford: Hart, 2010), pp. 3–8; Norman Marsh, 'Some Reflections on Legal Integration in Europe' (1963) 12(4) *International and Comparative Law Quarterly*, 1411–1416; Nial Fennelly, 'The Dangerous Idea of Europe? *Van Gend en Loos* (1963)' in Eoin O'Dell (ed.), *Leading Cases of the Twentieth Century* (Dublin: Round Hall Sweet & Maxwell, 2000), pp. 220–236; Andrew Oppenheimer, *The Relationship between European Community Law and National Law: The Cases* (Cambridge: Cambridge University Press, 1994), pp. 48–49.

4.2.3 *The Emergence of the Community National*

Perhaps this point is no better illustrated than by the use of the phrase 'Community national'. On one level it could be described as a purely convenient shorthand with little, if any, long-term discursive consequences. In practical terms it is clearly a shorthand as using 'national of a Member State of the Community' is lengthier than Community national. This 'shorthand' is illustrated in *Allué* where AG Lenz alludes to 'nationals of other Member States of the European Communities (hereinafter referred to as "Community nationals")'.[38] Indeed, it is possible to argue that in substance there is little difference between the phrase 'Community national' and 'national of a Member State of the Community'. By taking this perspective on the phrase, one could split the two words 'Community' and 'national' and imply that they are supposed to be read separately, one as referring to the Community and one as referring to nationality which had nothing to do with the then EEC. Putting it differently, the Community was not a nation and therefore little could be read into the use of the phrase. However, firstly, the phrase was never used in the Treaty and, secondly, it is possible, through an examination of the use of the phrase over several years of jurisprudence, to contend that the context leads to an understanding of it being a development from 'nationals of Member States of the Community' and not simply a synonym for it. This point is illustrated by AG Mayras in *Frilli* in 1972 when he states:

> Although the principle of equal treatment ... undeniably requires nationals of a Member State resident on the territory of another Member State to be treated in exactly the same way as nationals of that Member State, this does not mean *all* Community nationals whatever their occupation and whatever the circumstances in which they have come to settle in a country other than their own.[39]

What is immediately noticeable is how aspects of a much later debate on EU Citizenship emerge here in the context of the phrase 'Community

[38] Case 33/88, *Pilar Allué and Carmel Mary Coonan* v. *Università degli studi di Venezia* [1989] ECR 1591, p. 1602. In the French translation, the word 'ressortissants' is used for nationals. However, in AG Lenz's original version of his opinion, he alludes, in the initial part of the sentence to the German word 'Angehörige' (i.e. national) but then when referring to 'Community nationals' in brackets he actually uses the word Gemeinschaftsbürger' (i.e. Community citizen). In other words, there was an intentional difference made in this case not simply by the Court's translators but by an Advocate-General in the opinion's original language. For further analysis of the case, see Section 5.3.1.

[39] Case 1/72, *Rita Frilli* v. *Belgian State* [1972] ECR 457, p. 479. The word 'ressortissant' is used in the original French on both occasions. See Section 1.3.4 for an outline of the case.

national'. First, the link is immediately made between the principle of equal treatment and nationals of a Member State and, as has been previously maintained in Chapter 3, there is a clear link between the principle of equal treatment and citizenship. Indeed, AG Mayras makes a similar assertion in *Van Duyn* when he alludes to the 'Community national' in the context of the principle of non-discrimination and equal treatment.[40] This link is then made even more overtly in *Raulin* when AG Van Gerven refers to a 'Community national pursuant to Article 7 of the EEC Treaty'.[41] Second, one way of interpreting the above citation in *Frilli* is that the law as it then stood refers specifically to nationals of a Member State being entitled to derive protection from the principle of equal treatment but only in the context of having an 'occupation' that falls within the remit of one of free movement provisions of the Treaty. Third, therefore by implication AG Mayras was then claiming that Community law as it then stood did not apply to the economically inactive ('whatever their occupation and whatever their circumstances'); however, if it did, then all (note highlighted in italics) Community nationals would be entitled to derive rights based on the Treaty. By this a potential development of Community law would be to place emphasis on the individual rather than their position as an economic actor and this concept is best summed up by the phrase 'Community national'. Perhaps today AG Mayras may well have used the phrase EU Citizen instead but at the time he could only choose to use the phrase 'Community national' to illustrate the point that he was trying to make as it was simply not part of the everyday language within the Court in 1972. Therefore, this phrase must be seen as a development from the phrase 'national of a Member State'. This claim can be further illustrated in *Van Binsbergen, Watson and Belmann* and *Adoui*. In *Van Binsbergen*, AG Mayras states: 'a person resident abroad, who is privileged because he is a Community national, must undoubtedly enjoy the same treatment as nationals'.[42] Irrespective of whether it might be

[40] Case 41/74, *Yvonne van Duyn* v. *Home Office* [1974] ECR 1337, p. 1358. For further analysis of the case see Section 2.2.5.

[41] *Raulin*, p. 1042. In the original Dutch 'gemeenschapsonderdaan' (i.e. Community national) is used. In the French translation of the phrase, the word 'étudiant' is used. For commentary on the case see Section 1.6.

[42] Case 33/74, *Johannes Henricus Maria van Binsbergen* v. *Bestuur van de Bedrijfsvereniging voor de Metaalnijverheid* [1974] ECR 1299, p. 1316, p. 1316 and p. 1308 (below). The original French states: 'ce résident étranger, privilégié parce que communautaire, doit certes bénéficier de l'égalité de traitement'. It is noticeable, therefore, that Community national is not actually referred to (particularly the use of the word 'ressortissant') and

possible to alternate the phrase with the 'national of a Member State' orthodoxy and derive the same meaning, what cannot be ignored is that, for AG Mayras, being a Community national is a 'privilege'.[43] Underlying several academic perspectives on citizenship is its potential to emerge out of the then EEC to become a unique and uncharted form of post-national as well as supranational citizenship.[44] In this context, the term 'privilege' was a loaded one in the sense that it points towards a relationship between individuals (whether as workers or not) and the Member States that is qualitatively different from any other regional arrangement or free trade agreement. For this reason, the 'Community national' is privileged by comparison with any other national and this in part is so because of the principle of equal treatment that is alluded to in the second part of the sentence.[45] Moreover, AG Trabucchi states in *Watson and Belmann*:

> So long as there is no Community nationality, nationals of other Member States will always have a different status from that of a national of the State concerned even where he enjoys the right of free movement and residence on conditions of parity with such a nationals.[46]

instead the phrase roughly translates as a 'Community foreigner', itself a somewhat novel concept. The issue in the case concerned a Dutch law which required lawyers to reside in the Netherlands in order to practice. See also Morse, 'Direct Applicability', 67–69; March-Hunnings, 'European Community Law' 168–169.

[43] This privilege has, of course, now been lost to UK nationals and in the context of a potential second secession from a second union, in the form of potential Scottish independence, Shaw outlines the connection between such a privilege and being a national of a smaller Member State. As she suggests: 'Being born with, or subsequently acquiring, the citizenship of certain states currently conveys significant life opportunities not available to others. This was one reason why many saw the prospect of continued or renewed EU membership for Scotland after independence as a central element of the argument that a small Scotland could be a viable and prosperous state.' Jo Shaw, 'Union and Citizens: Membership Status and Political Rights in Scotland, the UK and the EU' in Carlos Closa (ed.), *Secession from a Member State and Withdrawal from the European Union: Troubled Membership* (Cambridge: Cambridge University Press, 2017), pp. 153–186 at p. 156.

[44] See Section 5.4 for a specific outline of the concept of postnational citizenship.

[45] Though Iglésias Sanchez questions the extent of this privilege in reality and criticizes the 'quality' of the right of EU Citizens to stay in other Member States. As he continues: The 'supranational right to stay never attains the level of protection recognised for the right to stay in the state of nationality'. Iglésias Sanchez, 'A Citizenship right to stay?', p. 384.

[46] Case 118/75, *Lynne Watson and Alessandro Belmann* [1976] ECR 1185, p. 1210. In the original Italian translation, it is particularly noticeable that the word 'cittadinanza' (followed by 'citiadino' in the singular) is used. In other words, a direct reference to Community Citizenship is made in the original version of the opinion. In the French translation, Community nationality is translated as 'nationalité communautaire', yet

This statement has several implications. First, for AG Trabucchi, there is a clear conceptual difference between Community nationality and being the mere national of another Member State, with the former evidently being seen as a development from the latter. Second, is there, or indeed was there at the time, truly 'no Community nationality' as AG Trabucchi seems to be suggesting? On one level, it could be maintained that he is right as his own understanding of what would need to happen, in terms of legal and political development, had clearly not been achieved in 1976.[47] Nonetheless, on a discursive level, the use of the phrase, even if intended as a shorthand, has a linguistic effect that would be hard to ignore. In other words, the more various different agents continually utter the phrase, the more it becomes real.[48] Third, implicitly what AG Trabucchi was suggesting was that the development towards such a supranational nationality can, in part, be achieved through the exponential expansion of the usage of the principle of equal treatment. On one level, AG Trabucchi is expressing cynicism by stating that nationals of other Member States 'will always' have a different status from home nationals. This 'difference' in his view cannot be circumvented through the mere enjoyment of equal treatment in free movement and residence alone. What he is pointing towards is a development towards 'parity' in all other aspects of socio-economic life and that it is only by doing so that Community nationality can become established as an independent social concept from being the mere national of a Member State.

Conversely, the Commission in *Auer* points towards the development of the Community national that potentially complements the vision of AG Trabucchi when it maintains:

> It cannot . . . be accepted that Community nationals who fulfil the conditions for the enjoyment of freedom of movement throughout the Community may move about, establish themselves and offer their services in all the Member States except the one in which they are nationals.[49]

ressortissant' is referred to on the two other occasions that the word 'nationality' is used. See Chapter 1 (n. 53) for analysis of this case.

47 See Section 5.2 for an expansion on this point.

48 See 'Introduction' for an outline of this important point.

49 Case 136/78, *Criminal proceedings against Vincent Auer* [1979] ECR 437, p. 443, p. 446 (facts). In the original French a distinction is made between 'Community nationals' which is translated as 'ressortissants de tous les États membres' (note with no reference to the Community) and 'nationals' (at the end of the above citation) which is written as 'nationalité'. The case formed part of a series of cases before the Court relating to criminal proceedings being brought against an Austrian national who had acquired

By contrast with the potential for the mere replication of nationality on a European level, this statement by the Commission illustrates the qualitatively different nature of the Community national. As has previously been outlined, the phrase 'national of a Member State of the Community' is commonly uttered in tandem with movement to an 'other' Member State. The Commission in *Auer*, by contrast, appears to be pointing towards a development of the term to identify a category of individuals who are entitled to protection against their own state, and perceive themselves as such. In this sense, the 'Community national' is filled with meaning beyond that of being a 'national of a Member State of the Community' as this type of individual is not actually the national of another Member state. Therefore, it is his/her position or status of simply being a 'Community national' that enables him/her to derive such protection. Furthermore, in *Adoui* there appear to be multiple references to in effect the same linguistic development. The UK, unsurprisingly, refers to 'nationals of a Member State within the Community', whereas the Commission and the French government use the phrase 'Community national'.[50] However, what is of note in the case is the use by the Belgian government of the phrase 'European national' (once again to express the same concept).[51] If ever there were a justification for the caution in the terminology used by the UK government, it is in the use of the phrase 'European national'. Put simply, all three phrases can have different meanings attributed to them. For instance, the phrase 'national of a Member State of the Community' is qualitatively not the same as a 'European national' and, likewise, neither is it the same as the 'Community national' (though there are points of comparison). By contrast with the 'Community national' it would be hard to suggest that the phrase 'European national' is a convenient shorthand for 'national of a Member State of the Community'. Ignoring the fact that 'Europe' is clearly territorially more extensive

French nationality for practising as a vet in France without prior authorization by a national committee. What was particularly contentious in the case was (a) the fact that the committee refused to recognize veterinary qualifications acquired in other Member States and (b) the fact that they treated him as a 'home national' for the purposes of the litigation which could, then, be seen as an early example of reverse discrimination.

[50] *Adoui*, p. 1698 (UK), p. 1690 (Commission and France).

[51] Ibid., p. 1686, pp. 1686–1698 (below). Here the translation into English almost exactly mirrors the original French (with the use of the word 'ressortissant' to mean 'national' in the English, i.e. the UK alludes to 'ressortissants des États membres', the Commission and the French state: 'ressortissants communautaire' and the Belgian government states: 'ressortissant européen'.

than the current Member States of the EU (let alone the then Member States of the EEC), what is also different is a form of nationality based upon a continent and not a 'Community'. As Shore claims, the concept of European nationality is a rather paradoxical aspiration as, in normative terms, the aspirations of the Community (then Union) should be to circumvent the problems associated with nationality, not replicate it on a continental level.[52] In this respect the 'Community national' and then EU Citizenship are much less problematic as, particularly in the case of the latter, the overt aim is not to recreate nationality but to find a form of unity on a Communitarian and value-led basis.[53] Nonetheless, what is clear is that in both cases the use of the phrases 'Community national' as well as more occasionally 'European nationality' are qualitatively not the same as 'national of a Member State of the Community' and it could be argued that their repeated utterance reflects either an unintentional development (i.e. discursive structural change) on the part of the utterer or that a deliberate normative point is being made that is designed to further the cause of closer integration.[54] Furthermore, what it is also noticeable is that at a much later stage in the Court's jurisprudence, the term had, to a certain extent, become the predominant way to describe individuals within the Community. Putting it differently, the phrase 'Community national' had simply become an innocuous way to describe the status of individuals within the Community. For instance, in *Netherlands* v. *Reed*, AG Lenz refers to it twice,[55] and in *Gullung*, AG Darmon alludes to it three times.[56] This seemingly innocuous and

[52] Chris Shore, *Building Europe: The Cultural Politics of European Integration* (London: Routledge, 2000), p. 21. See Sections 5.3 and 5.4.3 for further analysis of this point.

[53] See Section 5.4.

[54] See 'Introduction' for an outline of the important subjective role that agents play in discourse creation.

[55] Case 59/85, *State of the Netherlands* v. *Ann Florence Reed* [1986] ECR 1283, p. 1287, p. 1286 (facts). In the original German of the AG, he refers to 'EG-Staatsangehörige' (i.e. EC national). 'Ressortissants de la CEE' is used in the French translation. The case itself concerned an unmarried British couple, one of whom worked, and one of whom had been unsuccessful in finding work. The latter was refused a residence permit and an order for deportation was made. The applicant then relied on a claim of discrimination based on Article 7 of the Treaty on the grounds that an equivalent law for Dutch nationals with foreign partners would have allowed her to remain in the Netherlands or, alternatively, that she should be classified as a 'spouse' for the purposes of Regulation 1612/68. See further Robin White, 'Round-up of Cases', 147–153.

[56] Case 292/86, *Claude Gullung* v. *Conseil de l'ordre des avocats du barreau de Colmar et de Saverne* [1988] ECR 111, p. 124, p. 126, p. 127, p. 129 (below), pp. 132–133 (facts). 'Ressortissant communautaire' in the original French. It is also worth noting that further on in his opinion AG Darmon also alludes to 'Community colleagues' (in the English translation

predominant way to describe a concept belies its subjective origins. Thus, the 'Community national' became a form of social common sense but its origins lay not in the Treaty itself but in its continual usage by various protagonists throughout the early years of the Court's jurisprudence and beyond.

4.2.4 *The Community Worker*

What is perhaps also a clearly 'Communitized' concept in both substance and form is the 'Community worker'. In substance, Chapter 1 has been devoted to assessing the emergence of the 'worker' and outlining its development to the point where it became, unrecognizable from a conventional understanding of the worker. In this chapter, what are of relevance are the phrases for it or, in other words, mere utterances of it. It is clear that, on one level, there are references to the 'Community worker' throughout the Court's jurisprudence and that, as with the Community national, the phrase is not actually specifically used in the Treaty itself. Ex Article 48(2) of the Treaty, for instance, alludes to 'workers of the Member States' but not to the 'Community worker'. For instance, in *Sotgiu*, AG Mayras alludes to 'Community workers by comparison with national workers', in *Rutili*, AG Mayras once again refers to the phrase, and in *Pieck*, much later on in 1980, the Court uses the phrase three times, as well as in *Prodest*.[57] Such references span decades of the Court's jurisprudence and in this respect the phrase can be seen as dovetailing with the 'Community national' in terms of furthering the cause of closer integration. A 'Community worker' clearly has a powerful resonance and, as AG Mayras stated in *Rutili* (above), the comparison to be made is between Community workers and national

('confrères communautaires' in the original French)) and 'Community lawyer' ('avocat communautaire' in French). The case itself concerned a lawyer with dual French and German nationality who attempted to represent clients in France whilst practising from an office in Germany after having previously been disbarred in France on the grounds of bad character. See further Cathal O'Conaill, 'Community Lawyers Right to Practise within the E. C. Two Recent Decisions of the European Court of Justice' (1988) *Gazette of the Incorporated Law Society of Ireland*, 259–264; Julian Lonbay, 'Free Movement for Professionals' (1988) 13(4) *European Law Review*, 275–279.

[57] Case 152/73, *Giovanni Maria Sotgiu* v. *Deutsche Bundespost* [1974] ECR 153, p. 173; Case 36/75, *Roland Rutili* v. *Ministre de l'intérieur* [1975] ECR 1219, p. 1243; *Pieck*, pp. 2184–2188; Case 237/83, *SARL Prodest* v. *Caisse Primaire d'Assurance Maladie de Paris* [1984] ECR 3153, p. 3162. In *Sotgiu*, 'Travailleurs communautaires par rapport aux nationaux' in the original French, see Section 3.4 for an outline of the case. In *Rutilli, Pieck* and *Prodest*, 'Travailleurs communautaires' in the original French. See Sections 5.2.2, 2.2.2 and 3.6.5 for an outline of the cases.

workers and, as he also maintains in the case, what matters is the application of the principle of equal treatment between the two categories.[58] In other words, the purpose of the free movement provisions of the Treaty is to ultimately create a situation where all workers are treated alike irrespective of their Member State of origin. Moreover, such a phrase is also evidently a convenient shorthand. The long form for a 'Community worker' could perhaps be 'worker from another Member State of the Community' and it is therefore not surprising that the latter phrase was rarely, if ever, used whereas the former was. Moreover, the phrase also dovetails with the Community national as it is also used as an alternative to it. Thus, in *Rutili*, AG Mayras also alludes to Community nationals in addition to the Community worker and the Court does likewise in *Prodest* when it alludes to both the Community worker (discussed earlier) and then refers to the Community national in the following paragraph.[59]

However, on the other hand, what is also noticeable is that the 'Community worker' did *not* become the predominant term with which to describe individuals within the Community and that, by comparison, in qualitative terms, the 'Community national' appears to be a more visible and utilised phrase. There are important normative reasons for its limited use in that it is a limiting phrase by its very nature. As Chapter 1 outlined, the 'worker' ultimately became an (often derided) concept divorced quite extensively from *bona fide* work. In a sense, it became an inclusive phrase in which various categories of individuals could perceive themselves as 'counting' even if they were not workers. Moreover, the Treaty itself militates against such a limitation in that individuals within the then EEC could also derive protection on the basis of being self-employed or being the provider or recipient of a service. In this respect, the 'Community national' better summarizes the position of the individual than the 'Community worker'. Furthermore, there are normative or principled reasons for not allowing the 'Community worker' to become the predominant phrase to describe the position of individuals in that it is limited, overtly, to those engaging an economic activity.[60] This could, in part, limit any future development towards the citizen. By contrast, the citizen is better served, at least initially, by a development in the case-law

[58] *Rutili*, p. 1244.
[59] *Rutili*, p. 1243; *Prodest*, p. 3162. 'Ressortissants communautaires' in the original French.
[60] That is because it is a self-limiting phrase. See Section 5.2 for a detailed analysis of attempts to decouple the then EEC from its economic roots.

towards the concept of a worker that more closely resembles a non-economically active individual (or citizen) whilst at the same time describing the status of that individual as a 'Community national' rather than a worker. Thus, whilst the Community worker is clearly a Communitized term that was referred to, in qualitative terms it did not become the predominant way to describe the position of individuals within the then EEC.

4.2.5 *The Community Student*

By contrast with the Community worker, the emergence of the 'Community student' can be seen as a sign of progress, as it is not as self-limiting. Its emergence matters more in substance than form in that, as with the Community worker, there are not a multiplicity of references to the term. In *Commission* v. *Belgium*, for instance, the Court refers to 'Community students'.[61] However, what is of significance is the fact that the phrase is used in the first place given the fact that no reference is made to the phrase in not only the original Treaty but also even in the TFEU. In the latter, students are clearly explicitly given (to a certain extent extended) rights by virtue of Title XII of TFEU, but the phrase itself is not used. Putting it differently, in legal terms, the Community student should not have existed at all given the fact that rights were never explicitly created for students in the first place; *Gravier* itself had to in effect create or 'invent' such rights.[62] Therefore, to refer to such a phrase as a matter of fact as the Court did in *Commission* v. *Belgium* is a reflection of legal and linguistic progress. Perhaps to grapple with the unconventional nature and emergence of this new category of individual attempting to derive rights, the applicant in *Brown* refers to the 'Community national student'.[63] On one level, this legitimizes the phrase by tying it in with a clearly established phrase, the Community national. However, the meaning of such a statement needs to be seen in its context and the facts of the case allude to a home (UK) national (albeit

[61] Case C-293/85R, *Commission of the European Communities* v. *Kingdom of Belgium* [1985] ECJ 3521, p. 3525 at para. 11, pp. 3521–3525 (facts). The original French states: 'étudiants communautaires'. This was an application by the Commission to get an interim order from the Court for Belgium to apply the *Gravier* judgment prior to its final determination on the legality of the offending Belgium legislation that was at issue in the *Gravier* case.

[62] See Section 2.5 for detailed analysis of derived rights for students, including *Brown* and *Gravier*.

[63] Case 197/86, *Steven Malcolm Brown* v. *The Secretary of State for Scotland* [1988] ECR 3205, p. 3229.

with dual nationality and having been educated in France) attempting to derive rights to a student grant against his own state.[64] This, then, points towards an understanding of a Community national and therefore a Community national student as being supranational in its essence as his was not a case of being a student from another Member State. Putting it differently, the mere existence of the 'Community student' adds an additional layer of legal protection for a state's own nationals and at the same time provides the potential for the development of a novel form of post-national identification. Seen in this manner – as a term earmarking a clear legal and political development – the 'Community student' is as empowering as the 'Community worker' is limiting. Thus, whilst references to the Community student are not predominant (and are only referred to after *Gravier*) the significance of such utterances should not be missed.

4.3 The Birth of the Community Citizen: An Examination of Its Mere Utterance

It has been claimed earlier that a development towards the citizen can, in a linguistic sense be envisaged through the use of the phrase 'Community national'. Thus, as has been contended, it is perfectly conceivable to progress from a 'national of a Member State of the Community' to a 'Community national' ultimately ending up with a 'Community Citizen'. However, what is of equal if not greater relevance are mere utterances of the 'Community Citizen' itself and this section is devoted to examining such utterances. Three points need to be made in relation to such utterances from the outset.

First, that Community Citizenship literally did not exist nor has it ever existed. Whilst there was discussion from academic commentators as early as the 1970s, no aspect of the original EEC Treaty made any reference to citizenship in any form (be it national or supranational).[65] Moreover, Community Citizenship has never existed in a formal legal sense because the amended Treaty at Maastricht created *Union* and not *Community* Citizenship. Given the fact that a great deal of academic literature was (eventually) dedicated to Community Citizenship it may seem surprising to claim that it actually did not exist in a legal sense.[66]

[64] Ibid.
[65] See Plender, 'An Incipient Form'. See also Section 4.2.1 above.
[66] See Section 5.2.1.

What did exist, though, in an epistemological and discursive sense, was 'Community Citizenship speak' in that, as will be examined in this section, there was a great deal of 'talk' concerning Community Citizenship within Court judgments. In this respect, there is a linguistic (as well as a conceptual) difference between the phrase 'Community national' and 'Community Citizen' because, whether phrased a 'national of a Member State of the Community' or 'Community national' it is clear that the word 'national' is contained within the Treaty and thus forms part of the formal legal pre-existing lexicon at the genesis of the then EEC. Indeed, even the phrase 'Community national' is at least making use of such a pre-existing lexicon as the words 'Community' and 'national' are clearly referred to throughout the Treaty even if not fused together. By contrast any reference to the 'Citizen' would have to be something entirely new and thus indicative not only of a sociological progression but also reflective of the normative views of agents uttering such a phrase in the first place.[67]

The second, and related point, is that what has been particularly noticeable in relation to utterances of the Citizen is that such utterances, whilst not prolific, actually took place early on in the development of the Court's jurisprudence and that a subsequent and gradual tide of references eventually subsumed the common lexicon of the Court in the immediate build-up to the formal creation of the Citizen at Maastricht. Moreover, such references can only be understood in a discursive or non-legal sense as not only did the citizen not exist legally but also such a phrase was clearly a politically loaded and normative one in that there is an obvious difference between 'national of a Member State of the Community' and 'Community Citizen'. Whilst such utterances have to be seen in tandem with the other phrases outlined earlier or, in other words, various agents may well use 'Community Citizenship' as a shorthand alternative to other more Member State-orientated phrases, the significance of making such a statement or set of statements cannot be ignored, even if of no legal effect.

Third, a key issue of translation has also arisen in relation to such utterances.[68] For instance, one of the earliest (and most prominent) references to Community citizens was made in *Sagulo* yet appeared

[67] See 'Introduction'.

[68] A point that is equally applicable in relation to previous utterances of the phrase 'Community national' hence the original language versions of such statements were provided in the footnotes.

only in the English translation of the case.[69] In the French translation, the word 'ressortissant' was used as opposed to 'citoyen'.[70] Moreover, this issue of (mis)translation was also apparent in relation to citations (below) from *Hirardin* (1976), *Patrick* (1977), and *Thieffry* (1977) as all four of these cases (including *Sagulo*) were originally pleaded and reported in French.[71] It could then be suggested that what has actually taken place is a mere mistranslation of little significance. On one level, this contention has some veracity as one translation of the word 'ressortissant' is 'citizen' in English meant in a strictly legal sense.[72] It could therefore be suggested that the selection of the word 'citizen' is a seemingly value-neutral one by the translators of the judgment into English as it is a perfectly plausible translation.[73] However, the use of the word is inconsistent even in the cases themselves. In *Hirardin*, for example, whereas it is clear that, as will be outlined, the word 'Community citizen' was used in the English translation of the report in circumstances where 'ressortissant' was used in French, it is also clear that the word is also used in other circumstances. In a translation into English of the Commission's submissions, the phrases 'Community nationals' and 'French nationals' are used.[74] However, in the French translation the words 'ressortissants de la Communauté' are used to translate 'Community nationals' and 'les nationaux' to translate French nationals. This, then, raises two issues. First, on every occasion that the word 'ressortissant' is used, a subjective decision has to be made as to which word could be used to translate it. As will later be outlined in the same case, the word 'ressortissant' has been translated as either a 'Community citizen' or a 'Community national'.[75] As has also already been argued the 'Community citizen' is a more advanced (and

69 Case 8/77, *Concetta Sagulo, Gennaro Brenca and Addelmadjid Bakhouche* [1977] ECR 1495, p. 1495. See Section 2.3.2 for an outline of the facts.

70 Ibid.

71 See Section 4.3.4 for more detailed analysis of all these cases.

72 Larousse, 'Dictionnaires bilingues: "citizen"' (*Larousse*, 2014) www.larousse.fr/dictionnaires/anglais-francais/citizen/570230 accessed 7 August 2020.

73 See 'Introduction' for an outline of the notion of value-neutrality in the context of SC theory.

74 Case 112/75, *Directeur régional de la sécurité sociale de Nancy* v. *Auguste Hirardin and Caisse régionale d'assurance maladie du Nord-Est* [1976] ECR 553, p. 557, p. 559 (facts). The case itself was a pensions case in which the applicant, a Belgian national residing in France, was discriminated against on the grounds of nationality by virtue of a law which did not take into account periods of employment in colonial Algeria in circumstances where French nationals would have been able to do so.

75 See Section 4.3.4.

inherently political) term than the 'Community national'.[76] Thus, any translator using the two words would have been aware of the different implications of the two phrases.

Moreover, what is also apparent from the above citation is that there are in effect different hierarchies of words used in the original French version of the judgment, all of which have a subtle or nuanced meaning. For instance, as has already been outlined in *Hirardin*, the word 'nationaux' is not used in relation to what is translated as 'Community nationals' in French whereas it is used in relation to a French national. This is for a reason because, as will be discussed in Chapter 5, it is almost inconceivable for there to be a novel form of Community nationality; indeed, if anything, 'Community nationality' (better described as Community Citizenship as has also been already argued) is designed to replace the problems associated with nationality (for which the then EEC was founded in the first place), not replicate it.[77] By contrast, the phrase 'les nationaux' is rather emblematic, with a powerful normative resonance associated with the equally powerful nature of French nationality.[78] It is therefore not surprising to see that a much less linguistically 'loaded' term is used to describe 'Community nationals' (as in 'ressortissant' in the French) than French nationals.

Furthermore, a similar point can be made in relation to the use of the word 'citoyen'. The word 'citoyen' has a particularly powerful resonance in French culture in a way that the word 'citizen' does not in (UK) English culture because in the former the term is so inexorably bound

[76] See Section 4.2.3.

[77] See Section 5.4 for an outline of the dilemmas associated with EU Citizenship as a concept.

[78] See Edwidge Lefebvre, 'Republicanism and Universalism: Factors of Inclusion or Exclusion in the French Concept of Citizenship' (2003) 7(1) *Citizenship Studies*, 15–36 at 16. It should not be forgotten that 'Le Citoyen's' origins derive from a pre-revolutionary concept in which 'the word *citoyen* was synonymous with "national", used in the civil sense ... perceived in terms of allegiance and fidelity to the kingdom' (Lefebre). The Revolution itself did not change this notion but merely changed the subject of allegiance to the people and imposed a new and powerful ideological concept 'based on republican anti-particularism and the universalistic principle' (Lefebvre). Ever since the Revolution there has been a continuous debate as to how closely associated citizenship and nationality should be in France. However, in a modern context, the two are closely interconnected simply because national identity in France is constructed on the basis of associations with the core universal and secular values that are at the heart of French citizenship at the expense of a focus on particularist sensibilities of ethnic and other communities.

up in the nature of not only the French state but also the entire political project and infrastructure behind it;[79] whereas in the UK there is no such formal concept of citizenship as the UK's nature is still one of constitutional monarchy, not 'la république', in which individuals are subjects as opposed to citizens.[80] Therefore it would have been more acceptable to use the word 'citizen' in the English translations of the above cases than to have used the word 'citoyen' in the French language as the latter word is an inherently politically charged word that would have been objected to by the French government had it been consistently deployed as a synonym for national of a Member State. Thus, it is equally not surprising that the phrase was never deployed in the original French version of these early judgments.

However, merely because the phrase is not used in the original language of the case is not to dismiss it for being either irrelevant or the translator for simply doing a 'bad' job of translating. The reason for not being dismissive is both a question of agency and discursive structure. In terms of agency, it would be hard to dismiss outright these early references given, as will be outlined, how many times the phrase 'Community citizen' is used in a rather short burst in 1976–1977. This point then needs to be linked in with the above point in relation to

[79] For Lefebvre, the result of the French revolution, embodied in Article 3 of *La Déclaration des droits de l'Homme at du Citoyen* was that 'Citizenship had become a specific status' inexorably linked to an outright rejection of 'feudal and monarchic traditions' in which 'the new citizen possessed rights, freedoms and duties, and consequently was an active participant in a government in which justification would be imposed not from the top, as under the monarch, but from the bottom up'. Lefebvre, 17. See also François Borella, 'Nationalite´ et citoyennete´ en droit français' in Dominique Colas (ed.), *L'Etat de droit, travaux de la mission de la modernisation de l'Etat* (Paris: Presses Universitaires de France, 1987), pp. 27–51; Rogers Brubaker, 'De l'immigre´ au citoyen' (1993) 99 *Actes de la recherche en Sciences Sociales*, 3–25.

[80] As Everson put it: 'The modern Briton is no "fellow-traveller" in a state constituted exclusively for its needs by its citizenry. Rather, the "British subject" retains a feudal flavour, still linked, by simple virtue of common law and the constitutional "non-definition" of modern British citizenship, to an outmoded monarchical Sovereign'. Indeed, for Everson what minimalist notion there is of citizenship as a concept in the UK is defined as the very antithesis of the egalitarian notions that are at the heart of the French model: 'the examination of the philosophical thought that found its way into constitutional thinking to govern relations between Briton and state demonstrates UK rejection of every one of Rousseau's philosophical prescriptions for the *Citoyen*'. Michelle Everson, '"Subjects", or "Citizens of Erewhon"? Law and Non-Law in the Development of a "British Citizenship"' (2003) 7(1) *Citizenship Studies*, 57–83 at 57, 75. See also Ann Dummet and Andrew Nicol, *Subjects, Citizens, Aliens and Others* (London: Weidenfeld and Nicolson, 1990); Adrian Favell, *Philosophies of Integration: Immigration and the Idea of Citizenship in France and Britain* (Basingstoke: Macmillan, 1998).

subjectivity in that, as has already been outlined, a subjective decision has clearly been taken to use the phrase as opposed to less politically charged alternatives. Exemplary of this point was its use in *Sagulo* as the phrase 'right of residence for Community citizens' was used (see further) as the main phrase in which to describe the case: its most powerful linguistic aspect of the judgment.[81] Moreover, as the phrase forms neither part of the wording of the judgment nor part of summary of the facts that would have been written by the juge-rapporteur, it appears as if the sole discretion for what headline could be used to describe the case lay with the translators. In other words, this was a rare part of the judgment in which the translators had a degree of intellectual freedom and it is contended that such freedom was so exercised through using a phrase with evident linguistic ramifications. Thus, because the phrase 'citizen' does not have the same resonance in (UK) English, it would have been more acceptable to insert the phrase into the English translations of both *Sagulo* and *Hirardin*.

Finally, there are discursive implications for uttering something in one language even if it was not stated in the original judgment nor even specifically uttered by the Court's judges itself. For instance, as will be outlined later, what cannot simply be ignored is the number of times that the phrase is used in a relatively short period of time. It is uttered in seven different cases over two years and, as has already been argued, mere repetition can itself have an effect.[82] Putting it differently, the more something is said, the more it becomes 'real' – a form of social truth – and this can take place within an epistemic community of lawyers and students of Community law that primarily express themselves in the English language.[83] Moreover, in this context, whilst an utterance by the Court (in the form of its juge-rapporteur) may well carry greater significance, the subjective utterances of translators, translating from an original language into English, are worth assessing in and of themselves. If, for instance, a groundswell of discursive expression emerges using the phrase Community citizen then this can in effect create the citizen and, further, create an impetus for its formal inclusion in the original French language versions of the Court judgments. To illustrate this point, it is worth briefly assessing the context of the cases in which citizenship is uttered as will be outlined later. Whilst the original language of all Court

[81] *Sagulo*, p. 1495.
[82] See 'Introduction' on repetition.
[83] See 'Introduction' for an outline of the nature of epistemic communities.

judgments was French, many of the above-mentioned cases had little connection to France (or Belgium) or, if they did, they involved English-speaking applicants. Thus, in *Kermaschek*, the applicant was Dutch, *Jansen* was a German case, and *Watson and Belmann* was an Italian case. Furthermore, in *Watson and Belmann*, one of the applicants was from the UK and in *Patrick* even though the case was a French one the applicant was also from the UK. Thus, words uttered repeatedly on a page can have an effect even if uttered in the context of a translation from an original language as a multiplicity of agents would read and absorb the phrase, particularly if, as has been examined, it appears as the first phrase to describe the case (appearing underneath the title to it in the Court reports) as happened in *Sagulo*.[84] Thus, having set the framework in which analysis of the Community citizen will take place, there now follows a chronological and contextual assessment of utterances of the Community Citizen.

4.3.1 *References to the Citizen Other Than in the Form of Community Citizenship*

Prior to assessing literal utterances of the 'Community citizen' it is important to briefly assess other utterances of 'citizenship' without necessarily being linked to Community Citizenship and this is important for three reasons. First, it could be asserted that if reference is made to the phrase 'citizens of the Member States' then Community Citizenship could be seen to develop as a convenient shorthand in the same manner as the development from 'nationals of the Member States of the Community' developed into the 'Community national'. Second, there is a fundamental substantive difference between a 'national' and a 'citizen' even if references to 'Community Citizenship' are perceived by certain agents to be a seemingly inconsequential alternative to more orthodox phrases such as 'national of a Member State'.[85] In other words, literal references to any form of citizenship are relevant because such

[84] This point is further exemplified by utterances in Advocate- General's opinions in that translations from the original language into English can still have a discursive impact. The major difference between such opinions and Court judgments themselves is that the original text is not necessarily French. Where that has happened, the original language version will be alluded to. In addition, as the working language of the Court is still French, where such utterances are made, the French translation of the original text will also be referred to. See Mancini and Keeling (for a more detailed analysis of the process of translation at the Court).

[85] See Sections 5.2 and 5.3 for an analysis of such a distinction.

a distinction can be made. As an example of a more general reference to the citizen, the Commission in *Commission* v. *France* states:

> On the second point the Commission considers that the maintenance in office in the laws of a Member State of provisions which are incompatible with the provisions of the Community rules, constitutes in itself a failure to fulfil Community obligations. Such maintenance, contrary to the obligation expressed in Article 5 of the Treaty, would create in any event a doubt *in the mind of citizens* and would compel them to initiate judicial proceedings in the national courts.[86]

There are several aspects of this citation that are of relevance to a more general discussion of citizenship. First, the context in which it was stated is a case in which a Member State was being pursued by the Commission for failing to fulfil its obligations under (then) Article 5 of the Treaty and what matters for the Commission is the mind-set of individual litigants in terms of the decision to initiate proceedings. In other words, their *cognition* is important.[87] Therefore, and second, this in essence highlights the difference between the 'citizen' and the 'national'. The latter is in a sense a condition that you are born with and little if any effort on the part of the individual is required to be a national: it is a passive state of existence. Whilst it is perfectly conceivable to be the mere passive recipient of a form of citizenship, the nature of citizenship, with an emphasis on civic participation of individuals in society, is, by its very nature, an active concept.[88] Here the category of individuals that the Commission were trying to incentivize to pursue litigation were a group of active participants in the juridical process of the Community and, it is maintained, what matters is that they are in effect aware of the rights that they have through being equally aware of the rigid pursuit by the Commission of infringing Member States. This image being portrayed of a proactively aware citizen is further illuminated by the third point in that what is also evident is the lack of reference to citizens from any particular Member State. Putting it differently, the

[86] Case 167/73, *Commission of the European Communities* v. *French Republic* [1974] ECR 359, p. 364 (emphasis added), p. 366 (facts). 'Une équivoque dans l'esprit des justiciables', i.e., litigants in the original French. See Section 5.4.1 on this point as one argument that will be made is that the early litigants before the Court were in effect pioneer Community citizens. In the case, France was being pursued by the Commission for maintaining in force a law requiring that a certain proportion of sailors in a merchant fleet be French.

[87] See 'Introduction' for an outline of the interrelationship between SC and psychological methods.

[88] See Section 5.2 for an outline of differing conceptions of citizenship.

Commission is referring to citizens more generally throughout the Community and these archetypal Community citizens are the litigants pursuing matters in domestic courts that protect the rights that they are in theory entitled to under Community law. Thus, whilst no reference is made by the Commission to Community Citizenship, the mere utterance of the citizen and the picture painted of such 'citizens' is of relevance in and of itself.

However, references to 'citizens' more generally are not as frequent as references to citizens of the Member States. In literally the first case that was examined in research for the purposes of this book, the German government alludes, in *Van Gend*, to a 'citizen of a Member State of the Community'.[89] Likewise, in *Fiege*, AG Warner alludes to 'Citizens of the Member States'.[90] Whilst references to this particular phrase have not been prolific, by comparison with the 'Community national', such a phrase is also uttered much later on in the jurisprudence of the Court. For instance, AG Mancini states it twice in *Auer* ('Citizen of a Member State'),[91] and in *Commission* v. *Netherlands*, it is alluded to twice by the Dutch government (as summarized by AG Tesauro) and, on the second occasion it states:

> The status of citizen of Member State does not automatically confer the right to enter and stay in other Member States, since there is at least one class of Community nationals - those who are not in gainful employment - who do not, under the Community legislation in force, enjoy an independent right to enter and remain in a country.[92]

What this statement reveals is that the phrase 'citizen of a Member State' was intended by the Dutch government to be limited in its nature

89 Case 26/62, *van Gend en Loos (NV Algemene Transporten Expeitidie Onderneming)* v. *Nedelandse Administratie der Belastingen* [1963] ECR 1, p. 8, p. 17 (below). 'Citoyen' in the original French.

90 Case 110/73, *G. Fiege* v. *Caisse régionale d'assurance maladie de Strasbourg* [1973] ECR 1001, p. 1020, p. 1019 (below), p. 1009 (below). Interestingly, the translation into French from the original English uses the word 'citoyen'. The cases itself related to whether the applicant, a German national, resident in Algeria prior to its independence, was entitled to export his accrued pensions benefits to Germany under Regulation No. 3/63.

91 Case 271/82, *Vincent Rodolphe Auer* v. *Ministère public* [1983] ECR 2727, p. 2749, p. 2753. 'Cittadino di uno Stato membro' in the original Italian. 'Ressortissant' once again in the French translation.

92 Case C-68/89, *Commission of the European Communities* v. *Kingdom of the Netherlands* [1991] ECR I 2637, p. 2645, p. 2652 (facts). 'Cittadino' in the original Italian. 'Ressortissant' in the French translation. In the case, the Commission had pursued action against the Netherlands for having introduced legislation allowing border officials to ask Community citizens questions about the nature of their journeys and financial means.

and a mere alternative to both the 'Community national' (since it alludes to it in the same sentence) and the 'worker' as what is being envisaged is an economic contributor moving from one Member State to another. This point is further illustrated by AG Tesauro later on in his opinion where, by contrast and when not summarizing others' views, he maintains there to be a 'right of residence to all Community citizens' and then utters the phrase on two further occasions.[93] On one (albeit limited) reading of what the Dutch government stated, little can be read into alluding to a 'citizen of the Member State' and all of the phrases used are merely synonymous with each other. However, the use of the phrase can, on the other hand, be seen to be a precursor to the eventual emergence of the Community citizen. On another reading of the above statement, a linguistic distinction appears to be made between the 'citizen of a Member State' and a 'Community national' as the former phrase has a different resonance and linguistic significance from the latter. For the Dutch government, all individuals within the Community must be 'Community nationals' but non-workers do not count for the purposes of the Treaty. The essence of the phrase 'citizen of a Member State' is different in the context of the above statement as it is claimed to be more than just mere words but in actual fact a 'status' and one with clear significance. Thus, what is being suggested is that a concept is in the process of being constructed in which non-economic contributors can also claim a right of residence on the basis of the creation of a general right of residence and this point is further illustrated by AG Tesauro when he claims there to be a 'right of residence to all Community citizens' later on in the case.[94] In other words, the phrase 'citizen of a Member State' is itself a loaded one whose utterance cannot be so easily dismissed as an inconsequential synonym. Thus, whilst utterances of 'Citizen of the Member State' are evidently neither as evocative nor as obvious a sign of jurisprudential development as more specific assertions of 'Community Citizenship', references to the former phrase needed to be outlined prior to references to the latter as, to a certain extent, we can also see one as developing from the other.

[93] Ibid., p. 2647 at paras. 48–49. 'Cittadino di uno Stato membro' in the original Italian. However, the French translation differs and the words 'citoyens de la Communauté' is used instead in the first instance; whereas on the other two occasions the word 'ressortissants' is used.

[94] Ibid., p. 2647. See Section 2.3 for an expansion on this point.

4.3.2 *Utterances of the 'Community Citizen' Itself*

What follows is both a qualitative and quantitative assessment of utterances of the Community Citizen (or variants of it) from the Court's inception until the formal inclusion of the Citizenship provisions in the amended Treaty at Maastricht. By contrast with utterances of the 'worker' or the 'principle of equal treatment' it is necessary to comprehensively examine utterances of citizen because, firstly, it did not, as has already been maintained, exist in any formal legal capacity prior to 1992. The same could not be said of the worker or the principle of equal treatment. The second reason why such utterances are important is because a core tenet of SC theory is that the more something is uttered the more it becomes 'real'; in a sense a linguistic snowball effect.[95] The previous chapters of this book have attempted to examine the emergence of the Citizen in a contextual or consequential sense. By this what is meant is that the emergence of the Citizen can be better envisaged, by using SC methodology, through examining the context in which the citizen emerged and the context had its consequences in that, for instance, the emergence of an increasingly broad concept of the 'worker' necessitated a further debate on how to classify the economically inactive, one phrase for which arguably was the citizen. This is one aspect of a Community-specific concept of Citizenship that ultimately developed. Moreover, a second aspect of the development towards citizenship is an increasing jurisprudential recognition of concepts, such as the principle of equal treatment and fundamental human rights, that core citizenship rights are generally composed of. However, a third aspect of the incremental evolution of the Citizen has been its mere utterances. Indeed, this even differs from terms such as 'Community national' that, as has already been outlined, could be seen to be a linguistic stepping-stone towards citizenship. Here, merely stating the term itself can directly have that effect. Furthermore, what has also been suggested is that the analysis will be both quantitative and qualitative. In quantitative terms, what has been particularly noticeable is an exponential increase in usage of the term from rare or occasional use in the Court's early years to frequent use in the decade before the coming into force of the Maastricht Treaty. Yet, in qualitative terms, the context in which such utterances are made is fundamental in that what is of relevance is not just when the statement

[95] See 'Introduction' on repetition.

is said but who is saying it and what substantive linkages are being made with the phrase.

4.3.3 *The Earliest References to the Citizen*

The first references to the concept of Community Citizenship came in two cases in 1973, *Smieja* and *Vanderweghe*. In *Smieja*, the referring court asks the following question:

> Do ... Regulation No 3 and ... Regulation 1408/71, complement each other in such a way these provisions considered together broaden the requirements of nationality and residence into the citizenship and territory of the Community?[96]

The fact that the first utterance of such a concept is from an external actor with a host of ideas inherently from Dutch domestic law and politics should not be ignored.[97] In other words, a language game from a different context is influencing the epistemic community of the Court. Moreover, it is clear that the referring court was not envisaging Community Citizenship as a mere synonym for Community nationality as one can be seen to develop from the other, providing the possibility for a post-national form of citizenship based upon the wider territory of the Community. What is also noticeable is the

[96] Case 51/73, *Bestuur der Sociale Verzekeringsbank* v. *B. Smieja* [1973] ECR 1213, p. 1225, p. 1220 (facts). 'Cittadini' in the original Italian of the Advocate-General. 'Onderdaanschap' in the Dutch version (roughly translating as subjecthood, though it can also be translated as nationality). It should be noted that the Netherlands is a constitutional monarchy and therefore Dutch nationals are also subjects in the same way as UK nationals (van der Burg). This is exemplified by the law on Dutch citizenship of 1892 which treats citizenship and nationality as synonymous (Bryant). Whilst the word can be translated as nationality, it is noticeable that the word 'nationaliteit' is used in the same sentence when referring to 'nationality and residence in the English translation' that is, there is a deliberate distinction being made between the two concepts. 'Citoyenneté' in the French translation. The case itself concerned a German national residing in Germany having previously worked in the Netherlands and was denied a pension in Dutch law on the grounds of both nationality and residence.
Martijn Van der Burg, 'Transforming the Dutch Republic into the Kingdom of Holland: The Netherlands between Republicanism and Monarchy (1795–1815)' (2010) 17(2) *European Review of History: Revue europeenne d'histoire*, 151–170 at 158; Christopher Bryant, 'Citizenship, national identity and the accommodation of difference: Reflections on the German, French, Dutch and British cases' (1997) 23(2) *Journal of Ethnic and Migration Studies*, 157–172 at 166.

[97] In other words, posing such a radical a question is not un-typical from a Dutch perspective because of its avowedly pro-integration approach that it has consistently taken. Rey Koslowski, 'A Constructivist Approach to Understanding the European Union as a Federal Polity' (1999) 6(4) *Journal of European Public Policy*, 561–578 at 569.

immediate link made to citizenship and the issue of residence, something that was ultimately reflected in legislative form in Article 8a of the amended Treaty at Maastricht. Yet, as has been outlined earlier, what should not be forgotten is that this statement was made in 1973, not 1993 and thus is evidentially radical in its nature. To a certain extent this can be demonstrated by the response of other parties to this statement; namely, with the exception of the Dutch government, this issue was not only not dealt with, it was also simply not uttered. The Dutch government, by contrast, chose to take a proactive approach and dismiss the concept outright when it maintains:

> There is no support for the theory that the above provisions complement one another in such a way as to broaden the requirements of nationality and residence into the citizenship and territory of the Community. If that were so, anyone resident in the Community could obtain the benefits provided for in, say, the legislation considered in [*Frilli*]".[98]

There are several aspects of this citation that necessitate further specific examination. First, for the Dutch government what is being proposed by its own referring court is pure 'theory' and therefore what it is doing is attempting to dismiss this theory out of hand in order to prevent theory becoming reality. Second, though, there is irony in such an attempt by the Dutch government in that by 'talking' about such a matter, even if in a negative sense, it can start the process of becoming a form of social truth.[99] As has also been previously outlined, the better avenue is often to simply not utter anything at all in response to subjective attempts to create radical concepts, as the statement itself becomes linguistically isolated from the remaining 'debate' within the judgment and, implicitly, ridiculed.[100] Third, the Dutch government, once again ironically, is eerily prophetic in a much more specific way than even the referring court as to the manner and form in which citizenship eventually appears as it points to a potential future in which attempts would be made to obtain benefits on the basis of not being an economic participant in the Common Market in any way and simply on the basis of being a Community citizen.

[98] *Smieja*, pp. 1217–1218. Once again, the word 'onderdaanschap' is used, except this time this word was the original wording.

[99] See 'Introduction' on utterances.

[100] Ibid.

Furthermore, the only other reference to the citizen at this point in the development of the Court's jurisprudence is AG Trabucchi in *Vandeweghe* when he states:

> When interpreting the Community social rules one must bear in mind, in accordance with the general tendency of the case law of this Court, the need to avoid – as regards the application of the social laws of the individual States – any difference in the treatment of citizens of the Community on grounds of nationality.[101]

What is made immediately apparent, even this early on in the development of the Court's jurisprudence, is the importance of both the principle of non-discrimination (which is immediately linked to the citizen in the sentence) and the early social security cases to the eventual emergence of the citizen in 1992. In particular what cannot be ignored is that when AG Trabucchi is referring to 'the Community social rules' he is referring to, for the most part, Regulation Nos 1408/71 and 1612/68 and, as has been outlined in Chapter 2, these regulations from the outset dealt with the circumstances of individuals who were not necessarily economically active and either dealt with dependents' rights or an expanded concept of an 'assimilated worker'. In either case, though, the exponential expansion of the jurisprudence led, as has already been outlined, to an increased linguistic as well as legal need to find a 'label' to attach to such categories of individuals that could clearly not be termed workers. Moreover, what is equally noticeable about the above citation is that it was also being uttered not just in 1973 but almost immediately after *Smieja* and in circumstances where AG Trabbuchi was the Advocate-General for both references. In other words, the two cases can be seen to be part of a discursive bubble that marks the potential for the future but then does not reappear until three years later on in 1976.

4.3.4 *A Second Wave of Early References*

The second wave of early references took an entirely different linguistic form. Whereas the two cases in 1973 in the previous section used the phrase 'citizen of the Community', the first actual statement of the

[101] Case 130/73, *Magdalena Vandeweghe and others* v. *Berufsgenossenschaft für die chemische Industrie* [1973] ECR 1329, p. 1339, p. 1330 (facts). 'Cittadini' in the original Italian. 'Ressortissant' in the French translation. The plaintiffs in the case were Belgian nationals claiming a 'death grant' in Germany but denied it on the grounds of an ambiguity between the different translations of Regulation No. 3 and the local authority in German claiming that the German version of the Regulation did not include this particular grant.

phrase 'Community citizen' was made in *Hirardin* in 1976 by the French referring court when it asks whether 'discrimination provided for between French nationals and aliens ... be applied to a Community citizen'.[102] The Court itself then reiterates this question along with the phrase 'Community citizen'.[103] At almost the same time, in 1976, the phrase is also stated in *Watson and Belmann* by AG Trabucchi where he makes two references to it. In the first reference, he expresses concern that that there could be a development in Community law in which there would be 'an extension to all citizens of the Community of a right to freedom of movement which the Treaty intended to apply only to clearly defined categories of persons' and then goes on to claim that the case amounted to there being an 'intrusion into the private affairs of Community citizens'.[104] AG Trabucchi in both of these citations in addition to uttering the citizen has uttered it in a context that relates to the broader form that EU Citizenship eventually takes, that is, a generalized right of residence.[105] In the former citation, the concern that he expresses is that the general population of the Community could eventually benefit from the right to freedom of movement – once again irrespective of whether involvement in an economic activity takes place – and that the phrase to describe this 'new' status for individuals would be 'citizens of the Community'. In the latter citation, though, the link is clearly made between citizenship and fundamental rights, another core tenet of citizenship more generally as will be examined in Chapter 5. This contrasts with the Commission in *Kermaschek*, where it links the citizen directly to the worker when it states: 'The guarantee of freedom of movement of workers laid down by the EEC Treaty is in the economic interests of the Community and of its citizens'.[106] Nonetheless, this linkage is also important as, as has

[102] Case 112/75, *Directeur régional de la sécurité sociale de Nancy* v. *Auguste Hirardin and Caisse régionale d'assurance maladie du Nord-Est* [1976] ECR 553, p. 563, p. 555 (below). 'Ressortissant' in the original French.

[103] Ibid., p. 559 at para. 3. 'Ressortissant' in the original French.

[104] *Watson and Belmann*, pp. 1205–1206. 'Cittadini' in the original Italian for the first citation and 'soggetti' i.e. subject for the second.

[105] See Sections 2.3 and 5.2.8.

[106] Case 40/76, *Slavica Kermaschek* v. *Bundesanstalt für Arbeit* [1976] ECR 1669, p. 1674, p. 1675 (facts). 'Bürger' i.e. citizen in the original German. 'Citoyen' in the French translation. The case itself concerned a Yugoslav national who was refused unemployment benefit in Germany, after having worked in the Netherlands and subsequently moving to Germany to reside with her German husband. See also Derrick Wyatt, 'Rights of Members of a Worker's Family under Regulation 1408/71' (1977) 2(2) *European Law Review*, 125–126.

already been argued in Chapter 1, the worker can still be seen as an antecedent to the citizen. There then follow, in 1977, several repeated references to the Community citizen at an almost identical time in terms of where they are reported in the Court reports. In *Bozzone*, the Commission refers to 'citizens of the Community';[107] in *Jansen*, the referring court's questions referred to 'the right of citizen of the EEC to freedom of movement';[108] and in *Patrick*, AG Mayras alludes to 'Community citizens'.[109] Yet, perhaps the ultimate and rather extraordinary reference to the Citizen at this exact period of time was in *Sagulo* in 1977. The editor of the Court's judgments in the court reports had developed a habit of giving a one-line, seemingly neutral 'summary' of the case in inverted commas underneath the names of the parties and on the front page of the report. The 'summary' that was chosen is eerily reminiscent of not even *Sala* but in *Grzelczyk* (2001) over twenty years later was 'Right of residence for Community Citizens'.[110] The mere fact that this phrase was used in 1977 is extraordinary in and of itself but what makes this statement even more remarkable is the complete lack of any reference to the Community Citizen anywhere in the judgment either by the AG or the Court itself. Thus, whilst references to the Community citizen were not prolific in 1977, the citizen had now subjectively emerged into the linguistic arena at least, as has already been outlined, in the English language translation of the Court reports.

[107] Case 87/76, *Walter Bozzone* v. *Office de Sécurité sociale d'outre-mer* [1977] ECR 687, p. 694, p. 693 (below), p. 695 (facts). 'Ressortissant' in the original French. In the case, the applicant was an Italian worker residing in Belgium who was denied an entitlement to have insurance periods in which he was working in the Belgian Congo count for purposes of determining invalidity benefit.

[108] Case 104/76, *Gerda Jansen* v. *Landesversicherungsanstalt Rheinprovinz* [1977] ECR 829, p. 841, p. 839 (facts). 'Staatsbürger' in the original German. 'Ressortissants' in the French translation. The case itself was a pensions dispute between a German national and her local authority as a result of them ceasing to pay her when she moved to the Netherlands.

[109] Case 11/77, *Richard Hugh Patrick* v. *Ministre des affaires culturelles* [1977] ECR 1199, p. 1209, p. 1203 (facts). 'Ressortissants' in the original French. In the case, the French government refused to recognize the qualifications an architect from the UK. See also Rebecca Wallace, 'Recognition of Foreign Qualifications' (1977) 127 *New Law Journal*, 1007–1008; Catherine Crisham, 'Case 71/76, *Jean Thieffry* v. *Conseil de l'Ordre des Avocats à. la Cour de Paris* (1977) ECR 767' (1978) 15 *Common Market Law Review* 366–370 (note).

[110] *Sagulo*, p. 1495. 'Ressortissants' in the original French.

4.3.5 *A Further Linguistic Bubble of References in the Late 1970s and Early 1980s*

In a series of cases that are sufficiently distanced from the cases previously referred to 'count' as a self-contained 'discussion', a further linguistic momentum towards the creation of citizenship was created. In *Defrenne III*, the applicant states:

> As is shown by Articles 48 and 117 one of the aims of the EEC Treaty is the abolition of all discrimination as between nationals of the Member States. Several judgments of the Court of Justice have defined the concept of non-discrimination. Thus, within the Community, equal access to employment and to other working conditions may be achieved between Community citizens of different nations. It seems inconceivable, therefore, that the same equality should not exist as between the nationals of a single country as a result, in particular, of discriminatory conditions of employment.[111]

This is a significant statement which can be seen to be providing the linguistic framework in which the later EU Citizen can emerge for several reasons. First, the statement directly links (ex) Article 48 on free movement of workers with (ex) Article 117 on sex discrimination to make the argument that there is a broader concept of non-discrimination. As has already been outlined in Chapter 3, attempts to create such a broad principle can be seen to form part of the basis of citizenship more generally. Second, equal treatment is evidently being linked with citizenship as citizens are referred to in the same sentence as equal access to employment. Third, and most importantly, a distinction is made between 'Community citizens' and 'different nations'. In other words, Member State nationality and Community Citizenship are not the same concept. Fourth, therefore, the reason why such a distinction is important is because the case itself concerned sex discrimination against an individual by her own state with, then, no movement taking place within the EEC. Instead, the individual is trying to apply 'the same equality' as a non-national would expect when exercising his/her right to free movement and what is implicitly being suggested is that the best label to attach to this individual is the

[111] Case 149/77, *Gabrielle Defrenne* v. *Société anonyme belge de navigation aérienne Sabena* [1978] ECR 1365 (*Defrenne III*), p. 1368. The original text is somewhat contradictory. When alluding to 'nationals of the Member States', the original French states 'citoyens des États membres'. However, when referring to 'Community citizens of different nations' the word 'ressortissant' is used. See further Philip Allott, 'The European Court Ordains Equal Pay for Women' (1977) 36 *Cambridge Law Journal*, 7–10; L. Neville Brown, 'Air Hostesses and Discriminating Employers' (1984) 47 *The Modern Law Review*, 692–703.

'Community citizen'.[112] Putting it differently, Community Citizenship is being used in the above citation in an entirely different context from the workers' cases and provides for potential development towards a post-national form of civic awareness in which the Citizen becomes radically decoupled from preconceived concepts of national citizenship.[113] Finally, what is also noticeable is that the emphasis on the importance of the individual (whether as a national of another Member State or not) is further made when AG Capotorti also alludes to 'individual citizens of the Community'.[114] Thus, in 1978, citizenship was first linked to the sex discrimination cases.

However, the linguistic progression towards citizenship appeared to equally carry on unabated in the more straightforward free movement cases, though, on each occasion, a linguistic link is made with various different aspects of what the later EU Citizen eventually came to be understood as. In *Gillard*, the referring court alludes to 'citizens of the Community who satisfy those conditions only in relation to their own Member State' and AG Mayras states: 'Once again it is the Court's task to confirm the directly applicable nature of the principle of equality of treatment between nationals of a Member State and other Community Citizens'.[115] In relation to the first citation, what is evident is that a link

112 As the EU's own description of the history of the principle of equal treatment put it on the Europa website: 'Equality between women and men is one of the European Union's founding values. It goes back to 1957 when the principle of equal pay for equal work became part of the Treaty of Rome. The European Union's achievements in fostering equality between women and men have helped to change the lives of many European citizens for the better'. In other words, there is an intrinsic link between the principle (in the context of sex discrimination) and Citizenship. For Prechal, such linkages increased as a result the Union's attempt to embrace the principle of non-discrimination more generally as a result of the enactment of the Charter of Fundamental Rights. As she put it: 'broad anti-discrimination protection became part of the policy aiming at bridging the gap between the Union and "its" citizens.' This notion is not, however, without its critics. See, in particular, O'Brien's trenchant criticism of the evolution of EU Citizenship in which a gender bias is evidenced in its evolution by virtue of the constant link to the free market.

European Commission website, 'Gender Equality' (*Europa*, 2014) https://ec.europa.eu/info/policies/justice-and-fundamental-rights/gender-equality accessed 7 August 2020; Prechal, 550; Charlotte O'Brien, 'I Trade, Therefore I Am: Legal Personhood in the European Union' (2013) 50 *Common Market Law Review* 1643–1684.

113 See Section 5.4 for an outline of such a decoupling.

114 *Defrenne III*, p. 1389. 'Soggetti' i.e. subjects in the original Italian. 'Assujettis' in the French translation.

115 Case 9/78, *Directeur régional de la Sécurité sociale de Nancy* v. *Paulin Gillard and Caisse régionale d'assurance maladie du Nord-Est, Nancy* [1978] ECR 1661, p. 1670 (referring court), p. 1669 (AG Mayras), pp. 1670–1671 (below). The word 'ressortissant' is used in the original French. See Section 5.3.2 for an outline of the facts of the case.

has been made to the potential for citizenship to be an additional layer of identification for individuals against their own state (a point that has already been made earlier) and, in relation to the second citation, AG Mayras 'once again' alludes to a link between citizenship and the principle of equal treatment. Similarly, in *Choquet*, the referring Court states: 'citizens of the Community have a right of residence under Article 48', thereby making an immediate link between a key issue for the later citizen, the issue of the right of residence, and the worker.[116] Likewise, the summary of case in *Pieck* refers to 'right of residence for community citizens'.[117] However, what is also noticeable in relation to *Choquet* is another reference to the citizen when AG Reischl alludes to 'foreigners who are citizens of the EEC'.[118] Likewise, the Belgian government in *Van Wesemael* alludes to 'foreigners (who in the present case are Community citizens)'.[119] There is a contrast between AG Reischl's comment and the referring court in *Gillard* as in effect what the Advocate-General was doing was reverting to the 'orthodoxy' of understanding Community Citizenship as a mere synonym for a national of a Member State moving to another Member State. This more orthodox reference is also made by AG Mayras in *Überschär* when he alludes to 'Community citizens other

[116] Case 16/78, *Criminal proceedings against Michel Choquet* [1978] ECR 2293, p. 2305, p. 2306 (German), pp. 2305–2306 (French), p. 2300 (facts). 'Gemeinschaftsangehörige' in the original German i.e. Community dependents. Once again, there appears to be a reverse of the translation in the French when in relation to the phrase 'nationals of other Member States' in the English translation earlier on in the same paragraph the translation from the German into French uses the word 'citoyen'; whereas when the word 'citizen' is actually used in the English, the word 'ressortissant is used in the French'. In the case, a French national working in Germany was being prosecuted in Germany for driving without what the local authorities deemed to be a valid driving licence, despite the fact that he possessed a perfectly valid French licence.

[117] *Pieck*, p. 2171. 'Ressortissant' once again in the French. However, on this occasion, the attempt to examine references to the citizen in the English language is somewhat justified as, despite what the word may appear as in other languages in the Court reports, continual reference to the word in the English language can itself have a discursive effect. The reason such a point is made is because the case itself was a reference from Pontypridd Magistrates Court and therefore the original language of the case was English/Welsh.

[118] *Choquet*, p. 2309. 'EWG Ausländer' in the original German (i.e. EEC foreigner). 'Ressortisssant' once again in the French.

[119] Joined Cases 110 and 111/78, *Ministère public and 'Chambre syndicale des agents artistiques et impresarii de Belgique' ASBL* v. *Willy van Wesemael and others* [1979] ECR 35, p. 43, p. 57 (facts). 'Ressortissant' in the original French version. In the case, a Belgian café worker used a French agent (both of whom were the defendants) to provide entertainment in his café without adhering to a provision of Belgian law requiring the agent to be licensed in Belgium. See further Geoffrey Morse, 'Provision of Services: The Professional Supervision Exception' (1979) 5(4) *European Law Review*, 375–377.

than German nationals', and 'Community citizens other than nationals' (twice) in *Commission* v. *Belgium*, as well as the Commission in *Überschär* where it refers to 'a non-German migrant worker which is a Community citizen'.[120] It should be reiterated at this point that on one level mere utterances of the Citizen are still important in establishing a momentum towards Citizenship, even if it is used as a mere synonym for national of Member state.

However, on another level, its use in that capacity is by definition limiting as the logical corollary of all the above statements is that a 'home' national must therefore not be a Community Citizen. By contrast, to associate an individual attempting to derive protection based upon Community law against his own state and labelling such an individual a 'Community citizen' adds, as has been outlined, a novel intersubjective concept to the jurisprudence of the Court. In a similar vein, in *Auer*, multiple references are made to the Citizen. AG Warner links, on this occasion, freedom of establishment with the citizen when he states, firstly, 'What matters is that Dr Auer is a French citizen and therefore a Community citizen' and, then to the 'Community citizen's right of establishment'.[121] Once again the citizen is being used in the context of attempts to develop Community law in an entirely novel direction. Whilst the phrase 'Community citizen' is not actually uttered again in the same opinion, AG Warner also claims: 'the very purpose of Articles 7, 52 and 57 of the Treaty is to confer the same right on the citizens of all the Member States, and that the problem posed in this case is the same as it would have been if Dr Auer had been a citizen of another Member State'.[122] Here the link is made between the citizen

[120] Case 810/79, *Peter Überschär* v. *Bundesversicherungsanstalt für Angestellte* [1980] ECR 2747, p. 2771 (AG Mayras), p. 2758 (Commission), p. 2761 (facts); Case 149/79, *Commission of the European Communities* v. *Kingdom of Belgium* [1980] ECR 3881, p. 3909 and p. 3919 (AG Mayras), pp. 3898–3899 (facts). 'Ressortissant' in the original French (1980; 2771). *Überschär* concerned a German national who had periods of employment in Belgium and was in dispute with the German authorities over a pensions back-payment for a period of non-insurance. In *Commission* v. *Belgium*, the Commission was pursuing the Belgian government for allowing various railway boards and local municipalities to advertise jobs requiring Belgian nationality. See also Wyatt, 'Article 48(4)', 459–463.

[121] *Auer* [1978], p. 455, p. 459. It should be noted the original language of the text of the opinion was English.

[122] Ibid., p. 455, p. 455 (below). Whilst it has been overtly stated that the examination of the texts of the court judgments in this chapter has been restricted to the texts in the English language, AG Warner's opinion in *Auer* justifies such a restriction in three ways. First, because the intention of AG Warner on all the occasions cited here was to use the word 'citizen' because English was the original language of the text. Second, despite the fact that AG Warner amongst all AGs and employees of the Court would

and the entire legislative architecture of the free movement provisions of the Treaty, with the then Article 7 on Equal Treatment being at its forefront. Moreover, what is also apparent is a distinction being made between a 'citizen of another MS' and 'citizens of all the Member States'. Once again, this points towards a development in Community law in which individuals asserting rights against their own state could be classified as and perceive themselves as Community Citizens.[123] Moreover, the emergence of the citizen could, (implicitly) according to AG Warner, be seen as a way of resolving the so-called reverse-discrimination problem in the sense that 'all the Member States' could be seen to be a way of alluding to nationals pursing matters against their own state as all other nationals were 'citizens of another Member State' by definition.[124] Whilst none of these cases in the 1970s were pure

have to have good command of the French language, what appears to be undeniable is that the word 'citizen' is used subtly but also relatively frequently in the English language version of the Court reports and that this can have a cumulative effect on English language readers of the Court reports (including AGs), a fundamental aspect of discourse theory (see 'Introduction'). Finally, there is an evident reluctance to use the word 'citoyen' in the French language versions of the Court reports and, conversely, a lack of such reticence to do so in the English language (as evidenced by the frequency of citations of the word in this chapter). In the main text of this chapter, the word 'citizen' has been cited five times in the case. In addition, the word was used a sixth time. Immediately after the first citation alluding to Dr Auer as a French and Community citizen, AG Warner also states: 'His erstwhile Austrian citizenship could neither help nor hinder him in asserting a right under Community law.' Curiously, though, despite the fact that that the word was clearly intended to be used in all of the citations from the case, the French translation of each word differs with little, if any, justification, for so doing. In relation to the reference to French and Community citizenship, the word 'citoyen' is used. However, in relation to Austrian citizenship and the other two uses of the word in the context of Member States, the word 'ressortissant' is used instead. Whether there was a conscious attempt made on the part of the translators to avoid using a word that had obvious significance in the French language in a way that it did not in the English language, is partly speculative (though clearly shown in this case). However, what does matter, from a discursive perspective, is that a unique 'language game' (see 'Introduction') is taking place in the English language that is worthy of analysis in and of itself.

123 See Section 5.2 for an outline of perceptions of EU Citizenship.

124 Whilst the issue of so-called reverse discrimination or wholly internal situations is not the subject of this book, the commentary on it is prolific. As early as 1986, David Pickup wrote an article entitled 'Reverse Discrimination and Freedom of Movement for Workers' (1986) 23 *Common Market Law Review* 135–156. However, this issue became particularly prominent in the early 2000s as a result of Citizenship cases such as *Flemish Care Insurance*. See, in particular, Alina Tryfonidou, 'Reverse Discrimination in Purely Internal Situations: An Incongruity in a Citizens' Europe' (2008) 35(1) *Legal Issues of Economic Integration*, 43–67; Shuibhne, 'Time to Move On?', 731–771; Toner, 'Judicial Interpretation', 158–182.

reverse discrimination cases as they all involved a cross-border element (in Dr Auer's case a qualification from another Member State), this same rhetoric and legal argument was used in the *Flemish Care Insurance* case to justify the extension to all nationals, irrespective of movement, of the right to equal treatment.[125] Yet, even in this case, in 2006, the Court would not determine that Community law could extend to wholly internal situations.[126] Therefore what can be seen even in 1978 was the establishment of a momentum in which the issue of reverse discrimination could be radically assessed in the way that it was in 2006. Thus, mere utterances of the citizen in these circumstances played an important role in its later emergence.

4.3.6 *Its Increasing Usage in the Early 1980s*

By the early 1980s, references to the Community citizen had increasing become part of the Court's common lexicon. In *Webb* (1981) and *Levin* (1982), the Member States themselves were making reference to it. In *Webb*, the German government alludes to 'Community citizens',[127] and in *Levin* what was at issue was 'the scope of the phrase favoured EEC Citizen' contained within Dutch legislation.[128] Moreover, in *Levin* and *Adoui* (both of which were reported at similar times in 1982), its usage

[125] *Auer*, p. 452; Case C-212/06, *Government of Communauté française and Gouvernement walloon* v. *Gouvernement flamand* [2008] ECR I 1683 (*Flemish Care Insurance case*), p. 1748 at para. 40.

[126] Ibid., p. 1747 at para. 39.

[127] Case 279/80, *Criminal proceedings against Alfred John Webb* [1981] ECR 3305, p. 3314, p. 3321 (facts). The Dutch version of the judgment (as it was a Dutch case) makes no references to Community citizens at all. Choosing instead to state 'en op die van andere Lid-Staten' (i.e. 'and those from other Member States'). 'Ressortissants' is used in the French version and 'Ausländer aus den Europäischen Gemeinschaften' or EEC foreigner in the German version. It should be noted, though, that the English version of the case is not without its significance. The is because the case concerned a UK national, resident in the UK who, as a director of a British employment agency, was supplying agency workers in the Netherlands without prior authorization and was being prosecuted for so doing. In other words, the defendant in the case was an English speaker and, in addition, the Advocate-General for the case was AG Slynn.

[128] Case 53/81, *D. M. Levin* v. *Staatssecretaris van Justitie* [1982] ECR 1035, p. 1054, pp. 1054–1055 (below). 'Onderdaan' in the Dutch, which, therefore, was the wording in the original legislation. 'Ressortissant' in the French translation. Nonetheless, the original language of the opinion (from which the citation derived) was English as the opinion was written by AG Slynn. In addition, as has already been outlined in Chapter 2, the case concerned a UK national. Finally, it should be noted that the use of word 'citizen' by AG Slynn could, to a certain extent, be seen as deliberate. Below the citation itself, AG Slynn states 'Mrs Levin is a British subject'. The Dutch version of the opinion also uses the word 'onderdaan'. In other words, the same word is used twice in the Dutch translation; whereas AG Slynn appears to make a distinction between the two because of the context, i.e. 'EEC' on the one hand and 'British' on the other.

within both cases was frequent. In *Levin*, aside from the above reference to Dutch domestic legislation containing the phrase, the Danish government refers to both 'A citizen of the Community' and 'Community citizen', the French government refers to the latter phrase twice and the Commission alludes to an 'EEC Citizen'.[129] Likewise, in *Adoui*, the applicant makes repeated reference to the phrase, uttering it six times along with the French government that states it twice.[130] What is, though, of most significance is the statement of the phrase 'Citizens of the Community' as it is stated by the Court itself in its highlighted summary in bold at the end of the judgment.[131] Whilst the main body of the judgment did not allude to the phrase, this was the first time in which the phrase had been very specifically highlighted in bold at the end of a judgment and, it could be suggested this was, in part, a response to its repeated utterance throughout the text of the report of the case. Furthermore, there are two other aspects of the use of the phrase 'Community citizen' that are important to bear in mind in both cases. First, the facts of both cases are controversial. In *Levin*, the applicant, a UK national, admitted that she had taken up limited part-time employment as a chambermaid 'as a precaution' in order to derive the right to reside with her TCN husband in the Netherlands.[132] Likewise, the applicants in *Adoui* were both waitresses considered to be engaging in behaviour that was 'suspect from the point of view of morals'.[133] Therefore

[129] *Levin*, pp. 1041–1044. 'Onderdaan' in the Dutch. 'Ressoritissant' on all occasions in the French version of the report.

[130] *Adoui*, pp. 1680–1683, p. 1689.

[131] Ibid., p. 1712, pp. 1681–1712 (below). It is at this point, in 1982, becoming particularly noticeable that the word is 'ressortissant' is being consciously used in the original language version of the Court judgment on every occasion that 'Community citizen' has been uttered in the English translation. There are three other occasions in which the word 'citizen' is used but not in the context of Community Citizenship. On the first occasion, and on the same page as four of the citations of Community Citizenship by the applicant, a reference is made to 'citizens' freedom of movement'. However, in the French version, the word 'citoyen' is used. On the second occasion, the Belgian government states 'a State can clearly not expel its own citizens'. Once again, the word 'citoyen' is used in the French version. Finally, the French government alludes to 'citizen of another Member State' and, once again the word 'citoyen' is used. There are two conclusions that can be drawn from these other references. First, that there is an obvious reticence, evident from plain reading of the text of the report, to refer to the Community Citizenship in the French language in the Court reports. Second, a parallel, and important, language game is taking place in the English language in that on all occasions the word 'citizen' is used, ensuring that the use of the word in the text is prolific. A phenomenon that, in and of itself, should not be ignored.

[132] *Levin*, p. 1055. See Sections 2.6.1 and 5.3.2 for an outline of these controversies.

[133] *Adoui*, p. 1714.

the 'Community citizen' was being used in the context of individuals on the periphery of conventional working relationships. Second, what was also evident from *Adoui* was the intermingling of the phrase 'Community citizen' with various other phrases to describe the same concept. As has already been outlined earlier, the UK government utters the phrase 'nationals of a Member State within the Community' in a context in which all other parties, with the exception of the Court, use a different word.[134] The Belgian government, for instance, uses the phrase 'European national' and, likewise, the Commission refers to the 'Community national'.[135] Thus, at this stage in the Court's jurisprudence, the phrase Community Citizen was becoming increasingly used (and hence discursive) but in competition with a number of other phrases, none of which were entirely dominant.

Aside from the above references, there were no prolific references to the Citizen in the English language in the remainder of the middle part of the 1980s. In *Morson and Jhanjan*, the UK and Dutch governments referred to 'Community citizens' and 'citizen of the European Economic Community', respectively.[136] On one level, this could be seen to be an example of the UK government itself becoming entrapped by the rhetoric of the Court, since in the previous year, in *Adoui*, the UK referred to the 'nationals of a Member State' (as has already been outlined).[137] However, the Dutch and UK government views were both conflated and summarized by the juge rapporteur for the case and so it is not entirely certain that the UK itself intended to use the phrase (with all its connotations).

However, in *Meade*, AG Mancini made a more significant utterance of the phrase, when he states: 'I might add that workers referred to in Article 48 must be Community citizens. That article itself confirms it'.[138] This is a highly subjective, though important, statement by AG Mancini for several reasons. First, since a detailed assessment has taken

134 Ibid., p. 1698. See Section 4.2.1 above.

135 Ibid., p. 1702.

136 Joined Cases 35 and 36/82, *Elestina Esselina Christina Morson* v. *State of the Netherlands and Head of the Plaatselijke Politie within the meaning of the Vreemdelingenwet; Sweradjie Jhanjan* v. *State of the Netherlands* [1982] ECR 3723, pp. 3730–3701. 'Onderdaan' in the original Dutch. 'Ressortissant' in the French version. See Section 2.3.2 for an outline of the facts of the case.

137 See 'Introduction' for an outline of this concept.

138 Case 238/83, *Caisse d'Allocations Familiales de la Région Parisienne* v. *Mr and Mrs Richard Meade* [1984] ECR 2631, p. 2641. 'Cittadini' in the original Italian. The French translation of this sees an almost absurd distortion of AG Mancini's original wording as it alludes to 'nationaux des États membres' thereby not referring to the words

place of the wording in the original Treaty, it has already been stated that, with respect to (the late and great) Advocate-General, Article 48 does not 'confirm' the legal existence of Community Citizenship; instead, only workers are referred to. Second, the inherent subjectivity of such a statement can be seen from the almost superfluous reference to the Citizen in the first place. In the above statement he states 'I might add' that workers 'must' be citizens, which, give the impression that AG Mancini was himself attempting to construct the reality he was merely purporting to describe.[139] Finally, the fact that AG Mancini perceived himself as being able to make such a bold statement is indicative of a wider structural cultural change in which it was acceptable to make such a statement in the first place.[140] Similarly, in *Castelli*, the applicant refers to the citizen in a progressive manner when she refers to 'equality of treatment between citizens of one and the same Community', having previously alluded to the 'Community citizen'.[141] Arguably, the reason that such a statement is progressive or indicative of a gradual contextual transformation is that not only is a link made between equality of treatment and the citizen but also the concept of (post-national) solidarity is being implicitly alluded to as no distinction is made between nationals of the different Member States with, instead, a statement being made that all individuals *qua* citizens are part of 'one and the same Community'.[142] Moreover, in *Pinna*, AG Mancini alludes to 'The Community citizen who has decided to work in a country other than his own'.[143] This is also a progressive utterance in that implicitly what AG

'Community' or 'citizen' as was originally intended. See Section 1.4.1 for an outline of the facts of the case.

139 See 'Introduction' on this concept.

140 Ibid.

141 Case 26/83, *Carmela Castelli* v. *Office National des Pensions pour Travailleurs Salariés (ONPTS)* [1984] ECR 3199, p. 3203, p. 3201, pp. 3201–3203 (below). On the second occasion, the word 'ressortissante' is used. However, on the first occasion, the word 'citoyens' is used. This constitutes one of the first occasions in which the word 'citoyen' is overtly used in the French language and it is particularly significant that its use comes in the context of a linkage made with the principle of equal treatment. It also particularly noticeable that 'cittadini' is used in the Italian version of the Court judgment given the fact that the applicant was Italian (see Section 3.6.5 for an outline of the facts).

142 See Section 5.2 for an outline of the concept of solidarity in the concept of the early case law.

143 Case 41/84, *Pietro Pinna* v. *Caisse d'allocations familiales de la Savoie* [1986] ECR 1, p. 6, p. 10 (facts). 'Cittadino' in the original Italian. Once again, the word 'ressortissant' is used in the French translation. The case concerned an Italian worker in France who was denied benefits for his children on the grounds that they had stayed with their mother in Italy for an extended period of time. See also Derrick Wyatt, 'Prospective Invalidity

Mancini is also suggesting is that not only are individuals who exercise their right to free movement classified as Community citizens but also so are those who do not; they still have a conceptually novel post-national identity irrespective of whether the right to free movement is exercised or not.[144] Finally, AG Mancini once again refers to Community citizens in *Commission* v. *France*.[145] Thus, during this period, whilst utterances of the Citizen were infrequent, those that were made (most of which by AG Mancini) were progressive and therefore significant.

4.3.7 *The 'Citizen' as Firmly Established Rhetoric in the Late 1980s*

Having examined previous eras in the Court's jurisprudence a pattern emerged in the late 1980s of repeated use of the phrase 'Community citizen' in which it was evident that citizenship had become a core part of the Court's common language. Putting it differently, it simply became 'normal' to allude to the citizen and it was no longer a question of an agent asserting his/her subjectivity by doing so. It is maintained that this manifested itself in two ways.

First, a number of actors attempted to 'reflect back' on core Community provisions as if they already embodied Citizenship in the first place. For instance, in *Van Roosmalen*, AG Darmon, having already asked 'may a Community citizen defeat a residence requirement' (once again linking citizenship to residence), then claims that 'Community citizenship [has now] become ... "moored" to Regulation 1408/71'.[146] It has already been maintained in Chapter 2 that in substantive terms the jurisprudence on the early social security secondary legislative provisions, including Regulation

for the Discriminatory Family Allowances Rule' (1986) 23 *Common Market Law Review* 703–717; Philippa Watson, 'Equal Treatment in the Award of Family Allowances' (1989) 14(5) *European Law Review*, 346–349.

144 See Section 5.4 for an analysis of the notion of postnational identity.

145 *Commission* v. *France* [1986] ECR 273, p. 289, p. 300 (facts). 'Cittadino' in the Italian, 'ressortissant' in French. In the case, the Commission was pursuing France for granting tax credits on dividends for shareholders in France and four other Member States by bilateral agreements without having extended the benefit to shareholders in other Member States. See further Wouters, 'Case-Law on Direct Taxes', 179–220; Lyons, 27–51; David Edward, 'Establishment and Services: An Analysis of the Insurance Cases' (1987) 12(4) *European Law Review*, 231–256.

146 Case 300/84, *A. J. M. van Roosmalen* v. *Bestuur van de Bedrijfsvereniging voor de Gezondheid, Geestelijke en Maatschappelijke Belangen* [1986] ECR 3097, p. 3108, p. 3110, pp. 3108–3110 (below), p. 3118 (facts). 'Ressortissant' in the original French version. In the case, a Catholic priest moved to Zaire (via Belgium) in order to preach and contracted a disease, incapacitating him. The Dutch authorities refused to pay him incapacity benefit for the time in which he resided in Zaire.

No. 1408/71, played a vital role in forming part of the collective understanding of what EU Citizenship means today in the context of the evolution towards the three residency directives in 1990.[147] However, once again, it should be noted that no such wording was used in the regulation. Likewise, in *Heylens*, AG Mancini claims that Article 8 of Directive 64/221 concerned Community citizens, whereas, once again, there is no reference to the citizen in that directive.[148] In both cases an expanded understanding of individuals that 'count' for the purposes of Community law was necessary for which the term 'citizen' could be used.[149] As has already been argued, Regulation No. 1408/71 enabled such a diverse set of non-economic actors to derive Community law rights even though they could simply not be called workers in any conventional sense.[150] Likewise, Directive 64/211,

[147] See Sections 2.3 and 2.5.2. Specifically, in relation to the contribution that Regulation No. 1408/71 made to the emergence of EU Citizenship, Sindbjerg-Martinsen maintains: 'Regulation 1408/71 was adopted as a social complement to the free movement of workers and has developed in parallel with the gradually extended right of free movement' and then continues: 'The personal scope of Regulation 1408/71 has undergone a gradual, but continual development. From entitling only the worker *sensu stricto*, i.e., the market citizen, to cross-border welfare, its personal scope has been incrementally expanded to the point where by 29 April 2004 the Regulation has been extended to all European citizens and where, recently, legally residing third-country nationals have been included in its personal scope. The development is thus a specific reflection of the general development from economic community to political union.' Dorte Sindbjerg-Martinsen, 'Social Security Regulation in the EU: The De-Territorialisation of Welfare' in Gráinne de Búrca (ed.), *EU Law and the Welfare State: In Search of Solidarity* (Oxford: Oxford University Press, 2005), pp. 89–111 at p. 90, p. 95. See also A. Pieter Van der Mei, 'Regulation 1408/71 and Coordination of special Non-Contributory Benefit Schemes' (2002) 27(5) *European Law Review*, 551–556; S. Van Raepenbusch, 'Persons covered by Regulation (EEC) no. 1408/71 and European Citizenship: From Migrant Worker to European Citizen' in *25 Years of Regulation (EEC) no. 1408/71 on Social Security for Migrant Workers: Post Experiences, Present Problems and Future Perspectives* (Stockholm: Report from the European conference on social security, 1996), pp. 71–88.

[148] Case 222/86, *Union nationale des entraîneurs et cadres techniques professionnels du football (Unectef)* v. *Georges Heylens and others* [1987] ECR 4097, p. 4111, p. 4114 (facts). 'Cittadini' in the original Italian and 'citoyens' in the French translation. In the case, the applicant, a Belgian national, was appointed as the manager of Lille football club (OSC Lille) but was being prosecuted by the French footballing authorities for not having obtained a qualification equivalent to a French one in order to entitle him to work as a manager, despite the fact that he did hold a Belgian diploma. See further Rebecca Wallace, 'Remedies for Foul Play' (1988) 13(4) *European Law Review*, 267–270.

[149] See Chapters 1 and 2 for an outline of the differing types of categories of individuals that 'count' for the purposes of Community law (loosely under the definition of 'work'). See Chapter 5 for an outline of the ultimate linkages that were made between non-economic contributors and citizenship in the early case law of the Court specifically on EU Citizenship.

[150] See Section 1.4.2.

most famously discussed in *Van Duyn*, deals not with the nature of the work of an individual *per se* but their personal individual conduct leading to a purported claim for their detention and expulsion by a particular Member State.[151] Here, the discussion within *Van Duyn* and all other Directive 64/211 cases is not so much on the nature of their work – it is either accepted or not relevant to the facts of the case – but the nature of their behaviour as individuals within their host society. In both *Van Roosmalen* and *Heylens,* it is maintained that it is not surprising that a retrospective citizenship gloss was put on these legislative provisions, making it appear that they concerned the 'citizen' in the first place.

The second manifestation of this 'new era' for utterances of the citizen was its repeated use both between and within cases. In *Laborero and Sabato*, AG Mischo alludes to the Community citizen three times, once in the conclusion.[152] Likewise, in *Stanton*, there are multiple references to the citizen. The Headnote refers to the 'Community citizen' and the applicants utter it twice along with the Belgian government.[153] The Commission, though, is a particularly significant protagonist in the use of the phrase, referring to it four times.[154] Eventually, the Court itself uses the phrase in paragraph 13 of its judgment.[155] Moreover, such utterances have added significance because of the case that immediately followed it: *Wolf*, which, in effect, dealt with an almost identical set of facts.[156] Because the two

[151] See Section 2.2.5 for an outline of the facts of *Van Duyn* and the way in which Directive 64/211 was applied in the case. See further Ami Barav and Sandy Thomson, 'Deportation of EEC Nationals from the United Kingdom in the Light of the *Bouchereau* Case' (1977) 2(1) *Legal Issues of Economic Integration*, 1–37.

[152] Joined Cases 82 and 103/86, *Giancarlo Laborero and Francesca Sabato* v. *Office de sécurité sociale d'outre-mer (OSSOM)* [1987] ECR 3401, pp. 3415–3420, pp. 3423–3424 (facts). 'Ressortissant' in the original French. In the case, the two applicants were Italian nationals residing in Belgium when the local authorities refused to count a period of time working in newly independent Zaire for the purposes of calculating pensions contributions.

[153] Case 143/87, *Christopher Stanton and SA belge d'assurances 'L'Étoile 1905'* v. *Institut national d'assurances sociales pour travailleurs indépendants (Inasti)* [1988] ECR 3877, p. 3878, pp. 3882–3883, pp. 3878–3886 (French), p. 3892 (facts). 'Ressortissant' in the original French on all occasions. The use of the English language, though, takes on added significance in the case as the applicant was English. In the case the applicant was a director of a company in Belgium but was also a full-time employee in the UK. Had he been employed in Belgium he would have been entitled to a partial exemption from social security contributions in Belgium.

[154] *Stanton*, pp. 3884–3886.

[155] Ibid., p. 3894.

[156] Joined Cases 154 and 155/87, *Rijksinstituut voor de sociale verzekering des zelfstandigen (RSVZ)* v. *Heinrich Wolf and NV Microtherm Europe and others* [1988] ECR 3897, p. 3910 (facts). In the case, the applicant was a German national employed full time in

cases were so closely related the Commission's submissions were identical, along with the Court's judgment.[157] What ended up happening, then, were multiple repetitions of the citizen over the course of a few pages of the Court reports in the English language. A conventional legal approach to this issue of repetition may not read very much into such a repetition; however, from an SC perspective, the prolific utterance of such a phrase in any language, even if merely repeating a Court judgment based on similar facts, can have the effect of conveying to the reader of the report the importance of the phrase and further establish the existence of the Citizen even if it did not exist formally at that stage.[158] In other words, appearances on a page do matter, irrespective of the substance of what is being said.

Moreover, the context in which such utterances were being made can also not be ignored in that cases such as *Van Roosmalen*, *Huylens*, *Laborero* and *Wolf* were heard and reported at the same time as some of the most significant cases that, as has already been submitted in Chapters 1 and 2, provided the groundwork for the emergence of the citizen. For instance, 1988 was also the year in which *Brown* and *Cowan* were decided.[159] In both cases it has already been maintained that they were significant decisions by the Court in which the student and the tourist were able to derive rights which, in turn, created an impetus towards citizenship. Nonetheless, even in these two cases, utterances of the citizen were linguistically very visible. In *Brown*, the applicant maintains the need for there to be 'equality as between citizens of the Community', thereby again linking citizenship with equal treatment, and in *Cowan*, AG Lenz makes prolific reference to the citizen.[160] In total, AG Lenz refers to the citizen nine times throughout his opinion.[161] However, once again, the context in which some of these utterances were made necessitates

Germany whilst at the same time being a director of a company in Belgium. He also fell foul of the same piece of Belgium law as the applicant in *Stanton* and was required to make parallel contributions to the Belgian social security system.

[157] Ibid., pp. 3909–3914. With one exception being that because the case originated in Flanders, the original language of the case was Dutch and the word 'onderdaan' was used in the Dutch version.

[158] See 'Introduction' on utterances.

[159] The judgment for the latter was actually in 1989; however, AG Lenz's opinion, which is cited in this paragraph, was delivered on 6 December 1988.

[160] *Brown*, p. 3212. The case itself is a Scottish case and, in any case, the word 'citoyen' is used in the French version.

[161] Case 186/87, *Ian William Cowan* v. *Trésor Public* [1989] ECR 195, pp. 203–215. 'Gemeinschaftsbürger' on all occasions in the original German. In the French version

further examination. In only the second sentence of the Advocate-General's opinion, he states: 'The case raised fundamental questions regarding the freedom to provide services and the concomitant rights of Community citizens.'[162] This citation clearly links the 'fundamental' right to provide services with the citizen and also makes the point that the rights of Community citizens are 'concomitant'. In other words, the citizen provides a conceptual label to which additional rights can be attached; in addition, that is, to the rights that one can derive from the free movement provisions of the treaty (at least interpreted strictly). This understanding of Community Citizenship is novel. AG Lenz then expands on what he views the nature of Community Citizenship to be when he later maintains that 'a Community citizen who does not belong to a privileged category under Community law enjoys a reduced level of protection with regard to his most personal rights'.[163] This conceptualization of the citizen lays an important foundation for its eventual emergence in the '*Sala* revolution', as for AG Lenz the citizen is one that exists in addition to the rights that could be derived under the ordinary free movement provisions of the Treaty – the 'privileged' category; however such an existence is limited by comparison.[164] In other words, it is possible to derive additional rights for the non or limited economically active but those rights have to be limited in some way.[165] This then ties in with AG Lenz's previous assertion in his opinion (in the course of which he refers to the 'Community citizen') in which he states that 'a recipient of services must be capable of being an independent subject of Community rights and obligations'.[166] This statement, then, albeit in the context of being a recipient of services, makes the much broader point that Community citizen must be an independent subject in two senses: first, independently of being classified as a 'worker' and, second, that to derive economic rights on the basis of merely having the status of Community citizen necessitates obligations to be fulfilled on the part of the citizen, reflective, in turn, of the specific wording of the

of his opinion, the word ''ressortissants' is used on all occasions with one notable exception: on the fourth occasion the word 'citoyen' is used.

162 Ibid., p. 203.

163 Ibid., p. 212.

164 Jacqueson, 265.

165 For O'Brien, these caveats were and remain problematic in that whilst the law appears to move away from 'the single market paradigm', the Citizen, with its limitations still exists in a 'shallow' and ''malleable form as a ''facilitator of economic movement'. O'Brien, *Unity in Adversity*, p. 24.

166 *Cowan*, p. 205.

later amended Treaty in 1992. In this vein, an additional reference to the citizen by AG Lenz then demonstrates the emergence of the conceptually novel concept of the citizen when he alludes to 'Community citizens who are victims of crime'.[167] It is no longer, the 'recipient of services' who is the 'victim of crime' but the citizen directly. Therefore, AG Lenz is in part reflecting previous discussions of citizenship but also, in part, making a subjective assertion designed to effect radical change through the conceptual vehicle of the Community citizen.

Furthermore, there are several other references to the citizen in both significant and controversial cases. In *Bettray*, AG Jacobs refers to the need for 'equality of access ... for all Community citizens' and, in addition, to the position of an 'ordinary citizen of the Communities'.[168] However, the reference to the citizen was being made in the case of an individual who was attempting to claim he should be classified as a 'worker' on the basis of taking part in a drug rehabilitation scheme in which a limited amount to work took place.[169] Moreover, in *Roux*, AG Tesauro also makes continual reference to the citizen. In the course of his (rather short) opinion, he refers to the Community citizen five times.[170] Once again, though, the substance of such references closely resembled the emergence of the citizen post-Maastricht.[171] The case ultimately concerned the issue of right of residence and, specifically in relation to a residence permit, AG Tesauro states: 'It is clear therefore that the residence permit is exclusively declaratory of the rights of Community citizens, if certain conditions are met.'[172] This, then, cuts to the heart of what later evolved into in the early case law on citizenship in that, whilst the case admittedly concerned a worker, it ultimately turned on the nature of to a residence permit and, in the end by specifying that 'certain conditions' need to be met, AG Tesauro is not only making it clear that this principle applies to all Community nationals, irrespective of

167 Ibid., pp. 212–213.

168 Case 344/87, *I. Bettray* v. *Staatssecretaris van Justitie* [1989] ECR 1621, pp. 1637–1638. 'Citoyen' in the French translation (1989; 1637–1638). See Section 1.5.7 for an outline of the facts of the case.

169 Ibid., p. 1631.

170 Case C-363/89, *Danielle Roux* v. *Belgian State* [1991] ECR I 273, pp. 282–285. 'Cittadino' in the original Italian. 'Ressortissant' in the French on all occasions.

171 *Roux*, p. 275 (facts). To add a further light to this case, the facts were actually somewhat extraordinary. The Belgian authorities were threatening to deport the applicant, a French national, merely because she had classified herself for social security purposes, as self-employed; whereas the local social security office formed the view that she was employed.

172 *Roux*, p. 283.

whether an individual is or is not a worker, but also he is providing (self-imposed) limitations on such rights which, in turn pre-empts the much later Citizenship Directive.[173] In other words, one 'condition' of being entitled to reside in another Member State regardless of whether such an individual is making an economic contribution or not, is that they must not at the same time be parasitic and therefore be able to sustain themselves on their own resources.[174]

Finally, it became clear that by the end of the 1980s and beginning of the early 1990s, a wave of highly significant references was being made to the citizen, creating a linguistic momentum for the citizen's eventual creation. In addition to the cases already cited, utterances of the citizen arose in relation to two other in controversial cases in *Grogan* in 1991 and *Singh* in 1992 in the immediate build- up to the formal creation of the Citizen at Maastricht. In *Grogan*, the 'right of Community citizens to receive services' is uttered twice by AG Van Gerven,[175] and in *Singh*, the Court itself states:

> The provisions of the Treaty to the free movement of persons are intended to facilitate the pursuit by Community citizens of occupational activities of all kinds throughout the Community, and preclude measures which might place Community citizens at a disadvantage when they wish to pursue an economic activity in the territory of another Member State.[176]

Whilst the proviso of pursuing an economic activity is clearly being laid out by the Court, the fact that the Court itself is overtly uttering the citizen is indicative of a subtle linguistic change that has evolved since the citizen's first utterance. Moreover, the Court also referred to 'occupational activities of all kinds' which is sufficiently ambiguous to encompass non-economic activities as much as economic ones. Finally, what should not be forgotten are the facts of both cases. Whilst the issue in *Grogan* was of the rights that one could derive as a recipient of services, the applicants were hardly either 'ordinary'

173 See Chapter 5 for a detailed analysis of the linkages between the early free movement case law and the Citizenship Directive.

174 Also see Section 5.2 for analysis of this controversy within the concept of EU Citizenship.

175 Case C-159/90, *The Society for the Protection of Unborn Children Ireland Ltd* v. *Stephen Grogan and others.* [1991] ECR I 4685, p. 4712. 'Gemeenschapsburgers' i.e. 'Community Citizenship' in the original Dutch version and 'citoyen' in the French translation.

176 Case C-370/90, *The Queen* v. *Immigration Appeal Tribunal and Surinder Singh, ex parte Secretary of State for Home Department* [1992] ECR I 4265, p. 4293, p. 4292 (French). 'Ressortissant' is used in the French version of the court report. It should be noted, though, that the case was an English one, being a reference from the High Court.

recipients of services nor even recipients of services at all. The defendant applicants were simply members of Trinity College Dublin's student union being pursued by the Society for the Protection of the Unborn for being in breach of Ireland's constitution for openly advertising abortion clinics in the UK.[177] Thus, the student union members themselves were not actually the recipients of services as such; they were merely advertising services in another Member State that were highly controversial given the stance taken by both successive Irish governments and its constitution on the issue of abortion.[178] Nonetheless, even though the case ultimately, then, concerned mere potential recipients of services being discriminated against (by their own state), as far as AG Van Gerven was concerned, this was very visibly an issue for 'the citizen'. Moreover, in *Singh*, the applicant was a UK national, married to a TCN, though in the process of a divorce, attempting to claim permanent leave to remain for her soon-to-be divorced husband on the basis of her having worked for a brief period of time in Germany and then returning to the UK.[179] Whilst there clearly was an element of work and cross-border movement, it was also equally inexorably related to a core aspect of UK immigration policy and for this reason the case was controversial.[180] Despite this, for the Court, as has already been cited, this was a case concerning the 'citizen'. Thus, by the early 1990s, the 'citizen' had

[177] *Grogan*, pp. 4734–4735.

[178] It was, though clearly no longer, seen by many to be a fundamental and unchangeable aspect of Irish identity. As Smyth put it 'the stimulus for anti-abortion politics in Ireland has emerged from a concern to mark Ireland out, using the liberal apparatus of global human rights, as a morally distinct nation-state'. Lisa Smyth, *Abortion and Nation: The Politics of Reproduction in Contemporary Ireland* (Aldershot: Ashgate, 2005), p. 2. See also Juliane B. Kokott, 'European Community Case Note: *Society for the Protection of Unborn Children (Ireland) Ltd.* v. *Grogan* Case No. C-159/90' (1992) 86(2) *American Journal of International Law*, 367–370; Siofra O'Leary, 'The Court of Justice as a Reluctant Constitutional Adjudicator: An Examination of the Abortion Information Case' (1992) 17(2) *European Law Review*, 138–157; Brian Wilkinson, 'Abortion, the Irish Constitution and the EEC' [1992] (Spring) *Public Law*, 20–30; Catherine Barnard, 'An Irish Solution' (1992) 142 *New Law Journal*, 526–533; Cathleen Colvin, 'Irish Abortion Law and the Free Movement of Services in the European Community' (1991) 15(2) *Fordham International Law Journal*, 476–526; Diedre Curtin, 'Case C-159/90, *The Society for the Protection of Unborn Children Ireland Ltd* v. *Grogan*, Judgment of 4 October 1991' (1992) 29 *Common Market Law Review* 585–563.

[179] *Singh*, p. 4290.

[180] As Tryfonidou put it, 'the case has attracted an immense amount of criticism' and the reason for such criticism is that there is a perception that 'the cross-border element in *Singh* led the Court to give some nationals vis-à-vis their home State a "bonus" right that is in no way linked with the protection of their freedom of movement in another Member State' (citing then AG Poiares Maduro writing extra-judicially).

become such a common part of the Court's lexicon that it could be suggested that the citizen's formal creation was an inevitability.

4.4 The Citizen Is Born: Key References to the Citizen in the Immediate Build-up to Maastricht

Whilst it is clear that towards the end of the 1990s, references to the citizen had become recognized as a common and 'ordinary' part of the Court's everyday language, it is also clear that references were made to not just the citizen but to its soon-to-emerge form in a very specific, conceptually novel and inherently normative manner. In three key cases, *Commission* v. *France*, *Micheletti* and *Konstantinidis*, the citizen emerged as not merely a reflection of pre-existing economic rights but as a free-standing normative concept. In this respect, the role of two highly influential AGs – Mancini and Jacobs – played an important role in not simply pre-empting the soon-to-emerge amended Treaty but to specify the manner and form of such emergence. In *Commission* v. *France* (1986), AG Mancini, in clearly philosophical and normative overtones, states:

> The greatest danger of the action called for lies elsewhere: the danger of halting a process which, linked as it is to the aim of political unity which is being pursued by means of the integration of the European States and peoples, must be allowed to take its course with as few impediments as possible. It is indeed clear that in order to guarantee full freedom of movement it would be necessary to remove the obstacles deriving from the existence of different nationalities and to create a Community citizenship, which is no longer metaphorical, in the sense currently reflected by judgments of the court, but real.[181]

In the preamble to the Advocate-General's statement in relation to citizenship, he sets the citizenship project in its context. For AG Mancini, the emergence of the citizen has to herald a new era in the

Alina Tryfonidou, *Reverse discrimination in EC Law* (Alphen aan den Rijn: Kluwer Law International, 2009), pp. 99–100. See also Watson, 'One Way Ticket?', 68–77; Cullen, 77–82; Robin White, 'A Fresh Look at Reverse Discrimination?' (1993) 18(6) *European Law Review*, 527–532.

[181] Case 307/84, *Commission of the European Communities* v. *French Republic* [1986] ECR 1725, p. 1731, p. 1726 (facts). 'Cittadinanza' in the original Italian. 'Citoyenneté' in the French translation. In the case, France was being pursued by the Commission for making French nationality a requirement for being employed as a nurse in public hospitals. See further White, 'Round-up of Cases', 147–153.

'process' of European integration in which an explicit 'aim of political unity' is now conceivable. This political unity is manifested in the integration not of nationals of different Member States but 'peoples' more generally from European States as a whole.[182] This integration has its roots in the economic right to free movement but the development, in his mind, is towards the attainment of 'full' freedom of movement and this can only be achieved by 'removing obstacles deriving from the existence of different nationalities'. There remains an ambiguity as to the form envisaged by AG Mancini of the post-national nature of Community Citizenship.[183] On one interpretation of the above citation, his 'vision' of citizenship is monolithic in the sense that he could appear to be suggesting that the mere existence of particular nationalities is a barrier to closer integration and that it should be superseded by an all-encompassing identity construct.[184] It should also be noted that in this sense his assertions relate less to the legal nature of citizenship and more to the ideational effect it has on individual identities. However, on another level his vision could be seen to be more in line with many contemporary views of EU Citizenship in the sense that what is actually being proposed is a pluricultural overlapping identity in which one can identify with both national identities and a greater Community one.[185] This interpretation is also possible as AG Mancini's concern is not with national identities *per se* but the obstacles that can be derived from them. A pluricultural overlapping form of identity overcomes such obstacles through, in part, one not being seen as a 'threat' to the other but complementary to it. Such a statement by AG Mancini is inherently normative in the sense that what he is setting out is an almost utopian vision of how he envisaged a political and philosophical form of Community Citizenship *should* be. In perhaps an ironic twist to his vision is his view of the state of citizenship in the jurisprudence of the Court at the time. For AG Mancini, it is his utopian vision that is 'real' – a rather high standard to achieve – as the status of citizenship at the time in 1986 was mere metaphor with no 'real' existence. Arguably, AG Mancini was both right and wrong in making such a presumption. He was right in the sense that until such a grand statement had been

[182] See Section 5.4 for analysis of linkages made between citizenship and a unity of the peoples of Europe.

[183] See Section 5.4 for an analysis of postnational identity.

[184] See 'Introduction' for an outline of the relationship between the ideational (or ideology) and identity.

[185] See Section 5.4.4.

uttered there had been no attempt to even describe a future vision of the emergence of the Citizen in any other part of the Court's jurisprudence. It has already been outlined in this book that the citizen emerged indirectly through the development, for instance, of the concept of the worker that became increasingly divorced from its ordinary meaning that it began to appear more akin to citizenship. Moreover, many utterances of the citizen, whilst clearly loaded in their implications, have either been uttered (unwittingly) by some as a shorthand or synonym for the worker or the national of a Member State or the word has been deliberately used by various agents (such as the Commission) with a view to its inclusion in the ordinary language of the Court. However, in neither case was a vision actually set out for how the Citizen would fit into a wider project of political integration. In this respect, AG Mancini's utterances have a greater meaning than all previous utterances that could be dismissed as mere metaphor, rhetoric and 'puff'.[186]

Nonetheless, it is submitted that AG Mancini is wrong in making such an assumption as the basic assumption made in SC theory is that an individual is not prior to society; indeed he/she is continually immersed in it.[187] Thus, as has already been outlined, it is clear that the discursive cultural and structural context within which the Court and AG Mancini operated had radically changed such that it became acceptable for him to make such a far-reaching statement in 1986. In other words, he would not have felt that it was 'appropriate' to do so in 1964 in the early days of the Court's jurisprudence. Seen in this manner, mere rhetoric or metaphor plays an important role in the equally

[186] This is also not to ignore the fact that the person making the utterance was not only an Advocate-General (an important enough figure at the Court) but also a highly significant one. The role of the Advocate-General within the architecture of the Court is complex, undeniably significant and has been much commented on. See in particular Mortelmans' nuanced analysis of the influence that the AGs had on the Court on the early case law on the functioning of the internal market (which included free movement), Dashwood's excellent early analysis of the AG's role and Burrows and Greaves' comprehensive analysis of the AG's contribution to EC law more generally.

Kamiel Mortelmans, 'The Court under the influence of its Advocates General' (2005) 24(1) *Yearbook of European Law*, 130–131; Dashwood, 202–216; Burrows and Greaves, *Advocate-General*.

See also Kristen Borgsmidt, 'The Advocate General at the European Court of Justice: A Comparative Study' (1988) 13(2) *European Law Review*, 106–119; Marco Darmon, 'The Role of the Advocate General at the European Court of Justice' in Simon Shetreet (ed.), *The Role of Courts in Society* (Dordrecht: Martinus Nijhoff, 1988), pp. 425–436; L. Neville Brown and Tom Kennedy, *Brown and Jacobs: The Court of Justice of the European Communities* (5th edn, London: Sweet and Maxwell, 2000); Takis Tridimas, 'Role of AG', 1349–1387.

[187] See 'Introduction' on this concept.

linguistic development of European integration as much as the legal and political developments.[188] Therefore, a mere statement of a concept such as citizenship even if not intended to be anything other than a convenient shorthand or metaphor can collectively have the effect – depending upon the frequency of its utterance – of making something 'real'.[189] Thus, by the time of AG Mancini's grand statement (above) the Citizen had become real through its mere continual appearance on a page; what remained was the manner and form of its substantive appearance.[190]

Furthermore, where AG Mancini in *Commission* v. *France* differs from *Micheletti* and *Konstantinidis* is in its timing. In 1986, when AG Mancini made such a statement, the Single European Act was in the process of coming into force but the formal inclusion of citizenship into the Treaty in 1992 was some way off.[191] By contrast both *Micheletti* and *Konstantinidis* were decided explicitly under the shadow of the soon-to-come-into-force citizenship provisions of the Treaty which, in part, provided the manner and form of the soon-to-emerge EU, not Community, citizen. In *Micheletti*, the first reference is made in the Court reports by AG Tesauro to the amended and new Article 8 of the Treaty.[192] The case is not only significant in terms of such a reference but also in terms of the nature of the case brought before the court as it concerned not whether the applicant worked in any capacity (he clearly did, as he was a dentist) but whether his acquisition of Italian nationality through a historic and ancestral right, despite never having lived in Italy, should entitle him to practise as a dentist in Spain without being discriminated against on the grounds of nationality on the basis of being a Community citizen.[193] The conclusion of both the AG and the Court was a resounding yes to that question in that the simple point that Article 8 of the amended Treaty makes is that it is for the Member States to define whether an individual is or is not a national and should Italy, in this case, do just that, then the applicant should be entitled to derive protection under Community law.[194]

188 Ibid.

189 Ibid.

190 It should also be noted that, as has been outlined, the word frequently appears in the Italian version of the Court reports.

191 The opinion was delivered on 15 April 1986 under the shadow of the SEA which was signed in February 1986. The Act itself only came into force on 1 July 1987.

192 Case C-369/90, *Mario Vincente Micheletti and others* v. *Delegación del Govierno en Cantabria* [1992] ECR I 4239, p. 4254.

193 Ibid., pp. 4240–4241.

194 Ibid., p. 4254, p. 4262.

However, the issue itself was novel in the sense that something that is at the core of how the nation-state defines itself (through deciding who its own nationals are) is being openly discussed in the Court, which then sets the trend for a line of cases after the TEU then came into effect.[195] For this reason, the Spanish government in *Micheletti* took a dismissive approach to the soon-to-come-into-force citizenship provisions of the treaty by claiming that 'Community citizenship is still today an ambitious project' and that 'the impact of the Community provision on questions of nationality is very limited, indeed marginal'.[196] On a question of legal analysis the Spanish government is arguably correct that in their opinion the soon-to-come-into-force Article 8 of the Treaty would not affect the way in which a Member State determines its own nationals.[197] Seen in this manner, any reference to the citizen is, to coin AG Mancini's previous term, merely 'metaphorical' and of no substance. However, what the Spanish government was in effect suggesting was that the citizenship provisions of the Treaty were not merely limited in terms of allowing for any Community competence in defining Member State nationality but in terms of the citizenship project as a whole. Nonetheless, considerable discussion about citizenship creates an impetus for its eventual creation as a substantive legal right and, whilst the Spanish government was not alone in dismissing the potential impact of such provisions, their instrumental use by the Court in the post-*Sala* revolution proved the Spanish government to be decidedly wrong.[198]

[195] See, for instance, Case C-192/99, *The Queen* v. *Secretary of State for the Home Department, ex parte Manjit Kaur, intervener* [2001] ECR I 1237; Case C-138/02, *Brian Francis Collins* v. *Secretary of State for Work and Pensions* [2004] ECR I 2703; Case C-200/02, *Kunqian Catherine Zhu and Man Lavette Chen* v. *Secretary of State for the Home Department* [2004] ECR I 9925; Case C-135/08, *Janko Rottman* v. *Freistaat Bayern* [2008] ECR I 1449; Case C-434/09, *Shirley McCarthy* v. *Secretary of State for the Home Department* [2011] ECR I 3375; Case C-34/09, *Gerardo Ruiz Zambrano* v. *Office national de l'emploi (ONEm)* [2011] ECR I 1177. See further Hans Ulrich Jessurun D'Oliveira, 'Case C-369/90, *M. V. Micheletti and others* v. *Delegacion del Gobierno en Cantabria*, Judgment of 7 July 1992' (1993) 30 *Common Market Law Review* 623–637.

[196] *Micheletti*, pp. 4247–4248. ''Ciudadanía' in the Spanish and 'Citoyenneté' in the French versions of the case.

[197] This point was confirmed in *Kaur*, to the frustration of the applicant as, being from Kenya, he was only entitled to a British Overseas Passport which, to all intents and purposes, meant that in UK immigration law he did not count as a UK national, thereby not enabling him to also be an EU Citizen. Kaur, pp. 1267–1268. See also Shah, pp. 271–278; Hall, 'Determining the Scope', 355–360; Toner, 'Case C-192/99', 881–893.

[198] See Section 5.2.1 for an outline of other views that dismissed the citizenship provisions of the amended Treaty.

Furthermore, the view of the Spanish government in *Micheletti* stands at odds with that of AG Jacobs in *Konstantinidis* in what was the final and most significant statement on citizenship prior to the TEU coming into force. As with *Micheletti*, the issue was a novel one that would not have arisen in the course of an ordinary worker's case. The applicant, a Greek national, was a self-employed masseur and hydrotherapist in Germany and the German authorities forced his name to be transcribed as 'Hrestos Konstantinidis' in Roman character from its original Greek, even though this did not in any way reflect how it was supposed to be pronounced nor the wishes of the applicant to have the name transcribed as 'Christos'.[199] In this context, AG Jacobs states:

> In my opinion, a Community national who goes to another Member State as a worker or self-employed person under Articles 48, 52 or 59 of the Treaty is entitled not just to pursue his trade or profession and to enjoy the same living and working conditions as nationals of the host State; he is in addition entitled to assume that, wherever he goes to earn his living in the European Community, he will be treated in accordance with a common code of fundamental values, in particular those laid down in the European Convention on Human Rights. In other words, he is entitled to say 'civis europeus sum' and to invoke that status in order to oppose any violation of his fundamental rights.[200]

This clearly significant statement by AG Jacobs rebuts the 'minimalist' approach taken by the Spanish government in a number of ways.[201] What is immediately noticeable is that he uses the phrase 'Community national', that is, the orthodox phrase; but what is also evident is that there is also an entitlement to say '*civis europeus sum*' which, by his own words is 'an addition' to being simply a Community national. In other words, it is not merely a synonym for the Community national: it can be seen as a substantive development from it. What is also clear is that the substance of AG Jacobs' vision for citizenship is of adherence to a common set of values rooted in fundamental rights and the Convention. In this respect, the development in the jurisprudence on fundamental rights

[199] Case C-168/91, *Konstantinidis* v. *Stadt Altensteig* [1993] ECR I 1191, p. 1198.

[200] Ibid., p. 1211.

[201] Indeed, it has been widely commented on. Courthaut, for instance, sees the statement as part of Union folklore when he claims that one 'does not need a constitution to proclaim with Advocate General Jacobs "civis europeus sum" or to observe Europe Day on 9 May'. Significantly 'civis europeus sum' is stated verbatim in all translation of the opinion (including Greek). Tim Courthaut, 'Plus ça change, plus c'est la même chose? A Comparison with the Constitutional Treaty' (2008) 15(1) *Maastricht Journal of European and Comparative Law*, 21–34 at 24; *Konstantinidis*, p. 1212. See also O'Neill, 168–170; Lawson, 395–412; Haltern, 'The Dawn of the Political', 585–614.

dovetails with that of citizenship and can explicitly be seen to be one of its origins. Moreover, AG Jacobs' vision is also rooted in an identity construct as a Community national would be 'entitled to say' and feel that 'I am a European citizen'.[202] Seen in this manner what was particularly noticeable about AG Jacobs' opinion is the manner in which the applicant was humanized within the text. AG Jacobs firstly reiterates the applicant's view that being forced to spell his name 'Hrestos' is 'intensely distasteful … and does not convey an accurate impression of the way that his name is pronounced in the Greek'.[203] In other words, what is important in this case is not merely whether he is a worker or not but goes much deeper than that to his very essence. Moreover, AG Jacob's clearly expressed sympathy towards the applicant who was a litigant in person that 'presented with simple eloquence and brevity' and reiterated his views that what was being proposed in terms of the spelling of his name was 'an insulting, unpronounceable parody of his name, which was offensive to his religious sentiments'.[204] On one reading of AG Jacobs' vision of the citizen, as an addition to (and development from) the Community national, is an emphasis on going beyond seeing an individual within the Community as being merely entitled to a series of economic free movement rights but seeing the individual as a human being, first and foremost.[205] In this respect, AG Jacobs further claims, in a statement that can be seen as significant as his prior '*civis europeus sum*' statement:

> Community law does not regard the migrant worker (or the self-employed migrant) purely as an economic agent and a factor of production entitled to the same salary and working conditions as nationals of the host State; it regards him as a human being who is entitled to live in that State 'in freedom and dignity' (see the fifth recital in the preamble to Regulation No 1612/68 on freedom of movement for workers within the Community; OJ, English Special Edition, 1968 (II), p. 475) and to be spared any difference in treatment that would render his life less comfortable, physically or psychologically, than the lives of the native population.[206]

The above assertion summarizes, in essence, thirty years of jurisprudential development. Putting it differently, it is maintained that such an overt humanizing claim would not have been possible within the linguistic frame of reference during the early years of the Court's

[202] See 'Introduction' for an outline of the relationship between discourse and identity.
[203] *Konstantinidis*, p. 1199.
[204] Ibid., p. 1202.
[205] See Section 5.2.4.
[206] *Konstantinidis*, p. 1205.

jurisprudence. It took, instead, an incremental evolution over decades to get to the point where an individual was emphasized in his/her entirety and this, in AG Jacobs' view, is his normative vision of what the EU Citizen should then become.[207] Finally, this process of humanizing within the text focuses on the nature of identity and, therefore, implicitly the interrelationship between citizenship and identity.[208] After having examined various constitutional provisions of different nation-states, he then concludes that there is 'a principle according to which the State must respect not only the physical well-being of the individual but also his dignity, moral integrity and sense of personal identity' and then continues:

> A person's right to his name is fundamental in every sense of the word. After all, what are we without our name? It is our name that distinguishes each of us from the rest of humanity. It is our name that gives us a sense of identity, dignity and self-esteem. To strip a person of his rightful name is the ultimate degradation.[209]

These powerful and almost poetic pronouncements by AG Jacobs form the context behind his now famous utterance '*civis europeus sum*' and seen collectively convey a discursive 'snapshot' of a watershed moment in the history of the Court's jurisprudence.[210] There remain certain caveats behind this watershed moment in that the utterances by AG Jacobs were iterative in the sense they were reflective of cultural and structural jurisprudential development but, at the same time, were also normative in that they were expressing a hope by AG Jacobs as to the potential for the development of the EU Citizen. Putting it differently, AG Jacobs' remarks were both subjective utterances and reflective statements. In reflective terms, his illuminating opinion marks the end of an era of exponential expansion of 'Citizen-speak' in both quantitative and qualitative terms. In quantitative terms every utterance of the Citizen has been examined since the early days of the Court's jurisprudence and it has been maintained that its use increased during the mid-part of the 1980s to the point where it became a common part of the court's lexicon. However, in qualitative terms, AG Jacobs' opinion in *Konstantinidis* marks a point of transition from any suggestion that 'citizen-speak' was simply a meaningless synonym for clearly defined words such as the worker or Community national, to an increasing

[207] See 'Introduction' for an outline of the relationship between discourse and identity.
[208] Ibid.
[209] *Konstantinidis*, p. 1209.
[210] See 'Introduction' on discursive snapshots.

realization that EU Citizenship had the potential to develop into a substantive and distinct concept in which additional rights, as well as a sense of meaning and belonging, could be attached.[211] Thus, what such utterances in the late 1980s culminating in AG Jacobs' opinion in *Konstantinidis* serve to do is to not only add further impetus to the legislative inclusion of the Citizen in the Treaty at Maastricht but also to create an understanding of the citizen that is filled with meaning beyond the text of the amended Treaty that could, then, provide the cultural and discursive backdrop for the later '*Sala* Revolution'.

4.5 Conclusion

This Chapter essentially commenced on the basis of no references to citizenship at all and ended with '*civis europeus sum*'. What this Chapter has sought to do is to 'plot' the chart between these two points and to do so on the basis of examining mere utterances of citizenship alone. The analysis has been quantitative in terms of examining utterances of the word throughout thirty years of jurisprudence but it has also been qualitative and dialectical. In qualitative terms, the context of a number of utterances has been examined, particularly focusing on the timing of such utterances and the agent making the utterance.[212] In dialectical terms, this chapter has sought to outline the changing nature of normative acceptability from within the case law such that subjective utterance is followed by socio-cultural change which, in turn, is followed by more radical subjective utterances several years later. In addition, there is value in undertaking such an exercise in that there has been no previous attempt made to examine the use of the word 'citizen' in the early free movement case law because it was essentially the 'label' which attached, in the end, to individuals deriving protection based on free movement of persons law. This point is particularly well illustrated by virtue of this chapter's 'starting point' in that, by simply examining primary and secondary legislation prior to 1992 on free movement, citizenship did not exist.[213] Nonetheless, it is clear that the word *was* used and instead of dismissing such an utterance as, perhaps, a legally irrelevant choice of words, it has been claimed that

[211] This potential, in substantive terms, is examined in Section 5.4.

[212] Or, at least, the actor to whom the utterance is attributed from within the text of the judgment.

[213] Indeed, as has already been outlined, Community Citizenship never formally existed even after 1992. See also Section 5.2.1.

each utterance is of significance in different ways. In the opening part of this chapter, after having examined a number of 'others' to the citizen, a period of tentative references to citizenship in the 1970s, often done in 'bursts' over several cases, was examined. It was suggested that, whilst a number of such utterances were used as a synonym for phrases such as a 'Community national', their utterance, in the English language, was not without significance in that mere utterance itself has rhetorical effect. In the second part of this chapter, it was submitted that the 1980s constituted a fundamental transitory phase for the citizen because, firstly, utterances were more prolific and, secondly, the phrase was being used in circumstances of either significance (such as in *Levin*) or controversy (such as in *Singh*), often both. It has also been maintained that an understanding of citizenship had been implicitly outlined that was more than simply a synonym in that a number of the cases in which citizenship was uttered also related to the issue of reverse discrimination. In the final part of this chapter, a detailed and nuanced analysis of three key cases took place (more specifically the opinions of the AGs in them): *Commission* v. *France*, *Micheletti* and *Konstantinidis*. In particular, it has been suggested that AG Mancini in *Commission* v. *France* and AG Jacobs in *Konstantinidis*, in addition to uttering the citizen, did so in an inherently subjective manner by outlining a 'vision' of citizenship that had a profound impact. Nonetheless, it has also been argued that such a vision would not have been possible had the context within which the visions were uttered not changed. It has been submitted that, in addition to developments towards citizenship that have been (and will be) examined in other parts of this book, a partial contribution to such a changing context was made by utterances of the citizen with the case law prior to such 'grand' statements being made.[214]

Thus, using SC methodology, an entirely differently light has been shed on the case law that did not technically even concern citizenship.

[214] It should also be noted that, whilst beyond the scope of this chapter because the focus of it has been on utterances in the English language, a parallel language game in a number of different languages has also been examined. Whilst at times utterances of the citizen have roughly translated into the 'citizen' in French and other languages, at times, also, a reticence in uttering 'le citoyen' has also been noticeable. This stands in sharp contrast with utterances in English and Italian in particular, where citizenship was liberally stated. Nonetheless, as has also been outlined, towards the end of the 1980s, there appears to have been a 'reverse' effect of such utterances back into the French language as citizenship was, finally, more consistently stated in the French version of the Court reports.

However, such a light has arguably revealed further fissures within the edifice that is free movement of persons case law paradoxically at the same time as consolidating it. This book has outlined a structure of EU Citizenship law based partly in the vision outlined by the Treaty makers themselves of an edifice of a Greek Temple and has suggested that the roof of it constitutes contemporary citizenship and that this book has attempted to examine both the foundations of such a structure and two core pillars upon which the roof was placed. This second pillar has fissures within it that differ somewhat from that of Equal Treatment. Examining actual utterances of citizenship within the case law prior to citizenship technically existing reveals a crescendo ultimately culminating in the famous statement by AG Jacobs in *Konstantinidis*. Arguably the label 'citizen' was a convenient one upon which to describe all individuals who could derive protection based upon the various strands of law which have been outlined in the first two chapters. Nonetheless, a convenient 'label' could also potentially constitute a loaded one in the sense that it thus infers in the mind of the reader all of the problems inherent in the case law, as will be particularly exposed in Chapter 5. Seen in this manner, uttering citizenship frequently within the case law looks less like the noble achievement of lofty ambitions leading up to *Konstantinidis* itself and the eventual legal creation of EU Citizenship and more like an inappropriately small plaster over a gaping wound.

Part III

Could the Roof of the Temple Cave in?

5 Genealogy and the Potential for Dismantling EU Citizenship?

5.1 Introduction

This book has attempted to, in effect, go right back to where it all began and examine the case law on free movement in a genealogical sense to expose fissures: latent defects in the project that appear to have come to light fifty years later. Prior to Brexit, such latent defects were never even thought of as such, with the emphasis being, if anything, upon closer integration at all costs. Chapters 1 and 2 outlined a specific way in which the worker was outlined in a (then) Community context, leading to a further set of legal developments in how to conceptualize and legally protect those that did not count as workers. Chapters 3 and 4 then attempted something different by outlining the discursive infrastructure to solidify the construction of citizenship as understood today. These were all fundamental building blocks to the extent that today the evolution towards citizenship is almost unquestionable. This chapter will attempt to outline perhaps the greatest fissure of all within the early cases: a seam that perhaps runs straight through the very purpose of citizenship that arguably, if not tended to, could lead to its eventual dismantling. At the heart of this chapter are the concepts of solidarity and the inherent impossibility, perhaps, of postnational identification. The point here is not contemporary, but genealogical: that the problems were apparent from the outset and almost entirely overlooked as the pace of further integration (on a structural and elite level at least) increased exponentially. The first two parts of the chapter will outline two fissures that are inherent to the concept of EU Citizenship as understood today but with problems that can be traced back to the very infancy of the case law. The first fissure that will be outlined is that of solidarity. It will be argued that a concept which is so contested within contemporary understandings of EU Citizenship in actual fact has been contested for over thirty years and never meaningfully resolved. It will be suggested that the radicalism of the Court in cases such as *Gravier* in particular came at a significant cost because the Member States did not appear to be actively listened to and individuals were able to derive protection and at times significant financial benefits from host states without appearing to fulfil even the *de minimis* expectations of the market citizen. In addition, the case law appears to, ironically, both question whether postnational citizenship is attainable given how powerful national identity construction appears by comparison (and very visibly so in the case law) or even normatively desirable given the toxic legacy upon which the concept 'Europe' could be harnessed, particularly during an era of populism. The chapter then ends somewhat constructively by claiming, based on personal narratives within the early case law, that a new truly social form of citizenship needs to emerge partly based on the lived experiences of the millions of citizens who have quietly gone about their business of moving, have made subtle and important contributions to their host state and who, for the most part, do not need to litigate as a result.

5.2 The Fissure of Solidarity

The concept of solidarity remains core to contemporary understandings of EU Citizenship and is controversial. The traditional narrative on the concept sees it in the context of conceptualizing citizenship in the later post '*Sala* Revolution' cases and is at least seen to have been born in the seminal *Grzelczyk* case in 1999.[1] In the case, a French student in his fourth year studying in Belgium was denied a minimum subsistence allowance, the *minimex*, simply because he was not Belgian.[2] For the Court, this was not only an infringement of Article 12 but also constituted a 'social advantage' within the meaning of Regulation No. 1612/

[1] Jacqueson, 'Union Citizenship and the Court of Justice', 264. As Barnard put it: 'the principle … increasingly crept into the lexicon of the Court … [and was] used … to establish the parameters of Union Citizenship'. Catherine Barnard, 'EU Citizenship and the Principle of Solidarity' in Michael Dougan and Eleanor Spaventa (eds.), *Social Welfare and EU Law* (Oxford: Hart, 2005), pp. 157–180 at 157–158.

[2] Case C-184/99, *Rudy Grzelczyk* v. *Centre public d'aide sociale d'Ottignies-Louvain-la-Neuve* [2001] ECR I 6193, pp. 6236–6242 at paras. 10–12 and para. 29.

68.[3] The Court encountered, though, two additional problems. First, the specific wording of Directive 93/96 on student residence appeared to prohibit the claimant from claiming such a benefit.[4] A student was allowed to lawfully reside in another Member State without being economically active so long as he/she declared that he/she was able to live on his/her own resources during his/her time of study and therefore not be a burden on the state.[5] For the first three years of his course, this is exactly what the claimant did; it was only in his final year that he proved unable to do so.[6] The Court got around this problem by fudging the issue.[7] It stated that, in the interest of 'financial solidarity' amongst Europeans, what this Directive meant was that the claimant was only required to state that in his belief he would be self-sufficient - a merely paper declaration - the fact that he turned out not to be so was irrelevant *so long as* the claimant was not an '*unreasonable* burden' on the Member State.[8]

In the process, two core and interconnected tenets of the concept of solidarity arose in the case that will be of equal relevance to much of the pre-Maastricht jurisprudence which will be examined in turn. First, a Union-specific understanding of solidarity was articulated in the case; in fact, a multiple layered and rather complicated one.[9] The issue of

[3] Ibid., p. 6241 at para. 27.

[4] Ibid., p. 6244 at para. 39.

[5] Ibid., para. 38.

[6] Ibid., para. 11.

[7] Maas, *Creating European Citizens*, p. 65. Likewise, for de Waele, the case 'fudged the matter at stake' was full of 'hazy reasoning' and 'relied on a nebulous and noncommittal extract from the preamble to Directive 93/96'. Henri De Waele, 'EU Citizenship: Revisiting its Meaning, Place and Potential' (2010) 12(3) *European Journal of Migration and Law*, 319–336 at 324. See also White, *Workers, Establishment and Services*, pp. 134–135; Stephen Weatherill, 'Activism and Restraint in the European Court of Justice' in Patrick Capps, Malcolm Evans and Stratos Konstadinidis (eds.), *Asserting Jurisdiction: International and European Legal Perspectives* (Oxford: Hart, 2003), p. 490; Dora Kostakopoulou, 'European Union Citizenship: Writing the Future' (2007) 13(5) *European Law Journal*, 623–646 at 636–637; Barnard, *Four Freedoms*, pp. 444–445; Stefano Giubboni, 'Free Movement of Persons and European Solidarity' (2007) 13(3) *European Law Journal*, 360–379 at 369.

[8] *Grzelczyk*, pp. 6244–6245 at paras. 40–44.

[9] As Guibboni asserts: 'The solidarity model which emerged from this case law - and which is serving to legitimize cross border access to social and welfare rights for European citizens who are *economically inactive* - is indeed broader and more inclusive than, and in that sense qualitatively different from, that presumed by Article 39 EC. What is emerging, in effect, is a different solidarity paradigm, centered on the future of the citizen *as such*, which is increasingly general and universalistic and so not 'category-based' in that it is not governed by the individual's functional position in the trans-national production process or his economic roles in the common market.' Likewise, Dougan and Spaventa state: 'the introduction of Union citizenship shifts the focus away

solidarity also illustrates another aspect of EU Citizenship that necessitates critical reflection as it demonstrates the essentially contested, quite specific and distinct origins of EU Citizenship traced from the 'embryonic' market citizen to the emerging case law on EU Citizenship. Second, there has been a continual dilemma within the Court's jurisprudence from the outset in relation to what Community nationals that can be classified as a burden can expect to benefit from in terms of Community law.[10] In the aftermath of the line of cases dealing with the concept of solidarity precipitated by *Grzelczyk*, Somek famously and critically questioned whether the concept had 'decomposed'.[11] However, the fissure in relation to this issue occurred arguably much earlier than this period and is, thus, much deeper and inherently problematic than perhaps previously thought of in terms of the standard narrative on the evolution towards citizenship.

5.2.1 *What is the European Citizen or What Ought It to Be?*

A fundamental question prior to examining the role of solidarity in the early case law of the Court is one of definitions. In other words, what is or ought the European Citizen to be by contrast with other citizenship models? In general, citizenship is a concept that is complex[12] and, as has been repeatedly emphasized, is 'essentially

from a purely market-orientated notion of belonging, whereby entitlement to benefits is as a direct result of the economic output produced by the frontier worker, towards a broader notion of inclusion, whereby entitlement to benefits is recognized also for those whose claim to membership of the solidaristic community can be established through non-economic links'. What both citations have in common is a context-specific understanding or 'vision' of citizenship emerging in the case law of the Court that cannot be found in discourses on citizenship elsewhere.

Giubboni, 368; Michael Dougan and Eleanor Spaventa, '"Wish You Weren't Here . . . ": New Social Models of Social Solidarity in the European Union' in Michael Dougan and Eleanor Spaventa (eds.), *Social Welfare and EU Law* (Oxford: Hart, 2005), pp. 181–219 at p. 208. See also Barnard, *Four Freedoms*, p. 477; Gerard Delanty, 'European Citizenship: A Critical Assessment' (2007) 11(1) *Citizenship Studies*, 63–72 at 69.

10 White, *Workers, Establishment and Services*, p. 125. This debate took place within Court judgments, academic commentary and in the political arena beyond the courtroom resulting, for instance, partially in the 1990 residency directives, all of which placed an emphasis on not being burden on the host state (White). Similarly, the consequence of the Court's radical case law on non-economic actors post-*Sala* also resulted, in part, in the later Citizenship Directive which also adopted a non-burden criterion (Article 1(a)–(b)) (Barnard). Barnard, *Four Freedoms*, p. 265.

11 Somek, 'Solidarity Decomposed', p. 787.

12 As Douglas-Scott put it, it is 'far from a "simple idea", but rather a phenomenon to be perceived by process of induction from a myriad of empirical sources'. Douglas-Scott, *Constitutional Law of the European Union*, p. 479.

contested'.[13] Citizenship denotes a legal relationship between an individual and the state as well as a sociopolitical relationship between an individual and a national community. In other words, citizenship is both a legal concept and a continually evolving identity practice.[14] As will become evident elsewhere in this chapter, whilst EU Citizenship, by definition, does not involve a relationship between a state and an individual (instead a supranational entity), identity is still considered to be a core part of the EU Citizenship project (or at least attempts to engender it).[15] However, discussions of solidarity inevitably involve a hybrid analysis, if anything, between what could be conceived of a Roman and Athenian model. Put simply, citizenship can either be understood as conferring a status, involving rights and entitlements, or a more Athenian

[13] For Siim and Squires: 'Citizenship is a contested concept that is at the centre of policy debates within and across national borders ... [and] has different meanings ... The definition includes three different dimensions: (1) individual rights and obligations, (2) political participation including the right to vote, (3) belongings to nation states. Recently scholars included a fourth trans-national dimension'. Birte Siim and Judith Squires, 'Contesting Citizenship: Comparative Analyses' in Birte Siim and Judith Squires (eds.), *Contesting Citizenship* (London: Routledge, 2008), pp. 1–14 p. 2. Similarly, Sommers describes citizenship as a 'contested truth' in Margaret Sommers, 'Rights, Relationality and Membership: Rethinking the Making and Meaning of Citizenship', *Law and Social Inquiry (Journal of the American Bar Foundation)* (1994) 19(1) 63–112, p. 64.
See also Everson, 'The Legacy of the Market Citizen', p. 82 and Yasemin Nuhoğlu Soysal, *Limits of Citizenship: Migrants and Postnational Membership in Europe* (Chicago: Chicago University Press, 1994).

[14] As Lister maintains: 'One of the recurring themes of the literature is that citizenship is "an essentially contested concept". It is contested at every level from its very meaning to its political application, with implications for the kind of society to which we aspire ... At its lowest common denominator, we are talking about membership of a community ... and about the relationship between individuals and the state and between individuals citizens within that community'. For Delanty: 'Citizenship as membership of a political community involves a set of relationships between rights, duties, participation and identity. These may be termed the components of citizenship'. Ruth Lister, *Citizenship: Feminist Perspectives* (Basingstoke: Macmillan, 1997), p. 3; Gerard Delanty, *Citizenship in a Global Age – Society, Culture, Politics* (Buckingham: Open University Press, 2000), p. 10.

[15] As has been stated earlier, the wording was 'attempts to engender' and not necessarily indicative of success. This is what Shaw terms the 'idiosyncrasies of EU Citizenship' where she states: 'EU citizenship involves looking at the classic elements commonly associated with modelling citizenship as a form of full membership (e.g. status, rights, identity, duties). It is only in the sphere of rights that EU citizenship seems well developed. As to the issue of identity, the sense of "Europeanness" that exists across the collectivity of citizens is relatively thin in nature, again focused on rights, and it is hardly comparable with the form of societal glue that gives community cohesion to the national (and subnational) polities on which the EU is built.' Shaw, *EU Citizenship – Still a Fundamental Status*, p. 4.

concept involving active engagement.[16] However, this is where a divergence is evident between even a Roman concept of citizenship and contemporary EU Citizenship as the former, whilst a passive concept by comparison with the Athenian model, still necessitates a citizen fulfilling duties.[17] It is for this reason that the newly amended Article 8a of the Treaty at Maastricht alluded, to much derision, to duties as well as rights.[18] As will be outlined, it is not

[16] For Yuval Davies, a Roman tradition of citizenship can be understood in a legal sense and is rooted in the entitlement and rights that can be derived from having the mere status of citizenship. Whilst duties are also an aspect of the Roman tradition, it is a more passive concept than its Greek counterpart.

It should be noted that a distinction is made between the two traditions in order to illustrate citizenship as both a passive and active concept in the case law. This is not to suggest that there is either a simple distinction that can be made between a Greek and a Roman understanding of citizenship or that both traditions have 'active' and 'passive' elements.

Nonetheless, in its ancient Athenian form, as Lister maintains: 'Citizenship as obligation has its roots in the more ancient civic republican tradition of classical Greece in which political participation as civic duty and the expression of the citizen's full potential as a political being represented the essence of citizenship as articulated by Aristotle in particular'. This contrasts distinctly with the Roman tradition based upon status and rights.

Nira Yuval-Davies, 'Intersectionality, Citizenship and Contemporary Politics of Belonging' in Birte Siim and Judith Squires (eds.), *Contesting Citizenship* (London: Routledge, 2008), pp. 159–172, p. 160. Ruth Lister, *Citizenship: Feminist Perspectives*, p. 14.

[17] Seen holistically, citizenship expresses 'solidarity with the State as well as the reciprocity of rights and duties which are the foundation of the nationality link'. Similarly, Marshall's understanding of citizenship was that it was 'based upon principles of freedom, equality and solidarity' which includes being subject to the 'same rights and duties'. Carlos Closa, 'Citizenship of the Union and Nationality of the Member States' (1995) 32 *Common Market Law Review*, 487–518 at 506; Thomas H. Marshall, *Citizenship and social class* (Cambridge: Cambridge University Press, 1950), p. 43.

[18] As Shore contends: 'What exactly the *duties* are, Article 8 does not say, nor is there any indication in what direction the provisions may be leading – a point that has prompted criticism that governments of Europe have effectively signed a blank cheque for their citizens. The EU concept of citizenship focuses exclusively on rights without outlining a set of corresponding duties'. This seemingly hollow reference to duties in the then Article 8a also partially led to repeated criticism of the formal creation of EU Citizenship at Maastricht more generally. For instance, Guild derides the legislative provisions for being 'just some fancy words on a piece of paper', Jessurun d'Oliveira termed it 'nearly exclusively a symbolic plaything without substantive content' and Kostakopoulou summarized much of the commentary at the time of the formal creation of EU Citizenship as describing it as 'pie in the sky' and a 'purely decorative and symbolic institution'. Shore, pp. 75–77; Elspeth Guild, 'The Legal Framework of Citizenship of the European Union' in David Cesarini and Mary Fulbrook (eds.), *Citizenship, Nationality and Migration in Europe* (London: Routledge, 1996), pp. 30–56 at p. 30; Jessurun D'Oliveira, 'European Citizenship: Its Meaning', p. 149; Kostakopoulou, 'European Union Citizenship', 625.

evident that many of the embryonic citizens in the pre-1992 cases fulfilled any such duties and this controversy continued into (and arguably was exacerbated by) the later cases on EU Citizenship. Thus, early references, be they overt or implicit, to this contemporary debate in EU law, are highly relevant to understanding the evolution of EU Citizenship. As Barnard put it in terms of the later cases:

> The Union gives rights but – despite the wording of Article 20 (2) – demands little by way of duties from its citizens (e.g., to pay taxes, to participate in the defence of the country, to obey the law, to vote, willingness to work). These duties are owed to the Member States and thus it is the Member States which bear the burden – using taxpayers' money – of the rights.[19]

Thus, from the outset, by contrast with national models, the concept of solidarity involves the relationship between two states and an individual, not one, and was thus skewed in a manner which, as will be outlined, created a seemingly unavoidable dissonance.[20]

5.2.2 *Solidarity within the Early Case Law*

In *Grzelczyk*, one issue that arose was who is supposed to be exercising solidarity and to whom? The Court answered this question by stating that it is 'between nationals of a host Member State and nationals of other Member States'.[21] On one reading of this, what the Court is in effect suggesting is that home nationals will simply have to accept the fact that in certain circumstances an individual from another Member State that neither works nor resides as a worker in the host state will be entitled to derive a benefit that ordinarily they would not have been entitled to absent of being either being a home national or

See also Joseph Weiler, *The Constitution of Europe: 'Do the new clothes have an emperor?' and other essays on European integration* (Cambridge: Cambridge University Press, 1999), p. 324; Ulrike Liebert, 'The European Citizenship Paradox: Renegotiating Equality and Diversity in Europe' in Birte Siim and Judith Squires (eds.), *Contesting Citizenship* (London: Routledge, 2008), pp. 15–40 at p. 19; Hans Ulrich Jessurun d'Oliveira, 'Pie in the Sky', pp. 58–84; Tony Downes, 'Market Citizenship: Functionalism and Fig-Leaves' in Richard Bellamy and Alex Warleigh (eds.), *Citizenship and Governance in the European Union* (London: Continuum, 2001), pp. 93–107 at p. 93.

19 Barnard, *Four Freedoms*, p. 422.

20 Indeed, Vlad Perju arguably goes further in outlining an interpretation of Habermas' double sovereignty thesis in which it is suggested that asymmetry of the EU's origins, with a market emphasis, ensures that it does not (and arguably cannot) have a real concept of social solidarity. In other words, regardless of what the Court might say on the matter. Vlad Perju, 'The asymmetries of *pouvoir constituent mixte*' (2019) 25 *European Law Journal*, 515–520 at 518–519.

21 *Grzelczyk*, p. 6245 at para. 44.

a worker.[22] The reason why such home nationals should have to accept such a degree of solidarity was not elaborated by the Court in the case, nor whether it was really the home nationals that were supposed to display such solidarity or the Member States themselves. More specifically, could it be that the Court was suggesting that the *quid pro quo* of a citizen of one Member State going to study in another and being entitled to a benefit such as the *minimex* is that the same principle applies the other way around? Seen in this manner, solidarity could be understood as implying that the net loss of this particular benefit to the host state of an individual who has not actually contributed towards its finance in the form of taxation is a net gain elsewhere whenever, say, a Belgian national decides to study abroad and derive a similar type of benefit. Thus, it could therefore also be suggested that the Court's intended message was not to the ordinary citizen of the host state but to the Member States themselves in that, on this occasion, the Belgian social security authorities would have to shoulder the financial burden of paying out the *minimex* to the claimant for both the greater good of European integration and the potential for such a burden to be offset by Belgian nationals studying elsewhere.[23] As will be elaborated upon later, the extent of this solidarity, whether expressed as 'solidarity' or not, is controversial.

Prior to 1992, the Court's jurisprudence did not contain prolific overt references to the word 'solidarity'; though those that were made were significant. One early reference in *Biason* outlined a form of solidarity that took form several years later in the '*Sala* revolution' when AG Reischl states:

> Benefits which … retain 'need' as the essential criterion for their application, and are thus a form of social assistance, [show] that in fact these systems are the expression of a form of solidarity within the national community, a solidarity such that one is bound to ask whether it must extend to members, whether

[22] See n. 9.

[23] Barnard, for instance, explores the meaning of the principle of solidarity. Having defined solidarity as being a relationship of 'mutual dependence' which, in terms of citizenship, tends to mean a solidarity as expressed between peoples. However, in an EU context, it also has an additional layer of meaning; namely solidarity between the Member States, and this type of mutuality can be evidenced in cooperative legislation such as Regulation No.1101/89 dealing with overcapacity in the inland waterways sector and meaning something that was beneficial to the Union as a whole even if a particular piece of legislation appears to impact upon one Member State more than another. Barnard, 'Principle of Solidarity', p. 158.

nationals or not, who by reason of having established their residence in another country, are no longer part of that community?[24]

On an individual level this encapsulates the principle of solidarity as understood in a national context with application to the Community as a whole. The point being made by AG Reischl is that social assistance (thereby deliberately distinguished from social security), because it is based upon the need of a (usually impoverished) individual, is an expression of national solidarity. Putting it differently, it is the legislative expression of a moral form of collective consciousness in which a national community normatively should contribute financially to the disadvantaged in society as a form of equally collective burden sharing.[25] Whilst the case itself posed the question whether an individual who leaves a particular national community should be entitled to export such a benefit to another Member State, the logical corollary of AG Reischl's statement is that those 'whether nationals or not', that reside in a Member State of which they are not a national, should be entitled to have the same kind of solidarity expressed towards them. Thus what *Biason* is particularly illustrative of is how a subjective assertion, made decades prior to *Grzelczyk*, still explored an aspect of a contemporary understanding of EU Citizenship.

Moreover, in *Hurd* v. *Jones*, the applicant attempted to circumvent the wholly internal situations rule by arguing for a principle of 'Community solidarity'.[26] The applicant, a UK national, was the headmaster of the European School in Oxfordshire and claimed to be exempt from tax for the 'European supplement' he received and other allowances in addition to his UK salary.[27] Had he been a national of any other Member State, he would have been entitled to the exemption. The applicant attempted to 'circumvent' the wholly internal situation rule by claiming that to prevent him from obtaining such an exemption would be contrary to the 'principle of equality applicable to Community

[24] Case 24/74, *Caisse régionale d'assurance maladie de Paris* v. *Giuseppina Biason* [1974] ECR 999, p. 1005 (AG Reischl), p. 1004 (facts). The case concerned an Italian national that was precluded access to an invalidity pension in France on the grounds of nationality.

[25] Liebert, p. 30. It should be noted that O'Brien is critical of the meaningful possibility of achieving the aims of 'social justice' on a Europe basis with the legal regime as it currently exists: 'Whereas EU welfare law is about coordinating/permitting integration into national welfare regimes to promote free movement, those national welfare regimes are deeply intertwined with social justice objectives.' O'Brien, *Unity in Adversity*, p. 12.

[26] Case 44/84, *Derrick Guy Edmund Hurd* v. *Kenneth Jones (Her Majesty's Inspector of Taxes)* [1986] ECR 29, p. 384 at para. 44.

[27] Ibid.

employees'.[28] In other words, all Community workers should be treated alike in relation to this exemption. Another strand of argument, though, made by the applicant was that there was a principle of 'Community solidarity' and the non-application of this exemption was in breach of it.[29] This is then elaborated upon as a summary of the applicant's submissions by the Court when it states 'the refusal to accord the exemption is contrary to the principle of Community solidarity, which is an independent and fundamental principle of Community law'.[30] Here the object of solidarity is different from that being implicitly suggested in *Grzelczyk* in that the situation of the applicant was the opposite of that in *Grzelczyk* as he was a home national being in effect penalized for being such by his own state.[31] In *Grzelczyk*, the solidarity being expressed was, in part, directed in favour of the applicant against the Belgian social security authorities involving shouldering the burden of a payment made by the said authorities to the applicant from another Member State. By contrast, the applicant in *Hurd* was being forced to pay the (then) Inland Revenue in the UK more than he would have done had he been a national of any other Member State. The net loss was therefore the applicant's and not the Member State's. Therefore, the argument being made by the applicant in *Hurd* was that the applicant should be treated in the same manner as all other Community nationals and that this is an expression of solidarity towards him from other Community workers.

Comparing and contrasting *Biason* with *Hurd*, several points are clear. First, whilst neither replicates the facts of *Grzelczyk*, they both constitute a discussion of what then became a fundamental issue in the context of Citizenship law of the Union. Indeed, the facts and executor of a duty of solidarity were different in the three cases. In *Grzelczyk*, the applicant was from another Member State and was applying for social assistance explicitly not on the basis of being a 'worker'. In *Biason*, the applicant was a home national attempting to export social assistance to another Member State where he was residing and, finally, in *Hurd*, the applicant was a home national being refused a tax exemption by his own state that would ordinarily have applied had he been a national of another Member State. As has already been outlined earlier, therefore, the duty of solidarity is

[28] Ibid., paras. 43–44.
[29] Ibid.
[30] Ibid., p. 391 at para. 61.
[31] See also L. Neville Brown, 'Case 44/84, Hurd v. Jones (Inspector of Taxes)' (1986) 23 *Common Market Law Review* 895–907 at 901–907 (note).

owed by different parties. What is of particular significance, though, is the chronological difference between the two cases. *Biason* was a relatively early case in the Court's jurisprudence (in 1974); whereas *Hurd* was a 1986 case and, importantly, a case in which the then Francis Jacobs QC was the primary instigator of the principle of solidarity as he was counsel for the applicant. *Hurd* can then, from a discursive perspective, be seen to tie in more closely with the emergence of citizenship in the Treaty not only because it was AG Jacobs himself who made the '*civis europeus sum*' statement but also because the link is also made in the case with the principle of equality, another core aspect of the later citizen (see Chapter 3).[32] Thus, whilst references to the principle of solidarity are not prolific, they are qualitatively significant.

5.2.3 *The Substance of Solidarity: The Question of Rights and Obligations*

The second aspect of solidarity is the substantive debate that underlies the use of the word. The previous section has attempted to characterize solidarity by examining to whom this solidarity is supposed to be expressed (the worker or the non-economically active) and who is supposed to be expressing it (other EU Citizens, national workers or the Member States themselves)? This section, though, will assess the substantive discussion within the pre-Maastricht jurisprudence of what the issue in substance really is and why it is controversial. As has already been outlined in *Grzelczyk* (above), the expression of solidarity contained a proviso: that Union citizens attempting to derive rights on the basis of the Treaty in circumstances where they might not be a 'worker' must not become an 'unreasonable burden' on state resources. There is a debate that runs inexorably in tandem with the thorny question as to who can and cannot (or more appropriately should or should not) be classified as an unreasonable burden on state resources. This is the issue of what duties, if any, are owed by Union citizens as provided for in Article 8(2) of the amended Treaty at Maastricht?[33] Whilst the Treaty

[32] In *Konstantinidis*, see Section 4.4.

[33] In an ordinary (national) sense, citizenship inevitably involves a relationship between rights and duties. As Delanty put it: 'In return for rights, citizens had basic duties to perform, for the entitled citizen was also a dutiful citizen' and, likewise, White maintains: 'Citizenship in its classical sense involves duties as well as rights: typically to serve in the armed forces of the State of citizenship if called upon to do so and to pay taxes.' In general terms, to not have such a correlative obligation creates what Etzioni terms an 'imbalance between rights and responsibilities' and, for Selbourne, the 'politics of dutiless right' leads to what he calls the creation of 'civic deserts'. This is very much an issue in relation to EU Citizenship. As Barnard claims: 'The rights for migrants

reiterated a standard aspect of citizenship practice, namely that Citizens derive rights but are also subject to duties, the extent of such 'duties', if any, has not been elaborated upon by the Court and remains a continually unanswered question.

However, the discussion on this subject, without necessarily outlining an answer, arose within the Court's jurisprudence from the outset. In *Ciechelski*, in 1967, the applicant, a naturalized French citizen who had contributed towards an old-age pension in both France and Germany, was attempting to utilize Community law in a manner that, if applied, would have given him a comparative advantage over a French citizen that had simply remained throughout his/her working life in France.[34] In this context, the Commission felt the need to weigh up a dilemma:

> The Commission believes that it can extract two matters of concern from an analysis of the case-law of the Court [then referring to *Kalsbeek* and *Labots*]: it is necessary on the one hand to avoid depriving the migrant worker of rights which he has acquired outside the application of Community law, and on the other hand allowing this application to have the effect of giving him through accumulation the benefit of advantages to which he is not entitled.[35]

Therefore, from its inception the Court made implicit reference to a duty in addition to a right. The applicant was making a claim to a benefit – his pension – to which he was entitled (his right); yet, in a sense, he had also fulfilled a duty in order to derive his entitlement, namely, a long-standing contribution to the social security systems of both France and

are extensive. It is, however, surprising, how little reference is made to duties for those migrants. This suggests a structural imbalance in the EU's notion of citizenship.'

Gerard Delanty, *Citizenship in a Global Age*, p. 123; Amitai Etzioni, *The Spirit of Community – the Reinvention of American Society* (New York: Touchstone, 1993), p. 4; David Selbourne, *The Principle of Duty* (London: Faber and Faber, 1994), p. 31; Barnard, *Four Freedoms*, p. 461. For the frequent link made between the rights of citizens and their correlative obligation to pay taxes, see, for instance, Albert Weale, 'Citizenship Beyond Borders' in Ursula Vogel and Michael Moran (eds.), *The Frontiers of Citizenship* (Basingstoke: Macmillan, 1991), pp. 155–165 at pp. 158–159; Geoff Mulgan, 'Citizens and Responsibilities' in Geoff Andrews (ed.), *Citizenship* (London: Lawrence & Wishart, 1991), pp. 37–50; Samantha Besson and André Utzinger, 'Introduction: Future Challenges of European Citizenship – Facing a Wide-Open Pandora's Box' (2007) 13(5) *European Law Journal*, 573–590 at 577; Agustín José Menéndez, 'Taxing Europe: Two Cases for a European Power to Tax (with some comparative observations)' (2004) 10(2) *The Columbia Journal of European Law*, 297–338; Ruth Rubio-Marin, *Immigration as Democratic Challenge: Citizenship and Inclusion in Germany and the United States* (Cambridge: Cambridge University Press, 2000), p. 46.

[34] Case 1/67, *Stanislas Ciechelski* v. *Caisse régionale de sécurité sociale du Centre d'Orléans and directeur régional de la sécurité sociale d'Orléans* [1967] ECR 181, p. 192.

[35] Ibid., p. 184.

Germany and therefore, his 'entitlement' should be commensurate with what he contributed towards his pension *a priori*.[36] Therefore, the issue in the case was that the applicant could potentially have derived an advantage from having exercised his right to free movement by contrast with a domestic worker who had never exercised such a right. It is maintained that it is when there appears to be a fragmented or disjointed relationship between an (economic) duty to contribute and a correlating right to a benefit that a controversy arises and then becomes the subject of continual conjecture throughout the Court's jurisprudence.[37]

5.2.4 *The Inherent Problem of Seemingly Undeserving Applicants*

With the embryonic EU Citizen, by contrast with national models, there is a dissonance between rights and duties in that it is neither certain what the scope of any duty is, if there is any at all, and to whom this duty is owed. In other words, an impression can be created of a Community citizen as parasitic and not with any need to demonstrate loyalty towards the host state. It is at this point that the structural fault of EU Citizenship as a project is evident from the outset. For Bellamy, citizenship involves:

> The capacity, entitlement and obligation to participate as a full and equal member within the economy and the polity. For example, the right to vote was standardly tied to the payment of taxes ... Similarly, social and economic rights were linked to the duty and ability to work and to contribute to national schemes of social insurance. Those deemed socially irresponsible, a label applied at various times and places to lunatics, children, criminals, women, the propertyless and the indigent, either forfeited or were ineligible for most citizenship rights. The rights enjoyed by citizens of the member states ... extend way beyond the basic rights most people recognize they owe to humanity in general. Solidarity leads citizens to feel certain obligations towards their fellows, while trust gives them faith that others will reciprocate in fulfilling them. Without such sentiments, citizens will be tempted to free ride.[38]

What is at the heart of an inherently complicated concept of Union Citizenship is a reality in the early jurisprudence of the Court in which a

[36] See Michel Voirin, 'Sécurité sociale des travailleurs migrants. Commentaires des arrêts de la Cour de justice des Communautés européennes (*Kolditz, Ciechelski* et *de Moor*)' (1968) 4 *Droit social*, 329–346.

[37] See Section 5.2.1.

[38] Richard Bellamy, 'Evaluating Union Citizenship: Belonging, Rights and Participation within the EU' (2008) 12(6) *Citizenship Studies*, 597–611 at 599.

parasitic impression can be compounded by the circumstances of individuals' cases.[39] This fluctuating relationship between the Community national, his/her host Member State and potentially wider supranational obligations towards the Union manifests itself in terms of both the scope of the expected obligations of Community nationals and the relative merit-worthiness of individual litigants. One attempt to outline a potential set of duties – in an argument that ultimately failed – was made by the Dutch and Danish governments in *Levin* when they defined who, in their views, are the primary intended beneficiaries of the Treaty, namely those:

> Who are of importance to the economic life of Member States, or who contribute by their economic activity to the development of the Community and not for nationals of Member States in general, or those who engage in no economic activity or whose economic activity is insignificant.[40]

This is exemplary of a minimalist market citizenship concept. For two of the Member States, the Citizen's role is purely economic and his/her duty is therefore to 'engage in an economic activity' and, by doing so, the Citizen 'is of importance to the economic life of the Member States'. By inference, the sole yardstick upon which to judge the importance of the Citizen is in terms of economic contribution and thus the Citizen is not of importance to the civic life of a host state, only its economic life. Dismissed though this view may have ultimately been (see Chapters 1 and 2), this is evidently a paradigm that governed the views of at least some of the Member States and is what Everson terms 'the legacy of the market citizen' in that the people for whom some of the Member States perceived normatively *should* benefit from the provisions of the Treaty are solely economic actors and this is a troublesome legacy which the EU Citizen inevitably inherits.[41] Equally, the two governments were prepared to conceive of the duty being

[39] See, for instance, Claus Offe, 'The Democratic Welfare State in An Integrating Europe' in M. Green and L. Pauly (eds.), *Democracy Beyond the State? The European Dilemma and the Emerging Global Order* (Lanham: Rowman and Littlefield, 2000), pp. 63–89 at pp. 67–68; Jack Barbalet, *Citizenship: Rights, Struggle and Class Equality* (Milton Keynes: Open University Press, 1988).

[40] Case 53/81, *D. M. Levin* v. *Staatssecretaris van Justitie* [1982] ECR 1035, p. 1058 (as summarized by AG Slynn).

[41] Michelle Everson, 'Legacy of the Market Citizen', p. 83. As Meehan summarizes: 'The oldest criticism of EU citizenship starts from the limitations of the Treaty for some as a basis for rights. These being restricted to the freedom of movement of goods, capital, labour and services mean that European rights were restricted to the "citizen-as-worker" instead of reflecting the normative principle that people are citizens because

owed to either one or more of the Member States or the Community more generally ('Member States' in the plural) but, nevertheless, the duty is solely economic. Seen within this particular paradigm, there is a dissonance or schism between rights and duties because, for many categories of applicant, they could not be seen to be economic contributors.[42] As the applicant claimed in *Levin*, the underlying purpose behind what at the time was a proposed directive on residence (which in turn became a series of directives on residence as was discussed in Chapter 2) was that an individual would only be entitled to derive a right to reside if he/she could 'provide proof of adequate means of support' as, otherwise, a Community national who does little or no work becomes a burden on state resources without actually ever having contributed towards them in the form of social security and tax payments.[43] As Barnard maintains:

> The nascent citizenship cases involved those who were not economically active taking advantage of the fundamental Treaty provisions on free movement to gain access to welfare services in other Member States . . . [This] may,

they are human beings.' Elizabeth Meehan, 'Europeanization and Citizenship of the European Union' (2000) 14 *Yearbook of European Studies*, 157–177 at 166.

42 As Douglas-Scott states: 'The private notion of citizenship has been incipient in EC law from the outset. This model is generally perceived as being passive in nature, stressing not a capacity for engagement in public life, but rather human nature as a bundle of passions and interests satisfied in market relations . . . Even the expansive conception of citizenship delineated by Advocate-General Jacobs in the *Konstantinidis* case, which would allow an individual . . . to state loftily, "*civis Europeus sum*", must still involve migration within the framework of the EC Treaty, and thus, for the most part, rules on the notion of market citizenship.' Likewise, Closa claims that EU Citizenship is, for the most part, in reality 'a privilege for those citizens of the Union who intend to move to and reside in another Member State for economic purposes' and Barnard contends that there is a 'historical legacy of market citizenship, which essentially premised on self-interest'. For Everson, this legacy is particularly problematic from the perspective of creating a European identity based upon citizenship as an evolving project: 'the high productive character of the market citizen has also endowed Europe with a troublesome legacy. Having been so strongly instrumentalized with regard to the completion of the internal market, the market citizen had no choice but to become instrumentalist in that self-interest alone drove the European market citizen in his or her dealings with Europe, a general allegiance to the Communities was not established'.

Douglas-Scott, pp. 486–487; Closa, 'Citizenship of the Union', 496; Barnard, *Four Freedoms*, p. 463; Everson, 'Legacy of Market Citizen', p. 93.

See also Kostakopoulou, 'Ideas', 234–235; Percy Lehning, 'European Citizenship: A Mirage?' in Percy Lehning and Albert Weale (eds.), *Citizenship, Democracy and Justice in the New Europe*. (London: Routledge, 1997), pp. 175–200 at 175; Downes, 'Market Citizenship', pp. 93–107.

43 *Levin*, p. 1038.

in the long term, do more damage to any developing sense of solidarity gradually evolving in the Union than foster it.[44]

Thus, the embryonic 'market' citizen's duties, being embryonic, therefore also provided a critical yardstick by which to determine the meritworthiness of individual applicants.

5.2.5 *Examples of Seemingly Undeserving Cases*

Furthermore, what is evident from many of the cases is that they fell short of such a yardstick, appearing to lack either integration into their host state or to have made any meaningful contribution towards that state. As has been outlined in Chapter 1, one of the main controversies with many of the worker cases is that by extending an understanding of how a worker is defined, large categories of individuals who could not be seen as meaningful economic contributors were able derive a panoply of benefits from the host state (irrespective of whether that was an issue in the case or not).[45] The potential, therefore, was always there to claim such benefits once defined as a worker. In *Levin*, for instance, the applicant, a UK national, admitted to undertaking a minimal amount of work 'as a precaution' in the Netherlands in order to be allowed to obtain a residency permit, rather than out of any desire to make any meaningful contribution towards the tax system of the host state.[46] In *Kempf*, the applicant was a part-time music teacher that was earning so little that he had applied for supplementary benefit for those on minimal income.[47] By definition, therefore, he could not have been making a substantial contribution towards the tax system of the host state and was, instead, a financial burden, reliant upon the host state's social assistance in order to live. Indeed, in *Hoeckx*, it was never clear whether the applicant had ever worked but yet was claiming a raft of social welfare measures.[48] Exemplary of the apparent dissonance between rights and duties is illustrated in *Kenny*. The applicant, an Irish national, was convicted of assaulting his wife and had a suspended sentence imposed upon him which he then breached by, once again, assaulting his wife.[49] He was subsequently sentenced to a year's imprisonment

[44] Barnard, 'Principle of Solidarity', pp. 160–161.
[45] See Barnard (ibid.) and Section 5.2.4.
[46] *Levin*, p. 1055.
[47] Case 139/85, *R. H. Kempf* v. *Staatssecretaris van Justitie* [1986] ECR 1741, p. 1743.
[48] Case 249/83, *Vera Hoeckx* v. *Openbaar Centrum voor Maatschappelijk Welzijn, Kalmthout* [1985] ECR 973, p. 975.
[49] Case 1/78, *Patrick Christopher Kenny* v. *Insurance Officer* [1978] ECR 1489, p. 1493.

and, during his time in prison, he was found to be incapable of work.[50] After his release he then attempted to claim incapacity benefit for the entire time in which he was incarcerated.[51] Already, an issue has arisen in that the applicant is hardly the model Community citizen; however, his claim became even more controversial because a UK national would not have been entitled to receive such a benefit if the time of incapacity was during a term of imprisonment.[52] Nonetheless, a strict interpretation of Regulation No. 1408/71 entitled him to claim such a benefit.[53] To compound matters, even prior to the serving of his sentence, as AG Mayras observed 'It is not known exactly in what profession he was employed'.[54] Whilst the applicant was therefore successful in the case, the moral appropriateness of such a case was severely questioned by the UK government who submitted that the 'obligations' of the applicant that needed to be fulfilled were to contribute to the social security system in exactly the same way as home nationals – a form of social solidarity – which meant also being subject to 'any fact entailing disqualification from a right to benefits'.[55] However, AG Mayras took a completely different view of the scope of a worker's obligations under the Regulation when he maintains:

> For my part, I consider that the term "obligations" used in Article 3 of Regulation No. 1408/71 ... refers to the strict field of social security: they are conditions imposed by national legislation with regard to the acquisition, maintenance or recovery of the right to social security (for example the conditions for being subject to a social security scheme, the minimum number of working hours, whether the worker is an employed person or worker treats as such and the minimum registration period), and not detailed rules which are extraneous to social security and depend for example upon the "civic" status of the persons insured.[56]

At once, then, the controversies and dilemmas that have persistently underpinned the normative basis of later citizenship law become exposed.[57] By AG Mayras' own admission, the worker has no '"civic" status' and is therefore neither a civic participant nor subject to any civic duties in his/her host state. The scope of the obligations of the

[50] Ibid.
[51] Ibid.
[52] Ibid.
[53] Ibid.
[54] Ibid., p. 1501.
[55] Ibid., p. 1505.
[56] Ibid.
[57] See Section 5.2.4.

embryonic citizen is, by contrast, rather mundane. He/she was simply subject to the same rights and obligations as home nationals as regards the acquisition of the right, not its withdrawal. The obligation that he/she has to fulfil is to 'be subject to a social security scheme', in other words to make a financial contribution to the scheme and work for a set amount of hours. Every other aspect of domestic social security rules is somehow, by contrast, 'extraneous' to the field of Community social security law and, therefore, irrelevant. Thus, what many of the cases assessed in previous chapters have revealed is that an underclass of individuals existed making essentially parasitic claims and therefore not fulfilling any economic obligation or duty in the process.[58]

5.2.6 *The Controversy Underlying Student Cases*

Moreover, many of the student cases are illustrative of a similar problem as what in effect was being asked of the host state was for considerable financial support when the student or the family of the student had made no financial contribution to the host state.[59] In *Gravier* itself, the applicant, a French citizen, was studying a course in cartoon art in Belgium and charged the *minerval*, a fee only applicable to non-Belgians.[60] The applicant could not be construed as a worker and so was claiming a simple breach of the principle of equal treatment.[61] She therefore had made no financial contribution to the social security system in which she was attempting to obtain an exemption from the *minerval*. Thus, on one level, her claim could only be seen as parasitic and this fact, in tandem with the Court's use of the Common Vocational Treatment Policy to derive an entirely novel right, made the case controversial.[62] As AG Slynn maintained in *Commission* v. *Belgium*: '*Gravier* was a totally new development in Community law, since it recognized rights in respect of persons who could not be regarded as economically active'.[63] One aspect of

58 This is tied in with the concept of market citizenship, see Section 5.2.4.

59 See n. 80 for an analysis of this controversy.

60 Case 293/83, *Françoise Gravier* v. *City of Liège* [1985] ECR 593, p. 596.

61 Ibid.

62 See, for instance, Steiner, 'Recipients of Services', 348–352; Philippa Watson, 'Case 293/83, *Gravier* v. *City of Liège* and Case 293/85R, *Commission of the European Communities* v. *Kingdom of Belgium*' (1987) 24 *Common Market Law Review* 89–97 (note); Anthony Arnull, 'Institutional and jurisdictional questions: of Strip Cartoonists, Vets and Gunsmiths' (1988) 13(4) *European Law Review*, 260–267 at 260–267.

63 Case 293/85, *Commission of the European Communities* v. *Kingdom of Belgium* [1988] ECR 305, p. 331.

such controversy was a perceived disjuncture between rights and duties.[64] However, the Court's reasoning in the case also demonstrated an attempt to link the applicant's circumstances to work, in that it was not the case (at least in *Gravier*) that all students were entitled to an exemption from the *minerval*, the exemption applied to students specifically studying vocational subjects in preparation for the work world.[65] In other words, this was an investment in a future worker and, like all Belgian students studying in Belgium who were entitled to higher education free of charge, they may not be working at the time of their study, but would clearly do so after such a period and would, then, make a substantive contribution to the tax system within Belgium in the future. Thus, the relationship between the right to non-payment of the *minerval* and the duty to contribute towards its payment is simply extended for several years, pending the student's completion of his/her studies. Nonetheless, the applicant in *Gravier* could perfectly conceivably have gone to Belgium to study, then gone on to become a cartoon artist in France and thus have made no contribution towards the Belgium tax system at all. What is left is a *Grzelczyk*-type situation in which the Belgian state would have to shoulder the economic burden of non-nationals or residents studying for free in Belgium as an expression of 'solidarity' on the understanding that Belgian nationals would be entitled to study in other Member States under the same conditions.[66] As a result of being acutely aware of the dissonance between rights and duties, AG Slynn, in *Commission* v. *Belgium*, made a conscious attempt to delineate the type of student that should benefit from this new development in Community law and the type that should not. He firstly maintains the need for there to be a 'direct link' between a course and profession and contrasts this with other more classical degree courses such as 'mediaeval history' which, in his view, 'do not have a sufficiently direct link with the skills needed in those

[64] See Section 5.2.1.

[65] *Commission* v. *Belgium [1988]*, p. 595.

[66] This problem was in fact exacerbated by the *de facto* asymmetry between Community nationals coming to Belgium to study and Belgium nationals going elsewhere to study. As. Barnard points out, what makes the precedent set in *Gravier* particularly damaging for Belgium was the relationship was 'imbalanced between the number of foreign students studying in Belgium and the number of Belgian students living abroad . . . this had serious consequences for the national education budget'. Barnard, 'Principle of Solidarity', p. 177.

particular professions'.[67] The Commission was trying, by contrast, to argue that all university courses should be construed as vocational training and, in addition, that equal treatment should apply to all student finance, including a maintenance allowance.[68] In reply to this point, AG Slynn states: 'Belgium has no obligation to disburse public funds to support needy foreign students and the requirement that sufficient subsistence be available seems to me not to be one prohibited by the Treaty.'[69] In the process, AG Slynn adopted a position that was similar to that of the Court in *Grzelczyk* (and then reflected in the then unimplemented Citizenship Directive as well as the then implemented directives on residence) in relation to the need to not be a burden on public funds.[70]

It is this position, or its logical opposite – a perceived need for a student applicant or his/her family to make a meaningful contribution to the social security and tax system of their host state – that dominated much of the discussion on the purported rights of students during this period of the Court's jurisprudence. In *Lair*, the referring Court claimed that the applicant should only be entitled to obtain a student grant if she 'contributed by [her] own work to the gross national product and thus to the social fund out of which the grants were financed'.[71] In the case, the applicant's circumstances raised similar dilemmas to those of Gravier's potential to work in Belgium after the completion of her course. The applicant was a French national who had previously worked in Germany and then become unemployed.[72] She then resided in both France and Germany over several years before deciding to study an arts course in Hanover, for which she was refused an educational grant.[73] The local authorities refused her application on the grounds that she had not been in employment for five years and 'therefore [had not] paid tax and social security contributions'.[74] Whilst this was clearly the case, it could be suggested that an extended understanding of the interrelationship between rights and duties could conclude that rather than simply looking prospectively at the potential to contribute towards the German tax

67 *Commission* v. *Belgium [1988]*, p. 337.

68 Ibid., p. 334, p. 338.

69 Ibid., p. 424.

70 *Grzelczyk*, p. 6245 at para. 44. See also Section 5.2.8.

71 Case 39/86, *Sylvie Lair* v. *Universität Hannover* [1988] ECR 3161, p. 3180. See also Barnard, 'Case C-209/03', 1465–1489.

72 Ibid.

73 Ibid.

74 Ibid.

system in the future (which she could do as well), the applicant's fulfilment could also be seen retrospectively in that she clearly did make a meaningful contribution towards the system in the past, which contrasts with Gravier's circumstances.

Nonetheless, the momentum of this particular discourse (that of not being a burden on the state) continued unabated. In *Commission* v. *Belgium*, the Belgian authorities submitted that:

> As regards the condition concerning adequate means of support, the Belgian government maintains that it is normal for a State to admit a foreigner to its territory only if the persons concerned will not become a burden for the public purse, even if he is a national of a Member State of the Community.[75]

Likewise, the UK, in *Lair*, maintained that there is a fundamental distinction between non-discrimination against non-nationals or residents as regards the payment of a fee to study in higher education and a maintenance grant:

> Whereas it is right that such person should not be subject to discrimination with regard to entry fees, there is no fundamental freedom under the Treaty which requires that an individual who may be in the host State for the primary purpose of pursuing a course of vocational training should be maintained at the expense of the public purse in the host State.[76]

Ironically it is the Commission itself, in *Lair*, that contributed towards the establishment of this particular discourse when it stated:

> It is of little importance whether, and if so to what extent, the person concerned or their parents have increased the gross national product or public revenue by their occupational activity.
>
> If that 'taxpayer principle' were compatible with the prohibition of discrimination, a European system of social legislation based on the principle of equal treatment would cease to have much meaning, since no social benefits can possibly be paid otherwise than from the gross national product.[77]

In other words, even if to deride the principle, a convenient shorthand – the 'taxpayer principle' – was created. This point was then reiterated by the UK in *Humbel*:

> In this regard the United Kingdom emphasizes that every Member State has a particular obligation towards its own nationals who, by paying taxes, have contributed to the establishment of a system of social services which is

[75] *Commission* v. *Belgium [1988]*, p. 323.
[76] *Lair*, p. 3169.
[77] Ibid., p. 3165.

administered by the State. It would therefore be unacceptable that a national of a Member State who has not made any financial sacrifice in order to pursue certain types of education should be able to go to another Member State to receive instruction of his choice free of charge.[78]

In making such a statement, the UK also makes a direct link between duty and sacrifice, whilst, at the same time continuing the discursive development of the taxpayer principle.

This issue became even more problematic when the beneficiaries of the newly developed *Gravier*-type rights became in effect extended to include all university students. As has been outlined earlier, AG Slynn was at pains to demarcate what subjects counted as vocational and what did not, in part, arguably, because of an acute perception of the lack of moral validity behind the extension of rights to those that were not overtly economic contributors.[79] However, AG Slynn's argument on this matter was ultimately lost. The Commission, in *Commission* v. *Belgium,* simply claimed that any course at a university 'is always vocational training' by simply adopting a broad interpretation as to what counts as vocational.[80] Whilst the case itself was dismissed on the grounds of admissibility by the Court, the Court then took the opportunity, almost immediately after dismissing the Commission's enforcement action against Belgium, to rule in *Barra* that 'in general all university studies' can be construed as vocational training.[81] This new era was seen in a very different light by the Belgian government when it claimed that 'the majority of the plaintiffs, before commencing their studies in Liège, had no real connection with Belgium. After completing their studies, the majority returned to live in France'.[82] It would be hard to see the circumstances of these applicants as being anything other than parasitic.[83]

[78] Case 263/86, *Belgian State* v. *René Humbel and Marie-Thérèse Edel* [1988] ECR 5365, p. 5371, p. 5368 (facts). The applicant was the son of a French worker in Luxembourg who also went to study in Belgium and was charged the *minerval.*

[79] See Section 5.2.8.

[80] *Commission* v. *Belgium [1988]*, p. 334.

[81] Case 309/85, *Bruno Barra* v. *Belgian State and City of Liège* [1988] ECR 355, pp. 405–406 at para. 20 and para. 31, p. 370 (facts). The case was another one in which the *minerval* was charged by Belgium, this time involving gunsmiths.

[82] Ibid., pp. 361–362. For Barnard, the Belgian government's position was based fundamentally upon the principle of solidarity because, for them, there was a complete 'absence of a sufficient degree of solidarity between Belgian taxpayers and migrant students to justify demanding additional tuition fees from foreign students'. Barnard, 'Principle of Solidarity', p. 177.

[83] Belgian taxpayers were, instead, 'footing the bill – and seeing little in return'. Barnard, 'Principle of Solidarity', p. 180.

The controversy over the development of *Gravier*-type rights in Community law was also exacerbated by attempts by applicants to argue that, as an alternative to being construed as a *Gravier* type student, a period of minimal work in the host state, immediately prior to commencing a course of study, makes the applicant a 'worker' and entitled to the entire panoply of benefits that home national workers would be entitled to by virtue of simply residing on the territory.[84] This was a submission made in both *Brown* and commented on by AG Slynn in *Lair*. In *Brown*, the applicant, whose family resided and worked in France, had worked in Edinburgh for a matter of months and was asking for a maintenance grant to be paid to him throughout the entirety of his studies at Cambridge during a time when he would clearly have ceased to be a worker.[85]AG Slynn determined in the case:

> I do not find it possible to accept that working for however short a period is necessarily sufficient to give rights to a maintenance grant under Article 7. It is unacceptable that the person who honestly says, 'I am going as a student' should get no maintenance grant under the regulation whereas the person who gets a job for, say, a week or a month, in order essentially to be in the Member State to study should be able to say on day 1 or day 7 or day 31: 'I am now a worker; pay me a grant under Article 7'.[86]

What is relevant from a discursive perspective of these continuous discussions of the merits of students obtaining rights is that whether as a *Gravier*-type student who has made no prior economic contribution to the state or the *Brown*-type student who has undertaken a minimal period of work in order to derive rights as a worker, both types of situation were perceived by several Member States as lacking moral validity in their claims (and the extension of rights by the Court to include them), irrespective of the legal merits of their individual cases. This socially constructed paradigm was underpinned by a perception of a lack of correlation between rights and duties or, in other words, an obligation is being fulfilled by a Member State with no obligation being fulfilled by the recipient of a benefit in return. Thus, whilst clearly

84 See also the Court in Case 207/78, *Criminal proceedings against Gilbert Even and Office national des pensions pour travailleurs salariés (ONPTS)* [1979] ECR 2019, p. 2034 at para. 22.

85 See Section 1.5.7 for an outline of the facts in *Lair*. The case itself, unlike *Brown*, did not concern a Community national expressly moving from one Member State to another for the express purpose of working for a short period of time prior to studying in order to be classified as a 'worker' under the Treaty. See also Gould, 'Equality of Access', 540–550; Noreen Burrows, 'Wandering Scholars', 99–102.

86 Case 197/86, *Steven Malcolm Brown* v. *The Secretary of State for Scotland* [1988] ECR 3205, p. 3183.

being radical and, at times, hailed as development in Community law, the creation of *Gravier*-type rights also carried with it a legacy that provides a critical point of reflection on contemporary understandings of EU Citizenship.[87]

5.2.7 *Other Non-economic or Marginally Economic Contributors*

Furthermore, the issue of non-contribution to the tax system by a host migrant arose in cases that did not concern students. Whilst the merits of cases such as *Steymann* and *Levin* have been examined in Chapter 1, the point here is that what almost all of the cases concerned were applicants who had conducted a minimal amount of work but were claiming benefits of some form from the host state. Exemplary of such a dissonance between rights and duties is *Hoeckx*. The case concerned the *minimex*, the Belgian minimal subsistence allowance. One of the two applicants in the case was a Dutch citizen residing in Belgium and obtaining unemployment benefit.[88] The applicant then moved to France and received unemployment benefit there and subsequently returned to Belgium, applied for the *minimex* and was refused on the grounds of not having been employed for the last five years.[89] Irrespective of the legal merits of the reference to the Court, what is evident is that the case concerned a litigant who has never made any meaningful contribution towards the social security system of either of her host states but who was still attempting to derive a benefit from them.[90]

Moreover, this issue is not simply one of rights and duties: for some Member States, it is equally one of solidarity. In *Cowan*, the French government refused to pay the applicant, a victim of crime, compensation from a national fund because:

> It concerns a right which is a manifestation of the principle of national solidarity. Such a right presupposes a closer bond with the State than that of a recipient of services, and for that reason it may be restricted to persons who are either nationals of that State or foreign nationals on the territory of that State.[91]

87 It should also be stated that, as Barnard has implicitly alluded to, another fact is that the burden in these cases then falls unequally upon Member States that happen to have good universities teaching in an accessible language. Barnard, 'Principle of Solidarity', pp. 177–80.

88 *Hoeckx*, p. 975.

89 Ibid.

90 See Philippa Watson, 'Minimum Income Benefits: Social Security or Social Assistance?' (1985) 10 *European Law Review*, 335–343.

91 Case 186/87, *Ian William Cowan* v. *Trésor Public* [1989] ECR 195, p. 221.

What concerned both governments is that in *Hoeckx* the applicant lacked either any meaningful economic contribution towards or social integration within the host state.[92] Irrespective of the legal merits of both cases (the applicant in *Cowan* was seriously injured in a violent mugging on the Paris metro and was refused the compensation on the grounds of neither being a national nor a resident[93]), what arose during this key period of time in the jurisprudence of the Court throughout the 1980s was that a pervasive impression – or discourse – was created in which various Member States challenged the moral validity of some of the most radical developments in the Court's jurisprudence on the basis of there being a lack of connection or dissonance between rights and duties which was not the case with straightforward workers. Indeed, even the Commission, in *Cowan*, appeared to reflect this concern when it claimed that essentially there are two types of Community citizens: 'those persons ... integrated into the society of the host country, with all the consequent rights and obligations' and, conversely, those who 'remain integrated in the society of their country of origin ... [and] cannot therefore be regarded as having to be assimilated and integrated into the society of the host country'.[94] In other words, there are certain categories of individuals who are more morally deserving of the Court's attention than others because of the manner in which they have fully integrated into their host society.[95] This underlying assumption manifested itself, likewise, in discussions of solidarity or, in other words, the substance of discussions about the lack of moral validity of such legal developments was labelled as either an issue of a lack of duties/obligations being fulfilled or as an issue of solidarity.[96] Thus, if the image of the Community then Union citizen – its 'ideal type'[97] – were to have emerged as a result of the jurisprudence of non-contributors, it is submitted that a fracture is created between the citizen and the obligations that he/she is supposed to have fulfilled which, in turn, would cast a long shadow over the soon-to-be-created Citizen after the '*Sala* revolution'.[98] Such a shadow

[92] See, for instance, Arnull, 'Metropolitan Misfortune', 166–169; Weatherill, 'Case 186/87', 563–581.

[93] *Cowan*, p. 219.

[94] Ibid., p. 201.

[95] See Section 5.4.1 for a detailed outline of this point.

[96] See Section 5.2.4.

[97] See 'Introduction' on this point.

[98] The normative dissonance in terms of non-contribution to the economy of the host state by Community national is starkly outlined by Bellamy 'such matters go to the heart of the capacity for states to respond to their citizens priorities when setting their

would also affect the nature of solidarity as a Member State, such as Belgium, would fail to understand the need to express solidarity with them, other Member States or the interests of the Community given the enormous financial cost to it with comparatively little, if any, benefit to it or its citizens in return.[99]

5.2.8 *The Need for Legislative Change*

Furthermore, this pervasive understanding of a new reality that was being created by the Court resulted in legislative change in much the same way that a perceived dissension against the rights created by the Court in *Grzelczyk* in part resulted in the Citizenship Directive.[100] In *Commission* v. *Belgium*, immediately after the citation made above in which the Belgian government made it clear that students should not be a 'burden on the public purse', it then continues: 'that was recognized by the Commission itself in its proposal of a directive on the right of residence of persons not in employment on the territory of another Member State'.[101] In other words, this controversy resulted in a political impetus for such a directive. This point is made even more explicitly by the Danish government in *Brown* when it asserted that the substance of the proposed directive on right of residence was that it should be 'based on the principle that students must not be a financial burden to the country of residence'.[102] Ultimately, this paradigm, in which various categories of non-economically active actors combine, resulted in legislative change in the form of the three directives on residence in 1990.

budgets. Not to take them seriously, risks disturbing the reciprocal ties between citizens that make public spending sustainable'. In response to this problem, Liebert advocates the creation of a 'European social solidarity [which] would oblige citizens to assume the burden of redistributive policies with the ultimate solution, according to Menéndez, being the creation of a form of European taxation. Bellamy, 'Evaluating Union citizenship', 606; Liebert, p. 30; Menéndez, 'Taxing Europe', 297.

99 As Barnard put it, in relation to the student cases: 'the reality is that (poor and usually non-mobile) taxpayers from the host countries are supporting the education of (middle class) students from other Member States with whom they have little by way of community of interests. These taxpayers cannot even comfort themselves with the argument that these better educated students will contribute more to the economies of the host State since 75 percent of them subsequently return to their home state and, of those that do remain, many do so for only a relatively short period of time. If this were widely known it could do more to harm the nascent development of EU citizenship ... than to foster it'. Barnard, 'Principle of Solidarity', pp. 178–179.

100 See Section 5.3.5.

101 *Commission* v. *Belgium [1988]*, p. 323.

102 *Brown*, p. 3219.

Directive 90/364 created a general right of residence, under Article 1 (1) for:

> [Those] who do not enjoy this right under other provisions of Community law … provided that they themselves … are covered by sickness insurance in respect of all risks in the host Member State and have sufficient resources to avoid becoming a burden on the social assistance system of the host Member State during their period of residence.[103]

Directive 90/365 related to former workers and, similarly, Article 1(1) made the proviso that a former worker's pension and old-age benefits should be 'sufficient to avoid becoming a burden'.[104] Finally, Directive 90/366 granted a right of residence to students but, once again, on terms. Article 1(1) of the Directive makes it clear that students who are enrolled on a vocational course are granted a right of residence so long as they make a declaration that they have 'sufficient resources to avoid becoming a burden'.[105] This is, therefore, an example of legislative change taking place as result of concerns expressed by certain Member States (as evidenced within the text of court judgments) as to the extent of rights being granted by the Court which, in turn, arose as a result of the emergence of the discourse of the 'taxpayer principle'.

In 2004, the Citizenship Directive was enacted. This was, in part, a response to a more contemporary debate that emerged from *Grzelczyk* and this can be seen in Recital (3) of the Directive where it states that 'Union citizenship should be the fundamental status of nationals of the Member States when they exercise their right of free movement and residence', itself a similarly worded phrase to that adopted by the Court in paragraph 1 of the judgment in *Grzelczyk*.[106] However, Article 10 of the Directive also reiterates that, at least for an initial period of three months, a right of residence for all Union citizens exists but only on the proviso, that, once again, the citizen: 'should not … become an

[103] Council Directive 90/364/EEC of 28 June 1990 on the right of residence [1990] OJ L180/26.

[104] Council Directive 90/365/EEC of 28 June 1990 on the right of residence for employees and self-employed persons who have ceased their occupational activity [1990] OJ L180/28.

[105] Council Directive 90/366/EEC of 28 June 1990 on the right of residence for students [1990] OJ L180/30.

[106] Directive 2004/38/EC of 29 April 2004 on the right of citizens of the Union and their family members to move and reside freely within the territory of the Member States amending Regulation (EEC) No 1612/68 and repealing Directives 64/221/EEC, 68/360/EEC, 72/194/EEC, 73/148/EEC, 75/34/EEC, 75/35/EEC, 90/364/EEC, 90/365/EEC and 93/96/EEC [2004] OJ L158/77 ('The Citizenship Directive').

unreasonable burden on the social assistance system of the host Member State'.[107] The Citizenship Directive (Directive 2004/38) repealed all three directives on residence and Regulation Nos 1612/68 and 1408/71, the analysis of which has formed the background to much of this and to the emergence of citizenship itself. Arguably the value in using SC methodology to assess this key period of time in the jurisprudence of the Court is to holistically outline in effect a double debate taking place leading eventually to the Citizenship Directive. When the citizen had eventually crystallized into law in 1992, it inherited a debate that had commenced since the inception of the Court as to what to do with non-economic contributors. This was, then, still reflected in the Citizenship Directive as much as it was the previous residence directives. Yet, the Citizenship Directive was also reflective, as Article 3 demonstrates, of a much later debate on the specific content of citizenship which, itself, was infused by the earlier debate.

5.2.9 *The Toxic Legacy of Solidarity: Ignore the Member States at Their Peril*

Fundamentally the standard narrative on EU Citizenship law treats the concept of solidarity as almost self-contained within its (later) case law. This case law in what has been termed the post '*Sala* revolution' is, of course, itself not without its own controversies, particularly in relation to the instrumental use of the citizenship provisions of Treaty by non or partial economic contributors in cases such as *Grzelczyk* (2001), *Baumbast* (2002), *D'Hoop* (2002), *Ninni-Orasche* (2003) and, most controversially, *Collins* (2004).[108] Likewise, the standard narrative has a tendency to portray the Citizenship Directive as an almost emancipatory and constitutional document. The reality is that both the Citizenship case law and the Citizenship Directive itself are both intrinsically genealogical (with their roots in the case law from their infancy) and linked to the views of the Member States. Put simply, a large part of the fissure in the concept of solidarity within the case law appears to be a lack of meaningful engagement with the views of the Member States. Indeed, it appears that concept 'unreasonable burden' was articulated in its essence by the Member States from the outset and the controversies that underpin this concept remain to the present day. It is an unresolved dissonance right at the heart of the

[107] Ibid.
[108] Jacqueson, 'Union Citizenship and the Court of Justice' 265.

case law and relates intimately to a perception – where, as has been repeatedly stated, perception matters – that in many cases no kind of duty is being fulfilled by certain categories of EU Citizen, whether in the form of the narrative of sacrifice as has been outlined in relation to national citizenship models or even of the duty as a market citizen to contribute to the economic life of the host state. As Weiler put it: 'In "selling" European citizenship the vocabulary was always one of rights, never duties. One of benefits, never sacrifice or selflessness'.[109] As has also been repeatedly stated, a core tenet of this book is that 'vocabulary' matters.

Being, perhaps, truly genealogical, one way of illustrating this point is to start with the Citizenship Directive and work backwards. As has already been suggested in reality, the Citizenship Directive is clearly not an emancipatory constitution but arguably a pragmatic response by the Member States to prevent *Grzelczyk*-type litigants becoming an unreasonable burden on the host state. However, the Citizenship Directive itself is simply an amalgamation of the three prior residency directives, as has also already been outlined, and the unreasonable burden proviso not only can be traced back to much earlier case law in the 1980s but also is reflective of the objections of the Member States then to the evolution of both the 'worker' and to the evolving protection by the Court of those that could not be classified as workers. The outline of the views of the Member States within the case law was outlined in Chapters 2 and 3 as relevant in a descriptive sense to the evolution of the discourses that underpin the case law on free movement. Essentially, their contribution added to inherent contingency of such an evolution (a good example being the 'effective and genuine' proviso on the worker as elaborated in *Levin*).

However, such views are also relevant in a different, perhaps more critical and normative context in this chapter. A recurrent utterance of various Member States has been an objection to, in effect, the concept of solidarity as outlined in *Grzelczyk* in terms of essentially the Member State (and its tax payers) having to shoulder the economic burden of non or marginally economically active EU Citizens who have exercised their right to free movement. This was reflected as far back as Council minutes prior to the *Levin* case objecting to (then) Community nationals not becoming a burden on public funds, and, somewhat later, can also

[109] Joseph Weiler, 'Secessionism and Its Discontents', in Carlos Closa (ed.), *Secession from a Member State and Withdrawal from the European Union* (Cambridge: Cambridge University Press, 2017), pp. 12–31 at p. 31.

be traced to objections on similar lines by those exercising *Gravier* or *Cowan*-type rights by Belgium in *Commission* v. *Belgium* (with legislative development in the form of the three residency directives to follow).

Furthermore, by examining solidarity in a genealogical sense, its fissure arguably is further opened by posing a normative question: *should* the various objections of the Member States have been listened to more actively by the Court? A seemingly blind obedience to an integration narrative appeared to have sidelined such views. In the contemporary context of a significant Member State leaving the European Union, perhaps the fact that the Member States felt the need to create secondary legislation arguably to deal with the consequences of the adventurous approach of the Court over many years is part of the problem. As has already been outlined, the UK trenchantly objected to the development of the case law to incorporate non-economic actors as expressed by its views in *Commission* v. *Netherlands*. However, it should be noted that the fissure in this respect is not that of the relationship between the UK and the rest of the Union but within the concept of citizenship itself. The UK was far from alone in making its views plain to the Court and what is also noticeable is how several of the Member States, including some of the original founding states, appeared to share similar views. For instance, the Danish and German governments objected to such a development in *Levin* and *Lair* respectively, the Dutch government shared similar views to the UK government in *Commission* v. *Netherlands* itself and, finally, the German, Danish and Dutch governments all appeared to object to the creation of *Gravier*-type rights (where, of course, a considerable amount of taxpayer money was at stake). Whilst it is certainly the case that the Member States took their own course of action by enacting legislative change, what appears to have never been meaningfully questioned is whether their views should have been listened to more actively by the Court from the outset, or, in other words, to have prevented the need for the Member States to legislate in the first place.

Moreover, and finally, the fissure of solidarity goes even further back than even the so-called *Levin* era in the 1980s. As was also stated in Chapter 1, the Danish government was clearly concerned that the Court had developed the concept of the assimilated-worker to effectively mean that 'virtually the entire adult population of the Communities would have to be regarded as a worker'.[110] The concern

[110] *Brack*, p. 1462.

from the Danish government was based on an interpretation of a piece of legislation (Regulation No. 3/58) that is so old that it was replaced by Regulation No. 1612/68 (a provision of secondary legislation most scholars of EU law are more familiar with) and, indeed, is so old that it is not even available as a translation into the English language because by the time the UK joined it had ceased to be law. The concept of solidarity was undeniably controversial from the moment of its apparent creation in *Grzelcyk*. This is partly because of the apparent dissonance between rights and duties within the case law of the Court on citizenship. However, as is also equally evident the real controversy itself goes back much further to the very earliest cases on free movement with there being an apparent lack of economic contribution or duty fulfilled by many of the litigants in the early cases. Moreover, it is clear that some of the Member States did object profoundly to this type of evolution and had a significant Member State not decided to leave the Union, then perhaps these utterances would simply be confined to a dusty archive and overlooked.

In a contemporary climate, by contrast, a light has been shone on a fissure that was arguably not properly treated from the outset and, now, looks 'exquisite and glaring'.[111] Clearly, citizenship has technically now been dismantled in one (now) former Member State: UK nationals are no longer EU Citizens. Nonetheless, the issues underpinning the controversies in the concept of solidarity do not simply evaporate by virtue of one Member State leaving, particularly in an era of populist politics with Euroscepticism being expressed much more widely than simply within the UK.[112] If anything, the era of COVID-19, with borders being

[111] Chambon, 'Foucault's Approach', p. 60.

[112] As Bakker et al. state: 'Support for populist parties that claim to defend "the people" against the establishment has risen across Europe – and this sentiment appears to extend to the European Union (EU). From the Northern League in Italy and the Forum for Democracy in the Netherlands to the AfD in Germany, many populist parties denounce European integration as an elitist project that undermines the interests of ordinary people and the nation.' In addition, as the basis for the nuanced and detail empirical analysis that they then engage in, Kang and Oh refer to there being a 'proliferation of Euroscepticism as a phenomenon of declining support for EU integration' of Brexit is part but not the complete picture: as Euroscepticism has received intense attention before and after the Brexit referendum, accordingly, it has widened the negative influence against deeper integration of the EU'.

Ryan Bakker, Liesbet Hooghe, Seth Jolly, Gary Marks, Jonathan Polk, Jan Rovny, Marco Steenbergen and Milada Anna Vachudova, 'Who opposes the EU? Continuity and change in party Euroscepticism between 2014 and 2019' (London School of Economics: 2020) https://blogs.lse.ac.uk/europpblog/2020/06/01/who-opposes-the-eu-continuity-and-change-in-party-euroscepticism-between-2014-and-2019/ accessed 18

closed throughout the EU, has illustrated that entitlement to free movement in general is far from as sacrosanct as it once was: untrammelled movement has itself become the problem. Indeed, it is arguable, using the example of Hungary, that one of the Member States has instrumentally taken advantage of a seemingly temporary restriction on free movement on health grounds to attempt curtail free movement more generally in order to appease populist and Eurosceptic politics.[113] Thus, whilst Somek famously summarized that solidarity had 'decomposed' in the case law on free movement, it is perhaps questionable that it ever really meaningfully existed in the first place.

5.3 The Fissure of Seemingly Inherent Impossibility: The Problem with Postnational Identification

Whilst there is an inescapable interrelationship between citizenship and identity, the crucial link to postnational identification arguably remains elusive. Whilst it has been previously defined in this chapter as having many meanings, what the various definitions do have in common is contained in the Oxford English Dictionary itself; namely membership of a state.[114] In other words, the inherited legacy of citizenship prior to contemporary discussions about the possibility of supranational citizenship was always one of national citizenship and, therefore, there is a powerful normative bond between citizenship and nationality. Bosniak, for instance, defines 'citizenship as membership' denoting a collective belonging to something and inevitably citizenship as a concept becomes a question of identity.[115] The construction of identity within institutional environments is as important an aspect of SC theory as that of

September 2020. Yoo-Duk Kang and Chang-Rhyong Oh, 'Spreading Euroscepticism and its macro-level determinants: empirical analysis of the Eurobarometer survey in 2004–2017' (2020) 28(3) *Journal of Contemporary European Studies*, 348–365 at 348–349.

113 See 'Introduction', n. 4.

114 To be citizen, according to the dictionary, is to be 'a member of a state, an enfranchised inhabitant of a country, as opposed to an alien'.

115 Linda Bosniak, *The Citizen and the Alien* (Princeton: Princeton University Press, 2006), p. 18. Likewise, for Heater: 'Citizenship is more than a label. He who has no sense of a civic bond with his fellows or of some responsibility for civic welfare is not a true citizen whatever his legal status. Identity and culture invest the concept of citizenship with power' and for Closa 'rights and identity are the two component elements of citizenship'. Derek Heater, *Citizenship: The Civic Ideal in World History, Politics and Education* (London: Longman, 1990), p. 182; Carlos Closa, 'Between EU Constitution and Individuals' Self: European Citizenship' (2001) 20(3) *Law and Philosophy*, 345–371 at 365.

discourse (indeed, there is complex interrelationship between the three concepts).[116]

Whilst the majority of utterances on citizenship within the jurisprudence of the Court have related to a Roman (and legal) understanding of citizenship (with the occasional glimpses of an Athenian model), there are references to identity within the free movement cases that, perhaps inadvertently, delineate an inherent impossibility of postnational citizenship from the outset. Arguably, one of the other key controversies that relates specifically to EU Citizenship is how it is conceivable to replicate the strong bond that is associated between a national citizen and his/her state. Whilst a great deal of attention in the free movement cases is devoted to protecting, *inter alia*, the 'worker', what is also evident from the cases is that the text of the Court judgments also contains multiple references to the normative 'pull' of national identity.

This section relates to a fundamental tenet of discourse theory, namely that it is critical, and will problematize or deconstruct the partly inherited economic legacy of citizenship which contrasts with the strong interrelationship between national citizenship and identity. Whilst it may be conceivable to foresee the normative potential of EU Citizenship as a postnational form of identity construction, what many of the free movement cases illustrate is the continual juxtaposition between free movement rights and national identity. This, then, poses a significant problem for any future development of EU Citizenship as a project if the two concepts (the 'market citizen' and identity) are treated as conceptually distinct given the important relationship there is between citizenship and identity. In other words, the inherited legacy of the 'market citizen' as the *de facto* origins of contemporary EU Citizenship, regardless of attempts to manoeuvre the concept beyond such economic origins, meant that perhaps not only is there evidence of another fissure within the concept from the outset, but also that somewhat ironically the cases themselves illustrate the contrast between market citizenship and a fully fledged meaningful concept of citizenship on a national level.

This section will make essentially two points. First, that for EU Citizenship to have meaning for individuals, the types of identity practices that take place on a national level would have to, in part, be

[116] See 'Introduction' on this point.

replicated, itself a considerable task. As Hobson, Carson and Lawrence maintain:

> At the level of the national community, culture and identity have been seen as the precursor for nation building. The framing of citizenship is linked to nationalist projects, construction based on notions of origin and culture as well as ideologies that define who is to be included in the Collective We. National and citizenship identity are conflated in this process.[117]

Second, that by doing so problems inherent in national identity construction may then be equally replicated.[118] In terms of the types of cases in which issues of identity are discussed, the most fertile ground has proven to be the public service exception cases, as well as social security cases relating to military service. It was thus concluded that, ironically, the inability to replicate anything even approaching the level of a national identification on a supranational level was also starkly highlighted from the outset. Thus by examining contemporary controversies relating to EU Citizenship in the light of the pre-1992 case law,

[117] Barbara Hobson, Marcus Carson and Rebecca Lawrence, 'Recognition Struggles in Trans-National Arenas: Negotiating Identities and Framing Citizenship' (2007) 10(4) *Critical Review of International Social and Political Philosophy*, 443–470 at 443. Likewise, for Wiener 'citizenship invariably involves a notion of "stateness"' and as Meehan put it: 'Normally, the idea of citizenship involves full membership of a political community and that community is generally defined as a *national* political community.' Moreover, as Shore put it: 'Citizenship is . . . the legal conception of an individual who owes allegiance to, and receives protection from, a state' and for Bellamy, the inevitable link between citizenship and national identity is due to the role 'civic consciousness' plays in engendering allegiance and a sense of identity. Indeed, Maas goes so far as to claim: 'citizenship would be meaningless without states, and states would not be states without citizens'. Thus, what is illustrated in the above citations is the considerable challenge presented to EU Citizenship as a purported identity construct.

Antje Wiener, 'Citizenship' in Michelle Cini (ed.), *European Union Politics* (Oxford: Oxford University Press, 2003), pp. 397–414at p. 402; Elizabeth Meehan, 'European Citizenship and Social Policies' in Ursula Vogel and Michael Moran (eds.), *The Frontiers of Citizenship* (Basingstoke: Macmillan, 1991), pp. 125–154 at p. 126; Shore, p. 66; Bellamy, 'Evaluating Union citizenship', 599; Maas, *Creating European Citizens*, p. 1.

See also Dora Kostakopoulou, 'Citizenship Goes Public: The Institutional Design of Anational Citizenship' (2009) 17(3) *The Journal of Political Philosophy*, 275–306 at 276–277; Barnard, *Four Freedoms*, p. 461.

[118] For Shore, 'citizenship is a classificatory device; a way of ordering people in terms of boundaries of inclusion ("insiders") and exclusion ("aliens")'. This could then lead to the alienation of non-citizens on a given territory and overt and implicit ethnocentricism (Yuval-Davies). The end-point of citizenship is then the physical demarcation of self from 'other' in the form of borders; necessitating what Favell terms the 'dirty work of boundary maintenance'.

Shore, p. 71; Yuval-Davies, 'Intersectionality', p.161. Favell, *Philosophies of Integration*, p. 43.

Brexit and potentially further challenges to the integrity of the Union were clearly conceivable, even if not necessarily predictable in the sense that arguably there is an inherent dissonance between EU Citizenship as postnational identification by virtue of the *a priori* origins of the very concept of citizenship itself.

5.3.1 *Public Service Exception Cases*

From the outset, the provisions of free movement in relation to workers specifically excluded employment in the public service (ex Article 48 (4)). The trend of thirty years of jurisprudence has been to severely curtail such an exemption in order to circumvent Member States' repeated attempts to exclude vast sectors of the public sector from the reaches of workers from other Member States.[119] Thus limited, the Court, in *Commission* v. *Belgium*, settled on the notion that in order for the exemption to apply, the employment requires 'a special relationship of allegiance'; a standard clearly considerably higher than simply whether an institution can be classified as a public body (what White terms 'the classic definition of what constitutes employment in the public service').[120]

Nonetheless, what the Court did not do was to challenge the core principle that there are certain aspects of the way a nation-state

[119] See, for example, *Commission* v. *Belgium* (1980) in which Belgium claimed that not only should all national railway employees be covered by such an exemption (including 'painters assistants' and 'office cleaners' but also local government employees (especially in Brussels) (including gardeners, joiners and electricians). Case 149/79, *Commission of the European Communities* v. *Kingdom of Belgium* [1980] ECR 3881, 1847–1848. See also Case 307/84, *Commission of the European Communities* v. *French Republic* [1986] ECR 1725 (nurses); Case 225/85, *Commission of the European Communities* v. *Italian Republic* [1987] ECR 2625 (employees of a national research institute); Case 33/88, *Pilar Allué and Carmel Mary Coonan* v. *Università degli studi di Venezia* [1989] ECR 1591 (foreign language assistants); Case C-4/91, *Annegret Bleis* v. *Ministère de l'Education Nationale* [1991] ECR I 5627 (secondary school teachers) and Case C-42/92, *Adrianus Thijssen* v. *Controledienst voor de verzekeringen* [1993] ECR I 4047 (insurance inspectorate).

[120] *Commission* v. *Belgium [1980]*, p. 3900 at para. 10; White, *Workers, Establishment and Services*, p. 79. See also Handoll, 'Article 48(4) EEC', 223–241; O'Keeffe, 'Judicial Interpretation', p. 89; Anthony Arnull and Francis Jacobs, 'Applying the Common Rules on the Free Movement of Persons: The role of the national judiciary in the light of the jurisprudence of the European Court of Justice' in Henry Schermers (ed.), *Free Movement of Persons in Europe: Legal Problems and Experiences* (Dordrecht: Kluwer Academic Publishers, 1993), pp. 272–285; Jolanda Beenen, *Citizenship, Nationality and Access to Public Service Employment. The Impact of European Community Law* (Groningen: Europa Law Publishing, 2001), p. 48; and Birgit Friedl, 'Fixed Term Contracts for Foreign Language Lecturers – A Proportionate Restriction on Free Movement of Workers?' (1996) 25(1) *Industrial Law Journal*, 66–70.

functions, even within the then EEC, that necessitate reserving employment for its own nationals as it is part of different nation-states' very essence and how they define themselves.[121] In other words, it is a vital aspect of both a nation-state's identity and, therefore, its understanding of citizenship.[122] In *Sotgiu*, the applicant was an Italian national working as a postman in Stuttgart but with his family residing in Italy.[123] Under German law, he would have been entitled to a separation allowance of 10 DM a day had he resided in another part of Germany with his family; however, because he resided outside of Germany altogether he was only entitled to 7.50 DM a day instead.[124] The applicant argued that this provision discriminated against him on the grounds of nationality and the German government countered this by claiming that, as a postal worker, his employment was covered by the public service exemption.[125] In legal terms, the case set an early precedent in the Court's jurisprudence for the limited way in which the Court would allow the public service exception to apply in that it is only the substance of what the job entails that is of relevance not how it is classified (i.e. delivering post).[126] Equally, as the Court ruled in *Sotgiu*, the fact that a non-national was already employed in this particular aspect of the public sector effectively stops a Member State from maintaining the need for it to be the sole preserve of home nationals.[127] The case, though, also revealed the powerful nature of national identity constructs. The Italian government made two points to justify the public service exception in the first place. First, it asserts: 'This provision is justified by the need to be able to rely upon the special loyalties of the national.'[128] In other words, the criterion that

[121] As Barnard states 'It has been traditional for Member States, as part of the exercise of their sovereignty, to reserve certain public-service jobs to their own nationals'. Barnard, *Four Freedoms*, p. 500.

[122] Seen conversely by O'Keeffe: 'this view of the public service exception is founded on a conception of nationality which may face increasing strain. It is based on a very traditional notion of loyalty to the State and finds its parallel in the denial of foreigners of political rights'. O'Keeffe, 'Judicial Interpretation', p. 105.

[123] Case 152/73, *Giovanni Maria Sotgiu* v. *Deutsche Bundespost* [1974] ECR 153, p. 155.

[124] Ibid.

[125] Ibid.

[126] Ibid., p. 163 at para. 4.

[127] White, *Workers, Establishment and Services*, p. 80. See also Wyatt, 'Scope of Equal Treatment', 62–63; Gillian Morris, Sandra Fredman and Jon Hayes, 'Free Movement and the Public Sector' (1990) 19(1) *Industrial Law Journal*, 20–28; Barnard, *Four Freedoms*, p. 500; Brigitte Lenz, 'The Public Service in Article 48 (4) EEC with Special Reference to the Law in England and in the Federal Republic of Germany' (1989) 16(2) *Legal Issues in Economic Integration*, 75–112.

[128] *Sotgiu*, pp. 157–158.

needs to be satisfied in order to be allowed to be employed in the public service is of loyalty to a particular nation and that loyalty is not only a non-legal concept (though clearly appearing within a legal text) but also it is the demonstrable evidence of the success of a particular manifestation of identity construction. This would be hard to replicate on an EU-wide basis.[129] Second, the Italian government also claimed that it would not be appropriate for a non-national to be employed within the public service because, should that happen: 'such an employee remains a stranger to the organization, to which he is not integrated by any organic bond'.[130] This demonstrates both the powerful nature of national identity constructs and, paradoxically, the problems with such a construction. Thus far, a core aspect of national identity has been shown to be that of loyalty: a national is expected to be loyal to his/her state.[131]

However, shedding further light on this construction is that such loyalty emanates from a 'bond' that is 'organic'. It is not elaborated upon as to what that 'bond' consists of (i.e. what is the social glue by which individuals' identities are knitted together),[132] but what is suggested is that such a bond emerges in an organic fashion. In other words, national identities emerge almost naturally over a considerable period of time through, in part, the construction of a particular national narrative.[133] On one level, EU Citizenship does have this potential in that the thrust of this book examines the emergence of a commonly understood narrative of the Citizen (being complex and context-specific) and this development could

[129] As Harty and Murphy maintain: 'without this sense of attachment or solidarity, it may be very difficult, if not impossible, to sustain levels of mutual understanding, self-sacrifice, accommodation and cooperation necessary for a healthy, stable and governable multi-national polity'. Siobhán Harty and Michael Murphy, *In Defence of Multinational Citizenship* (Cardiff: University of Wales Press, 2005), pp. 89–90. See also n. 130.

[130] *Sotgiu*, p. 158.

[131] Whether that is the case or not in reality is not the point, what matters is how the concept is socially constructed. See 'Introduction' on this point.

[132] See Section 5.4 for an elaboration of this point in the context of EU Citizenship. As Barnard put it, part of the purpose behind it was 'to provide the glue to help bind together nationals of all the Member States'. Likewise, Shore opines that 'national identity derives from a *deep-rooted* sense of ethnic community', thereby emphasizing how entrenched and powerful such a 'bond' is. Barnard, *Four Freedoms*, p. 418; Shore, p. 17 (emphasis added).

[133] As Harty and Murphy state: 'national identities are political-historical contingencies formed by a combination of factors, including deliberate state policy . . . habit formation arising from shared practices and common enterprises and sheer accident (wars, treaties, conquests, etc.) The story involving the particular blend and sequence of these various factors can be told in numerous plausible versions'. Harty and Murphy, p. 152.

very much be seen as organic in that it has emerged over more than fifty years. This, though, compares poorly with national narratives that have often emerged over centuries[134] and, indeed, it is questionable as to whether there is even a commonly agreed narrative upon which an identity construction could be built.[135] Moreover, the alienation and ethnocentricism[136] that is at the heart of problematic aspects of identity construction should not, it is submitted, be seen to be replicated on an EU-wide supranational level as the point of EU Citizenship was to provide a novel post-national status that avoids the common pitfalls of national identity practices.[137] As the Italian government put it in the above statement, anyone that is not integrated into a state by an organic bond is, therefore, a 'stranger' to it: an alien that will simply never fit in.

Furthermore, in effect a process of loyalty, bond, narrative and alienation is repeated in *Commission* v. *Belgium* (1980). As has already been cited earlier, the governing criterion for determining what types of professions fell within the scope of employment in public service was outlined in the case. However, the Court's reference to allegiance was actually made in the context of a bigger citation which stated: 'Such posts in fact presume on the part of those occupying them the existence of a special relationship of allegiance to the State and reciprocity of rights and duties which form the foundations of the bond of

[134] For Heater 'the myth of distorted history provide the necessary emotional adhesive for such civic feelings as pride and patriotism'. Likewise, Harty and Murphy allude to the 'age old' connection with territory and narrative and Closa assesses that national identity and national narrative have 'traditionally been linked, at least in the last two centuries'. Heater, p. 184; Harty and Murphy, p. 149; Closa, 'Citizenship of the Union', 487.

[135] As Delanty claims: 'Europe lacks the core components of national culture: language, a shared history, religion, and educational system and press or media.' Delanty, *Citizenship in a Global Age*, p. 96.

[136] As Closa contends: 'Historical narratives (which are a source of identity) transmit a perception of the other and these narratives probably foster or reinforce mythical elements of national identities.' Closa, 'Between EU Constitution', 362.

[137] This was a fundamental question posed by Bellamy in relation to the project of EU Citizenship: 'Is a shared nationality necessary to bind people to each other and to the state? If so, what are the sources of such national feelings? Can their less appealing aspects, such as xenophobia and racism, be avoided?' An attempt will be made to answer this question based upon utterances within the text of pre-1992 free movement cases. Richard Bellamy, 'Introduction: The Making of Modern Citizenship' in Richard Bellamy, Dario Castiglione and Emilio Santoro (eds.), *Lineages of European Citizenship: Rights, Belonging and Participation in Eleven Nation-States* (Basingstoke: Palgrave Macmillan, 2004), pp. 1–21 at p. 1. See Section 5.4.

nationality'.[138] This utterance by the Court is clearly as much political and rhetorical as it is a powerful yardstick in which to judge future applications of the principle and is also reflected in *Allué*, where foreign language teachers in Italy were being claimed to be subject to a public service exception from the provisions on free movement.[139] In dismissing such a contention, AG Lenz claimed that: 'The persons occupying such posts ... have no special allegiance to the State, nor is there any reciprocity of rights and duties which form the foundation of the bond of nationality.'[140] The strength of loyalty to the nation-state is specifically outlined as a 'special relationship of allegiance' to the state. Once again, the depth of such identity practices would be hard to replicate on a supranational level. Likewise, such an allegiance is created by a 'bond of nationality': an underlying and pervasive social fabric in which such a relation of allegiance is created.[141] Equally, such a 'bond' is rooted in 'foundations' and such foundations are inherently discursive in the sense that an identity emerges through socially constructed practices.[142] Such practices are evidenced, in part, through citizenship, as one aspect of such an identity is rooted in a 'reciprocity of rights and duties'.[143] Therefore, given that rights and duties are context and nation-state specific (i.e. each state defines such rights and duties differently), they form an aspect of a national narrative upon which an identity is, in part, based.[144] Indeed the UK government, in *Commission* v. *Belgium* (1980), implicitly acknowledged the importance of a national narrative when it stated that: '"employment in the public sector" varies from one Member State to another according to the laws or traditions of each of them'.[145]

Nonetheless, there are, once again, two aspects of such identity construction that should be laid bare. The Commission, in the same case,

[138] *Commission* v. *Belgium [1980]*, p. 3900 at para. 10. See also Wyatt, 'Article 48(4) EEC', 459–463.
[139] *Allué*, p. 1593.
[140] Ibid., p. 1601. See also Philippa Watson, 'Free Movement of Workers: Recent Cases' (1989) 14(6) *European Law Review*, 417–422; Friedl, 66–70.
[141] Yuval-Davies, 'Intersectionality', p. 162. See also n. 130.
[142] Maurice Roche, *Exploring the Sociology of Europe* (London: Sage, 2010), p. 76.
[143] See Section 5.2.1.
[144] For Harty and Murphy they are 'an expression of an individual's legal membership in a polity'. In terms of the context-specific origins rights-based citizenship Bellamy maintains that 'there has been no single trajectory for the development of citizenship. It has been played out very differently in different states'. Harty and Murphy, p. 7; Bellamy, 'Introduction', p. 14.
[145] *Commission* v. *Belgium [1980]*, pp. 3892–3893.

submitted that to be a core civil servant in the public service: 'requires devotion and loyalty from officials which is more readily to be expected from nationals than from aliens'.[146] Thus, a non-national is, by definition, considerably less capable of displaying such devotion and loyalty than a home national: he/she is both an 'alien' and, as has already been stated in *Sotgiu*, a 'stranger'.[147] Moreover, for AG Mancini in *Commission* v. *France*, a national narrative can be inherently problematic and a stumbling block for social change. The Advocate-General expressed exasperation at the submissions being made by the French government as the case concerned nurses (with, once again, a nationality requirement and a claimed public service exception) and effectively the same submissions were being made by the French government as were made by the Belgian government in *Commission* v. *Belgium* (1980):

> I have already stated that the points of defence which I have just described coincide exactly with those already relied upon in Case 149/79, which were rejected in the judgments delivered by the Court. Is this a case of faithful adherence to a centuries-old heritage of ideas or, more simply, of difficulty in presenting to the Court a fresh and more cogent line of argument?[148]

The point that is firstly being made by AG Mancini is that a national narrative matters even in the context of legal analysis. The contents of such a narrative both dictate the specific aspects, viewed narrowly, of a national discourse on employment in the public service and (viewed broadly) form a fundamental aspect of national identity.[149] Putting it differently, particular national contexts differ as to what types of professions necessitate a form of national loyalty and which do not, and this is based upon a context-specific 'heritage of ideas'.[150] In *Moser*, for instance, a German national was refused a contract of employment as a teacher in Germany on the grounds that because he was a member of the German Communist Party this put 'his loyalty to the democratic principles of the Federal Republic

146 Ibid., p. 3891.

147 See Section 5.3.1.

148 *Commission* v. *Belgium [1980]*, p. 1729.

149 As Shore states: 'history is central to the imagination of community, for how people experience the past is intrinsic to their perception for the present. It is also fundamental to their conception of *themselves* as subjects and members of a collectivity'. Likewise, for Roche, history, being 'socially constructed [is] . . . a form of collective consciousness connected with distinctive cultural identities'. Shore, p. 41; Maurice Roche, p. 76.

150 See Section 5.3.1.

of Germany in doubt'.[151] Viewed narrowly in order to be a teacher in Germany a loyal adherence to a set of core national values was necessary. By contrast in the UK, for instance, no such loyal adherence is necessary in that no overt or implicit adherence to a set of core values is necessitated in order to become a teacher.[152] In other words, each national context differs in terms of employment However, viewed broadly a context-specific set of national values that are a composite part of a national narrative and hence identity are also outlined in the same sentence.[153] The applicant was supposed to adhere to 'the democratic principles' not generally but of the 'Federal Republic of Germany'.

Moreover, an explicit link is made between discourse and national narrative by AG Mancini in *Commission* v. *France* itself as he effectively terms such a narrative (or indeed set of narratives) a 'heritage of ideas'. Furthermore, a stumbling block is evidently being presented that seems to be preventing the French government in *Commission* v. *France* from advancing something that is either new or 'fresh' or rational ('a cogent line of argument'). This therefore is an example of agency being influenced by something that cannot be reduced to pure rationality and acting accordingly.[154] This tacit influence is made clear by the reference to 'faithful adherence' and, further, it can be linked to individual national identities as such identities have already been described as being dependent on loyalty. Once again, the ethnocentrism underlying the French government's submissions is problematic. First, an almost unthinking adherence to a national narrative is directly preventing the expansion of the law on free movement of persons (in the eyes of the French government at least): such seeming irrationality is worthy of academic analysis in and of itself.[155] Second, a stumbling block for EU Citizenship is also implicitly outlined by AG Mancini as the core of national identity is defined as a 'centuries old heritage';

[151] Case 180/83, *Hans Moser* v. *Land Baden-Württemberg* [1984] ECR 2539, p. 2549. See also Robin White, *Workers, Establishment and Services*, p. 44.

[152] UK Department for Education, 'Basic Requirements to Become a Qualified Teacher' (*Department for Education*, 2014) www.education.gov.uk/get-into-teaching/apply-for-teacher-training/basic-requirements accessed 11 December 2014.

[153] See notes to Section 5.3.1.

[154] See subsequent note.

[155] As Shore claims, 'ideological constructs not only define individuals ... but, more importantly, seeks to infiltrate their subjectivity and consciousness'. Shore, p. 71.

something which would simply not be possible to establish on a supranational level over a considerably shorter period of time.[156]

5.3.2 *Military Service and Social Security*

In addition to cases relating to the public service exception, the line of jurisprudence that exposes at once the strength of national identities and paradoxical frailties of Union Citizenship is that of military service, where arguably the two concepts can be seen within the case law to be mutually exclusive. In *Ugliola*, the applicant was an Italian national employed in a German dairy that had his employment interrupted in Germany in order to perform military service in Italy.[157] Had he been German and called up to perform military service for the Bundeswehr, his conscripted year would have counted as a year of employment in order to derive various social security benefits.[158] In answering the question whether this constituted discrimination on the grounds of nationality AG Gand states: 'The performance of military service in the army of the State other than that of which one is a national is a hypothesis which even [the German government] considers to be somewhat theoretical.'[159] The reason why the AG made such a point is because the German government was trying to claim that this did not constitute discrimination as technically anyone could perform military service for a state in which one is not a national.[160] However, from a critical discursive perspective this 'somewhat theoretical' proposition can be seen to be problematic. In other words, why is it purely a matter of theory that an individual could commit to serve in a national army to which he/she is not a national or even a supranational one? The answer to this question relates inexorably to the potency of national identity construction and issues of loyalty. Putting it differently, an individual's service in the armed forces is considered to be the ultimate expression of loyalty to the state and therefore exemplary of being a 'good citizen'.[161] Even

[156] For this reason, Siim and Squires question 'whether citizenship can be transferred from the nation-state to the trans-national level, and whether it is possible to combine citizenship rights tied to the nation-state to global citizenship and human rights'. Siim and Squires, 'Contesting Citizenship: Comparative Analyses', p. 5.

[157] Case 15–59, *Württembergische Milchverwertung-Südmilch AG* v. *Salvatore Ugliola* [1969] ECR 363, p. 365. See Section 3.5.2 for a summary of the facts.

[158] Ibid.

[159] Ibid., p. 375.

[160] Ibid.

[161] Heater, *Citizenship*, p. 192.

in the context of a conscript, an individual is expected, when called upon, to perform the ultimate act of sacrifice or duty to one's nation by bravely dying in conflict (itself forming a profound aspect of a nation's narrative). As Shore maintains: 'Since classical times the main obligation of citizens (their "first duty") was not simply to participate actively in the life of the *polis*, but to take up arms when called to its defence'.[162] The controversy, then, in relation to the above proposition is whether it is possible to in effect transfer loyalty of individuals, much like that of social security benefits, from one Member State to another, and to whom would such loyalty be owed?

AG Mayras in *Gillard* attempts to answer this seemingly 'theoretical proposition'. The applicant was a Belgian national living in Belgium but employed in France, having previously been a member of the Belgian army and become a Prisoner of War.[163] He attempted to obtain a benefit for ex-servicemen in France which would have entitled him to draw on his pension five years early had he been in captivity for at least fifty-four months (which he was) and been French (which he was not).[164] The referring court asked the following question:

> Does the principle of non-discrimination as laid down with regard to social security in Article 3 (1) of that Regulation prevent a national law such as the French Law . . . from excluding from old-age benefits accorded to ex-servicemen and former prisoners of the 1939–1945 war, on the grounds of the hardship suffered by them and for services rendered by them to their country, citizens of the Community who satisfy those conditions only in relation to their own Member State?[165]

In other words, as has already been suggested, is it possible for 'Citizens of the Community' [*sic*] to use the principle of non-discrimination to allow a non-national to in effect have the loyalty that he/she displayed to his/her own nation transferred to another Member State in order derive a particular benefit? The answer that AG Mayras gives (namely in the affirmative) paradoxically poses critical questions in relation to the normative aspirations of Union Citizenship and, once again, reveals the inherent potency of national identity construction. AG Mayras firstly maintained that the case concerns 'the principle of equality of

162 Shore, p. 78. Likewise, for Yuval-Davies: 'fighting for one's country is one of the major signifiers of citizenship'. Yuval-Davies, 'Intersectionality' p. 162.

163 Case 9/78, *Directeur régional de la Sécurité sociale de Nancy* v. *Paulin Gillard and Caisse régionale d'assurance maladie du Nord-Est, Nancy* [1978] ECR 1661, p. 1664.

164 Ibid. See also Wyatt, 'Discrimination on Grounds', 369–371.

165 *Gillard*, p. 1670.

treatment between nationals of a Member State and other Community Citizens'.[166] By contrast, he claims that it is 'pointless to inquire whether the law in question *also* has the character of benefit schemes for victims of war or its consequences and whether it relates to national solidarity'.[167] With respect to the learned Advocate-General to dismiss such a fundamental aspect of 'national solidarity' [*sic*] as being of no relevance to determining whether a matter falls within the scope of the principle of equal treatment is both politically insensitive and to underestimate the power of such schemes in the context of national narratives.[168]

Instead, though, AG Mayras projects a novel, radical and rather problematic concept of supranational citizenship when he states:

> As workers are not free agents in respect of the fortune of arms and have no choice as the army in which they fight it might be thought that employed persons from *any* Member State who suffer hardship as a result of the last war in the field of the acquisition of rights to old-age pension should have the right, under whatever colours they served, to benefit from the provisions laid down in *any* Member State under which they have a right to benefit.[169]

On the one hand, AG Mayras admits that nation-states still retain control over their own nationals (and in turn identities) when it comes to military service. Contradicting the assertion that the German government made in *Ugliola* in respect of the ability for a non-national to serve in a host Member State's army, the one core aspect of a worker that is restricted is in which army to fight.[170] This, in part, reveals the inherent structural power that a nation-state holds over its own citizens.[171] On the other hand, for AG Mayras, the potential for a form of supranational attributable rights is laid out even in such sensitive area for the Member States. Whilst the choice of army may still be retained within the preserve of the nation-state, in the context of Community law, the 'hardship' 'suffered' can seemingly be transferred from one Member State to another in relation to the receipt of benefits. A form of multiple-layered identity is outlined in that on one level the 'colours' in which a worker serves are still relevant (i.e. national identity constructs still

[166] Ibid., p. 1669.
[167] Ibid., p. 1671.
[168] See, for instance, Maurice Roche, pp. 107–115.
[169] *Gillard*, p. 1671.
[170] For Heater it is the ultimate expression of 'loyalty' and therefore part of being a 'good citizen'. Heater, *Citizenship*, p. 192.
[171] Harty and Murphy, *In Defence of Multinational Citizenship*, p. 1.

exist); except that they do not matter in relation to the receipt of benefits for war pensions as such a benefit can be obtained in '*any* Member State' in which such a right exists (i.e. a form of supranationalism).[172] Furthermore, AG Mayras (in *Gillard*) justifies such a radical claim by attempting to equate one form of suffering with another in accordance with the principle of equal treatment:

> There can be no doubt that a scheme such as that set out in Article L 332 (2) of the social security code extends to workers of a nation other than France who are subjects of a Member State (Belgium) which was one of the Allied nations, and who served in the uniform of that State.[173]

On one level, this may seem to be a tempting basis upon which a form of post-nationalism can develop in that what AG Mayras is effectively suggesting is that the two nations (Belgium and France) suffered in the same manner during the Second World War and therefore there is a collective narrative of suffering that can form the basis of supranational solidarity.

On another level, though, such a form of identification is inherently and irretrievably problematic.[174] Such reasoning has been applied here to two Allied nations. However, the reasoning behind such an extension of the principle of equal treatment could equally be applied to, say, a German national claiming the payment of a war pension from the Belgian security system. Therefore, laudable though the normative aspirations of such a proposition were, they were deeply politically insensitive.[175] Arguably being more acutely aware of such a lack of sensitivity, the Court (in *Gillard*) entirely dismisses AG Mayras'

[172] See Section 5.4.1.

[173] *Gillard*, p. 1672.

[174] For Weiler, AG Mayras' reasoning is not without context or moral force but ultimately failed as normative vision. The notion of being able to communitize and collectivize something as sensitive as suffering is what was intended by European integrations. As he states: 'This was in fact the project of the enlightenment taken to the international level, as the Kant himself had dreamt. To embrace the Schuman Plan was to tap into one of the most powerful idealistic seams in Europe's civilisational mines.' Nonetheless, as he continues, this vision was bound to fail because: 'The deep tragedy of the European construct has been its failure to engrain itself, implant itself in the social and political consciousness as a community of fate'. Weiler, 'Secessionism and its Discontents', pp. 27–31.

[175] Gerber, for instance, makes a repeated distinction between pensions for civilians and war pensions for disabled veterans in which the latter have historically been treated as operating entirely outside the normal framework for state pensions (and involving much more generous terms) to take account of the sacrifice of such individuals. David Gerber, 'Disabled Veterans and Public Welfare Policy: Comparative and Transnational

suggestion. It firstly refuses to extend the principle of equal treatment to war pensions and then states:

It appears from the file that the benefit granted in pursuance of the national provisions in question has the essential purpose of providing for former prisoners of war who prove that they underwent a long period of captivity, testimony of national gratitude for the hardships endured between 1939 and 1945 on behalf of France and its Allies and thus granting them, by an increases in the rate of old-age pension, a *quid pro quo* for the services rendered.[176]

Instead, therefore, what the Court has (rein)stated, by contrast with AG Mayras, is the powerful interrelationship between national citizenship, national identity and national narrative. A narrative of suffering is outlined, one of long periods of captivity and hardships endured, the nation is grateful for the duty fulfilled and the granting of a reward is a '*quid quo pro* for the services rendered' (citizenship) and, implicitly, the interrelationship between a national narrative and the individual forms part of both a collective and individual consciousness in particular nation-states (identity).[177] Once again what the Court in the end concludes is that there is an almost impenetrable potency to such a cultural narrative that would be almost impossible to replicate on a Union-wide basis.[178] Equally, though, the end-point of ethnocentricism implicitly underlies such a line of jurisprudence as what is attempting to be harmonized or equated on a supranational level is suffering and, ultimately death.[179] Given the fact that the main purpose of the construction of the then EEC was to entirely avoid a return to war between nations,[180] it would seem futile to collectively pool such suffering as an extension of the principle of equal treatment and, thereby, to form part of an early basis for the Citizen and to confine it, instead, to being a matter extraneous to Community law and reflective of a period of time prior to the EEC's creation.

Nonetheless, the military service cases also reveal, at their core, the latent power of national identity construction that would seem to leave

Perspectives on Western States in the Twentieth Century' (2001) 11(1) *Transnational Law & Contemporary Problems*, 77–106 at 78–81.

176 *Gillard*, p. 1666 at para. 3 (war pensions), p. 1668 at para. 13.

177 See Gerber, 85–86.

178 For an outline of such a challenge in the context of EU Citizenship, see Douglas-Scott, pp. 580–582.

179 Yuval-Davies, 'Intersectionality', p. 162. For Shore, war is 'parochial' and simply the expression of 'animalistic loyalties', something which the EEC was created to avoid. Shore, *Building Europe*, p. 21.

180 Shore, p. 15.

little discursive residue for an alternative construct loaded with content and meaning in which an EU Citizen can positively identify him/herself as such.[181] The applicant in *Even* was suffering the reverse problem from the applicant in *Gillard* in that he was a French national attempting to obtain the early receipt of a war pension in Belgium.[182] The Commission, like AG Mayras, attempted to extend the remit of the principle of equal treatment:

> It is moreover impossible in the present case to obstruct the application of the principle of equality of treatment either by the consideration of the special link between a national and a Member State as regards the performance of the duty of military service and its consequences or by the consideration of the special protection and aid owed by a Member State to its nationals as regards the after-effects of war.[183]

The Court, though, dismisses this proposition in its entirety by repeating the statement it made in *Gillard* in which emphasis was placed on 'the services which those in receipt of the benefit have rendered in wartime to their own country and its essential objective is to give those nationals an advantage by reason of the hardships suffered for that country'.[184] By doing so the Court was ruling that it was simply not possible to transfer over such hardships to another Member State; the relationship remains uniquely between the individual and his/her home state. For the Commission, it was seemingly 'impossible' to 'obstruct the application of the principle of equality of treatment' even in such a sensitive area as recognition of military service during a time of war. In reality, though, the Court, by entirely dismissing such a suggestion, has offered a proposition to the contrary; namely that there is a 'special link between a national and a Member State' that should be prioritized above and beyond that of equal treatment. Indeed, the 'special link' or 'organic bond' (as has been referred to earlier) is explicitly spelled out by the Commission: the individual has performed a 'duty of military service' and for that reason the 'quid pro quo' of such a sacrifice is that 'special protection and aid' is 'owed by a Member State to its nationals'.

Seen in this manner, the challenges of Union Citizenship in terms of engendering an identity upon which individuals can derive an embedded meaning are enormous. As Shore asserts: 'the challenge is to find a

[181] See Section 5.4.
[182] *Even*, p. 2020.
[183] *Even*, pp. 2027–2028.
[184] Ibid., p. 2034 at para. 23.

European alternative to the axiomatic and hegemonic grip that the nation-state continues to hold over the mindsets of the peoples of Europe'.[185] A strong and organic bond based on (often) a centuries-old narrative upon which national identities are constructed contrasts poorly with that of Union Citizenship. The EU Citizen by contrast appears hollow and vacuous, embodied by a series of essentially parasitic rights which form the core of what EU Citizenship can be collectively understood, in part, to mean, but which do little to engender any kind of loyalty on the part of those benefitting from a right derived from Union law, let alone those who have never exercised any right to free movement.[186] As Shaw critically assesses:

> Another way of highlighting the idiosyncracies of EU citizenship involves looking at the classic elements commonly associated with modelling citizenship as a form of full membership (e.g. status, rights, identity, duties). It is only in the sphere of rights that EU citizenship seems well developed. As to the issue of identity, the sense of 'Europeanness' that exists across the collectivity of citizens is relatively thin in nature, again focused on rights, and it is hardly comparable with the form of societal glue that gives community cohesion to the national (and subnational) polities on which the EU is built.[187]

Thus, what is evident is that the normative 'pull' of national identity is equally outlined within the cases on free movement (in terms of the public service exception and war pensions cases) and serves as a critical point of reflection for the future development of EU Citizenship as a potential form of identity construction.[188] Ironically, therefore, the inability to replicate anything even approaching the level of a national identification on a supranational level was also starkly highlighted from the outset. Thus, by examining contemporary controversies relating to EU Citizenship in the light of the pre-1992 case law, Brexit and potentially further challenges to the integrity of the Union were clearly conceivable, even if not necessarily predictable.

[185] Shore, p. 17. See also Section 5.4.
[186] For Douglas-Scott this is one aspect of the 'torturous problem of European citizenship'. Douglas-Scott, p. 480.
[187] Shaw, 'EU Citizenship – Still Fundamental Status', p. 4.
[188] By contrast with such a 'pull' in terms of national identity, one critical problem with EU Citizenship for Kostakopoulou is that it has a 'weak affective dimension'. Kostakopoulou, 'Writing the Future', 625.

5.4 The Fissure of Seemingly Inherent Impossibility: The (Lack of) Desirability of Postnational Identification

Whilst the previous section of this chapter focussed on the seemingly inherent impossibility of postnational identification simply by virtue of comparing the market citizen within the case law on national identification, this section poses a slightly different question: *should* EU Citizenship be used as a vehicle for engendering a form of postnational identification? To a certain extent posing this question constitutes trashing one of the sacred bulls of European integration. Arguably, EU Citizenship is somewhat loftily portrayed as being part of a vision towards a postnational future, thus ridding at least one part of the globe of the problems inherent in national identification and nationalism. Achieving the seemingly impossible would require a form of narrative or discursive construction upon which such an identity can be based. The earlier case law on free movement offers several options on the discursive menu of identification, all of which are arguably problematic from a normative, as opposed to practical, perspective.

5.4.1 *Identity Based upon Shared Values*

Firstly, one possible form of postnational identification is based on a commonality of values. The applicant in *Burton* v. *British Rail* makes such a point when outlining the purpose of the equal treatment provisions of the Treaty: 'Article 119 forms part of the social objectives of the Community, intended, by common action, to ensure social progress and seeks the constant improvement of the living and working conditions of the people of Europe.'[189] The applicant had thus outlined the fact that there exists a 'people of Europe' and such people could identify themselves as having a commonality based upon the norms of social progress and the improvement of living and working conditions. Likewise, in *Dekker*, AG Darmon refers to 'our community of European societies' and therefore implicitly alludes to a complex web of epistemic communities upon which a form of identity can be

[189] Case 19/81, *Arthur Burton* v. *British Railways Board* [1982] ECR 554, p. 560. See also Frank Wooldridge and Joseph Thomson, 'Railway Travel Permits, Voluntary Redundancy Schemes and EEC Law' (1982) 32 *Scots Law Times*, 261–263; Kieran Bradley, 'Case 12/81, *Garland* v. *British Rail Engineering Limited* and Case 19/81, *Burton* v. *British Railways Board*" (1982) 19 *Common Market Law Review* 629–634 (note); Nigel Foster, 'Sex Discrimination: The Effect of EEC Law on Sex Discrimination in Relation to Early Retirements and Redundancy Payments Schemes' (1987) 14(1) *Legal Issues of Economic Integration*, 111–120.

based.[190] As has already been asserted in Chapters 3 and 4, one aspect of Union Citizenship as it evolved relates to equal treatment and another relates to fundamental rights. In this respect, the incorporation of fundamental rights into the TFEU by virtue of the Charter on Fundamental Rights – expressly identified to be part of an EU Citizen's bundle of rights[191] – has been portrayed as a positive step towards a form of postnational identification and there have been a number of academic commentators that have advocated fundamental rights as a basis for an inclusive and pluricultural (as opposed to ethnocentric and based upon demarcating 'self' from 'other') form of Citizenship.[192]

There are, though, undoubted pitfalls with such an approach. For instance, fundamental rights may be protected on a Union-wide basis but it is not necessarily the case that individuals within the Union even recognize such universal values as relating to the Union *a priori*, let alone basing an aspect of their identities upon

[190] Case C-177/88, *Elisabeth Johanna Pacifica Dekker* v. *Stichting Vormingscentrum voor Jong Volwassenen (VJV-Centrum) Plus* [1990] ECR I 3941, p. 3960 (AG Darmon). See 'Introduction' for an outline of the interrelationship between epistemic communities and identity. See also Josephine Steiner, 'Pregnancy Discrimination in Sex Discrimination' (1991) 16(4) *European Law Review*, 313–320; Ruth Nielsen, 'Case C-177/88, *Elisabeth Johanna Pacifica Dekker* v. *Stichting Vormingscentrum voor Jong Volwassenen (VJV Centrum) Plus*, and Case C-179/88, *Handels-og Kontorfunktionærernes Forbund i Danmark (acting for Birthe Hertz)* v. *Dansk Arbejdsgiverforning (acting for Aldi Marked A/S)*' (1992) 29 *Common Market Law Review* 160–169 (note); Gillian More, 'Reflections on Pregnancy Discrimination under European Community Law' (1992) 14(1) *The Journal of Social Welfare Law*, 48–56.

[191] The preamble to the Charter makes an explicit link between universal values, fundamental rights and citizenship when it states: 'Conscious of its spiritual and moral heritage, the Union is founded on the indivisible, universal values of human dignity, freedom, equality and solidarity; it is based on the principles of democracy and the rule of law. It places the individual at the heart of its activities, by establishing the citizenship of the Union and by creating an area of freedom, security and justice' and Title V of the Charter is explicitly titled 'Citizens' Rights'.

[192] Moreover, as Maas contends: 'The common European identity putatively flowing from common EU citizenship might advance the mutual understanding and trust that enable democratic citizenship, transforming the EU into a multinational or supranational political community in which feelings of common loyalty reflect a shared patriotism rather than a common national identity.' Likewise, for Shore, EU citizenship's normative potential lies in the fact that from it 'collective identity' can be formed that can, in turn, 'lay the foundations for a higher level of consciousness based on allegiance to European, rather than national, institutions and ideals'. For Siim and Squires, its potential as a project is similar in its aims to the notion of global cosmopolitan citizenship, centered, for Harty and Murphy, on the universal concepts of freedom and democracy. Maas, *Creating European Citizens*, p. 96; Shore, p. 21; Siim and Squires, p. 10; Harty and Murphy, pp. 81–83. See also 'Introduction' for an outline of the notion of 'self' and 'other'.

them.[193] Conversely, it could also be suggested that it is not necessarily normatively desirable to base any identity upon fundamental rights in the wake of a number of politically controversial decisions of the Strasbourg court which are then either ignorantly or deliberately conflated within Union policy by Eurosceptics such as UKIP.[194] Despite, this, there was emphasis in the early case law upon common values being an aspect of EU Citizenship and hence identity. In *Lawrie-Blum*, for instance, the applicant, a UK national born in Portugal, had applied to study a teacher training course in Freiburg and was refused on the grounds that in order to be a teacher, one had to be a civil servant and in order to be a civil servant one had to be a German national.[195] One justification for such discrimination was based upon what being a civil servant of any description in Germany entails, namely the necessity for a declaration to commit to 'the principles of the free and democratic social order'.[196] With respect to such submissions by the German government, arguably such values are universal and not necessarily solely an aspect of a distinct national narrative.[197] In other words, there appears, at least somewhat superficially, firstly, no reason why the applicant could not equally commit to such values and, secondly, why such values (i.e. a commitment to democratic principles) cannot form part of a postnational narrative. Nonetheless, even at this point,

193 In Antonsich's view, after an extensive survey, what emerges is a view amongst a minority of the survey's respondents that the EU represents a 'space that protects human rights, a space of democracy and tolerance, and a space at peace' but the problem is that even for this minority such values do not form the core upon which a form of European identity could be based. Marco Antonsich, 'The narration of Europe in "national" and "post-national" terms: Gauging the gap between normative discourses and people's views' (2008) 11(4) *European Journal of Social Theory*, 505–522 at 514–518.

194 Exemplary of this is the response by UKIP to the *Hirst* v. *UK (No. 2)* case where the ECtHR held that a blanket ban by the UK of prisoners' entitlement to vote violated Article 3 of Protocol No.1. In commenting on the UK government's attempt to implement the ruling, UKIP MEP Paul Nuttall commented 'Quite frankly we should not even be contemplating appeasing the Strasbourg court, our own Parliament should decide who can and cannot vote in this country. We must stand up to this Mickey Mouse court and we must withdraw from the EU as a matter of urgency'.

Case of Hirst v. *The United Kingdom (No. 2)* [2005] ECHR 681; Paul Nuttall, 'No Votes for Prisoners' (*UKIP*, December 18th 2013) http://ukipnw.org.uk/no-votes-for-prisoners accessed 11 December 2014.

195 Case 66/85, *Deborah Lawrie-Blum* v. *Land Baden-Württemberg* [1986] ECR 2121, p. 2122.

196 Ibid.

197 See n. 187. See also White, 'Round-up of Cases', 147–153; and Handoll, Article 48(4) EEC', 223–241.

the context of such statements cannot be ignored with continual emphasis being placed upon such seemingly universal values also being inherently European.

5.4.2 *Citizenship and Education*

A second potential avenue for postnational reconstruction relates to education. There were important sociopolitical and contextual reasons behind the radical development of the Common Vocational Training Policy by the Court in *Gravier* and beyond. AG Slynn, in *Commission* v. *Belgium*, when alluding to *Gravier*, stated: 'This case is also important to the Commission since, to adapt Disraeli, "upon the education of the people of this Community the fate of this Community depends"'.[198] This development in (then) Community law was not simply concerned with a perceived unfairness of such an obvious discrimination on the grounds of nationality. The consequences of such a development would inevitably lead to a great increase in students in one Member State choosing to be educated in higher education in another Member State (or indeed multiple Member States) and then forming a truly postnational, multinational and young set of novel epistemic communities in which the peoples of Europe can literally be brought closer together in accordance with the Treaty's original aims.[199] Indeed, this point is emphasized by the Court in deciding the legislative basis of the *Erasmus* scheme (*Commission* v. *Council*) when it alludes to the scheme as being 'in keeping with the general objectives of the Community, such as the achievement of people's Europe'.[200] This itself is reflective of one of the bases for the Decision to adopt the *Erasmus* scheme when it is stated that the: 'Commission, in following up the People's Europe initiative of the European Council, has attached the highest priority to university cooperation'. Moreover, another basis for the Decision alludes to: 'the intellectual potential of the individual universities throughout the Community [which] could be much more effectively exploited by providing a network for increasing student and university teacher mobility and other forms of inter-university cooperation throughout the

[198] *Commission* v. *Belgium [1988]*, p. 333. See also Arnull, 'Institutional and jurisdictional questions', 260–267.

[199] Namely an 'ever-closer union among the peoples of Europe' as contained in the preamble to the original Treaty. For Maas, the CVP was developed by the Commission to reflect a 'people's Europe concept [in which] education, free movement and EU citizenship are linked'. Maas, *Creating European Citizens*, p. 109.

[200] Case 242/87, *Commission of the European Communities* v. *Council of the European Communities* [1989] ECR 1425, p. 1456 at para. 29.

Community'. In other words there is potential for the creation and expansion of a numerous and novel postnational form of epistemic communities, of which students are one.[201] Indeed, Wolff, commenting on the Erasmus scheme in an article in the New York Times, alludes to the 'Erasmus generation' and highlights such potential when he maintains:

> For the first time in history, we're seeing the seeds of a truly European identity . . . Give it 15, 20 or 25 years, and Europe will be run by leaders with a completely different socialization from those of today . . . I'm quite optimistic that in the future there will be less national wrangling, less Brussels-bashing and more unity in EU policy making – even if that is hard to picture today.[202]

In other words, the expansion of the scope of the Union's policies in the post-*Gravier* era heralded the potential for future identification based upon the shared values and experiences of over 1.2 million young people exercising their rights under the scheme to study abroad over twenty-five years since the scheme's inception.[203] Thus, whilst the *Erasmus* scheme (and other students moving to study from one Member State to another) may only occupy a minority of the EU's population, there at least appears, so the argument goes, to be the potential, over a long period of time, for the creation of a postnational identity in the form of EU Citizenship based upon a pan-European education policy.

However, arguably Wolff's predictions have simply not come to pass in that over fifteen years after making such a prediction it would be hard to suggest that there is 'less national wrangling', 'Brussels bashing' or, indeed, policy unity in an era of challenges from populism that Wolff clearly did not predict. Indeed, what Brexit arguably also reveals is that, to an extent, whether an epistemic community of elite and educated individuals has a sense of European identity engendered within them over time does not impact upon feelings of more widespread postnational identification amongst EU Citizens more

201 For Maas, the *Erasmus* scheme enables 'national authorities . . . [to] use education to foster civic engagement and a shared sense of community. Education has played a similar dual role on the process of European integration . . . [by] promoting student mobility . . . it was also intended to foster a European cultural identity and created a shared sense of European citizenship'. Maas, *Creating European Citizens*, p. 109. See also Wiener, 'Citizenship', p. 408.

202 Katrin Bennhold, 'Quietly sprouting: A European Identity' *The New York Times* (New York, 26 April 2005) www.nytimes.com/2005/04/26/world/europe/26iht-enlarge2.html?pagewanted=all&_r=0 accessed 7 August 2020 (interviewed by Bennhold).

203 See notes to Section 5.4.1.

generally.[204] Fundamentally the 'Remain' campaign in the UK was supported by the leaders of all the major political parties but yet this clearly did not, ultimately, do enough to persuade the UK's population that this was a project of postnational identification that they could themselves could identify with.[205] More profoundly, though, there is arguably a problem inherent in such seemingly lofty ambitions in the first place. If, under SC theory, there is an inherent link between identity and norms/discourse then the question remains as to what the syllabus for the so-called peoples of Europe would contain? In addition, to summarize what has been outlined earlier, the 'seeds' of a 'truly European identity' are based on a Community people linked to specific territory: Europe. Both of these issues will be examined in turn.

5.4.3 *Cultural Heritage as a Basis for Citizenship*

Fundamentally, it could be suggested that the end-point of such a European Citizen's syllabus – at least one that could lead a form of postnational identification – is that of a shared heritage. The final potential for postnational identification that is identified within the pre-1992 case law for the construction of a postnational identity based upon EU Citizenship relates to Europe's cultural heritage. One criticism of an approach to citizenship based upon a universal set of values is that such universalism, conversely, makes it difficult to construct identities with profound meaning because of a lack of link to a deeply embedded narrative which, in a national sense, forms the bedrock of citizenship as an identity project.[206] In this context, various statements within the

[204] See n.112.

[205] With, it should be noted, an enormous caveat as outlined by Favell, in terms of how close the Brexit vote actually was and what it in reality represented. As he put it: 'Fifty-two per cent – or to be more precise, the victorious 35 per cent or so of the British electorate who bothered to show up to vote 'leave' – is no more a verdict on the behavioural foundations of a society than it is an expression of truly democratic politics. Democracy, and Britain's extensive Europeanization, have both been silenced by a show of hands in a moronic inferno orchestrated by Daily Mail and Daily Telegraph headlines – democracy and the definition of Britain sitting in the crabby hands of a few Fleet Street editors.' Favell, Adrian, 'European Union versus European Society: Sociologists on "Brexit" and the "Failure" of Europeanization' in William Outhwaite (ed.), *Brexit: Sociological Responses* (London: Anthem Press, 2017), pp. 193–200, p. 196. That being said, a so-called moronic inferno orchestrated by national newspapers could itself be construed as discursive in in this respect impressions count and in circumstances where the official case for Remain was made principally on economic grounds lacking any attempt to engender postnational identification as reason for remaining.

[206] See Section 5.3.

text of the case law demonstrate the potential for an identity based upon a European narrative.[207] In *Bond van Adverteerders*, AG Mancini advocates the inclusion within ex Article 59 of the Treaty of services provided by cable distributors of programmes emanating from another Member State but with advertisements specifically targeted at the Member State in which such services were being received.[208] The first reason that AG Mancini gives is that to do so is 'more consistent than any other with the philosophy on which the Community edifice, above all, recognition of the "four great freedoms" are based'.[209] Such a statement can easily be seen in SC terms in that AG Mancini is alluding to both a philosophy and a discourse on which an edifice or sociocultural institution is based.[210] The second reason why AG Mancini is particularly enthusiastic about affording protection to such cable providers is that it enables 'access of Community citizens to cultural programmes of other Member States'.[211] For the Advocate-General, this has a huge amount of potential as:

> It corresponds to the aims of the Community that national cultural features available, no matter by what organization they are supplied, should be accessible to everyone in the whole Community. If interpenetration and integration of national cultures by means of trade in goods (books, periodicals, films, fashions), tourism and freedom of movement for creative artists ... do not arouse

[207] There are a number of advocates for engendering a form of EU Citizenship based upon a common European cultural heritage. Tasliki, for instance, emphasizes the need to bring 'a common cultural heritage to the fore' in establishing citizenship. Harty and Murphy, likewise envisage EU Citizenship as an alternative to nationality (with all its pitfalls) based on 'cultural postnationalism'. Preuß terms the concept a 'civilizational entity' and Shore suggests that there is a: 'possibility of a European consciousness leading to feelings of obligation to the European commonwealth as an imagined historical community'.

Liza Tasliki, 'The Construction of European Identity and Citizenship through Cultural Policy' (2007) 24(2) *European Studies*, 157–182 at 176; Harty and Murphy, pp. 141–143; Ulrich K Preuß, 'Problems of a Concept of European Citizenship' (1995) 1(1) *European Law Journal*, 267–281 at 269; Shore, p. 67. See also Bellamy, 'Evaluating Union citizenship', 597.

[208] Case 353/85, *Bond van Adverteerders and others* v. *The Netherlands State* [1988] ECR 2085, p. 2115.

[209] Ibid. See also Matthijs De Blois, 'Case 352/85, *Bond van Adverteerders* v. *The Netherlands State*, Judgment of 26 April 1988' (1990) 27 *Common Market Law Review* 371–381 (note); Georges Friden, 'The *Bond van Adverteerders* Case and Recent Legal Developments in EEC "Television Law"' (1990) 3(2) *Leiden Journal of International Law*, 231–238 at 231–234.

[210] See 'Introduction' for an outline of the interrelationship between discourse, culture and philosophy.

[211] *Bond van Adverteerders*, p. 2115.

concern the position cannot be any different for broadcasting as a cultural medium.[212]

Thus, Union Citizenship as an identity construct could potentially be based upon a multilayered cultural structure of 'interpenetration and integration of national cultures'.[213]

The layered aspect of such a construct can also be seen as a unique form of pluriculturalism. In *Groener*, AG Darmon maintained that 'it is essential to preserve Europe's cultural richness and to ensure the diversity of its linguistic heritage'.[214] The case concerned a Dutch national in Dublin who was refused the opportunity of a full-time job at a state-funded college of marketing and design on the basis of a requirement to speak Gaelic.[215] The applicant could speak English and Dutch and argued that given the fact that in practice the English language would be used in the college, such a provision simply constituted discrimination on the grounds of nationality.[216] The struggle against the English both physically and linguistically in terms of re-establishing Gaelic in Ireland is a fundamental aspect of the Republic's cultural history and is therefore also a core aspect of Irish identity.[217] As the Court stated in *Groener*, these efforts have for 'many years ... been designed not only to maintain but also to promote the use of Irish as a means of expressing national identity and culture'.[218] Nonetheless, what has in effect taken

212 Ibid., pp. 2115–2116.

213 The nature of a European culture as a potential for a form of postnational identification is outlined by Shore when he states: 'it is located ... in traditions like Roman law, Greek philosophy Hebraic ethics and Christian theology, as well as their Renaissance and Enlightenment successors. These traditions have permeated the European continent to produce a "Europe culture-area"'. Heater, likewise, alludes to an 'EU discourse on European culture' as a potential basis for EU Citizenship, particular given the Greco-Roman origins of the very notion of citizenship. Shore, pp. 16–17; Heater, pp. 2–27.

214 Case C-379/87, *Anita Groener* v. *Minister for Education and the City of Dublin Vocational Educational Committee* [1989] ECR 3967, p. 3982.

215 Ibid. See also Bryan McMahon, 'Case 379/87, *Groener* v. *Minister for Education and The City of Dublin Vocational Education Committee (CDVEC)*, Judgment of 28 November 1989' (1990) 27 *Common Market Law Review* 129–139 (note).

216 Ibid.

217 This is exemplified by the Friel play *Translations*. Brian Friel, *Translations* (London: Faber and Faber, 1981). See also Lionel Pilkington, 'Language and Politics in Brian Friel's *Translations*' (1990) 20(2) *Irish University Review*, 282–298; Collin Meissner, 'Words between Worlds: The Irish Language, the English Army and the Violence of Translation in Brian Friel's *Translations*' (1992) 28(3) *Colby Quarterly*, 164–173; Anthony Roche, *Brian Friel: Theatre and Politics* (Basingstoke: Palgrave Macmillan, 2012), pp. 130–152.

218 *Groener*, p. 3992 at para. 18.

place in the case is a preference in favour of a cultural policy in Ireland designed to re-establish Gaelic as a spoken language and against a Community Citizen's right to free movement. Despite this apparent limitation, though, on the Citizen's individual rights, for AG Darmon, a scheme such as that in the Republic of Ireland can be seen to establish rather than detract from a European culture. He firstly states:

> The preservation of languages is one of those questions of principle which one cannot dismiss without striking at the very heart of cultural identity. Is it therefore for the Community to decide whether or not a particular language should survive? Is the Community to set Europe's linguistic heritage in its present state for all time? Is it to fossilize it?[219]

The answer that AG Darmon gives to such a set of questions is to suggest that it should be part of Community policy to attempt to preserve the linguistic diversity of peoples within the Union.[220] In other words, a key aspect of an additional layer of identification in a postnational sense should be to emphasize unity in difference and this is what EU Citizenship should be rooted in. He further maintains:

> At this point I would like to quote from *Le degree de l'écriture* by Roland Barthes:'il n'y a pas de pensée sans langage', he states after having written 'la lange ... est l'aire d'une action, la definition et l'attent d'un possible'. To limit the requirement of a knowledge of Irish to posts involving the actual teaching of Irish would be to treat it like ancient Greek or Latin, and as a language incapable of further development, or, at least, as a confidential language whose use is restricted to a small circle of initiates.[221]

Immediately the link is made between individuals' thoughts being dictated by language or discourse.[222] AG Darmon also makes an appeal against the restriction of the Irish language to simply Irish language classes for want of it being 'restricted to a small circle of initiates'.[223] Indeed, what is being proposed in this book is that for Union Citizenship to develop it cannot be restricted to a small circle of initiates. In this respect the appeal by AG Darmon to Greek and Latin is deliberate in that it is making an explicit link to Europe's cultural heritage based partly upon its Greco-Roman origins.[224] The difference, though, is that AG Darmon is

219 Ibid., p. 3982.
220 Ibid.
221 Ibid.
222 See 'Introduction' for an outline of the link between language and discourse.
223 *Groener*, p. 3982.
224 See notes to Section 5.4.3.

effectively making an appeal to a Community body – the Court – to not make the same mistakes as were made with ancient Greek and Latin and allow the language to not be a living one. Instead of 'fossilising' Gaelic's development, what AG Darmon was implicitly asserting was that it should be the Union's role to foster the development of diverse languages. In this respect, what cannot be ignored in the case is that there was a political movement in Ireland to establish the European Office on Minority Languages in Dublin.[225]

Perhaps, so the argument goes, an emphasis on unity through diversity could form the potential for a dynamic and evolving postnational form of identification based upon EU Citizenship because it both creates a layered supranational narrative based upon shared values whilst at the same time avoiding the ethnocentricism that tends to be at the heart of such a narrative.[226] It is clear that there had been an attempt by the Union as a whole to encourage inclusive and postnational forms of

[225] AG Darmon was actually referring to the now defunct European Bureau for Lesser-Used Languages (based in Dublin), a project jointly funded by the Commission and the Council of Europe. European Bureau for Lesser-Used Languages, 'About Us' (*EBLUL*, 2010) http://eblul.eurolang.net/index.php?option=com_content&task=view&id=14&Itemid=33 accessed 11 December 2014.

See also Niamh Nic Shuibhne, 'The European Union and Minority Language Rights' (2001) 3(2) *International Journal on Multicultural Societies*, 61–77; J Fishman, 'The New Linguistic Order' (1998) 113 *Foreign Policy*, 26–40; François Grin, 'European Economic Integration and the Fate of Lesser Used Languages' (1993) 17(1) *Language Problems and Language Planning*, 101–116.

[226] For Siim and Squires, this 'vision' of EU Citizenship is a 'differentiated citizenship ... [an] inclusionary and multi-layered citizenship that is able to reconcile national belonging with a transnational notion of citizenship'. Likewise, for Liebert, this vision is a: 'European citizenship conception defining democratic inclusiveness while keeping with fundamental concerns about the rights and diversity of "others" ... [and] denotes a multi-layered construction of a new form of transnational membership that aims at reconciling equality with diversity.' It is also, for Liebert, a form of 'active political citizenship in a deliberative European policy ... acknowledging different spheres of belonging that are relevant for citizens in Europe within a shared framework for equal European citizenship rights'. Indeed, for De Búrca 'the legitimacy of the Union should be founded on a concept of citizenship and identity which is neither exclusionary nor linked to national ties, but which is defined inclusively by reference to political and civic participation'. One final aspect of this notion of citizenship is its evolving and adaptive inclusivity. As Kostakopoulou opines: 'It should resist closure and be more at ease with the infinitude of the social that accompanies institutionalised projects.'

Siim and Squires, p. 133; Liebert, pp. 16–17, p. 28; Gráinne De Búrca, 'The Quest for Legitimacy in the European Union' (1996) 59 MLR 349–376 at 360; Dora Kostakopoulou, 'Towards a Theory of Constructive Citizenship in Europe' (1996) 4(4) *The Journal of Political Philosophy*, 337–358 at 358.

identity through the creation of institutions such as the Committee of the Regions and, as has been identified earlier, an office designed to protect minority languages.[227] Seen as a commensurate whole, Union Citizenship has, it seems, a great deal of potential in a pluricultural melting pot within the Union in which individuals are given conceptual space to have multiple and overlapping identities and that AG Darmon in *Groener* implicitly illustrates this point.[228] For instance, a Catalan may have more in common with a Frenchman from Biarritz than with a fellow Spaniard from Madrid.[229] Such an individual may, for instance, perceive him/herself as being both Catalan and an EU Citizen above and beyond being Spanish. Likewise, in Belgium, where *French Community and Walloon Government* v. *Flemish Government* (2008) itself demonstrated evident tensions between the French and Flemish speaking regions, emphasis may be placed on EU Citizenship above and beyond Member State nationality.[230] Thus, whilst certain sections of the populations of the Member States may still primarily identify themselves based upon nationality, there may be a number of areas within the EU that would find EU Citizenship as a liberating form of postnational identification.-[231] The encouragement of both regionalization and linguistic diversity

[227] For further analysis of the important role that the Committee of the Regions plays in engendering EU Citizenship based upon the Union's cultural policy see Juan Delgado Moreira, 'Cohesion and Citizenship in EU Cultural Policy' (2000) 38(3) *Journal of Common Market Studies*, 449–470. See also Ekaterina Domorenok, 'The Committee of the Regions: in Search of Identity' (2009) 19(1) *Regional and Federal Studies*, 143–163; Alex Warleigh, 'A committee of no importance? Assessing the Relevance of the Committee of the Regions' (1997) 17(2) *Politics*, 101–107.

[228] See n. 193.

[229] For Harty and Murphy, this form of 'multinational citizenship' constitutes a 'political mobilization in favour of self-determination for substate . . . peoples should be conceptualized as part of the broader trend towards democratization that has been sweeping the globe'. Likewise, for Siim and Squire: 'membership of a community allows for a broader discourse about local and global levels of citizenship'. Finally, Delanty maintains: 'The most important challenges for citizenship are the double task of devolving national citizenship downwards to subnational units such as regions, cities and localities, on the one side, and on the other side transferring citizenship upwards to the European Union'.

Harty and Murphy, p. 163; Siim and Squires, p. 10; Delanty, *Citizenship in a Global Age*, p. 121.

[230] See also Dennis Martin, 'Comments on *Gouvernement de la Communauté française and Gouvernement wallon* (Case C-212/06 of 1 April 2008) and *Eind* (Case C-291/05 of 11 December 2007)' (2008) 10(3) *European Journal of Migration and Law*, 365–379.

[231] For further analysis of the emancipatory potential of EU Citizenship as a form of postnational identity see Bellamy, 'Evaluating Union citizenship', 610 (claims that EU Citizenship will simply fail as a project if such an identity does not emerge); Yuval-Davies, 'Intersectionality' (in the context of globalization); Siim and Squires, p. 160;

could therefore in part create a unique cultural narrative for the Union itself, upon which a novel and inclusive form of identity could be based. Whilst an extensive discussion of identity based upon Union Citizenship is beyond the scope of this book, what is clear is that there is both an implicit and overt discussion of it emanating from the Court's jurisprudence and such utterances within judgments can potentially conceptualize the ultimate form upon which a living identity based on Union Citizenship may emerge.

Fundamentally, though, the emergence of a form of supranational citizenship based such a cultural heritage is inherently problematic. Despite such seemingly emancipatory visions being outlined within the early case law on free movement, a lingering issue remains – a normative fissure – as to whether underpinning EU Citizenship with meaning in a thick sense based upon shared cultural heritage, even if presented in a pluricultural way, is desirable even if attainable. Unavoidably an emphasis on shared heritage as a form of identity is based upon identification with an entire continent, as opposed to a nation, but can thus be criticized (and has been by many commentators) as simply replicating the same problems of a national ethnocentricism on a much larger scale. For Lister, the problem with trying to embed a form of European identity is that 'to be European is to be white, Christian and holding to a Eurocentric view of the world, and that to be other than this is to be "other", to be outside'.[232] Likewise, for Ward, the fundamental problem with EU Citizenship is that it ultimately replicates 'them and us' and Hansen, whilst being broadly in favour of the concept, stresses the need to avoid the impression of cultural superiority.[233] If anything, this particular vision of EU Citizenship encounters a relatively novel contemporary development in the form of the Black Lives Matter movement. One key aspect of the movement, at least within Europe, has been an attempt to force some of the key Member States of the EU to come terms with, critique and holistically understand the brutal implications of their colonial legacies and European integration, with citizenship deposited at the very top of a very European Greek temple, and the Union institutions and

Yasemin Nuhoğlu Soysal, *Limits of Citizenship*, pp. 17–27; Delanty, *Citizenship in a Global Age*, pp. 65–67; Preuß, 267–281.

232 Ruth Lister, *Citizenship: Feminist Perspectives*, pp. 46–47.

233 Ward, pp. 155–156; Peo Hansen, '"European Citizenship", or where Neoliberalism meets Ethnoculturalism: Analysing the European Union's citizenship discourse' (2000) 2(2) *European Societies*, 139–165 at 154.

some of its Member States appear to be epistemologically blind to this issue.[234] As Linke put it:

> As Europe strives to achieve political and economic unity, we see a concurrent push toward inequality, exclusion and marginalization. The legacies of colonialism and nationalism not only continue to imprint the privilege of whiteness onto the new map of Europe, but sustain the political fortification of Europe as a hegemonic white space.[235]

Being European in this context is simply a synonym for 'white, Anglophone and Christian'.[236] The Black Lives Matter movements have arguably crystallized this issue and brought what was 'exquisite and glaring' to the fore.[237] Begum, for instance, states: 'people in European countries have been taking part in Black Lives Matter protests. Many have been condemning Europe's colonial past, not least in Belgium, where the EU has its headquarters' and continues: 'People working in European Union institutions regularly remark on its whiteness. Many even use the hashtag #BrusselsSoWhite to record their experiences.'[238] Thus arguably, attempts to engender identification with shared 'European' values, even if seen in a universalist or emancipatory manner, could be seen to simply collectivize a culturally loaded legacy, simply on a supranational level.

Moreover, in the light of Brexit (and the populism that underpins it), a further word of caution needs to be uttered in terms of outlining the emancipatory potential of EU Citizenship as a form of postnational identity based on 'humanizing' free movement and embedding citizenship in shared values and cultural experiences. Arguably in the light of

[234] Roger Tooze and Craig N. Murphy, 'The Epistemology of Poverty and the Poverty of Epistemology in IPE: Mystery, Blindness and Invisibility', *Millennium* 25 (3), (1996), pp. 681–707.

[235] Uli Linke 'Technologies of Othering: Black Masculinities in the Carceral Zones of European Whiteness' in Manuela Ribeiro Sanches, Fernando Clara, João Ferreira Duarte and Leonor Pires Martins (eds.), *Europe in Black and White: Immigration, Race and Identity in the 'Old Continent'* (Bristol: Intellect, 2011), pp. 123–142, p.125.

[236] Vron Ware, 'White Resentment: The Other Side of Belonging' in Manuela Ribeiro Sanches, Fernando Clara, João Ferreira Duarte and Leonor Pires Martins (eds.), *Europe in Black and White: Immigration, Race and Identity in the 'Old Continent'* (Bristol: Intellect, 2011), pp. 155–172, p.169.

[237] Chambon, p. 60.

[238] Neema Begum, 'Is being European a white identity? Brussels needs deep reflection in the wake of the Black Lives Matter movement', (The Conversation, 2020), https://theconversation.com/is-being-european-a-white-identity-brussels-needs-deep-reflection-in-the-wake-of-the-black-lives-matter-movement-141902, accessed on 19 September 2020.

recent developments since the 2016 referendum in particular, the emancipatory potential of EU Citizenship is on a knife-edge and the self-same proclaimed values could also sow the seeds for its potential destruction. The argument is this: if citizenship was built on weak foundations from the outset by protecting the 'undeserving' for instance, then its saving grace is in emphasizing the counterbalance of deserving litigants (see further on this issue), combined with an inclusive vision of a common future based on shared values and a shared history. It could certainly be suggested that the arguments in favour of articulating the benefits to the host state of EU migrants remain. They will, though, potentially be drowned out by those articulating the self-same values – of a common European heritage – in the name of populism and far-right nationalism. The concept of 'Fortress Europe' has existed for quite some time. However, the articulation of so-called European values not in the name of inclusion and empathy for the 'other' but in order to justify the continual exclusion of non-EU Citizens from the territory of the EU renders a development in this direction at least potentially problematic. As Jünemann et al. maintain:

> Nationalist, anti-migrant parties from Slovakia over Germany to the UK are gaining increased support among the electorate, challenging not only the political "establishment" but also ideas of an open and humanitarian society ... While the search for solutions has not yet ended, a pattern seems to be emerging: Border fences are getting higher and higher. Fortress Europe is in the making.[239]

If anything, the oft-cited *Ruiz Zambrano* case illustrates this problem. Whilst it is clear that the Court emphasized the derivative rights for the parents of two of the Ruiz Zambrano children based on their EU Citizenship (contrasting therefore with AG Sharpston who emphasized their potential reliance directly on Article 8 ECHR), what is left entirely unresolved is the situation of those who simply could not derive any parasitic rights at all based on family members acquiring nationality of a Member State.[240] In other words, those not fortunate enough to be in

[239] Annette Jünemann, Nicolas Fromm and Nikolas Scherer, 'The kaleidoscope of migration – Theoretical perspectives and conceptual considerations', in Annette Jünemann, Nicolas Fromm and Nikolas Scherer (eds.) *Fortress Europe? Challenges and Failures of Migration and Asylum Policies* (Wiesbaden, Springer, 2017), pp. 1–11, p. 1.

[240] Case C-34/09 *Gerardo Ruiz Zambrano* v. *Office national de l'emploi (ONEm)*. [2011] ECR I- 1177. For extensive commentary on the implications of the case see Dimitry Kochenov (Ed.) *EU Citizenship and Federalism: The Role of Rights* (Cambridge: Cambridge University Press, 2017).

the position of the Ruiz Zambrano family would very much feel the hard edge of a European form of 'othering'. Seen in this manner EU Citizenship is as problematic as both the Roman and Athenian models. Both models fundamentally only created entitlements for a relatively small number of individuals within both empires in the sense that women, slaves and anyone not considered to be either Roman or Athenian were not citizens.[241] Thus, in addition to suggesting that aspects of the early case law on free movement reveal a fissure of inherent impossibility, it could also perhaps be maintained that, if not managed carefully at least, postnational identification based on 'European' citizen is not even normatively desirable.

5.5 A Form of Postnational Reconstruction? What of the Citizen?

This chapter, from the outset, outlined two fissures that appear to emanate from within the early case law that could potentially play a significant role in the dismantling of the entire project of EU Citizenship. It has been suggested that a somewhat twisted and controversial notion of solidarity emerged early on in this case law, in which applicants who could be construed as underserving (for want of fulfilling any correlative 'duty' in their host state) derived protection from the court. This can be seen to be particularly controversial in a contemporary environment. Likewise, the fact that the inherent 'normative pull' of nationality (contrasting markedly with the 'market citizen') appears to somewhat ironically illustrate the inherent impossibility of postnational identification based on EU Citizenship (or even its desirability) appears poignant in an era of increased populism and nationalism (of which Brexit is simply one part). Nonetheless, this chapter laid bare such fissures in the case law from the outset but only in the context of illustrating the *potential* for the dismantling of citizenship. In this respect, deconstruction can serve a purpose by virtue of attempting to prompt further discussion and evolution towards EU Citizenship that sheds itself of its loaded and, to a certain extent, ethnocentric legacy.

241 In relation to Roman Citizenship see Aude Chatelard and Anne Stevens, 'Women as legal minors and their citizenship in Republican Rome', *Clio. Women, Gender, History* 43 (2016), pp. 24–47. In relation to Athenian Citizenship see Kostas Vlassopoulos, 'Identity, Experience and Democracy in Classical Athens', *The Classical Quarterly* 57(1) (2007), pp. 33–52.

By way of a tentative conclusion to this book, it could certainly be suggested that critique based on solidarity grounds is at least somewhat unfair and taken entirely out of context. Whilst many of the applicants in the cases examined in the context of the principle of solidarity have been criticized for their apparent lack of contribution to their host state, there is an equal number, if not more, of morally deserving applicants who have both contributed significantly to the host state and fully integrated themselves with it. As has already been outlined, the concept of so-called benefit tourism as a reason to critique EU Citizens who have exercised a right to free movement was simply a myth not substantiated by empirical evidence.[242] However, this issue also can be traced to the very early cases on free movement as what is also evident from the case law is that there were many examples of 'good' contributors who were worthy of analysis in their own right as they can be seen to be exemplary EU Citizens as envisaged by the Treaty by exercising their right to free movement to a significant extent. Moreover, such cases are highly relevant to a contemporary understanding of EU Citizenship because, in a legal sense, in cases on citizenship such as *Bidar*, the yardstick by which to determine whether an applicant should be entitled to a particular benefit in the host state was determined by the Court to be the degree to which an individual has been integrated within the host state.[243]

5.5.1 *The 'Deserving' Applicants*

In the early free movement cases, an informal moral spectrum, under the predominant shadow of the 'taxpayer principle', arose in which an engendered sympathy within the text was evident in favour of heavily integrated applicants within their host Member States. In *Casagrande*, for instance, the applicant was an Italian national residing in Germany who applied for an education grant that was only open to German nationals.[244] However, he could not have been more integrated as a Community national within a host state as he had'lived since his birth in Munich' (a point that AG Warner immediately points out).[245] AG Warner then goes into specific detail about the applicant's circumstances, outlining the fact that if he did not get this grant he would have to quit education altogether and that the only reason that in reality

[242] See Section 2.2.3.
[243] *Bidar*, p. 2119.
[244] Case 9/74, *Donato Casagrande* v. *Landeshauptstadt München* [1974] ECR 773, p. 775.
[245] Ibid., p. 782.

he would ordinarily have been able to claim the entitlement to it as a dependent of his father, who was a worker, was because his father had already died.[246] This engendered sympathy because the degree of integration of the applicant played a role in the outcome of the case as AG Warner emphasized that 'The spirit of Regulation 1612 and of Article 12 in particular' (i.e. the principle of non-discrimination) involves 'equality of treatment ... between the children of ... fellow workers ... [and] equality of opportunity as between those children'.[247] It should also be noted that, given the fact that the applicant's claim was in principle at the time dependent upon his deceased father's rights as a worker, then, given the fact that he was born in Germany, his father would therefore have made many years of economic contribution towards the German tax and social security systems. Putting it simply, the applicant was clearly a deserving case and is treated as such by AG Warner.

Similarly, in *Di Paolo*, the applicant was Italian but had been brought up for most her life in Belgium, where she had been schooled.[248] After school, she then went to study English and work, over the summer, in England and subsequently applied for unemployment benefit in Belgium upon her return.[249] The Belgian authorities refused her application and claimed, instead, that she would either have to have claimed such a benefit from the UK (where she had only worked temporarily) or Italy (where she had never resided).[250] The applicant was, likewise, given an enormous degree of sympathy within the text of the judgment. For AG Capotorti, what was taken into account was not simply where the applicant's last place of employment was, or what her nationality was but where the applicant *felt* she was permanently settled, which was Belgium.[251] Likewise, the Italian government claimed that: 'residence is not determined merely by the material fact of establishing a place of stay but also by the intention of giving that stay a degree of stability, which may be discerned from the person's way of life and from the development of normal social relations'.[252] Equally, the Court itself held in the applicant's favour, emphasizing the fact that, in the case,

[246] Ibid.
[247] Ibid., p. 784.
[248] Case 76/76, *Silvana di Paolo* v. *Office national de l'emploi* [1977] ECR 315, p. 317.
[249] Ibid.
[250] Ibid.
[251] Ibid., p. 331.
[252] Ibid., p. 332.

the applicant 'retain[s] close ties with the country where [she had] settled'.[253]

This tendency equally took place within the later cases. In *Matteucci*, the applicant was the daughter of an Italian worker in Belgium. She was a teacher of 'rhythmics' in Namur and wanted to expand the repertoire of what she could teach by undertaking a singing course in Berlin.[254] She applied for a scholarship in Belgium in which three Belgian and three German students were funded to undertake a year of a course in Germany and Belgium respectively.[255] She was refused such a scholarship on the grounds of her nationality.[256] The defence raised by the Belgian government was, in part, based upon the suggestion that the underlying purpose of the scholarship was to 'bring their own national culture and absorb that of the Member States to which they go' and, by definition, a non-Belgian national would not be able to bring Belgian culture to Germany.[257] However, for AG Slynn, the position of the applicant was that she was so integrated that she was almost akin to being a national:

> It seems to me that it cannot be said of a candidate born and wholly educated in Belgium, that she cannot be eligible for such a scholarship, solely on the grounds of her nationality, on the basis that she is not someone who has experience or understanding of Belgian culture.[258]

Ultimately it was this that persuaded AG Slynn to favour the applicant: once again an example of a merit-worthy litigant.

In *Echternach*, the applicant, a German national, was employed by the European Space Agency in the Netherlands and resided there for many years. Consequently, his son had spent almost the entirety of his life being educated in the Netherlands and had applied to study at university in the Netherlands.[259] The applicant's father, though, had returned to live in Germany with his family for one year and, on this basis, the applicant was unsuccessful in applying for student finance.[260] Once

[253] Ibid., p. 324 at para. 12.
[254] Case 235/87, *Annunziata Matteucci* v. *Communauté française of Belgium and Commissariat général aux relations internationales of the Communauté française of Belgium* [1988] ECR 5589, p. 5591.
[255] Ibid.
[256] Ibid.
[257] Ibid., p. 5604.
[258] Ibid., pp. 5603–5604.
[259] Joined Cases 389/87 and 390/87, *G. B. C. Echternach and A. Moritz* v. *Minister van Onderwijs en Wetenschappen* [1989] ECR 723, p. 727.
[260] Ibid.

again, there appeared to be an engendered sympathy towards the applicant displayed in the text. For AG Darmon, the applicant was the exemplary Union citizen:

> Mr Moritz's case provides a perfect illustration of what the integration of a family, and in particular a child, in the host state ordinarily means. Mr Mortiz completed most of his education in the Netherlands because his father was working there and the possibility of his satisfactorily continuing his education there cannot, in my view, depend solely on the place where his father happens to pursue his occupation.[261]

In other words, he illustrates perfectly the normative aspirations of the then Community in which, now, a generation of children have benefited from their parents' right to free movement at the then EEC's inception and have now, therefore, been brought up entirely integrated within another Member State. Thus, again, a clear sympathy is demonstrated towards the personal circumstances of the applicant and, subsequently, they were successful in their application.

Indeed, in *Di Leo*, AG Darmon explicitly referred to the need to protect what he terms 'second generation immigrants' which, by 1990 when the case was heard, were a conceptually novel category of individuals that had integrated within a host state, society and community but still retained the nationality of their parents.[262] In *Di Leo*, the applicant was the daughter of an Italian migrant worker who had been working in Germany for twenty-five years.[263] She applied for a maintenance grant for studying a course abroad and was refused because, in part, she had chosen to study in Italy.[264] The German government argued that they were entitled to refuse such a grant as returning to her (technical) state of origin to study renders the matter 'unconnected' with integration.[265] In other words, the purpose of Community law is to facilitate integration within a host state and if the applicant had chosen to study in her own state, it was not necessary for the German authorities to pay for it as her doing so was not facilitating integration. There then followed a repeated and humanizing rebuttal of this suggestion by AG Darmon. He firstly, asks how the applicant would feel at being refused such a grant:

261 Ibid., p. 750.
262 Case C-308/89, *Carmina di Leo* v. *Land Berlin* [1990] ECR I 4185, p. 4200.
263 Ibid., p. 4189.
264 Ibid.
265 Ibid., p. 4194.

> Is the [applicant], at the time when the refusal is notified to [her], likely to experience a feeling of being integrated in the host Member State, a feeling that [she] was being treated by that State no differently from [her] fellow students whose nationality is different from his own? Integration is not simply a legal concept; it is also something which must be lived and experienced personally and intimately. Hence it is far from certain in my view, that the actual possibility of a migrant worker's child pursing a course outside the host State, which may depend on the award of a grant by the State is *a priori* unconnected with the aim of integration in that State.[266]

In other words, it is fundamental to the migrant worker's child to be allowed this grant, even if going to study in the Member State whose nationality she possesses, because to do otherwise would make her feel as if, despite her twenty-five years in the country, she had never truly integrated. Moreover, AG Darmon is as concerned with the feelings of the applicant as with the technical legal merits of the application when he continues:

> If a person has lived since birth or early childhood in a given place with his family, going to study in another country leads to a comparable change in the conditions of existence, both physical and emotional, whether or not that person is a national of the country left behind. The award or otherwise of a grant by that country in order to cope with that change must, in that respect as well, surely be relevant to the feeling of being integrated in that country.[267]

Having thus empathized with the applicant on the basis of his feeling of integration, AG Darmon finally, once again, emphasizes the fact that the applicant had 'spent more than 20 years with his parents in a Member State of which he is not a national'.[268]

Moreover, AG Darmon outlines an entirely novel form of identification by individuals within the (then) Community which has arisen because of the success of the integration project, something which the mindsets of governments of nation-states would find hard to comprehend: 'The governments of the Federal Republic of Germany and the Netherlands have referred to the abstract image of a student returning to his homeland and immersing himself in its society and culture as if he were entirely at home there.'[269] For AG Darmon, this 'image' misunderstands how 'second generation immigrants' actually feel:

[266] Ibid., p. 4195.
[267] Ibid.
[268] Ibid.
[269] Ibid.

There are also some very well-attested case of children who were born in a Member State other than that of which they are nationals or moved there when they were very young, received all their schooling there, made friends there with nationals of that State and who only returned to their country of origin for brief periods in order to spend their holidays there. It is often said that 'second generation immigrants' do not feel they belong entirely to their host country or to their country of origin.[270]

Ultimately a collective picture is thus painted of an applicant in *Di Leo* (and all the previous cases) that is clearly morally merit-worthy and therefore deserving of the Court's attention and are, in a sense, the prototype EU Citizens.

In addition, what can also not be forgotten is that the cases themselves are, by definition, skewed. Only the EU Citizens who have needed to litigate by definition are the ones who appear in the Court reports. EU Citizens exercising their right to free movement who encounter no problems and indeed make positive contributions (in both an economic and social sense) to not only their host state but communities within them are not frequently written about in a legal sense at least because there is no matter to litigate. However, this issue does not simply concern legal reporting but can also be seen to be part of the multiple issues in relation to the negative newspaper coverage of free movement in the UK at least in the build-up to the 2016 referendum. Fundamentally, there appears an 'epistemological blindness' to so-called success stories. Indeed, one of the many criticisms of the Remain campaign during the referendum was that it simply failed to make a positive case for free movement, choosing to focus on the economic repercussions of leaving.[271] Focus instead, perhaps, should have been on the positive effects of closer integration in a micro (as well as macro) sense. In other words, there is no better time, arguably, to make the 'personal political'.[272] Perhaps a narrative should have been

[270] Ibid., p. 4200.

[271] The UK Government's official remain campaign leaflet (deposited in the doors of every household in the UK) made no mention of EU Citizenship at all and its primary focus was on convincing voters to vote remain because of the perception that the UK's economy would be 'stronger' in the Single Market. HM Government, 'Why the Government believes that voting to remain in the European Union is the best decision for the UK', (2016) https://assets.publishing.service.gov.uk/government/uploads/system/uploads/attachment_data/file/515068/why-the-government-believes-that-voting-to-remain-in-the-european-union-is-the-best-decision-for-the-uk.pdf, accessed 19 September 2020.

[272] Susan Armitage, 'Making the Personal Political: Women's History and Oral History', *Oral History Review* 17(2) (1989), pp. 107–116, p. 107.

constructed based on lived experiences and one that, crucially, links the mobile Citizen exercising his/her right to free movement to the immobile or static citizen, constituting the majority of EU Citizens. This link is crucial to the future success of the project, as Bauböck quite rightly implicitly identifies: static citizens need to identify and show solidarity with moving ones.[273] Two contrasts will be used by way of illustration. Boris Johnson's intervention in the Brexit referendum campaign has been assessed by many as being decisive.[274] Yet the same Boris Johnson, then prime minister of the UK, contracted COVID-19 in March 2020, was clearly in a very serious condition and installed in an intensive care unit at St Thomas' Hospital in central London.[275] Johnson thanked, in particular, two nurses, one of whom stayed by his bedside for forty-eight hours when 'things could have gone either way'.[276] Whilst the other nurse who he credited was Jenny McGee, a TCN nurse from New Zealand (and thus this book is not ignoring the impact of TCNs on the Member States), what cannot be ignored is the nurse who stayed by his bedside for forty-eight hours was Luis Pitarma, a Portuguese national, thus clearly being one of last EU Citizens to have exercised his rights to free movement as an EU Citizen to the UK.[277] There is almost no public discussion about the fact that one of the key protagonists in helping a Brexit-supporting prime minister to return to full health was an EU Citizen exercising the very rights that Johnson himself is attempting to curtail. Equally, he is described as having resided in West London for over four years and clearly pays tax as an employee of the UK's National Health Service.[278] Any notion of solidarity is clearly fulfilled in his case: indeed he sacrificed two nights of sleep in order to ensure the full return to health of Johnson. After four years of residence, tax paying and sheer hard work (clearly well beyond his contractual hours), if he chose to undertake a period of study and wanted to derive an entitlement to access to study on the same terms as UK nationals, it would be morally

[273] Bauböck, 'The New Cleavage Between Mobile and Immobile Europeans', p.127.
[274] Rajeev Syal, 'A celebrity, not a leader': how Vote Leave harnessed the Johnson effect', The Guardian (2019), www.theguardian.com/politics/2019/jul/17/celebrity-leader-how-vote-leave-harnessed-boris-johnson-effect, accessed 19 September 2020.
[275] James Wood, 'NHS nurse who helped save Boris Johnson's life from coronavirus in intensive care confirms: 'He absolutely needed to be there', *Daily Mail* (2020), www.dailymail.co.uk/news/article-8248513/NHS-intensive-care-nurse-helped-save-Boris-Johnsons-life-says-just-patient.html, accessed 19 September 2020.
[276] Ibid.
[277] Ibid.
[278] Ibid.

absurd to claim he lacked such an entitlement. Moreover, it should also be pointed out that the situation of Johnson is not unique or, indeed, elitist and is replicated in thousands, if not millions, of patient/nurse relationships around the UK. As Jude Diggins, the London regional director of the Royal College Nursing, put it in December 2018: 'Without EU nursing staff, the health service would be unable to provide safe and effective care.'[279] In a sense, there is a direct link between the mobile and the literally immobile right at the heart of a public health service that is considered by many to be a core part of British identity.[280] Yet arguably a successful narrative based on such interrelationships in an EU context is yet to exist in a meaningful sense. As Recchi put it:

> One of the things that Brexit proved is that Europe's root problem is Europeans' self-identification. It is not by chance that the only (or the first?) country that has seceded from the European Union (EU) is the UK. For decades, Britons have scored on top of Eurobarometer as the EU citizens least willing to call themselves 'European'. Collective identification matters. A poor sense of 'Europeanness' means no solidarity with other Europeans.[281]

Beyond Brexit, an attempt to engender a meaningful form of identification between movers and the immobile in the types of scenarios outlined earlier may well prove crucial to preventing the dismantling of the project of EU Citizenship in the remaining twenty-seven Member States. It should, perhaps, also be pointed out that, somewhat ironically, at least in the UK, solidarity is very much 'decomposed' in relation to a particular strand of privileged elites by virtue of declaring either themselves or members of their family to not be domiciled in the UK for tax purposes (and thus avoid paying tax in any meaningful sense).[282] Thus in some circumstances, EU Citizens exercising their right to free movement exercise more solidarity with their host state than even home nationals.

Furthermore, beyond Brexit, interpersonal narrative can arguably be extended to a meta-narrative running for generations. As has already

[279] In Steve Ford, '"Huge" drop in EU nurses coming to London since Brexit vote', Nursing Times (2018), www.nursingtimes.net/news/workforce/huge-drop-in-eu-nurses-coming-to-london-since-brexit-vote-21-12-2018/, accessed 19 September 2020.

[280] For instance see Stephanie Snow, 'A Source of Pride: The NHS and the Nation', *The Fabian Society* (2018), https://fabians.org.uk/a-source-of-pride-the-nhs-and-the-nation/, accessed 19 September 2020.

[281] Recchi, 'The Engine of Europeanness', p. 135.

[282] See, for instance, Jen Birks, 'Tax avoidance as an Anti-austerity Issue: The Progress of a Protest Issue Through the Public Sphere' (2017) 32 (4) *European Journal of Communication*, 296–311.

been outlined, many of the later free movement cases involved needing to protect a second (and arguably now even third) generation of successful and integrated EU Citizens in a manner that is entirely novel. In some cases, EU Citizens eschewed obtaining host state nationality. In some cases (such as the Netherlands or Austria), this is because of a prohibition of dual nationality.[283] However, in other cases (such as Belgium) this was simply because obtaining the nationality of host state was simply not considered necessary because, with a few notable exceptions (such as voting in national elections), the panoply of rights that EU Citizens derive is almost identical to those of nationals of a host state. In other words, the fact that some EU Citizens simply did not acquire dual nationality when they might have been entitled to it is illustrative, if anything, of the partial success of closer integration, in a meaningful sense, in some parts of Europe. Thus, the potential for EU Citizenship as a project to not be dismantled, in an era of enormous challenges, could, to a certain extent, depend on the success of weaving a narrative bonding the mobile to the immobile, in which a positive discursive construction based upon contribution and integration, irrespective of nationality or background, leads to the engendering of a postnational identity. This was a task which the UK government simply failed to even attempt to meaningfully achieve (in terms of the construction of a counter-narrative) in terms of its campaign in the build-up to the 2016 referendum. The challenge, now, over a prolonged period of time but with an imminent sense of urgency by virtue of the rise in populism throughout several of the current Member States, is to create such a counter-narrative to prevent the citizenship project eventually dismantling over time with a corresponding retreat to nationalism.

5.6 Conclusion

This chapter has sought to question whether citizenship as a concept could be dismantled in a tense contemporary environment due to fissures that are evident in the current case law on citizenship but that can traced back to a much earlier period. After having defined citizenship to incorporate, at the very least, a reciprocity of rights and duties, this chapter firstly outlined, within the early case law, the

[283] See, for instance, European Parliament, 'Acquisition and loss of Citizenship in EU Member States' (2018), www.europarl.europa.eu/RegData/etudes/BRIE/2018/625116/EPRS_BRI(2018)625116_EN.pdf, accessed 19 September 2020.

thorny issue of solidarity that emerged from the post-1998 case law on citizenship. The rest of this section of the chapter then focusses on the dissonance between rights and duties that is evident from the numerous seemingly 'undeserving' applicants that have appeared before the Court. The second section of the critical part of this chapter then focussed on the fundamental barriers to a genuine form of citizenship understood in terms of identity that have flowed from the text of Court judgments, particularly emphasizing the powerful and seemingly irreplaceable hold of national identity as evidenced in the public service exception and war pensions cases. It is submitted that such cases, particularly those relating to war pensions (that related to sacrifice of an individual for one's nation) provide a sharp point of contrast with applicants who, instead, can be portrayed as parasitic and that this contrast asks critical questions of Union Citizenship. The third part of the chapter reveals a further fissure within the structure of citizenship which questions not only the realistic possibility of EU Citizenship as a postnational identity construct but whether it is *even* normatively desirable. It was argued that citizenship viewed as an identity construct could, if not managed extremely delicately, merely evolve, particularly during an era of populism, to simply replicate the ethnocentrism of national citizenship constructs merely on a Europe-wide basis. In other words, a meaningful concept of EU Citizenship cannot evolve without grappling with the ethnocentric and toxic legacy of 'Europe' itself as a concept, particularly with its roots in colonial injustices. If all of these dilemmas are tied together it certainly raises the possibility of the dismantling of EU Citizenship altogether and the final part attempts at least to reconstruct citizenship in a manner that is based on the individual experiences of the millions of EU Citizens who have exercised their right to free movement, become wholly integrated in their host state and are not visible in cases or newspapers because they are success stories. In other words, a bottom-up approach to EU Citizenship is needed to prevent the crumbling of its entire edifice.

Concluding Remarks

Europe (and its Union) has famously been described as a 'constitutional mosaic'.[1] Perhaps now it might be better described as an unconstitutional mess full of controversies, asymmetries and multiple fissures right at the heart of one of its core concepts: EU Citizenship. This book has focussed for the most part on areas of law in the form of the pre-Maastricht case law on free movement of persons because, as was outlined in the Introduction, Plender and Evans famously claimed that citizenship existed in 'incipient' and 'embryonic' form because of these early cases.[2] In a sense, their predictions proved to be correct in that the Treaty was amended at Maastricht to formally create citizenship and, indeed, AG Jacobs alluded to the phrase '*civis europeus sum*' even prior to 1992. This book has attempted to 'trace' the origins of the Citizen from an explicitly Social Constructivist perspective (or at least one of many versions of it). This type of research into this area of law is arguably much needed. As Favell put it, it is a:

> Cliché that sociologists only come out at dusk. Sociology was 'absent' from EU studies during the 'golden years of the European Union' (around 1986 – 1992) . . . 'Nobody was interested in whether there needed to be an actual European society underpinning the political/legal construction. (p. 193)

What this book has attempted to do is shine a light in the dusk to such an extent that the case law reveals 'exquisite and glaring' aspects of an inherently contingent concept of EU Citizenship. In so doing it has been

[1] Neil Walker and Stephen Tierney, 'A Constitutional Mosaic? Exploring the New Frontiers of Europe's Constitutionalism' in Neil Walker, Jo Shaw and Stephen Tierney (eds.), *Europe's Constitutional Mosaic* (Oxford: Hart, 2011), p. 1.

[2] Plender, 'An Incipient Form of European Citizenship', p. 39; Evans, 'European Citizenship', 497.

claimed that undetected fissures were evident in the free movement of persons case law from its infancy, that such fissures were compounded by building more structures on top of them with even more fissures to the extent that now it is at least possible to suggest that the entire edifice of EU Citizenship might be crumbling and could even collapse or be dismantled.

Part I of the book outlined specific and contingent discursive structures (in addition to legal concepts) that paved the way for the later Citizen to emerge in 1992 and constitutes the foundations of the Greek Temple façade that symbolizes citizenship as a structure. In Chapter 1, it was submitted that what emerged from the case law on the 'worker' was a powerful discourse of the concept that was conceptually distinct from ordinary definitions of the word. In Chapter 2, the opposite proposition was outlined, namely that vast categories of individuals who were either not workers or, at best, partial economic contributors, were collectively constituted by the Court as 'counting' in both an epistemological and legal sense without a pervasive discourse in which to describe them. It was suggested that, instead, a conceptual label which could be attached to such individuals was citizenship and that contemporary dilemmas relating to a Union-specific understanding of the concept could equally be traced to this aspect of the early free movement case law. In relation to both chapters, this specific evolution towards citizenship is inherently controversial. A supranational concept of the 'worker' evolved to such an extent that work appeared to be terminologically divorced from it necessitating a further evolution in the case law to create legal protections for individuals that could not be classified as workers even with the Court's extended understanding of the phrase. Ultimately a combination of legal evolution and Member State objection resulted in three residency directives to deal with non-economic actors which, in turn, became the Citizens' Rights Directive. Thus EU Citizenship as understood today, with all its controversies, can be traced back to a period of time with fissures evident in the very foundations of EU free movement law.

In Part II of the book, mere utterances of both equal treatment (in Chapter 3) and citizenship (in Chapter 4) were examined and construed as the pillars upon which the roof of citizenship was placed whilst at the same time being placed on top of the foundations outlined in Part I. In Chapter 3 it was suggested that a discursive structural evolution could be traced from a paradigm of non-discrimination to that of equal treatment. In Chapter 4 an evolution towards a crescendo of 'citizen-speak' was evident. This is particularly important to assess because technically citizenship did not exist as a legal concept prior to 1992 and yet a vibrant set of utterances were evident in a manner not properly analysed by conventional legal approaches. Both chapters are, though, also clearly critical. In Chapter 3 it was claimed that some are clearly more equal than others and, as has been suggested, equal treatment as a concept, predicated on nationality and movement, prioritizes the exercise of economic rights over other forms of discrimination and leaves the (often less wealthy) immobile majority of EU Citizens behind in the path towards closer integration. In short it is an inherently loaded concept with a large fissure running straight through it. In relation to utterances of citizenship in Chapter 4 the fissure inherent within it is the fact that it is equally an inherently loaded concept based on an evolution to incorporate non-economic actors, often pejoratively perceived to be 'freeloaders' as encapsulating what citizenship means. Thus the reality of Citizenship linguistically is, sadly, far from the lofty ambitions of AG Jacobs in *Konstantinidis*.

Part III of the book incorporating Chapter 5 outlines the potential for the unravelling and dismantling of citizenship in a contemporary climate of Brexit, populism and ethnocentrism. In this respect, the conclusions are unavoidably pessimistic but with a glimmer of hope being projected as food for critical thought in the future evolution of both EU Citizenship and European integration more generally. It has been claimed that EU Citizenship as postnational membership is inherently problematic and that a set of fissures running through it have been evident from the very early case law. Firstly, it was suggested that solidarity did not 'decompose' in the mid-2000s but was rotting from the infancy of the case law. In particular, persistent objections from key Member States were ignored in order to not obstruct a seemingly never-ending juggernaut towards closer integration. In this context it should be said that Member States reacting to the case law in the form of legislative change is not exactly illustrative of active consent which perhaps may have been an issue that would have never emerged had one key Member State not decided to leave the Union altogether. It was also suggested that supranational citizenship, based on utterances in the case law alone, appears to be inherently impossible to achieve given the roots of citizenship in national models. Moreover, even if it was, it is questionable whether it is normatively desirable to achieve supranational EU-specific Citizenship given the possibility of replicating national ethnocentricity and a colonial legacy on a Europe-wide level.

The European Union (and its Citizenship) is currently in the middle of one the most challenging periods in its history with consequences that will undoubtedly be felt for many years to come. The final part of the book pointed tentatively towards some shoots of recovery. It is not easy to fill in so many fissures within the edifice of citizenship. It might perhaps be better to deconstruct it, go back to 'square one' and start again. Arguably the loaded legacy of market citizenship is EU Citizenship's ultimate fissure. For O'Brien, such a legacy has made EU Citizenship 'incoherent', 'stratified', 'fragmented' and, crucially, with 'little attachment to a coherent sense of social justice'.[3] Achieving a meaningful concept of EU Citizenship, one which individuals can identify with, with a lasting and positive legacy, is not going to be easy. On the one hand, EU Citizenship has to evolve to embrace a true sense of social justice, become genuinely meaningful to the immobile citizen and finally decouple itself from its fissure-ridden economic origins. On the other hand, it has to do so in a way in which Member States perceive themselves to be active participants in this process and not having their views overridden by adventurous judicial interpretation. This is a difficult task that EU law and policymakers have to grapple with, and urgently. The fate of millions of not only current but future EU Citizens is dependent on it.

[3] O'Brien, *Unity in Adversity*, pp. 269–270.

Bibliography

Cases

Court of Justice of the European Union

Case 26/62 *van Gend en Loos (NV Algemene Transporten Expeitidie Onderneming)* v. *Nedelandse Administratie der Belastingen* [1963] ECR 1

Case 75/63 *Mrs M. K. H. Hoekstra (née Unger)* v. *Bestuur der Bedrijfsvereniging voor Detailhandel en Ambachten (Administration of the Industrial Board for Retail Trades and Businesses)* [1964] ECR 177

Case 31/64 *'De Sociale Voorzorg' Mutual Insurance Fund* v. *W. H. Bertholet* [1965] ECR 81

Case 6/65 *Flaminio Costa* v. *E.N.E.L.* [1964] ECR 585

Case 44/65 *Hessische Knappschaft* v. *Maison Singer et fils* [1965] ECR 965

Case 1/67 *Stanislas Ciechelski* v. *Caisse régionale de sécurité sociale du Centre d'Orléans and directeur régional de la sécurité sociale d'Orléans* [1967] ECR 181

Case 6/67 *Teresa Guerra, widow of Pietro Pace* v. *Institut national d'assurance maladie-invalidité* [1967] ECR 219

Case 18/67 *Argia Pagotto (née Cossutta)* v. *Office National des Pensions pour Ouvriers* [1967] ECR 309

Case 19/68 *Giovanni de Cicco* v. *Landesversicherungsanstalt Schwaben* [1968] ECR 473

Case 27/69 *Caisse de maladie des C.F.L. 'Entr'aide médicale' and Société nationale des chemins de fer luxembourgeois* v. *Compagnie belge d'assurances générales sur la vie et contre les accidents* [1969] ECR 405

Case 29/69 *Erich Stauder* v. *City of Ulm – Sozialamt* [1969] ECR 419

Case 34/69 *Caisse d'assurance vieillesse des travailleurs salariés de Paris* v. *Jeanne Duffy* [1969] ECR 597

Case 32/70 *Union nationale des mutualités socialistes* v. *La Marca Stéphanie* [1970] ECR 987

Case 11/70 *Internationale Handelsgesellschaft mbH* v. *Einfuhr- und Vorratsstelle für Getreide und Futtermittel* [1970] ECR 1125

Case 80/70 *Gabrielle Defrenne* v. *Belgian State* [1971] ECR 445

Case 23/71 *Michel Janssen* v. *Landsbond der christelijke mutualiteiten* [1971] ECR 859

Case 80/71 *Adalgisa Merluzzi* v. *Caisse primaire centrale d'assurance maladie de la région parisienne* [1972] ECR 175
Case 1/72 *Rita Frilli* v. *Belgian State* [1972] ECR 457
Case 2/72 *Salvatore Murru* v. *Caisse régionale d'assurance maladie de Paris* [1972] ECR 333
Case 44/72 *Pieter Marsman* v. *M. Rosskamp* [1972] ECR 1243
Case 45/72 *Giuseppe Merola* v. *Nationaal Pensioenfonds voor Mijnwerkers* [1972] ECR 1255
Case 76/72 *Michel S.* v. *Fonds national de reclassement social des handicapés* [1973] ECR 457
Case 110/73 *G. Fiege* v. *Caisse régionale d'assurance maladie de Strasbourg* [1973] ECR 1001
Case 51/73 *Bestuur der Sociale Verzekeringsbank* v. *B. Smieja* [1973] ECR 1213
Case 130/73 *Magdalena Vandeweghe and others* v. *Berufsgenossenschaft für die chemische Industrie* [1973] ECR 1329
Case 140/73 *Direction régionale de la sécurité sociale de la région parisienne and Caisse régionale d'assurance maladie de Paris* v. *Carmela Mancuso and Caisse nationale d'assurance vieillesse des travailleurs salaries* [1973] ECR 1449
Case 152/73 *Giovanni Maria Sotgiu* v. *Deutsche Bundespost* [1974] ECR 153
Case 167/73 *Commission of the European Communities* v. *French Republic* [1974] ECR 359
Case 4/73 *J. Nold, Kohlen- und Baustoffgroßhandlung* v. *Commission of the European Communities* [1974] ECR 491
Case 9/74 *Donato Casagrande* v. *Landeshauptstadt München* [1974] ECR 773
Case 2/74 *Jean Reyners* v. *Belgian State* [1974] ECR 631
Case 24/74 *Caisse régionale d'assurance maladie de Paris* v. *Giuseppina Biason* [1974] ECR 999
Case 33/74 *Johannes Henricus Maria van Binsbergen* v. *Bestuur van de Bedrijfsvereniging voor de Metaalnijverheid* [1974] ECR 1299
Case 39/74 *Luciana Costa, spouse Mazzier* v. *Belgian State* [1974] ECR 1251
Case 41/74 *Yvonne van Duyn* v. *Home Office* [1974] ECR 1337
Case 36/74 *B. N. O. Walrave and L. J. N. Koch* v. *Association Union cycliste internationale, Koninklijke Nederlandsche Wielren Unie and Federación Española Ciclismo* [1974] ECR 1405
Case 68/74 *Angelo Alaimo* v. *Préfet du Rhône* [1975] ECR 109
Case 66/74 *Alfonso Farrauto* v. *Bau-Berufsgenossenschaft* [1975] ECR 157
Case 67/74 *Carmelo Angelo Bonsignore* v. *Oberstadtdirektor der Stadt Köln* [1975] ECR 297
Case 7/75 *Mr. and Mrs. F.* v. *Belgian State* [1975] 679
Case 17/75 *Antonio Anselmetti* v. *Caisse de compensation des allocations familiales de l'industrie charbonnière* [1975] ECR 781
Case 20/75 *Gaetano d'Amico* v. *Landesversicherungsanstalt Rheinland-Pfalz* [1975] ECR 891
Case 27/75 *Gaetano Bonaffini and others* v. *Istituto Nazionale della Previdenza Sociale (INPS)* [1975] ECR 971

Case 32/75 *Anita Cristini* v. *Société nationale des chemins de fer français* [1975] ECR 1085
Case 33/75 *Benito Galati* v. *Landesversicherungsanstalt Schwaben* [1975] ECR 1323
Case 24/75 *Teresa and Silvana Petroni* v. *Office national des pensions pour travailleurs salariés (ONPTS)* [1975] ECR 1149
Case 36/75 *Roland Rutili* v. *Ministre de l'intérieur* [1975] ECR 1219
Case 49/75 *Camilla Borella* v. *Landesversicherungsanstalt Schwaben* [1975] ECR 1461
Case 39/75 *Robert-Gerardus Coenen and others* v. *Sociaal-Economische Raad* [1975] ECR 1547
Case 108/75 *Giovanni Balsamo* v. *Institut national d'assurance maladie-invalidité* [1976] ECR 375
Case 43/75 *Gabrielle Defrenne* v. *Société anonyme belge de navigation aérienne Sabena* [1976] ECR 455
Case 48/75 *Jean Noël Royer* [1976] ECR 497
Case 112/75 *Directeur régional de la sécurité sociale de Nancy* v. *Auguste Hirardin and Caisse régionale d'assurance maladie du Nord-Est* [1976] ECR 553
Case 118/75 *Lynne Watson and Alessandro Belmann* [1976] ECR 1185
Case 17/76 *M. L. E. Brack, widow of R. J. Brack,* v. *Insurance Officer* [1976] ECR 1429
Case 40/76 *Slavica Kermaschek* v. *Bundesanstalt für Arbeit* [1976] ECR 1669
Case 63/76 *Vito Inzirillo* v. *Caisse d'allocations familiales de l'arrondissement de Lyon* [1976] ECR 2057
Case 76/76 *Silvana di Paolo* v. *Office national de l'emploi* [1977] ECR 315
Case 79/76 *Carlo Fossi* v. *Bundesknappschaft* [1977] ECR 667
Case 87/76 *Walter Bozzone* v. *Office de Sécurité sociale d'outre-mer* [1977] ECR 687
Case 71/76 *Jean Thieffry* v. *Conseil de l'ordre des avocats à la cour de Paris* [1977] ECR 765
Case 104/76 *Gerda Jansen* v. *Landesversicherungsanstalt Rheinprovinz* [1977] ECR 829
Case 11/77 *Richard Hugh Patrick* v. *Ministre des affaires culturelles* [1977] ECR 1199
Case 8/77 *Concetta Sagulo, Gennaro Brenca and Addelmadjid Bakhouche* [1977] ECR 1495
Case 112/76 *Renato Manzoni* v. *Fonds national de retraite des ouvriers mineurs* [1977] ECR 1647
Joined Cases 117/76 and 16/77 *Albert Ruckdeschel & Co. and Hansa-Lagerhaus Ströh & Co.* v. *Hauptzollamt Hamburg-St. Annen; Diamalt AG* v. *Hauptzollamt Itzehoe* [1977] ECR 1753
Case 22/77 *Fonds national de retraite des ouvriers mineurs* v. *Giovanni Mura* [1977] ECR 1699
Case 32/77 *Antonio Giuliani* v. *Landesversicherungsanstalt Schwaben* [1977] ECR 1857
Case 30/77 *Regina* v. *Pierre Bouchereau* [1977] ECR 1999
Case 36/77 *Azienda di Stato per gli interventi sul mercato agricolo (AIMA)* v. *Rocco Michele Greco* [1977] ECR 2059
Case 64/77 *Mario Torri* v. *Office national des pensions pour travailleurs salaries* [1977] ECR 2299
Case 66/77 *Petrus Kuyken* v. *Rijksdienst voor Arbeidsvoorziening* [1977] ECR 2311

Case 83/77 *Giovanni Naselli* v. *Caisse Auxiliaire d'Assurance Maladie-Invalidité and l'Institut National d'Assurance Maladie-Invalidité* [1978] ECR 683
Case 126/77 *Maria Frangiamore* v. *Office National de l'Emploi* [1978] ECR 725
Case 115/77 *Gert Laumann and Anja Laumann* v. *Landesversicherungsanstalt Rheinprovinz* [1978] ECR 805
Case 134/77 *Silvio Ragazzoni* v. *Caisse de compensation pour allocations familiales 'Assubel'* [1978] ECR 963
Case 149/77 *Gabrielle Defrenne* v. *Société anonyme belge de navigation aérienne Sabena* [1978] ECR 1365
Case 1/78 *Patrick Christopher Kenny* v. *Insurance Officer* [1978] ECR 1489
Case 9/78 *Directeur régional de la Sécurité sociale de Nancy* v. *Paulin Gillard and Caisse régionale d'assurance maladie du Nord-Est, Nancy* [1978] ECR 1661
Case 10/78 *Tayeb Belbouab* v. *Bundesknappschaft* [1978] ECR 1915
Case 26/78 *Institut national d'assurance maladie-invalidité and Union nationale des fédérations mutualistes neutres* v. *Antonio Viola* [1978] ECR 1771
Joined Cases 103 and 145/77 *Royal Scholten-Honig (Holdings) Limited* v. *Intervention Board for Agricultural Produce; Tunnel Refineries Limited* v. *Intervention Board for Agricultural Produce* [1978] ECR 2037
Case 16/78 *Criminal proceedings against Michel Choquet* [1978] ECR 2293
Joined Cases 110 and 111/78 *Ministère public and 'Chambre syndicale des agents artistiques et impresarii de Belgique' ASBL* v. *Willy van Wesemael and others* [1979] ECR 35
Case 136/78 *Criminal proceedings against Vincent Auer* [1979] ECR 437
Case 100/78 *Claudino Rossi* v. *Caisse de compensation pour allocations familiales des régions de Charleroi et Namur* [1979] ECR 831
Case 139/78 *Giovanni Coccioli* v. *Bundesanstalt für Arbeit* [1979] ECR 991
Case 182/78 *Bestuur van het Algemeen Ziekenfonds, Drenthe-Platteland, Zwolle,* v. *Mrs G. Pierik* [1979] ECR 1977
Case 207/78 *Criminal proceedings against Gilbert Even and Office national des pensions pour travailleurs salariés (ONPTS)* [1979] ECR 2019
Case 237/78 *Caisse régionale d'assurance maladie de Lille (CRAM)* v. *Diamante Palermo, née Toia* [1979] ECR 2645
Case 266/78 *Bruno Brunori* v. *Landesversicherungsanstalt Rheinprovinz* [1979] ECR 2705
Case 98/79 *Josette Pecastaing* v. *Belgian State* [1980] ECR 691
Case 129/79 *Macarthys Ltd* v. *Wendy Smith* [1980] ECR 1275
Case 143/79 *Margaret Walsh* v. *National Insurance Officer* [1980] ECR 1639
Joined Cases 41/79, 121/79 and 796/79 *Vittorio Testa, Salvino Maggio and Carmine Vitale* v. *Bundesanstalt für Arbeit.*[1980] ECR 1979
Case 157/79 *Regina* v. *Stanislaus Pieck* [1980] ECR 2171
Case 810/79 *Peter Überschär* v. *Bundesversicherungsanstalt für Angestellte* [1980] ECR 2747
Case 149/79 *Commission of the European Communities* v. *Kingdom of Belgium* [1980] ECR 3881
Case 279/80 *Criminal proceedings against Alfred John Webb* [1981] ECR 3305

Case 65/81 *Francesco Reina and Letizia Reina* v. *Landeskreditbank Baden-Württemberg* [1982] ECR 33
Case 12/81 *Eileen Garland* v. *British Rail Engineering Limited* [1982] ECR 359
Case 19/81 *Arthur Burton* v. *British Railways Board* [1982] ECR 554
Case 53/81 *D. M. Levin* v. *Staatssecretaris van Justitie* [1982] ECR 1035
Case 79/81 *Margherita Baccini* v. *Office national de l'emploi (ONEM)* [1982] ECR 1063
Joined Cases 115 and 116/81 *Rezguia Adoui* v. *Belgian State and City of Liège; Dominique Cornuaille* v. *Belgian State* [1982] ECR 1665
Joined Cases 35 and 36/82 *Elestina Esselina Christina Morson* v. *State of the Netherlands and Head of the Plaatselijke Politie within the meaning of the Vreemdelingenwet; Sweradjie Jhanjan* v. *State of the Netherlands* [1982] ECR 3723
Case 152/82 *Sandro Forcheri and his wife Marisa Forcheri, née Marino,* v. *Belgian State and asbl Institut Supérieur de Sciences Humaines Appliquées – Ecole Ouvrière Supérieure* [1983] ECR 2323
Case 165/82 *Commission of the European Communities* v. *United Kingdom of Great Britain and Northern Ireland* [1983] ECR 3431
Case 26/83 *Carmela Castelli* v. *Office National des Pensions pour Travailleurs Salariés (ONPTS)* [1984] ECR 3199
Joined Cases 286/82 and 26/83 *Graziana Luisi and Giuseppe Carbone* v. *Ministero del Tesoro* [1984] ECR 377
Case 180/83 *Hans Moser* v. *Land Baden-Württemberg* [1984] ECR 2539
Case 182/83 *Robert Fearon & Company Limited* v. *Irish Land Commission* [1984] ECR 3677
Case 238/83 *Caisse d'Allocations Familiales de la Région Parisienne* v. *Mr and Mrs Richard Meade* [1984] ECR 2631
Case 184/83 *Ulrich Hofmann* v. *Barmer Ersatzkasse* [1984] ECR 3047
Case 237/83 *SARL Prodest* v. *Caisse Primaire d'Assurance Maladie de Paris* [1984] ECR 3153
Case 293/83 *Françoise Gravier* v. *City of Liège* [1985] ECR 593
Case 249/83 *Vera Hoeckx* v. *Openbaar Centrum voor Maatschappelijk Welzijn, Kalmthout* [1985] ECR 973
Case 122/84 *Kenneth Scrivner and Carol Cole* v. *Centre public d'aide sociale de Chastre* [1985] ECR 1027
Case 29/84 *Commission of the European Communities* v. *Federal Republic of Germany* [1985] ECR 1661
Case 94/84 *Office national de l'emploi* v. *Joszef Deak* [1985] ECR 1873
Case 137/84 *Criminal proceedings against Robert Heinrich Maria Mutsch* [1985] ECR 2681
Case 41/84 *Pietro Pinna* v. *Caisse d'allocations familiales de la Savoie* [1986] ECR 1
Case 44/84 *Derrick Guy Edmund Hurd* v. *Kenneth Jones (Her Majesty's Inspector of Taxes)* [1986] ECR 29
Case 270/73 *Commission of the European Communities* v. *French Republic* [1986] ECR 273
Case 152/84 *M. H. Marshall* v. *Southampton and South-West Hampshire Area Health Authority (Teaching)* [1986] ECR 723

Case 59/85 *State of the Netherlands* v. *Ann Florence Reed* [1986] ECR 1283
Case 222/84 *Marguerite Johnston* v. *Chief Constable of the Royal Ulster Constabulary* [1986] ECR 1651
Case 307/84 *Commission of the European Communities* v. *French Republic* [1986] ECR 1725
Case 139/85 *R. H. Kempf* v. *Staatssecretaris van Justitie* [1986] ECR 1741
Case 1/85 *Horst Miethe* v. *Bundesanstalt für Arbeit* [1986] ECR 1837
Case 66/85 *Deborah Lawrie-Blum* v. *Land Baden-Württemberg* [1986] ECR 2121
Case 79/85 *D. H. M. Segers* v. *Bestuur van de Bedrijfsvereniging voor Bank- en Verzekeringswezen, Groothandel en Vrije Beroepen* [1986] ECR 2375
Case 168/85 *Commission of the European Communities* v. *Italian Republic* [1986] ECR 2945
Case 300/84 *A. J. M. van Roosmalen* v. *Bestuur van de Bedrijfsvereniging voor de Gezondheid, Geestelijke en Maatschappelijke Belangen* [1986] ECR 3097
Joined Cases 82 and 103/86 *Giancarlo Laborero and Francesca Sabato* v. *Office de sécurité sociale d'outre-mer (OSSOM)* [1987] ECR 3401
Joined Cases 201 and 202/85 *Marthe Klensch and others* v. *Secrétaire d'État à l'Agriculture et à la Viticulture* [1986] ECR 3477
Case 225/85 *Commission of the European Communities* v. *Italian Republic* [1987] ECR 2625
Case 316/85 *Centre public d'aide sociale de Courcelles* v. *Marie-Christine Lebon* [1987] ECR 2811
Case 222/86 *Union nationale des entraîneurs et cadres techniques professionnels du football (Unectef)* v. *Georges Heylens and others* [1987] ECR 4097
Case 63/86 *Commission of the European Communities* v. *Italian Republic* [1988] ECR 29
Case 292/86 *Claude Gullung* v. *Conseil de l'ordre des avocats du barreau de Colmar et de Saverne* [1988] ECR 111
Case 293/85 *Commission of the European Communities* v. *Kingdom of Belgium* [1988] ECR 305
Case 309/85 *Bruno Barra* v. *Belgian State and City of Liège* [1988] ECR 355
Case 353/85 *Bond van Adverteerders and others* v. *The Netherlands State* [1988] ECR 2085
Case 84/87 *Marcel Erpelding* v. *Secrétaire d'État à l'Agriculture et à la Viticulture* [1988] ECR 2647
Case 39/86 *Sylvie Lair* v. *Universität Hannover* [1988] ECR 3161
Case 197/86 *Steven Malcolm Brown* v. *The Secretary of State for Scotland* [1988] ECR 3205
Case 143/87 *Christopher Stanton and SA belge d'assurances 'L'Étoile 1905'* v. *Institut national d'assurances sociales pour travailleurs indépendants (Inasti)* [1988] ECR 3877
Joined Cases 154 and 155/87 *Rijksinstituut voor de sociale verzekering des zelfstandigen (RSVZ)* v. *Heinrich Wolf and NV Microtherm Europe and others* [1988] ECR 3897
Case 236/87 *Anna Bergemann* v. *Bundesanstalt für Arbeit* [1988] ECR 5125
Case 263/86 *Belgian State* v. *René Humbel and Marie-Thérèse Edel* [1988] ECR 5365
Case 313/86 *O. Lenoir* v. *Caisse d'allocations familiales des Alpes-Maritimes* [1988] ECR 5391

Case 235/87 *Annunziata Matteucci* v. *Communauté française of Belgium and Commissariat général aux relations internationales of the Communauté française of Belgium* [1988] ECR 5589
Case 196/87 *Udo Steymann* v. *Staatssecretaris van Justitie* [1988] ECR 6159
Case 186/87 *Ian William Cowan* v. *Trésor Public* [1989] ECR 195
Joined Cases 389/87 and 390/87 *G. B. C. Echternach and A. Moritz* v. *Minister van Onderwijs en Wetenschappen* [1989] ECR 723
Case 249/86 *Commission of the European Communities* v. *Federal Republic of Germany* [1989] ECR 1263
Case 242/87 *Commission of the European Communities* v. *Council of the European Communities* [1989] ECR 1425
Case 305/87 *Commission of the European Communities* v. *Hellenic Republic* [1989] ECR 1461
Case 33/88 *Pilar Allué and Carmel Mary Coonan* v. *Università degli studi di Venezia* [1989] ECR 1591
Case 344/87 *I. Bettray* v. *Staatssecretaris van Justitie* [1989] ECR 1621
Case C-379/87*Anita Groener* v. *Minister for Education and the City of Dublin Vocational Educational Committee* [1989] ECR 3967
Case C-175/88 *Klaus Biehl* v. *Administration des contributions du grand-duché de Luxembourg* [1990] ECR I 1779
Case C-2/89 *Bestuur van de Sociale Verzekeringsbank* v. *M. G. J. Kits van Heijningen* [1990] ECR I 1755
Case C-177/88 *Elisabeth Johanna Pacifica Dekker* v. *Stichting Vormingscentrum voor Jong Volwassenen (VJV-Centrum) Plus* [1990] ECR I 3941
Case C-308/89 *Carmina di Leo* v. *Land Berlin* [1990] ECR I 4185
Case C-363/89 *Danielle Roux* v. *Belgian State* [1991] ECR I 273
Case C-292/89 *The Queen* v. *Immigration Appeal Tribunal, ex parte Gustaff Desiderius Antonissen* [1991] ECR I 745
Case C-68/89 *Commission of the European Communities* v. *Kingdom of the Netherlands* [1991] ECR I 2637
Case C-221/89 *The Queen* v. *Secretary of State for Transport, ex parte Factortame Ltd and others* [1991] ECR I 3905
Case C-208/90 *Theresa Emmott* v. *Minister for Social Welfare and Attorney General* [1991] ECR I 4269
Case C-159/90 *The Society for the Protection of Unborn Children Ireland Ltd* v. *Stephen Grogan and others* [1991] ECR I 4685
Case C-27/91 *Union de Recouvrement des Cotisations de Sécurité Sociale et d'Allocations Familiales de la Savoie (URSSAF)* v. *Hostellerie Le Manoir SARL* [1991] ECR I 5531
Case C-4/91 *Annegret Bleis* v. *Ministère de l'Education Nationale* [1991] ECR I 5627
Opinion 1/91 [1991] ECR I 6079
Case C-357/89 *V. J. M. Raulin* v. *Minister van Onderwijs en Wetenschappen* [1992] ECR I 1027
Case C-3/90 *M. J. E. Bernini* v. *Minister van Onderwijs en Wetenschappen* [1992] ECR I 1071

Case C-370/90 *The Queen* v. *Immigration Appeal Tribunal and Surinder Singh, ex parte Secretary of State for Home Department* [1992] ECR I 4265
Case C-9/91 *The Queen* v. *Secretary of State for Social Security, ex parte Equal Opportunities Commission* [1992] ECR I 4297
Case C-369/90 *Mario Vincente Micheletti and others* v. *Delegación del Govierno en Cantabria* [1992] ECR I 4239
Case C-295/90 *Council of the European Communities* v. *European Parliament, Commission of the European Communities, United Kingdom and Kingdom of the Netherlands* [1992] ECR I 5299
Case C-168/91 *Konstantinidis* v. *Stadt Altensteig* [1993] ECR I 1191
Case C-42/92 *Adrianus Thijssen* v. *Controledienst voor de verzekeringen* [1993] ECR I 4047
Case C-109/92 *Stephan Max Wirth* v. *Landeshauptstadt Hannover* [1993] ECR I 6447
Case C-85/96 *María Martínez Sala* v. *Freistaat Bayern* [1998] ECR I 2691
Case C-192/99 *The Queen* v. *Secretary of State for the Home Department, ex parte: Manjit Kaur, intervener* [2001] ECR I 1237
Case C-184/99 *Rudy Grzelczyk* v. *Centre public d'aide sociale d'Ottignies-Louvain-la-Neuve* [2001] ECR I 6193
Case C-224/98 *Marie-Nathalie D'Hoop* v. *Office national de l'emploi* [2002] ECR I 6191
Case C-413/99 *Baumbast and R* v. *Secretary of State for the Home Department* [2002] ECR I 7091
Case C-413/01 *Franca Ninni-Orasche* v. *Bundesminister für Wissenschaft, Verkehr und Kunst* [2003] ECR I 13187
Case C-138/02 *Brian Francis Collins* v. *Secretary of State for Work and Pensions* [2004] ECR I 2703
Case C-200/02 *Kunqian Catherine Zhu and Man Lavette Chen* v. *Secretary of State for the Home Department* [2004] ECR I 9925
Case C-209/03 *The Queen (on the application of Dany Bidar)* v. *London Borough of Ealing, Secretary of State for Education and Skills* [2005] ECR I 2119
Case C-135/08 *Janko Rottman* v. *Freistaat Bayern* [2008] ECR I 1449
Case C-212/06 *Government of Communauté française and Gouvernement wallon* v. *Gouvernement flamand* [2008] ECR I 1683
Case C-34/09 *Gerardo Ruiz Zambrano* v. *Office national de l'emploi (ONEm)* [2011] ECR I 1177
Case C-434/09 *Shirley McCarthy* v. *Secretary of State for the Home Department* [2011] ECR I 3375

European Court of Human Rights

Case of Hirst v. *The United Kingdom (No. 2)* [2005] ECHR 681

Legislation

Treaty establishing the European Community [2002] OJ C325/1 (EEC Treaty)

Council Regulation No 3/58 of 16 December 1958 concerning social security for migrant workers [1958] OJ 30/561 (translated from the original French)

Council Regulation No 15/61 of 16 August 1961 on the first measures for the achievement of free movement of workers within the Community [1961] OJ 57/1073 (translated from the original French)

Council Directive 64/220/EEC of 25 February 1964 on the abolition of restrictions on movement and residence within the Community for nationals of Member States with regard to establishment and the provision of services [1964] OJ Spec Ed 115

Council Directive 64/221/EEC of 25 February 1964 on the co-ordination of special measures concerning the movement and residence of foreign nationals which are justified on grounds of public policy, public security or public health [1964] OJ Spec Ed 117

Council Directive 68/360/EEC of 15 October 1968 on the abolition of restrictions on movement and residence within the Community for workers of Member States and their families [1968] OJ L257/13

Council Regulation 1612/68/EEC of 15 October 1968 on free movement of workers within the Community [1968] OJ L257/2

Council Regulation No 1251/70 of 29 June 1970 on the right of workers to remain in the territory of a Member State after having been employed in that State [1970] OJ Spec Ed 402

Council Regulation 1408/71/EEC of 14 June 1971 on the application of social security schemes to employed persons and their families moving within the Community [1971] OJ L149/2

Council Directive 73/148/EEC of 21 May 1973 on the abolition of restrictions on movement and residence within the Community for nationals of Member States with regard to establishment and the provision of services [1973] OJ L172/14

Council Directive 90/364/EEC of 28 June 1990 on the right of residence [1990] OJ L180/26

Council Directive 90/365/EEC of 28 June 1990 on the right of residence for employees and self-employed persons who have ceased their occupational activity [1990] OJ L180/28

Council Directive 90/366/EEC of 28 June 1990 on the right of residence for students [1990] OJ L180/30

Council Directive 93/96/EEC of 29 October 1993 on the right of residence for students [1993] OJ L317/59

Consolidated Version of the Treaty on European Union [2012] OJ C326/13 (TEU)

Directive 2004/38/EC on the right of citizens of the Union and their family members to move and reside freely within the territory of the Member States amending Regulation (EEC) No 1612/68 and repealing Directives 64/221/EEC, 68/360/EEC, 72/194/EEC, 73/148/EEC, 75/34/EEC, 75/35/EEC, 90/364/EEC, 90/365/EEC and 93/96/EEC [2004] OJ L158/77 ('The Citizenship Directive')

Other Sources

Acosta-Arcarazo, Diego and Geddes, Andrew (2013) 'The Development, Application and Implications of an EU Rule of Law in the Area of Migration Policy', *Journal of Common Market Studies* 51(2), 179–193.

Adler, Emanuel (1997) 'Seizing the Middle Ground: Constructivism in World Politics', *European Journal of International Relations* 3(3), 319–363.

(2002) 'Constructivism in International Relations', in Walter Carlsnaes, Thomas Risse and Beth Simmons (eds.), *Handbook of International Relations* (London: Sage), 95–110.

Adler, Emanuel and Bernstein, Steven (2005) 'Knowledge in Power: The Epistemic Construction of Global Governance', in Michael Barnett and Raymond Duvall (eds.), *Power in Global Governance* (Cambridge: Cambridge University Press), 294–318.

Adler, Emanuel and Haas, Peter (1992) 'Conclusion: Epistemic Communities, World Order, and the Creation of a Reflective Research Program', *International Organization* 46(1), 367–390.

Albors-Llorens, Albertina (1998) 'A Broader Construction of the EC Treaty Provisions on Citizenship?', *The Cambridge Law Journal 1998* 57(3), 461–463.

Alemanno, Alberto (2020) 'We Lived the European Dream. Will Any Politician Stand Up for Open Borders?' [online] (*The Guardian*, 22 May 2020) Available at: www.theguardian.com/world/commentisfree/2020/may/22/european-dream-politician-stand-up-for-free-movement. Accessed 10 September 2020.

Allott, Philip (1977) 'The European Court Ordains Equal Pay for Women', *The Cambridge Law Journal* 36(1), 7–10.

Anderson, Malcolm and Bigo, Didier (2003) 'What are EU Frontiers for and What Do They Mean?', in Kees Groenendijk, Elspeth Guild and Paul Minderhoud (eds.), *In Search of Europe's Borders* (The Hague: Kluwer Law International), 7–26.

Antonsich, Marco (2008) 'The Narration of Europe in "National" and "Post-National" Terms: Gauging the Gap between Normative Discourses and People's Views', *European Journal of Social Theory* 11(4), 505–522.

Armitage, Susan (1989) 'Making the Personal Political: Women's History and Oral History', *Oral History Review* 17(2), 107–116.

Arnull, Anthony (1985) 'Social Advantages and the Language Barrier', *European Law Review* 10(5), 346–348.

(1988) 'Institutional and Jurisdictional Questions: Of Strip Cartoonists, Vets and Gunsmiths', *European Law Review* 13(4), 260–267.

(1989) 'Metropolitan Misfortune', *European Law Review* 14(3), 166–169.

(1990) *The General Principles of EEC Law and the Individual* (Leicester: Leicester University Press).

Arnull, Anthony and Jacobs, Francis (1993) 'Applying the Common Rules on the Free Movement of Persons – The Role of the National Judiciary in the Light of the Jurisprudence of the European Court of Justice', in Henry Schermers (ed.), *Free Movement of Persons in Europe: Legal Problems and Experiences* (Dordrecht, Netherlands: Kluwer Academic Publishers), 272–285.

Asen, Robert (2004) 'A Discourse Theory of Citizenship', *Quarterly Journal of Speech* 90(2), 189–211.

Aspinwall, Mark (2004) *Rethinking Britain and Europe – Plurality Elections, Party Management and British Policy on European Integration* (Manchester: Manchester University Press).

Azmanova, Albena and Dakwar, Azar (2019) 'The Inverted Postnational Constellation: Identitarian Populism in Context', *European Law Journal Special Issue* 25(5), 493–501.

Baker, David and Seawright, David (1998) 'Introduction', in David Baker and David Seawright (eds.), *Britain for and against Europe* (Oxford: Clarendon), 1–11.

Bakker, Ryan, Hooghe, Liesbet, Jolly, Seth, Marks, Gary, Polk, Jonathan, Rovny, Jan, Steenbergen, Marco and Vachudova, Milada Anna (2020) 'Who Opposes the EU? Continuity and Change in party Euroscepticism between 2014 and 2019' (London School of Economics) Available at: https://blogs.lse.ac.uk/europpblog/2020/06/01/who-opposes-the-eu-continuity-and-change-in-party-euroscepticism-between-2014-and-2019/. Accessed 18 September 2020.

Baldwin-Edwards, Martin (1992) 'Immigration and migrants in the Europe of the 1990s', *European Access* 3, 14–16.

Bamforth, Nicholas (1996) 'Limits of Anti-Discrimination Law', in Janet Dine and Bob Watt (eds.), *Discrimination Law: Concepts, Limitations and Justifications* (London: Longman), 49–63.

Barav, Ami (1981) 'Court Recommendation to Deport and the Free Movement of Workers in EEC Law', *European Law Review* 6(3), 139–161.

Barav, Ami and Thomson, Sandy (1977) 'Deportation of EEC Nationals from the United Kingdom in the Light of the *Bouchereau* Case', *Legal Issues of Economic Integration* 2(1), 1–37.

Barbalet, Jack (1988) *Citizenship: Rights, Struggle and Class Equality* (Milton Keynes: Open University Press).

Barber, Nicholas (2002) 'Citizenship, Nationalism and the European Union', *European Law Review* 27(3), 241–259.

Barents, René (1994) 'The Court of Justice and the EEA-Agreement. Between Constitutional Values and Political Realities', in Jules Stuyck and Anne Looijertijn-Clearie (eds.), *The European Economic Area EC-EFTA: Institutional Aspects and Financial Services* (Deventer: Kluwer), 57–71.

Barnard, Catherine (1992) 'An Irish Solution', *New Law Journal* 142(6548), 526–533.

(1996) *EC Employment Law* (Chichester: Wiley).

(1998) 'The Principle of Equality in the Community Context: *P, Grant, Kalanke* and *Marshall*: Four Uneasy Bedfellows?', *Cambridge Law Journal* 67(2), 362–373.

(2005) 'Case C-209/03, *R (on the application of Danny Bidar) v. London Borough of Ealing, Secretary of State for Education and Skills*', *Common Market Law Review* 42 (5), 1465–1489.

(2005) 'EU Citizenship and the Principle of Solidarity', in Michael Dougan and Eleanor Spaventa (eds.), *Social Welfare and EU Law* (Oxford: Hart), 157–180.

(2005) 'Of Students and Babies', *The Cambridge Law Journal* 64(3), 560–563.

(2010) *The Substantive Law of the EU – The Four Freedoms* (Oxford: Oxford University Press).

Barnett, Michael and Finnemore, Martha (1999) 'The Politics, Power, and Pathologies of International Organizations', *International Organization* 53(4), 699–732.

(2004) *Rules for the World – International Organizations in Global Politics* (New York: Cornell University Press).

Barrett, Gavin (2003) 'Re-examining the Concept and Principle of Equality in EC Law', *Yearbook of European Law* 22 (1), 117–153.

Barrington, Donal (1992) 'The Emergence of a Constitutional Court', in James O'Reilly (ed.), *Human Rights and Constitutional Law – Essays in honour of Brian Walsh* (Dublin: Round Hall Press), 251–263.

Bauböck, Rainer (2019) 'The New Cleavage Between Mobile and Immobile Europeans', in Rainer Bauböck (ed.), *Debating European Citizenship* (Cham: Springer), 125–127.

Beenen, Jolanda (2001) *Citizenship, Nationality and Access to Public Service Employment. The Impact of European Community Law* (Groningen: Europa Law Publishing).

Begum, Neema (2020) 'Is being European a white identity? Brussels needs deep reflection in the wake of the Black Lives Matter movement' (The Conversation) Available at: https://theconversation.com/is-being-european-a-white-identity-brussels-needs-deep-reflection-in-the-wake-of-the-black-lives-matter-movement-141902, Accessed 19 September 2020.

Bell, Mark (2002) *Anti-Discrimination Law and the European Union* (Oxford: Oxford University Press).

(2008) *Racism and Equality in the European Union* (Oxford: Oxford University Press).

Bellamy, Richard (2004) 'Introduction: The Making of Modern Citizenship', in Richard Bellamy, Dario Castiglione and Emilio Santoro (eds.), *Lineages of European Citizenship – Rights, Belonging and Participation in Eleven Nation-States* (Basingstoke: Palgrave Macmillan), 1–21.

(2008) 'Evaluating Union Citizenship: Belonging, Rights and Participation within the EU', *Citizenship Studies* 12(6), 597–611.

Bennhold, Katrin (2005) 'Quietly sprouting: A European Identity' [online]; Available at: www.nytimes.com/2005/04/26/world/europe/26iht-enlarge2.html?pagewanted=all&_r=0, Accessed 11 December 2014.

Bernard (1996) 'Discrimination and Free Movement in EC Law', *International and Comparative Law Quarterly* 45(1), 82–108.

Besson, Samantha and Utzinger André (2007) 'Introduction: Future Challenges of European Citizenship – Facing a Wide-Open Pandora's Box', *European Law Journal* 13(5), 573–590.

Betten, Lammy (2000) 'New Equality Provisions in European Law: Some Thoughts on the Fundamental Value of Equality as a Legal Principle', in Kim Economides, Lammy Betten, John Bridge, Andrew Tettenborn and Vivien Shrubsall (eds.), *Fundamental Values* (Oxford: Hart).

Beyless, Natalie (1975) 'Recent Developments – EEC Court of Justice: *H. P. Bulmer, Ltd.* v. *Bollinger, S. A.*, (1974) 2 ALL E.R. 1226 (C.A.)', *Texas International Law Journal* 10 (2)419–428.

Bierbach, Jeremy (2008) 'European Citizens' Third-Country Family Members and Community Law', *European Constitutional Law Review* 5(2), 344–362.

Birks, Jen (2017) 'Tax Avoidance as an Anti-austerity Issue: The Progress of a Protest Issue Through the Public Sphere', *European Journal of Communication* 32 (4), 296–311.

Boerzel, Tanja (1999), 'Toward Convergence in Europe? Institutional Adaptation to Europeanisation in Germany and Spain', *Journal of Common Market Studies* 37(4), 573–596.

Bogdan, Michael (1977) 'Free Movement of Tourists within the EEC?', *Journal of World Trade* 11(5), 468–475.

Böhning, Wolf (1972) *The Migration of Workers in the United Kingdom and the European Community* (Oxford: Oxford University Press).

Borella, François (1987) 'Nationalité et citoyenneté en droit français', in Dominique Colas (ed.), *L'Etat de droit, travaux de la mission de la modernisation de l'Etat* (Paris: Presses Universitaires de France), 27–51.

Borgsmidt, Kirsten (1988) 'The Advocate General at the European Court of Justice: A Comparative Study', *European Law Review* 13(2), 106–119.

Bosniak, Linda (2006) *The Citizen and the Alien* (Princeton: Princeton University Press).

Bradley, Kieran St.C. (1982) 'Case 12/81, *Garland v. British Rail Engineering Limited*, Judgment of 9 February 1982 and Case 19/81, *Burton* v. *British Railways Board*. Judgment of 16 February 1982', *Common Market Law Review* 19(4), 629–634.

Brand, Michiel (2005) 'Case Law: Case C-209/03, *the Queen (on the Application of Dany Bidar)* v. *London Borough of Ealing, Secretary of State for Education and Skills*, 2005 E.C.R. I-2119', *The Columbia Journal of European Law* 12(1), 293–304.

Brown, Christopher (2001) 'The Race Directive: Towards Equality for All the Peoples of Europe?', *Yearbook of European Law* 21 (1), 195–227.

Brown, L. Neville (1984) 'Air Hostesses and Discriminating Employers', *The Modern Law Review* 47(6), 692–703.

(1986) 'Case 44/84, Hurd v. Jones (Inspector of Taxes), preliminary ruling under Article 177 (EEC) and Article 150 (Euratom) of the Court of Justice of 15 January 1986', *Common Market Law Review* 23(4), 895–907.

Brown, L. Neville and Kennedy, Tom (2000) *Brown and Jacobs: The Court of Justice of the European Communities* – fifth edition (London: Sweet and Maxwell).

Brubaker, Rogers (1993) 'De l'immigré au citoyen', *Actes de la recherche en Sciences Sociales* 99 (September), 3–25.
Bryant, Christopher (1997) 'Citizenship, National Identity and the Accommodation of Difference: Reflections on the German, French, Dutch and British Cases', *Journal of Ethnic and Migration Studies* 23(2), 157–172.
Bulmer, Simon (1992) 'Britain and European Integration: Of Sovereignty, Slow Adaptation, and Semi-Detachment', in Stephen George (ed.), *Britain in the European Community* (Oxford: Clarendon), 1–30.
Burchfield, Robert (ed.) (1994) *The Oxford English Dictionary* (Oxford: Clarendon).
Burley, Anne-Marie and Mattli, Walter (1993) 'Europe Before the Court: A Political Theory of Legal Integration', *International Organization* 47(1), 41–76.
Burrows, Noreen (1989) 'Wandering Scholars', *The Juridical Review* 34(1), 99–102.
Burrows, Noreen and Greaves, Rosa (2007) *The Advocate-General and EC Law* (Oxford: Oxford University Press).
Cahill, Maria (2012) 'European Integration and European Constitutionalism: Consonances and Dissonances', in Daniel Augenstein (ed.), *'Integration through Law Revisited' – The Making of the European Polity* (Farnham: Ashgate) 11–28.
Caldeira, Gregory and Gibson, James (1995) 'The Legitimacy of the Court of Justice in the European Union', *International Social Science Journal* 49(2), 1053–1064.
Cappelletti, Mauro (1987) 'Is the European Court of Justice "running wild"?', *European Law Review* 12(1), 3–17.
Caracciolo di Torella and Masselot, Annick (2004) 'Under Construction: EU Family Law', *European Law Review* 29(1), 32–51.
Caro de Sousa, Pedro (2015) *The European Fundamental Freedoms: A Contextual Approach* (Oxford: Oxford University Press).
Chambon, Adrienne (1995) 'Foucault's Approach: Making the Familiar Visible', in Adrienne Chambon, Allan Irving and Laura Epstein (eds.), *Reading Foucault for Social Work* (New York: Columbia University Press).
Chatelard, Aude and Stevens, Anne (2016) 'Women as Legal Minors and their Citizenship in Republican Rome', *Clio. Women, Gender, History* 43, 24–47.
Checkel, Jeffrey T. (2001) 'Social Construction and European Integration', in Thomas Christiansen, Knud Erik Jørgensen and Antje Wiener (eds.), *The Social Construction of Europe* (London: Sage).
Choate, Mark (2007) 'Sending States' Transnational Interventions in Politics, Culture, and Economics: The Historical Example of Italy', *International Migration Review* 41 (3) 728–768.
(2008) *Emigrant nation – The Making of Italy abroad* (Cambridge, Massachusetts: Harvard University Press).
Churchill, Robin (1992) 'Case 221/89, *R* v. *Secretary of State for Transport ex p. Factortame*, Judgment of 25 July 1991, [I991] 3 All ER 769; Case 246/89, *Commission* v. *United Kingdom*, Judgment of 4 October 1991; Case 93/89,

Commission v. *Ireland*, Judgment of 4 October 1991', *Common Market Law Review* 29 (2), 405–414.

Closa, Carlos (1995) 'Citizenship of the Union and Nationality of the Member States', *Common Market Law Review* 32(2), 487–518.

(2001) 'Between EU Constitution and Individuals' Self: European Citizenship', *Law and Philosophy* 20(3), 345–371.

(2010) '*Martínez Sala* and *Baumbast*: An Institutionalist Analysis, The Past and Future of EU Law', in Miguel Poiares Maduro and Loïc Azoulai (eds.), *The Classics of EU Law Revisited on the 50th Anniversary of the Rome Treaty* (Oxford: Hart), 394–401.

Cole, Alistair and Drake, Helen (2000) 'The Europeanization of the French Polity: Continuity, Change and Adaptation', *Journal of European Public Policy* 7(1), 26–43.

Colvin, Cathleen (1991) 'Irish Abortion Law and the Free Movement of Services in the European Community', *Fordham International Law Journal* 15(2), 476–526.

Condinanzi, Massimo, Lang, Allessandra and Bruno Nascimbene (2008) *Citizenship of the Union and Freedom of Movement of Persons* (Leiden: Brill).

Costello, Cathryn (2009) '*Metock*: Free Movement and "Normal Family Life" in the Union', *Common Market Law Review* 46 (2)587–622.

Courthaut, Tim (2008) 'Plus ça change, plus c'est la même chose? A Comparison with the Constitutional Treaty', *Maastricht Journal of European and Comparative Law* 15(1), 21–34.

Crisham, Catherine (1978) 'Case 71/76, *Jean Thieffry* v. *Conseil de l'Ordre des Avocats à. la Cour de Paris*. Preliminary ruling of 28 April 1977 at the request of the Cour d'Appel, Paris. (1977) ECR 767', *Common Market Law Review* 1978 15(3), 366–370.

Crosby, Margaret (2008) *The Making of a German Constitution: A Slow Revolution* (London: Bloomsbury).

Crowley, John (2003) 'Locating Europe's Borders', in Kees Groenendijk, Elspeth Guild and Paul Minderhoud (eds.), *In Search of Europe's Borders* (The Hague: Kluwer Law International), 27–44.

Cullen, Holly (1993) 'Spouses' Rights to Free Movement – Community Rules Prevail', *The Journal of Social Welfare Law* 15(1), 77–82.

Curtin, Deidre (1992) 'Case C-159/90, *The Society for the Protection of Unborn Children Ireland Ltd* v. *Grogan*, Judgment of 4 October 1991', *Common Market Law Review* 29(3), 585–563.

Curtin, Deidre and Meijers, Herman 'The Principle of Open Government in Schengen and the European Union: Democratic Retrogression', *Common Market Law Review* 32(1), 391–442.

Dahlberg, Kenneth (1967) 'The EEC Commission and the Politics of Free Movement of Labour', *Journal of Common Market Studies* 6(4), 310–333.

Darmon, Marco (1988) 'The Role of the Advocate General at the European Court of Justice', in Simon Shetreet (ed.), *The Role of Courts in Society* (Dordrecht: Martinus Nijhoff), 425–436.

Dashwood, Alan (1982) 'The Advocate General in the Court of Justice of the European Communities', *Legal Studies* 2(2), 202–216.

De Blois, Matthijs (1990) 'Case 352/85, *Bond van Adverteerders* v. *The Netherlands State*, Judgment of 26 April 1988, [1988] E.C.R. 2085. Reference to the Court by the Gerechtshof (regional Court of Appeal) The Hague on the interpretation of Article 59 et seq., of the EEC Treaty', *Common Market Law Review* 27(2), 371–381.

de Búrca, Gráinne (1996) 'The Quest for Legitimacy in the European Union', *Modern Law Review* 59(3), 349–376.

(1997) 'The Role of Equality in European Community Law', in Alan Dashwood and Siofra O'Leary (eds.), *The Principle of Equal Treatment in EC Law* (London: Sweet & Maxwell), 137–152.

De Groot, Gerard-René and Seling, Anja (2011) 'Decision of 2 March 2010, Case C-135/08, *Janko Rottman v. Freistaat Bayern* – Case Note II – The Consequences of the *Rottman* Judgment on Member State Autonomy – The European Court of Justice's Avant-Gardism in Nationality Matters', *European Constitutional Law Review* 7(1), 150–160.

Delanty, Gerard (2000) *Citizenship in a Global Age – Society, Culture, Politics* (Buckingham: Open University Press).

(2007) 'European Citizenship: A Critical Assessment', *Citizenship Studies* 11(1), 63–72.

Delgado Moreira, Juan (2000) 'Cohesion and Citizenship in EU Cultural Policy', *Journal of Common Market Studies* 38(3), 449–470.

De Moor, Adrienne (1985) 'Article 7 of the Treaty of Rome Bites', *Modern Law Review* 48(4), 452–459.

Department for Education (2014) *Basic Requirements to become a Qualified Teacher* [online]; Available at: www.education.gov.uk/get-into-teaching/apply-for-teacher-training/basic-requirements, Accessed 11th December 2014.

Derrida, Jacques (1992) *The Other Heading: Reflections on Today's Europe* (Bloomington, Indiana: Indiana University Press).

De Waele, Henri de (2010) 'EU Citizenship: Revisiting its Meaning, Place and Potential', *European Journal of Migration and Law* 12(3), 319–336.

De Witte, Bruno (2010) 'The Continuous Significance of *Van Gend en Loos*, The Past and Future of EU Law', in Miguel Poiares Maduro and Loïc, Azoulai (eds.), *The Classics of EU Law Revisited on the 50th Anniversary of the Rome Treaty* (Oxford: Hart), 9–15.

(2019) 'Freedom of Movement Needs to Be Defended as the Core of EU Citizenship' in Rainer Bauböck (ed.), *Debating European Citizenship* (Cham: Springer), 93–99.

Diez, Thomas (2001) 'Europe as a Discursive Battleground – Discourse Analysis and European Integration Studies', *Cooperation and Conflict* 36 (1), 5–38.

Dine, Janet and Watt, Bob (1996) 'Introduction', in Janet Dine and Bob Watt (eds.), *Discrimination Law: Concepts, Limitations and Justifications* (London: Longman), 3–13.

Docksey, Chris (1991) 'The Principle of Equality between Women and Men as a Fundamental Right Under Community Law', *Industrial Law Journal* 20 (4), 258–280.

Domorenok, Ekaterina (2009) 'The Committee of the Regions: In Search of Identity', *Regional and Federal Studies* 19(1), 143–163.

Dougan, Michael (2006) 'The Constitutional Dimension to the Case Law on Union Citizenship', *European Law Review* 31(5), 613–641.

Dougan, Michael, Shuibhne, Niamh Nic and Spaventa, Eleanor (2012) 'Introduction', in Michael Dougan, Niahm Nic Shuibhne and Eleanor Spaventa (eds.), *Empowerment and Disempowerment of the European Citizen* (Oxford: Hart), 2–7.

Dougan, Michael and Spaventa, Eleanor (2005) '"Wish You Weren't Here . . ." New Social Models of Social Solidarity in the European Union', in Michael Dougan and Eleanor Spaventa (eds.), *Social Welfare and EU Law* (Oxford: Hart), 181–219.

Douglas-Scott, Sionaidh (2002) *Constitutional Law of the European Union* (London: Longman).

Downes, Tony (2001) 'Market Citizenship: Functionalism and Fig-Leaves', in Richard Bellamy and Alex Warleigh (eds.), *Citizenship and Governance in the European Union* (London: Continuum), 93–107.

Dummet, Ann and Nicol, Andrew (1990) *Subjects, Citizens, Aliens and Others* (London: Weidenfeld and Nicolson).

Edward, David (1987) 'Establishment and Services: An Analysis of the Insurance Cases', *European Law Review* 12(4), 231–256.

Ellis, Evelyn (1996) 'Gender Discrimination in the European Community', in Janet Dine and Bob Watt (eds.), *Discrimination Law: Concepts, Limitations and Justifications* (London: Longman), 14–30.

(1997) 'The Principle of Equality of Opportunity Irrespective of Sex: Some Reflections on the Present and Future Development of European Community Law' in Alan Dashwood and Siofra O'Leary (eds.), *The Principle of Equal Treatment in EC Law* (London: Sweet & Maxwell), 172–188.

Etzioni, Amitai (1993) *The Spirit of Community – the Reinvention of American Society* (New York: Touchstone).

European Bureau for Lesser-Used Languages (2010) *About Us* [online]; Available at: http://eblul.eurolang.net/index.php?option=com_content&task=view&id=14&Itemid=33, Accessed 11 December 2014.

European Commission (2014) *Gender Equality* [online]; Available at: http://ec.europa.eu/justice/gender-equality/, Accessed 1 December 2014.

European Council (2016), 'Decision of the Heads of State or Government, meeting within the European Council, concerning a new settlement for the United Kingdom within the European Union' in 'Conclusions – 18 and 19 February 2016', pp. 8–24. Available at: www.consilium.europa.eu/media/21787/0216-euco-conclusions.pdf, Accessed 15 September 2020.

European Parliament – Directorate-General for Research and Documentation (1979) *Proceedings of the Round Table on 'Special rights and a charter of the rights of*

the citizens of the European Community' and related documents (Florence, 26 to 28 October 1978) (Luxembourg: European Parliament).
(2018) 'Acquisition and Loss of Citizenship in EU Member States' (2018), Available at: www.europarl.europa.eu/RegData/etudes/BRIE/2018/625116/EPRS_BRI(2018)625116_EN.pdf, accessed 19 September 2020.
Evans, Andrew (1982) 'European Citizenship', *Modern Law Review* 45(5), 497–515.
Everson, Michelle (1995) 'The Legacy of the Market Citizen' in Jo Shaw and Gillian More (eds.), *New Legal Dynamics of European Union* (Oxford: Clarendon Press), 73–90.
(2003) '"Subjects", or 'Citizens of Erewhon'? Law and Non-Law in the Development of a "British Citizenship"', *Citizenship Studies* 7(1), 57–83.
Fabbrini, Sergio and Piattoni, Simona (2004) 'Introduction: Italy in the EU – Pigmy or Giant?', *Modern Italy* 9(2) 149–157.
Faini, Riccardo and Sapir, André (2009) 'An Obsolete Model? Growth and Specialisation in the Italian Economy', in Marco Buti (ed.), *Italy in EMU – The Challenges of Adjustment and Growth* (Basingstoke: Palgrave Macmillan), 1–36.
Favell, Adrian (1998) *Philosophies of Integration: Immigration and the Idea of Citizenship in France and Britain* (Basingstoke: Macmillan).
(2008) *Eurostars and Eurocities – Free Movement and Mobility in an Integrating Europe* (Oxford, Blackwell).
(2017) 'European Union versus European Society: Sociologists on "Brexit" and the "Failure" of Europeanization' in William Outhwaite (ed.), *Brexit: Sociological Responses* (London: Anthem Press, 2017), 193–200.
Favell, Adrian and Barbulescu, Roxana (2018) 'Brexit, "Immigration" and Anti-Discrimination' in Patrick Diamon, Peter Nedergaard and Ben Rosamond (eds.), *The Routledge Handbook of Politics of Brexit* (Routledge, London), 118–133.
Fennelly, Nial (2000) 'The Dangerous Idea of Europe? *Van Gend en Loos* (1963)', in Eoin O'Dell (ed.), *Leading Cases of the Twentieth Century* (Dublin: Round Hall Sweet & Maxwell), 220–236.
Ferguson, James (1994) *The Anti-Politics Machine: Development, Depolitization, and Bureaucratic Power in Lesotho* (Cambridge: Cambridge University Press).
Finnemore, Martha (1996) *National Interests in International Society* (Ithaca, New York: Cornell University Press).
(2000) 'Are Legal Norms Distinctive?', *N. Y. U. Journal of International Law and Politics* 32, 699–710.
Finnemore, Martha and Sikkink Kathryn (1998) 'International Norm Dynamics and Political Change', *International Organization* 52(4), 887–917.
(2001) 'Taking Stock: The Constructivist Research Program in International Relations and Comparative Politics', *Annual Review of Political Science* 4, 391–416.
Fishman, J. (1998) 'The New Linguistic Order', *Foreign Policy* 113 (Winter), 26–40.
Flynn, James (1988) 'Vocational Training in Community Law and Practice', *Yearbook of European Law* 8(1), 59–85.
Ford, Steve (2018) '"Huge" drop in EU nurses coming to London since Brexit vote', Nursing Times (2018), Available at: www.nursingtimes.net/news/wo

rkforce/huge-drop-in-eu-nurses-coming-to-london-since-brexit-vote-21-12-2018/, Accessed 19 September 2020.

Forman, John (1977) '*R. J. Brack v. Insurance Officer*. Case 17/76. Preliminary Ruling of 29 September 1976 on request of the National Insurance Commissioner', *Common Market Law Review* 14(2), 231–240.

Foster, Nigel (1987) 'Sex Discrimination: The Effect of EEC Law on Sex Discrimination in Relation to Early Retirements and Redundancy Payments Schemes', *Legal Issues of Economic Integration* 14(1), 111–120.

Fox, Carole (1991) 'European Community Migrant Workers: The Right to Remain and Look for Work', *The Journal of Social Welfare Law* 13(2), 85–89.

Franklin, Michael and Wilke, Michael (1990) *Britain's Future in Europe* (London: Pinter).

Friden, Georges (1990)'The "*Bond van Adverteerders*" Case and Recent Legal Developments in EEC 'Television Law'; *Leiden Journal of International Law* 3(2), 231–238.

Friel, Brian (1981) *Translations* (London: Faber and Faber).

Fries, Sybilla and Shaw, Jo (1998) 'Citizenship of the Union: First Steps in the European Court of Justice', *European Public Law* 4(4), 533–559.

Friedl, Birgit (1996) 'Fixed Term Contracts for Foreign Language Lecturers – A Proportionate Restriction on Free Movement of Workers?', *Industrial Law Journal* 25(1), 66–70.

Gabaccia, Donna (2000) *Italy's Many Diasporas* (London: University College London).

Gallo, Flaminia and Birgit, Hanny (2003) 'Italy: Progress Behind Complexity', in Wolfgang Wessels, Andreas Maurer and Jürgen Mittag (eds.), *Fifteen Into One? The European Union and Its Member States* (Manchester: Manchester University Press), 271–297.

Gamble, Andrew (1988) 'The European Issue in British Politics', in David Baker and David Seawright (eds.), *Britain for and against Europe* (Oxford: Clarendon), 11–30.

George, Stephen (1998) *An Awkward Partner: Britain in Europe* (Oxford: Oxford University Press).

Gerber, David (2001) 'Disabled Veterans and Public Welfare Policy: Comparative and Transnational Perspectives on Western States in the Twentieth Century', *Transnational Law & Contemporary Problems* 11(1), 77–106.

Giubboni, Stefano (2007) 'Free Movement of Persons and European Solidarity', *European Law Journal* 13 (3), 360–79.

Gormley, Lawrence (1986) 'The Application of Community Law in the United Kingdom', *Common Market Law Review* 23(2), 287–323.

Gould, Mark (1989) 'Equality of Access to Education', *Modern Law Review* 52(4), 540–550.

Gowland, David, Turner, Arthur and Wright, Alex (2010) *Britain and European Integration Since 1945 – on the sidelines* (Abingdon, Oxfordshire: Routledge).

Gravells, Nigel (1983) 'Article 177 EEC: References in Interlocutory Proceedings', *European Law Review* 8(4), 250–251.

Greaves, Rosa (1988) 'Who is a Dependent Member of a Worker's Family?', *European Law Review* 13(4), 270–275.

Green, Nicholas, Hartley, Trevor and Usher, John (1991) *The Legal Foundations of the Single Market* (Oxford: Oxford University Press).

Greenwood, Christopher (1983) 'Free Movement of Workers under EEC Law and English Law', *New Law Journal* 133, 933–934.

Greve, Bent (1991) 'Economics and Social Security in Europe', in Danny Pieters (ed.), *Social Security in Europe: Miscellanea of the Erasmus-Programme Social Security in the E.C* (Brussels: Bruylant), 191–216.

The Guardian (2020) 'Jamaican-born deportees mount last-minute challenges against the Home Office', Available at: www.theguardian.com/uk-news/2020/feb/10/jamaican-born-deportees-mount-last-minute-challenges-against-home-office. Accessed on 15 September 2020.

Guild, Elspeth (1996) 'The Legal Framework of Citizenship of the European Union', in David Cesarini and Mary Fulbrook (eds.), *Citizenship, Nationality and Migration in Europe* (London: Routledge), 30–56.

(1997) 'EC Law and the Means to Combat Racism and Xenophobia', in Alan Dashwood and Siofra O'Leary (eds.), *The Principle of Equal Treatment in EC Law* (London: Sweet & Maxwell), 189–213.

(2001) *Immigration Law in the European Community* (The Hague: Kluwer Law International).

(2003) 'The Border Abroad – Visas and Border Controls', in Kees Groenendijk, Elspeth Guild and Paul Minderhoud (eds.), *In Search of Europe's Borders* (The Hague: Kluwer Law International), 87–105.

Haas, Peter (1992) 'Introduction: Epistemic Communities and International Policy Coordination', *International Organization* 46(1), 1–35.

Habermas, Jürgen (1995) 'Citizenship and National Identity: Some Reflections on the Future of Europe', in Ronald Beiner (ed.), *Theorizing Citizenship* (New York: State University of New York Press), 255–283.

Hall, Stephen (1985) *Nationality, Migration Rights and Citizenship of the Union* (Alphen aan den Rijn: Kluwer Law International).

(1996) ''Loss of Union Citizenship in Breach of Fundamental Rights', *European Law Review* 21(2), 129–143.

(2001) 'Determining the Scope *ratione personae* of European Citizenship: Customary International Law Prevails for Now. ECJ, Judgment, 20 February 2001, Case C-192/99, *The Queen* v. *Secretary of State for the Home Department ex parte Kaur*'', *Legal Issues of Economic Integration* 28(3), 355–360.

Haltern, Ulrich (2004) 'Integration through Law', in Antje Wiener and Thomas Diez (eds.), *European Integration Theory* (Oxford: Oxford University Press).

(2004) 'The Dawn of the Political: Rethinking the Meaning of Law in European Integration', *Schweizerische Zeitschrift für Internationales und Europäisches Recht* 14(4), 585–614.

Handoll, John (1988) 'Article 48(4) EEC and Non-National Access to Public Employment', *European Law Review* 13(4), 223–241.

(1995) *Free Movement of Persons in the EU* (Chichester: John Wiley).

Hansen, Peo (2000) '"European Citizenship", or Where Neoliberalism Meets Ethnoculturalism: Analysing the European Union's Citizenship Discourse', *European Societies* 2(2), 139–165.

Hartley, Trevor (1996) 'The European Court, Judicial Objectivity and the Constitution of the European Union', *Law Quarterly Review* 112(1), 95–109.

Harty, Siobhán and Murphy, Michael (2005) *In Defence of Multinational Citizenship* (Cardiff: University of Wales Press).

Hepple, Bob (1997) 'The Principle of Equal Treatment in Article 119 EEC and the Possibilities for Reform', in Alan Dashwood and Siofra O'Leary (eds.), *The Principle of Equal Treatment in EC Law* (London: Sweet & Maxwell), 137–152.

Heun, Werner (2011) *The Constitution of Germany: A Contextual Analysis* (Oxford: Hart).

HM Government (2016), 'Why the Government believes that voting to remain in the European Union is the best decision for the UK', Available at: https://assets.publishing.service.gov.uk/government/uploads/system/uploads/attachment_data/file/515068/why-the-government-believes-that-voting-to-remain-in-the-european-union-is-the-best-decision-for-the-uk.pdf, Accessed 19 September 2020.

Home Office (2014) *UK Visas and Immigration* [online], Available at: www.gov.uk/government/organisations/uk-visas-and-immigration, Accessed 4 November 2014.

Home Office (2021) UK Visas and Immigration [online]; Available at: www.gov.uk/government/organisations/uk-visas-and-immigration, Accessed 8 March 2021.

Hopkins, N. (1994) 'Education and the European Community: Education as a Service and the Principle of Non-Discrimination', *The Journal of Social Welfare and Family Law* 16(4), 486–491.

Iglésias, Sanchez, Sara (2017) 'A Citizenship Right to Stay? The Right Not to Move in a Union Based on Free Movement' in Dimitry Kochenov (ed.), *EU Citizenship and Federalism: The Role of Rights* (Cambridge: Cambridge University Press, 2017), 371–393.

Ignatieff, Michael (1995) 'The Myth of Citizenship', in Ronald Beiner (ed.), *Theorizing Citizenship* (New York: State University of New York Press), 53–78.

ILGA Europe (2015), 'Equality for All – Joint NGO Statement', www.ilga-europe.org/sites/default/files/Attachments/2015-06 17_joint_ngo_statement_on_horizontal_directive_before_junes_epsco_council.pdf, Accessed 16 September 2020.

Iliopoulou, Anastasia and Toner, Helen (2003) 'Case Comment: A New Approach to Discrimination Against Free Movers?', *European Law Review* 28(3), 389–397.

The Independent (2017), *Brexit: Deportations of EU citizens soar since referendum* (2017) www.independent.co.uk/news/uk/politics/brexit-latest-eu-citizens-

deportations-rise-uk-home-office-referendum-a7935266.html. Accessed 15 September 2020.
International Student Team, The University of Cambridge (2014) *Tier 4 visa (entry clearance)* [online]; Available at: www.internationalstudents.cam.ac.uk/applying/uk-immigration/tier-4-entry-clearance, Accessed 4 November 2014.
Jacobs, Francis 1997) 'An Introduction to the General Principle of Equality in EC Law', in Alan Dashwood and Siofra O'Leary (eds.), *The Principle of Equal Treatment in EC Law* (London: Sweet & Maxwell), 1–12.
(2004) ''The Evolution of the European Legal Order', *Common Market Law Review* 41(2), 303–316.
Jacqueson, Catherine (2002) 'Union Citizenship and the Court of Justice: Something New under the Sun? Towards Social Citizenship', *European Law Review* 27(3), 260–281.
Jessurun D' Oliveira, Hans Ulrich (1993) 'Case C-369/90, *M. V. Micheletti and others* v. *Delegacion del Gobierno en Cantabria*, Judgment of 7 July 1992', *Common Market Law Review* 30(3), 623–637.
(1994) 'European Citizenship: Its Meaning, Its Potential', in Renaud Delhousse (ed.), *Europe After Maastricht – An Ever Closer Union?* (Munich: Law Books in Europe) 126–149.
(1995) ''Union Citizenship: Pie in the Sky', in Allan Rosas and Esko Antola (eds.), *A Citizen's Europe: In Search of a New Order* (London: Sage), 58–84.
(2011) 'Decision of 2 March 2010, Case C-135/08, *Janko Rottman* v. *Freistaat Bayern* – Case Note I – Decoupling Nationality and Union Citizenship?', *European Constitutional Law Review* 7(1), 138–149.
Johnson, Esther and O'Keeffe, David (1994) 'From Discrimination to Obstacles to Free Movement: Recent Developments Concerning the Free Movement of Workers 1989–1994', *Common Market Law Review* 31(6), 1313–1346.
Johnstone, Ian (2004) 'The Power of Interpretive Communities', in Michael Barnett and Raymond Duvall (eds.), *Power in Global Governance* (Cambridge: Cambridge University Press) 185–204.
Jünemann, Annette, Fromm, Nicolas and Scherer, Nikolas (2017) 'The Kaleidoscope of Migration – Theoretical Perspectives and Conceptual Considerations', in Annette Jünemann, Nicolas Fromm and Nikolas Scherer (eds.), *Fortress Europe? Challenges and Failures of Migration and Asylum Policies* (Wiesbaden: Springer), 1–11.
Kang, Yoo-Duk and Oh. Chang-Rhyong (2020), 'Spreading Euroscepticism and Its Macro-level Determinants: Empirical Analysis of the Eurobarometer Survey in 2004–2017', *Journal of Contemporary European Studies* 28 (3), 348–365.
Kendall, Gavin and Wickham, Gary (1999) *Using Foucault's Methods* (Guilford: Sage).
Knill, Christoph (2001) *The Europeanisation of National Administrations. Patterns of Institutional Change and Persistence* (Cambridge: Cambridge University Press).
Kochenov, Dimitry (2017), 'EU Citizenship and Withdrawals from the Union: How Inevitable is the Radical Downgrading of Rights?' in Carlos Closa (ed.), *Secession from a Member State and Withdrawal from the European Union: Trouble Membership* (Cambridge: Cambridge University Press), 257–286.

(2017) (ed.) *EU Citizenship and Federalism: The Role of Rights* (Cambridge: Cambridge University Press).

Kokott, Juliane B (1992) 'European Community Case Note: *Society for the Protection of Unborn Children (Ireland) Ltd.* v. *Grogan* Case No. C-159/90', *American Journal of International Law* 86(2), 367–370.

Koslowski, Rey (1994) 'Intra-EU Migration, Citizenship, and Political Union', *Journal of Common Market Studies* 32 (3), 369–402.

(1999) 'A Constructivist Approach to Understanding the European Union as a Federal Polity', *Journal of European Public Policy* 6(4), 561–578.

(2000) *Migrants and Citizens – Demographic Change in the European State System* (Ithaca, New York: Cornell University Press).

Kostakopoulou, Dora (1996) 'Towards a Theory of Constructive Citizenship in Europe', *The Journal of Political Philosophy* 4(4), 337–358.

(2001) *Citizenship, Identity and Immigration in the European Union: Between Past and Future* (Manchester: Manchester University Press).

(2005) ''Ideas, Norms and European Citizenship: Explaining Institutional Change', *The Modern Law Review* 68(2), 233–267.

(2007) 'European Union Citizenship: Writing the Future', *European Law Journal* 13 (5), 623–646.

(2009) 'Citizenship Goes Public: The Institutional Design of Anational Citizenship', *The Journal of Political Philosophy* 17(3), 275–306.

Kratochwil, Friedrich (2000) 'How Do Norms Matter?' in: Michael Byers (ed.), *The Role of Law in International Politics* (Oxford: Oxford University Press, 2000), 35–68.

Kritzinger Sylvia, Cavatorta, Francesco and Chari Raj S. (2004) 'Continuity and Change in Party Positions towards Europe in Italian Parties: An Examination of Parties' Manifestos', *Journal of European Public Policy* 11(6), 954–974.

Kruma, Kristine (2012) 'How Do We Get More out of the EU Citizenship? Which Integration Policies for Migrants? Interaction between the EU and its Member States', in Yyves. Pascouau and Tineke. Strik (eds.), *Which Integration Policies for Migrants? Interaction between the EU and its Member States* (Nijmegen, The Netherlands: Wolf Legal Publishers), 185–207.

Larousse (2014) *Dictionnaires bilingues: 'citizen'* [online]; Available at www.larousse.fr /dictionnaires/anglais-francais/citizen/570230, Accessed 28 November 2014.

Laske, Caroline (1993) 'The Impact of the Single European Market on Social Protection for Migrant Workers', *Common Market Law Review* 30(3), 515–539.

Lasok, Dominik (1991) 'Deporting Unemployed Immigrants', *The Law Society's Gazette* 88 (17)18 September, 17–18.

Lawson, Rick (1994) 'Case C- 168/91, *Christos Konstantinidis* v. *Stadt Altensteig-Standesamt*, Judgment of 30 March 1993, [1993] 3 C. M. L. R. 401', *Common Market Law Review*, 31(2), 395–412.

Lefebvre, Edwidge (2003) 'Republicanism and Universalism: Factors of Inclusion or Exclusion in the French Concept of Citizenship', *Citizenship Studies* 7(1), 15–36.

Lehning, Percy (1997) 'European Citizenship: A Mirage?', in Percy Lehning and Albert Weale (eds.), *Citizenship, Democracy and Justice in the New Europe* (London: Routledge), 175–200.

Lenz, Brigitte (1989) 'The Public Service in Article 48 (4) EEC with Special Reference to the Law in England and in the Federal Republic of Germany', *Legal Issues in Economic Integration* 16(2), 75–112.

Lessig, Lawrence (1995) 'The Regulation of Social Meaning', *University of Chicago Law Review*, 943–1045.

Liebert, Ulrike (2008) 'The European Citizenship Paradox: Renegotiating Equality and Diversity in Europe', in Birte Siim and Judith Squires (eds.), *Contesting Citizenship* (London: Routledge), 15–40.

Linke, Uli (2011), 'Technologies of Othering: Black Masculinities in the Carceral Zones of European Whiteness' in Manuela Ribeiro Sanches, Fernando Clara, João Ferreira Duarte and Leonor Pires Martins (eds.), *Europe in Black and White: Immigration, Race and Identity in the 'Old Continent'* (Bristol: Intellect), 123–42.

Lister, Ruth (1997), *Citizenship: Feminist Perspectives* (Basingstoke: Macmillan).

Lonbay, Julian (1988) 'Free Movement for Professionals', *European Law Review* 13 (4), 275–279.

Louis, Jean-Victor (1984) 'Free Movement of Tourists and Freedom of Payments in the Community: The Luisi-Carbone Judgment', *Common Market Law Review* 21(4), 625–637.

Lundström, Karin (1996) 'Family Life and Freedom of Movement of Workers in the European Union', *International Journal of Law, Policy and the Family* 10(3), 250–280.

Lyons, Timothy (1995) 'Discrimination against Individuals and Enterprises on Grounds of Nationality: Direct Taxation and the European Court of Justice', *EC Tax Journal* 1(1.3), 27–51.

Maas, Willem (2007) *Creating European Citizens* (Rowman and Littlefield; Lanham, Maryland).

(2008) 'Migrants, States, and EU Citizenship's Unfulfilled Promise', *Citizenship Studies* 12(6) 583–596.

Major, Claudia (2005) 'Europeanization and Foreign and Security Policy: Undermining or Rescuing the Nation State?', *Politics* 25(3), 175–190.

Mancini, Federico (1989) 'The Making of A Constitution For Europe', *Common Market Law Review* 26(4), 595–614.

(1992) 'The Free Movement of Workers in the Case-Law of the European Court of Justice', in Deidre Curtin and David O'Keefe (eds.), *Constitutional Adjudication in European Community and National Law – Essays for the Hon. Mr Justice TF O'Higgins* (Dublin: Butterworths).

Mancini, Federico and Keeling, David (1994) 'Democracy and the European Court of Justice', *The Modern Law Review* 57(2), 175–190.

(1995) 'Language, Culture and Politics in the Life of the European Court of Justice', *Columbia Journal of European Law* 1(3), 397–414.

Manolkidis, Sotirios (1997) 'The Principle of Equality from a Comparative Constitutional Perspective: Lessons from the EU', in Alan Dashwood and Siofra O'Leary (eds.), *The Principle of Equal Treatment in EC Law* (London: Sweet & Maxwell), 80–104.

March-Hunnings, Neville (1975) 'European Community Law: Nationality Discrimination', *The Journal of Business Law*, 168–171.

Marsh, Norman (1963) 'Some Reflections on Legal Integration in Europe', *International and Comparative Law Quarterly* 12(4), 1411–1416.

Marshall, Thomas H. (1950) *Citizenship and Social Class* (Cambridge: Cambridge University Press).

Martens, Albert (1973) *25 Jaar Wegwerparbeiders. Het Belgisch Immigratiebeleid na 1945* (Leuven: KULeuven).

Martin, Dennis (2008) 'Comments on *Gouvernement de la Communauté Française and Gouvernement Wallon* (Case C-212/06 of 1 April 2008) and *Eind* (Case C-291/05 of 11 December 2007)', *European Journal of Migration and Law* 10(3), 365–379.

Martin, Dennis and Elspeth Guild (1996) *Free Movement of Persons in the European Union* (London: Butterworths).

Marxen, Christian (2019) 'Discourse Theory of Law in Times of Populism', *European Law Journal Special Issue* 25(5), 480–486.

Mazzi-Zissis, Sabina (1999) 'Les Accords de Schengen et la libre circulation des personnes dans l'Union européenne: exemple á suivre ou dangereux precedent?', in Claus Ehlerman (ed.), *Multi-Speed Europe – the Legal Framework of Variable Geometry in the European Union* (Bonn: Bundesanzeiger), 47–66.

McKean, Warwick (1983) *Equality and Discrimination Under International Law* (Oxford: Clarendon).

McMahon, Bryan (1990) 'Case 379/87, *Groener* v. *Minister for Education and The City of Dublin Vocational Education Committee (CDVEC)*, Judgment of 28 November 1989', *Common Market Law Review* 27(1), 129–139.

Meehan, Elizabeth (1991) 'European Citizenship and Social Policies', in Ursula Vogel and Michael Moran (eds.), *The Frontiers of Citizenship* (Basingstoke: Macmillan), 125–154.

(2000) Europeanization and Citizenship of the European Union, *Yearbook of European Studies* 14, 157–177.

Meissner, Collin (1992) 'Words Between Worlds: The Irish Language, the English Army and the Violence of Translation in Brian Friel's *Translations*'', *Colby Quarterly* 28(3), 164–173.

Menéndez, Agustín José (2004) 'Taxing Europe: Two Cases for a European Power to Tax (with some comparative observations)', *The Columbia Journal of European Law* 10(2), 297–338.

(2010) 'European Citizenship after Martínez Sala and Baumbast: Has European Law Become More Human but Less Social?', in Miguel Poiares Maduro and Loïc Azoulai (eds.), *The Past and Future of EU Law: The Classics of EU Law Revisited on the 50th Anniversary of the Rome Treaty* (Oxford: Hart) 363–393.

Michalowski, Sabine and Woods, Lorna (1999) *German Constitutional Law: The Protection of Civil Liberties* (Dartmouth: Ashgate).
Miers, David (2004) 'Britain in Europe - Community to Union: 1973–2001', in Phillip Giddings and Gavin Drewry (eds.), *Britain in the European Union - Law, Policy and Parliaments* (Basingstoke: Palgrave), 12–36.
Molle, Wellem and Van Morik, Aad (1988) 'International Movements of Labour under Conditions of Economic Integration: The Case of Western Europe', *Journal of Common Market Studies* 26(3), 317–340.
Monaghan, Karen (2007) *Equality Law* (Oxford: Oxford University Press).
More, Gillian (1992) 'Reflections on Pregnancy Discrimination under European Community Law', *The Journal of Social Welfare Law* 14(1), 48–56.
Morris, Gillian, Fredman, Sandra and Hayes, Jon (1990) 'Free Movement and the Public Sector', *Industrial Law Journal* 19(1), 20–28.
Morse, Geoffrey (1975) 'Direct Applicability of Main Treaty Provisions and Scope of Safeguard Clauses', *European Law Review* 1(1), 67–69.
(1976) 'Residence Requirements and the Provision of Services', *European Law Review* 2(4), 227–229.
(1979) 'Provision of Services: The Professional Supervision Exception', *European Law Review* 5(4), 375–377.
Mortelmans, Kamiel (2005) 'The Court under the Influence of its Advocates General', *Yearbook of European Law* 24(1), 130–131.
Mulgan, Geoff (1991) 'Citizens and Responsibilities', in Geoff Andrews (ed.), *Citizenship* (London: Lawrence & Wishart), 37–50.
Mutschler, Max (2013) *Arms Control in Space: Exploring Conditions for Preventive Arms Control* (London: Palgrave Macmillan).
NAFTA Secretariat (2014) *North America Free Trade Agreement* [online]; Available at www.nafta-sec-alena.org/Default.aspx?tabid=97&ctl=FullView&mid=1588&language=en-US, Accessed 4 November 2014.
Nielsen, Ruth (1992) 'Case C-177/88, *Elisabeth Johanna Pacifica Dekker* v. *Stichting Vormingscentrum voor Jong Volwassenen (VJV Centrum) Plus*, Preliminary reference under Article 177 EEC by Hoge Raad der Nederlanden, Decision of the European Court of Justice of 8 November 1990; and Case C-179/88, *Handels-og Kontorfunktionærernes Forbund i Danmark (acting for Birthe Hertz)* v. *Dansk Arbejdsgiverforning (acting for Aldi Marked A/S)*, Preliminary Reference under Article 177 EEC by Højesteret, Denmark, Judgment of the European Court of Justice of 8 November 1990', *Common Market Law Review* 29(1), 160–169.
Noirfalisse, Catherine (1992) 'The Community System of Fisheries Management and the *Factortame* Case', *Yearbook of European Law* 12(1), 325–351.
Nuttall, Paul (2013) *No Votes For Prisoners - 18 December* 2013 [online], Available at http://ukipnw.org.uk/no-votes-for-prisoners, Accessed 11 December 2014.
Oberman, Kieran (2019) 'What to Say to Those Who Stay? Free Movement is a Human Right of Universal Value' in Rainer Bauböck (ed.), *Debating European Citizenship* (Cham: Springer), 145–148.

O'Brien, Charlotte (2009) 'Social Blind Spots and Monocular Policy Making: The ECJ's Migrant Worker Model', *Common Market Law Review* 46(4), 1107–1141.

(2013) 'I Trade, Therefore I Am: Legal Personhood in the European Union', *Common Market Law Review* 50(6), 1643–1684.

(2017) *Unity in Adversity: EU Citizenship, Social Justice and the Cautionary Tale of the UK* (Oxford: Hart).

O'Conaill, Cathal (1988) 'Community Lawyers Right to Practise within the E.C. Two Recent Decisions of the European Court of Justice', *Gazette of the Incorporated Law Society of Ireland*, 259–264.

Offe, Claus (2000) 'The Democratic Welfare State in an Integrating Europe', in M. Green and L. Pauly (eds.), *Democracy Beyond the State? The European Dilemma and the Emerging Global Order* (Lanham: Rowman and Littlefield), 63–89.

Office of the United States Trade Representative (2020), 'Agreement between the United States of America, the United Mexican States and Canada 12/ 13/ 19Text' (2020) https://ustr.gov/trade-agreements/free-trade-agreements/united-states-mexico-canada-agreement/agreement-between, Accessed 14 September 2020.

O'Keeffe, David (1984) 'The Free Movement of Workers. An Annotation of the *Levin* Case', *Journal of the Irish Society for Labour Law* 3(1), 17–22.

(1985) 'Equal Rights for Migrants: The Concept of Social Advantages in Article 7 (2), Regulation 1612/68', *Yearbook of European Law* 5(1), 95–123.

(1991) 'The Schengen Convention: A Suitable Model for European Integration', *Yearbook of European Law* 11(1), 185–219.

(1992) 'The Free Movement of Persons and the Single Market', *European Law Review* 17(1), 3–19.

(1992) 'Case C-357/89, *Raulin* v. *Netherlands Ministry of Education and Science*, and Case C-3/90, *Bernini* v. *Netherlands Ministry of Education and Science*, Judgments of 26 February 1992', *Common Market Law Review* 29(6), 1215–1228.

(1992) 'Judicial Interpretation of the Public Services Exception to the Free Movement of Workers' in Deidre Curtin, and David O'Keeffe (eds.), *Constitutional Adjudication in European Community and National Law* (Dublin: Butterworths).

O'Leary, Siofra (1992) 'The Court of Justice as a Reluctant Constitutional Adjudicator: An Examination of the Abortion Information Case', *European Law Review* 17(2), 138–157.

(1995) 'The Social Dimension of Community Citizenship' in Allan Rosas and Esko Antola (eds.), *A Citizen's Europe – In Search of a New Order* (London: Sage).

(1996) *The Evolving Concept of Community Citizenship* (The Hague: Kluwer Law International).

(1999) 'Putting Flesh on the Bones of European Union Citizenship', *European Law Review* 24(1), 68–79.

Oliveira, À. Castro (2002) 'Workers and Other Persons: Step-by-Step from Movement to Citizenship – Case Law 1995–2001', *Common Market Law Review* 39(1), 77–127.

O'Neill, Michael (1995) 'The Expansion of the ECJ's Fundamental Rights Jurisdiction: A Recipe for Tensions with Strasbourg?', *Irish Law Times and Solicitors' Journal* 129, 168–170.

Oppenheimer, Andrew (1994) *The Relationship between European Community Law and National Law: The Cases* (Cambridge: Cambridge University Press).

Paltridge, Brian (2006) *Discourse Analysis: an Introduction* (London: Continuum).

Papagianni, Georgia (2001) 'Free Movement of Persons in the Light of the New Title IV TEC: From Intergovernmentalism towards a Community Policy', *Yearbook of European Law* 21(1), 107–162.

Paskalia, Vicki (2007) *Free Movement, Social Security and Gender in the EU* (Oxford: Hart).

(2009) 'Co-ordination of Social Security in the European Union: An Overview of Recent Case Law', *Common Market Law Review* 46(4), 1177–1218.

Pennings, Frans (2003) *Introduction to European Social Security Law* (Antwerp: Intersentia).

Perju, Vlad (2019) 'The asymmetries of pouvoir constituent mixte', *European Law Journal Special Issue*, 25 (5), 515–520.

Perl, Gabriel (1972) 'Règlement n 3 du Conseil de la C. E. E. relatif à la sécurité sociale des travailleurs migrants', *Revue belge de sécurité sociale* 1972(5), 591–595.

Pescatore, Pierre (1983) '"The Doctrine of "Direct Effect": An Infant Disease of Community Law', *European Law Review*, 155–177.

(2010) 'Van Gend en Loos, 3 February 1963 – A View from Within, The Past and Future of EU Law', in Miguel Poiares Maduro and Loïc Azoulai (eds.), *The Classics of EU Law Revisited on the 50th Anniversary of the Rome Treaty* (Oxford: Hart), 3–8.

Phalet, Karen and Swyngedouw, Marc (2003) 'Measuring Immigrant Integration: The Case of Belgium', *Studi Emigrazione XL* (152),773–803.

Pickup, David (1986) 'Reverse Discrimination and Freedom of Movement for Workers', *Common Market Law Review* 23(1), 135–156.

Pilkington, Lionel (1990) 'Language and Politics in Brian Friel's *Translations*'', *Irish University Review* 20(2), 282–298.

Piris, Jean-Claude (2006) *The Constitution for Europe: A Legal Analysis* (Cambridge: Cambridge University Press).

Plender, Richard (1976) 'An Incipient Form of European Citizenship', in Francis Jacobs (ed.), *European Law and the Individual* (Amsterdam: North Holland Publishing).

Pomoell, Jutta (2000) *European Union Citizenship in Focus: The Legal Position of the Individual in EC Law* (Helsinki: The Erik Castrén Institute of International Law and Human Rights Research Reports).

Powell, Jason (2006) 'Chapter Three: The Development of Post-Structuralism and Aging', in Jared Jaworski (ed.), *Advances in Sociology: Volume 3* (Hauppauge, New York: Nova Science Publishers), 53–68.

Prechal, Sacha (2004) 'Equality of Treatment, Non-Discrimination and Social Policy: Achievements in Three Themes', *Common Market Law Review* 41(2), 533–551.

Preuß, Ulrich K. (1995) 'Problems of a Concept of European Citizenship', *European Law Journal* 1(1), 267–281.

Prime Minister's Office (2015), 'PM letter to President of the European Council Donald Tusk' www.gov.uk/government/publications/eu-reform-pms-letter-to-president-of-the-european-council-donald-tusk, accessed 1 September 2020.

Rasmussen, Hjalte (1986) *On Law and Policy in the European Court of Justice – A Comparative Study in Judicial Policymaking* (Dordrecht: Martinus Nijhoff).

(1998) *The European Court of Justice* (Copenhagen: GadJura).

Rasmussen, Morten (2008) 'The Origins of Legal Revolution – The Early History of the European Court of Justice', *Zeitschrift für Geschichte der Europäischen Integration* 14(2), 77–98.

Raz, Joseph (1998) 'On the Authority and Interpretation of Constitution: Some Preliminaries', in Larry Alexander (ed.), *Constitutionalism – Philosophical Foundations* (Cambridge: Cambridge University Press), 152–193.

Recchi, Ettore (2017) 'The Engine of "Europeanness"? Free Movement, Social Transnationalism and European Identification' in Daniel Thym (ed.), *Questioning EU Citizenship: Judges and the Limits of Free Movement and Solidarity in the EU* (Oxford: Hart), 135–48.

Reich, Norbert and Harbacevica, Solvita (2003) 'Citizenship and Family on Trial: A Fairly Optimistic Overview of Recent Court Practice with Regard to Free Movement of Persons', *Common Market Law Review* 40(3), 615–638.

Risse, Thomas (1994) 'Ideas Do Not Float Freely: Transnational Coalitions, Domestic Structures, and the End of the Cold War', *International Organization* 48(2), 185–214.

(2004) 'Social Constructivism and European Integration', in Antje Wiener and Thomas Diez (eds.), *European Integration Theory* (Oxford: Oxford University Press).

Risse, Thomas and Antje Wiener (2001) 'The Social Construction of Social Constructivism', in Thomas Christiansen, Knud Erik Jørgensen and Antje Wiener (eds.), *The Social Construction of Europe* (London: Sage), 199–205.

Robin-Olivier, Sophie (2020)'Free Movement of Workers in the Light of the Covid-19 Sanitary Crisis: From Restrictive Selection to Selective Mobility' (2020) *European Papers* 5(1), 613–619.

Roche, Anthony (2012) *Brian Friel: Theatre and Politics* (Basingstoke: Palgrave Macmillan).

Roche, Maurice (2010) *Exploring the Sociology of Europe* (London: Sage).

Rogers, Nicola, Scannell, Rick and Walsh, John (2012) *Free Movement of Persons in the Enlarged European Union* (London: Sweet & Maxwell).

Rohrbach, Heidi (1976) 'European Communities – Free Movement of Workers – Court of Justice Sets Guidelines for Use by Member States of the Public Policy Exception in Article 48', *Vanderbilt Journal of Transnational Law* 9(3), 651–658.

Romero, Federico (1990) 'Cross-Border Population Movements', in William Wallace (ed.), *The Dynamics of European Integration* (London: Pinter), 171–191.

(1993), 'Migration as an Issue In European Interdependence and Integration: The Case of Italy', in Alan Milward, Frances Lynch and Ruggero Ranieri (eds.), *The Frontier of National Sovereignty: History and Theory 1945–1992* (London: Longman), 33–58.

Rubio-Marin, Ruth (2000) *Immigration as Democratic Challenge: Citizenship and Inclusion in Germany and the United States* (Cambridge: Cambridge University Press).

Ruggie, John (1998) 'What Makes the World Hang Together? Neo-utilitarianism and the Social Constructivist Challenge', *International Organization* 52(4), 855–885.

Rumford, Chris (2003) 'European Civil Society or Transnational Social Space? Conceptions of Society in Discourses of EU Citizenship, Governance and the Democratic Deficit: An Emerging Agenda', *European Journal of Social Theory* 6 (1), 25–43.

Schaar, John (1967) 'Equality of Opportunity and Beyond', in J. Roland Pennock and John Chapman (eds.), *Nomo IX: Equality* (New York: Atherton Press), 228–249.

Schermers, Henry (1990) 'The European Communities Bound by Fundamental Human Rights', *Common Market Law Review* 27(2), 249–258.

Séché, Jean-Claude (1969) 'The Revision of Regulations Nos. 3 and 4 (Social Security of Migrant Workers) in the Light of their Interpretation by the Court of Justice', *Common Market Law Review* 6(2) 170–192.

(1977) 'Free Movement of Workers under Community Law', *Common Market Law Review* 14(4), 385–420.

Secretariat of the Commission for Labor Cooperation (2014) *North American Agreement on Labor Cooperation between the Government of the United States of America, the Government of Canada and the Government of the United Mexican States, 13 September 1993* [online], Available at: www.naalc.org/naalc/naalc-full-text.htm, Accessed 4 November 2014.

Selbourne, David (1994) *The Principle of Duty* (London: Faber and Faber).

Seling, Anja (2010) 'Case C-135/08 *Janko Rottmann v. Freistaat Bayern*, Judgment of the Court of Justice (Grand Chamber) of 2 March 2010, nyr – Towards a direct "droit de regard"?', *Maastricht Journal of European and Comparative Law* 17(4), 470–478.

Shah, Prakash (2001) 'British Nationals under Community Law: The *Kaur* Case', *European Journal of Migration and Law* 3(2), 271–278.

Shaw, Jo (1997) 'The Many Pasts and Futures of Citizenship in the European Union' *European Law Review* 22(6), 554–572.

(1998) '*Citizenship of the Union: Towards Post-National Membership?*'; *in Collected Courses of the Academy of European Law – 1995 European Community Law, Vol VI, Book 1, European University Institute, Florence, Academy of European Law* (The Hague: Martinus Nijhoff).

(2010) 'A View of the Citizenship Classics: *Martínez Sala* and Subsequent Cases on Citizenship of the Union', in Miguel Poiares Maduro and Loïc Azoulai (eds.), *The Past and Future of EU Law: The Classics of EU Law Revisited on the 50th Anniversary of the Rome Treaty* (Oxford: Hart), 356–362.

(2017) 'Union and Citizens: Membership Status and Political Rights in Scotland, the UK and the EU' in Carlos Closa (ed.), *Secession from a Member State and Withdrawal from the European Union: Trouble Membership* (Cambridge: Cambridge University Press), 153–86.

(2019) 'EU Citizenship: Still a Fundamental Status?' in Rainer Bauböck (ed.), *Debating European Citizenship* (Cham: Springer, 2019), 1–17.

Shore, Chris (2000) *Building Europe – The Cultural Politics of European Integration* (London: Routledge).

Shuibhne, Niamh Nic (2001) 'The European Union and Minority Language Rights', *International Journal on Multicultural Societies* 3(2), 61–77.

(2002) 'Free Movement of Persons and the Wholly Internal Rule: Time to Move On?', *Common Market Law Review* 39(4), 731–771.

Sieberson, Stephen C. (2004) 'The Proposed European Union Constitution – Will it Eliminate the EU's Democratic Deficit?', *The Columbia Journal of European Law* 10(2) 173–264.

Siim, Birte and Squires, Judith (2008) 'Contesting Citizenship: Comparative Analyses', in Birte Siim and Judith Squires (eds.), *Contesting Citizenship* (London: Routledge), 1–14.

Sindbjerg-Martinsen, Dorte (2005) 'Social Security Regulation in the EU: The De-Territorialisation of Welfare', in Gráinne de Búrca (ed.), *EU Law and the Welfare State: In Search of Solidarity* (Oxford: Oxford University Press), 89–111.

Smith, Robert (2003) 'Diasporic Memberships in Historical Perspective: Comparative Insights on the Mexican, Italian und Polish Cases', *International Migration Review* 37(3), 724–759.

Smyth, Lisa (2005) *Abortion and Nation: The Politics of Reproduction in Contemporary Ireland* (Aldershot: Ashgate).

Snow, Stephanie (2018) 'A Source of Pride: the NHS and the Nation', The Fabian Society (2018), Available at: https://fabians.org.uk/a-source-of-pride-the-nhs-and-the-nation/, Accessed 19 September 2020.

Somek, Alexander (2007) 'Solidarity Decomposed: Being and Time in European Citizenship', *European Law Review* 32(6), 787–818.

Sommers, Margaret (1994), 'Rights, Relationality and Membership: Rethinking the Making and Meaning of Citizenship', *Law and Social Inquiry (Journal of the American Bar Foundation)* 19(1) 63–112.

Soysal, Yasemin Nuhoğlu (1994) *Limits of Citizenship: Migrants and Postnational Membership in Europe* (Chicago: Chicago University Press).

(1996) 'Changing Citizenship in Europe: Remarks on Postnational Membership and the National State', in David Cesarini and Mary Fulbrook (eds.), *Citizenship, Nationality and Migration in Europe* (London: Routledge), 17–29.

Starck, Christian (1987) 'Constitutional Definition and Protection of Rights and Freedoms', in Christian Starck (ed.), *Rights, Institutions and Impact of International Law according to the German Basic Law* (Baden-Baden: Nomos Verlagsgesellschaft).

Steiner, Josephine (1985) 'Recipients of Services – Some More Equal than Others', *European Law Review*, 348–352.

(1991) 'Pregnancy Discrimination in Sex Discrimination', *European Law Review* 16(4), 313–320.

Stillar, Glenn (1998) *Analyzing Everyday Texts: Discourse, Rhetoric and Social Perspectives* (California: Sage).

Stone-Sweet, Alec (2004) *The Judicial Construction of Europe* (Oxford: Oxford University Press).

Sufrin, Brenda (1983) 'When is a Worker a Worker?', *The Modern Law Review* 46(4), 495–499.

Syal, Rajeev (2019) '"A celebrity, not a leader": how Vote Leave harnessed the Johnson effect', *The Guardian*. Available at: www.theguardian.com/politics/2019/jul/17/celebrity-leader-how-vote-leave-harnessed-boris-johnson-effect, Accessed on 19 September 2020.

Szyszczak, Erika (1997) 'Building a European Constitutional Order: Prospects for a General Non-Discrimination Standard', in Alan Dashwood and Siofra O'Leary (eds.), *The Principle of Equal Treatment in EC Law* (London: Sweet & Maxwell), 80–104.

(2000) *EC Labour Law* (Harlow: Longman).

Taschner (1993) 'Free Movement of Students, Retired Persons and other European Citizens – A Difficult Legislative Process', in Henry Schermers (ed.), *Free Movement of Persons in Europe: Legal Problems and Experiences* (Dordrecht, Netherlands: Kluwer Academic Publishers), 427–436.

Tasliki, Liza (2007) 'The Construction of European Identity and Citizenship through Cultural Policy', *European Studies* 24(2), 157–182.

ter Heide, Harm (1969) 'The Free Movement of Workers in the Final Phase', *Common Market Law Review* 6(4), 466–477.

Timmermans, Christiaan (2010) '*Martínez Sala* and *Baumbast* Revisited', in Miguel Poiares Maduro and Loïc, Azoulai (eds.), *The Past and Future of EU Law: The Classics of EU Law Revisited on the 50th Anniversary of the Rome Treaty* (Oxford: Hart Publishing) 345–355.

Titscher, Stefan, Meyer, Michael, Wodak, Ruth and Vetter, Eva (2000) *Methods of Text and Discourse Analysis* (London: Sage).

Tomuschat, Christian (2000) 'Case C-85/96, *María Martínez Sala* v. *Freistaat Bayern*, Judgment of 12 May 1998, Full Court [1998] ECR I-2691' *Common Market Law Review* 37(2), 449–457.

Toner, Helen (2000) 'Judicial Interpretation of European Union Citizenship – Transformation or Consolidation?' *Maastricht Journal of European and Comparative Law* 7(2), 158–182.

(2002) 'Case C-192/99, *R* v. *Secretary of State for the Home Department, ex parte Kaur*, Judgment of the Full Court of 20 February 2001, [2001] ECR I-1237', *Common Market Law Review* 39(4), 881–893.

Tooze, Roger and Murphy, Craing N (1996), 'The Epistemology of Poverty and the Poverty of Epistemology in IPE: Mystery, Blindness and Invisibility', *Millennium* 25 (3), 681–707.

Torfing, Jacob (2005) 'Discourse Theory: Achievements, Arguments and Challenges', in David Howarth and Jacob Torfing (eds.), *Discourse Theory in European Politics: Identity, Policy and Governance* (Basingstoke: Palgrave Macmillan), 1–32.

Traversa, Enrico (1989) 'L'Interdiction de Discrimination en Raison de la Nationalité en Matière d'Accès à l'Enseignement', *Revue Trimestrielle de Droit Européen* 25(1), 45–69.

Tridimas, Takis (1996) 'The Court of Justice and Judicial Activism', *European Law Review* 21(3), 199–210.

(1997) 'The Application of the Principle of Equality to Community Measures', in Alan Dashwood and Siofra O'Leary (eds.), *The Principle of Equal Treatment in EC Law* (London: Sweet & Maxwell), 214–242.

(1997) 'The Role of the Advocate General in the Development of Community Law: Some Reflections', *Common Market Law Review* 34(6), 1349–1387.

(1999) *The General Principles of EC Law* (Oxford: Oxford University Press).

(2006) *The General Principles of EC Law – Third Edition* (Oxford: Oxford University Press).

Tryfonidou, Alina (2008) 'Reverse Discrimination in Purely Internal Situations: An Incongruity in a Citizens' Europe', *Legal Issues of Economic Integration* 35(1), 43–67.

(2009) *Reverse Discrimination in EC Law* (Alphen aan den Rijn: Kluwer Law International).

UCL Centre for Research and Analysis of Migration (2014), 'Positive economic impact of UK immigration from the European Union: new evidence' www.ucl.ac.uk/news/2014/nov/positive-economic-impact-uk-immigration-european-union-new-evidence, accessed 15 September 2020.

Ulbert, Cornelia and Risse, Thomas (2005) 'Deliberately Changing the Discourse: What Does Make Arguing Effective?', *Acta Politica* 40 (3), 351–367.

US Department of State, 'Visas for Canadian and Mexican NAFTA Professional Workers' (*Travel State Gov*) https://travel.state.gov/content/travel/en/us-visas/employment/visas-canadian-mexican-nafta-professional-workers.html accessed 6 August 2020.

Usher, John (1998) *General Principles of EC Law* (London: Longman).

Vandenhole, Wouter (2005) *Non-Discrimination and Equality in the View of the UN Human Rights Treaties* (Antwerp: Intersentia).

Van der Burg, Martijn (2010) 'Transforming the Dutch Republic into the Kingdom of Holland: The Netherlands between Republicanism and Monarchy (1795–1815)', *European Review of History: Revue europeenne d'histoire* 17(2), 151–170.

Van der Mei, A. Pieter (2002) 'Regulation 1408/71 and Coordination of Special Non-Contributory Benefit Schemes', *European Law Review* 27(5), 551–556.

(2003) *Free Movement of Persons within the European Community – Cross-Border Access to Public Benefit* (Oxford: Hart).

(2005) 'Union Citizenship and the "De-Nationalisation" of the Territorial Welfare State. Comments on Case C-456/02 *Trojani* and Case C-209/03 *Bidar*', *European Journal of Migration and Law* 7(2), 207–211.

Van Der Woude, Marc and Mead, Phillip (1988) 'Free Movement of the Tourist in Community Law', *Common Market Law Review* 25(1), 117–140.

Van Dijk, Teun (1985) ''Introduction: The Role of Discourse Analysis in Society', in Teun Van Dijk (ed.), *Discourse Analysis in Society: Handbook of Discourse Analysis Volume 4* (London: Academic Press).

Van Dyke, Vernon (1985) *Human Rights, Ethnicity and Discrimination* (Westport, Connecticut: Greenwood Press).

Van Raepenbusch, S. (1997) 'Persons covered by Regulation (EEC) no. 1408/71 and European Citizenship: From Migrant Worker to European Citizen', in *25 Years of Regulation (EEC) no. 1408/71 on Social Security for Migrant Workers: Post Experiences, Present Problems and Future Perspectives* (Stockholm: Report for from the European conference on Social Security, June 1996), 71–88.

Verdicchio, Pasquale (1997) *Bound by Distance: Rethinking Nationalisms through the Italian Diaspora* (Madison, New Jersey: Fairleigh Dickinson University Press).

Vlassopoulos, Kostas (2007) 'Identity, Experience and Democracy in Classical Athens', *The Classical Quarterly* 57(1), 33–52.

Voirin, Michel (1968) 'Sécurité sociale des travailleurs migrants. Commentaires des arrêts de la Cour de justice des Communautés européennes (*Kolditz, Ciechelski* et *de Moor*)', *Droit Social* (4), 329–346.

Wæver, Ole (2004) 'Discursive Approaches', in Antje Wiener and Thomas Diez (eds.), *European Integration Theory* (Oxford: Oxford University Press), 197–215.

Walker, Neil and Tierney, Stephen (2011) 'Introduction: A Constitutional Mosaic? Exploring the New Frontiers of Europe's Constitutionalism', in Neil Walker, Jo Shaw and Stephen Tierney (eds.), *Europe's Constitutional Mosaic* (Oxford: Hart).

Wallace, Rebecca (1977) 'Recognition of Foreign Qualifications', *New Law Journal* 127, 1007–1008.

(1988) 'Remedies for Foul Play', *European Law Review* 13(4), 267–270.

Ward, Ian (2009) *A Critical Introduction to European Law* (Cambridge: Cambridge University Press).

Ware, Vron (2011) 'White Resentment: The Other Side of Belonging', in Manuela Ribeiro Sanches, Fernando Clara, João Ferreira Duarte and Leonor Pires Martins (eds.), *Europe in Black and White: Immigration, Race and Identity in the 'Old Continent'* (Bristol: Intellect), 155–172.

Warleigh, Alex (1997) 'A Committee of No Importance? Assessing the Relevance of the Committee of the Regions', *Politics* 17(2), 101–107.

Watson, Philippa (1979) 'Social Security Rights of Non-EEC Nationals', *European Law Review* 4(1), 106–109.

(1980) *Social Security Law of the European Communities* (London: Mansell Publications).

(1984) 'Family Allowances: Persons Covered', *European Law Review* 9(6), 434–435.

(1987) 'Case 293/83, *Gravier v. City of Liège*, Judgment of 13 February 1985. Reference to the Court by the Tribunal de Première Instance, Liège, for a preliminary ruling on the interpretation of Articles 7 and 59 of the EEC Treaty. Case 293/85 R, *Commission of the European Communities* v. *Kingdom of Belgium*: Order of the President of the Court of 25 October 1985', *Common Market Law Review* 24(1), 89–97.

(1989) 'Equal Treatment in the Award of Family Allowances', *European Law Review* 14(5), 346–349.

(1989) 'Free Movement of Workers: Recent Cases', *European Law Review* 14(6) 417–422.

(1993) 'Free Movement of Workers: A One-Way Ticket?', *Industrial Law Journal* 22(1), 68–77.

Watts, Duncan and Pilkington, Colin (2005) *Britain in the European Union Today* (Manchester: Manchester University Press).

Weale, Albert (1991) 'Citizenship Beyond Borders', in Ursula Vogel and Michael Moran (eds.), *The Frontiers of Citizenship* (Basingstoke: Macmillan), 155–165.

Weatherill, Stephen (1989) 'Case 186/87, *Cowan v. Le Trésor Public*. Preliminary reference under Art. 177 EEC by the Commission d'indemnisation des victimes des infraction du Tribunal de Grande Instance de Paris, on the interpretation of Art. 7 EEC. Decision of the European Court of Justice of 2 February 1989', *Common Market Law Review* 26(3), 563–581.

(1990) 'Case Comment: The Scope of Article 7 EEC', *European Law Review* 15(4) 334–340.

(2003) 'Activism and Restraint in the European Court of Justice', in Patrick Capps, Malcolm Evans and Stratos Konstadinidis (eds.), *Asserting Jurisdiction: International and European Legal Perspectives* (Oxford: Hart).

Weiler, Joseph (1995) 'Does Europe Need a Constitution? Reflections on Demos, Telos and the German Maastricht Decision', *European Law Journal* 1(2), 5–30.

(1997) 'The European Union Belongs to its Citizens: Three Immodest Proposals', *European Law Review* 22(1), 150–156.

(1999) *The Constitution of Europe: 'Do the new clothes have an emperor?' and Other Essays on European Integration* (Cambridge: Cambridge University Press).

(2017) 'Secessionism and Its Discontents', in Carlos Closa (ed.), *Secession from a Member State and Withdrawal from the European Union* (Cambridge: Cambridge University Press, 2017), 12–31.

Weiss, Freidl and Wooldridge, Frank (2002) *Free Movement of Persons within the European Community* (The Hague: Kluwer Law International).

Wendt, Alexander (1992) 'Anarchy is What States Make of it: The Social Construction of Power Politics', *International Organization* 46(2), 391–425.

(1999) *Social Theory of International Politics* (Cambridge: Cambridge University Press).

Westen, Peter (1982) 'The Empty Idea of Equality', *Harvard Law Review* 95(3), 537–596.

Whelan, Anthony (2000) 'Union Citizenship and The Free Movement of Persons', *The Bar Review* 5, 179–185.

White, Robin (1987) 'A Round-up of Cases on Free Movement of Workers', *European Law Review* 12(2), 147–153.

(1993) 'A Fresh Look at Reverse Discrimination?', *European Law Review* 18(6), 527–532.

(1999) *EC Social Security Law* (London: Longman).

(2004) *Workers, Establishment and Services in the European Union* (Oxford: Oxford University Press).

Wiener, Antje (1998) *'European' Citizenship Practice: Building Institutions of a Non-State* (Boulder, Colorado: Westview Press).

(2003) 'Citizenship', in Michelle Cini (ed.), *European Union Politics* (Oxford: Oxford University Press), 397–414.

Wilkinson, Brian (1992) 'Abortion, the Irish Constitution and the EEC', *Public Law* (Spring), 20–30.

Wilsher, Daniel (2001) 'Economic Migration into the European Union: Standing at the Crossroads', *Yearbook of European Law* 21(1), 163–193.

Wincott, Daniel (1995) 'Political Theory, Law and European Union', in Jo Shaw and Gillian More (eds.), *New Legal Dynamic of European Union* (Oxford: Clarendon Press).

(2001) 'The Court of Justice and the European Policy Process', in Jeremy Richardson (ed.), *European Union, Power and Policy Making – Second Edition* (London: Routledge).

Wodak, Ruth (2004) 'National and Transnational Identities: European and other Identities Oriented to in Interviews with EU Officials', in Richard Hermann, Thomas Risse and Marilynn Brewer (eds.), *Transnational Identities* (Lanham, Maryland: Rowman and Littlefield), 97–128.

Wood, James (2020), 'NHS nurse who helped save Boris Johnson's life from coronavirus in intensive care confirms: "He absolutely needed to be there"', *Daily Mail*, Available online at: www.dailymail.co.uk/news/article-8248513/NHS-intensive-care-nurse-helped-save-Boris-Johnsons-life-says-just-patient.html, Accessed 19 September 2020.

Wooldridge, Frank (1977) 'Free Movement of EEC Nationals: Limits Based on Public Policy and Public Service', *European Law Review* 2(2), 139.

Wooldridge, Frank and Thomson, Joseph (1982) 'Railway Travel Permits, Voluntary Redundancy Schemes and EEC Law', *The Scots Law Times* 32, 261–263.

Worbs, Susanne (2003) 'The Second Generation in Germany: Between School and Labor Market', *International Migration Review* 37(4), 1011–1038.

Wouters, Jan (1994) 'European Citizenship and the Case-Law of the EC Court of Justice on the Free Movement of Persons', in Epaminondas Marias (ed.),

European Citizenship (Maastricht: European Institute of Public Administration), 25–61.
(1994) 'The Case-Law of the European Court of Justice on Direct Taxes: Variations upon a Theme', *Maastricht Journal of European and Comparative Law* 1(2), 179–220.
Wyatt, Derrick (1975) 'The Scope of "Equal Treatment" under Articles 7 and 12 of Regulation 1612/68', *European Law Review* 1(1), 62–63.
(1976) 'Alien's Duty to Notify National Authorities of His Presence', *European Law Review* 1(6), 556–560.
(1976) 'Article 119 EEC: Definition of "Pay" – Towards the Elimination of Sex Discrimination', *European Law Review* 1(6), 414–420.
(1976) 'Rights of Employment and Residence: Some Further Clarification', *European Law Review* 1(6), 406–410.
(1977) 'Rights of Members of a Worker's Family under Regulation 1408/71', *European Law Review* 2(2), 125–126.
(1977) 'The Social Security Rights of Migrant Workers and their Families', *Common Market Law Review* 14(4), 411–433.
(1978) 'Recent Cases on Regulation 1408/71. Unemployment Benefit for School-leavers', *European Law Review* 3(5), 398–399.
(1978) 'Regulation 1408/71: Duplication of Orphans' Benefits and Family Allowances', *European Law Review* 3(5), 371–373.
(1979) 'Discrimination on Grounds of Nationality: Schemes for the Victims of War or its Consequences', *European Law Review* 4(5), 369–371.
(1980) 'Article 48: Permissible Entry Formalities for Nationals of Member States', *European Law Review* 5(5), 380–388.
(1981) 'Article 48 (4)EEC: Scope of the Public Service Proviso', *European Law Review* 6(6) 459–463.
(1981) 'Current Survey: Contrasting Cases On Non-Discrimination', *European Law Review* 6(1), 42–51.
(1986) 'Case 41/84, *Pietro Pinna* v. *Caisse d'Allocations familiales de la Savoie*", Judgment of 15 January 1986: Prospective Invalidity for the Discriminatory Family Allowances Rule', *Common Market Law Review* 23(3), 703–717.
Wyatt, Derrick, Dashwood, Alan, Ross, Malcolm and Arnull, Anthony (2000) *Wyatt & Dashwood's European Union Law (Fourth Edition)* (London: Sweet & Maxwell).
Yeo, Colin (2019) *Theresa May's Immigration Legacy* www.freemovement.org.uk/theresa-mays-immigration-legacy/, Accessed 15 September 2020.
Young, Hugo (1998) *The Blessed Plot* (London: Macmillan).
Yuval-Davies, Nira (1997) *Gender and Nation* (London: Sage).
(2008) 'Intersectionality, Citizenship and Contemporary Politics of Belonging', in Birte Siim and Judith Squires (eds.), *Contesting Citizenship* (London: Routledge), 159–172.

Index

Human Rights in the Council of Europe and the European Union: Achievements, Trends and Challenges
Steven Greer, Janneke Gerards and Rosie Slowe

Core Socio-Economic Rights and the European Court of Human Rights
Ingrid Leijten

Green Trade and Fair Trade in and with the EU: Process-based Measures within the EU Legal Order
Laurens Ankersmit

New Labour Laws in Old Member States: Trade Union Responses to European Enlargement
Rebecca Zahn

The Governance of EU Fundamental Rights
Mark Dawson

The International Responsibility of the European Union: From Competence to Normative Control
Andrés Delgado Casteleiro

Frontex and Non-Refoulement: The International Responsibility of the EU
Roberta Mungianu

Gendering European Working Time Regimes: The Working Time Directive and the Case of Poland
Ania Zbyszewska

EU Renewable Electricity Law and Policy: From National Targets to a Common Market
Tim Maxian Rusche

European Constitutionalism
Kaarlo Tuori

Brokering Europe: Euro-Lawyers and the Making of a Transnational Polity
Antoine Vauchez

Services Liberalization in the EU and the WTO: Concepts, Standards and Regulatory Approaches
Marcus Klamert

Referendums and the European Union: A Comparative Enquiry
Fernando Mendez, Mario Mendez and Vasiliki Triga

The Allocation of Regulatory Competence in the EU Emissions Trading Scheme
Jospehine van Zeben

The Eurozone Crisis: A Constitutional Analysis
Kaarlo Tuori and Klaus Tuori

International Trade Disputes and EU Liability
Anne Thies

The Limits of Legal Reasoning and the European Court of Justice
Gerard Conway

New Governance and the Transformation of European Law: Coordinating EU Social Law and Policy
Mark Dawson

The Lisbon Treaty: A Legal and Political Analysis
Jean-Claude Piris

The European Union's Fight against Corruption: The Evolving Policy towards Member States and Candidate Countries
Patrycja Szarek-Mason

The Ethos of Europe: Values, Law and Justice in the EU
Andrew Williams

State and Market in European Union Law: The Public and Private Spheres of the Internal Market before the EU Courts
Wolf Sauter and Harm Schepel

The European Civil Code: The Way Forward
Hugh Collins

Ethical Dimensions of the Foreign Policy of the European Union: A Legal Appraisal
Urfan Khaliq

Implementing EU Pollution Control: Law and Integration
Bettina Lange

European Broadcasting Law and Policy
Jackie Harrison and Lorna Woods

The Transformation of Citizenship in the European Union: Electoral Rights and the Restructuring of Political Space
Jo Shaw

The Constitution for Europe: A Legal Analysis
Jean-Claude Piris

The European Convention on Human Rights: Achievements, Problems and Prospects
Steven Greer

Social Rights and Market Freedom in the European Constitution: A Labour Law Perspective
Stefano Giubboni

EU Enlargement and the Constitutions of Central and Eastern Europe
Anneli Albi

For EU product safety concerns, contact us at Calle de José Abascal, 56–1°,
28003 Madrid, Spain or eugpsr@cambridge.org.

www.ingramcontent.com/pod-product-compliance
Lightning Source LLC
LaVergne TN
LVHW011700200926
848484LV00004B/1014
* 9 7 8 1 1 0 8 4 9 0 8 9 4 *